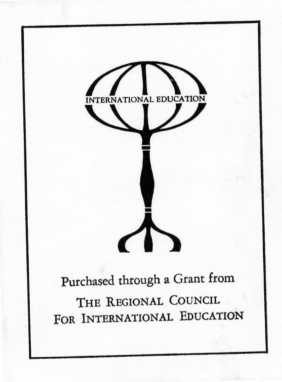

NATIONAL DEVELOPMENT

AND LOCAL REFORM

POLITICAL PARTICIPATION IN MOROCCO,
TUNISIA, AND PAKISTAN

BY DOUGLAS E. ASHFORD

PRINCETON, NEW JERSEY

PRINCETON UNIVERSITY PRESS

1967

PREFACE

THE STUDY OF LOCAL government in developing countries, and in more advanced countries as well, has suffered from our concentration on the formalities of government. In the modern nation the locality tends to be divested of power and in the developing country the locality is isolated from the central power structure. In both instances the revival of the locality as an appropriate focus of analysis requires a careful reexamination of the institutional assumptions in much of political science. This process has already begun in the study of modern communities and cities. My hope is that this book will help to cast a new light on the significance of the locality in the study of political development, in part by the use of some of the concepts applied to the more advanced political systems.

Because I am not prepared to take on the whole field of political science, the problem has been stated in the book in terms of participation. Largely under the stimulus of the voting-behavior studies, political scientists have been forced to reconsider many of their notions about participation, and the rudiments of a more accurate model of the citizen have begun to emerge. The community-power studies have also compelled us to reconsider the relation between individual and government. These discoveries were made possible in fairly recent times by the readiness of the political scientist to engage in research at the micro-level—in brief, to examine very carefully the validity of his institutional assumptions. Although there have been some pioneering studies attempting this examination of developing countries with aggregate data, there are few inquiries dealing with localized politics in the full complexity reflected in studies of American cities and communities.

To make the break in the study of American politics, the scholars involved have generally adopted some radically new conceptual tools, and much of sterile disputation in political science stems from their courage to do so. The results are now acquiring sufficient weight to judge them increasingly on their own merit, which, one hopes, will lead to a more productive kind of controversy. The reader will find that this study also introduces some unfamiliar, perhaps alarming, notions into the study of participation in developing countries. I have done so because even the assumptions of micro-level political studies in America are open to doubt when applied to the developing country. However, I have tried to make clear my indebtedness to efforts to examine participation in complex political systems.

There are two more caveats to be inserted in introducing the book. I have found that it is very easy to become transfixed with the use of coercion when one discusses power. The fact that this is indeed the last resort of every government makes it a common concern. However, there are persuasive common-sense reasons for treating coercion as a special case in the exercise of power rather than as the definition of power. The most obvious of these is that when any government is reduced to the application of coercion to implement its decisions, we agree quite sensibly that something is wrong. Participation, whatever substantive form it may take, is part of every political system, and when there is no reciprocal relationship in the exchange of power we are, I feel, dealing with a situation that can be seen to be unlike all complex power relationships. My approach, then, is to put aside the limiting case and to look for better ways of describing what in fact does occur between the governed and the governor in an operating society. In my view the best approach is to look for better ways of describing complex situations, rather than making complex relationships into simple ones.

The second observation is treated at several points in the book, but deserves some preliminary notice. Anthropologists have been involved in the systematic study of small communities much longer than have political scientists. I have tried to acknowledge their work, but have used the notion of the community or locality in a very different sense than that in which it normally appears in anthropological research. The developing country has villages and towns wherein power can be studied and where a power structure of great importance to the development process rests. But precisely because participation most meaningfully includes some allowance for reciprocity, relevance to national problems can only be described if power *outside* the village can be allowed for. The ideas suggested in this book may not do so adequately, but they are certainly not to be viewed as a repudiation of anthropological concerns. Some of the most important insights into the problem of participation discussed in the book have been taken from anthropology.

The book has been in preparation over four years and the task of acknowledging support, not to mention inspiration, is formidable. The field work began in 1961-1962 with a grant from the Joint Committee on the Near East of the Social Science Research Council and the American Council of Learned Societies. I am especially indebted to them for accepting a proposal that was, not to be immodest, rather freewheeling. They are not responsible for omissions or errors. The first draft of the manuscript would not have been possible without the unencumbered year made possible in 1963-1964 by the Center of International Studies, Cornell University. Though the poverty-stricken state of the social sciences has ended, unconditional and generous support for writing is still looked upon in many quarters as academic self-indulgence. The Center also gave support for the typing and reproduction of the early drafts of the book.

Many persons have read portions or all of the book in manuscript and it is not possible to list them all. I am especially indebted to the

PREFACE

members of Cornell's Modernization Workshop, which provided an uninhibited and demanding group for trying out the basic concepts. Among the persons who have read parts of the manuscript and made helpful comments are Khalid Ben Sayeed, Wayne Wilcox, Karl Von Vorys, Clement Moore, Jack Montgomery, and Eqbal Ahmed. Steven Muller was a constant source of encouragement whose unobtrusive sensitivity was invaluable. A final note of appreciation is well earned by the editors of Princeton University Press, whose precision and care have added immeasurably to the quality of this book. I particularly appreciate the contribution of Mary Tozer, who has diligently scrutinized my prose after a similar effort with my earlier Morocco book. The large number of North Africans and Pakistanis whose confidence and cooperation made this book possible will remain anonymous, but I hope the book will contribute to the exciting experiment they have undertaken.

Douglas E. Ashford

Ithaca, November 1965

CONTENTS

CONTENTS

CONTENTS

NATIONAL DEVELOPMENT
AND LOCAL REFORM

SECTION I:

NATIONAL DEVELOPMENT AND LOCAL REFORM

"The capacity of a people to sense the existence of ordered systems of human relationships is a crucial achievement in the nation-building process. It is this sense for an elaboration of systematic relationships that makes it possible for a people to accept the concept that an economy can be developed, a polity strengthened, and a society opened to constant innovation. Without it economic activity becomes the enrichment of some at the expense of others, political action becomes little more than personal aggrandizement of power, and social relations become essentially matters of relative status."[1]

[1] Lucian W. Pye, *Politics, Personality, and Nation-Building: Burma's Search for Identity*, New Haven, Yale University Press, 1962, p. 292.

CHAPTER I

POLITICAL PARTICIPATION AND DEVELOPMENT

POLITICAL ANALYSIS OF THE DEVELOPMENT process has tended to gravitate into two schools of thought. The first is that the major obstacle to development is acquiring the skills and techniques for the manipulation of the physical environment. The political implications of this approach, very simply, are that strong governments are desirable and that the sponsoring nations should reconcile themselves to, if not actually encourage, firm rule in order that development can take place in a stable political setting. The argument is very persuasive. The Western nations have seen how disruptive social upheaval can be in the development process. Moreover, where there has been unmanageable political conflict in developing countries, our disciplinary skills are most adept at measuring the economic costs and material losses.

A second viewpoint has gained ground as the faulty logic of the environmentalist approach has been exposed by the experience of the past decade. While the Western nations never doubted that the developmental process involved a struggle for the minds of men, the modern democracies have on the whole neglected the ideological component in development. More recently the democracies have been less modest in championing the values that are indeed basic to our societies, and a greater appreciation has emerged for the vital role of ideas in the developmental process. The democracies have begun to realize that the highly romantic disassociation of political values and social change that characterized their own development under historically fortuitous conditions is not likely to be repeated in Africa and Asia.

There are perhaps three particularly important factors that have contributed to this reexamination. First has been the simple demonstration that many rich countries do not achieve political stability.[1] The obvious neglect of European experience might be excused by our own unfamiliarity with the developmental process and our consequent hesitance to make sweeping inferences from Western experience. But we can now also observe that many developing countries that have made substantial increments in their control over their environments are still plagued with political unrest and turmoil. Indeed, as this study will argue, it may well be that the initial phases of development contribute to political instability. Quite possibly the modesty of democratic nations has also

[1] James S. Coleman, "Conclusion: The Political Systems of Developing Areas," in Almond and Coleman, eds., *The Politics of the Developing Areas*, Princeton, Princeton University Press, 1960, p. 542. See also Phillips Cutwright, "National Political Development," *American Sociological Review*, vol. 28, no. 2, April 1963, pp. 253-264.

been a form of self-deception. The social fabric of the new nation cannot be rewoven without proportionate dislocations in all aspects of the social system. The inadequacy of an economic system may be mirrored in the dissent and insecurity of a people who find comparable faults in their forms of political expression.

A second factor has been a renewed appreciation for the cultural inertia that constantly handicaps the developmental process. Impressive as the developmental gap may be in per capita income figures, it is even more dramatic when we compare the "maps of problematic social reality and matrices for the creation of collective conscience"[2] in the more and less developed nations. In concentrating on the most readily identifiable aspects of development, we have very likely been blinding ourselves to the full dimensions of the task, thereby creating as many false expectations for ourselves as for the developing nation. Cultural anthropology has made a major contribution to this realization and some of the most revealing studies of the full complexity of development have been anthropological studies.[3]

Lastly, more attention has been given in recent years to the psychological dimensions of the developmental process. More than any other social science discipline, psychology is concerned with how values are internalized and how the environment is perceived. Psychologists have always acknowledged the extent to which reality is self-determined, but only recently has there begun to appear a series of works on how various schools of psychology might explain the developmental process. The student of developing nations can now select, from among a fairly straightforward application of Freudian thought, an interpretation based on neo-Freudian analysis, a motivational study, and a study derived from cognition theory.[4] Without our choosing among them, we can state that these works have made us more aware of the profound individual impact that development entails, and that the acquisition of new belief systems can itself be explained in many ways.

[2] Clifford Geertz, "Ideology as a Cultural System," in D. Apter, ed., *Ideology and Discontent*, Glencoe, Free Press, 1964, p. 64.

[3] Reference is made here to those anthropological studies that have paid particular attention to the relationship of tribal or traditional political systems to the nation. See, for example, Frederick G. Bailey, *Politics and Social Change: Orissa in 1959*, Berkeley, University of California Press, 1963; A. L. Epstein, *Politics in an Urban African Community*, Manchester, Manchester University Press, 1958; and Lloyd Fallers, *Bantu Bureaucracy; A Study of Integration and Conflict in the Political Institutions of an East African People*, Cambridge, Heffer, 1956.

[4] Examples, in the order referred to in the text, are Everett E. Hagen, *On the Theory of Social Change*, Homewood, Dorsey Press, 1962; Lucian W. Pye, *Politics, Personality, and Nation Building: Burma's Search for Identity*, New Haven, Yale University Press, 1962; David C. McClelland, *The Achieving Society*, Princeton, Van Nostrand, 1961; and Gabriel A. Almond and Sidney Verba, *The Civic Culture: Political Attitudes and Democracy in Five Nations*, Princeton, Princeton University Press, 1963.

The upshot of these three influences on the analysis of development might be summarized as a new concern with the citizen in the developing country. The emergence of modern democracy, curiously enough, also began with the notion of the citizen—a man who acquired certain rights and obligations in a new social unit, the nation-state. In a sense, then, our thinking about the developmental process has gone the full cycle and returned to a concern with how individuals will play political roles as well as economically productive roles in the new nations. The nation as a new source of values is universally accepted in the world today, perhaps even more enthusiastically among the less developed nations than among the more highly industrialized nations. The critical premise for the following analysis, however, is that the developmental process represents the conjunction of political values advocated by the various governments of the new nations and a massive effort to rebuild the social structure of each nation. For this reason the title of the book is "national development" rather than the more conventional "political development," and the emphasis should rightfully be placed on the adjective. Above all, the goal of development is to make the nation a meaningful frame of reference for millions of subjects, who are citizens in only the most elementary and formal sense.

GOVERNMENT: ARBITRATOR OF DEVELOPMENT

If development or major social change is the constant in a comparison among new nations, the major variable becomes the political orientation of the government. There have been some notable attempts at devising typologies for the types of government in developing countries.[5] The reason for these endeavors to reorganize our thinking about government in developing countries is not only that the conventional classifications seem inappropriate, but also that the old categories do not allow for the diversity found among the governments of the new countries. Although the purpose of this study is not to add to the typologies that have already been suggested, comparative analysis requires this kind of conceptual short cut in order to make high-order generalizations.

The three governments discussed in the study were chosen not so much because they represent three distinct forms that national politics may take in developing countries, but because each is a government that has made a major developmental effort. The political orientation of each is very different, but the reason for their inclusion is that each country has been actively engaged for a decade or more in adapting its

[5] See, for example, Edward Shils, *Political Development in New States*, The Hague, Mouton, 1963, and Gabriel A. Almond, "Comparative Political Systems," *Journal of Politics*, vol. 18, 1956, pp. 391-409, and reprinted in Ulmer, ed., *Introductory Readings in Political Behavior*, New York, Rand McNally, 1961, pp. 147-157.

political and social values to the developmental process. A government does not constitute a nation any more than achieving national independence assures continued development. The goal of government may be to make development a national concern, which is why these three governments were selected, but evidence is hardly needed to assert that few, if any, of the new governments have yet made the relatively sophisticated and abstract notions of politics that operate among the educated elite indeed part of the political life of the new citizens.

Hence the new governments have been described as "arbitrators" in the developmental process. Though varying greatly in political orientation, they are very much alike when confronted with the developmental challenge. As the nation-state concept demands, each is most concerned with law and order. As developmental needs begin to displace the law-and-order structure that most new nations have acquired from colonial regimes, government decides how much will be spent, where it will be spent, and what priorities will be recognized. Although the government of the new nation is remote from the citizen both as an organization and as a concept, it does in fact make the critical decisions about how the society will be reconstructed, and it does this with almost no consultation with the vast proportion of the citizens. The dilemma of government in the new nation is that it is all-powerful in the decision-making sense, but that it is utterly devoid of structural relationships to the society that make it possible to extend the meaning of development.

Two observations may make this apparent paradox clearer. Time after time the citizens of developing countries indicate the fervor of their national loyalty in opinion surveys.[6] Their identity with the nation supersedes all other loyalties. From time to time they are prepared to give their lives for the most absurd national causes. A good many new citizens have actually seen their standard of living decline since independence and many of the most elementary promises of nationalist leaders remain unfulfilled. The most amazing aspect of national political life in most developing countries is that the new citizens have endured so much incompetence and procrastination and have still been able to sustain their devotion to the nation. The answer, of course, is that the nation is largely an emotional identity. Government is not part of an intricate pattern of social relationships to the new citizen, but a source of considerable symbolic gratification. The national identity has indeed been firmly internalized as the evidence suggests, but only as a value bereft of operational meaning and content. So long as government does not tamper with the nation's social fabric, this is by far the easiest way to rule a country.

A second observation that may shed some light on the dilemma of government that seeks to reconstruct a society is the relation of the new

[6] For example, Almond and Verba, *Civic Culture, op.cit.*, pp. 101-122.

government's monopoly of coercion to development. There is no better disproof of the Hobbesian formula than futility of coercion in the developmental process. As Von Vorys has pointed out in the case of Pakistan,[7] the government can easily bring preponderant force to bear at any given point within the nation, but the sum of all this power is not equal to the potential violence of the retarded society. Where the government is not determined to remodel the society, the governmental process may indeed be reduced to a sequence of frantic moves to checkmate the outbursts of tension and discontent in one part of the country or another. Thus begins the downward spiral of cumulative alienation from government and increasing dissipation of governmental resources so that development is never launched. The three governments analyzed in this study have not yet become the victims of their own ineffectiveness, but the crucial point is that the monopoly of legitimacy and coercion are simply not enough to bring about massive social change.

If development represents the process by which government and nation are brought into some kind of harmony, how then are we to describe the variety of governments to be found? Once it is understood that the government of the developing country seldom represents the focus of beliefs that actually operate throughout the society, the problem becomes much simpler. Government has what will be termed an "orientation" to the use of power. In a highly developed society the government's orientation to power is not only shared and understood by most citizens, but it may actually become part of the individual's belief system and serve to structure his thinking over a wide range of subjects rarely thought of as "political."[8] Government of the advanced society enjoys, of course, the loyalty of its citizens and most people continue to receive purely emotional gratification from the display of national symbols. Legitimacy still represents adherence to a common set of national values, but nation and government have been brought much closer together by the latent meaning of national identity and usefulness of the national framework in structuring an intricate and highly specialized enviroment.

A government's political orientation, then, is the way in which it interprets the symbolic national identity in order to promote social change. There is in fact no other agency to do this, just as there is no other agency to make the essentially arbitrary decisions about how development will take place. The two changes are obviously interdepend-

[7] Karl Von Vorys, *Political Development in Pakistan*, Princeton, Princeton University Press, 1965.

[8] Perhaps the most ambitious effort to study the latent attitudinal effects of ideology is Ulf Himmelstrand, *Social Pressures, Attitudes and Democracy*, Stockholm, Almquist and Wicksell, 1960. See also his article, "A Theoretical and Empirical Approach to Depolitization and Political Development," *Acta Sociologica*, vol. 6, fasc. 1-2, 1962, pp. 83-110.

ent and only distinguishable analytically. The present inquiry includes three orientations: the traditional approach of the Moroccan monarchy, the activist solution advocated by the Tunisian single-party system, and the highly professional view of politics represented by Pakistan. Elaborate paradigms could be prepared to underscore the differences in these political orientations, but these have been left out because the burden of the inquiry is to elaborate and describe how each government does indeed respond to the developmental challenge. The evidence collected in this study suggests that there is a remarkable similarity in the way in which each government has gone about development, and that these similarities can best be explained by reference to each government's political orientation.

LOCAL REFORM: FOCUS OF DEVELOPMENT

The governmental response to the developmental challenge implies that there is some unit of operation outside the national government which can be utilized as a focus for the new activities. Most new governments acquire some kind of local unit from the earlier colonial regime, although it is by no means clear that the Indian district or the French *cercle* are in fact the most appropriate divisions. Because this study is more concerned with the process of development and its psychological implications than with organizational questions, the issue of the optimum-sized unit will not be discussed in detail. In practice the optimum unit is difficult to determine until the arbitrator of development decides what kind of program it wishes to implement and what role it is prepared to assign to the new citizen.

For these reasons the phrase "local reform" will simply refer to the continuing process in every new nation of seeking a way to bring the activities of government closer to the citizen. Since the ultimate criterion in the following analysis is the extent to which the new government succeeds in bringing about social change enabling the citizen to contribute to the developmental process, an empirical test would, in the final analysis, have to be some form of attitudinal measurement. Some suggestions along these lines will be made in the final chapters of the book.

Because the analysis argues that local reform will be greatly influenced by the political orientation of the new government, and the orientation differs from government to government, it is not proposed that decentralization itself is a virtue. In fact, local reform implies administrative decentralization and very little developmental activity can begin at the local level until some decentralization takes place.[9] But

[9] See Henry Maddick, *Democracy, Decentralisation and Development*, London, Asia Publishing House, 1963; also Ursula Hicks, *Development from Below*, Oxford, Oxford University Press, 1961.

there are no organizational panaceas to the diffusion of power through more intricate social structures, and, like the emphasis on economic development as the solution for all national problems, the stress placed on simple organizational devices to resolve local conflict can be extremely misleading. Despite the fact that administration is a tangible and generally a manageable aspect of the developmental process, two serious errors can be made if the inherent political problems of nation-building are slighted.

The first is that the government may create the illusion of change without there being any substantial reconciliation of the image of government and nation in the mind of the citizen. The costs are twofold because such an experiment may be costly for the new nation and may only reinforce the new citizen's apprehension and distrust of the more complex political relationship involved in developmental activities. The second, and less readily observed, error is to use administrative expediency to rationalize inaction when a people is indeed prepared to assume more responsibility. The psychological interpretation placed on the developmental process permits one to observe that a government may be doing too little rather than too much to involve the new citizen in developmental activities. Since the nature of most governments is to be both arbitrary and cautious, the reader will not be surprised to find that all three governments compared in this study have displayed characteristic forms of reluctance.

In the terms of the present analysis the second error is a much greater hazard to national development than the first. If a government decides that it prefers the *status quo* and does not wish to press development vigorously—itself a dangerous decision in the world of underdeveloped nations—the ritualized response to local reform may suffice. The government, or more likely a new government, may revive the developmental process at a later date without encountering serious psychological handicaps among the citizens. The locality in every neglected region of the world has developed ageless structures to fill existing political and social requirements, and, as Apter has pointed out, there can hardly be a system of accountability for a government that must itself determine the pace of change.[10] The potential hazard is that although the community is generally self-contained, if not self-sufficient, in the new nation, the people have acquired some notion of national existence and usually have a tenuous emotional identity with the nation. The conservative government almost always wishes to utilize this identity, but finds, as psychologists have long recognized, that simple repetition of symbolic gratification soon palls. Hence the stage is set for the exploitation of patriotic maneuvers to accentuate national fervor, which, in

[10] "Nationalism, Government and Economics," *Economic Development and Cultural Change*, vol. 7, 1959, p. 124.

turn, become the rationalization for even further neglect of local reform.

In the analysis of national development, however, the argument will be that in the case of countries where there has been a continuing effort to bring about local reform, the most difficult problem has been assessing how rapidly concessions can be made. A government that does not wish only to nurse a fragile, emotional association with its new citizens has a very different problem from the country making a ritualized response. Where the arbitrator of development is greatly concerned with performance and change, a fundamental but neglected question is how to transform an affective relationship to the isolated governing process. Moreover, the transformation is not simply one of stimulating national loyalty, but one of enlarging on an emotional attachment to the nation and using the developmental process to assist the new citizen in articulating the meaning of government itself. This process has both cognitive and affective aspects and requires learning as well as devotion.

Two specific qualifications should be made to the approach being suggested. The more common sequence for assessing local capacities to undergo change is to begin with an analysis of the community. There have been some excellent studies by anthropologists which incorporate many of the ideas advanced here, and which acknowledge the significance of more remote frameworks of action in the transformation of communities.[11] These analyses are essential to determining from one locality to another how best a government might select specific programs and implement policies. The author fully agrees that many development programs are launched with very little, if any, consideration of the psychological conditions existing in localities, and clearly future empirical research along the lines suggested would entail some comparative analysis of villagers' perception of government.

The author's reluctance to accept the anthropological-perspective approach in dealing with national development involves a classic problem of social science for which there are as yet no easy solutions. The qualities that are found in concrete subordinate units of a society cannot be added up in order to constitute a nation. For reasons that are at the very core of social science disciplines, the macrocosm is not an arithmetical function of the microcosm. Hence the analyst must state his unit of analysis in order to measure variance, and in the process of national development this unit is government, not the community. The device for the description of variance in this comparative analysis is the political orientation of the government.

The problem can be stated in somewhat different form by pointing out that some anthropological studies imply even more conservative

---

[11] For example, Oscar Lewis, *Life in a Mexican Village: Tepoztlán Restudied*, Urbana, University of Illinois Press, 1951.

approaches to development than those chosen by uncertain new governments.[12] Local reform has been used intentionally in order to suggest that the concrete unit wherein the citizen best expresses the relation of nation and government does change as a society becomes more complex. The purpose is not to identify what specific unit of social organization is most appropriate, for this must be determined by taking into account all of the factors affecting government and citizen. The problem is not that government *or* the community change, but that *both* are changing in the developmental process. The particular concern of this study is not to suggest how either unit might be stabilized, which has already been suggested to be a relatively easy task, but to indicate how one might assess the relationship between locality and nation as government presses for rapid social change.

The second qualification is less directly related to the following analysis, but may help to clarify the kind of relationship on which this study focuses. Because the community in the developing society is obviously remote from government in both a physical and psychological sense, the temptation is great to resolve their differences simply by changing the environment. However, a converse situation may help to explicate the reversible quality of the orientation of locality to government even where a society has achieved a high level of development. Thus a study of a depressed community in Australia demonstrates that a community of educated and articulate citizens can be estranged from political life. The citizens lost their capacity to relate national values to their daily lives, and the town of Malle became unresponsive and dull. Despite the fact that many factors contributed to this situation, the important point is that political relationships to the government lost their meaning for the citizen, and politics, not unlike the prevailing condition in most developing societies, became "mainly an activity for parliamentarians or would-be parliamentarians."[13]

ATTITUDINAL INTEGRATION: GOAL OF DEVELOPMENT

National development, as has been stated, is a process whereby the citizen begins to reconstruct the values placed on the nation in such a way as to enhance his chances of leading a more productive life and living happily in a more complex environment. For the comparative analysis of this process the political orientation of the arbitrator of development has been selected as the major variable. On the condition

[12] This viewpoint generally centers around analyses attaching very high value to the solidarity of the traditional community and casting some doubt on the value on external influences. See, for example, Robert Redfield, *The Primitive World and Its Transformation*, Ithaca, Cornell University Press, 1953, pp. 11-21.

[13] This exemplary study of the community in relationship to the outside world would bear repetition in developing countries. See O. A. Oeser and F. E. Emery, *Social Structure and Personality in a Rural Community*, New York, Macmillan, 1954.

that the locality not be predetermined as a concrete unit, it has been suggested the relationship between a government's effort to promote social change and the citizen's task of transforming his view of the nation might be local reform. The notion of local reform that has been advanced is not so much the manipulation of the environment in some localized setting, as the way in which the new citizen finds his concept of the nation transformed as he tries to reconcile his views on politics and the nation with the various developmental programs.

Thus the developmental process depends heavily on the successful integration of the values governing the citizen's family, community, and nation. The problem could be more easily approached if there were more precise studies of the way in which this feat is accomplished in the more advanced societies. The available evidence is provocative if incomplete. Thus it has been found that ideology becomes a structuring factor in the electoral process of the United States, and that those who perceive political ideology unrelated to their life situation, i.e., the most pure ideologists, have considerable difficulty in deciding how to cast their vote.[14] Not unlike that of the nationalist fanatic in the developing country, their perception of government has become so purely a matter of national value that even to apply the value becomes a painful and difficult process. Other studies have demonstrated that although the American citizen professes uniformity in his assertion of national values, there is wide variation in the way in which these values are indeed attached to issues and problems in everyday life.[15] In Almond's words, the American "cuts authority down to his own size."[16] For the American political process this means that the distinction between locality and government virtually disappears, much to the distress of ideologically inclined groups in American politics. From the position of the citizen in a democratic society, it means that he himself is selecting the issues and problems to which political significance is to be attached and that he manifests remarkable flexibility in reconciling within his own pattern of values the activity of government and the many concerns of his daily life.

[14] In the opinion of this writer, one of the most serious deficiencies in our attempts to conceptualize non-Western political processes is that so little is known of the political behavior and attitudes composing the relatively effective, advanced systems. One of the richest available sources is the voting studies, of which the last, *The American Voter*, Angus Campbell, et al., New York, Wiley, 1960, contains, especially chapters 9 and 10, some extremely imaginative and suggestive accounts of how the voting process is perceived in the United States.

[15] James M. Prothro and Charles M. Grigg, "Fundamental Principles of Democracy: Bases of Agreement and Disagreement," *Journal of Politics*, vol. 22, 1960, pp. 276-295. Using a very different method, the writer made similar conclusions on the consensual process in Morocco. See "Patterns of Consensus in Developing Countries," *American Behavioral Scientist*, vols. 4, 1961, pp. 7-10.

[16] *The American People and Foreign Policy*, New York, Harcourt, Brace, 1951, p. 51.

The unusual skill with which the citizen of the advanced nation moves from one frame of reference to another when dealing with political problems represents a high degree of attitudinal integration. His values are not insulated from one another nor from the environment in which they operate. This is a familiar problem to the psychologist, whose early inquiries into authoritarian personality have provided ample evidence of the perceptual rigidity and cognitive distortion characterizing the person with fixed values.[17] More recently clinical studies have focused on the manner in which individuals do reconcile conflicting values and, most important in the developmental process, the way persons "re-examine previously terminal values with regard to their instrumental implications for other values."[18]

Although clinical studies are only beginning to explore the psychological functions of conceptual systems, it is increasingly evident that our more general notions about the nation and the world do more than help to organize a complex body of information. Efficiency and flexibility of learning is, of course, an important benefit derived from the acquisition of more complex ideas. The person who can deal with remote frameworks of action or act in reference to processes and procedures that he himself cannot manipulate is better suited for modern life. To perform such acts he needs concepts which "serve the critical cognitive function of providing a system of ordering by means of which the environment is broken down and organized, is differentiated and integrated, into its many relevant psychological facets."[19] The process of national development will supply such concepts if the government hopes to create flexible citizens. In fact, it appears that the person who fails to acquire the mental constructs with which to make his environment intelligible and rewarding is less productive and more discontented. He tends to regard stimuli in a categorical way, cannot exercise his own judgment, and attributes an excessively dichotomous quality to the external world. The person prepared to take an active role in na-

[17] See T. W. Adorno, et al., *The Authoritarian Personality*, New York, Harper, 1950. Also, Sidney Pally, "Cognitive Rigidity as a Function of Threat," *Journal of Personality*, vol. 23, 1955, pp. 346-355, and Milton Rokeach, "Generalized Mental Rigidity as a Factor in Ethnocentrism," *Journal of Abnormal and Social Psychology*, vol. 43, 1948, pp. 259-278. For some political interpretations, see Morris Janowitz and Duane Marvick, "Authoritarianism and Political Behavior," *Public Opinion Quarterly*, vol. 17, 1953, pp. 195-201, and Charles D. Farris, "Selected Attitudes on Foreign Affairs as Correlates of Authoritarianism and Political Anomie," *Journal of Politics*, vol. 22, 1960, pp. 50-67.

[18] Milton J. Rosenberg, et al., *Attitude Organization and Change: An Analysis of Consistency Among Attitude Components*, New Haven, Yale University Press, 1960, p. 34. This study and Leon Festinger's *A Theory of Cognitive Dissonance*, Evanston, Row Peterson, 1957, are two rich sources of empirical findings concerning the impact of affective feelings or beliefs on perception and attitude formation.

[19] O. J. Harvey, et al., *Conceptual Systems and Personality Organization*, New York, Wiley, 1961, p. 4.

tional development needs to understand the relative character of many problems and to be aware of the multiplicity of alternatives in most policy-making situations.

The problems of learning under strain are quite well known, and have direct relevance to national development. It is clear, first, that "events which do not seem to have any relationship to self are likely to be ignored." Furthermore, it also seems clear that mental rigidity is "a concomitant of the individual's experience of threat and shows itself in decreased efficiency on intellectual tasks, an intolerance of ambiguous situations, and an inability to 'shift gears' appropriately in moving from one situation to another."[20] The person who is preoccupied with self-defense cannot adapt to change so readily as the person who is confident that change is desirable. The rigid person will tend to take refuge in reactionary associations and authoritarian institutions to spare himself the psychological stress of adaptation. While he can be approached only by driving a wedge into the perceptual world in which he lives, an adjustment ultimately requires a reconciliation with the more intricate pattern of relationships demanded by change. Such a contact can be made only at the local level, and is perhaps the most important reason why this study will be especially concerned with change through local reform.

Although the nationalist movements have helped to create national values, serious questions can be raised as to the suitability of such value systems to the more complex process of development. Indeed, it is quite possible that extreme nationalism may create intolerable situations for those most able to assist, while doing little to give a more elaborate, flexible set of values to those unfamiliar with the national context. Thus it is perhaps indicative of the dilemmas of modernization that Egyptian civil servants have tended to take ambivalent positions on treating their country's problems, although they have very definite notions as to the source of the country's problems. Their judgments concerning Egyptian affairs expressed considerable agreement on whom to blame, but they did not attach meaningful courses of action to such agreements.[21] It is not enough to acquire the external signs of modernity without also acquiring the confidence and desire to express one's ideas and to apply one's learning. The highly affective orientation to national affairs generated in many new nations paralyzes individual adaptation and inhibits participation.

The discussion of attitudinal change is not in the more familiar motivational terms, but in terms of cognitive psychology. Although the

[20] Arthur W. Coombs and Donald Snygg, *Individual Behavior: A Perceptual Approach to Behavior*, rev. edn., New York, Harper, 1959, pp. 148 and 195.
[21] Patricia L. Kendall, "The Ambivalent Character of Nationalism Among Egyptian Professionals," *Public Opinion Quarterly*, vol. 20, no. 1, Spring 1956, pp. 277-292.

properly motivated individual will clearly contribute to development,[22] the approach is difficult to relate to existing conditions in Africa and Asia. There are undoubtedly common attitudinal and ideological characteristics among individuals who have acquired achievement motives, but we also need to know how such motives relate to the political values being offered new citizens and how the diverse programs for changing environments in developing programs may converge in different social patterns to create such individuals. A cognitive approach may also provide us with some leverage on the difficult problem of consensus formation as the political system itself adapts, or fails to adapt, to the individual change it has promoted.

Perhaps the best illustration of the application of cognition theory in political studies is the Almond-Verba book, which describes the feelings and the knowledge of governmental processes in five democracies.[23] Although the study does not go so far as one might wish in devising indices of change in attitudinal structure, there is dramatic evidence on how varied views on politics may be in comparable institutional settings. Moreover, the book collects important data in terms of affective and cognitive aspects of political perception. One of the most revealing findings is the close identification and pride the Mexican feels for his government, although he has little confidence that the nation will change his life or that administrative channels are capable of handling his immediate problems. This pioneering work has certainly pointed the way toward further comparative studies of attitudinal change in developing countries.

The underlying assumptions of the theory of attitudinal change are by no means unfamiliar, nor do they alone provide the basis for radical changes in general knowledge of the way in which individuals adapt to change in their social and physical environment. The particular attraction of the affective-cognitive formulation is that it enables us to trace the relationship of new values and behavior in individual perception, while also following the effects of increased learning and skill that are equally a part of the developmental process. In terms of national development the intriguing problem is the way the injection of demanding loyalties and powerful values from the nation will relate to the individual's capacity not only to relate new knowledge of his environment to his everyday life—a critical component of successful change—but also the way the growing range and diversity of his cognitive skills will

[22] The most ambitious attempt to devise a single motivational index is, of course, David C. McClelland, *The Achieving Society*, Princeton, Van Nostrand, 1961. See also the short presentation of his findings, McClelland, "The School and Social Development," in Hobert W. Burns, ed., *Education and the Development of Nations*, Syracuse, Syracuse University Press, 1963, pp. 60-78; and the response by Robert Jacobs, *ibid.*, pp. 79-82.

[23] Almond and Verba, *Civic Culture, op.cit.*

relate to his expression and participation in the political system. In brief, the countries intent on rapid social revolutions have inverted the development process of European nations, where political institutions gradually evolved over a century or more of development. The citizen in the new nation is being asked to change his values first, and learn about his environment later.

A more systematic inquiry into the attitudinal components of national integration would require more careful delimitation of the frameworks of perception and the intensity of the forces affecting these frameworks. This study can touch on only two such backdrops for individual involvement in the developmental processes: the community and the nation. The problem has been further simplified by dwelling mainly on the impact of the nation on the locality, because the major efforts to modify environments at the local level will certainly be undertaken by government. This is not to suggest that there are not numerous differences in local-structures power and individual capacities to work in the remote framework of national government. Such studies are essential in dealing with specific communities, and may reveal highly useful qualities in the local political and social life relevant to national efforts.[24] However, research has tended to neglect the full range of interaction which the villager must eventually understand, and it is for this reason that we shall be primarily concerned with the way in which the actions of the national government relate to the citizen.

With no intent to neglect more ambitious schemes of assessing the power variable in development, the readily available evidence on the way a country goes about national reconstruction is relatively easy to accumulate and to interpret. First, does the government demonstrate conceptual skill in formulating the development problem, and does it, in turn, bring the best of its skills and effort to bear on such analyses? The first step is certainly the realization that change cannot be segmented, either in governmental efforts to sponsor change or in the villager's mind. Once the concept of broad development is communicated, the next indicator is evidence of sustained, planned action. Where changes must be carefully phased or where the preferable sequence of development is known, one can derive some indications of the seriousness of the government's intentions. Third, and more controversial, is whether the country anticipates the modernizing citizen's growing capacity to participate in various facets of development. Pro-

---

[24] It should be noted that the national framework is taken to include international forces that may also reach the village level. Some of the attitudinal repercussions of international phenomena on the villager will be discussed in the concluding section dealing with attitudinal change under conditions of rapid development. A highly suggestive study of some of the similarities of life in international and local environment is Roger D. Master, "World Politics as a Primitive Political System," *World Politics*, vol. 16, July 1964, pp. 595-619.

grams to mobilize popular energies and interests must be sustained. Once interpersonal contact is understood at more remote levels of activity, the gains must be consolidated by reinforcing actions, both social and psychological. Probably the most difficult decision to make, if indeed it can be made explicitly, is to proceed with the diffusion of power and the delegation of responsibility that characterize many aspects of productive, flexible social systems. Despite the similarities of advanced nations, the fact that no two have achieved their level of development in the same way may be a hopeful sign to those undergoing national reconstruction. These considerations will enter into the first portion of the book as the efforts at local government reorganization in each country are described.

The second factor, the impact of developmental programs at the local level, is one which is discussed in voluminous literature on technical assistance and foreign aid programs. Most of this literature is useless to the social scientist because he cannot relate it directly to social change. Part of the purpose of this study is to suggest the relevance of this literature, most easily formulated in comparative terms in its cumulative impact on the citizen's attitudes toward government and other remote agencies of national reconstruction. All the modifications of the village environment, from straight-line furrows to smallpox inoculations, relate to the changing attitudes of the peasant. There are no easy methods for interrelating the bewildering changes perceived in the village,[25] but the direction of change is obvious and the failure of efforts to introduce change in piecemeal fashion is the subject of increasing agreement, by both social scientists and technicians in the field. What we know much less about, in part because many of the governmental agencies of change are segmented administratively, is how well the government interrelates these programs.

A serious planning effort does not guarantee a successful national reconstruction. The expansion of primary education does not mean that farming techniques will be improved, nor do birth-control efforts necessarily stem the flow of rural unemployed to the cities. If we are to deal intelligently with the complexities of the social revolutions in Africa and Asia, much better methods must be devised to indicate the interdependence of developmental programs. The next section of the book does not succeed in advancing the methodology, but it is hoped that it suggests how a variety of research might assess the way in which gov-

[25] There have been several notable attempts to devise cross-national indices of development. See, for example, James Coleman, *Politics of the Developing Areas, op.cit.*, pp. 532-576; Lyle W. Shannon, ed., *Underdeveloped Areas: A Book of Readings and Research*, Harper, 1957, pp. 445-476; Phillips Cutwright, "National Political Development," *op.cit.*; and Karl W. Deutsch, "Social Mobilization and Political Development," *American Political Science Review*, vol. 55, 1961, pp. 493-514.

ernment acquires significance at the local level. The immediate aim is only to arrive at a rough estimate of how well the three governmental systems anticipated the problems of dealing with a more complex society by judging the character of various programs to modernize the rural segment of the populace. One of the encouraging results of the inquiry was the extent to which each government's approach to a wide variety of developmental programs encounters problems similar to their difficulties in reorganizing local government.

Establishing the interdependence of the specific attempts at nation-building in agriculture, education, local administration, et cetera, and a nation's political orientation is indeed an immensely complicated task. This study will succeed in the mind of the author if it does no more than raise the problem of critically evaluating not only the immediate benefits of national reconstruction efforts, but also the structural qualities of development. The complexity is twofold, because investigations hoping to anticipate political development must deal not only with success in specific areas of endeavor, but with the interrelationship of success and failure in the mind of the citizen as he is thrust into a new environment. The author feels that there are opportunities for assessing individuals' response to change over time by learning more about the perception of political affairs in the new national context, both as it has direct impact in local reorganization and indirect impact in a variety of developmental schemes. The relevance of attitudinal change in studying the integration of national, regional, and local developmental efforts will be discussed in the final section of the book. The structure of the book is to some extent dictated by the author's desire to force the reader to recognize the severe discontinuities, and the importance of space and time dimensions in modernization as perceived by the individual citizen. Each government's political orientation toward the locality is presented first; comparisons of multiple efforts to change the local environment next; and, finally, the interrelationship of the emergent forms of participation and the nation-building programs is analyzed as a problem of attitudinal change.

SECTION II:

NATIONAL POLITICS AND
LOCALIZED AUTHORITY

"Modernization implies not only the development of these various indices of social mobilization and of growing structural differentiations, but also the development of a social, economic, or political system which not only generates continuous change, but unlike many other types of social and political systems, is capable of absorbing changes beyond its own initial institutional premises."[1]

A critical step in creating new attitudes toward development is to convince the villager that political life beyond the local setting is related to his everyday concerns. The symbolic meaning of the new nation is easily communicated simply because it can be accepted without making major changes in traditional patterns of living. Self-sustained, adaptive behavior, essential to the developmental process, places new demands for versatility and exchange on the political system. Nowhere is this new dimension of national political life more in evidence than in the attempts to accommodate local government to the expanding role of government. In this section the effort to reorganize local government will be examined as it has taken place in a traditional regime, the Moroccan monarchy; an action-oriented regime, the Tunisian Socialist Destour; and a professionally oriented regime, the military-bureaucratic alliance of Pakistan.

In this section of the inquiry special attention will be given to attempts to communicate the meaning of a national political system to the locality. Though all states are treated as comparable units for diplomatic purposes, it has become clear that they vary greatly in their capacity to involve the citizen in national affairs, and to persuade him that events at the governmental level are relevant to life in the village. This section will deal largely with the affective component of more informed, diversified participation. The various local government schemes include, of course, both new behavior and the communication of new values. But the major obstacle to expanding the role of local government, and with it the role of the citizen, has been establishing confidence in the national political system.

Understanding and feeling are mixed in every psychological relationship, and it will be apparent that local government also includes some efforts to bring about new behavior as well as establish common ground

[1] S. N. Eisenstadt, *Modernization: Growth and Diversity*, Bloomington, Indiana University, Department of Government, 1963, p. 5.

for a new identification with government. It is one of the main purposes of this inquiry to indicate that these two efforts are indeed inseparable, although the second section of the study deals at more length with the cognitive aspects of transforming the village and integrating the individual into a more productive society. Within the psychological framework of the study, then, these sections represent rough approximations of two forces converging on the individual in every developing country. His feelings about the nation are inextricably entwined with his understanding of his environment and his capacity to manipulate the forces in his environment. Differing political systems represent differing mixtures of these affective and cognitive components, faith and understanding. Although the final purpose of the study will be to clarify how we might assess the convergence of these elements in the human being, the preliminary step is to compare how the three governments have sought to identify the citizen with the nation by communicating new political values through the local government.

CHAPTER 2

THE MOROCCAN COMMUNE: LIMITS OF FAITH

ALTHOUGH BOTH MOHAMMED V and the present king, Hasan II, have repeatedy endorsed major social and political reforms, the Moroccan government has achieved little in the way of fundamental change at the local level to hasten the developmental process. The most impressive concessions have been in the less controversial areas. Like most new countries Morocco began her reconstruction with great faith in industrialization. The entire range of political opinion, the Palace, the more conservative Istiqlal, and the progressive National Union, were able to agree on measures to attract investment and to hasten capital formation through the relatively simple devices of financial and monetary privileges and guarantees. For those who already had money, or for foreigners who found attractive openings, such measures were helpful and did contribute to Moroccan development in a restricted sense. However, these measures are of limited importance because they involved only small segments of an already urbanized, relatively advanced minority of Moroccans. The most important proposal for more widespread social reform was the organization of rural communes, which were to pave the way for a major social transformation. The communes have been set up, but the transformation has been very slow in getting under way.

The explanation for the procrastination and stagnation probably rests more squarely on the character of the political system in the Moroccan case than do the shortcomings of the developmental effort in the other two countries to be evaluated. Though certainly working within many of the limitations found throughout the non-Western world, Morocco was relatively well endowed with human and material resources at the time of independence. Under the Protectorate Morocco acquired an impressive infrastructure of roads, ports, and railways. An industrial complex was begun in Casablanca and nearby cities, and the mining industry had prospered over the past decade. Roughly a fifth of the school-age Muslims were in school, and the more advanced regions had secondary schools and basic technical schools. Moroccan per capita income was considerably over a hundred dollars a person, although disproportionately distributed.[1] Although the French had made sure their own nationals received many of the benefits of economic growth, there was a substantial commercial and industrial class of Moroccans.

[1] The Moroccan government has not done analyses of income distribution comparable to those made in the Tunisian Ten Year Plan. The best available study is the United Nations document, *Structure and Growth of Selected African Economies*, New York, 1958.

Compared to many of the new nations, Morocco was quite well off in 1956, and to some extent has been living off early achievements under French tutelage.

The traditional orientation of the Moroccan political system has not been conducive to impartial rule or effective government. Both economically and politically Morocco was probably ready to enter a phase of "competitive" activity[2] at the time of independence. The historic nationalist movement, the Istiqlal, had organized about half the country, but with varying degrees of thoroughness.[3] There were many nationalist militants prepared to step into positions of responsibility, and a large number of experienced political leaders. These men had led the Istiqlal and its predecessor organizations since the early 1930's, and since World War II had received the active support of the late Mohammed V. Both the monarch and the nationalists developed their political skills in the postwar period. When independence was finally won in early 1956, the king returned triumphantly from exile and assumed his role as absolute monarch.

There are two major sources of the monarch's traditional influence. He is, first, *imam* or spiritual leader of his people. Even less orthodox varieties of Islam recognize his primacy spiritually, and many tribal peoples attribute magical powers to him.[4] Neither Mohammed V or Hassan II have supported measures that might compromise their religious influence. Indeed, recently the monarchy has been associated more intimately with tribal festivals that once were regarded as somewhat heretical by religious reformers and were used by the French to rally tribal support against the nationalists. Islamic ceremonies and rituals involving the *imam* are given much publicity, and are often public holidays. Secondly, the king is the supreme official of the *maghzen* or royal palace and associated agencies and representatives throughout the land. Through this device the late king kept personal control of the army, police, and rural administration. The premier was only the first among equals in the cabinet, whom the king pronounced "individually and collectively" responsible to him. Despite a royal charter issued in

---

[2] Unfortunately the concept of "competitiveness" has not been developed beyond the highly suggestive essay of James S. Coleman in *The Politics of the Developing Areas*, Almond and Coleman, eds., Princeton, Princeton University Press, 1960. Certainly there are other measures of competitive relationships than the economic.

[3] For an analysis of the social base of the Istiqlal see the author's *Political Change in Morocco*, Princeton, Princeton University Press, 1961, pp. 243-259. The preindependence Istiqlal is analyzed in Robert Rezette's *Les Partis Politiques Marocaines*, Paris, Colin, 1955.

[4] See Jean and Simonne Lacouture, *Le Maroc à l'Epreuve*, Paris, Editions du Seuil, 1958, an example of how the keen observer can often surpass the specialist in conveying subtle relationships. Also, see Roger Le Tourneau, *Evolution Politique de l'Afrique du Nord Musulmane 1920-1961*, Paris, Colin, 1962, for historical background.

1958 by Mohammed V and the creation of a constitutional monarchy in 1962, the role of the Palace remained unchanged and gained power relative to other potential competitors, who began to fall into factional disputes.

There is little doubt but that both conservative, old guard leaders of the Istiqlal as well as the younger, more progressive party officials were surprised by the "government by dialogue" which developed after 1956. Often the dialogue was so prolonged that the issue lost its significance or was forgotten. Many times there were so many voices to be heard and so many viewpoints to be considered that nothing was done. Even the conservative Balafrej was driven to request the "necessary means to govern" when he became premier in 1958.[5] But the impatience of the reformist leaders, strongly backed by the unions, was vented on their party rather than on the monarchy. In early 1959 the more aggressive modernizers broke off from the Istiqlal and formed the National Union of Popular Forces.[6] A tribally based party, the Popular Movement, also emerged around leaders loyal to the monarchy and entered a shaky coalition with a royalist group in 1963. The division of political forces in the advanced regions of the country and the revival of some traditional political patterns focusing on the Palace has served to postpone institutional reform on both the national and the local level.

While this inquiry is not concerned with placing responsibility for the failure to exploit opportunities fully, it is directed toward an assessment of the suitability of the three political systems as the central vehicles of change. In the Moroccan case it is evident that the growing suspicion between the Palace and other political forces contributed to an increasingly serious stalemate in government. The monarch was reluctant to enact reforms that might compromise his authority or detract from his religious prestige. To some extent there developed a classical case of resistance to secularization on the part of a figure exercising some charismatic influence.[7] Even though local reform was advocated by the king, it could not proceed without initiating locally based institutions that would indirectly, and perhaps eventually more directly, detract from the central government's powers, which remain concentrated in the Palace. The development of the rural communes is probably the most revealing as a display of the dilemmas of a traditionally oriented political system undergoing transformation.

[5] *Le Monde*, October 21, 1958.

[6] *Political Change in Morocco, op.cit.*, pp. 334-343.

[7] The notion of conflicting requisites for the exercise of charismatic influence in a modern setting is obviously taken in part from Weber. The problem has received special attention in relation to economic development from Edward A. Shils, "The Concentration and Dispersion of Charisma," *World Politics*, vol. 11, 1958, pp. 1-19.

POLITICS AND LOCALIZED AUTHORITY

DILEMMAS OF COLONIAL LOCAL REFORM

The Moroccan experience in reorganizing local communities is particularly significant given the abuse of local reform under the French Protectorate. The nationalists had received their first impulse from resentment created by French attempts to divide the rural and generally tribal populace from the more advanced regions of the country.[8] The king had found himself cut off from the remote countryside by the French administration, which used the tribal councils and other devices to threaten the monarch and the nationalists. The French efforts to advance the less privileged to a point where they could more effectively counteract the influence of the advanced areas would be more easily excused if it had not become increasingly clear that the French ultimately intended to use the "assimilated" areas against Moroccans of the advanced areas. Steps were taken to exclude Islamic influences and to magnify ethnic differences. There were undoubtedly many sincere and well-intentioned persons associated with the effort to improve the Berber areas, especially after World War II, but the program became a tool of a corrupt and irresponsible colonial administration in the last years of the Protectorate.

From the beginning of the Protectorate the French were concerned with cultivating the tribal councils as instruments of rural administration. Marshal Lyautey greatly admired many facets of Moroccan civilization and took steps to preserve and record its history. He recognized the tribal *jemaâ* or council as a critical element of Moroccan tribal life, and, like Lugard in Nigeria, studied its possible relationship to colonial administration. The first law recognizing the tribal councils dates from 1914, and in 1915 a Committee on Berber Studies was founded. From the beginning the potential political use of the tribal institutions did not escape French officials. A report of 1914 notes the importance of avoiding "Islamicizing, Arabizing the Berbers" and considers it "necessary that they evolve toward a basically European culture, and not a purely Muslim culture."[9]

In fact, the Protectorate was so busy pacifying tribal uprisings against their rule that little more could be done with the councils until the early 1930's. The first concern of the Protectorate was to survive, and to this

---

[8] The attempt centered around the "Berber *dahir*" of 1930, which established the customary tribal courts in the remote areas independent of the Muslim court system in the coastal areas. The move was accompanied by more intensive efforts to proselytize among the Berbers and to cut them off from Arabic. Many Protectorate officials lamented this arbitrary abuse of Moroccan institutions, but the French still retained a certain affection for the *l'homme brave* of the Atlas mountains.

[9] Quoted from the "Rapport sur la situation du Protectorate au 31 juillet 1914," Service de la Résidence Générale, 1914, in Alain Plantey, *La Réforme de la Justice Marocaine*, Paris, Librairie Générale de Droit et de Jurisprudence, 1952, p. 197.

end the rural administration, partly civilian and partly military, appears to have undermined the councils. In restoring peace and order *caids* or Palace representatives were placed throughout the countryside to collect taxes, keep order, and perform minimal civic functions. Although the *caids* had functioned as royal delegates for centuries, they were made part of a modern bureaucracy extending throughout the realm. The representatives of central authority, both French and monarchial, inescapably clashed with tribal views. Indeed, some authorities on the Protectorace feel that the French lost an important opportunity to institutionalize a divided Morocco. One exasperated colonialist student of the epoch writes, "From concern with efficiency, by lack of imagination, by reducing ancient democratic institutions to the level of village *palabres*, and by installing tribal chiefs whose docility compensated poorly for their faults, the French administration perhaps destroyed one of the best chances of an effective Berber policy."[10]

The French dilemma was, therefore, twofold. The first requirement of an effective colonial administration was in effect not too different from that of the newly independent country. Law and order had to be maintained. To do this the Protectorate devised a system of rural administration based on the pattern of the old *maghzen*, and extended it to the entire country—something which the Moroccan monarch had seldom been able to do before 1912. As often happens in colonial empires, the French sowed the seeds of their own destruction; they did this by creating the rural administrative framework on which the emergent nation would rest. The crucial difference is that the nation would presumably be able to avoid the second obstacle, on which the Protectorate inescapably stumbled. Many of the tribal groups did not wish to be controlled by any kind of central government. No matter how sincere the French might be in their designs to protect tribal life, these designs could not be communicated persuasively to a retarded people. French reforms made it easier for Moroccan nationalists to exploit tribal tensions and to persuade fiercely independent tribal leaders of the advantages of national unity and independence.[11]

Had the French embarked on an energetic program to adapt the Berbers to modern conditions at this time, they might have succeeded in dividing the country. But their policy became more and more one of "de-Islamization,"[12] coupled with the policy of the "great *caids*" or sheer tribal manipulation. Both the attempted cultural penetration and the crude power play with tribal lords such as Al-Glaoui in the south

[10] *Ibid.*, pp. 199-200. For a more detached view of the Protectorate administration see Frédéric Brémard, *L'Organisation Régionale du Maroc*, Paris, Librairie Générale de Droit et de Jurisprudence, 1949, especially pp. 302-321 on the *jemaâ*.

[11] Plantey, *op.cit.*, p. 209.

[12] Discussed in Charles-André Julien, *L'Afrique du Nord en Marche*, Paris, Julliard, 1952, pp. 142-147.

discredited French aims and, more important, provided fuel for the growing nationalist movement. The full exposure of French intent was the famous Berber *dahir* (law) of 1930, which was aimed at the eventual division of the country between Muslim and Western law. Nothing could have more thoroughly alarmed the young nationalists or more openly exposed the Protectorate's interest in using local reform for divisive purposes. Officials who later sought to revive the councils on the eve of independence admit that nothing was accomplished after the early 1930's, although a law was passed in 1937 giving them some responsibility for collective property other than land. One French officer wrote that their "sole role has been to furnish the authorities with opinions that one no longer asks of them."[13]

Only once during the Protectorate was there an opportunity for coordinated, massive social reorganization. With the liberal government in France after World War II, more farsighted officials were appointed to many colonies. One of these men, Eric Labonne, was resident general from March 1946 to May 1947. His program of reforms ranged from a reorganization of the *maghzen* to the beginnings of agrarian reform. However, by 1947 vigorous opposition was forthcoming not only from the reactionary French *colon* group, but also from the nationalists, who were unable to imagine serious reform under French auspices. Labonne was aided by a small group of liberal intellectuals, among them Jacques Berque, Julien Couleau, and Marc Bloch.[14] Berque's views strongly influenced postwar plans for revival of the *jemaâs* and for agrarian modernization, which will be discussed below.

The essentials of the law, finally passed in 1951, were contained in a circular to the rural administration in 1945 and 1948. The earlier circulars outlined a plan for the establishment of rural modernization centers, which were to concentrate on the Moroccan *fellahiin*. The second circular was even more ambitious and spoke of the need "to interest the rural masses in the management of local affairs" and "to create a harmonious equilibrium between local authority and collective representation."[15] These ideas never penetrated the Protectorate bureaucracy, and with the arrival of the oppressive resident general, Alphonse Juin, in 1947 there was no hope of widespread local reform. Conditions steadily deteriorated as the nationalist movement grew. One

---

[13] Capt. Jacques Romieu, *Les Jemmas depuis le dahir de 1951*, Rabat, Service des Affaires Indigenes, 1953, p. 2. This remarkable document is the commentary of a young, idealistic officer caught between his enthusiasm for the French empire and the abuses of the Protectorate administration. When his colleagues found themselves in a similar situation in Algeria nearly ten years later, they took matters into their own hands.

[14] These early efforts are discussed in Julien, *op.cit.*, pp. 356-358, and more recently in Jacques Berque, *Le Maghreb entre Deux Guerres*, Paris, Espirit, 1962, pp. 351-353, where he recalls his association with Labonne.

[15] Romieu, *op.cit.*, p. 4.

of the pieces of legislation over which the resident general and Moham-med V were deadlocked was local reform, and the late king's refusal to sign the *dahir* contributed to his enforced exile in 1953.

The 1951 law inspired considerable enthusiasm among some of the French officers and *controleurs civiles*, who worked close to the tribes and thought the tribal qualities of independence and resourcefulness could be converted to good use in a more modern setting. Thus it is possible to find an officer writing in 1953 that the reorganized tribal councils are the "keystone to the entire system destined to lead the country to internal autonomy on a democratic foundation."[16] In a strange way French efforts to divide the country became a perceptual block in their own evaluations of the country—a drama that was later to be repeated in Algeria. The remote, devoted young officer could speak in idealistic terms without taking into consideration the brutal suppression of the nationalists then underway.

Mohammed V consented to the reorganization of the tribal councils in July 1951, although he refused to agree to the establishment of mu-nicipal councils in the larger cities, where the French would dominate affairs as they did in the similar system used in Tunisia. The new law contained certain confusions concerning the council's role in applying customary law and also on their relation to the ancient *jemaâs* selected by tribal consent. But there were, nevertheless, important concessions, some of them more substantial than those contained in the Moroccan rural commune legislation after independence. The formation of the council and its size were decided by the central bureaucracy. The *caid* or local *sheikh* could sit as chairman.[17] Like the communes organized after independence, there was no realm of activity reserved to the coun-cils and all acts had to be submitted to the authorities. However, the 1951 law did permit the councils to plead cases in court, a privilege reserved to the municipal councils after independence. Later circulars on implementing the law provided for a centrally managed system of accounts and suggested that the president be someone capable of "ad-dressing himself against the *caidal* authority." Unfortunately, by the time the local reform was put into effect there were very few Moroccans outside prison who dared to challenge the Protectorate's authority in the new councils.

Where the councils were permitted to develop, however, there were still a few sympathetic officials, whose writings provide some idea of the initial concept of local reform in Morocco. Their writing stresses the need to demonstrate confidence in the councils, and tries to show how administrative tasks might be simplified with the councils' help. The importance of a real election is also noted, with the suggestion that it will be more effective if held in the familiar surroundings of the *souk*

---

[16] *Ibid.*, p. 5.   [17] *Ibid.*, pp. 8-10.

(market), rather than in the more austere setting of the official's bureau. The need to encourage respected villagers to take office and to restrain the police from embarrassing the council is also underlined. Acknowledging the uncertainty of the younger rural officials and the "bad habits" of the older ones, the writings reassure the administrator that his position will not be jeopardized.

By mid-1952 there were 507 of a planned 2,500 councils formed. The councils in operation included roughly half the rural population, but progress was admittedly slow because of lack of funds and the officials' preoccupation with more pressing duties. The councils were distributed by province as follows: Agadir, 75; Casablanca, 135; Rabat, 55; Oujda, 34; Fez, 63; Meknes, 125; and Marrakech, 20.[18] Although the Protectorate provided a grant of about $300 to each council, the shortage of local funds and the need to hire a secretary, if one could be found, meant that little more could be done than fill the minimal administrative obligations. Experienced local officials had little free time, especially once terrorist opposition was begun by the nationalists. By the mid-1950's the Istiqlal had made some inroads into the closely watched countryside, and the Protectorate began to sense that the tribes could no longer be so easily manipulated as before the war. Local French officials became convinced that "the controlling authorities do not believe in the *jemaâs*," and the question of local reform under the Protectorate became increasingly academic as the threat of rural uprisings increased on the eve of Moroccan independence.

There is little doubt but that the French hoped to use the local councils to buttress their claim that the nationalist movement was not sufficiently "national" to represent the country, and also that the Protectorate was making a substantial contribution to the country's modernization process. The racial aspect of the *jemaâs* probably increased as the French saw themselves excluded from the Arab world and defeated at Suez in the midst of the Algerian adventure. It is revealing that as late as 1952 a reputable French scholar should write that Berber social patterns were "more meaningful in relation to Western social forms than to Arab traditions."[19] Oblivious to the abuses and sheer disintegration of the Protectorate under *colon* infiltration of police and bu-

---

[18] *Ibid.*, p. 17. It should be noted that the provincial organization has changed twice since independence, while the Protectorate provinces were larger than anything used since then. The commune system was never implemented in the northern, Spanish zone.

[19] Plantey, *op.cit.*, p. 291. The parallel with the Kabylie in Algeria would be worth exploring. Although more directly exposed to modern life through labor migration to France, the tribal structures proved just as amenable to nationalist exploitation as to French, once loyalties were shifted. There is nothing about tribal structures per se that makes them essentially conservative, except that they are more easily manipulated if conservatives can manage to sustain their positions outside the tribe that make manipulation possible.

reaucracy, Metropolitan France clung to the unreal but highly logical concept of development suited to its political needs. The mixture of Arab and Berber for nearly a millennium was ignored, as was the penetration of Islam to nearly all tribal communities, even though sometimes adapted to the more precarious life of the tribesman.

Thus it did not seem incongruous to the best-intentioned Frenchman that Morocco would be divided in order that it might be integrated. The less advanced regions would be given their chance to "catch up" by being culturally isolated from the more advanced regions, including both Arabs and Arabized Berbers. Customary law and the French language would institutionalize the estrangement of the tribal areas, possibly followed with Christian proselytizing. That a colonial regime would hope to make such a profound break with the past after not being able to undertake even simple steps to relieve social and economic ills of one Moroccan generation is symptomatic of a declining regime that is rapidly losing contact with real issues. By the time independence negotiations began in mid-1955 the Protectorate was no longer able to hold the tribes in check. In the regions most often cited as strongholds of tribal custom, the Rif and the Middle Atlas, tribesmen rallied to the Liberation Army and joined in terrorist attacks on French settlers.[20]

More important for the Moroccan concept of local development, the Protectorate policy served to alarm the nationalists over the potential abuses of local activity without demonstrating its benefits. The independent government inherited a colonialist-inspired scheme in which Marrakech, for example, was almost totally ignored, to the advantage of Al-Glaoui's personal empire, despite the tribal groups suitable for such development in the south. The reluctance of the Moroccan government to assign more powers to the communes is very likely explained in part by apprehensions aroused by the nationalists' Protectorate experience. Postindependence procrastination in devising the rural commune plan, although fundamentally a problem of a defective decision-making procedure, was probably influenced by the feeling that all Moroccans should be included before any program could be started. Thus the Moroccans' caution in dealing with local reform was compounded by inherited French habits of centralized administration and their own difficulties in adapting the monarchy to the needs of effective national government.

There were also gains for the Moroccans compared to the other two plans to be discussed below. In Tunisia the notion of a nationally organized institution for local participation was never introduced, and the government has used the standard French system as adapted to the needs of the single-party system. The exclusion of the Tunisian coun-

[20] For the role of Moroccan tribesmen in the nationalist struggle see *Political Change in Morocco, op.cit.*, pp. 157-184.

cilors from political expression at any higher level of government has not been considered a deprivation by most citizens. More important from the developmental viewpoint, the broader interpretation of the local community or village as the framework for development projects and regional improvement has not caught on. Likewise, the highly varied pattern of local administration in British India has meant that a uniform plan geared to the requirements of national participation was slow to emerge. The developmental role of local councils was not clearly spelled out in Pakistan until after the 1958 revolution.

LOCAL REFORM AS A NATIONAL ISSUE

In all three countries local reform raised certain dilemmas for the existing political system. How each system responded to these problems and thereby revealed its views on the broader issues of massive development and political participation recommends the localized focus. Of the three systems, however, the Moroccans found themselves projected into the most profound examination of existing political institutions and values. The delicacy of local reform as a political issue is, in part, a function of the more traditional system based on an absolute monarchy. As will be outlined in later chapters, the monarchy encountered similar difficulties in dealing with other aspects of national reconstruction. In the traditional system the regime finds the character of political relationships altered, and possibly threatened, as power is diffused and individual capacities are developed. The explanation does not rest solely with the personality of traditional leaders, although those who acquire their authority through divine or customary channels are likely to be alarmed with the notion of sharing power or accepting controls. As achievement begins to outweigh ascribed moral superiority, the traditional figure finds his influence restricted and sometimes discredited.

The steps leading up to the rural-commune legislation in Morocco reveal one important advantage and one important disadvantage of the traditional system in the process of change. Both the royal charter of mid-1958, under Mohammed V, and the Fundamental Law of mid-1961, under Hassan II, were evidence of the growing pressure for institutional development, which was the product of the diverse political forces contesting the monarchial authority. Thus Morocco to some extent shared the benefits of traditional institutions, which Apter and others have suggested might play important roles in introducing modern institutional forms.[21] Fundamental institutional reform is, at least in the initial stages, facilitated by customary and religious allegiances that may serve to reduce the apprehensions aroused by introducing strange,

---

[21] The possible functional harmony of traditional elements in the process of modernization was analyzed in relation to Ghana in Apter's *Gold Coast in Transition*, Princeton, Princeton University Press, 1956.

less easily observed patterns of behavior. The rural-commune question, however, posed the issue of delegating power and guaranteeing fundamental rights more sharply than any other event in Moroccan development. The existence of the monarchy made these adjustments easier, while it raised certain problems for the monarchy.

The problems of the monarchy as an institution center on the difficulty of creating a specialized agency or a limited role for any traditional institution. The Moroccan monarchs saw fit to share their power, but they were not prepared to do so without careful preparation. The value of the reform was reduced by procrastination and precaution. By the time the historic institutions could adjust, social needs had already begun to outdistance the limited reform. The same problem existed for Bourguiba and the Tunisian political system in this period, but the reaction was very different where the government was based on a highly secularized single-party system.

Since independence the Moroccan monarch has found himself surrounded with parties, from whom most of the demands for local reform have come. The king was excluded from party activities by virtue of his office, although the Istiqlal continued to support the king without reservation until 1960. Nevertheless, opinion within the major nationalist party was divided even before the party split in early 1959. Younger, activist leaders of the Istiqlal realized that only major institutional reforms would enable them to play an effective role in government. They were not content with the vague promises of constitutional government which Mohammed V had made on his triumphal return to his country in November 1955. However, at the party congress the next month both the speeches and the motions emphasized the need to reform the rural administration more than to make plans for participation in local government. The speeches of the party elders phrased the local reform issue only in terms of administrative reorganization, and it is only in the speech of the younger leader, Bouabid, that a clear statement on locally elected bodies is found. Bouabid, who was to become one of the opposition leaders of the National Union Party in 1959, asked for the "creation of locally elected assembles with sufficient guarantees to assure free elections."[22]

The king was certainly aware of these claims, although the country was still preoccupied with the more pressing problems of organizing the essential services of an independent country and concluding negotiations with France. However, Mohammed V clearly stated his intentions, as did the leaders of the other two countries included in this comparison. In the Speech from the Throne the king spoke of "the creation of democratic institutions based on free elections," and when the first cabinet was installed in December 1955, he defined one of its goals as

[22] *Al-Istiqlal*, August 17, 1956.

laying "the foundations of a new regime which will enable the people to administer their own affairs by means of local assemblies and a parliament." Neither the king nor the party leaders appear to have had a well-defined concept of local reform, nor did they appear to understand the complexity of the task they set for themselves.

Over 1956 and 1957 competition between the monarchy and the nationalist party grew, especially after the Istiqlal saw that its predominance might be eclipsed by new parties of little import in the independence struggle. As the elder Istiqlal leaders worried about their past, the younger Istiqlal leaders, many of them now ministers, felt constrained and ineffective under monarchial supervision. The question of local reform became a central issue in the broader question of "separation of powers."[23] It is not surprising that questions so vital to the character of the political system also raised extremely delicate problems about the future of the monarchy. The Moroccan regime could not muster the kind of specific concentration produced in both the Tunisian and Pakistani systems. Institutional reform at the central level could not precede local concerns, as it did in the other two cases, nor could it become the product of local reform unless the traditional system was prepared to make substantial concessions. Indeed, none of the political forces in Morocco could begin to have constructive effect of a cumulative nature until changes in the regime took place. The king's good intentions could not overcome inertia and apprehension. As the Ministry of the Interior began to explore the questions of reforming the old jemaâ system, the king made his son first chief of staff of the royal army and later the hereditary prince of the dynasty.

The investigations of the Ministry of the Interior were jealously guarded from the other ministries, who might have eventual responsibilities in an expanding program of rural improvement, and from the politicians. Both Mohammed V and Hassan II have kept a strong hold on the Ministries of Defense, Justice, and Interior, where tribal affairs had been concentrated under the Protectorate. This did not keep younger Istiqlal leaders from advancing a more ambitious concept of local reform, which inescapably harmonized with their ambitions to limit the monarch's role. The articles on the rural commune which appeared in the Istiqlal party papers in early 1957 suggest the influence of Ben Barka, the energetic president of the Consultative National Assembly. The young progressives, chafing within the conservative Istiqlal, saw the rural commune as the "cell for the complete evolution of the country," a notion that was hardly shared by their elders within

[23] The Moroccan speaks of *separation des pouvoirs* in at least three senses: the reorganization of the courts, the provinces, and the monarchy. More recently the issue of who should control the police and royal army has also been discussed under this general heading, which is indeed a tribute to French cultural penetration.

or outside the party. The young leaders conceived of the commune as part of a representative system of government, rather like the original concept of Basic Democracies in Pakistan. They were clearly impatient with the bureaucratic aspects of the commune system imposed by the French and with the tribal vestiges incorporated into many of the Protectorate's *jemaâs*.

The progressives' plan was based on the market town, which would incorporate ten to twenty villages (*douars* or *ksars*), much like the plan that finally emerged in 1959. However, the party officials had an overly optimistic view of the potential resources of the commune, in part because they based their estimates largely on the wealthier regions of Chaouia. There was a clear sequence of representation outside administrative channels. The commune would send representatives to the subprovincial level, and the intermediate bodies would contribute to a provincial council.[24] The unspoken but fairly clear implication was that the provincial assemblies would enlarge their representative functions to take on some kind of national significance. The progressives' proposition was just a bit too neat and orderly to be convincing. They clearly saw the need to reorient the local authorities of the Ministry of the Interior to developmental needs, and even suggested that their titles be changed to suggest a clean break with the past. While recognizing the tribal limits on the social and economic development of the country, they did not have a clear idea how the communes, once rid of tribal vestiges, would take on broader welfare or developmental functions. They certainly overestimated the numbers of skilled technicians and advisers available to guide and assist the communes.

If the proposals revealed a degree of political opportunism, it should be remembered that the traditional system did not provide many attractive opportunities for politically ambitious men. Their ideas were certainly not revolutionary. The examples used in a subsequent Istiqlal series on the commune system in other countries included France, Yugoslavia, Turkey, and Greece. There was still the overlapping administrative and representative aspect of local self-government inherited from France, probably necessary in the developing country. The young Istiqlal officials were still too much under the spell of their French education to depart radically from the French model, and, given the restrictions of the Moroccan political system, a more revolu-

---

[24] There are two administrative levels of full-time officials between the provincial governor and the village: the *super-caid* (about 70) at the circle and then the *caid* (about 300), each responsible for perhaps twenty villages. Part-time administrative officials at the village level were usually paid from market taxes and appointed by the *caid*. The progressives were considering committees of elected representatives at the *caid* level, which is the working level for most villagers. The *super-caid* is occupied more with liaison with the other ministerial representatives in the area and with supervision of the *caids*, some of whom are of very poor quality.

tionary concept—along Pakistani lines, for example—would be highly suspect to more conservative ears. Even the relatively cautious views exposed in the party paper produced letters to the editor warning against burdening the initial communes with duties at higher levels and advising a reduced role for the provincial body. Even so, the more radical politicians continued to speak of the communes as the "driving element in the total transformation of the country." Despite the short-comings of their plan, they had clearly grasped the need to integrate local reform with national political life and to engage the country in a social transformation in harmony with the more complex political system needed in a widespread developmental effort. The ability and desire to propose such renovations is very likely an essential prerequisite to the rapid development of any retarded country.

Once the existence of the new nation was assured by its international recognition, the question of internal reform lost some of its urgency. It became apparent that the country could exist without radical internal reorganization, and that many of the Protectorate devices for control and exploitation worked quite well in the setting of independence. With this trend the opposed views on local reform were examined and elaborated in a broader perspective. With none of the systematic, concentrated effort of the Tunisian or Pakistani regimes, the Moroccans began to realize how difficult it would be to mobilize their country for a major modernization effort. The psychological obstacles received more attention as old social patterns of peasant and tribesman reasserted their self-sufficiency and isolation from the modern segments of Morocco. An F.A.O. mission early in 1957 raised the broad issue very clearly when its leader noted "the necessity that the *fellah* (peasant) actively participate in economic improvement by realizing that his interest and the national interest coincide. If he remains indifferent the success will be very limited no matter what governmental effort, technical assistance or external aid is applied."[25] The social aspect of local reform did not receive attention again until nearly the end of 1957, when Thami Ammar, who was to be Minister of Agriculture when the progressives took control of the cabinet in 1959, wrote on the need for a rural mobilization. As a provincial agricultural inspector he saw the possible benefits of public-works projects designed to engage the peasants in cooperative effort for the improvement of their lands and crops.

But interest in the commune as a developmental structure was overshadowed with increased party competition and new promises of elections from the king. Speaking before the Casablanca workers on May Day 1957, Mohammed V announced that elections would be held on a communal basis by the end of the year. However, the king unfortunately was raising false hopes because the preparations proved much

[25] *Al-Istiqlal,* March 30, 1957.

more difficult than his advisers had anticipated. Nevertheless, the political aspect of the communes immediately took on great importance, which grew as the Istiqlal found itself confronted with a rurally based party late in 1957, the Popular Movement. The resultant conflict within the monarchial regime is worth stressing, for it contributed to continued procrastination in organizing the local bodies.

The parties could not be made more responsible or more confident of the future without giving them major concessions in the operation of the government. If the king were to do this in the absence of even rudimentary local government, he would be virtually abdicating his throne, and would risk shattering the traditional framework of control that centered on the monarchy. Simultaneously, as the parties saw the elections from intensely partisan positions, the communes became less suitable as the vehicle for a meaningful reorientation of local life and a moderate presentation of the problems of government to the isolated segments of the population. An atmosphere of incrimination and bitterness overcame the capital, while the villages and tribes were neglected. The full measure of the loss in terms of Morocco's over-all development will be analyzed in later chapters dealing with specific aspects of national and local reform.

The effect of this treatment of the local-reform problem, still hardly conceived of as a "problem" in the Moroccan mind in 1958, was to politicize the transitional process. All attention was placed on elections, and elections were dominated by centrally located parties having only fragmentary roots in the countryside. The issue was politicized in terms of the existing pattern of political relationships, which was not oriented to change or very effective outside the urban setting where parties were known well. In relation to the integration of her highly differentiated social structure it is possible to argue that Morocco lost ground. Parties were not compelled to focus their attention on the isolated citizen of the *douar*, and the king was understandably reluctant to compromise his traditional appeal. If "politicized" is taken to mean involvement in national affairs, both socially and psychologically, the Moroccan experience seems very clearly one that would underscore a feeling of isolation from politics in the national sense, and confirm opinions that the breach between the political life of the Moroccan substrata and the privileged moderns could not be filled.

The most dramatic evidence of how the issue suffered as a result of interparty squabbling is the Istiqlal's comment on local reorganization, once it was no longer in the cabinet and, thereby, without direct representation in the decision-making apparatus. When the party split in January 1959, the king decided to form a cabinet using the more progressive leaders, now associated with the National Union of Popular

Forces.[26] Ibrahim was asked to become premier and to prepare for the long-promised elections. Suddenly village elections and rural reform became vitally important to the excluded Istiqlal, who protested placing such momentous programs in the hands of an opposition group. In the intensely emotional bickering of the past two years the Istiqlal had seldom voiced such a concern for the minority groups it had excluded from power, although the party paper could fervently claim that "it had never ceased to denounce delay" in organizing rural communes.

Perhaps for the first time the Istiqlal old guard realized that the nation could continue without them, and this realization had the natural effect of making them seek to reestablish the party's preeminence in local political life. The party's historic leader, Allal al-Fassi, who for the past three years had seldom had a word for anything but recovering Mauritania, began stressing the need for local reform. His early statements were more vague than the ambitious proposals of Ben Barka in 1957. Al-Fassi called for local and regional institutions "conforming to the natural and social conditions of the countryside" and enabling participation in "economic and social affairs."[27] Although the forces converging to make the issue of constitutional monarchy central to Moroccan politics will be analyzed in a later chapter, the shift in Istiqlal interest to the monarchy and the communes in 1959 is telling evidence of the way in which the political system interlocks with the developmental process in a traditional setting. The elder leaders had been willing, and possibly relieved, to sacrifice nationalist unity rather than accommodate the radical group in their ranks. But they remained steadfastly devoted to the monarchy, even though their inaction in the face of pressing developmental problems—partly due to the king's equivocation—might hurt the party much more than a reluctant monarch.

As the old guard Istiqlal saw the party going into decline as a result of the stagnation of the early years of independence, they also saw how the traditional influence of the Palace could prevail while they were isolated. Some of the party elders felt they were being abandoned by Mohammed V, whose reputation had in part been built by the Istiqlal. But the clash of leadership is not so pertinent to present considerations as the way in which the party was the victim of a more complex pattern of political relationships connected with the transformation of the country as a whole. Thus the party could only defend its reservations on the organization of the rural communes by itself raising the delicate questions concerning the regime in its entirety. Its claims to direct voice

[26] The U.N.F.P. (*Union Nationale des Forces Populaires*) was formally initiated in September 1959, about nine months after the progressive faction broke from the Istiqlal to form what they called the "Democratic Istiqlal." The name indicated their dissatisfaction with the old party; but once the rudiments of a local organization were laid, a name more appropriate to the party's appeal was selected.

[27] *Al-Istiqlal*, May 9, 1959.

in the planning of the communes—a process which it had done little to assist during two years in office—partially repudiated the monarchial framework. Indeed, the Istiqlal had once regarded the tribal councils as potentially heretical institutions. They now wrote that the *jemaâs* were established in "traditions of the Moroccan people who have confided the management of local affairs to elected councils for centuries."[28]

By the elections in May 1960 the Istiqlal had adopted as enthusiastic an outlook on local reform as the progressives, now excluded from the government, had proposed three years earlier. As the elections approached, the bitter exchanges within the limited and intense world of the parties led the king to take charge of his cabinet for the first time. The elder nationalists could now endorse the commune as the "instrument to raise the standards of living and basic education . . . to select local projects and to organize citizens for collective work . . . , and to manage local affairs and vote the budgets."[29] Their support represented a dramatic shift in policy, and implied an entirely new approach to the development of Moroccan society. Possibly they themselves did not immediately realize the full implication of their commitment to a new regime, although their increasingly outspoken statements on the need for a constitutional monarchy over the following two years demonstrate the inescapable pressures for adjustment to developmental requirements.

ORGANIZING LOCAL AUTHORITIES

While the parties were trying to orient themselves in the elusive but changing pattern of Moroccan internal affairs, the government went forward with its plans for the communes. Like Tunisia, Morocco has a highly centralized administration, and one which is still run much the same as in the Protectorate. Responsibility for law and order in the countryside rests with the Ministry of the Interior. Although the king's directions to the ministry made it very clear that the new communes were to be economically viable and independent of tribal considerations except as they coincided with other requirements of communication and transportation, there was very little consideration as to how the broad concept of the commune as a reform agency would mesh with the plans and operations of the other ministries. While local reform was also isolated from developmental planning in the Tunisian government, the single-party system was able to overcome ministerial rivalries more easily than was Morocco. But the Moroccan communal organization rested almost wholly with the Ministry of the Interior, whose views generally prevailed in the case of conflict. Other agencies and ministries were consulted at the local level, but there was no lateral exchange of

[28] *Ibid.*, January 1, 1960.   [29] *Ibid.*, January 16, 1960.

ideas or interministerial consultation in Rabat. The explanation for this is quite simple: any exchange would very likely have completely bogged down the entire process of planning communes.[30]

The king's promise to hold elections by the end of 1957 was only the first in a series of public disappointments. Mohammed V was apparently acting on the advice of his Minister of the Interior, Mohammedi, who tended to take a rather cavalier view of the electoral process. However, the king made it clear in a cabinet meeting of July 1957 that he would not support improvised elections which would become the focus of party complaints and local discontent. By the end of the year several French consultants had been called in, and the minister visited Tunisia to study preparations for municipal and national elections. Once the issue was seriously considered within the government, it was clear that plans would have to be made from the local level up, or the commune system would be weighted down with vestiges of the Protectorate system and unmanageable disputes over the selection process. This alone was a novel experience for the Moroccan, as for most other, newly established governments. To lay the groundwork for the communes the king appointed an Itinerant Commission, which was to work in conjunction with the governor of each province to reorganize the entire commune system, virtually untouched since the 1953 speculations on new elections under the aegis of the Protectorate. For all practical purposes the local councils had totally disintegrated and lost contact with national affairs.

The Itinerant Commission began its provincial meetings in August 1957. The minutes of these meetings[31] provide excellent evidence on the problems of local reform in Morocco, aspects of which still plague efforts to develop the Moroccan countryside. Compared to Tunisia and Pakistan, Morocco has had great difficulty in bringing governmental effort to bear on specific developmental problems. In the commune planning the representatives of the service ministries would attend provincial planning sessions, and they often sharply differed with the views

[30] For additional materials on the organization and execution of the first commune elections in Morocco see Paul Chambergeat, pseud., "Les Elections Communales Marocaines du 29 Mai 1960," *Revue Française de Science Politique*, vol. 11, no. 1, March 1961, pp. 89-117; Douglas E. Ashford, "Elections in Morocco: Progress or Confusion?" *Middle East Journal*, vol. 15, no. 3, Spring 1961, pp. 1-15; I. William Zartman, *Problems of a New Power: Morocco*, New York, Atherton, 1964, pp. 196-242; and William H. Lewis, "Rural Administration in Morocco," *Middle East Journal*, vol. 14, no. 1, Winter 1960, pp. 45-60.

[31] The minutes of the planning sessions were made available to the author by the Ministry of the Interior during his second visit to Morocco in 1960. They are an invaluable record of the grass-roots considerations that are part of any local reorganization and reflect the myriad local and national forces that come into play in such a reorganization. The comparative value of the minutes is much greater than their direct use in the following description conveys. Individual citations of each province's proceedings will not be made.

of the rural administrative officials. Apparently little had been done to clarify the relative importance of various goals of local reorganization, nor were there defined channels for settling more serious conflicts as areas were broken down into communal regions. Nothing had been done to rectify such conflicts of interest at the central level, and, as has appeared in other programs as well, the vague lines of administrative authority leading from the monarchy produced confusion and costly interministerial rivalry. Even among personnel of the Ministry of the Interior there were obvious differences in the conception and purpose of the new commune reorganization. Since the governors were, and still are, appointed by the monarch and responsible to him through the minister, there was a tendency to regard other representatives as superfluous and to distrust their advice or directions in the absence of clear indications from the king or the minister.

There were, of course, general guidelines for the governors' preparations. Each commune was supposed to include from ten to fifteen thousand persons, and have a central community with a market or *souk* to provide a taxable source of revenue. Stress was placed on creating a commune that would be economically viable, and that would also contribute to breaking down tribal lines of organization. The last goal was stressed in particular by the commission chairman, Hassan Zemmouri, and met with fairly outspoken resistance from several governors, who still viewed tribal lines as the only meaningful divisions in their provinces. Zemmouri, on the other hand, tended to treat the old tribal *jemaâs* with some disdain, and in his introductions to the various meetings often repeated the need to give the communes "an administrative role and political significance." In fact, these were requirements that would be filled only if the officials had some idea of what powers and plans awaited the new councils. The traditional orientation of the Moroccan political system made it impossible to provide such guidelines, and the planning officials worked without clear directions as to the ultimate purpose of their handiwork.

If the authorities in Rabat hoped to create economically sound units, more attention should have been given to what the economic role of the commune was to be and what funds might be needed. Possibly encouraged by the highly centralized character of the French-inspired administrative system, there was a touch of unreality about the entire scheme. The hope was to provide each commune with a market capable of providing up to a million francs or about $2,000 a year from indirect taxes. In practice it was difficult to come close to this goal for the entire country, although there were some wealthy regions where market income was five and even ten million francs a year.[32] There was also a serious

---

[32] Although the Moroccan government still makes many calculations in francs, roughly equivalent to the French franc, the currency was "reformed" in 1960 to

obstacle to any program hoping to encourage localized activity in the Ministry of Finance, which guarded its crucial powers over the collection and disbursement of funds with great jealousy.

The minutes reflect the varying reception that the Itinerant Commission received. Although the Ministry of the Interior was clearly committed to the planning mission, the provinces varied greatly in their ability to outline new communes, and in several cases the provincial administrations appear to have viewed the new scheme with some skepticism. In the northern provinces, Tetouan, Al-Hoceima, and Nador, the Spanish administration failed to provide a precedent for local government and the new Moroccan state had relied heavily on military rule, especially after the 1958-1959 tribal uprisings. In the provinces where tribal structures were still preserved there were especially knotty problems of reconciling economic and administrative needs with ethnic boundaries. The provincial officials tended to think in terms of their own convenience and efficiency, and thereby supported the less ambitious course, which generally followed the tribally based communes of the Protectorate. For example, several meetings were needed to iron out differences over the tribal regions of Meknes. Most provinces followed the pattern of Chaouia, where there were both advanced and retarded areas. In the more advanced plains region the report notes that "economic criteria were applied exclusively," but in the isolated area of the Tadla plain, ethnic considerations were given precedence and the communes were based on existing tribal *jemaâs*. In several instances the local authorities consulted the tribal councils in preference to other local leaders.

Perhaps the most progressive province was Fez, where the governor and secretary general had taken a personal interest in community improvement well before the rural-commune plan took shape. It was the only province where the provincial administration had been adapted to the needs of local government. While other provinces still used a conventional staff organization with each major officer responsible to his parallel ministry in Rabat, the governor of Fez had created a section of rural affairs, where budgets, personnel problems, and records of all kinds from the communes were handled. This enabled him, for example, to specify the amount of funds and the projects being provided by the communes. None of the other provincial headquarters visited during the study were able to extricate commune finances from the cumbersome records designed to serve only Rabat, and in Rabat only the needs of the Ministry of Finance. Furthermore, the governor was able to keep fairly close tabs on the work of the various service agencies

---

create the *dirham*, equivalent to 100 old French francs. The exchange rate with the dollar has varied between 400 and 500 francs since independence, and converted officially at 420 francs to the dollar.

—rural development, water and forestry, public health, education, urban affairs, telephone and telegraph—as they made improvements in the province.

None of the other governors were in a position to coordinate ministerial plans with provincial needs, and sometimes the capital would proceed with work in the province quite unknown to the governor. By supervising project lists and budgets the governor in Fez could see that improvements were equitably distributed and phased to yield maximum results. Local resources and interests could be directed to the benefit of nationally sponsored work. In 1961, for example, the communal budgets were known to have supplied an additional 250 million francs or about $500,000 for local improvements.[33] Shortly after independence, an administrative committee had been formed of the service-agency chiefs and the *super-caids*. The committee met to discuss local budgets early in the year, and to review progress and needs late in the year. When the communal councils were elected, their presidents were added to the committee. The fact that the Ministry of the Interior was unable or unwilling to persuade other governors to adopt this practice in other provinces suggests how poorly coordinated and supervised the rural administration had become.

Despite the failure to mobilize existing administrative services or to give full meaning to the communal program, the commission managed to complete its work by late 1958. The obstacles that it encountered at the local level fall under three categories. The first category might be thought of as the strictly technical hurdles, although this estimate is less accurate if one takes a comprehensive view of the relation of human and technical change. Severe conflict of interest arose over the best size for communes that had undergone some intensive modernization, usually irrigation. As happens so frequently in developing countries, the technical services adopted a highly mechanical evaluation of the human resources involved in their projects, and placed their organizational goals above the more vague but higher-order political and social goals of the community. The fact that national goals were especially vague in Morocco may have contributed to the bureaucracy's determination to clarify its task in material terms. The most difficult cases were the irrigated regions in the Triffa plain of Oujda province and the Beni Mellal complex, both projects started under French rule. In the latter area it appeared that the governor was "not opposed" to having the irrigation sectors coincide with communes, but also felt that the irrigation services had not yet sufficiently outlined their own structure to follow such a course. The technicians stated very clearly their prefer-

[33] "Liste des travaux inscrits aux budgets primitifs et additionnels 1961 des communes rurales de la province de Fes," Bureau of Communal Affairs, Office of the Governor, Fez, 1962. This was an increase of 25 per cent over the communal budget for 1960.

ence for "a reduced number of interlocutors," although very good arguments could be made for the opposite view if the irrigation officials were to place more emphasis on the human problems of their program. The extension service (*génie rural*) expressed reservations on the commune in several of the provincial meetings, though this may have been partly due to a long-standing and utterly fruitless rivalry between the Ministries of Agriculture and the Interior over supervision of rural modernization.

A second group of problems was concerned with the way to provide the communes with the necessary resources. This question was closely related to the problem of how the commune boundaries were drawn, because there were numerous instances of a single market serving many more people than would normally be placed in one commune. Commercial concentration occurred in both more and less advanced parts of the country. For example, Saida on the rich Triffa plain tended to draw market income away from the relatively rich nearby villages and prevent the development of local markets. In the Middle Atlas mountains the tribal groups around Khenifra, still relatively intact, tended to make most of their purchases in the center, which did not come under the control of any of the surrounding communes. Another example in a fairly wealthy area was Souk al-Arba in the rich Gharb plain of Rabat province, where five adjoining communes relied wholly on the town's markets and thereby were deprived of the indirect taxes that might otherwise accrue to the local councils.

Although there could be no fixed rules for dealing with problems of this kind, it was evident that the Protectorate administrative system, which had not been changed, multiplied the difficulties. The French had organized "autonomous centers" and "urban centers" in the countryside as refuges for their nationals and centers of communication and control. As the country grew, these small towns—or sometimes mere outposts—became the focus for all new activity in a remote area, but the changes were never integrated with life in the surrounding villages or tribes. Even without the colonial experience there would probably have been islands of modernity in the tribal areas, and consequent problems of relating their unavoidable prosperity relative to the tribes to development in the region.

In areas where modern agriculture was well established, however, the colonial impact also left awkward situations. In the Sais plain between Meknes and Fez, for example, the tribal villages were crushed against the surrounding foothills and in the ravines, while the rich land was occupied by large French and Moroccan landowners. The local populace was in many respects more deprived and often poorer than those living under much more isolated circumstances. It would be unfair, of course, to place all responsibility on the French, for the Moroccans are now the masters of their own destiny and have not shown un-usual energy in resolving such problems. Nor were all such problems created by the Protectorate alone. North of Fez the rich olive farms are largely the property of Moroccan landlords residing in the ancient city. For example, around Karia ba Mohammed the local councils found their income restricted due to absentee ownership, which drained off much local income that might otherwise change hands in the market place.

The third category of organizational problems clusters around the ethnic and geographic barriers which could not be summarily removed. In the areas still greatly influenced by tribal life it might well be dis-astrous to ask bordering tribes or tribal clans to unite in a single coun-cil. The problems were especially difficult in the Middle Atlas regions, such as Sefrou in Fez province or Azrou and Khenifra in Meknes prov-ince. It is often difficult to judge to what extent provincial officials themselves preferred the old system, with its assurances of order and minimum demands, over a community reorganization that would create strains and ask more of the officials. One provincial aide, a Frenchman like many of the second-echelon officials throughout Morocco, noted that "the tribal framework best provided the communes with sufficient funds . . . [and was] an educational force having group support." Both these contentions are open to serious doubt, and they reflect the failure of the government to state clearly the purpose of the reorganization. Although the Itinerant Commission was often outspoken in its dis-approval of ethnically based communes, the local officials generally managed to prevail, and smaller clan or tribally defined communes were often formed in remote areas. If the government was prepared to use the commune organization to transform the isolated group rather than to put it aside, the use of ethnic boundaries would be easier to defend.

In a country so varied geographically as Morocco, it is not surprising that there were also a multitude of strictly physical limitations to form-ing communes. The rule of thumb was that a commune should not be so large that an elected councilor could not ride by horseback to and from the meeting in one day. In the mountainous regions of the north this requirement imposed severe restrictions. In the southern border areas there were comparable limits because of the distribution of the populace along miles of river beds in the midst of an otherwise arid region. The over-all effect of such limitations was to outweigh factors of size and to form communes of 5,000 and occasionally fewer persons. While sev-eral communes in some of the rich plains included as many as 25,000 persons, there were also a few of only two or three thousand. Again, the formation of such communes must be accepted, given the physical conditions, although it would be unfortunate if the decision results in even further neglect of the outlying areas.

DECLINE AND NEGLECT OF THE COMMUNE

Moroccan authorities gave relatively little thought to the developmental role that might be assigned to the commune system. The elections were held more in response to partisan demands for monarchial concessions than with any larger developmental goal in mind. Indeed, the discussion of the communes became increasingly involved with party politics by mid-1960. This, combined with the monarch's reluctance to raise the more complex questions of major institutional reforms, meant that the developmental role of the commune received little attention. Although it would be unfair to place all responsibility for inaction and evasion on the Palace, it is quite true that only the king could change the increasingly bitter and fruitless tone of the election discussions. The more heated the arguments over the new communal system became, the more delicate became the king's position. If he permitted others to voice opinions and take actions that detracted from

TABLE I

Communes per Province under Protectorate and Moroccan Plans[a]

	Protectorate	Itinerant Commission	1960 Elections
Agadir	180	90	91
Al-Hoceima	—	19	21
Beni-Mellal	181	48	44
Chaouia[b]	130	99	104
Fez	—	54	61
Ksar es-Souk	72	66	43
Marrakech	—	124	126
Meknes	64	27	31
Nador	—	26	28
Ouazarzate	52	40	40
Oujda	45	38	35
Rabat	125	65	72
Tangier	—	—	4
Tarfaya	—	—	1
Taza	39	31	34
Tetouan	—	62	62

[a] The prefectures of Casablanca and Rabat are omitted. The commune figures for the Protectorate and the Itinerant Commission are taken from the latter's reports for each province. The electoral figure is from a Ministry of Interior report, "Etat par province pour prefecture des candidatures en vue de l'election des conseils communaux," n.d. (1960).

[b] Chaouia province included two regions, Chaouia and Al-Jadiida (Mazagan), now merged. The Protectorate plan conformed more closely to the Moroccan plan in Chaouia, where 88 Protectorate communes became 77 under the commission report. In Al-Jadiida 42 Protectorate communes became 22 under the reorganization.

his monarchial position, he might lose control of events. The tendency was, therefore, to settle for minor changes. To raise more fundamental questions about modifying the regime would focus popular attention on possible inadequacies of the Palace, and constitute an implicit admission of the party claims.

The result was irreconcilable conflict and governmental stagnation. The trend was exemplified in the king's unwillingness to define the role of the new communes until after the communal councils had been selected, and his insistence that the elections should be "nonpolitical." The unavoidable result was that the elections took on even greater political significance as each party or community sought the hidden political meaning of the votes. Indeed, the Ministry of the Interior was itself engrossed in making a confidential estimate of party strengths before final action was taken on the law defining the commune's powers. By trying to minimize the political role of the communes, the Moroccan authorities in fact tended to exaggerate it. More important for the framework of this inquiry, they also reduced the potential impact of the commune as a developmental device and as a phase in the psychological transition to a more advanced society. The traditional system could accommodate "politics" in neither the narrower sense of meaningful party affiliation nor the broader sense of a general political mobilization applicable to many social problems facing Morocco.

The law defining the powers of the communes was promulgated about a month after the elections.[34] The Moroccan statute is probably the most conservative of all three local government laws considered in this study. The sole unqualified power given to the commune is that of discussing the communal budget. Given the local community's dependence on subsidies from the central government and the local citizens' unfamiliarity with budget procedures, this power is certainly more apparent than real. The only other explicit powers are those to approve the accounts according to procedures already in force and "to give its opinion as requested by laws and regulations or as asked by the administration" (art. 19). The commune may also express its approval, if it so desires, on fifteen additional matters after they have first been approved by superior authorities. Most of these consultative subjects concern minor financial affairs, which are controlled by the Ministry of Finance.

The fact that a group of popularly selected representatives could meet regularly with government officials meant, however, that pressure might be brought against the administration. The commune law took several measures to see that this did not happen. In the same way as in the Tunisian communes, the councils were explicitly "forbidden to

[34] "Dahir no. 1-59-315 du 28 hija 1379 (23 juin 1960) relatif à l'organisation communale," *Bulletin Officiel*, no. 2487, June 6, 1960, pp. 1230-1235.

formulate views of a political character or foreign to objects of local interest" (art. 25). This sweeping restraint is interpreted in the first instance by the local official of the Ministry of the Interior and in the event of a dispute by the minister himself. It is impossible for the commune to establish influence outside the bureaucracy and, until the country develops representative institutions, impossible to appeal through independent channels. The discussions of the council are further circumscribed by the requirement of administrative approval of the agenda for each meeting. Any discussion which touches on matters not already approved in the meeting's agenda can be forbidden by the local authority.

In addition to the above specific limitations, there are a number of procedures that must prove extremely burdensome to those being introduced to local government. The local *pasha* or *caid* must always be in attendance, even if the council votes itself into closed session. The council may appoint commissions only in accordance with directions in the law and in proportion to the population. The local authorities must also be represented on these commissions. The long list of obligatory expenses (art. 27) exhausts the meager resources of most communes, and precludes consideration of more constructive use of resources as the local people might desire. The time, place, and arrangements of the meetings are all carefully defined. As an ultimate check, the local authority or the Minister of the Interior can arbitrarily suspend any council for three months.

The significance of the Moroccan approach to commune organization is not so much that it retains the cumbersome practices of the Protectorate, but that it has accepted them without examination. The regime could not muster sufficient imagination to assess the suitability of its own structure to the possible goals of the communal system. The result is that the purpose of the commune has never been made clear beyond its usefulness as a political expedient. Thus the communal system was left to the Ministry of the Interior, which looked upon it as an extension of the fragmentary system devised before independence. In fact, the first directions regulating the financial procedures of the communes were those established for tribal councils in 1956,[35] and there had been no reexamination of the accounting procedures in the light of new events.

A few adjustments that have been made have been toward delegating some financial authority to the provincial governors. The governor is now authorized, for example, to resolve disputes over the communal budgets.[36] He cannot, however, make any changes in a budget once it

[35] "Arrête interministeriel portant reglément sur la compatabilité des communes rurales," Ministry of the Interior, dated December 29, 1956.

[36] "Décision des ministre portant délégation de pouvoirs au profite des Gouverneurs des Provinces," Ministry of the Interior, dated September 12, 1960.

is approved and is being executed. Administrative rigidity has been one of the important factors contributing to the lapse of funds as the commune finds it impossible to receive the essential technical advice and other administrative support for projects included in the budget. With the present procedures it is impossible to calculate how much has been turned back to the treasury, but the commune minutes often cite projects that have been repeatedly approved in the budget over three or four years. Though the procedural requirements remain unchanged, there has been a minor attempt to facilitate local planning by doubling the amount the local commune, in conjunction with the governor, could expend for one project without approval from Rabat. The limit has been raised from five hundred thousand to a million francs—about $2,000.

But increased authority to approve expenditures locally means little if the accountability procedures remain as intricate as before, and if the commune is too poor to spend more than a few thousand francs a year in any event. The willingness of the national government to increase local funds is one of the critical indications of the intent of the local reorganization scheme. In Morocco nothing was done to increase local revenues, and no steps were taken to have the various service ministries adapt their budgets to local desires or even to establish a means of consultation. The income of the commune was limited to the *tertib*, a land tax created in the late nineteenth century and despised by all variety of landowners, local market taxes, and any income from community property. Since the *tertib* was abolished by Hassan II in 1961, the communes are now wholly dependent on meager local resources and governmental subsidies.

From the psychological viewpoint, the commune minutes are perhaps the best available evidence of the untapped energies and unused cognitive skill at the local level.[37] This is not to suggest that complex development programs will be spontaneously supported by villagers, but that the local citizen may be much more prepared to evaluate his position in life and to relate his affairs to the needs and goals of the higher echelons of political affairs than most Moroccans and Westerners have been willing to admit. The fact that the Moroccan citizen has had this small chance to participate in regulating his own community means, of

---

[37] As in the case of the minutes dealing with commune planning, the individual *procès-verbal* will not be cited in the following pages. The ministry's records varied greatly from province to province, and later field work indicated that even where communes had been filing their minutes as directed, the records did not always reach Rabat because of other administrative tangles. There were nearly complete minutes on file for roughly half the communes, and these are used as indicated. The sampling within the ministry does not represent a predisposition toward more progressive councils, since by the ministry's own complaint, verified by the author, more National Union than Istiqlal councils had been delinquent in filing their records. The author is indebted to the ministry and its officials for their cooperation.

course, that he has taken an irremovable step toward the operation of a modern community.

The communal meetings have centered on the budget, but this has provided an opportunity to raise many issues about community life and also about the services and procedures of the governmental agencies affecting the village. First, the local councils proved themselves quite aware of the nature of their financial contribution to the country, and were prepared to ask embarrassing questions about services yet to be received. In Meknes province a council observed that although they were obliged to pay for the services of a *cadi* or minor judge for their weekly market, he did not appear. In several provinces there were complaints that the locally paid market officials, a long-time sinecure for friends of the local authority, were not doing their job well and that the commune lost market revenue as the result of their laziness. One of the communes near Fez simply declined to appropriate funds for several minor officials whose services were poorly performed, although this action can be overruled by Rabat.

There were, secondly, a variety of indications that Moroccans from many walks of life were learning to challenge traditional authority. One *caid* was criticized by several councilors for monopolizing the commune's secretary, who was supposed to be working on community business. In another the council decided that the *mokhaznis* or administrative police of the Ministry of the Interior could henceforth purchase their own water as did other members of the community. In some of the larger towns, like Safi, there were major disputes over the local subsidy to the police, whom the councils felt should be partially accountable to the local body. Some of the police criticism was certainly aroused by the National Union, which felt quite rightly that the police were unaccountable and sometimes overbearing. However, there were similar complaints from strong Istiqlal regions, where the police allegedly overlooked prostitution and liquor sales to Muslims. These grievances were very likely voiced by the members of the council who were already more accustomed to modern forms of controversy and governmental procedures, but they were still part of the demonstration that a virtually defenseless villager could successfully withstand the force of government within legally constituted channels.

The integrated budgetary procedures of the French-inspired administration may have placed certain obstacles in the way of efficient local action, but this also meant that the local council could debate the work of a variety of ministries. The comments in this third area of discussion show that the villager was able to relate his life to affairs in Rabat, and willing to use whatever opportunities might be given him to find out why Rabat was not dealing with local problems effectively. For example, near Al-Jadiida the Ministry of Public Works had built a road across local fields without compensating or informing the owners. The local *caid* himself professed ignorance of how this happened and had not been informed of the construction. In several communes funds had been appropriated for school construction since 1959, but the Ministry of Education had not yet authorized the work and provided a teacher. The Ministry of Habous (religious foundations), which operates directly from the Palace, was criticized by both liberals and conservatives for the poor services it provided for mosques, while receiving local subsidies and privileges because of its religious functions. These comments suggest that many local councilors realized that the pattern of the past fifty years could be changed, and that the social forms of the past two millennia were open to modification.

The most encouraging signs of an increased concern with the community's potential development role were the discussions that displayed the council's willingness to take on new responsibilities and its awareness of its independent position in political life. Thus one town undertook to patrol its own streets at night, and laid plans to provide better street lighting. Several towns announced their intention of hiring Moroccan experts to replace French advisers. In other communes in tribal areas the councils asked that their control over collective tribal lands be restored so that these lands could be exploited to the community's benefit. In addition to asserting their authority over officials paid by the commune, some councils asked that they have assured means for confidential communication between communes and that all correspondence between themselves and Rabat officials travel direct rather than through the Ministry of the Interior. In Souk al-Arba in Rabat province there were especially firm objections to central interference and subsequent delay in rezoning and development of the town. Although the communes were certainly not ready to undertake complex developmental tasks, they were aware of many of the problems of reconstructing their communities, knew a good deal of the requirements of their communities, and had their grievances concerning the central government firmly in mind.

THE POLITICAL IMPASSE OF PARTICIPATION

The monarchial system encourages the politically active, mostly from the modern segment of society, to cluster around the center of power. Most new countries are characterized by the concentration of the political strength in the capital city and, perhaps, a few regional cities. The consequent rarefied atmosphere makes governmental action at the local level less likely, but it also means in the monarchy that those excluded from the system as a result of the necessary exclusiveness of a kingship seek other ways to justify their influence and gain more strength in the system. Thus in Morocco the local reform has tended to become a rationalization for delegating the monarch's power. In Morocco after the communal elections of 1960 the communes constituted a threat to the monarchy insofar as they offered legitimate grounds for such opposition.

But the elections constituted a step toward fundamental reform that could not be withdrawn, however far they may have been from elections of more advanced countries. Even the proceedings of the defunct Consultative National Assembly could not compare with the elections as evidence of popular interest and aspirations. Both the Istiqlal and the National Union used the election results to fortify their claims for a more active role in government. The reactions of the more conservative Istiqlal are especially noteworthy, because the party was ostensibly supporting Mohammed V and later Hassan II, and had several representatives in the cabinet throughout the period to be discussed. The National Union was in violent opposition to the monarchy throughout the period, and so its views are strongly influenced by strictly partisan concerns. Although the Istiqlal was also concerned with preserving its identity and following, it remained a strong supporter of the monarchy until 1963, and was, therefore, acutely aware of the potential conflict between institutional development at the local level and monarchial frame of action.

Until the 1960 elections the Istiqlal had spent over a year as the opposition party, and was intent on solidifying its position, once it enjoyed the privileges accruing to those accepted in the government. Even before the law on communal powers was published, the Istiqlal wrote that it should not be a "suffocating structure" but an "effective implement for the exercise of democracy."[38] Their bitter disappointment over the highly circumscribed role assigned to the commune indicates how far short of expectations the law must have been for more energetic advocates of local reform. The party denounced the new law as "the negation of all the attributions and powers which should be given to elected councils," and concluded that it was "not even a timid step toward democracy."[39] The party's position in the government notwithstanding, the criticism of the local administration and even veiled comment about constitutional reform became increasingly common in 1961. All the parties were very likely eager to use the communal councils they controlled to build more party strength and, conversely, to direct their influence in the government to the advantage of councils favorable to the party. Whether or not such a competitive approach to local development would have been desirable at such an early phase in local reorganization became an academic question, because King Hassan had no intention of using the communes to encourage more individual participation in political and social affairs at any level.

[38] *Al-Istiqlal*, June 25, 1960.   [39] *Ibid.*, July 9, 1960.

Late in 1961 the Istiqlal went so far as to endorse the similar objections of its bitter rival, the National Union. In a long article it noted the revisions needed in the municipal councils of Fez, Marrakech, Meknes, and Casablanca, only two of which it controlled.[40] Specifying the objectionable articles, the party outlined the essential extensions of power. First, the communes should be given some functions independent of the local officials of the Ministry of the Interior, including control of its own agents, presentation of its budget, and specific supervisory powers over police and minor judges (arts. 36, 38, 39). Second, the financial powers of the commune should be sufficient to provide some leverage over the technical services. The party noted that some officials had actually prevented the local councils from contacting representatives of the service ministries, and also admitted that no one was really able to influence them at the local level (art. 18). Third, the obligatory three-month delay in the execution of all decisions tended to limit the usefulness of the council, and often became six months or more in practice (Arts. 21, 22). Fourth, the commune should have some avenue of recourse outside the Ministry of the Interior in order to provide an impartial judge of disputes and to ensure full discussion (arts. 23, 24, 31, 11). The party hoped that all the arbitrary powers of the ministry might be qualified. Finally, the Istiqlal objected to the obligatory local taxes, especially for police services, which were inherited from the Protectorate and were considered excessive (arts. 27, 28). Almost the same criticisms were forthcoming from the Nation Union during this period.

In 1962 the Istiqlal, as well as the National Union, began to seek a way to bring popular pressure to bear on the monarchy. At the Istiqlal congress in early 1962 the party claimed that 500 council chairmen belonged to the party, and again attacked the rural-commune law.[41] The party suggested that a ministry be organized for commune affairs —the first time such a proposal appeared publicly. Soon after the congress the party formed the "Istiqlal Federation of Rural and Municipal Communes"—almost an *ad hoc* legislature to challenge the king. The group was particularly firm in its objections to the rural administration. It also raised the need to have rural public-works projects evaluated by the councils, and asked for regional and national bodies made up of local councilors. For the first time the party clearly identified the problem of undertaking widespread local reform without some way of exchanging views and presenting common problems. The party noted that for "two years the councils have lived and worked in isolation, separately seeking to resolve their problems and to overcome many difficulties, always thinking separately on problems of common interest

[40] *Ibid.*, November 11, 1961.
[41] *Ibid.*, January 17, 1961.

because there was no liaison or coordination between them."[42] The concept of community interaction and cooperation emerged much more clearly in the discussion than in earlier planning papers of 1957 and 1958. The Istiqlal's thinking was still strongly influenced by its desire to preserve its association with the monarchy, but it also presented more definitely the notion of introducing an entirely new framework of action into the lives of the isolated Moroccan.

In a political system strongly predisposed to affective thought and action, the Istiqlal was relatively less reliant on emotional appeal in the realm of local reform. In this critical area at least the party held promise of breaking through the morass of capital-city politics and making contact with its base in a way that was meaningful to the peasant. This was possible, in part, because the Istiqlal shared the traditional orientation of the political system, and could act within it more easily than the aggressively modern National Union. The communes became a constant concern of the Istiqlal, while the National Union considered them sporadically and emotionally. Nevertheless, in their congress in the spring of 1962 there was almost no mention of specific needs of the communes despite the recent efforts to rally councilmen to the party's cause.

Although generally more deeply opposed to the government and the monarchy than the Istiqlal, the National Union was less precise and often less rational in its criticisms of the commune system. The more progressive party was greatly influenced by its needs and desires in Casablanca, the major industrial and commercial city in Morocco, which it controlled and which occupied the thoughts of most of the party leaders. The new party was also more inflammatory in its presentation and discussion of local reform. Their reaction is similar to the Istiqlal's in that both parties took more radical positions than their leaders' established positions would indicate. Both parties were driven to greater extremes to establish a framework for political exchange in a setting that minimized opportunities for organized political expression, and where only the firmest beliefs could succeed in overcoming the traditional pattern.

By 1962 it was clear to the progressive group that Hassan II was firmly in power, and that he had no intention of voluntarily sharing his authority. A constitution had been promised for 1962, and the party's concern for its popular base in any subsequent elections was revived. In March, two months after a similar meeting of the Istiqlal, the National Union assembled 350 representatives of rural communes in Casablanca. The speeches played more heavily on the frustrations and failures of the communal system than did those delivered at the Istiqlal meeting.[43] Bouabid and others sought to tie the question of increased

[42] *Ibid.*, April 21, 1962.   [43] *At-Tahrir*, March 21 and 22, 1962.

– 54 –

powers for the communes into questions of the monarchy, constitutional reform, and an effective national assembly. Though fundamentally in agreement with the Istiqlal, the National Union stressed the arbitrary character of the local officials and mistreatment at the hands of the police. The more inflammatory themes of abuse, injustice, and rejection were again picked up in a second regional meeting of National Union councilors in Marrakech several months later. The communes were considered almost wholly in reference to the national regime, and seldom as a new framework for localized activity.

Despite Hassan II's intentions to establish a more effective government, the role of the communes failed to evolve over 1963 and 1964. The chronic detachment of the parties from the social fabric of the country was only increased by a series of plots, trials, and new external threats. Though Morocco held more elections in 1963 than either Tunisia or Pakistan have held in their history, the formalities of participation were divorced of local meaning, and the spiritual appeal of the monarch became the major device to win approval by acclamation for the regime. The second round of rural-commune elections in mid-1963 found the Ministry of the Interior firmly in the hands of the king, with few ministers from opposing parties in the cabinet to challenge procedures or results.[44] As a result the local *caids* and governors were virtually unrestrained in their manipulation of the elections to put a majority of royalist-front candidates in office. How political participation at the local level could be integrated with political affairs at the regional and national level was no longer a significant issue in Moroccan political life.

The Moroccan rural communes provide the first and one of the most instructive examples of local reform under three political systems. In the hypothesis of the inquiry the political variable in Moroccan society is the monarchial system, modified by the demands of operating a modern state.[45] The appeal of the monarchy is primarily affective, be-

[44] Early in 1963 the Istiqlal joined the National Union in opposition to the monarchy. A government was formed with Hassan II as president of the cabinet and Ahmed Guedira, his close collaborator, the main spokesman for the monarch. The royalist front, the Front for the Defense of Constitutional Institutions (F.D.I.C.), included the Popular Movement, but their uneasy alliance broke in 1964. When Guedira was replaced and a new government formed in 1964, he created a Socialist Party. The local elections in 1963 caused little notice. See *Le Monde*, July 30, 1963, and *Jeune Afrique*, August 5-11, 1963. The first councils were organized early in 1964. See *New York Times*, March 15, 1964.

[45] There have been two accounts of the state of the Moroccan government at the time the Protectorate was created, one presenting a French view and another the Moroccan. Both are highly colored by French concern for the legal considerations of the occupation. See Mohamed Lahbabi, *Le Gouvernment Marocain à l'Aube du XXè Siècle*, Rabat, Editions Techniques Nord-Africaines, 1957, and Jacques Bonjean, *L'Unité de L'Empire Chérifien*, Paris, Librairie Générale de Droit et de Jurisprudence, 1955.

ing built on religious beliefs and historic traditions. So long as the Moroccan response to the European impact was limited to the reactions of a few privileged persons it entailed very little social upheaval. Only with independence did the Moroccan political system, like those of Africa and Asia generally, have to deal with the specific problems of development. Even relatively intensive development could be carried on for many years at a level sufficiently remote from the populace to forestall any new confrontation of villager and ruler. The government did not become fully aware of the need for a rural mobilization until several years after independence, and then it was undertaken with hesitance and misgivings.

A full understanding of Moroccan uncertainty when confronted with the problems of development at the local level requires digging beneath the intrigue and rivalries of the leaders. That intrigue was, on the whole, more prevalent in high-level Moroccan politics than in Tunisia or Pakistan is, perhaps, also a function of the traditional orientation of the country, but it is more significant as corroborative evidence of the pattern of political action in a system that has difficulty engaging in instrumental, concretely oriented activities involving large numbers of citizens. Intrigue and conniving are the result of a political setting in which politicians are not encouraged to direct their energies along more useful lines; it is a symptom more than a cause in the present framework.

At the national level a traditional structure must rely heavily on affective appeals and communications with the populace, or face gradual erosion by parties and other new institutions created to meet the needs of modernization. The potential conflict is much more acute than that found in Pakistan or Tunisia, where the existing political systems could adjust to the needs of local reform without abdicating authority. A full explanation of Moroccan uncertainties requires consideration of this dilemma, which was manifested in a variety of ways as programs involving widespread participation arose. First, all Moroccan leaders had great difficulty focusing their attention on the more prosaic, intricate projects associated with the creating of a complex, modern society. With the automatic consent the traditional system could generally evoke from the mass of Moroccans for more superficial treatment of national affairs, there was relatively little pressure to be concerned with the village and tribe. The limitations of the more easily evoked response only became apparent when the nation began to embark on a development program that anticipated individual support and cooperation.

Once the monarchy took a more active interest in local improvement, the tendency was to erect formidable barriers among the ministers and other political forces concerned. The Protectorate tradition of concentrating local administration in the Ministry of the Interior was not questioned, even though planning activities had been undertaken in the Ministry of the National Economy, and, later, the problems of channeling localized action via the Ministry of the Interior became obvious under the National Promotion scheme. More important than the choice of central administrative vehicle is the fact that no interministerial effort at the local level was called for. In a few provinces, Fez being the only striking example, some efforts were made to bring representatives of the service ministries together with the control activities of the rural administrators, but there was no interest in a major overhaul of the administrative system, whose roots extend back into pre-Protectorate practices.

Nor were other institutional reforms related to the communes to encourage them to fill the gap between community and nation. The original concept of the commune was simply that of adding another administrative unit beneath the *caid*, rationalized in part on the historic role of the *jemaâ*. Even the relatively routine but detailed act of delimiting the new communes was separated from, and prior to, review of the commune's functions either at the local level or at higher levels in the political system. Approximately two years elapsed between marking out the commune's borders and holding the elections. Once the elections were held, there was no thought of more actively engaging the local governments in development work until aid directed specifically toward that end was offered by the United States. As will be discussed later, even then the local communes had only a minor role, and there were no plans for enlarging it either within or without the Ministry of the Interior.

The Moroccan experience does not mean that traditional influence cannot profitably be used for reforms of a very specific nature. For example, when it appeared that villagers were not taking a sufficiently keen interest in the local elections of 1960, Mohammed V toured parts of the countryside and called upon peasants and tribesmen to join in the national effort to reform local government. But the highly affective appeal is hard to apply to situations where uniform action is inappropriate, and it cannot be used repeatedly without external justification based on crises, religious imperatives, or external threat to the nation. The traditional appeal rested on the use of ultimate values. Individuals might vary in their day-to-day application of such values, but the action equivalent of such an appeal from Rabat did not and could not lead to the kind of sustained, adaptive behavior that more intensive development at the local level required. As a result the Moroccan local-reform effort tended to become bogged down in the ministerial quarrels and party rivalries engendered, and sometimes encouraged, by the monarchy. The initial impulse provided by the country's central traditional institutions could not be shaped and expanded at the local level.

The insistence that local development be kept within the monarchial sphere of influence meant that party alignments were officially forbidden at the local level and, therefore, legally excluded from becoming a contributing force between community and capital. In practice, both the Istiqlal and the National Union were active in the elections, and the effect of their exclusion only made them less responsible to both the locality and the central government than they might otherwise have been. Without yielding full control of the local governments to the parties, it would have been possible to give them some local responsibility and to direct some of their energy to the community. As the commune scheme worked out, the parties did indeed become an important, though unofficial, link between the local councils and Rabat. Both the Istiqlal and the National Union actively advanced arguments for enlarged powers at the local level, but neither could be called to account for their actions at the local level by either the council or the Ministry of the Interior. It is interesting that the Istiqlal, whose principles most easily accommodated the monarchial system of government, was able to make more constructive proposals for improved local reform.

The National Union's more inflammatory, sporadic response is an intriguing example of how extremist appeals relate to a country's political and social life. The affective appeal can be based on secular grounds as easily as on religious grounds. In its offensive against the monarchy, the National Union relied more and more on highly affective appeals, based in part on charges of injustice from within and in part on fears of plots from without. The net effect was to create alarm and suspicion, which was no more suitable to the day-to-day needs of local development than the uniform, submissive action the *imam* of the faithful could evoke. In what seems almost a classic example of radicalism of the left and right,[46] the Moroccan organized political forces were driven farther and farther apart, with the result that neither could afford to concentrate on the tedious business of putting individual energies to work at the local level.

The Moroccan approach to local reform, especially the increasing reliance on affective appeals by organized political groups and parties, meant that the psychological impact of local reform was minimized. The chances of diffuse, self-sustaining action at the local level were obviously restrained by the conditions laid down in the law and by the failure to enlarge upon the foundations of local government. In this way there was little encouragement for the local citizen to enlarge his own framework of action and evaluation. National affairs were still

[46] This observation has been most carefully documented in the study of Communism and its supporters in the United States, and also in the earlier authoritarian inquiries. See, for example, Edward A. Shils, "Authoritarianism: 'Right' and 'Left,'" in Christie and Jahoda, eds., *Studies in Scope and Method of the Authoritarian Personality*, Glencoe, Free Press, 1954.

presented to him as accomplished facts and handled by institutions long known to be inefficient and arbitrary. The sense of urgency that was created in some stages of local reform was not utilized to increase the range of local activities in concert with national developmental needs. In a very real sense the repeated disillusion of aroused expectations meant that the country was gradually closing off psychological channels of mobilization. Subsequent efforts to arouse local interest would need to be slightly more extreme and urgent, thereby further widening the gap between the emotional appeal and the realm of reasonable accomplishment.

CHAPTER 3

THE TUNISIAN COUNCIL: LIMITED
RISK AND LIMITED IMPACT

ALTHOUGH TUNISIA LACKED THE wealth that might have supported Moroccan development, the Republic of Tunisia made organizational gains that far surpassed Morocco's effort. The political setting in Tunisia consists of a powerful single party, the Socialist Destour, under the dynamic leadership of President Habib Bourguiba. Bourguiba's frequently repeated slogan, "A sole party, a sole nation," suggests both the advantages and the disadvantages of the Tunisian political system as the vehicle of social change and rural reorganization. The need for national solidarity in the postindependence period is undisputed, and arguments in favor of the single-party system are persuasive. But uniformity and subordination to superior designs do not terminate at this relatively high level in the political system. Insistence on conformity to party, basically presidential wishes to the very roots of Tunisian society has placed certain handicaps on the country's development. The limitations of the single-party scheme have become increasingly apparent as Bourguiba increasingly, and unavoidably, becomes more involved in improvements affecting life at the local level.

While the traditionally oriented political system may hesitate when confronted with the development of more complex social patterns that are not governed by the moral superiority of the traditional figure, the single-party regime suffers other apprehensions. It is not unresponsive to secular patterns of behavior, efficient bureaucratic operations, and long-range planning of economic and social problems. The creation and continued success of the single-party system depends on the skillful use of modern organizational skills. Indeed, it is the similarity between single-party government and the organizational forms of more advanced societies that very likely makes them attractive to Western officials and apparently as adaptive and flexible as their counterpart in the more advanced setting.[1] The Socialist Destour, for example, has

[1] The recent collection of essays by Gwendolyn Carter, ed., *African One-Party States*, Ithaca, Cornell University Press, 1962, is a good example of renewed interest in this phenomenon. While the essays are individually of a very high caliber, the volume fails to elicit the particular significance of this kind of party organization, and, given the very great effort of Duverger and others to analyze systems in terms of party characteristics with little success, it seems unlikely that there are indeed reliable conclusions to be drawn. A more critical and more systematic treatment is Martin Kilson's "Authoritarianism and Single-Party Tendencies in African Politics," *World Politics*, vol. 15, no. 2, 1963, pp. 262-294. The simple existence of the single-party regime has so narrowed the field of theoretical vision that it would seem that more fruitful results might be had by mixing party regimes in reference to better defined goals of political development. For a psychological

been virtually unchallenged in Tunisian politics since 1934, and has managed to keep nearly all interest groups within the fold of the "national organization." Though Tunisian unity has not been so profound as Western observers have often concluded from their talks with the party elite, which holds all the high offices in the party and the government, the Tunisian government is certainly less corrupt and more effective than the Moroccan.

Thus the traditional relationships established between the Moroccan government and its people through the monarchy and Islam may be lacking in versatility as the modernization process advances, but the traditional ties can also accommodate hierarchical authority in development. As the treatment of parties and interest groups in Morocco suggests, there are indeed some assurances for the royal regime in keeping the contenders for power active but separate. The values of the Moroccan political system can adapt to social diversity if new political institutions are not added to the royal *équipe*. Unfortunately, in Morocco decisions have been delayed and institutions that might have diffused influence have been slow to emerge. It is indicative of the monarchy's apprehensions that the Moroccan constitution specifically forbids a one-party regime. The political requirements of the single-party system are less adaptable to social diversity and political differentiation at higher levels in the political system. This fact is a source of strength and weakness in the Tunisian developmental effort.

The strength of the activist regime is its ability to try out developmental suggestions on a limited scale, to organize specialized agencies to meet specific developmental programs, and to communicate specific directions to the local level. The Tunisian republic is highly effective in day-to-day operations from the central government, but the shortcomings of the regime appear in the flow of ideas and information from the local level to the government. The party can maintain its supremacy only if new political participants at any level in the society first accept the primacy of central authority.

The result is to impose severe restrictions on political behavior at all levels. In the government and the party one finds a classic case of "democratic centralism." Differences of opinion are only aired prior to the decision, and the decision of the Socialist Destour Political Bureau is final and undisputed.[2] The fact that the party has fallen short of this

---

interpretation of the single-party system see the author's *The Elusiveness of Power: The African Single Party State*, Ithaca, Center of International Studies, 1965.

[2] The Socialist Destour became the party's name in 1964. In 1934 it adopted the name "Neo-Destour" in opposition to the Destour or Constitutionalist Party. The 1964 designation has been used generally throughout this book, however, for purposes of simplification. General studies of the Socialist Destour regime are Charles F. Gallagher, Jr., "Tunisia," in *African One-Party States, op.cit.*, pp. 11-

utopian idea of political life is evidence of the shortcomings of the single-party system, particularly where large numbers of citizens are being asked to make major changes in their daily lives. At the center governmental effectiveness can become confused with socially based initiative. As the Tunisian experience with planning has demonstrated, the creation of a plan and its application was only the first step in the more intensive reorganization of the society, and the single-party regime's decisiveness does not necessarily allay the fears and passive resistance of many Tunisians. The danger in relying heavily on the executive powers of government is, of course, that control and surveillance may become oppressive and discourage local enterprise.

The potential shortcomings of the Bourguibist regime at the central level are on the whole relatively easy to identify. The single-party regime cannot divide responsibility for decisions so easily as either the monarchial or the military governments. Despite the paternal aspects of Bourguiba's rule, he never tires of asserting his similarity to all Tunisians, his everyday origins, and his political equality in the republic. At the same time, Bourguiba and the ruling elite are committed to the improvement of their people in a much more direct way than are Hassan II in Morocco and President Ayub in Pakistan. The magnitude of Bourguiba's commitment is conveyed in the president's innovation of a new party doctrine to engage the country in the development effort. "Destourian socialism" is not only an example of the president's remarkable flexibility as a political tactician, but it is also his personal stake in the future on which his reputation and the regime's destiny are dependent.

But the Tunisian political system exacts a price from its people for the decisiveness of their government. The Socialist Destour, and Bourguiba himself, expect that institutions will reflect the uniform purposefulness of the government and party machinery. The single-party system operates to assure that political responses will be known in advance and that the dominant party will not be publicly challenged. Given the elite's awareness of their concentrated responsibility, the tendency is to use new institutions to echo decisions already made in the Political Bureau, and to demonstrate popular enthusiasm. The long-term effects of the development process are in some ways more of a threat to the single-party regime than to the monarchy or the military, whose social values and institutional roots offer hope of successfully surviving social transformation. The single-party system, however, is severely strained

---

86, and Clement Henry Moore, "The Neo-Destour Party of Tunisia: A Structure for Democracy," *World Politics*, vol. 14, no. 3, April 1962, pp. 461-482. See also Moore's essay in Charles Micaud, ed., *Modernization in Tunisia*, New York, Praeger, 1963, pp. 69-128, and his book, *Tunisia Since Independence*, Berkeley, University of California Press, 1965.

as social complexities or popular demands begin to be expressed in ways not already endorsed by superiors. The Pakistan military have their professional detachment, and the Moroccan monarchs have their religious imperatives. The Socialist Destour will sink or rise with the regime as a whole.

The difficulties of the single-party regime in accommodating diversity have both social and psychological implications. The cumulative, self-supported economic growth to which the new nation aspires has as its corollary a pattern of political relationships that can adjust to the intricacies of a complex, innovating social system. Likewise, the kind of individual evaluation and application that is needed in the self-propelled society is not compatible with the constraints the single-party scheme imposes. The Socialist Destour seeks to penetrate every aspect of Tunisian life, though it has not been wholly successful in even the comparatively small country.

With no intention of minimizing Bourguiba's diplomatic skill in relations with France or the Algerian revolutionaries, it appears that much of the political mastery and ingenuity of "Bourguibism" is in fact the president's skill at working within self-imposed restraints. Were he free to call upon nore spontaneous popular energies and to apply his undoubted personal magnetism unrestricted by fears of losing the close control of Tunisian affairs required by the Socialist Destour, the Tunisian development effort might well be even more impressive than it has been. The municipal-council system is an excellent illustration of lost opportunity to mobilize local villages and towns in support of Tunisian development. Although the Tunisian government is a much more effective instrument than the Moroccan government, it was slow to take full advantage of the political energies mobilized to support it or of the opportunities the relatively more advanced state of Tunisian society offered.

COLONIAL USE AND ABUSE OF MUNICIPAL COUNCILS

The Tunisian experience under colonial rule in regard to local development is almost the reverse of the Protectorate's effort to exploit the Moroccan *jemaâ*. The area around Tunis has a history of administrative cohesion dating back to Roman days, and modern Tunisia predates the French occupation as a political entity. The fortunes of the Moroccan *maghzen* can be followed through a series of dynasties starting with the Almoravides. The dynasties always ruled, however, where they were able to suppress the tribes by virtue of superior force and with an administrative system designed to do little more than collect taxes. The Ottoman administration of Algeria and Tunisia brought to those areas a somewhat more advanced notion of the relation between ruler and ruled. Although dissidence continued in the southern regions of Tunisia, the bey of Tunis was virtually independent of the Ottoman Empire after 1705 and became a hereditary office. Professor Julien has noted that "apart from a few administrative terms and Turkish usages, the beys and their officials could be considered *gens du pays*."[3]

The net result was to provide Tunisia with an administrative and political structure better suited to the needs of running an independent country than Morocco. Well before the French occupation of 1881 the Tunisian bey was affected by the French pressures from Algeria, and attempted to establish good relations with other European powers. For example, Ahmed Bey established a military school in 1828, which was supplied with a French faculty several years later.[4] In mid-century a uniform currency was established, and a constitution promulgated in 1861 brought together a council of sixty notables. But the belated attempts at reform could not overcome the sapping of Tunisian strength through intrigue and indulgence at court. The establishment of the Protectorate forcefully carried the European impact to Tunisia a full generation before similar developments in Morocco.

The precedents for internal reorganization in response to the needs of modernization extended into the realm of local affairs, an area which was almost untouched by the Moroccan monarchy until after independence. Tunisia first experienced local reform well before the French occupation, when Mohammed Bey established a municipal council for Tunis in 1858. Although the Tunis council, like other efforts for political reform, was dominated by the *grandes familles*,[5] some specific regulations were issued concerning sanitation and *quartier* councils. The Tunis council was reorganized by the French in 1883, and representation was divided among Tunisian (8), Jewish (1), and French (8) residents. The reorganization of the capital city was followed up with municipal councils built on similar lines in Bizerte, Sousse, Sfax, La Goulette, and Kef. Thus a full generation before Morocco, each of the more densely populated regions of Tunisia had felt the impact of modern bureaucratic forms at the local level.

The historic precedent for local organization was not entirely beneficial in effect, for it also created a deep division between the urban and rural patterns of Tunisian local government. Although similar differences had existed in Morocco, where municipal councils had also been organized in the major regional cities and French-dominated towns, the distinction proved less important in postindependence thinking. For

---

[3] *Histoire de l'Afrique du Nord*, vol. 2, Paris, Payot, 1956, p. 302.

[4] A. Pellégrin, *Histoire de la Tunisie depuis les Origines jusqu'a nos Jours*, Tunis, Libraire Namura, 1948, p. 160.

[5] *Ibid.*, p. 188. It is remarkable how many of the families mentioned have successfully survived the nationalist period, which fact confirms this author's view that nationalists are seldom as revolutionary as they are portrayed in the foreign press.

the Moroccans none of the local-organization system was of their own design, and the nationalists had seen the entire administrative structure imposed by the colonial power within their lifetime. The Tunisians have taken a very different attitude toward the vestiges of colonial local government. Through the Protectorate the French Municipal Law of 1884 was applied to Tunisia, and continues to influence Tunisian legislation to the present day. It was used as the model for the first Tunisian Municipal Charter of 1885, under which the original councils actually lost powers. The Tunisian members were henceforth to be appointed by Protectorate authorities.

By 1914 there were thirty-eight municipal councils in Tunisia, including about a fourth of the population.[6] The scale of the municipal organization at a comparatively early date indicates that the local activities extended well beyond what would be regarded as "municipal" in the common sense of the term. Indeed, as will be stressed later in this chapter, by World War I the scale of Tunisian activity at the local level had reached heights that were unsurpassed in the independent period. The second Municipal Charter was decreed by the Protectorate in 1914.[7] and it is important to note that it too represented a net loss in the powers of the councils. The decision to establish a council was put wholly within the control of the Protectorate (previously there had been provision for a joint commission), and the number of council members was to be fixed arbitrarily rather than in ratio to the local population. The 1914 law also provided that the local Tunisian administrator could assign vice-presidential powers to a Frenchman, a device that could be used to authorize considerable abuse of the council system.

The period between the wars was barren of further improvements at the local level, a phenomenon that did not go unnoticed by the rising nationalist movement in North Africa. Under the 1914 law Tunisians found themselves excluded more and more from council activities, and increasingly the victims of injustices made official through local government. Additional expenses were assigned to the councils, and towns that were wholly Tunisian were excluded from the system. The composition of the Tunis council was changed to twelve Europeans and eight Tunisians, but remained the only council with elected members. Even so, the number of councils increased, probably in response to increased Protectorate needs to service the growing French community. The num-

---

[6] Mohamed Senoussi, *Les Collectivités Locales en Tunisie*, Tunis, n.p., 1958, p. 7. Senoussi has been judicial and legislative adviser to the president since independence, and his study is one of the most complete and instructive accounts of how the Socialist Destour viewed the problem of local government after independence.

[7] *Direction Générale de l'Intérieur, Monographie des Services*, Tunis, 1931, pp. 87-115. The 1914 law follows the postindependence law very closely in organization and powers, and generally represents the level of advancement in local government legislation that Morocco only achieved after World War II.

ber of councils grew from 38 in 1914 to 58 in 1931, distributed by region as follows: Bizerte, 9; Tunis, 17; Kef, 5; Sousse, 14; Sfax, 9; and southern territories, 4.[8] The concentration of local activities in the more advanced communities of the north and the central Sahel plain was characteristic of the Protectorate organization at an early time, and has proved difficult to remove since independence. Just prior to World War II attempts were made to establish rural counterparts of the councils for Djerba and three other southern towns, but these efforts were abandoned during the war and never revived.

Like the French regime in Morocco, the Tunisian Protectorate did not consider far-reaching local reform until all hope of preserving the colonial superstructure was lost. The attempt to invigorate the neglected councils was made several weeks after the assassination of Farhat Hached, the Tunisian union leader, in December 1952. By that time Bourguiba's efforts to negotiate for autonomy through the Chenik government had totally failed,[9] and the new local reforms were rejected out of hand by the Socialist Destour. Nevertheless, there was in Tunisia, as in Morocco, a small number of well-intentioned, rather idealistic colonial officials who sincerely advocated further reform, while the conservative French, who dominated North African affairs from this time, were not adverse to raising a façade of participation in order to defend their policies to the world, and in particular in the United Nations.

The law of December 1952 reverted to some of the practices of the original 1885 charter, and ostensibly opened the way for more Tunisian participation. The number of municipal councils, sometimes referred to as urban communes, was increased to 64. Of this number 37 councils were composed equally of French and Tunisian members, 15 were entirely Tunisian, and 10 were a majority Tunisian.[10] The Tunisian was allowed to vote if he were male, twenty-one years of age, had no police convictions, and filled a residency or tax requirement. For all practical purposes the 1952 reforms were never applied. When elections were held in 1953 the nationalist boycott kept roughly two thirds of the voters away from the polls despite intensive police suppression.[11] In twenty of the elections there were no Tunisians willing to run for

---

[8] *Ibid.*, p. 85.

[9] The best accounts of these troubled days are in Julien's *L'Afrique du Nord en Marche*, Paris, Julliard, 1952, pp. 217-276, and more briefly in Roger Le Tourneau's *Evolution Politique de l'Afrique du Nord Musulmane 1920-1961*, Paris, Colin, 1962, pp. 114-131.

[10] Victor Silvera, *Organisation Politique et Administrative de la Tunisie*, Tunis, Ecole Nationale d'Administration, n.d., p. 237. Also, Senuossi, *op.cit.*, pp. 10-11.

[11] This was an extraordinary performance compared to Istiqlal ineffectiveness at this time. For an account of the Istiqlal's disintegration during the early 1950's see Ashford, *Political Change in Morocco*, Princeton, Princeton University Press, 1961, pp. 57-74.

office, particularly in the Sahel area, a historic party stronghold. In the summer of 1954 Mendes-France made his offer of autonomy, and all further internal reorganization was suspended.

In the subsequent negotiations French representation on the municipal councils became a major stumbling block. After Bourguiba directly intervened, a formula was found by which the French representative in Tunisia would submit a list of councilors, from which the Tunisian government would select representatives of the French community.[12] In ten specified cases, including the major Tunisian cities, three sevenths of the council would be French; where the French population was 10 per cent or more of the municipality it would be entitled to a third of the representatives, and where less than 10 per cent it would have one councilor. No sooner had this agreement been put into effect than the Moroccan negotiations for full independence got under way. Tunisia demanded that the convention be abolished, and the local provisions of the Franco-Tunisian Convention were superseded by the independence agreement of March 20, 1956.

As a vehicle for postindependence development the Tunisian municipal-council system had decided shortcomings. It was strongly oriented to the housekeeping functions of the community, and the habits of procedural submission to a central government were reinforced with nearly sixty years' practice. The Tunisian experience provided the minimum administrative understanding at the local level, without which any development effort tends to flounder, but the bureaucratic grip was deeply ingrained by a much longer experience than that of Morocco. In this respect the Tunisian experience is similar to Pakistani efforts to mobilize the villages, where over two centuries of colonial rule had all but destroyed local initiative and confidence.

The essential aspect of any national mobilization scheme is its focus on increasing both the scope and the intensity of the development effort. Like political life in the society as a whole, development involves committing more people, and committing them in more ways in the country's social and economic problems. Unfortunately, the Tunisian experience held a strong precedent for discriminating between those communities ready to enjoy the privileges of municipal status, as defined by law, and those still under the direct supervision of agents of the central government. Communities that have achieved municipal status are painfully circumscribed, and directly supervised communities are not encouraged to expand their activities. Although the Tunisian single-party system has shown itself willing to undertake certain major reforms, it has been slow to remedy these fundamental shortcomings.

---

[12] The interim system is outlined in article 21, "Convention sur la situation des personnes," *Convention entre la France et la Tunisie*, Paris, 1955, p. 38.

To understand the historic proportions of the distinction between the municipal and rural community in Tunisia, it is necessary to trace the development of the rural administration. The French kept the bey's rural organization virtually intact, buttressed with civil-affairs officers similar to those who worked in Morocco. The bey had had a number of *caids* stationed in the major towns, from where rural affairs were managed through tribal delegates or *shioukh* (sing., *sheikh*). The similarity of titles between Morocco and Tunisia does not imply similarity of function. From 1705 on, there are numerous precedents of the appointment of *caids* by the bey, and there developed a relatively coherent, centralized system except for areas of dissidence in the south. In an attempt to strengthen the regime against the European threat, the bey required the *caids* to keep a set of accounts after 1875, and the next year assured the *caids* of a regular income from the tribal clans they were assigned to supervise. As in more recent times, limited reform only produced more abuse, and the pre-Protectorate system does not appear to have operated any more impartially than the colonial system.

Under the Protectorate the *caids* continued to be elected by the tribe or tribal clans they governed, but by the late nineteenth century tribal patterns began to disappear and the *caids* were selected more and more by a council of notables of the region. The Protectorate was divided into thirty-six *circonscriptions*, which remained the basic unit of rural organization until independence. By the turn of the century the tribes had sufficiently disintegrated to make the selection of their *sheikh* the subject of great acrimony. In 1905 the ethnic basis of selection was abandoned in favor of territorial units within the *circonscription*, for which the *caid* would make a list of qualified candidates for *sheikh* positions. The list was submitted to central authorities, who arbitrarily appointed the *shioukh* on the *caid's* recommendations.[13] Thus a tradition of centralized authority was introduced at a time when the tribal patterns were beginning to break down enough to permit more effective local participation in affairs outside the tribal framework. Centralization was not unusual among colonial practices of the time, however, and after 1925 the local officials were all appointed by the Protectorate without the doubtful help of the *caid's* nominations.

These officials were clearly not suited to the challenge of modernization, and they came eventually to pose an obstacle to even the relatively low level of activity needed to operate the Protectorate. In 1922 the regime introduced Caidat Councils, Regional Councils, and the Grand Council. The development of the *caids'* assembles represented a halfhearted attempt to decentralize the administration and to improve the quality of local government. The change was accompanied by in-

---

[13] Senoussi, *op.cit.*, p. 16.

creased specialization in Tunis, where the secretary general's office was divided into a Directorate of the Interior and a Directorate of Tunisian Justice.[14] The Caidat Council was selected by the *caid* from his list of local notables, an interesting continuation of the *grandes familles* pattern of rule.

The regional and national councils never enjoyed substantial powers, but they could handle requests from the *caid* level and discuss the annual budgets. Certainly Tunisia can be credited with a much more advanced system of local administration than Morocco had at the time, although the Protectorate was not eager to see a massive mobilization of Tunisian energies for developmental or any other purpose. Very little more was done except to make the local *shioukh* elective in 1945, part of the battery of reforms that then affected the municipal councils as well. However, the French did introduce an examination system for *caids,* but then failed to use it. With the growth of the nationalist movement the *caid's* role was shaped more and more to the police needs of the Protectorate. He was also assigned a variety of additional functions. When the rural administration was being overhauled shortly after independence, an official of the Ministry of the Interior described a *caid* as "accountant and judge, police officer, civil representative and finally mayor of the commune."[15]

In comparison with the Moroccan experience almost the reverse policy governed at the local level. Partly because of the greater rural wealth and larger *colon* group in Morocco, the Protectorate tried to advance the remote areas to a point where they could hold their own, hopefully to include French interests, against the rising tide of nationalism in the coastal regions. The equilibrium was never achieved, but it left an entirely different precedent for local reform than that of the Tunisian Protectorate. The French in Tunisia were quite content to leave the less promising Sahel plain and arid south to the Tunisians, and saw little chance of using the remnants of tribal life to resist the vigorous Socialist Destour. The resultant discrimination between the more articulate, more advanced centers and the rest of the countryside was harmonious with colonial needs. For different reasons it has also proved to be harmonious with the needs of the postindependence single-party regime. Despite the long experience with local government in Tunisia, the basic pattern remains unchanged. Relative to the society as a whole, it could even be argued that ground has been lost. The minority of the population enjoying the council system finds its interests and expression

---

[14] This early articulation of the Tunisian Protectorate's administrative organization contrasts with events in Morocco, where the secretary general remained a powerful administrative figure at the time of independence and has kept much of his colonial power in the new Moroccan government. On the Tunisian reorganization see Pellegrin, *op.cit.,* p. 198, and Silvera, *op.cit.,* pp. 279-291.

[15] *Action Tunisienne,* June 25, 1956.

as restrained as under the Protectorate, if not more so, while its capacity to participate in local activities has increased. From a developmental viewpoint the uniform views of the present supervisors of local government, emanating from the Socialists Destour's Political Bureau, can be just as stultifying as the earlier abuses of the *caids*.

THE PARTY CHALLENGED BY DIVERSITY

There are essential political differences between the developmental processes of Morocco and Tunisia. For the monarchy in a relatively heterogeneous social setting new institutions were devised to fit new social demands. Despite the procrastination and apprehension apparent in the system's response, the Palace did accommodate increasing diversity and changing demands from one developmental phase to the next. In the single-party system emphasis on accommodation of social difference is replaced with anticipation of how differences might be expressed. The Socialist Destour did not seek a reconciliation with the social forces of the country so much as it sought to superimpose party-inspired solutions.

For Bourguiba development did not mean finding new institutional solutions for existing social realities, but seeking to force social realities within the mold of the single-party system. In the political realm creativity and spontaneity were suspect. Simultaneously, the regime had to make considerable concession to entrenched social and political forces in order to protect the veneer of political harmony. The Bourguibist tactic is characterized by its method of isolating and eliminating one group at a time after carefully placating and isolating other groups that might support the potential threat to the republic. The political system must always operate along predetermined paths and decisions can be announced only after alliances and rewards are agreed upon.[16]

The Bourguibist system is replete with paradox. Though more is done to mobilize the mass than in Morocco or Pakistan, the individual citizen is kept more distant from effective power. The personal dynamism of *le grand combattant* is some compensation, but is no substitute for institutional patterns for the modernization of the society. The Moroccan citizen can derive some feeling of participation from religious sentiments attached to the *imam*, but he is also comparatively free to engage in new organizations, parties, and associations for other purposes. For the Tunisian citizen there is participation on the grounds

[16] This interpretation attributes more significance to the differences among Tunisian leadership than does the account of Moore in *World Politics, op.cit.* For more details on these differences and their implications for development see the author's "Tunisian Leadership and the 'Confiscated Revolution,'" *World Politics*, vol. 27, no. 2, January 1965, pp. 215-231.

offered by the Socialist Destour or none at all. It is not surprising, therefore, that opposition should be expressed in the attempted coup and passive resistance.[17] The Tunisian regime can be changed only by its partial destruction.

President Bourguiba has shown great personal courage in undertaking some major reforms in his country, and they are nearly all reforms basic to the speedy development of the country. It must be asked, however, whether these reforms have significance for the expanding role of the individual in a more intricate society, or if they were inspired by their potential or real threat to Socialist Destour unanimity. The municipal councils, for example, have not expanded to a degree that the comparatively advanced state of the society might have supported. Presidential daring is exercised with guile and charm so that fundamental changes are always harmonious with the single-party scheme. Institutions are established only when it is certain the party and its supporting associations can control them, and final decisions are made only when all powerful social groups have been reconciled. It is important to note that this deceptively smooth mode of operation has been seriously upset only since Bourguiba has firmly committed himself to economic development. "Bourguibism" meant having no doctrine and favoring no group. The demands of rapid development have removed these requisites to political maneuverability. Tunisia must now fashion more lasting, self-regulating institutions to deal with the complexities of a modern society.

The party's reaction to the councils on the eve of independence was similar to that seen in Morocco, although it did reveal one of the persistent shortcomings of the single-party system. There were strongly Arab extremist elements within the Socialist Destour in 1955 who favored continuing the battle for North African independence with Nasser's support.[18] The Arabist faction also objected to the terms for

[17] *Jeune Afrique*, December 19-26, 1962. The self-examinations following the attempts to assassinate the president are one of the few candid and public periods of criticism of the regime. It was virtually admitted that the party had become so transfixed by its orientation to party needs, and, ultimately, the president's demands, that it was no longer a reliable vehicle for communication between the people and the government. Even so, Bourguiba's first action was to engage in a new purge and a bitter exchange with Algeria for sheltering one of the schemers.

[18] Relations were delicate with Morocco at this time where there was a similar division of opinion. The old guard of the Istiqlal, especially Al-Fassi, felt that the younger Istiqlal leaders were abandoning the North African independence movement. Both Al-Fassi and Tunisian Islamic groups with comparable views favored continued fighting, which Nasser was apparently prepared to support. Salah Ben Youssef represents the entirely harmonious group on the extreme left, whose secular and Nasserist leanings could be overlooked in the struggle against the French. It was one of the few moments of open association of extreme progressive and extreme conservative forces, which was precluded from taking on larger proportions in Tunisia by Ben Youssef's exile. Even so, there remained much sympathy for him among the Islamic groups.

autonomy and reliance on France. Salah Ben Youssef, who was vanquished by Bourguiba in the party congress of November 1955, later went into exile and became the center of a series of conspiracies. One of the president's critically important supporters during his struggle for supremacy in the Socialist Destour was Mongi Slim.[19] Although Slim disliked the detailed tasks of internal reorganization, he was personally reliable and qualified for a high post by virtue of his party prestige. Therefore, he became Minister of the Interior and was one of the six Socialist Destour members of the interim cabinet formed by Tahar Ben Ammar after the convention was signed. In fact, Slim was not suited to the task, nor did the party seem to have a very clear notion of what it hoped to accomplish at the local level.

The old municipal councils, selected where possible under the Protectorate in 1953, were dissolved soon after Slim took office. Until new elections could be held, the councils were to be appointed by the Minister of the Interior. Quite clearly the interim councils were to be composed of party militants. For reasons that are not entirely clear, Slim was obstructed in the reorganization, although the party had decided that municipal posts would be parceled out through the local cell and other representatives of "national organizations."[20] Bourguiba was undoubtedly still encountering opposition from Youssefite supporters as well as from France, whose embassy asked to be consulted until independence negotiations were finished. The Socialist Destour did manage to replace the most important council, Tunis, but little else seems to have been accomplished.

The colonial onus was closely associated with the rural administration. The relative advancement of Tunisian society is reflected in the protests that were raised over continuing the Protectorate system, and Slim was subjected to severe criticism. The discussion is particularly noteworthy for it is one of the few public controversies concerning the administration, and one of the few times that a major party figure has been openly criticized. Five especially objectionable *caids* were removed in November, several months after Slim took office, but newspaper reports expressed doubt that the rural administrative conversion was being pursued with "vigor and desirable energy." No action had been taken a month later, and the minister was reminded of his promise to revise the *caid* system at the Sfax party congress. Reports implied that he might be sheltering pro-French *caids*, and asked if the minister might not be "sleeping on his laurels."[21] It is unbelievable, of course,

[19] The rules of Mongi Slim and Bahi Ladghdam during late 1955 are most clearly outlined in Lorna Hahn's *Nationalism and Nationhood in North Africa*, Washington, Public Affairs Press, 1960, pp. 166-176.

[20] *Action Tunisienne*, October 19, 1955.

[21] These are among the most outspoken criticisms of the Socialist Destour to appear in the press during this period. See *ibid.*, November 11, 1955, and

that Slim was purposefully delaying the conversion of the administrative machinery.

The incident is indicative of the responsiveness of the Tunisian political system in the national context, something which is yet to be achieved in Morocco and Pakistan. As the Socialist Destour gained momentum, however, the political arena became smaller. By the time more sweeping reorganization took place, the party machinery was in place and Bourguiba had added another triumph to his victory over Ben Youssef at the party congress. Under the aegis of the National Front, composed of the Socialist Destour and its auxiliary organizations, the single-party regime received popular endorsement. Shortly after independence was formally granted, the National Constituent Assembly was elected, with Bourguiba heading the list from his home town, Monastir. In the midst of independence celebrations and an alleged assassination plot engineered from Cairo by Ben Youssef, the election of April 1956 was more of a plebiscite for Bourguiba than a party contest. The Socialist Destour, the trade unions, and party organizations united in a National Front that easily swept away all opposition. The nationalist leader took his first step toward displacing the bey when he became premier shortly after the elections and organized a new cabinet with himself officially in charge for the first time.

These events will be analyzed in more detail below, but they are part of the necessary background to the ingenious process of building national institutions in proportion to the party's predetermined strength that characterizes the single-party regime in the developing country. The major reorganization at the local level took place about a month after the elections. Bourguiba appointed a new Minister of the Interior, Taib Mehiri, who is one of the few ministers to survive all cabinet shuffles until his death in 1965. One of his first acts was to handpick fourteen governors (*wali*), who became the heads of the new provincial system. The old *circonscription* system was abandoned, and over half the *caids* (105 of 160) were released.[22]

Like Morocco, Tunisia has had difficulties finding capable, reliable provincial chiefs. The first group of fifteen governors, which included the Director of Regional Administration, included two acceptable

---

December 12, 1955. It is evidence of Tunisia's relative advancement that such a sharp reaction against the Protectorate system should be voiced at such a critical juncture in Tunisian development.

[22] This was one of the first tasks of the new Minister of the Interior, Mehiri, whose press conferences at the time clearly indicate the importance the Socialist Destour attached to the new system. See *Action Tunisienne*, June 25, 1956, and *Petit-Matin*, June 22, 1956. It is indicative of Tunisian capacity for political organization that the rural administration was reorganized at the same time as the police force. Morocco managed to reconstruct her police at this time, but virtually nothing was done to reorient the rural administration.

caids from the old system, five men selected from within the government, and eight entirely new officials. They were hand-picked by the president, and their powers have never been legally defined. A top official of the ministry once described their powers as "draconian," and many responsible officials consider their office more influential than that of minister. The governors are in undisputed control of the police and all government services in their territory, and generally meet once a month with the president himself.

When Mehiri undertook the rural reorganization in early 1956 there was still sporadic fighting between Youssefists and Tunisians in parts of the south, and the threat of a Youssefist-inspired infiltration of the Socialist Destour through the party cells was quite real. Salah Ben Youssef had been in charge of the internal operations of the party since Bourguiba went into exile in 1952. He had also played a major role in organizing the Tunisian *fellagha*, who have been a constant source of discontent.[23] Furthermore, the rural administrators were also very concerned with keeping order and providing support for the Algerian revolutionaries who occupied most of the frontier regions. Not until 1961 was serious thought given to recasting the governors' roles, and by then the pattern of local government had been so firmly planted that the notion of a rural mobilization might easily have appeared alarming to rural officials.

Nothing could be done in the way of local reform without a thorough renovation of the regional and local administrative system. In comparison with Morocco, Tunisia promptly equipped herself with an effective, modernized organization. Though both governments were most concerned with surveillance of the populace, it is indicative of the single-party system's potential that Tunisia totally discarded the Protectorate and beylical structure. The thought of such a sweeping change did not even occur in Morocco, nor was there such an energetic reorientation of personnel. However, the Tunisian adaptation, like other major changes in the political system, was closely tuned to the needs of the single-party system and was used to staff key posts with party reliables. The president was fully capable of making popular contact in support of an articulated range of goals, and the Tunisian people were better prepared than most to work with the conceptual complexities of locally focused development activities. But the renovation never reached the local level with sufficient impact to dislodge energies and initiative appropriate to national developmental needs.

[23] The conspiracy to assassinate Bourguiba involved several ex-*fellagha* leaders, whose devotion to Ben Youssef and Nasserist ideas contributed to their discontent in armed forces. Although the guerilla movement organized by Ben Youssef in southern Tunisia and western Lybia was much smaller than the Moroccan Army of Liberation, it was much more heavily affected by revolutionary zeal, and continued to operate for several months after independence under Youssefist leadership.

The explanation of this failure centers on the overriding requirement that all political activity be kept within the scope of the single-party system. Early in 1956 the government withdrew budgetary powers from the interim councils, and began to reorganize the Tunis council. Since Tunis is the focus of Tunisian political life, including some elements critical of party policy, and constitutes nearly a tenth of the nation's populace, its council had obvious importance. In addition, the strength of the party cadre in Tunis and the presence of many high party leaders meant that the renovated municipal council would not easily escape party management. Even so, the transition went slowly and it was not until the late fall of 1956 that the Ministry of the Interior announced that the Tunis council would soon resume activities.[24] The appointed mayor was the late Ali Belhaouane, an intimate friend of the president. At that time it was also revealed that new elections for the other municipal councils had been planned first for October, and then later for December. Local elections were eventually postponed until May 1957.

Preparation for the local elections posed grave problems for the party. It was not organized to fight local elections. There were 39 regional federations grouping about 1,300 cells in 1957.[25] The federations were located roughly in proportion to population density, although the Sahel and Tunis areas were more highly organized. Though not widely known at the time, it appeared later that the party headquarters did not always prevail in cell and federation activities.[26] Any vestiges of Youssefite support or more traditional Islamic sentiment that might protest Bourguiba's relentless attack on religious institutions was much more likely to manifest itself in local elections than in the more fervent nationalist setting of the Constituent Assembly vote. Given these circumstances, it is not surprising that the Socialist Destour was reluctant to hold local elections. The strong historical precedent for the municipal councils, plus the relatively active community life of the Tunisian towns, may have pressed the party into action at the local level before it was fully prepared.

The party's organizational limitations, as well as possible doubts over its local solidarity, meant that local elections could not be organized

[24] *Petit-Matin*, November 11, 1956. After Bourguiba became president in the summer of 1957, the title of "Minister" was abolished in favor of "Secretary of State." For consistency and clarity the initial title will be used throughout this study, even though the change in title did correspond to a slight downgrading of the cabinet office. Bourguiba quite clearly intended that the president of the republic be more than *primus inter pares* in cabinet meetings and in the public eye.

[25] These figures are based on interviews with party officials in 1958. There was also one federation for Parisian-based Tunisians, mostly students, and one in Cairo.

[26] The clearest statement to this effect was Bourguiba's weekly speech of October 8, 1958, when the question of the party reorganization was first presented publicly. The speech is reprinted in *Les Congrès du Néo-Destour*, Tunis, 1959, especially pp. 89-91.

along National Front lines. The decision to disassociate local elections from national affairs is, therefore, implicit in Tunisian preparations. The slogan for the local elections first appeared in a party talk of Bahi Ladgham in late 1956, when he announced the program of *relèvement social* or social recovery. In cooperation with the national groups allied to the Socialist Destour, each cell was supposed to initiate a local project for community improvement. The program was intended to work in cooperation with the public-relief program, and hoped to direct such relief toward community needs, as will be discussed in more detail below. In fact, the public-relief program and the party's community-project scheme did not get under way on a national scale for several years, but the early interest in stimulating localities was manifested and, at the same time, presented serious dilemmas for the single-party regime.

In April 1957 Mehiri reported to the party's National Council[27] on the government's election plans, and explained the new Municipal Law. As in the national elections, the list voting system would be used, with the party cells encouraged to form *relèvement social* lists wherever possible. He acknowledged that the National Front would not be used, but did not stop to explain why it was inappropriate. The cell lists would be passed on to the federations and the Political Bureau, which would have the final word. Municipal councilors were elected for 94 communes, 30 more than existed under the Protectorate law of 1952. There were a total of 770 seats to be filled. An opposition list was filed in nearly a fourth of the municipalities, a remarkable indication of variety of viewpoint given the apparent prevalence of the Socialist Destour.

The number of opposition lists helps explain the party's hesitance to commit the National Front and its nationally focused prestige to the local contests. Indeed, it might have been most difficult to revive the Front because of the trade-union split of late 1956, which was repaired only a week before the local elections. The party's uneasiness is detectable in a preelection decision of the National Council to permit candidates "not having responsibility in cells or federations" to run in such cases as the federations judged the candidates "efficient and of a reliable background." Given the constant assertion of party solidarity with the auxiliary organizations, the decision to endorse individuals who did not have impressive party histories was a considerable concession to local forces. Except for a Communist list run in Tunis, the opposition lists were without party identification and ran simply as "independents." There were fifteen independent opposition lists, of which five were elected. In only two instances did the Socialist Destour

27 *Petit-Matin*, April 4, 1957.

authorize the inclusion of candidates on *relèvement* lists in the absence of party backgrounds.[28]

The electoral experience of May 1957 confirmed the party's apprehensions, and it is noticeable that the election results were not announced with the blare of publicity given to the more definite victories of the president and his colleagues in national elections. The fact that Tunisia had approximately an 80 per cent turnout for local elections, without anything approaching the vigorous appeal to vote that was made in Morocco in 1960, testifies to the relatively high degree of integration already achieved in Tunisia. For the party, however, the 20 to 25 per cent rate of abstention represented individuals who could not be mobilized by the party organization even though they had sufficient civic awareness to register. The turnout was sufficiently less than in the national elections to suggest a substantial opposition. In some communities, like Msaken in Sousse province, only 60 per cent of the registered voters came out, and there was vigorous competition among three lists of candidates.[29]

The social significance of this opposition is important in relating the elections to the development problems of the country. First, the party did not hold elections where it was not reasonably certain it could win. There is no way of estimating how many communities lacking strong party cells or hostile to the Socialist Destour have not been given the status of municipal council. Thus there may be some additional, uncounted opposition. Second, where the municipal councils are established, the community is supposed to be sufficiently advanced to manage its own affairs. It must also have certain minimal financial resources. Thus the dissent expressed in the local elections is much more likely to be an articulate, socially significant dissent than that of Morocco.

Bourguiba's introduction of the proposed changes in party organization at the 1959 congress reveals that the Socialist Destour may never have had as direct lines to the base of the party as the president desired. He characterized the role of the militants as "executing the

[28] Details on the 1957 elections were obtained from the Ministry of the Interior during visits to Tunisia in both 1958 and 1962. Additional information can be found in Senoussi, *op.cit.*, p. 35, and the newspaper accounts in *Action Tunisienne*, May 6, 1957, and *Petit-Matin*, April 30, 1957. The latter are useful as an index to the importance attached to the local elections by the government. It is noteworthy that the Socialist Destour was much more concerned about local elections in 1957, when there was a chance that the party would suffer a public defeat, than in 1960, when party hegemony was more secure and development problems had multiplied.

[29] Government officials are reluctant to discuss some of the problems that came up during the 1957 elections, and government regional figures blur some of the important differences in turnout. The newspapers of the period recapture some of the uncertainty of the election process, an experience that clearly caused great discomfort for the Socialist Destour leaders.

directives of the party and guiding the people toward a healthy orientation, conforming to these directives."[30] After outlining how the cell
structure had proliferated and how the membership had grown in the
postindependence enthusiasm, he pointed out how these popular energies were difficult to direct toward party objectives. In the president's
words, "One no longer finds the same spirit of sacrifice and the same
wish for abnegation. Victory achieved, it appears that numerous elements, undoubtedly insufficiently trained, are intoxicated by prestige
and do not know how to conduct themselves." This indirect admission
of party irresponsibility and disinterest at the local level helps explain
why the government had not been able to do more with the municipal
councils, and reminds one that the single-party scheme is not infallible
in handling more complex social problems.

With reference to preparations for coping with a rural mobilization,
Bourguiba's comments on the new party structure are particularly
significant. He admitted that the old system of federations had been
based on the *caidats*, with an attempt at organizing one or more cells
for each *sheikhat*. The diffusion of party strength and dilution of party
cadre greatly weakened the party.[31] The revised Socialist Destour organization still followed the pattern of the rural administration, but
with the Political Bureau acting as the party's Minister of the Interior.
The bureau appointed a party delegate for each governorate, who was
to represent the party in government activities at the provincial level.
The party cells would be responsible to him, although a provincial
committee would still exist for consultative purposes. The 1,300 party
cells would be reduced in number to be roughly equal to the number of
sheikats (700), and party membership would be confined to more
active persons. The old federations, whose committees had sometimes
been too parochial to bend to party directives, were dissolved. Although
there were some grumblings over the demise of the familiar structure,
henceforth Bourguiba had at his disposal a parallel organization of
party and state to communicate his wishes to the Tunisian people. The
advantages of smooth administration and central control are indisputable, but a certain price was paid in the loss of local initiative and
spontaneous development. The dimensions of such a loss are difficult
to measure, but are suggested by the relatively minor role assigned to
the municipal councils and other localized activity.

Subsequent chapters will explore in more detail other aspects of how
the single-party system manifests distrust of independent community
action. The impact of the new party organization on local elections,

---

[30] *Les Congrès du Néo-Destour, op.cit.*, p. 89.
[31] With somewhat greater regional disparities of organizational strength, the
Istiqlal faced very similar problems of reorganization after independence. See
Political Change in Morocco, op.cit., pp. 243-259.

however, is quite clear. The 1960 municipal elections were originally announced for May Day in order to coincide with the annual trade-union festivities, but were later held in mid-May. Despite the new party organization the number of councils was not substantially increased. Only 22 new towns and villages were added, making a total of 116 councils. Although the 1959 National Assembly elections had provided evidence of Bourguiba's popularity, it was again decided that the National Front would not be associated with local activities. The slogan of the local elections once again was *relevement social*, although there are no indications that the Socialist Destour lists again accepted candidates lacking experience in the party or one of the national organizations. The Communist party of Tunis was the only opposition group that appeared, and their list was withdrawn shortly before the elections. The over-all level of voting was higher than in 1957.[32] Only in Sfax did less than two thirds of the registered voters turn out, although the number of voters in the Kef, Kasserine, Gafsa, and Tunis regions was substantially below the 90 per cent or better voting in the rest of the country. These are the same regions where abstentions ran high in 1957, and where there are some historic sources of discontent. The Ministry of the Interior lacks figures on how many incumbent councilors the party chose to nominate for reelection, but interviews with regional officials indicate that approximately half of the 1957 councilors were replaced in 1960. The rate of attrition suggests that the 1957 councils may not have been too well qualified, although it is impossible to allow for party considerations in the nomination process.

Like the Moroccan rural-commune elections of 1963, the Tunisian municipal-council elections in 1963 aroused little interest. The basic format of the earlier elections was maintained, and the lists were, for the first time, entirely unopposed.[33] Considering the important modifications of party organization and the changes in rural administration in the preceding four years, the apparent satisfaction with self-justifying unanimity created at the local level again suggests the apprehension of the single-party regime. The routinization of local elections also created the possibility that the party would be embarrassed by the high rate of abstention, which was severely condemned in the visitations to the communities. A notable change was that the president gave up his historic seat at Monastir in favor of his son, Bourguiba, Jr.

ORGANIZED RESTRAINT AT THE LOCAL LEVEL

The local council can easily become an unpredictable group within the single-party system. As the preceding section has indicated, the Socialist

[32] The official results of the 1960 elections can be found in *Petit-Matin*, May 10, 1960.
[33] *Jeune Afrique*, May 13-18, 1963.

Destour's organization and leadership have imposed certain restraints on the councils to make sure that harmony prevails, at least on the surface, in the political system. If institutions are used only to reflect unanimity and to bestow national prestige, it is difficult to shape them to the widely differing local conditions to which operating national institutions of more advanced nations adapt. The reconciliation of local needs and desires with national capabilities and requirements is achieved at the price of an imposed uniformity from the center of power. The parallel system of control creates an illusion of more effective government because the government does not in fact deal with the human complexity of Tunisian society. An attempt is made to resolve problems and conflicts within the party and by the skillful use of Bourguiba's charm and power. While the Moroccan monarchial system has difficulty in making local contacts because its mode of operation is simply unrelated to developmental needs, the Tunisian system fails to make local contact in a meaningful way because it cannot risk being committed in an unpredictable situation.

With a hundred years of experience the Tunisian local-government structure is hardly more advanced than Morocco's innovations since 1956. The trend has followed that established within the Protectorate period. Powers have gradually been eroded or removed as they posed a threat to the central authority. Notice appeared early in 1956 that the municipal councils would no longer exercise authority over special budgets once assigned to the local level. While the act was probably necessitated by the exigencies of the moment, there is no record of this power having been restored. The austerity program following independence also led to the relieving of the councils of the obligatory contribution to local hospital expenses. This act was first announced by the president at the installation of the new local council at Sousse, and later appeared to be applied to all the municipalities.[34]

With all due regard to the limited resources of the municipalities, the government's attitude toward the councils is summed up in the following inaugural address to the Msaken council in 1957. The governor hoped that the new council would "consecrate themselves to [the community's] urban, esthetic and general well-being" and, thereby, "contribute to concord and national unity."[35] The sharp distinction between national and local affairs has been reinforced and the councils have been directed toward local improvements in only the most limited spheres. Discord at the local level has been treated as a neglect of the

[34] *Action Tunisienne*, June 12 and 19, 1957.
[35] *Petit-Matin*, May 21, 1957. It will be remembered that this was one of the councils where an independent slate had been run, and was also one of the councils to be dissolved before the 1960 elections. The history of discontent continued into 1964, when Msaken was the scene of violent opposition to agricultural reforms.

council's obligation to reflect the prearranged harmony of the regime. Any expressed reservations as to how the nation might better assist local efforts or more accurately respond to local desires were forbidden.

The Tunisian Municipal Law of 1957[36] imposes much more stringent restrictions on the councils than the similar legislation of Morocco, the administrative efficiency and political cohesion of the single-party regime notwithstanding. From an administrative viewpoint the critical qualification is the community's financial viability, and no steps have been taken within the framework of the local-government legislation to assist those communities falling short of the government's expectations. The exact criteria have never been made public, and it is, therefore, difficult to determine how financial and other qualifications are judged in practice. Officials of the Ministry of the Interior feel that all qualified communities have been given councils, and they do not foresee a major extension of the local-government system to the entire population. Under the law the president of the republic and the Minister of the Interior exercise all powers over the creation, delimitation, and suppression of the councils (art. 2).

The provisions designed to restrict the councils' activities to local affairs in the most narrow sense are numerous. First, the council is permitted to give views on laws and regulations only as requested by the administration (art. 44). The council is to express views only on objects of "local interest." Any deliberation affecting an object "foreign to its attributions or taken outside its legal meeting" is automatically annulled, as are any decisions in conflict with existing laws or regulations (art. 46). Furthermore, the council is forbidden "to publish proclamations or addresses, to emit political views, or put itself in communication with one or more councils except as defined by law" (art. 55). Although the proceedings of the council meetings are publicly posted, there is no indication of how the government has interpreted the sweeping terms of the law. It is quite clear from meeting with local officials, however, that nothing is suggested or discussed without previous clearance from Tunis. In explaining the apparent reluctance to give the councils autonomous powers, ministry officials immediately fall back on the *autorité tutelle* or guardianship of the central government. Given the institutional patterns of the regime, the Tunisian councils have even less opportunity to express local needs or desires than the Moroccan rural communes.

[36] All local-government legislation and local-election procedures are contained in a brochure, *Loi Municipale*, 2d edn., Tunis, 1960. It is interesting to note that although the Tunisian legislation applies less widely than the Moroccan, the Tunisians have done a better job in bringing all applicable laws, regulations, and decrees into one publication for the use of officials and the public. The implication for more effective government is fairly obvious, but it also suggests the Tunisians' concern for uniformity.

Having listed all the actions the councils are forbidden to take, the law next gives all the actions which must be approved by superior authority: the communal budget, supplementary credits, loans, local tax changes, the transfer of communal property, and numerous other acts affecting the internal affairs of the municipality (art. 50). These are the day-to-day activities of municipal management, which are supposed to be the primary responsibility of the council. Although the list of activities is longer than that found in Morocco, the reservations of the central government are just as great. The attitude toward local government is much the same as in Morocco, but in Tunisia explicit steps are taken to outline the council's relationship to all the supervisory agencies.

For example, the president of the council is given certain police powers in chairing meetings and in the management of the community streets, markets, et cetera. However, extremely detailed instructions are provided in the law as to how the commune may make requests of the police, who explicitly remain agents of the state (arts. 79-82). Although the council's attention is directed toward the management of the local budget and the municipal facilities, very little can be done without the permission of the Finance and Public Works Ministries in Tunis. In communities of under 10,000 persons the governor has been assigned power to regulate some of these matters—a fact which thereby acknowledges that excessive ministerial control at the local level might be obstructive in even the modest operations assigned to the local councils. However, actions affecting the defined local matters in municipalities of over 10,000 must be submitted to the Ministry of the Interior, a more onerous check than exists for the large municipalities of Morocco (art. 51). The councils undoubtedly found it extremely difficult to conduct business under these conditions, and in 1958 the governors were given the authority to approve budgets under 75,000 *dinars* or approximately $150,000. This authority is much greater than that given to similar Moroccan officials, who have very little influence in the financial matters of their provinces, and applies in over a hundred of the municipalities. In effect, the regulations make nearly all the councils responsible to the governors, while the dozen or so large towns and cities must submit their actions to the Director of Regional and Communal Affairs in the Ministry of the Interior.

If the councils were to begin to exercise their financial initiative with the encouragement of the government, the present restrictions would not be burdensome. The Tunisian councils are designed to enable the community to undertake major projects, although in practice these provisions have been applied conservatively. With the permission of the Ministry of the Interior and other ministries concerned, a council can accept loans for local improvements. When the system was revised in 1957 the government found that sixteen councils were devoting from

10 to 25 per cent of their income to paying old debts, and that four councils were paying from 25 to 50 per cent of their income. Early in 1958 the government refunded this debt in order to relieve the burden on the debtor councils, mostly the large towns and cities, and gave them new loans at low interest. There have also been a fairly large number of new loans to more prosperous communities for drainage (2), electrification (5), and public transport (12). In all cases these loans must be endorsed by a decree of the Ministry of the Interior, and there is little evidence that councils are encouraged to initiate projects.[37]

The Municipal Law is very specific, like the Moroccan law, on the sources and uses of local revenue. The Tunisian councils are obliged to bear the costs of the meeting house, the operation of the council's office and staff, the maintenance of municipal property and installations, and the care of the streets, fountains, and waterways within the community (art. 105). At the same time the councils have more substantial sources of income, including a share of Common Funds or regional subsidy, income from communal property and installations, real-estate taxes, and indirect taxes on beverages, cartage, entertainment, and other enterprises relying on the community for support (art. 106). Thus the municipal councils have a considerable realm of activity, but their realm is closely circumscribed by the details of the Municipal Law and other legislation. The responsibilities of housekeeping are so many that the municipal council is unlikely to think of local activities of significance in the economic development of the country. Nothing has been done to channel local energies along lines defined by the community, although there are numerous *chantiers* or public-relief projects working under the governors' supervision. With the exception of one legal device the municipal councils are confined to the bureaucratic mold laid down by the Protectorate during the Third Republic.

The single exception to this approach to local reform is the law on syndicates of municipal councils passed early in 1959.[38] With the permission of the Ministry of the Interior and also Finance, a group of municipal councils were empowered to pool their property, revenues, loans, or other funds for major improvements. The economies of some joint effort first became apparent in the administration of the bordering towns to the north of Tunis. Under the law they were able to share certain services and utilities. Since 1957 there has been increasing attention focused on cooperative enterprise. According to officials in the ministry there were fifteen syndicates operating in 1962, some engaged in tourist projects, fishing, and transportation services. To some extent these enterprises appear to have been formed in response to

[37] Senoussi, *op.cit.*, pp. 66-67.
[38] *Loi Municipal, op.cit.*, pp. 37-43.

efforts by the trade unions to expand the use of cooperatives and other popularly owned and operated businesses. The scale of the response indicates, however, that the local councils have been encouraged to participate in developmental activities under close central control and supervision.

The Tunisian Municipal Law is not intended to contribute to the rural-mobilization effort in the way that the Moroccan and Pakistani laws seek to provide new stimuli for neglected segments of the populace. Of course, there is no reason why conceptual innovation must focus on the local government, but it will become apparent in later chapters that the Tunisian political system has exercised similar precaution in all its developmental efforts. Being a somewhat better integrated, more specialized society, one might expect that local reform would have become more institutionalized, and that new needs would be met by innovation in other areas of local activity. In fact, this did not occur until the pressures for widespread change and social revolution threatened to destroy party harmony and to cause irreparable damage to Tunisian society, thereby handicapping any future development effort. At the local level, however, there was even less adaptation to developmental demands, conceived in either the social or psychological sense, than in Morocco and Pakistan.

SINGLE-PARTY REQUIREMENTS FOR PARTICIPATION

The hesitance of the Tunisian political system is more apparent in comparing the postindependence legislation with the earlier Protectorate laws. It is understandable that the French colonial government found it advisable to withdraw powers from the municipal councils, as was done in 1914 and 1931. But the independent government has not restored functions and powers removed from the councils since 1884, and the present law is very like the Protectorate decree of 1914.[39] Fifty years ago the councils could call on the police for municipal matters, enter into intercommunal syndicates if resources were available, accept loans for approved purposes, and levy roughly the same taxes being levied in 1962. The advisory and consultative role of the local councils appears to have been much larger than it is today. Like the Minister of the Interior under the new Municipal Law, the Protectorate could annul most acts of the council or summarily suspend its activities, but the old system did permit the councils to plead certain conflicts in court—an important device to communicate new problems at the local level and to seek solutions through institutional channels open to all citizens.

In addition to the allocation of resources the patterns of creaitng and distributing the councils provides some insight into their relationship

[39] *Monographie des Services, op.cit.*

to the political system as a whole. The rate of establishment of municipal councils has not changed noticeably since independence. Between 1956 and the first elections, about twenty new councils were formed, and twenty-two councils were established between the 1957 and 1960 elections. Although officials prefer to pass off the arbitrary suspension of councils, the *Journal Officiel* also records six dissolutions through 1961. Three of the five independent lists elected in 1957 were dissolved. The decrees generally provide short statements of the local difficulty. In Sousse, for example, it appeared that the "conduct of the municipal councilors was of a kind likely to harm administrative operations," while for Megrine a more direct statement revealed that "dissensions existed within the council . . . to a degree of sharpness likely to hurt local operations." In several relatively important towns, like La Goulette and Nabeul, councilors were removed for misconduct or dishonesty. These cases indicate the comparative advancement of the Tunisian system. Abuse at the local level seems to be detected and remedied to a greater extent than in the less advanced societies of Pakistan and Morocco. The simple fact that these cases are routinely reported in government publications suggests the relative sophistication of the administrative process in some spheres.

The obvious deficiency of the Tunisian local-government scheme as a development vehicle is its limited application. However, even a limited scheme can have important developmental impact and contribute to national integration if its energies are focused on the less advanced regions. Despite political slogans about the "disinherited regions," the Tunisian municipal-council system has not distinguished itself by concentrating either financially or organizationally on the neglected areas or provinces. In connection with the organizational aspect first, it should be recalled that the council system was well established in the Protectorate period. There are now thirty-two towns over 10,000 in Tunisia, for example, and all but three have had municipal councils since 1921.[40] Thus nearly every major community in Tunisia has had nearly forty years' experience with regulating municipal affairs in the restricted context of the Protectorate, and this framework has been extended in contemporary Tunisia with little modification. The organizational experience on which Bourguiba might have called extends well beyond the large towns. There are twenty-five municipal councils dating from before 1900, and twenty-eight more were added by 1922. Roughly two thirds of the present councils had been established prior to Tunisian independence.[41] This being the case, the government's very

[40] *Annuaire Statistique de la Tunisie*, Tunis, Service des Statistiques, 11ème vol., 1959, p. 16.

[41] This calculation is based on the list of communes published in 1956, which also gives date of establishment. See *Recensement Général de la Population de la Tunisie* (*Répartition Géographique de la Population*), Tunis, Service des

cautious approach to the creation of additional councils warrants careful examination.

The calculations presented in Table II reveal several aspects of municipal organization. First, the tendency has been to concentrate the councils in those provinces where the Socialist Destour has historic strongholds. The provinces of Tunis, Nabeul, and Sousse, areas dominated by the nationalist *bourgeoisie* prior to independence, include almost half the municipal councils. A comparison of the 1956 and 1960 lists of councils shows that Sousse has been particularly favored. Of the forty-one councils formed since independence eleven were estab-

TABLE II

Regional and Population Distribution of the Tunisian Councils in 1960

Province	Councils in 1960[a]	Council Pop. (th)[b]	Provincial Pop. (th)	Per Cent Pop. Organized
Tunis	18	445	582	76
Béja	6	48	235	21
Bizerte	8	127	222	57
Gabès	7	49	188	26
Gafsa[c]	7	73	288	25
Kairouan	7	38	203	19
Kef	9	41	248	17
Médenine	7	34	171	20
Nabeul[c]	11	93	231	40
Sbeitla[c]	5	15	159	9
Sfax	5	84	326	26
Souk al-Arba	6	16	190	8
Sousse	20	224	434	52
Totals	116	1,287	3,477	37

[a] The number of communes by province is taken from the *Loi Municipale*, Tunis, Ministry of the Interior, 1960, pp. 34-36.

[b] The population figures are all from the 1956 census. Since population movements tend to be toward the cities, changes since then would most probably be biased toward further concentration in more advanced, more urbanized provinces. The population figures by commune are given in *Recensement Général de la Population de la Tunisie* (*Répartition Geographique*), Tunis, Service des Statistiques, 1956, pp. 116-119. For councils created since 1956 it is necessary to look at the list of all towns and villages, *ibid.*, pp. 120-191.

[c] Gafsa includes most of Tozeur province, which was abolished shortly after independence. Nabeul is sometimes referred to as Cap Bon, and Sbeitla as Kasserine.

Statistiques, 1956, pp. 116-119. The data contained in the list was also used in compiling the regional distribution used in the following paragraph. It should perhaps be noted that the structural features of the councils on the national level do not indicate that there were no vigorous differences at the local level, but only the difficulty in relating such differences to national problems. See Clement H. Moore, "Politics in a Tunisian Village," *Middle East Journal*, vol. 17, no. 4, Late Autumn 1963, pp. 527-540.

lished for Soussi towns. Five more were formed in Nabeul, although some effort was also made in the less advanced provinces of Gabès and Kairouan, where the former was assigned five more councils and the latter six more. The prevailing pattern has been to build up the council system in the provinces where the party has had a powerful organization for many years, which are also areas that tend to be more highly developed.

The calculations in Table II of the proportions of the various provinces encompassed in the 1960 municipal-council system reveal additional disparities. Although Tunisian officials often claim that "nearly half" the population participates in the councils, it appears unlikely that more than two fifths actually do so. Furthermore, if the large council of Tunis with its appointed mayor is subtracted, only a third of the total Tunisian population now finds opportunities in the municipal system. The provincial figures for Tunis province are, of course, distorted by the importance of the capital city (272,000 Tunisians in 1956). The national distribution of the scheme emerges more clearly by holding aside the more highly urbanized, more developed provinces of Tunis, Bizerte, Nabeul, and Sousse. If this is done, no more than about a fifth of the Tunisian citizens receive the careful privileges of the council system. The municipalities certainly do not exhaust Tunisian efforts to assist the more remote, less advanced provinces, but it is quite clear that the municipality scheme has not been enlarged upon in areas where a favorable setting did not already exist. This means that potential benefits of generating civic awareness and mobilizing community resources have been lost, though there have been other centrally directed efforts to help such regions.

Barring a significant change of policy, the majority of Tunisians are represented by their governor, and their local needs and desires must be communicated through him to the Ministry of the Interior. To assist him in these duties the Governorate Councils were established in 1957. These councils, like the municipal councils, have a long history. Even before the Protectorate there were distinguished families in the various regions that provided services and support for the bey. These relationships provided a basis for the rudimentary representative institutions found in Tunisia, and have continuing significance in Tunisian politics. From 1891 the Protectorate maintained contact with many regional aristocrats through the Consultative Conference. When this institution underwent reorganization in 1922, Regional and Caidat Councils were established.[42] Although the councils were certainly subordinated to the Protectorate's wishes, the Governorate Councils have clear organizational precedents and are no doubt familiar to most Tunisians.

[42] Elie Fitoussi and Aristide Benazet, *L'Etat Tunisien et la Protectorate Francaise 1825-1931*, Paris, Libraire Arthur Rousseau, tome I, 1931, pp. 270-280.

The Tunisian government's interest in reviving the regional councils reflects the party's concern that diffusion of power be accompanied with well-defined channels of control and supervision. Unlike Morocco, where the communes arrived before other institutional adjustments were even considered, and Pakistan, where the Union Councils are helpless to overcome the gap between rural and urban society, the Tunisian effort was a natural sequence to the central consolidation of power. When the governor's councils were first announced in 1957,[43] they were entirely at the command of the governor. They had no independent powers of appeal, of formulating their agenda, or of selecting priority among local needs. It was further stipulated that "discussion of all questions of a political order is forbidden" (art. 15).

The pressures of development for greater decentralization of authority can be traced in the evolution of the councils. In the late 1950's Bourguiba was consolidating the regime, and in 1958 he announced that governors were to be given even greater powers and were to be the personal representatives of the chief of state.[44] Though some members of municipal councils were undoubtedly appointed to the governors' councils, they were in no sense a representative body and, like the municipal councils, were burdened with carefully enumerated housekeeping chores. The experience of the early 1960's demonstrated to the Tunisian government that more popular participation was needed in development programs, and major changes were made in 1963. The earlier legislation was superseded by an entirely new concept of the regional council, responding, in part, to the need to decentralize the vigorous planning activities begun in 1961.

The regional or Governorate Councils were to include the governor, as presiding officer, the regional committee of the Socialist Destour, representatives of each "national organization," and the presidents of any syndicates among municipal councils.[45] This was the first occasion on which the local councils received even indirect recognition at higher levels in the regime. The governor retained his control over the agenda of the meetings, but the Governorate Councils were given budgetary responsibilities and financial autonomy. The regional councils represent a substantial advance over the 1957 bodies, but are still obviously shaped to the interests of the single-party state. The interaction of party representatives and government officials in the new councils will be

[43] "Loi no. 57-12 de 17 aout 1957 (20 moharem 1377) portant création de conseils de gouvernorat," *Journal Officiel de la République Tunisienne*, August 23, 1957, pp. 80-82.

[44] *Petit-Matin*, January 9, 1958.

[45] Loi no. 63-54 du 30 décembre 1963 (14 chaabane 1,383), relative aux Conseils de Gouvernorate," *Journal Officiel de la République Tunisienne*, vol. 101, no. 60, December 31, 1963, pp. 1,873-1,875. The legislation, unlike many Tunisian reforms, was first discussed in the National Assembly meetings of December 1963. See also *New York Times*, March 15, 1964.

closely supervised, but will provide a focal point for exchange of views much closer to the locality than has ever existed before in Tunisia.

Despite the evidence that political differences could exist and were expressed at the local level,[46] the Tunisian political system has remained hesitant when confronted with the larger question of how political differences might manifest themselves throughout the system. The Socialist Destour enjoyed the advantages of unanimity in government while paying a price in its refusal to integrate political differences to enlarge individual awareness and capacity to make developmental adjustments. The Bizerte congress of 1964 expanded group representation at the local level by establishing provincial party committees, but the rigid power structure was only reproduced anew at higher levels in a more tightly organized central party bureaucracy.[47] Unlike the traditionalist orientation of Moroccan politics, the active and responsive qualities of the single-party regime demanded concessions. Such concessions were made to developmental realities, but it is too soon to predict if they represent retrenchment of the regime or the beginnings of the evolution of a more complex power structure to facilitate the developmental process.

If we view economic and social development as a process, it is significant that by the time the single-party system found the challenge of more intensive development efforts unavoidable, the political system had created rigidities and tensions detrimental to rapid societal growth. Like the Moroccan monarchy, the one-party regime anticipated correctly that development would focus on the expression of social differences at the national level while placing more power in the hands of groups and organizations beyond the embrace of the party. It is interesting to note in this regard that Bourguiba has been even more reluctant than Hassan II to create new institutional lines between the locality and the government. Given Morocco's less developed state, her rural-commune scheme, though not fully exploited for developmental purposes, was a much more significant institutional innovation than Tunisia's cautious revision of the Protectorate's municipal-council plan and enlargement of regional councils. Furthermore, the Moroccan councilors have been given the minor but significant stimulus of constitutional recognition. Their powers are legally defined outside the

---

[46] See Clement H. Moore, "Politics in a Tunisian Village," *op.cit.*, and also *New York Times*, June 8, 1964. Also the author's *Elusiveness of Power, op.cit.*

[47] One should not estimate the organizational capacity of the Socialist Destour, and the possibility that conflict may indeed be "managed" more skillfully in the less developed country. There is some evidence that this occurred in the 1964 congress. The congress was postponed from July, in part to give time for reconciliation of local party differences, and the president himself admitted in the congress that several ministerial candidates for the Political Bureau had been severely criticized. See *New York Times*, October 24, 1965, and *Jeune Afrique*, November 1, 1964.

administrative process and their positions are integrated into national political life in several ways. The Pakistani program, to be discussed in the following chapter, goes much farther toward integrating the community and the nation than either of the schemes in North Africa, but must operate in a more retarded social setting.

It would be unfair to assert that President Bourguiba has been less sensitive to the problems of his villages and towns than Hassan II or President Ayub, but his perceptions and judgments have been colored by dependence on the single-party system. Very early in Tunisia's development planning there were presidential speeches acknowledging the expanded role of the community, but as a party leader Bourguiba has had reason to distrust the self-regulated community. The political system was suited to an appeal to the nation or to the party, so often referred to as the "framework of the nation" in the president's speeches. Since Tunisia is the most extremely nationalist of the three systems in this inquiry's comparison, it is perhaps not surprising that political activity should be concentrated at the national level and that political values should be oriented to the national affairs to the exclusion of other concerns. However, it has become increasingly apparent in the attempts to begin a social reconstruction of the developing nations that human action cannot be explicitly oriented toward national goals as social complexities are purposefully multiplied in the developmental process.

Like Nasser, Nkrumah, and other highly charismatic figures in the developing nations, Bourguiba experiences serious dilemmas as he seeks to convert an "act of homage to an act of participation."[48] The conflict arises not only because of the very different individual character of these two acts, but also because the latter is virtually infinite in its diversity in any context of social interaction. Political issues aside, if this is possible in any operating society, the demands of a productive economy and adaptive society must be acknowledged. Bourguiba has made substantial concessions, but only where such concessions could more easily be watched over by the party. Progress in areas like administrative reorganization, for example, is much greater than in Morocco or Pakistan. What is not so widely recognized is that these improvements are accompanied by an increasingly acute nationalist appeal. The threat of Youssefist plots, the removal of the bey, the quarrel with Nasser, the Bizerte crisis, and the trial of Tahar ben Ammar are only a few of the dramatic issues that have sustained the single-party regime's nationalist pitch. These appeals have been used to justify further concentration of power in the central government, to eliminate rivals, and to enable the safe manipulation of national institutions within the single-party frame-

---

[48] From the highly instructive study of Fatma Mansur, *Process of Independence*, London, Kegan Paul, 1962, p. 164.

work. The president has relied more heavily on highly affective devices and has dampened localized activity in order to maintain political stability. Had Bourguiba been operating in a more primitive society or one in an earlier phase of its development, the beneficial effects of such a mobilization effort might be more easily justified. But Tunisia has been in the hands of a well-organized party since the mid-1930's and has a labor movement dating back to the early 1920's. There is a sizeable *bourgeoisie*, and the country's notables have distinct recollections of managing local affairs for several generations.

The Tunisian political system fails to build on existing institutional foundations because further institutional diversification might threaten party hegemony, while the Moroccan monarchy hesitates to provide institutional foundations because their sheer existence may detract from the *imam's* position. In both cases the developmental process is retarded, but it is retarded at rather different stages. As noted above, Morocco may lose time and wealth by procrastinating over a social revolution, but Tunisia must also absorb the tensions of capable citizens who find themselves deprived of expression and familiar means of action. The local-reform problem presents some of the best social evidence of the loss in human energy and talent to the developmental process as a result of an extremely cautious approach to local government. While countries like Pakistan and India desperately worked at creating the minimal civic awareness and local managerial skills now generated in Tunisia, the Socialist Destour allowed these assets to languish and indirectly justified local inactivity by stressing new crises and dangers at the national level.

The psychological effects of this pattern of control need more detailed investigation, but the broad impact can be inferred from our general knowledge. The repeated use of crises in communicating with others tends to generate fatigue and eventual disinterest. Given the relatively advanced state of Tunisian society and its long experience with several kinds of organizational activity, it seems entirely possible that serious apathy may be generated. These were precisely the concerns voiced by responsible party leaders after the unsuccessful plot on Bourguiba's life late in 1962.[49] Indeed, the statements of party leaders and conversations with young officials suggest that the Socialist Destour was well aware of the self-induced rigidities of the party's communication system and the party's diminished meaning in the lives of many capable, perfectly loyal Tunisians. The adjustments made in 1963 and

[49] The communication difficulties of the Socialist Destour in early 1963 are reminiscent of the rigidities and distortions introduced into Soviet communications during the Stalin era, as described and analyzed by Alex Inkeles, *Public Opinion in Soviet Russia*, Cambridge, Harvard University Press, 1950. Comparisons between the political systems in their entirety are, of course, easily misleading.

1964 do not represent a fundamental reorientation in Tunisian political life.

Compared to political communications in more developed societies, all the political systems of the new nations rely heavily on affective devices. But the charismatic leaders are more dependent than others on emotional appeals, especially when they are supported with a single-party regime, like Bourguiba. The effects of strain and pressure on the cognitive process are well known in clinical circumstances.[50] The extent to which the Tunisian development effort may be impeded by comparable perceptual rigidities and distortions is, of course, entirely a matter for conjecture, but the similarity is unmistakable. Given the knowledge of more instrumental, concretely oriented patterns of behavior generated over the past two generations, the imposition of more highly affective orientations, sometimes at the expense of established instrumental patterns of action, can lead to withdrawal and disinterest. Psychologically as well as sociologically the orientation of the Tunisian political system may create new obstacles for future developmental efforts in the name of the single-party system.

The grounds of comparison emerge more clearly with an account of the local-reform effort in two countries. As was outlined in the first chapter of this study, it is being argued that national development cannot be confined to one specific structure or one level of activity. The cognitive skills accompanying institutional development represent the psychological capacity to live in such a diverse system. Though this is a considerable oversimplification, it may be stated that the psychological rigidities noted on one level of analysis have an equivalent in social behavior in the form of violence, discontent, and apathy. While this hypothesis is sufficiently general to apply to any society, the question at hand means that the developing nation will become the focus for unusually severe apprehensions and conflict as more citizens are brought into a more active political life by the developmental process.

The Tunisian case has made the institutional dimensions of the problem clearer than the less advanced Moroccan system. It seems very likely that, as development takes place, social interaction increases geometrically and very soon outdistances the observational capacity of even the most determined political leaders. On the national level institutions are, of course, governed by certain ultimate values about the nation, but these values become less and less pertinent to the citi-

---

[50] There is a wide variety of literature examining the effects of strain on perception, though it is still difficult to determine the possible impact significance of such general attitudes as nationalism, creeds, et cetera. The reader interested in exploring the possible effects might read M. J. Rosenberg, "A Structural Theory of Attitudinal Chance," *Public Opinion Quarterly*, vol. 24, 1960, pp. 319-340, or Irving Sarnoff and Daniel Katz, "The Motivational Bases of Attitudinal Change," *Journal of Abnormal and Social Psychology*, vol. 49, 1954, pp. 115-124.

zen's everyday life as modernization takes place. Such values are also very remote from the more traditional pattern of living, but insofar as such patterns are integrated at the national level they rely almost wholly on national imperatives. The social pattern of the tribe is disconnected from the nation, just as theological systems of action also may be. In theory this is the critical distinction between the Moroccan and Tunisian political systems as they undertake more intense developmental phases.

Thus it would be misleading to state categorically that either country has surpassed the other. Morocco is in a period of her development when national values need to be articulated in the lives of individual citizens. The universally applied scheme for rural communes is itself evidence of the different institutional needs of the monarchial system, although little has been done to exploit fully the promise of the rural commune. In a sense Bourguiba's choice is more fateful, for his country appears to be reaching a phase where institutional patterns may become self-sustaining and self-regulating. More energetic development of the Tunisian municipal-council system would hasten this leap into the infinitely complex institutional world of the more advanced nations. Institutional concessions within the narrow world of the Socialist Destour are limited by the structure of the party itself. The party risks submersion into the society and loss of identity, as threatened to occur in 1958, or it must constantly seek issues for disciplining its following and justifying its monopoly of government. For this reason it is not surprising that Bourguiba has found it much easier to be bold in international than in national affairs. Hassan II, on the other hand, can afford to design a plan having more far-reaching implications in social action. The lower level of advancement means that the scheme is much less likely to swamp the monarchy, and the social structure permits more procrastination while isolated villagers continue on their separate ways relatively unaware of the problems of development.

CHAPTER 4

THE PAKISTANI UNION COUNCIL:
LIMITS OF REASON

THE ELABORATE SYSTEM OF councils organized by the Pakistani military-bureaucratic oligarchy is certainly the most ambitious of the three schemes for local reform discussed in this inquiry. The aims of Tunisian local-government structure have never been explicit, and the single-party system operates best where explicit goals are seldom announced. The Moroccan rural commune can be said to have at least implicit goals, for the scheme was applied to the entire country and publicly associated with the country's social and economic reconstruction. Pakistan, however, presents the most extreme case. The ruling oligarchy has made local reform the keystone of its domestic policy, and President Ayub Khan has regarded the Basic Democracies program as his most important reform.

The primary reason for leaping to another continent in order to complete the comparison of local-development schemes is fairly simple.[1] The Moroccan example demonstrates the use of monarchial and religious prestige in the development process, and Tunisia is an outstanding example of the activating effects of a single-party structure. Pakistan may be characterized as the professional approach to political and economic reconstruction, which very likely accounts for much of Ayub's popularity in Western eyes.[2] Behind the military-administrative coalition that made Pakistan's 1958 revolution possible stand two of the most highly professional organizations known to man—the British Indian Civil Service and the British Indian Army. Only by their supreme self-confidence and organizational skills were a handful of carefully selected British able to manage an entire continent for nearly

[1] A comparison that might seem more desirable would be Algeria, where there have been indications of a collegial, military body evolving as the ruling force. However, Algeria has been preoccupied in the first years of independence with problems stemming directly from the colonial past and the maintenance of order. There are reasons for expecting the rural mobilization to move more rapidly in Algeria, including the scale of the revolutionary organization, the large number of workers having rural origins who go to France, and the effects of the war. See, for example, Xavier de Planhol, *Nouveaux Villages Algérois*, Paris, Presses Universitaires de France, 1961.

[2] Until the border crisis in India, United States sympathy for Pakistan certainly had a great effect on our view of the Asian subcontinent and the programs for internal reconstruction under way there. But even if we put policy considerations aside, it is apparent that the Indian *panchayat* scheme, especially those strains derived from Gandhi's thoughts on village self-sufficiency, lacked organizational coherence. See S. C. Dube, *India's Changing Villages: Human Factors in Community Development*, Ithaca, Cornell University Press, 1958, ch. 4; also, S. K. Dey, *Panchayati Raj: a Synthesis*, London, Asia Publishing House, 1961, ch. 7.

two hundred years. The present rulers of Pakistan are the immediate successors to this regime, and it is important to remember that the tradition they represent was not without undemocratic features.

The viceregal system was fully developed in the nineteenth century, when the colonial officials were translating the highly applicable maxims of Bentham and Mill into systems of government. Although the intellectual origins of political values are seldom sufficient to understand how such values may be applied, the lacunae in the utilitarians' carefully spun theories went unquestioned. India was ruled by men who believed that reason could maximize human happiness, and the same convenient simplification still permeates the Ayub regime. Of course, the setting has changed, and in the midst of the postindependence chaos and stagnation reason seemed doubly compelling. The rational aspect of Pakistani government is nowhere more clearly championed than in the Basic Democracies scheme. This may be its fatal flaw as well as its great strength.

If one can imagine a dimension for rationality, the Basic Democracies scheme represents a distinct departure from the approaches discussed in the two previous chapters. While there are important differences between the monarchy and the Socialist Destour in respect to development, both political and economic, the Pakistani case introduces a variation in political orientation that has become increasingly popular in both Asia and Africa. A distinction should be made from the outset, however, between military elites who are reluctant to engage in social action and those who actively commit themselves to national reconstruction. Unfortunately, there has sometimes been implicit in our thinking an assumption as to the inevitable virtue of military government. When we are considering cases of unmistakably severe disorder, this may be a defensible assumption for the policy maker,[3] but there is certainly enough prima facie evidence of military bungling in Latin America and the Middle East to suggest some caution in adopting such an interpretation in all cases. The focus of the present study is not chaos, but the interplay of the political process and development. In all three cases the study deals with countries where life has not become "nasty, short and brutish."[4]

[3] It is interesting to note that sympathy for military regimes was first generated in dealing with the defense of Southeast Asia under war conditions. For Americans this was possibly one of the least understood parts of the underdeveloped world, and the fragmentation of leadership and parties was extraordinary in the face of pressing organizational needs. See the discussion of this problem in Guy Pauker's "Southeast Asia as a Problem Area in the Next Decade," World Politics, vol. 9, no. 3, 1959, pp. 325-345.

[4] The degeneration of political relationships to taking human life capriciously introduces compulsive elements into an analysis. A society must have identifiable, known standards for the taking of human life. The failure of many developing countries to achieve even this minimal degree of order has led to a confusion

The Ayub regime has shown itself to be seriously and energetically devoted to the restoration of civilian government. The most persuasive proof is that reforms were enacted leading to a new constitution, the revival of party activity, and intense legislative activity at both the national and provincial levels. Pakistan's institutional fruition was designed to be the culminating step in the reconstruction effort involved in Basic Democracies. With true professional perspective the president saw that irresponsible politics at the center, and the consequent corruption and economic stagnation, could only be prevented if new leadership was introduced and a more solid basis for political participation was constructed. His answer was the Basic Democracies plan, which was to provide an interlude for village instruction and revival. Elected village leaders were organized into Union Councils, the first tier of the Basic Democracies plan. Nearly 80,000 Pakistanis from the two provinces were organized into slightly more than 8,000 councils. These were to be the building blocks of the new regime for both political and developmental purposes. With the possible exception of the Indian *panchayat* organization, there has seldom been such an ambitious, and essentially optimistic, approach to local reform.

The attractions of the Pakistani experience for this inquiry are, therefore, reasonably obvious. The military regime acknowledged the social complexity of modern society and attempted to allow for it in the local-reform program. Although Ayub most often refers to political stability as the requisite for economic development, rather than the more intricate problems of politics created by development, his understanding of politics goes beyond the coffee-shop variety of politics that has contributed to the intense, urbanized political life of much of the Muslim world. Ayub hoped that increased awareness at the village level, stimulated by both economic and political devices, would act to restrain and moderate Pakistani political behavior in a less coercive regime to follow. Thus it may be argued that Basic Democracies by intent, and perhaps by accident, incorporates a concept of political life that is indeed closer to what we know of the social and psychological roots of a participant society under modern conditions than either of the other two approaches.

A word of caution should be injected because Pakistan has both stanch supporters and bitter critics on the American scene. Our British heritage has made the Pakistanis better known to Americans than the Moroccans or the Tunisians, and the CENTO military alliance created reserves of good will which do not exist in judging North African

---

of the prerequisite for orderly growth, with social and economic development. While a widely applicable approach to political development needs to deal with both problems, this study is clearly more concerned with development once societal requisites exist.

events. Therefore the analytical arguments favoring the Basic Democracies scheme do not constitute blanket approval of the military regime, which should be quite apparent from other observations in this inquiry. Nor does the scope of Ayub's experiment mean that it will necessarily succeed in any given time period or in any particular sense. Development is an ongoing process in all three countries, and like all human endeavors can have only mixed success, measured in arbitrarily determined periods of time.

The size and population of Pakistan do not preclude comparison of developmental experience with that of other countries. Indeed, it is important to learn if scale does have a noticeable or distinct effect on development, and this can be done only by making comparisons of this kind. In Pakistan there must be some allowance for individual and independent modification because the channels of government are extended. Minor adjustments are hard to make on the national level when one must contact 8,000 Union Councils, for example, as opposed to 100 municipal councils of tested party members. The best development plans must anticipate the changing relationship between government and locality in order that the effects of increased diversification and productivity can be accommodated without proportional increases in the scope of government, which is clearly impossible in a country of over 90 million people. It is not surprising that the larger developing nations have in fact embarked on the most daring experiments in local reform.[5] Much can be learned from them of importance to smaller nations who tend to adopt less flexible and often less imaginative proposals for local reform.

The division of Pakistan into two provinces or wings separated by 1,000 miles of Indian territory also creates peculiar problems, though such problems are not so removed from the concern of the present analysis as may appear to be the case at first glance.[6] The acute pro-

[5] Although this will be discussed further in the concluding chapters, there are very likely more severe pressures for local reform where the process of moderation, coordination, and innovation cannot easily be supervised by the central government. However, even when the distinct effects of larger-scale operations are allowed for, it seems that the rural-mobilization schemes run into similar obstacles. The higher organizational echelons are easier to control and supervise regardless of size. In both India and China, as well as Pakistan, the most difficult problems have been changing attitudes and practices at roughly the same level as where the North Africans have experienced difficulty: the intermediate working level of the *super-caid*, the *delegué*, or the district official. On the Chinese experience see, for example, Chao Kuo-Chun, *Agrarian Policy of the Chinese Communist Party 1921-1959*, London, Asia Publishing House, 1960. The popularity of Chinese Communist effort among developing nations makes it particularly important that the student of local reform in non-Communist countries be aware of the strengths and weaknesses of the Communist experiment.

[6] The geographical division of Pakistan is not so difficult to allow for in the present framework of analysis as the problem of scale, discussed above. It becomes comparable to other highly emotional issues in its effects on the develop-

vincialism of East Pakistan, and to a somewhat lesser extent West Pakistan, is an example of political differentiation on distinctions inappropriate to the developmental process and obstructive to political integration. Provincialism is maintained, in part, by a volatile and ingenious political faction which has often failed to resolve many development problems locally, especially in East Pakistan, and chooses to blame the central government. Aside from its intriguing social characteristics, which are certainly not unrelated to its political plight, East Pakistan is an outstanding example of the divorce of development effort from village life. The explosive character of East Pakistan politics, and more recently West Pakistan as well, can only be reduced in the long run by focusing political energies on the local level and by creating a pattern of political life that makes more comprehensive, diversified participation possible.

For purposes of tracing the roots of local government and the problems of development, however, there are important distinctions between the two wings which must be maintained in the following analysis. Hopefully, a constructive solution to Pakistan's provincial problems would mean that each wing would be able to proceed to exploit human and material resources at the village level without intense rivalries. The nature of British administration was such that very little direct intervention took place in rural life, although it is possible to exaggerate the impact of French colonial administration in the rural setting. The historic provinces of imperial India were virtually independent, and the recommendations of the viceroy and royal commissions were shaped to the provincial official's views. The length of the impact, however slight, also varies appreciably between the two wings. Whereas the British were present in force in Bengal from the late eighteenth century, the Punjab region was subdued later and divided among a variety of British-approved regimes. East Pakistan has kept its lead in the development of local government, and the first locally based service organizations in India were the Bengali Committees of Public Instruction organized in 1832.[7] An attempt was made nearly a generation later in 1862 to introduce some localized police supervision in the Punjab. Neither experiment met with great success, but they set the relative

---

mental process—a problem to be discussed in a later chapter. It is sufficient to note here that there is no reason why physical barriers necessarily detract from national unity, and there are many cases where the material obstacles have had integrative effect.

[7] Hugh Tinker, *The Foundations of Local Self-Government in India, Pakistan and Burma*, London, University of London, Athlone Press, 1954, pp. 33-35. One of the great attractions of the Pakistani comparisons is the body of excellent basic literature. There is nothing comparable to the Tinker book, for example, on the Middle East, and similar materials on Africa are by no means complete. For a classical critique of British shortcomings in dealing with Indian communities see Sir Henry Maine, *Village Communities in the East and West*, New York, Henry Holt, 1889, especially ch. 4.

pace of advance for the two provinces. The differences still exist, and will be acknowledged as materials permit in subsequent discussion.

THE BRITISH RAJ AND THE PANCHAYAT: INDECISIVE RECONSTRUCTION

The long period of British rule in the Indian subcontinent has given Pakistan and India more important precedents for local government than exist in either Tunisia or Morocco. However, it is problematical whether the early British experiments, often at the mercy of the viceroy, were any more significant in the lives of the people. Although Pakistan is in some ways the least advanced of the cases being examined herein, the heritage of experimentation and legislation has had an important impact on postindependence leaders, and the early achievements of the British in this field provide a crude measure of Pakistani success. Even so, the general conclusion is the same for both French and British territories. In no case were major efforts toward local reform made until nationalist activities spread and the complexities of national development became clear to the new governments.

Although more research has been done into the origins of the *panchayat* than the North African *jemaâ*, authorities seem to agree that it provided no firm foundation for local government in the late Moghul period, and was generally neglected throughout the British period. From the villagers' viewpoint it appears that the colonial regime was essentially a continuation of Moghul rule, both forms being indirect and mainly interested in law and order. In both periods the *panchayats* "seem to have been no more than agents of the royal government [and] over very considerable areas no trace at all can be found that they ever existed."[8] Not until early in the nineteenth century did the British administrators discover the Indian *panchayat*, and even then British rule only contributed to the further disintegration of the remaining vestiges of village government. Thus Tinker concludes that "while the *panchayat* is an ancient institution of unique prestige, it provides no precedent for the village council of today. During the greater part of recorded time *panchayats* were ignored by officials and official chroniclers until after the arrival of the British. Thereafter, attempts to endow the *panchayat* with some kind of formal status failed, partly because the British had no firm policy, but mainly because the *panchayat* could not resist the assaults of the modern age."[9]

The pattern of political reorganization followed that of most colonial empires. The British were most interested in the urban strongholds as bases for commercial activity, and the viceregal cities of Bombay, New Delhi, Calcutta, and Madras first enjoyed an illusory form of self-

[8] Sir George Schuster and Guy Wint, *India and Democracy*, London, Macmillan, 1941, p. 19.
[9] Hugh Tinker, "Authority and Community in Village India," *Pacific Affairs*, vol. 32, no. 4, 1959, p. 358.

government. By 1870 there were 65 municipalities in undivided Bengal, and 127 in the Punjab, but the vast majority were appointed. A British official reported in 1881 that "the population of a municipality does not in any sense govern himself."[10] The first important impulse for local reform under British rule was the Sepoy Mutiny, an indication of the kind of local conflicts and awareness created by the British regime. An effort was made to organize district committees in the Punjab, though this never filtered down to the village level and was itself soon forgotten. The important reform for modern Pakistan was the Bengal Village Chaukidari Act of 1870, from which stems the history of local rule in East Pakistan. Under the act villagers were taxed to provide local police services, while local councils were also established to facilitate collecting funds and provide an agency for subsequent local reforms. Although the act succeeded in organizing a number of union committees at the district level, its imposed character and limited functions doomed it to failure.[11]

The most forceful exponent of locally based reform was Lord Ripon, whose Local Self-Government Resolution of 1882 marks the turning point in local administration of the subcontinent. He hoped that local government would become "an instrument of political and popular education," producing "an intelligent class of public spirited men." Although his efforts revived administrative levels below the district, the *thana-tahsil* level,[12] and introduced the notion of appointing non-officials to local boards, there was minimal compliance at the district level, and what few subordinate boards were created were "shadows with little more than a nominal existence." The subsequent viceroy did little to bolster local authorities, despite the growing body of legislation from England on promoting self-government. Tinker concludes that under Lords Curzon and Elgin "the only dynamic influence . . . was directed against the extension of local authority."[13] In Punjab the *tahsil* boards had been allowed to deteriorate steadily until only two existed in 1908, and these were inactive. In one district now in India there were only 62 voters forthcoming of 400,000 on the rolls for a populace of three million. Only in Bengal did the union committees manage to sur-

[10] Tinker, *Foundations . . . op.cit.*, p. 38.

[11] The fact that the British introduced numerous administrative reforms can give the impression that the earlier regime had few controls. Although the Moghul empire had deteriorated greatly by the eighteenth century. Tinker writes that it "incorporated the village into the administration as a unit for revenue and police purposes only," *ibid.*, p. 19. This is not unlike the British administrative purposes, and to some extent mitigates the difference between the length of the North African and Indian colonial periods.

[12] The subdistrict level took on different names in different parts of India. The *thana* prevailed in the Punjab, the *tahsil* in northern India and the Bengal, and the *taluka* in southern India. As will be discussed in more detail below, they were not comparable in size or function.

[13] Tinker, *ibid.*, pp. 44-45 and 61.

vive in any number, although there were only 58 in 1904 in a province of over 70,000 villages.[14] British local officials were too sensitive to their people to remain ignorant of the growing neglect. One Bengali district officer noted "the enormous untapped resources of energy and intelligence which can be used for the local service of the people."[15] However, the Morley-Minto (Decentralization) Report of 1909 did little but reassert the aims of the 1882 resolution, although it did advise that half the district-level income be allocated to subdistrict bodies.

After World War I the furious struggle began to keep the nationalists in check through piecemeal concessions, while officials hoped to stem their growing popularity. Further local reform was plagued with the growing issue of communal representation that eventually exploded into the creation of Pakistan. The Montagu-Chelmsford Report of 1918 sought relief by establishing a greater degree of provincial autonomy. The Rural Self-Government Act of 1921, a product of the report, established district and subdistrict councils for the entire subcontinent, but the comparatively advanced state of local government in Bengal was used to justify similar reforms two years in advance of the act. The Bengal Village and Self-Government Act of 1919 constituted the "most complete system of 'rural authorities' " known to India prior to partition.[16] Union Boards were established for roughly every 8,000 persons. Again, a mixed body of elected and nominated members was formed, and local police supervision and support was the major function. They appear to have taken root and spread rapidly until nearly 1,600 existed in 1920, and they reached a peak in their activity about 1930. Bengal was also the only province of present-day Pakistan to maintain district boards after World War II. Although the Punjab complied with the Act of 1921, the new boards were kept small and generally confined to a single village.

Communal friction mounted in the 1920's, although the Muslims continued to increase their representation on local bodies. They were a minority in all district boards in Bengal in 1920, and had only 32 per cent of the members. By 1937 Muslim membership had risen to 43 per cent, and they were a majority in ten of the 26 Bengali Union Boards.[17] Despite the intense Muslim-Hindu-Sikh rivalry in Punjab province, which handicapped the growth of local self-government

[14] J. G. Drummond, *Panchayats in India*, London, Oxford University Press, 1937, p. 12.

[15] Quoted from the *Local Government of Bengal Report* in Drummond, *op.cit.*, p. 12. See also similar reports in A. T. R. Rahman, *Basic Democracy at the Grassroots*, Technical Publication No. 3. Comilla, Pakistan Academy of Village Development, 1962, pp. 7-9.

[16] Tinker, *Foundations* . . . , *op.cit.*, pp. 118-119.

[17] The Bengali statistics in this paragraph are taken from *ibid.*, p. 156 and pp. 199-200. Additional figures and information on the relative advance in Bengal will be found in Drummond, *op.cit.*, pp. 28-38.

there, the Muslims managed to take control of two municipalities, including Lahore, prior to World War II. Simultaneously, local activity was dying out in rural Punjab, where half the surviving *thana-tahsil* boards were abolished in 1919, and the small remaining number died out from neglect in the interwar period. Hence Professor Tinker concludes that while Bengal had a "complete net-work of village authorities" on the eve of the war, Punjab had managed to extend some form of local participation to no more than a tenth of the countryside.

The combination of Hindu passive resistance and explosive Islamic feelings made community action next to impossible. Given the emphasis of the entire administrative organization on law and order, it is no surprise that few independent efforts were made at village reconstruction. Nevertheless, several devoted Britishers began "rural uplift" experiments between the wars that became the models from which later village reconstruction efforts stemmed. Brayne and Darling were regarded as mavericks among the district officials of the interwar period. In the extremely unpromising region of Gurgaon, now in India, Brayne tried almost singlehandedly to interest the villagers in improved agrarian practices and village betterment. He devised a scheme of village guides not unlike the plan that later emerged in prerevolution Pakistan as the Village Level Worker (VLW) in the Village AID program. These "multipurpose" organizers were to become the contact for more intensive village-level programs in the "nation-building" departments, i.e., those departments engaged in social services such as agriculture, education, public health, et cetera.

Brayne himself realized that he was trying to accomplish too much in a very short period of time,[18] but he also foresaw some of the problems that were to plague the Village AID program as well as Basic Democracies. He saw, first, that conversion of the villager meant adjustment of a wide range of beliefs affecting many areas of action outside the specific goals of a rural-improvement program. He wrote that the peasant's attitude must change toward "his family, his work, his neighbors and his government."[19] There would be no permanence unless change was accompanied with a degree of "spontaneity," which represented the villager's assimilation of a new value system enabling him to participate confidently in activities extending beyond his village. Second, Brayne was candid in his remarks concerning the stagnation and decline of the *panchayat*, recognizing that it has generally managed to survive only in large villages as the focus of discord among factions and personal rivalries. In no instance had it become the vehicle of change, although in some instances certain judicial functions had been assigned to

[18] F. L. Brayne, *Socrates in an India Village*, 3d edn., Madras, 1937, pp. 116-119, quoted in Tinker, "Authority and Community in Village India," *op.cit.*, p. 360.

[19] F. L. Brayne, *Better Villages*, London, Oxford University Press, 1937, p. 3.

it.[20] While village councils would be needed, Brayne was under no romantic illusions about converting indigenous institutions to the methodical ways of modern life.

Sir Malcolm Darling was deeply inpressed by the inexorable burden of debt carried by the Punjab peasant despite the remarkable increase in prosperity brought about by British irrigation of the Punjabi plains. In investigations conducted around Rawalpindi, Multan and other towns in relatively prosperous regions, he found the small proprietors sometimes had debts over twenty times their average annual income. At the going interest rates it was not unusual for such debts to double in five years, so that a series of natural calamities or family crises could leave a relatively prosperous farmer in debt for several generations.[21] He felt strongly that expanded activity by cooperative credit societies would alleviate the peasant's plight before the moneylender. He foresaw some of the problems of later rural mobilization, however, in his recognition that many specialized agencies would need to make a local impact, and he advocated increased use of arbitration courts, animal-breeding centers, and many other devices to raise the villager's level of prosperity.

These early attempts at administrative reform and community development at the local level are important in two respects. They suggest, first, how inappropriate the colonial administration was for the tasks of social reconstruction, which the British never considered so important as did the culturally self-conscious French. But the implied significance of these efforts is important in the framework of the inquiry. The villager needed a stimulus more powerful than the familiar restraints of the colonial regime in order to participate in a fuller life. Apathy, suspicion, and fear could not be overcome simply by offering material benefits—something which was further demonstrated in the Village AID program of prerevolution Pakistan. Embellishing the traditional society might bring smiles of gratitude from the peasant but lasting, self-supported development at the local level involved reconstructing the cognitive framework within which the peasant operated. The first step in this reorientation is to persuade the villager to adopt loyalties outside the village, whether they be religious, political, or economic. In Pakistan there have been two powerful affective appeals, Islam and the Muslim League, the two almost inextricably interwoven. The period from 1947 to the 1958 revolution[22] represents the ordeal of trying to

[20] *Ibid.*, pp. 141-151.

[21] For a remarkable study of the village finances see Sir Malcolm Darling, *The Punjab Peasant in Prosperity and Debt*, 4th edn., London, Oxford University Press, 1947.

[22] The Ayub regime likes to call the military coup of October 1958 a "revolution," although no shots were fired. Their preference for the revolutionary vocabulary, while they represent very moderate, if not conservative, views on

differentiate these appeals and to orient the new nation to the tasks of national reconstruction.

The extraordinary fragility of the Pakistani political system prior to the 1958 revolution indicates how weak the lines of authority between people and government had become over the preceding two hundred years. Unfortunately, we do not yet have a complete social history of the partition period, but the indications of steadily increasing chaos are unmistakable. No doubt, the one great chance for a degree of political integration at the national level was the Muslim League, but even Jinnah did not realize the importance of organization until the late 1930's. By then the war was approaching and further political organization impossible. At the close of the war independence came so fast and in the midst of such intense feelings that the prosaic tasks of party organization were never considered. The Muslim League was divided among five virtually self-sufficient groups of leaders in the four provinces (Punjab, Sind, North-west Frontier, and Bengal) and the National Assembly. The League had even less experience with the concrete chores of government than the nationalist movements of Morocco and Tunisia. Each group looked upon the League as their personal instrument for political aggrandizement, which naturally focused on the provincial and national capitals. So long as the government did not become seriously committed to the nation's reconstruction, which was almost impossible in the atmosphere of intrigue and bitterness dominating Pakistani politics, local organizations and popular support meant nothing.[23]

The Pakistani experience is an even more attractive subject for comparative analysis because of prolonged detachment between politics on the national and local levels. Institutional abuse and personal rivalries at the national level are only a partial and formal manifestation of political disintegration. Simultaneously the country's developmental problems were multiplying and the burdens of social reform mounting as a result of neglect. A generation of political stagnation at the local level is doubly costly. Not only does the country forfeit the material benefits of constructively orienting the local populace to political and social issues, but any subsequent government is even farther removed by the injustices and disappointments of neglect.

---

social reconstruction, reveals their sensitivity to politics in other developing countries. A good, brief account of the gradual rise of the military and the final takeover is K. J. Newman's "Pakistan's Preventive Autocracy and Its Causes," *Pacific Affairs*, vol. 32, no. 1, 1959, pp. 18-33.

[23] For an account of the League's early history see Keith Callard, *Pakistan: A Political Study*, London, Allen and Unwin, 1947, pp. 34-76. See also Khalid Bin Sayeed, *Pakistan: the Formative Phase*, Karachi, Pakistan Publishing House, 1960; Mushtaq Ahmad, *Government and Politics in Pakistan*, Karachi, Pakistan Publishing House, 1959; and Karl Von Vorys, *Political Development in Pakistan*, Princeton, Princeton University Press, 1965.

THE PAKISTANI UNION COUNCIL

THE VILLAGE AID EXPERIMENT: INDECISIVE LOCAL REFORM

Pakistan's community-development program, now absorbed into the Basic Democracies scheme, represented an important phase in her re-orientation to the problems of national development. Indeed, part of the clarity of the Basic Democracies program is no doubt derived from the country's experience with Village AID (Agricultural and Industrial Development). For comparative purposes it should be noted that the government's first recognition of the villager's plight came at roughly the same time after Pakistan's independence as in Morocco and Tunisia. The first three or four years of independence were used to erect the minimal structure of government in a new nation. In 1947 Pakistan was excluded from nearly all the major centers of British rule by the partition and sorely lacked administrative cadre of all kinds. In addition there was the influx of approximately eight million impoverished refugees, a mass mobilization that is surpassed only by the similar migration taking place in Europe, where massive aid and an industrial complex relieved the problems of assimilating the new population. By the early 1950's Pakistan was able to turn to its chronic domestic problems, and the Sufi Report of 1951 is generally regarded as the first official notice of the need for local reform having a broad social impact.

To understand the first effort at local reform requires a brief sketch of how the village fared under the British. The basic pattern for rural administration for India was devised under the British East India Company. The company's main concern, like that of the subsequent colonial regime, was to collect land revenue. At the height of the Moghul Empire a relatively effective system of rent collection had been devised using revenue agents or *zamindari*. Land records and assessments apparently were made efficiently and fairly. By the time the British arrived in India this historic system had deteriorated and the *zamindari* had become hereditary officials excaping the control of the central government.

After several false starts the undermanned East India Company in consultation with Lord Cornwallis decided to auction the revenue-collection rights. Several proposals were made to lease such rights for determined periods, but later collection rights were given in perpetuity. This became the Permanent Settlement of 1793, which the British hoped would lay the foundations for a rural squirearchy similar to the one in England. In fact, they provided the foundations "for that absenteeism amongst landlords which in later times was to deprive Bengal of any natural leadership, and in due course to stir up a demand for the abolition of the *zamandari* system."[24] Although the system sur-

---

[24] For a short description of the transfer see Sir Percival Griffiths, *The British Impact on India*, London, MacDonald, 1952, pp. 379-390 and 166-179. The quotation is from Griffiths, p. 172. See also Sir Henry Maine, *op.cit.*, pp. 104-106.

vived almost intact for 250 years, there were two major shortcomings. First, the arbitrary method of payment produced a number of abuses to lighten the risk of the official ultimately responsible, while the villager remained subject to all the risks and hazards of working in primitive village society.

The second major injustice originated from the arbitrary manner in which the Permanent Settlement came about. The British took as reliable the Moghul records, which had been neglected for years. The original assessments were often too high or absurdly low. As agriculture began to prosper with the restoration of peace and order in Bengal, income multiplied and the proliferation of rental agents began. The increase in revenue was absorbed by a collection system unsuited to the villager's needs or to the expanding role of government. Under the rigors of the law an increasing number of less desirable *zamindari* tended to prevail, little was done in the way of land improvement, and the peasant faced a hopeless tangle of litigation if he wished to protect his interests or alter records. Little wonder that one of the most frequently heard grievances of Union Council members is the need to enlarge the locality's role in the maintenance of land records, assessments, and rent collections.

Very little mutual understanding or complex organization was possible so long as the burdensome tiers of rent collectors stood between the villager and the administrator. The influence of the *zamindars* was undoubtedly great, and it was not until 1950 that the system was abolished. By then many of the large Hindu landlords had abandoned their claims, though all were affected when their base of operations, Calcutta, was placed outside Pakistan. Under the new legislation only one lessee was permitted, which, in effect, meant that land rental could not become more complex than sharecropping. Since the arable land in Bengal was occupied by the mid-nineteenth century, and there was a large floating peasant population by the turn of the century, the 1950 reform established small peasant proprietors in most cases.

Benefiting from their experience in Bengal, the British devised a system for the Punjab that was supposed to avoid the abuses of the *zamindari* system. In practice it became an even greater obstacle to the development of local self-government than the Bengal scheme. In the Punjab, and today in West Pakistan, the district officer became known as the Deputy Commissioner, the title derived in neat and logical order from the immediately superior level found in both wings, the Division. Beneath the Deputy Commissioner is the *tahsildar*. There were many fewer intermediate-level officers, Assistant Commissioners comparable to the Subdivisional Officer of East Pakistan. The over-all effect is a much more orderly administrative system, and one which brings the powerful district official much closer to the village than in Bengal.

There are three officers responsible to the district: the police, the registrar, (*patwari*) and the collecting agent (*lambardar*).

The collector and registrar both report indirectly through the *tahsildar*, who is clearly in a much more influential position than the recently created tax official bearing the same title in Bengal. Furthermore, the British learned from the cumbersome land-tenure system in the east, and from the start of the British occupation land could be subleased only once. The Punjabi peasant has consequently been caught up in a three-pronged dilemma. The peasant could not risk offending *patwari* or *lambardar* or landlord. He had no other avenue of communication to higher officialdom, nor was there the tradition of a village self-rule that provided a measure of relief and self-confidence in Bengal. Certainly it would be incorrect to convey an image of the happy peasant in either wing, but the precedents for individual or collective initative are much fewer in the west.

The more orderly pattern of revenue collection in the Punjab did not contribute to the development of more vigorous local development or even to the creation of local councils. Even after partition a belated effort to revive *panchayat* councils in the Punjab failed. The Punjabi Local Government Reforms Committee reported in 1951 that the existing local bodies had "not been able to awaken civic consciousness among the people or to train the more intelligent out of them for civic leadership."[25] The report estimated that there were no more than 4,000 *panchayat* committees functioning for the more than 20,000 villages in the Punjab province of independent Pakistan. This is undoubtedly an optimistic estimate, and the report added that the vast majority had no income.

The Sufi Report came from the Food and Agriculture Department. Appearing about the same time that the early community-development experiments were being made in India, it may have been inspired in part by Pakistan's reluctance to see her major rival introduce reforms where Pakistan was deficient.[26] The Sufi Report was largely con-

[25] Local Government Reform Committee, *First Interim Report*, Lahore, Government of Pakistan, 1951, p. 3. See also the subsequent reports, *Local Government Reforms Committee Report*, vol. 1, "Reorganization of the Structure of Local Government," and vol. 2, "Relationship between the Provincial Government and Local Bodies," Lahore, Government of Pakistan, 1952. These are very slim reports, and there is no available evidence that they were ever put into practice. In contrast, Bengali legislation created Union Boards long before government tax collectors appeared in the village—a factor contributing to the vigor of local self-government in the eastern wing. Although there are land registrars (*patwaris*) and revenue agents (*tahsildars*) at the base of the system in East Pakistan, these are relatively new officials compared to the Union Boards. Unlike their counterparts in West Pakistan, they have been largely confined to official duties.

[26] There are voluminous writings on the Indian community development, rural extension, and village revival efforts. Despite the ample and often excellent writing on Indian experience, few persons concerned with local reform in other developing countries appear to be familiar with their work in any detail. Among others, one

cerned with agrarian reform, and was heavily influenced by American agricultural extension-service experience. Under the proposal all local agents were to be trained in agricultural extension work or animal husbandry, although the need for popular participation and other social improvements was recognized. The report is important testimony to the inadequacy of the existing development agencies of the government. It describes the local agricultural agent as "an insignificant person . . . with poor technical background . . . out of touch with research workers . . . inadequate remuneration [and without] much local prestige or influence." Like the community-development approach, represented by Village AID, the Sufti Report made implicit assumptions about the nature of the integration process. There was only minimal acknowledgment of the political complications of preparing an isolated citizen to contribute to national development, and uncritical acceptance of the existing bureaucracy plus the creation of social revolutions at the local level.

The Pakistan experience with Village AID is an important demonstration of the inability of community-development programs to achieve their most important goal—to enable the isolated villager to participate in a fuller life socially and politically. This is not to deny the fundamentals of community-development theory. Arousing the villager is certainly an integral part of the developmental process, but the initial stimulation is the easiest step in local reform. The local reorientation and reconstruction also create new psychological needs and require more effective societal integration beyond the village. Development unavoidably involves activity over a wider area. Some community-development experts have acknowledged this. For example, Batten writes, "What is important is that to the degree that the solidarity of the local communities becomes less all-embracing of mens' interest and less intensely felt, there shall be a compensating growth of a sense of community between local communities, i.e., that men shall create effective communities at the higher levels of region and the nation."[27]

One of the most important lessons to be drawn from the Village AID effort in Pakistan is that any program affecting the grass roots of a

---

might read S. C. Dube's *India's Changing Villages: Human Factors in Community Development*, op.cit.; B. Rambhai, *The Silent Revolution*, 2d edn., New Delhi, Jiwar Prakashan, 1959; Albert Mayer et al., *Pilot Project India*, Berkeley, University of California Press, 1958; *Report of the Team for the Study of Community Projects and National Extension Service*, Mehta Report, 3 vols., New Delhi, Committee on Plan Projects, 1957-1958; Ralph H. Retzlaff, *Village Government in India*, London, Asia Publishing House, 1962; and Planning Commission, Government of India, *The New India: Progress through Democracy*, New York, Macmillan, 1958.

[27] T. R. Batten, "Social Values and Community Development," in Phillips Ruopp, ed., *Approaches to Community Development*, The Hague, Van Hoeve, 1953, p. 83. See also T. R. Batten, *Communities and their Development*, London, Oxford University Press, 1957, for a general discussion of community-development principles and techniques.

society is constantly in jeopardy if it is not the product of some agreement at the national level. Even the so-called "nonpolitical" approaches to development are subject to national politics, and it is in some respects even more naïve to undertake a nationwide program of village reform without central agreement than to begin to reconstruct village life without anticipating national repercussions. By the time the Village AID notion appeared in Pakistan ministerial rivalries were playing the role of party competition in determining broad policy matters. The Muslim League was in decline, and looked more and more to favors and corruption to maintain an identity in parliamentary politics. Thus the Village AID scheme was always seriously estranged from the focus of national politics and, like many other problems of reconstruction, was left at the mercy of the bureaucracy so long as a modicum of graft was made available for party purposes.

The Village AID program had the support of Prime Minister Chaudri Mohammed Ali on its inception in 1955, but soon became embroiled in the bureaucratic struggle of the decline of the parliamentary regime and the formation of the military regime. Initially an attached department under the Ministry of Economic Affairs, the program enjoyed some autonomy. In 1958 it was shifted to the Community Development Division of the Ministry of Health and Labor. As a temporary agency the program never received full support from high-level civil servants. Despite the enthusiasm created in the ranks of Village AID most of the program's administrators were on loan and did not foresee attractive careers in community work. The fact that the program was almost entirely dependent on American aid made it acutely vulnerable to bureaucratic infighting, while this gave the devoted members of the higher staff little leverage in government.[28]

The convergence of unfavorable forces in the revolutionary regime is a useful reminder that military governments are not immune to the same kind of ministerial rivalry that saps the energy of civilian governments in developing countries. The Bureau of National Reconstruction, charged with marshaling popular support for the Ayub regime and watching over political activities, was initially directed by a general of xenophobic tendencies, who particularly dislike the appearance of American influence at the local level. Early in 1959 Village AID was transferred to the Ministry of Information and Broadcasting, where the

[28] The best analysis of the experience of the Village AID program is an unpublished paper of its chief administrator and enthusiastic advocate, Masihuzzaman, "Community Development: Lessons from Pakistan's Experience." See also Faqir Mohammed Chaudri, "Administrative Structure in Pakistan," in S. M. Z. Rizvi, ed., *A Reader in Basic Democracies*, Peshawar, West Pakistan Academy for Village Development, 1961, p. 44, and Brig. Gulzar Ahmad, "Basic Problems Related to the Evaluation of Extension and Rural Development Activities in Pakistan," paper read to I.C.A. Regional Seminar, New Delhi, January 11-23, 1960, p. 13.

minister was equally suspicious of American intentions. By the time the program returned to the Ministry of Health a little over a year later, its staff was discouraged and the government was placing more emphasis on the Basic Democracies program. Throughout this period the classical rivalry of Ministry of Agriculture, favoring extension methods, and community approach distracted the Village AID leaders.[29]

The Village Level Worker (V.L.W.) was in charge of approximately seven villages having a total population of about 5,000. Groupings of 30 village workers, including roughly 200 villages or 150,000 persons, constituted a Development Area. The area corresponded roughly to the *thana-tahsil* and was supervised by a Development Officer, assisted by a staff of more specialized workers, women workers, and literacy teachers, whose services were to be distributed among the V.L.W.'s of the Development Area. There were also eleven Village AID Training Institutes. The first Development Areas were established in 1954, and increased at the rate of from 15 to 25 areas a year until the military revolution in 1958. From then the rate of growth was noticeably stepped up, and from 30 to 40 new areas were being opened up in the last four years of the program's existence, 1958-1961.[30] By the time it was discontinued the program included about a fourth of the Pakistani population. Given the plan's rate of expansion in the four years prior to the revolution, it may well be that excessive demands were being made to enlarge the program when it might have more profitably taken stock of its progress and methods while improving the quality of the organizations already established.

Once the Ayub regime decided to abandon the Village AID scheme, it became almost fashionable to criticize it. However, the available evidence provides a general picture of the results, which are in most respects rather what one would expect to follow from the assumptions of community-development theory. Possibly the most complete survey was done using a control group of families outside the Village AID areas, although it was confined to West Pakistan.[31] The control group, which had

[29] See the comment in the *Food and Agriculture Report*, Lahore, Government of Pakistan, 1960, pp. 221 and 260-261. The alternatives for rural development suggested by the Ministry of Agriculture will be discussed in later chapters, but the fact that it has required nearly five years to develope comparable alternatives suggests that officials may have been hasty on dissolving the Village AID organization.

[30] These estimates of growth have been made from the quarterly reports, first appearing in September 1959 and entitled *Physical Achievements of Village AID Development Areas in East Pakistan, West Pakistan, Azad, Kashmir, Gilgit and Baltistan*. Those dated September 30, 1959, December 31, 1959, and March 31, 1960 were published by the National Development (V-AID) Organization; those dated June 30, 1960, September 30, 1960, and March 31, 1961 by the Ministry of National Reconstruction and Information.

[31] Dr. S. M. Akhtar, *A Report on the Contribution of Community Development to National Economic Development Particularly in Agriculture*, Lahore, University of Panjab, 1960.

available the regular services of the other government ministries, appears to have made comparable progress in the more concrete improvements, but seems to have made less progress in alleviating some of the historic conflicts of village family and social life. For example, there were no significant differences in the use of fertilizer, sowing methods, or crop patterns, although both test areas had made important changes. The important advantages of the Village AID areas appeared in reduction of family debt and de-emphasis of costly ceremonies. The debt in the Village AID region was half that of the unorganized area, and 60 per cent of debt in the Village AID region was for productive purposes compared to 30 per cent for productive investment in the less privileged villages. The Village AID regions also had higher aspirations for offspring, and had contributed sizable sums for local improvements. The Village AID program was weakest in handling those problems that involved coordination of villages, such as flooding and salinity.

A study done in East Pakistan confirms the continued resistance to agricultural improvements under Village AID, although there was no control group of unaffected villages.[32] About four fifths of the 120 farmers interviewed had made no adjustment to improve farm practices. Only about half thought the new village council erected by the VLW was "effective," which compares very unfavorably with the respondents' recollection of their old Union Board. Little had been accomplished in improving the village water supply, school, or sanitation. The findings are consistent with the widely held opinion that the East Pakistani tended to view the Village AID program as a poor substitute for his once vigorous Union Board. His resentment became even more pronounced when the Union Board was replaced arbitrarily with the Union Council of the Basic Democracies scheme. In contrast, the more primitive village of the Punjab responded with somewhat more enthusiasm and is generally conceded to have made more progress under Village AID.

A more vital question in reference to this inquiry is whether the Village AID program was perceived as a political concession or as a means whereby the villager could expand his influence in a larger social system. A study done in West Pakistan shows that although 90 per cent of the respondents knew of the VLW's presence, about half of these persons considered him an extension worker and the others saw him as a member of a social-welfare or sanitation agency.[33] Two thirds

[32] Program Analysis Unit, National Development Organization, *Evaluation Report: Tangail Development Area, Mymensingh District, East Pakistan,* 1961.

[33] Program Analysis Unit, National Development Organization, *Evaluation Report: Chichawatni Development Area, Montgomery District, West Pakistan,* 1961. By far the most critical reports were submitted by partisans of extension-service methods and others who championed increased agricultural production as the most important goal. See, for example, Dr. Carl C. Taylor, "National Development Organization and V-AID," in *Village Aid: Some Articles and Reports,* Lahore,

of the respondents could not name a major accomplishment of the program in their community.

Disappointing as these results may be, it should be remembered that understanding of national framework for development is slow to accumulate where government is uncertain. Only a few years before Nehru's death the vast majority of Indian peasants in some provinces could not name the prime minister. Unfortunately, there are no comparable studies of accomplishments under Basic Democracies, nor the cost of abandoning the nucleus of village leadership organized under Village AID.

The final decision to dissolve Village AID came abruptly. The first draft of the Second Five Year Plan appeared in June 1960, and it contained plans for extending Village AID to 85 per cent of the rural populace and assigning Development Officers to all the areas.[34] The plan also acknowedged that the VLW's had encountered difficulties in West Pakistan, and that the temporary nature of the agency made it difficult to recruit top-quality people. The planners were disappointed in the program's development role, and noted that the Rs.800,000 allocated as development expenditure had not been used, and consequently suggested that roughly half this sum be used over the next ten years. When the report was filed, the relatively high officials involved in planning still thought that the Village AID program would grow in cooperation with the Basic Democracies scheme. The evidence in the Second Plan, though by no means a hearty endorsement of the Village AID program, does not account for the decision taken in late 1960 to absorb the entire scheme into Basic Democracies.

There were allegations that the Village AID organization was dominated by political groups in some areas, as well as by the eternal rivalry between the two wings. The figures indicate that approximately two thirds of the benefits were directed to the western wing up to 1959.[35]

Village AID Administration, 1960, pp. 139-149. He estimated that of the two million farm families under Village AID only 100,000 had adopted improved practices after an expenditure of nearly three million dollars. There were then and continue to be persuasive reasons for concentrating on agriculture, although a later chapter will seek to demonstrate that the politics of agrarian reform is one of the most difficult hurdles in the development process.

[34] Government of Pakistan, Planning Commission, *The Second Five Year Plan (1960-1965)*, 1960, pp. 393-396.

[35] Reports to the end of 1958 indicate that 69 of 99 Development Areas, 11,291 of 17,274 villages, and 8.1 million of 12.2 organized peasants were in the west wing. The noteworthy disparity is that the higher level of organization notwithstanding, the East Pakistanis were much more successful in creating local councils. There were 9,884 village councils in East Pakistan, compared to 5,817 in West Pakistan. There are, of course, geographical and other features affecting this performance, but the Bengali experience in village government appeared to have some lasting effects. See S. M. Akhtar, *A Report on the Contribution of Community Development to National Economic Development Particularly in Agriculture*, Lahore,

Given East Pakistan's suspicions, the rapid expansion of Village AID in the east after 1958 must have detracted from the quality of the program. But the greatest handicap of the Village AID scheme under the Ayub regime was undoubtedly the mentality of the military officials themselves and the hostility of the civil service. The uncertain, yielding character of the whole community-development concept must have seemed strange to men trained in military logistics and discipline. Furthermore, they made themselves the emphatic guardians of the country's welfare. The unavoidable administrative indulgences and developmental disparities inherent in any program depending so wholly on village revival very likely offended their sense of professional symmetry and almost puritanical insistence on the need for sacrifice, forbearance, and morality.

The Basic Democracies Order appeared in October 1959, and two months later the Basic Democrats were elected. This created an obvious duplication of effort at the local level, and one that could be especially harmful as village factions learned to use the two organizations against each other. The new scheme, interestingly enough, was slower getting started than the military had anticipated, but by the spring of 1961 the new system was well enough established to take over appropriate aspects of the community-development program, and allow certain specialized Village AID activities to revert to ministerial and departmental control. With the Basic Democracies scheme the entire concept of local reform and rural mobilization for developmental purposes was changed.

THE BAFFLING SIMPLICITY OF BASIC DEMOCRACIES

Village AID failed above all because it could not generate effective relations with the national government; its ultimate rejection is dramatic testimony to the necessity of finding a shared frame of reference in the developmental process. Local reform is an integral part of an expanding development program, but development is greatly influenced by the character of the governing regime. Therefore it is important that we establish more clearly the limitations and advantages of the type of government committed to development. Nearly all the new nations will have reached a critical phase in their political development when the mobilization of rural energies and support impinges on the political system. Most countries can be expected to achieve a relatively advanced state of internal political organization prior to thinking about their long-range plans. Concern with a "national" program means that the pattern of internal politics has become sufficiently complex to consider accommodating some sort of participation and initiating sustained development activities. Often the economy has reached a point where more of

University of Panjab, 1960. It should be noted that the village-council figures compiled for this study are not consistent with those appearing in Table III.

the population's energies and talents must be integrated into development if new growth is to take place. National politics becomes increasingly dependent on mutually accepted specialization and sustained though less intense interest. The government can fall back on its authoritarian ways only at a steadily increasing risk of incurring popular disfavor, and failures in the developmental realm can be spectacular.

Perhaps the most obvious reason for evaluating military governments skeptically, particularly when they deal with local problems, is that the military may be socially and politically isolated in the developing country.[36] The military leadership varies greatly, of course, from country to country, but even the most romantic French assimilationist would marvel at the British achievements among the elite of India and Pakistan. In forging a new national identity their virtue may also be their major handicap. Though the Pakistani army is proud of its familiarity with the peasant, partly from the enlisted ranks and partly from periodic maneuvers in the countryside, the officers have tended to be the offspring of landed families once favored by the British. Their devotion to rank and position may exceed that of the British *raj* mentality, and their concern with order may be more rigid. These considerations enter into understanding the military's evaluation of Pakistan's ills in 1958, and into their earlier involvement in politics. Their psychology of human relations is probably most clearly revealed in the Basic Democracies plan.

The most impressive characteristic of the military discussion of local reform was the moralizing quality of their pronouncements. This may have been partly in response to the problems of communicating with villagers, but Moroccan and Tunisian leaders encounter comparable obstacles and use different methods. Ayub frequently asks his people to "work ceaselessly," to beware of "indulging" in politics, and to desist from "childish" acts. Boundless faith in the common man is professed, but there is great suspicion, if not loathing, for the political intermediary or the "manipulator" of political life. For example, when the Basic Democracies Order was issued, the field marshal denounced doubts expressed in the eastern wing and called provincial feelings the "cowardly aberration of diseased minds."[37] Naturally the Moroccan and Tunisian leaders have posed moral imperatives, but it is interesting to note that patriotic discussions seldom exclude a segment of their own countrymen.

The military have not graduated from the turbulent school of mass

---

[36] There has recently been a move toward reexamining some of our thoughts on the military in developing countries. See, for example, John J. Johnson, ed., *The Role of the Military in Underdeveloped Countries*, Princeton, Princeton University Press, 1962, and S. E. Finer, *The Man on Horseback*, London, Pall Mall, 1963.

[37] *Pakistan Times*, October 1, 1959. Karachi edition unless otherwise indicated.

politics, and in Pakistan they witnessed the degeneration of the Muslim League and its successors until national politics was almost totally divorced from real problems. What the military forgot was that the growing chaos was not simply political intrigue, but also a meaningful reflection of Pakistan's ills. After four years of military rule many of the same obstacles to political integration still existed. No amount of manipulation of the bureaucracy, careful allocation of funds, or sane appeals to reason and moderation would simplify the nation-building process. However, the military regime must also be given credit for identifying the weak areas of Pakistani political life, and forcefully giving the villager his due importance in national policy. One can only be impressed when Ayub acknowledges that "democratic institutions should be related to the people's intellectual level and their mental horizon."[38] But having grasped this simple truth does not necessarily mean that the military will achieve integration where their predecessors failed.

In all three cases of local reform it is apparent that political leadership is quite aware of the potential political importance of the rural populace and is making some concession to its welfare. Because of the long period of rural neglect, coupled with the politicians' appetites for intrigue and corruption, the military regime was firmly convinced that more widespread participation would produce economic and political benefits. Although they may have had rather naïve notions about the vigor of the emergent patterns of political behavior, they had some very down-to-earth views on local reform. The approach is neatly summed up in President Ayub's address introducing Basic Democracies. He claimed that the new scheme would "not be foisted upon the people from above"; that in the neighborhood elections ignorance and "unfair pressure" would be eliminated; and that the new councils would be "free from the curse of party intrigues."[39] Though none of these things were fully achieved under Basic Democracies, there is a clear and public identification of the obstacles to the development of local leadership and rural confidence in the new nation.

The other explicit characteristic of the Basic Democracies plan of particular importance in the framework of this analysis is the direct concern with local reform as a device to further national development. In this respect, the leaders' military regard for detail and contingency may have had a most pronounced effect. They saw that family patterns, local legal practices, agriculture, health, and the entire array of service functions must be attached to the local level to have maximum effect.

[38] *Ibid.*, November 29, 1959.

[39] Field Marshal Mohammed Ayub Khan, *Speeches and Statements*, (*July 1959-June 1960*), vol. 2, Karachi, Pakistan Publications, 1961, pp. 34-35. His concern is slightly naïve because several of the Village AID evaluations had shown that half or more of the village councils organized under the program were influenced by party considerations even though parties were outlawed.

The Ayub regime had some of the same difficulties selling this to the bureaucracy as did the Village AID planners. But the military added the additional quality of structure to local-reform plans. They realized that the central government needed to have some idea of the local impact of economic development, and that 50,000 village councils unrelated to the country's administrative or political institutions would not only be fatally fragmented, but chaotic.

From October 1958 until the new National Assembly took office in June 1962, Pakistan was ruled by martial law. It is important to remember that because of the administrative and political purges subsequent to the revolution the privileged segment of Pakistani society was sensitive to the powers concentrated in the military courts, and also the enhanced authority of the bureaucracy. Although there is little evidence that the military regime abused its power, its propaganda agencies were active in creating a favorable foreign image and competing with India for international prestige. These considerations certainly influenced the regime's views on the importance of Basic Democracies. Furthermore, until the constitution was promulgated the military skillfully censored the press and forbade public meetings. All political organizations were outlawed, except the activities of the religious scholars whose public services could not be curtailed. Ayub seems to have been particularly embittered over the role of political parties, which were originally forbidden under the constitution, and once called them "a source of mischief and an instrument of exploitation."[40] Several of the ministers enthusiastically followed Ayub's lead, and more than one of his close advisers allegedly leaned heavily toward more dictatorial methods than the president would permit.

The organization of Basic Democracies rests on a five-tiered system.[41] At the base are the Union Councils, representing a population of about 10,000 persons. The populations vary from four to fifteen thousand for reasons similar to those limiting demarcation in Morocco. The number of villages within a Union varies, and the general practice was to try to make the village the constituency of 800 to 1,500 persons. The Union Council was designed to have fifteen members, ten of whom were to be elected and five nominated nonofficials. The nominated members were to be selected by the district officer, often with the recommendation of police, education, and other officials. The nominated members do not appear to have performed their expected role of aiding the council by

[40] *Pakistan Times*, October 4, 1961. See also Von Vorys, *op.cit.*, chs. 11 and 12.
[41] *The Basic Democracies Order, 1959, The Gazette of Pakistan Extraordinary*, October 27, 1959. There are several good accounts of the early organization of Basic Democracies. See Harry J. Friedman, "Pakistan's Experiment in Basic Democracies," *Pacific Affairs*, vol. 33, no. 2, 1960, pp. 107-125; Khalid Ben Sayeed, "Pakistan's Basic Democracy," *The Middle East Journal*, vol. 15, no. 3, 1961, pp. 249-263; Von Vorys, *op.cit.*, pp. 196-207.

assuring representation of respected community members, partly because the influence of government officials in their selection weakened their positions greatly. The Union Council is the only level in the scheme where elected members are in a majority, and their acts are all subject to review by the district officer. Not unlike the provisions for the operation of local councils in Morocco and Tunisia, the controlling authority can annul proceedings, suspend any motion, prohibit any agreed action, and require that specified matters be considered or certain actions performed.

The next tier is the *thana-tahsil* council, which was designed to coordinate the activities of several Union Councils as its urban counterpart, the Town Committee, at the next level of rural administration. These councils are composed of all the chairmen of the subordinate Union-Town local bodies and of appointed officials selected by the district officer, who are supposed to be half the total membership. This has meant that the *thana-tahsil* councils have had from 30 to 40 members. The chairman is designated as the Subdivisional Officer, an official subordinate to the District Magistrate in East Pakistan. Because he is found less frequently in West Pakistan, the *tahsildar* has often been asked to serve as *tahsil* council chairman, which has very likely introduced many additional tensions and disputes into the council's activities. Although the district officer is relatively unhampered in delegating responsibilities to the *thana-tahsil* level, this has seldom been done. The reason for introducing the official members at this level was that agents of the "nation-building departments" (a Pakistani term for the service ministries) have generally functioned from this level. The *thana-tahsil* includes about 150,000 persons, 13 unions or 165 villages, though the ratios differ greatly for the two wings, and corresponds roughly to the Development Area in the Village AID program. When the two schemes for local development were merged, many Village AID officials became Development Officers at this level.

At the district level the role of the elected Basic Democrat becomes minor. The District Council is composed of the chairmen of *thana-tahsil* councils, representatives of the nation-building departments, and an appointed group which must be half the membership. At least half of the nonofficial members must be chairmen of Union Councils and Town Committees, and the remainder may be the nominated members. Thus elected members may constitute no more than a fourth of the membership at the district level. The District Council is obliged to provide and maintain primary schools, hospitals, and a wide variety of developmental services in agriculture, public health, community work, et cetera. Needless to say, most of these duties have remained with the District Officers, who have shown reluctance to assign authority to the District Councils, and often lack the trained personnel to whom such a delegation could be made. There is in addition a list of some seventy optional powers, but few District Councils progressed sufficiently over the early years of the program to do more than discuss plans presented by the respective departments.

Very clearly the very large number of technical responsibilities given the District Council has meant that very few elected members and only a small number of more influential nominated members would question the opinion of the district officer, who still holds a virtually unchallengeable position in the supervision of his area. The district averages about one and a half million persons, including roughly nine *thana-tahsil* bodies and 1,500 villages. It compares to the provincial level of activity in Morocco and Tunisia. The district has been the working level for development problems in Pakistan, much like the province in North Africa.

At the third tier, the Division, the chairmen of all District Councils, i.e., all district officers and departmental representatives, are again combined with an equal number of appointed members. However, the fifty-fifty division is misleading, since no more than a fourth of the appointed members at this level are chairmen of Union Councils or Town Committees—a situation which thereby dilutes the maximum possible elected membership to an eighth. With an average population of six and a half million, a good deal larger than Tunisia, the division can obviously do little more than act as a coordinating and reviewing level. The eleven divisions in West Pakistan, not including Karachi, could perform important functions, but it is difficult to see how East Pakistan, divided into only three divisions for nearly fifty million persons, can relate divisional activities to the local level. Operating control necessarily remains at the district in both wings, although there have been several proposals to lower the critical level of activity to the *thana* or *tahsil*, especially for developmental planning and eventually for project design.

At the top of the Basic Democracies hierarchy was the Provincial Development Advisory Council under the chairmanship of the governor. With the return to constitutional rule, the provincial assemblies were revived and the Basic Democracies provincial councils were disbanded. Although the role of the Provincial Development Advisory Council was limited, it is significant that important modifications in the Basic Democracies plan stemmed from its discussions. Indeed, one of the similarities of the three political systems in handling problems of local development is their inability to lower the level at which discussions meaningful in both national and local politics take place. As in the two North African countries, the ruling order has relied heavily on the provincial governors. The fact that the governor is proportionately much farther removed from the affairs of the village in the Pakistani hierarchy is itself indicative of how difficult is her problem of national integration.

There were major differences between the Basic Democracies organizational structure in the two wings, given in Table III. In their desire to have a standard, neat system for local development, the military appear to have created two very different organizations, and then, as will become more apparent in subsequent materials, to have proceeded as though the similar organizational charts really constituted similar local-reform structures. In a very important respect Ayub so reduced the integrative capacity of local institutions that they were severely handicapped from the start. The table also clarifies why East Pakistani officials tend to discount the District Council as too unwieldy for local-reform purposes and to stress the Subdivision Officer or *tahsil* council as an alternative.

Despite the difficulties of using local-government legislation as an indicator of a new government's capacity to bring about a social revolution, the basic law reveals how a government conceived the problem of creating a more complex society and at least the minimal role they foresaw for local bodies. The systematic nature of the military mind certainly accounts for part of the minute detail of ninety-nine articles in the Basic Democracies Order.[42] Indeed, one might argue that conceptual clarity was its major virtue, blinding the military regime to the vast disparities among villages that had to be minimized before more effective local government could emerge in concert with national and provincial government.

A careful reading of the Basic Democracies Order helps to elaborate the sense in which the Ayub government committed itself to a much more ambitious program than even they may have realized. The Basic Democrats were first to have the role of a legislative body, both in handling local problems and in acting as the electoral body for provincial and national assemblies. It is sufficient to note at this point that some 6,500 politicians of the previous regime were disqualified for office under purge legislation.[43] They provide the basis for an articulate and rather persuasive appeal for revision of the scheme, as events subsequent to the constitution's promulgation have demonstrated. The Union Councils were also given substantial executive assignments, generally at

[42] Those desiring a full exposition of the law, very much influenced by the wishes of the regime, might read Masud-ul-Hasan, *Law and Principles of Basic Democracies*, Lahore, Pakistan Social Service Foundation, 1960. The book is helpful in tracing some of the administrative and legal references for the Basic Democracies.

[43] The government has been very reluctant to release any precise figures on the numbers affected by the disqualification investigations, a subject that will be treated in more detail below. The estimate given here appears in Sayeed, *op.cit.*, p. 255, and is very likely based on reliable information. There have, of course, been subsequent investigations. See also Von Vorys, *op.cit.*, p. 190.

TABLE III

Village and Population Ratios of Basic Democracies Organization[a]

	West Pakistan			East Pakistan		
	Units	Village Ratio[b]	Pop. Ratio (ths.)[c]	Units	Village Ratio	Pop. Ratio (ths.)
District[d]	58	670	573	17	2,941	2,835
Thana-Tahsil	187	214	188	411	124	117
Union[e]	3,055	13	10.9	4,053	12	11.9

[a] Organizational figures taken from *Scope and Functions of Basic Democracies and Their Contribution to Development*, Rawalpindi, Government of Pakistan, Ministry of National Reconstruction and Information, n.d. (1960), Appendix I, p. 11.

[b] West Pakistan included 14 Agency Councils organized in tribal areas, and East Pakistan included the Chittagong Hill Tracts.

[c] The East Pakistan figure includes 39 Union Councils planned for the Chittagong Hill Tracts, but not organized when Basic Democracies elections were held. It should be noted that this table is adjusted to rural Pakistan, and therefore omits the Town Committees, Union Committees, Cantonment Boards, and Municipal Committees. In the *Law and Principles of Basic Democracies, op.cit.*, p. 43, Masud-al-Husan gives the average population per Union Council as 8,000 in West Pakistan and 11,000 in East Pakistan.

[d] It is extremely difficult to find accurate figures on the number of villages in the two wings. Village AID officials estimated 40,000 for West Pakistan; Tinker, *Foundations of Local Government . . . , op.cit.*, p. 56, gives 70,000 for pre-partition Bengal, which has been reduced to 50,000 for these calculations.

[e] The 1961 census provides relatively good population figures. See *Final Tables of Population*, Karachi, Ministry of Home Affairs, Office of the Census Commissioner, 1961, which gives the rural population (communities under 5,000) as 33.2 million for West Pakistan and 48.2 million for East Pakistan.

the discretion of the district officer. In this regard the regime's insistence on the development of responsible local leaders may have exceeded reasonable possibilities. For example, the chairmen were to assist village revenue officials in the collection of taxes, the assessment of land, and the maintenance of public order (sect. 29). This is all well and good where there is some tradition of local cooperation with officials and where some substantial concession can be made without jeopardizing the minimal order needed to embark on development activities. But the tax and police officials had been a historic threat to the villager, and the government was in no way prepared to give the Union Council real authority over local taxation.

Local reform is a cumulative process, and the process must take place within the limits placed by the existing political system. The military regime appears to have created a degree of harmony and order that was artificial in both its foundations and its self-sustaining qualities. For example, section 29 of the Basic Democracies Order concluded with the statement that the various functions of the Union Council chairman in no way "authorized the Chairman to interfere in the performance by any official of his official duties." Considering that Pakistan probably has less nationally oriented political activity at the local level than Morocco or Tunisia, the very cautious tone of this reservation appears to reflect the attitude of the military-bureaucratic coalition more than conditions at the local level. Of course, "interference" can mean many things. Sheer obstructionism would be intolerable, but most discussions of village life suggest that political expression at this level is a good deal more sophisticated than this, and does indeed involve some ingenious maneuvers to protect village interests in dealing with the rural administration. These interests center on revenue collection and its associated tasks, the historic role of the district officer and his subordinates. The effect of the Basic Democracies Order, then, is to place the Union Council chairman in an equivocal position on the very issues that are most likely to arise between officials and villagers.

The law is similar to the Tunisian law in permitting a variety of devices to encourage local development efforts. In section 36 the Union Council is authorized to engage in commercial enterprise; section 41 establishes their right to enter into contracts; section 55 permits the local councils to accept loans; and there is even provision in section 80 for joint committees of councils as may be needed for development purposes. In practice, most villagers have been reluctant to obligate themselves under these provisions, and very few have received sufficient consultation to make it possible for them to enter into any such agreements. Nearly all developmental activity in rural areas has been confined to a single village or Union Council. The reservations contained in the Basic Democracies Order may make more elaborate contracts difficult to arrange. For example, section 37 provides that any institution or service being carried on at the local level may be transferred to government. While the intent may be only to preserve a minimal degree of order in certain kinds of activity, it again reflects the regime's cautious approach and insistence on expertise at all costs.

THE SEARCH FOR INTERMEDIATE-LEVEL LEADERS

The central flaw of President Ayub's plan to breach the gap between village and capital proved to be not that he underestimated the peasant, but that he ignored the politician. His almost pathological distrust of the politician may stem from the same bureaucratic-professional convictions that led him to hedge on his commitment to the Basic Democrats. Political parties, for all their shortcomings and abuses, had always existed in Pakistan, and there is evidence that their influence was felt locally, perhaps not in important ways, in even the Village AID program.[44] The parties in East Pakistan had relatively well-developed lines

[44] *Evaluation Report: Tangail Development Area*, Mymensingh District, East Pakistan, pp. 21-25.

of communication to the villages, and West Pakistan had known sufficient agitation, if not political organization, in many areas to be familiar with party action. However, until the new constitution came into effect with the election of the National Assembly, party activity was suppressed and many major party figures were under arrest or barred from political life. Not only did Ayub lose the opportunity to seek a new *rapprochement* between villager and politician, but he so angered the politicians that when they recovered their positions in 1962 they had little sympathy for the Basic Democrats' potential political role, and very little understanding of the Basic Democrats' broader significance in the developmental process.

There can be no political system extending to all levels of a society without citizens prepared to accept responsibility and confident that the obligations and rewards inherent in such activity will be honored. The first task of the Ayub regime was to find 80,000 citizens prepared to enter into such a relationship. The problem confronting the Ayub regime was not so much the villagers' rejection of government, because few villages in Pakistan could remember a time where government had not existed and where the minimal services of government in time of distress and war had not been provided. The problem was rather one of having no confidence in government and no conception of government's role in nation-building. As it was stated in a report dealing with the local level, the villager "may not be afraid of them [government officers], but generally he will not believe them."[45] The military regime had a relatively short period to establish such confidence, and the evidence indicates that it did not succeed in making full use of the advantages offered by the subdued tempo of national politics during the first three years of Ayub's government.

The elections of Basic Democrats were the first nationwide elections in Pakistan's history. As has been demonstrated many times, the developing countries have much less difficulty in holding elections than in attaching significance to them. There were few reports of injustices in the elections, and available reports indicate that the elections transpired in an orderly fashion. The major distraction was that few persons appear to have had a clear notion of what the elections involved, and the regulations so stringently enforced by the military made it almost impossible for an exploratory dialogue to take place. Indeed, it was necessary to amend martial-law regulations in order to permit the modest processions and subdued meetings of the candidates a month before elections. They were not permitted to enter controversy involving the Basic Democracies scheme itself, nor, of course, could political discussion touch on regional issues, religious beliefs, foreign policy, or old party loyalties. In the

[45] A. K. M. Mohsen, *Report on a Rural Public Works Programme in Comilla Kotwali Thana*, Pakistan Academy for Rural Development, Comilla, East Pakistan, p. 44.

countryside campaign expenditure was limited to 200 rupees. The effect was to limit discussion to the individual candidate's village where he tried to impress his neighbors with his superior "goodness" over other candidates.[46]

Studies of the 1959 elections create some doubts as to whether any commonly accepted political issues were ever involved in local elections in West Pakistan. The last District Board elections had been held in 1951, and plans for new elections in 1957 were repeatedly postponed, finally to be abandoned when the revolution took place. A third of 221 Punjabis interviewed concerning their recollections of the last elections knew nothing about them; another third voted on the basis of caste, village headman, and Islamic considerations; and the remainder, except for a small percentage of nonvoters, decided on the basis of either their personal acquaintanceship with the candidate or his social position. The degree of sophistication in the Basic Democracies election was no greater, and there appeared to be considerable confusion. Some thought that the old District Board elections were now being completed, and several respondents thought they were voting for a provincial assembly. Two fifths of the respondents did not know the name of the new council, and only one fifth knew how many members were being elected to their Union Council. The inquiry made the extremely revealing conclusion that "to most villagers a Union Council appeared to represent more a court of law than a corporate representative body capable of undertaking social welfare activities in the area . . . the village folk are predominantly non-political in their process of thinking."[47]

However, it should be noted that citizens of more advanced nations also display their ignorance when asked how members sit in the House of Representatives or how many candidates were on a primary ballot. The more vital point, which the surveys do not cover, is what changes, if any, the voter expected to come about as a result of his participation. In all probability he expected little change, and the turnout, which does not reflect great enthusiasm for the scheme, was no doubt heavily influenced by Ayub's energetic barnstorming and general interest in the revolutionary regime. The voters were given little choice in attaching significance to candidates. They had never been accustomed to the notion that perceived differences among candidates were likely to be manifested in changes in the participant's environment. In the absence of a sense of political efficacy among the vast majority of Pakistani voters, it is meaningless to speak of what the voter hoped the elections would provide or what he perceived the election to represent. The

[46] Harry J. Friedman, "Pakistan's Experiment in Basic Democracies," *Pacific Affairs*, vol. 33, no. 2, June 1960, p. 118.

[47] Social Sciences Research Center, *Village Life in Lahore District* (*A Study of Selected Political Aspects*), Lahore, University of Punjab, 1960, pp. 16 and 22.

burden of proof in this election, as in most elections in developing countries, is with the government, whose subsequent actions reassure the few aroused voters or stimulate the disinterested to attach some value to their privilege. Ayub's election in 1959, like others in Morocco and Tunisia, was designed to protect the central government against direct impact, and, by so doing, it minimized chances of persuading the voter that this election was any different from more corrupt versions known under earlier regimes.

The Pakistanis did not face as difficult problems of delimiting electoral districts and Union Councils as did Morocco and Tunisia. Although the first Pakistani government had never managed to hold national elections, there had been several provincial elections and local elections in East Pakistan. In this respect the East Pakistanis appear to have been better prepared, and subsequent preparation of regulations and procedures was more promptly accomplished in East Pakistan. At a governors' conference in September 1959 it was decided to use the electoral rolls prepared for the national elections. During the year the West Pakistan provincial government outlined its constituencies, and the decision was made to hold the elections during December 1959 and January 1960. Orders went out to district officials to encourage qualified persons to become candidates. The effects of the official management of the elections, no doubt apparent to the voters, are hard to gauge, but must have created skepticism.

The use of the 1957 election rolls had been the center of several controversies. First, the established politicians, most of whom were excluded, found a certain irony in the adaptation of the election preparations they had made for their own use by the new regime, which had replaced the parliamentary government on the eve of national elections. The West Pakistan provincial government faced special problems in the tribal areas, which had not been included in the 1957 preparations. Ayub was eager to include the more remote areas in both wings, but the tribal areas did not participate until the 1964 elections. Each *tahsil* was divided into constituencies of about 8,000, in an attempt to use traditional boundaries. Although an attempt was made to use single-member constituencies throughout West Pakistan, the final arrangements provided 19,448 wards returning 31,821 members in rural areas. For the entire province there were 21,511 wards for 38,457 Basic Democrats. There were some complaints because voters coming of age since 1957 were excluded, and also because the parliamentary manipulators had created a sizable number of fictitious names. In at least one district the number of registered voters exceeded the population.

On the whole the East Pakistan provincial government encountered fewer obstacles than did the western wing. The Chittagong Hill Tracts and Sylhet had not been included under the Bengali Village Self-

Government Act, but provisions were made to incorporate them in the elections by using the existing police districts. With fewer large towns and only one major city nearly all the wards were for rural representation on Union Councils, rather than for Union or Town Committees. For the entire wing there were 26,012 wards for 40,000 Basic Democrats.[48] In many cases time was not available to divide the 1957 rolls into small constituencies, and the election authorities were compelled to form multimember constituencies. There were reportedly numerous cases of two- and three-member constituencies, and in one case as many as sixteen.[49]

Although the significance of voter turnout is no easier to fathom in a developing country than in an advanced country, there were large differences in voter participation among Divisions and between the provinces. Just over 20,000,000 voters came to the polls, although 32,000,-000 were registered. The highest turnout was in West Pakistan, where almost nine million or about three fourths of the voters appeared. In East Pakistan, where reportedly there was discontent over the elections as well as an accumulation of provincial grievances, participation dropped to only a little over half the registered voters, or about twelve million. The difference has particular meaning because of the eastern wing's advantage in experience with local self-government and more widespread participation in party politics for many years. The more articulate voter tended to discredit the Basic Democracies elections. The turnout among the very active voters of Karachi was only 35 per cent.

The candidates were carefully screened by the authorities for their qualifications as representatives, and also under the provisions for political disqualification. The sweeping terms of the Elective Bodies Disqualification Order (1959) allowed investigating bodies to bar individuals involved in "subversive activity, action contributing to political instability, bribery, favoritism or abetment of any such activity" since August 14, 1947. Nearly anyone related to the parliamentary regime could be disqualified under these provisions. Although the EBDO procedures were not designed specifically for the Basic Democracies elections, the East Pakistan election report notes that lists of politically barred individuals were received very late in the nomination

---

[48] Most of the figures cited on the elections come from *Scope and Functions of Basic Democracies and their Contribution to Development*, Government of Pakistan, Ministry of National Reconstruction and Information, 1961, Appendix I, "Statistics in respect of important items concerning Elections to Basic Democracies, held in December, 1959," pp. 10-11. For West Pakistan see Government of West Pakistan, *The West Pakistan Basic Democracies Election Report 1959-1960*, Lahore, 1960.

[49] For full election details see *Comprehensive Report on Basic Democracies in East Pakistan*, Government of East Pakistan, Health, Social Welfare and Local Government Department, 1960, pp. 4-6.

process, and that many nomination papers had to be rejected at a very late stage in the elections.

There were also bitter rivalries among political leaders in some of the old provincial regions of West Pakistan, which had had repercussions at the local level. Rejection of nomination papers could be either for technical errors or under the disqualification decree. Again, it is significant that the rejection rate was nearly three times as high in West Pakistan. The military regime left most casualties in the politically volatile city of Karachi, where nearly a third of all candidates were eliminated. As shown in Table IV, the Ayub regime made a monumental effort to exclude those familiar with party politics, paying a price in experience for the purity of the candidates.

TABLE IV

Nominations Filed, Withdrawn, and Rejected in Basic Democracies Elections[a]

	West Pakistan	East Pakistan	Karachi	Total
Field	92,730	87,190	3,359	183,279
Withdrawn	20,977	6,040	607	27,624
Rejected	6,345	2,274	596	9,215
Candidates	51,318	78,974	2,156	132,448
Seats	38,457	40,000	1,389	79,846
Unopposed[b]	10,311	7,083		

[a] Figures taken from Appendix I, "Statistics in respect of important items concerning Elections to Basic Democracies, held in December, 1959," *Scope and Functions of Basic Democracies and their Contribution to Development*, Government of Pakistan, Ministry of National Reconstruction and Information, 1960.

[b] There is a discrepancy between the provincial election reports and the figures given in the above report, where unopposed candidates are given only as 12 per cent for West Pakistan and 18 per cent for East Pakistan. However, the *Annual Report on Basic Democracy in East Pakistan*, Government of East Pakistan, Home Secretary, 1960, p. 3, gives the above number of uncontested seats. The West Pakistan figure is taken from Government of West Pakistan, *The West Pakistan Basic Democracy Election Report 1959-60*, p. 15. These two figures reverse the relative rate of unopposed seats in the two wings, and also indicate a much higher percentage of uncontested constituencies in both wings.

There were three possible sources of political experience for the Basic Democrats: Village AID councils, District Boards, and political parties. The West Pakistan secretariat for Basic Democracies has calculated the number of Village Council officials under the Village AID program who were reelected to positions in Union Councils.[50] In the four Divisions where the Village AID program had five or more Development Areas (Peshawar, Sargodha, Lahore, and Bahawalpur) about a third of the Union Council chairmen elected under Basic Democ-

[50] Table prepared for the author by the Basic Democracies and Local Government Department, Lahore, West Pakistan, dated April 16, 1962.

racies held comparable office under the earlier program. In Lahore and Peshawar the over-all record was somewhat better, and approximately two thirds of the chairmen, secretaries, and members had participated in Village AID councils. In Sargodha and Bahawalpur divisions about half the newly elected chairmen and members had Village AID experience. Although the Village AID program certainly had mixed results, it appears that it made an important contribution to village-level leadership.

In a study concerned with over 300 members and chairmen of Union Councils in Comilla *thana* of East Pakistan, roughly a third of the members and two thirds of the chairmen had experience under the old boards. There was a small element with extended experience, for about 15 per cent of the Union Council chairmen had had over five years' experience as presidents of Union boards. In another study of three East Pakistan Union Councils, the proportion of old Union board members varied from 40 per cent in one case to only one ex-Union board in another. As the author of this study concludes,[51] the evidence does not bear out the common criticism that the members of the Union boards were simply transferred to the new Union Councils, although the experience and popularity that might have been acquired may have some effect.

Despite the vigorous efforts of the Ayub government to discourage politicians from participating in the new councils, it appears that a sizable proportion of Basic Democrats have political affiliations. There were about 2,800 Basic Democrats in East Pakistan with past political affiliations, and about 5,000 in West Pakistan. This means that about a tenth of the Basic Democrats have political lines to parties,[52] which would seem an ample number to revive party activity at the lower levels of the political system as restrictions are lifted and party activity resumes. The fact that the more highly organized and more experienced East Pakistanis selected a much smaller number of ex-politicians suggests that, first, more local leaders could be found and, second, that the voters were more prepared to select local leaders without the guidance of old party affiliations. This is one of many indications that the

[51] Bureau of National Reconstruction and Pakistan Academy for Village Development (Comilla), *An Analysis of the Working of Basic Democracy Institutions in East Pakistan*, Dacca, 1961, p. 42, and A. T. R. Rahman, *Basic Democracies at the Grassroots* (*A Study of Three Union Councils of Kotwali Thana, Comilla*), Comilla, Pakistan Academy for Village Development, 1962, pp. 20-25. Hereafter cited as the Comilla and Kotwali Studies, respectively.

[52] *Comprehensive Report* . . . , *op.cit.*, p. 3, and *The West Pakistan Basic Democracies Election* . . . , *op.cit.*, Annex, Table 6. These figures differ from those given by Khalid Ben Sayeed, "Pakistan's Basic Democracy," *Middle East Journal*, vol. 15, no. 3, 1961, p. 258. Professor Sayeed's figure is taken from *Scope and Functions* . . . , *op.cit.*, while larger numbers of politicians were noted in *The West Pakistan Basic Democracies Election* . . . , *op.cit.*

East Pakistanis possess considerable political skill, and have benefited from the concessions made to the villages in the interwar period.

Ayub must be given credit for introducing the peasants to politics on a scale that has only been paralleled in India. The old parties had little time for the villager, and party organizations at the village level were rudimentary. Under Basic Democracies the overwhelming majority of the new local representatives were occupied with agriculture. For the country as a whole nearly 50,000 of the Basic Democrats were classified as agriculturally employed, although there is no breakdown of the size of holding or distribution of the farmers. Another 12,000 were classified as small landholders and small businessmen, though there were about twice as many in the latter category in West Pakistan—most likely a result of the relative concentration of industry and more commercialized agriculture in the western wing. The western wing was also able to provide more professional persons as Basic Democrats—over 11,000 compared to about 7,000 in the east. The large numbers of small entrepreneurs and professional persons available in the western wing meant that there were fewer farmers—about 16,000 in the west as compared to over 32,000 in the east. The curious aspect of the results was that, although Basic Democracies was most appropriate in its design and eventually its operation for conditions in West Pakistan, there were more farmers brought into the Union Councils in the east. The explanation rests with the very different agrarian and village patterns of the two wings.[53]

IN SEARCH OF A COMMON PATTERN OF PARTICIPATION

The comparative framework of this study hopes to underscore the complementary relationship between the developmental process and increased political participation. Once a country has made a firm commitment to the material improvement of its populace, it has also made a commitment to create a new relationship between government and governed. Most of the first year was spent adapting the Basic Democracies program to local needs, and establishing a basic organizational design. At the Governors' Conference a year after the Basic Democracies elections it was recognized that the lower tiers of the organization were beginning to stagnate.[54] The concession to local reform had begun to have independent influence on government, and the Ayub regime clearly felt that participation had to be made meaningful to the individual Basic Democrats.

[53] See Inayatullah, "An Analysis of the Functioning of Seven Union Councils in Peshawar Tehsil," mimeo., West Pakistan Academy for Village Development, Peshawar. See also his "Study of Selected Union Councils in Rawalpindi Division," mimeo., and *Study of Union Councils in Nowshera Tehsil*, Peshawar, West Pakistan Academy for Village Development, 1961. Hereafter cited as the Peshawar, Rawalpindi, and Nowshera Studies, respectively.
[54] *Pakistan Times*, October 24 and 25, 1960.

Nevertheless, there was a curious reluctance on the part of the military-bureaucratic alliance to make significant and explicit concessions of power. Ayub thought more along lines of creating a "healthy rivalry" at the local level, which might have the desirable effect of stimulating interest and initiative at the local level without undue complications at higher levels in the political system. Suggestions were made that "model" Union Councils be selected, and that cash prizes should be given to the more effective local bodies. While these measures might have some impact, one also senses that the Ayub regime still looked upon the Basic Democrats as Boy Scouts.

By the end of 1960 the government had decided that the nominated members, generally representing wealthier, more influential local interests, were having a deadening effect on the councils. The Minister of the Interior confessed in a speech in late 1960 that Basic Democrats often acted like "dummies" in the presence of the nominated members. Shortly afterward it was decided that appointed members for the higher tiers of the Basic Democracies hierarchy should come from elected members only.[55] It is quite possible that numerous conflicts between the elected and appointed members, both nominated and officials, had taken place. Early in 1961 the Basic Democracies law was amended to permit the nonofficial members of a lower tier to appeal to the next higher tier when a majority of them disagreed with official members, and after May 1961 the appointment of nominated members was discontinued.[56]

The crux of the national integration problem was to create new patterns of influence having local roots, but such a diffusion of power would require as much forbearance and restraint on the part of the military-bureaucratic regime as it would from a parliamentary regime. Indeed, it may well be that the parliamentary regime failed to integrate the nation through neglect, while the Ayub regime hesitated, with full awareness and some reluctance, over compromising the professional ease made possible by the military regime. Thus in mid-1960 Ayub replied angrily to press charges that Basic Democracies was "not alive." He sent a letter to Union Council chairmen and supervisory officials asking "tact, practice and persuasion of the highest order" and encouraging frank discussion.[57]

The need to orient Basic Democracies to the national political system came about, significantly, when the Ayub government was seeking to enlarge its developmental role. It was one thing to bar the new leaders from party politics because of the way in which the old parliamentary

[55] *Ibid.*, November 1, 1960.
[56] Government of West Pakistan, Department of Basic Democracies and Local Government, *Monthly Report*, May 1961, p. 2.
[57] *Pakistan Times*, May 18 and 19, 1960.

system operated, but Ayub was not able to keep national politics out of Basic Democracies. In late 1960 the president endorsed replacing higher-tier Basic Democracies chairmen who did not cooperate in enlarging the councils' activities. He also stated that officials who domineered communities in their areas should be removed. Still viewing the participant in a passive role, he acknowledged that "government operations should be discussed in the councils so as to make the administration accountable to the people and responsive to their actual needs and aspirations." He noted further that councils presided over by officials as chairmen had "not been productive of the best results."[58] Although these second thoughts did not constitute a major overhaul of the Basic Democracies scheme, they reveal the growing realization that participation without effective influence is senseless.

The problems of creating a coherent political unit within the new Union Councils were no greater than those of finding a new working relationship between the Basic Democrats and the administration. The "law and order" tradition of the bureaucracy, plus the obviously experimental character of the entire scheme, made most rural officials cautious. As plans were made to expand the role of the local councils, and as the potential development role of the local bodies was explored, the government urged officials to mix with the people in their areas.[59] It was apparent in case studies that the chairmen of the Union Councils seldom thought of the local program as the product of the community, and still looked upon the Union Council as the "handmaiden of government."[60] In very few cases did the councils feel that they had full authority, or that they were free of the constant surveillance of the district official. Many councils felt that they were fully occupied simply handling the correspondence from higher authorities.

With the merger of Village AID and Basic Democracies fully completed by mid-1961, the problem of supervising development activity at the local level made the government-Union Council relationship more urgent. In East Pakistan a plan was devised to appoint development officers within the Basic Democracies organization.[61] For each of the 410 *thanas* there was to be a Circle Officer (Development), who was relieved of all judicial and revenue functions. At the district level Assistant Directors were to be appointed, and at the division level Deputy Directors. However, these plans were slow in taking concrete form because the government lacked appropriately trained officials. The East Pakistan plan was put forward in September 1961, and in mid-1962

[58] *Ibid.*, December 6, 1960.
[59] *Ibid.*, November 22, 1961.   [60] Kotwali Study, *op.cit.*, p. 58.
[61] Government of East Pakistan, Department for Basic Democracies and Local Government, "Five Year Financial Plan for Basic Democracies" and "Scheme for Supervisory Staff for Basic Democracies and Provincial Advisory Councils," mimeo., both dated September 28, 1961.

there were still only 115 Circle Officers (Development) available to assist over 4,000 Union Councils in the province. In effect, less than a third of the councils received the guidance authorized under existing legislation. Similar steps were taken to provide officials solely concerned with Basic Democracies in West Pakistan.[62]

Like the Moroccan and Tunisian governments, the Ayub regime realized the need for local concessions to stimulate developmental activity, but the organizational complexity of the Basic Democrats' role in no way corresponded to comparable complexity in political structure within the system. The highly professional orientation of the military-bureaucratic alliance did not lend itself to generating political relationships appropriate to a more complex society. The president agreed to lift the ban on parties with great reluctance during the election of the National Assembly in mid-1962. The Basic Democrats served as electors and were accepted as the expedient device to establish workable constituencies for the implementation of the new constitution. The failure of Ayub's views in building new political relationships was immediately apparent. There was no preference for Basic Democrats as members of the National or Provincial Assemblies, nor did the experience of the past three years enable the Basic Democrats to arrive at clear majorities in selecting legislators.[63]

The conceptual clarity of Basic Democracy was no substitute for a framework by which individuals could more effectively relate themselves to political life. Ayub himself had no choice but to join the Conventionist Muslim League in June 1962, and the chief party organizer was later appointed to the cabinet. The inability of the government to translate its political orientation into action was again revealed in the second election of Basic Democrats in November 1964. The disparities that persisted in the nation are suggested by Von Vory's observation that both candidates for president were stronger than their party organizations.[64] Moreover, the emotional quality of the campaign was obvious, and the symbolic role of Miss Jinnah evident in her immediate withdrawal from politics after the campaign. In the subsequent selection of the president by the Basic Democrats, Ayub received the votes of nearly 50,000 electors. Though the president's accomplishment in holding elections should not be minimized, it is difficult to argue that the precision and foresight of the professional had changed the nature of political participation in Pakistan.

[62] *Pakistan Times*, November 29, 1960.

[63] Von Vorys, *op.cit.*, p. 237. The entire drama of how best to bring national political values into action was again played out in the Report of the Constitution Commission, representing more closely the views critical of the regime, and a government committee, representing Ayub's views. See Government of Pakistan, *Report of the Constitution Commission*, Karachi, Government of Pakistan Press, 1961. Also Von Vorys, *op.cit.*, pp. 220-221.

[64] *Ibid.*, p. 280.

As in the case of Morocco, the argument is more than simply asserting that certain kinds of government can do only certain kinds of things. The political orientation of a regime also becomes the justification for encouraging certain kinds of relationships. Ayub's response to Pakistan's problems, and to local reform in particular, was candid and rational in the extreme. The careful calculation of means and ends that the regime performed so well were, however, irrelevant to the calculations that everyday life demanded in Pakistan and even farther removed from the prevailing values of the citizens than the orientation of the Moroccan and Tunisian governments. There are grounds for arguing that Ayub found himself in a society where values are not easily attached to performance, but this hardly rationalized the regime's detachment from the question.

Ayub's attitude toward the developmental problem, and inescapably the view which also influenced Basic Democracies in the early stages, was suggested when he returned from East Pakistan in the fall of 1959. When asked how he found the people there, he replied that they are "cheerful and have clean clothes."[65] A similar orientation to local reform and to development more generally was exposed by a military officer in a meeting of the Development Advisory Council of West Pakistan. He suggested, first, that tea-drinking, smoking, and chewing betel nut (*pan*) should be abolished because such practices are unhealthy and waste agricultural resources. Later on he advocated a system of compulsory labor, not for development purposes, but "to eliminate possible obstacles which may crop up from time to time as a result of the covert and overt action of the mischievous and dissident elements in the society."[66] These may well be extreme views, but they represent the moral tone of the revolutionary regime—one which was much in evidence under martial law.

Simply setting up the Basic Democracies organization, important as the initial step was, did not give the new government any kind of self-propelling organization at the local level. Moreover, some of the attempts to use this organization to deal with local customs that were an obstacle to the development process, e.g., the Family Laws, could not be expected to work until a measure of confidence and familiarity with the impersonal world of national politics was acquired. Obviously, the transformation meant changing values and goals of individuals throughout Pakistani political life, and it is for this reason that the political aspect of the development process must be viewed as essentially a problem in national politics despite the self-evident and limiting problems seen in the villages.

The military-bureaucratic alliance had difficulty getting political and

[65] *Pakistan Times*, September 7, 1959.   [66] *Ibid.*, April 8, 1961.

social action structured at various levels, as several problems considered in this chapter suggest. The meetings of the Development Advisory Councils tended to be perfunctory and subdued until constitutional government was revived. It was noticeable that in a meeting of the West Pakistan council the nonofficial members had nothing to say, and that the number of speakers on any particular point was very small. The government was reluctant even to grant the members power to convene the council themselves, and preferred to withhold parliamentary immunity from the members.[67] The reluctance to give the Basic Democracies scheme the prestige and privileges associated with political activity in the parliamentary regime tended to lower the value of the program in Pakistani eyes, and, in turn, made it more likely that the program would be neglected in the renewed parliamentary system in 1962.

All local-reform measures are arbitrary by virtue of their origins, and all countries have problems evading the essentially authoritarian aspect of rural administration. The question is to see how the new government shows promise of escaping the rigid atmosphere of local-national relations that has been ingrained over generations of colonial rule and reinforced in the struggle for independence. Although the military-bureaucratic coalition in Pakistan exposed their professionalism by adhering closely to the organizational lines of the revenue administration, they acknowledged much more openly than Morocco and Tunisia that local leaders should gain confidence and acquire conceptual skills needed to deal with many levels in the political system. The monarchy, by comparison, adapted to local conditions very slowly, and preferred to disconnect nationally oriented political activities. The Tunisian single-party regime fulfilled the coordinating role of national politics through the judicious use of party militants, although this has placed substantial limits on how much specialized activity could be done in the municipal councils. In the Basic Democracies scheme the village and town leaders were openly accepted in theory, which is, after all, the only kind of reform one has in the early stages of development.

Although the Ayub regime went a step farther, they were not prepared to encourage the Basic Democrats to act outside the framework of the rural administration. The restriction was largely self-imposed. The military regime could perceive the decline of professional standards through corruption and waste, but they could not see that full local development requires patterns of behavior approved outside administrative channels. Of course, the Basic Democracies scheme had within it some implicit assumptions about national institutions, and the ultimate test of the program has been the postconstitutional period. National politics cannot operate on prearranged plans or be confined to administrative channels, however reasonable and efficient such methods

[67] *Ibid.*, July 20, 1961.

may be. This has been demonstrated in all the developing countries as more comprehensive patterns of political participation emerge, and as political relationships adapt to the demands of a more intricate society.

In each of the three proposals for reorganizing local government the realm of new political activity was restricted by devices characteristic of the regime itself. Thus the Pakistan military saw that political communication within the village was to some extent dependent on increased and improved communication with officials outside the villages and at levels of government heretofore generally closed to local leaders. However, the military had reservations about sharing power with any group that did not accept its highly professional view of national politics, which restrained the villager just as definitely as it had the disqualified political figures of the prerevolutionary regime. The Basic Democrats were combined with officials in the representative hierarchy in increasing proportions as one approached the provincial government. They could have no direct voice in central government, and the control given them as the electoral body for the new legislature was the subject of great controversy and ran against the grain of Pakistani political experience. The Ayub government was suspicious of competition in political life, but they hoped that the newly elected local leaders would accept political responsibilities. Furthermore, the government realized that local development was a prerequisite to the widespread impact of the economic and social revolution they wished to bring about, but they would not trust the new local leaders to make important decisions about the process of development.

Though each political system encountered peculiar institutional problems, there was in each case a desire to simplify political relationships while also building a more complex society. Individuals were expected to become both more responsive and responsible, but meaningful political concessions were difficult to fit into more rigid political patterns. While the Pakistanis were able to mobilize their officials, in part by making them the government, they simultaneously found it more difficult to accommodate differences that were not amenable to their professional outlook. The Tunisians divorced local politics from other aspects of political life, compartmentalizing localized activities in much the same way as other developmental programs have been compartmentalized. In Morocco the rural-commune program lost momentum for lack of political support, and the monarchy sought a substitute in nationally organized schemes for mass participation in development. In this way each national development effort encountered political obstacles stemming from the character of the regime, as each perceived the political hazards of accommodating new forms of participation.

SECTION III:

NATIONAL POLITICS AND LOCALIZED DEVELOPMENT

"Man does not live by technology alone. Any changes, even of far lesser scope than those required for rapid nation building and socio-economic development, threaten important interests. It is only the rich, the privileged and the well-born (the traditional elites) who feel the threats of change and resist them. The middle class man, entrenched in his small business, farm or government job; the poor man, deriving security from familiar institutions and relationships—they also fear the uncertainty of measures that may cause changes in economic functions or social status. The more precarious their security, the more they fear change."[1]

Local reform refers not only to the transformation of political values to create working relationships between villager and governor, but also to the array of social forces pressing the villager to engage himself in national development. The repercussions of radical environmental changes at the local level rapidly extend beyond the capacity of the existing political system, and place demands on government infinitely more diverse and subtle than the requirements of the early stages of independence. In this section the three governments' readiness to encourage widespread change and their anticipation of its political impact will be examined in some areas directly affecting village life. Only by recognizing the cumulative nature of development can government prepare to deal with the more articulate citizen, and persuade the isolated individual to enter a psychological world based on calculated risk, deferred gratification, and reliance on remote, impersonal processes.

In this section of the study the three governments' efforts to deal more directly with the environment of the citizen will be examined. Though these programs affect many aspects of the village life that involved deep emotions, the major goal of development is to teach the peasant that individual judgment and knowledge can indeed have an impact on conditions in the countryside. In introducing new behavior the assumption has often been that understanding alone produces change. Perhaps the greatest disservice Westerners have imposed on the developing nation is our belief that knowledge is self-justifying, perhaps even self-sufficient. The peasant lives in a world where feelings and understanding are not so conveniently differentiated, and our naïve assumption that his

[1] Milton Esman, *The Politics of Development Administration*, mimeo., Pittsburgh, University of Pittsburgh, Graduate School of Public and International Affairs, 1963, p. 28.

values and loyalties will simply keep pace with the complex new behavior involved in development has often been proved incorrect. In many instances the villager would prefer to remain poor rather than destroy the framework of his entire existence.

The fact that most of the chapters in this section deal with problems that make good sense to the Western reader jeopardizes his full comprehension of the individual reconciliation the new behavior entails for the villager. The same could be said of many governments of developing countries, staffed by the products of Western education and intent on producing material evidence of progress. The reluctance that most new governments display in communicating political values is not accompanied with nearly the same hesitance over making the villager more productive. One of the purposes of the inquiry is to indicate how these two components are interdependent in the transformation of the villager —a problem which will be taken up in more detail after reviewing some of the efforts to increase the villager's understanding in hopes that enlightenment itself would be persuasive.

Though a vast generalization, there is some evidence that a political system that cannot establish some confidence in the workability of the national values cannot begin to implement the programs needed to bring about new behavior. In real life the convenient limiting situation does not exist, and all political systems enjoy some degree of confidence in the form of legitimacy. Nevertheless, expanding the rudimentary and emotional basis for legitimacy into a more complex working relationship is essential to national development. Thus the focal point for this section may represent a fairly abrupt break when considered in terms of the conventional distinctions about the role of government. But in terms of the relationship between the system and the citizen it is not a major disparity, nor is there nearly the same discontinuity in the mind of the villager, who seeks to relate the behavioral aspect of development with the values advocated by his country. He may not succeed in reconciling and integrating his understanding and feeling, but the problem is immediate and may very likely determine how well he responds to the increasingly complex tasks the developmental process imposes on him.

CHAPTER 5

THE DECISION TO PLAN
AND POPULAR CONSENT

EACH OF THE regimes has found great difficulty in extending governmental activity to the local level through the more conventional channels of local government. Simultaneously, the three governments under examination, and most of the other African and Asian governments, are pledged to improve living conditions at the local level and irrevocably committed to massive programs of social change. The problems of development are curiously, and perhaps conveniently, divorced from the political system. The result may be a confirmation of the leaders' apprehensions in a self-fulfilling prophecy. Local government is not an adequate vehicle for creating a more diverse society because the citizens are socially retarded. The direct impact of social and economic programs is constantly handicapped by the inability of the villager to interrelate these efforts in the political system. Hence the national government is less prepared to seek a versatile basis for development or political life as it experiences new failures in each endeavor.

If the conditions advancing the development process and those affecting political life could be easily separated, it might be possible to explore the point at which advance in one area compelled adaptation in the other. Working governments are not easily described in terms permitting such an evaluation, nor are the variety of developmental efforts easily reduced to a common factor. However, each of the three governments described in this study is deeply involved in a series of programs to impress the locality with the regime's devotion to the welfare of each citizen. In turn, the citizen is asked to express his confidence in government by delaying immediate gratifications in the form of saving, by altering time-honored habits of cultivation, marketing, and storing his products, and by cooperating with the government in introducing modern ideas into once sheltered areas of education, family life, and marriage.

In their commitment to social revolution the new governments undertake a transformation that is not so easily postponed as the reorganization of local government, where the institutional channels of authority are relatively well defined. Each effort to change the villager represents a change in his capacity and inclination to participate in politics outside the traditional framework. It is at least logically possible that a government might so alter its social base that the political system would become irrelevant to the needs and desires of the populace. Certainly the highly affective devices for participation will become less meaningful as the populace acquires new understanding of life outside the village, and accumulates new institutional channels to express such desires.

The attitudinal component of this transformation is the decreasing usefulness of the symbolic attachment to the nation. The acquisition of new cognitive skills is part of the social change and inextricably part of the developmental process. This is not to imply that the citizen of a modern country is less patriotic, but only that he relies much less on patriotic outbursts to relate his personal life to politics. Political activity, like much other behavior, is sustained and moderated by the advanced citizen's ability to work in a variety of frameworks and to accommodate diversity in his environment. The emotional forms of attachment to one's country do not diminish in intensity necessarily, but they are supplemented with a vastly increased individual capacity to understand how the locality, the family, and the region fit into the pattern of national politics.

An important ingredient in confronting the villager with this more complex environment is the government's own views on how change will take place, the priority on different aspects of change, and the new institutions that will be formed to integrate social change with the role of government. Perhaps the most useful document in acquiring an overview of the regime's orientation to widespread efforts to change the environment is the plan or plans produced to envisage how the nation-building process will take place. Like most of the governments of Africa and Asia, the three governments of this inquiry have produced a variety of documents to indicate the paths of future development. Their utility in the context of this inquiry is not so much their economic feasibility, but the extent to which they provide a new concept of the relation between citizen and government.

There is a burgeoning literature on planning in developing countries, and it deserves more careful analysis in terms of the political systems from which it emanates as well as more conventional analysis in economic terms. Is it wholly coincidence, for example, that the planning effort of the Lybian monarchy has been evaluated as "drifting" and "indecisive" by the I.B.R.D.,[1] one of the major objections that also might be raised in criticism of Moroccan planning? The heavily doctrinaire character of early Indonesian planning was certainly characteristic of the type of government Sukarno preferred. The result was that the plan became only a "shopping list" of projects, which the president considered suitable and more easily managed for political purposes.[2] Even some of the economically more successful planning endeavors

[1] International Bank for Reconstruction and Development, *The Economic Development of Lybia*, Baltimore, Johns Hopkins Press, 1960, pp. 86-89.

[2] Guy Paulker, "The Indonesian Eight Year Plan," *Pacific Affairs*, vol. 34, 1960, pp. 115-130. The Indonesian plan consists of seventeen volumes, largely devoted to Sukarno's Marxist rhetoric and philosophy.

have failed to bring about the integration of the populace needed to enter into a more advanced phase of growth.

Although there have been some explorations in the comparative analysis of planning,[3] the political variable has seldom taken on primary importance in existing analyses. The three countries of this inquiry are a challenging comparison, and the first part of the chapter will be devoted to a review of how each came to be involved in planning. The planning activity of the Moroccan monarchy has, on the whole, been the most arbitrary and capricious of the three countries. The more traditional government has encountered more difficulties in reconciling different political views in planning discussions, and significantly has ended by being attacked by both the more conservative Istiqlal and the socialist-oriented U.N.F.P. Like most other major decisions in Tunisia, the commitment to planning was part of a long period of probing and preparation by the president. When the single-party regime did decide to engage wholeheartedly in planning, action was thorough and firm despite remarkable resistance from some quarters. Judged solely on its merits as a plan, the Pakistani effort is quite clearly the most successful, but it remains highly significant that planning has been conducted with little or no contact with existing political forces in the country, and with almost no attempt to present the plan to the Pakistani people. The military-bureaucratic alliance kept the plan very much to themselves, and it is only with the revival of organized political activity under the new constitution that economic reconstruction of the country has become a subject of political discussion.

To the extent that the values of the reconstructed society are made explicit and put into a form having meaning to the populace, the new government will be encouraging the kind of individual reorientation that is an essential aspect of the developmental process. Such an endeavor would be necessarily controversial, but it is perhaps the willingness to enter into controversy and to discuss political values that is the critical element in a self-generating, innovative society. Without a value system appropriate to both the political and economic challenge of a modern society, it is difficult to see how any plan can accomplish its ultimate purpose of creating a self-sufficient social system. Responsibility may not fall directly and wholly on the planning apparatus, but the

---

[3] Very few attempts have been made to evaluate planning in the Middle East, where there has been a large supply of foreign currency from oil. A short commentary will be found in A. J. Meyer's *Middle Eastern Capitalism*, Cambridge, Harvard University Press, 1959, pp. 93-109. The peculiar planning problems of less developed countries, both Muslim and non-Muslim, have received somewhat more attention from continental writers. See, for example, Jacques Austruy, *Islam en face au développement économique*, Paris, Les Editions Ouvrières, 1961, and also Charles Bettelheim, "Sous-développement et planification," *Politique Etrangère*, vol. 22, 1957, pp. 287-300.

plan is one of the most important opportunities to lay the groundwork for a coherent system of national values enabling the citizen to differentiate the intricate pattern of roles as entrepreneur, voter, father, and critic that are requisite to the vigorous, productive society.

THE LEAP INTO RELATIVE CERTAINTY

Moroccan politicians had great difficulty in coming to grips with the concrete issues of their country's future. To the uncertainties of the governing process were added the factionalism of the multiparty system and the distractions of a growing irredentist movement under the Istiqlal leader, Allal Al-Fassi. Moreover, the Protectorate administrative structure, burdensome and top-heavy as it might be, was designed to avoid disaster rather than initiate change. The French bureaucracy at home and overseas had long acted as the country's managerial agent. There were many offices from Protectorate days that ostensibly provided the coordination that a planning agency hopefully brings to a country's economic life. Only with time did the Moroccan leaders realize that the effectiveness of these offices depended on accepting the colonial presuppositions and purposes for which they were first erected.

Under the French Protectorate Morocco had been developed by an intricate mosaic of private, public, and semipublic corporations much like those found in France herself. The first resident general, Marshal Lyautey, set a precedent for planned national development by setting aside Morocco's rich phosphate deposits as a state monopoly in 1923. A few years later a governmental agency was created to attract mining companies for the exploitation of lead, manganese, zinc, and other mineral deposits. However, neither agency was used with the imagination needed to promote the economy as a whole.

French budgetary procedures contain a deceptive element of planned organization. The budget is normally presented in two parts, the ordinary or operating budget and the equipment or capital budget. In practice the French have negated this very logical division of funds by allowing investment funds to be used for operating expenses, and by including cost in the operating budget that might be more reasonably classified as capital investment. Each ministry also prepares a public-works program—a practice that was adopted by the Moroccan services and directorates in 1944. The program is approved piecemeal as the ministry concerned can convince the government, or can smuggle parts of the program into either of the two budgets. Needless to add, the orderliness of this procedure is more apparent than real. Integrated development programs are almost impossible, and interministry feuding can have paralytic effects.

The French economic reforms of 1946 failed to dislodge an entrenched Protectorate administration. The Parisian Commissariat

Général au Plan was quite rightly regarded by most Protectorate officials as too heavily staffed with persons whose ideas, political and otherwise, might upset the Protectorate and who might mingle too freely with the growing numbers of nationalist politicians. All three North African countries were exclueded from the French Ten Year Plan (1947-1956). Morocco proceeded to work from compilations of ministerial public-works programs, while receiving French investment funds.

Under the Marshall Plan two modernization and investment programs were devised for Morocco, using the French Ten Year Plan as a model. The first was to run from 1949 to 1952, and was later extended to 1953, while the second operated from 1954 to 1957.[4] Under the circumstances the first plan was largely an amalgamation of existing schemes, but the second plan surveyed Moroccan needs and Protectorate policy more critically. The report noted the nearly total neglect of the traditional agricultural sector of the economy, and at the same time the building of large-scale irrigation schemes and machinery centers that did little to help the Moroccan peasant. The report also noted the disruptive effect of administrative infighting in the Moroccan government, and the Pro-tectorate's failure to enlist the collaboration of the Moroccans in eco-nomic development.[5]

Compared to many of the more recently independent countries, Morocco had a considerable experience in national planning at the time of independence. Admittedly this experience was largely under the supervision of French officials, many of whom left in 1956, but there were many individuals in the Moroccan ministries and Metropole agencies familiar with Moroccan developmental problems. Many of the economists connected with French planning agencies were of liberal, if not socialist, tendencies, and as such were generally trusted by the nationalists. Thus it is probably fair to evaluate Morocco as quite well off in terms of experienced personnel and cumulative developmental effort in 1956. The fact that the independent government largely ignored this experience and failed to build on previous planning efforts can only be explained by examining the politics of a liberated Morocco.

On the Protectorate model, economic affairs were split among three ministries, Finance, Commerce and Industry, and Industrial Production and Mining. The consequent administrative tangles were further compli-cated by party divisions among the three ministers given these areas.

[4] For more detail on planning in the Protectorate see the careful study of Albert Waterston, *Planning in Morocco*, Baltimore, Johns Hopkins Press, 1962. This is part of a series of planning studies sponsored by the Economic Develop-ment Institute of the International Bank for Reconstruction and Development.

[5] France, President of the Council, General Commissariat of the Plan, Deuxième Plan de Modernisation et d'Equipment, *Rapport Général de la Commission d'Etude et de Coordination des Plans de Modernisation et d'Equipment de l'Algérie, de la Tunisie et du Maroc*, Maroc, 1954, pp. 6 and 17.

Agriculture was initially placed in the hands of one of the major land-holders of the Gharb plain. For reasons of political pride more than concern over the increasing economic disintegration of the country, the Istiqlal demanded more representation in the cabinet in the fall of 1956. Two changes were made at this time that would facilitate planned change, and were no doubt partly inspired by the growing administrative chaos. The three ministries concerned with economic problems were assigned to a single "superministry" under Abderahim Bouabid. Public works and housing were also merged in one ministry under a bright young Istiqlal engineer, Mohammed Douiri. Agriculture was given to an esteemed elder of the Istiqlal, whose infirmities and nationalist preoccupations left little time for the office.

Bouabid was almost certainly the leading figure in the reorganization for increased effectiveness in the dealing with the country's sagging economy, and he remained the most outspoken exponent of national planning. The Planning Office was moved to his ministry in November 1956, along with the statistical and publications services of the secretary general. Bouabid's proposal for a Superior Planning Council (*Conseil Supérieur du Plan*) was contained in a law passed in June 1957.[6] The twenty-four members of the council included most of the cabinet, representatives of the National Consultative Assembly, three agricultural representatives, three union representatives, and one each for handicrafts, industry, and commerce. The outside representatives were selected by the three pressure groups for agriculture (*Union Marocaine d'Agriculture*), for labor (*Union Marocaine de Travail*), and for business (*Union Marocaine des Commerçants, des Industrialistes et des Artisanats*). The council was to be supported by a committee on finance and by a series of specialized commissions. The planning organization was almost identical to the French organization.[7] The new organization was completed in the fall of 1957, when a special division (*Division de la Coordination Economique et du Plan*) was created to prepare working papers, conduct research, and supervise the execution of the Superior Planning Council's decisions.

Having gone through all the motions of serious planning, the Moroccan government simply failed to use the new agencies or to follow through with its announced intentions. This failure to use valuable human and organizational resources is characteristic of Moroccan politics and the explanation can only be found by viewing the developing political system broadly. The concessions made to Bouabid were in part to placate a political viewpoint, and were typical of the relatively

[6] *Bulletin Officiel du Maroc*, no. 2333, July 12, 1957, "Dahir no. 1-57-183 (22 juin 1957) préscrivant l'établissement d'un plan de développement économique et social et instituant un conseil superieur du plan," p. 861.
[7] See the almost identical organizational charts given in Waterston, *op.cit.*, p. 17.

complex pattern of bargaining and compromise that has continually gone on in the higher levels of the Moroccan government. The ostensible maturity and impressive moderation of this activity is misleading, because it has not led to effective decision-making. Morocco is sufficiently wealthy to permit this sort of indulgence, while Tunisia and Pakistan are not. The Moroccan people find themselves caught in an unproductive political pattern from which they cannot emerge.

Almost nothing was done for two years. The Division for Economic Coordination and the Plan produced a Biennial Plan for the years 1958-1959,[8] which was largely an interim document compiled from existing uncoordinated plans from the various ministries. The Superior Planning Council did not meet, nor were there any demands from the parties that it should meet. The National Consultative Assembly held perfunctory debates on the Biennial Plan, but no substantial criticism was made. The more progressive political forces, centered around Bouabid, Ben Barka, then president of the National Consultative Assembly, and Maghjub Ben Seddiq, president of the U.M.T., found themselves increasingly isolated in the government. Within the Istiqlal the progressive faction was viewed with skepticism, if not apprehension, by the nationalist elders.

Late in 1959 Bouabid assembled the long-neglected Superior Planning Council and its fifteen specialized commissions. Each commission had received a note of "orientation" early in 1959, and work was supposed to be proceeding on the projected Five Year Plan for 1960-1964. It became apparent that each commission had become the instrument of the dominant interest it represented, and that the projects were being designed with no consideration of financial or related needs of the economy. In his speech to the commissions Bouabid admitted that the country had not yet "undertaken planning in the rigorous sense of the term," and that previous efforts had been little more than consolidated investment budgets. He strongly criticized the commission's "complete indifference" to the problems of finance, and stressed the need to use local materials and skill.[9]

Under the chairmanship of the prince, now King Moulay Hassan II, the Superior Planning Council met to discuss the Five Year Plan in August 1960. The minutes of the meetings make clear how divided the council's members were, and how totally lacking the plan was of any central concept or purpose. Even the Istiqlal minister who had replaced Bouabid was not in accord with the prince. In Douiri's opening state-

[8] Morocco, Division of Economic Coordination and Planning, Ministry of the National Economy and Finance, *Plan Biennal d'Equipment, 1958-1959*, Rabat, 1958, p. 78.

[9] Morocco, Conseil Supérieur du Plan, *Exposé de M. Bouabid, Vice President du Conseil, 23 Novembre 1959*, mimeo., Rabat, 1959. Also reported in *L'Avante-garde*, November 29, 1959, p. 5.

ment he virtually admitted that the plan had not yet been evaluated for its impact on the economy as a whole, and confessed that more effective planning would be impossible unless the Division of Economic Coordination and Planning was given real powers.[10] Since he was Minister of National Economy, the revelation suggests that the internal operation of the government had not changed noticeably from the confused months following independence.

The most outspoken rejection came from the labor representatives. Their complaints, however, were directed more against the prince and their political rivals than against the plan.[11] The representatives of the landowners and of business also made pleas for their particular interests. The meeting closed with another speech from the prince that served to confuse the proceedings by introducing a proposal for an arms industry, which was not mentioned in the plan, and making suggestions on possible sources of foreign capital that were also new. The meeting ended arbitrarily and the council has not been convened since. Without further discussion the Five Year Plan was approved by the king and issued as a law.[12]

Although the Moroccans were intent on developing their country, the plan, like many other detailed aspects of development, became the focus for rival political forces. Even the monarch could not find a way to advance planning without making substantial concessions to political critics. For several years planning was done on an *ad hoc* basis, largely under the supervision of a trusted friend of the Palace, Laghzaoui, and concentrated largely on industrial projects. In the new constitution, however, planning was raised to national importance and combined with the rural-mobilization scheme. *Promotion Nationale*. Late in 1963 the new High Council for National Promotion and the Plan was appointed, and Morocco began once again to take stock of her future development.[13]

[10] Morocco, Division of Economic Coordination and Planning, Ministry of the National Economy and Finance, *Compte Rendu des Délibérations du Conseil Supérieur du Plan, 1-5 Août 1960*, mimeo., Rabat, p. 19.

[11] For the U.M.T. position, which is based very heavily on the plan's failure to provide any specific material on agrarian reform see *Les travailleurs et le plan*, Casablanca, U.M.T., April 1960; *L'U.M.T. rejette le Plan gouvernemental*, Casablanca, U.M.T., August 1960.

[12] Morocco, Division of Economic Coordination and Planning, Ministry of the National Economy and Planning, *Plan Quinquennal 1960-1964*, Rabat, 1960.

[13] During most of 1962 and 1963 the major spokesman for the Palace on internal developement was Guedira, who became Director of the Royal Cabinet, Minister of Agriculture, and Minister of the Interior. It was clearly impossible to perform all these tasks adequately, and Guedira gradually lost favor as it became apparent that his highly emotional approach seldom led to effective action. In a reorganization in 1963 he became foreign minister, and then in 1964 he was dropped. Shortly afterward the new council was appointed. See *Bulletin Officiel du Maroc*, "Dahir no. 1-63-322 du 13 novembre 1963 portant loi organique rélative à la composition du Conseil supérieur de la promotion nationale et du plan," November 9, 1963, p. 1758.

Like Morocco, Tunisia's needs were examined under the postwar planning activities of France and the Marshall Plan. As in the rest of the Maghrib, the plans were strongly influenced by the needs of the French population, especially the settlers and commercial farmers, whose interests were concentrated in the north. Two four-year plans were made, one for 1948-1952 and another for 1953-1957. Although consultative commissions were organized, the center and south were represented by only one person from Sfax and another from Sousse, the two major cities of Tunisia's eastern coastline.

The geographical disparities of French planning had a deep effect on the Tunisian nationalists.[14] Unlike the Istiqlal, which was practically confined to the agriculturally rich areas before independence, the Socialist Destour had strong support from the center and south. In the central coastal plains, known as the Sahel, the party had historic roots and Bourguiba himself came from a small town south of Sousse. The Sousse region is still a Socialist Destour stronghold. Farther south, Tunisia's active trade-union movement had its foundations in the phosphate industry, which spread from inland mines around Ghafsa to the port of Sfax. The Tunisian labor movement has much earlier origins than the Moroccan U.M.T., and was a key nationalist organization immediately after the war under the vigorous leadership of Farhat Hached.

The more even dispersion of nationalist influence in Tunisia has had important effects on the development of the Socialist Destour since independence, and especially on planning activity. There has never been any doubt of the need to assist the areas neglected under the Protectorate. Furthermore, the neglected areas had influential representation in the party and in the unions. Because of the labor organization's activity in the south, Tunisian workers were not preoccupied with a single industrial concentration like Casablanca. Therefore it was possible to get labor support for regional development, and union leaders were aware of the hardships of life in Tunisia's remote provinces.

The Tunisian approach to planning since independence differs greatly from the Moroccan experience. Bourguiba did not participate in the first interim government, and economic affairs were left largely in the hands of respected merchant and business families. In late 1955 Bourguiba was fully occupied repelling Salah Ben Youssef's attack on his policies. He emerged victorious at the Sfax congress of November 1955, where first mention appears of the need to engage in national planning. Unlike the Istiqlal congress of this period, which only agreed on an innocuous motion concerning the need for economic improvement and social justice, the Socialist Destour congress specifically endorsed planning. The motion on economic affairs "urged the elaboration of a

[14] Charles F. Gallagher, "Two Tunisias: The Plan for the Development of the Center-South," *American Universities Field Staff Reports*, August 15, 1956, p. 7.

national program of economic expansion and social progress," and the party's Political Bureau was explicitly charged with designing such a program.[15]

Although Bourguiba enjoyed undisputed preeminence among the nationalist forces in Tunisia, there were still wide differences of opinion concerning the country's future. His tactic of bargaining for gradual concessions from the French was made possible by the support he received from the influential Tunisian *bourgeoisie* of the large towns. At the same time he had to guard against the creation of a left-wing Arabist or socialist party. The Arabist threat was removed with Ben Youssef's defeat, but the socialist appeal was strong in union ranks. With ample support from American unions, the General Union of Tunisian Workers (Union Générale des Travailleurs Tunisiennes) had developed a strong organization and imaginative leadership. The U.G.T.T.'s secretary general, Ahmed Ben Salah, advocated a distinctly socialist line of economic development and felt that the workers were entitled to special recognition for their sacrifices on behalf of the party. His views were all the more conspicuous because of Bourguiba's disinterest in economic affairs and distrust of doctrine of any kind, which was basically incompatible with his style of leadership.

Preoccupied with reforms of immediate political significance, Bourguiba lost his grip on the labor movement and the U.G.T.T. congress of September 1956 challenged his policies. Central to the congress' report was the establishment of a powerful planning agency and a variety of new controls on the economy. The report was pointedly addressed to those who "distrust improvisation" and wish to "regard the future lucidly."[16] Bourguiba's government was openly charged with finding "endless pretexts to put off the moment when it might consecrate itself" and with having a "certain ignorance of the power of economic and social forces." The remnants of French planning activity that were part of the premier's office were described as "small and derisory." The proposal for a planning agency is very similar to the position created for Ben Salah five years after his critical report was issued.

Bourguiba was not prepared to undertake such an ambitious proposal in late 1956, much less to organize another office that might threaten his own before the bey's position had been dissolved. The result

[15] Neo-Destour, *Les Congrès du Neo-Destour*, Tunis, 1958, p. 79. For an analysis of the growth of the Tunisian economy in relation to Protectorate activities see Claude Zarka, "L'Economie Tunisienne à l'Heure de la Planification Impérative," *Annuaire d'Afrique du Nord: 1962*, Centre National de Recherche Scientifique, Paris, 1963, pp. 207-241.

[16] "Rapport Economique," *6ème Congrès National de l'U.G.T.T.*, September 20-23, 1956, pp. 7-8. This report compares dramatically with the much more subdued observations of the U.G.T.T. when it returned to Socialist-Destour auspices. See *Rapport d'Activité: 8ème Congrès National*, April 1-3, 1960, p. 24, and also the U.G.T.T.'s *Sur le Dur Chemin du Développement*, n.d. (1960?).

of the crisis was a scission of the U.G.T.T. between factions under Ben Salah and Tilili.[17] The split was not healed until late 1957. By then the bey had been removed, and Ben Salah had agreed to take the Ministry of Public Health and Labor, where he could keep contact with the workers and also use his organizational skill to the nation's advantage. However, Bourguiba, by then president of the republic, is much too capable a politician to allow an opponent's appeal to go unheeded. Early in 1958 the National Planning Council was established, quite possibly as part of the compromise to end the trade-union quarrel and reconcile Ben Salah to his new post.

The law establishing the council acknowledged the aims of planning much more clearly than the similar Moroccan law. The council was to fix economic goals, to elaborate programs to achieve them, to decide on priorities and rates of growth, to propose which sectors should receive attention and how funds might be obtained, and to suggest measures to stimulate private initiative as well.[18] The council was composed of key members of the president's office, the ministers concerned with economic and social affairs, two representatives of the National Assembly, and four representatives of national organizations (labor, commerce, agriculture, and banking). By omitting discussion of general goals or doctrine at the council's first meeting, Bourguiba reassured those elements who might consider the new agency as an approval of Ben Salah's 1956 report. The president noted that the plan would not eliminate or obstruct private initiative. He suggested that it start with more promising projects and did not mention the more controversial commercial and industrial sectors.

The process of establishing the confidence of influential Tunisians constitutes a revealing comparison with the Moroccan and Pakistani experience. In Morocco the Superior Planning Council was the expression of a political stalemate. The progressives placed great hopes on planning, but had neither the influence with the Palace or the informed body of followers to make planning activities acceptable. Planning in Pakistan has been carefully insulated from political forces, although the regime has had the support of wealthy groups. Tunisian officials were also well aware that there were strong backers for the *status quo* in their

---

[17] The split of the Tunisian trade unions has yet to be carefully studied. For some background see Clement Moore, "The Neo-Destour Party of Tunisia: A Structure for Democracy?" *World Politics*, vol. 15, April 1962, p. 466, and also the author's "Transitional Politics in Morocco and Tunisia," *Princeton University Conference Series*, 1959, pp. 14-35. A more complete study is being prepared by Eqbal Ahmad, doctoral candidate at Princeton University.

[18] The law appears in a brochure, *Le Conseil National du Plan*, Tunis, Secretary of State for Information, Tunis, n.d. (1958?) with the president's first address to the planning group. See also the *Journal Officiel de la République Tunisienne*, "Loi no. 58-2 du 16 janvier 1958 (24 joumade II 1377), portant création du Conseil National du Plan," January 17, 1958, p. 68.

country. However, they were able to mobilize opinion and to create an efficient planning group in less time.

Bourguiba is an experienced infighter. His experience is displayed in his willingness to forego combat until the most advantageous moment, and in his skill in keeping his opponents separated. While there is no evidence that he looked upon the National Planning Council as anything more than a political concesssion to progressive critics in 1958, it became the bulwark of his policy in 1961. To understand the change of view during this period it is necessary to note the transformation of the party that the president created in the interim. Certainly the president was aware of the growing economic misery of his country, but he also became increasingly aware that the small entrepreneur and merchant was a greater threat to party hegemony than the few urban radicals he pacified with the planning agency.

Perhaps the turning point came in the fall of 1958, when Bourguiba encountered resistance to his plan for reorganizing the party. He had planned to replace the provincial committees, consisting largely of local party elders and influential citizens, with *délégués* or centrally appointed officials.[19] The objections were lodged so effectively that the congress was postponed until the spring of 1959, by which time the party had managed to pacify or remove the centers of resistance. The incident very likely served to alert the president to the conservative and parochial views of the party militants. If the party became sufficiently localized, the single-party structure would collapse and the president's authority would be compromised. Although a diffusion of power might be desirable for the development, the conservative outlook of most provincial and cell committees outside Tunis also meant that the party organization, the most important force in Tunisia, would not respond to the needs of planned economic growth.[20] During the party's Sousse congress and the campaign for the National Assembly elections in late 1959 Bourguiba stressed these concrete benefits of governmental intervention

[19] Tunisian party officials were quite outspoken in the fall of 1958 concerning the difficulty of working with the provincial committees. They seem to have represented a body of opinion not unlike that now found in the Istiqlal. Perhaps the most revealing commentary on the proposed reorganization is Bourguiba's speech to local party officials, *Les Congrés du Neo-Destour*, op.cit., pp. 86-95. For an analysis of the various schools of opinion within the Socialist Destour see the author's "Tunisian Leadership and the 'Confiscated Revolution,'" *World Politics*, vol. 18, January 1965.

[20] The dilemma of economic growth versus political development is by no means inevitable, but this is one of the clearest examples known to the author of a place where a clear choice had to be made. The old guard Neo-Destourians quite clearly represented grass-roots opinion, which did not share much of the president's impatience to reform religious institutions or the economy. At the same time they were valuable interlocutors between the government and the villages, an asset which relatively few new countries have. Their subordination to centrally conceived plans sacrificed opportunities of less easily controlled but possibly just as effective development from the local level.

in social and economic affairs, but he did not publicly advocate more energetic planning.[21]

The second public bid for increased planning again came from the unions in their Eighth National Congress of April 1960.[22] While the U.G.T.T. has always maintained that it is not subordinate to the Socialist Destour, it has seldom disagreed publicly with the party and is amply represented on high party committees. The report noted that the U.G.T.T. preferred "an economic system based on cooperation and popular association of investment funds assuring the socialization of the means of production." The report also conceded that the capitalist-inspired groups of businessmen and landowners had begun to recognize the country's proletarian base and to subscribe to more progressive policies. In a brochure entitled "On the Difficult Road to Development" the union spokesman noted that the National Planning Council had "unhappily" not met since its creation in 1958."[23] It was also mentioned that the special funds promised for the development of the central and southern regions had not been forthcoming. The paper ended by stressing planning as the sole solution to Tunisia's problems. Such a plan must include all sectors of economy for at least a period of ten years. The plan must also be administered directly under the authority of the president and govern the policies of the various ministries.

Without minimizing the increasing economic pressures on Tunisia, and her increasing disillusionment with France, it is important to note the strength of Bourguiba's position before he was prepared to make the planning decision in early 1961. A little over a year before, he emerged virtually unchallenged in national elections. The party had been reorganized as he wished, using provincial and regional officers selected by the central headquarters. The problem had been raised, at least, with the party's most important auxiliary national organizations. The president had put off the final decision for three years, but he had used those years to make the public realize the importance of the "economic battle" and to ensure the support of the major organizations. The delay was just as great as in Morocco, but the monarchy did not succeed in mobilizing either popular opinion or in acquiring organized support.

Ben Salah came very close to receiving the powers of a second vice-

[21] Bourguiba's speeches are widely distributed, and after his periodical regional tours they are printed in small books. For example, see Habib Bourguiba, *Electoral Campaign Speeches, 26 October-5 November 1959*, Tunis, Secretary of State for Information, 1960; also *Le Discours de Victoire*, Tunis, Secretary of State for Information, 1959, the president's speech to the Sousse congress of March 1959.

[22] Union Générale des Travailleurs Tunisiens, *Rapport d'Activité: 8ème Congrès National, 1-3 Avril 1960*, Tunis, n.d., pp. 10-11.

[23] Union Générale des Travailleurs Tunisiens, *Sur le Chemin du Développement*, Tunis, n.d., p. 31. To compare their position with business see Union Tunisienne de l'Industrie et du Commerce, *Vème Congrès National: Rapport Economique (28-30 October 1960)*, pp. 10-15.

president, as outlined in the U.G.T.T. proposal of 1956. A new "super-ministry" was created, the Secretary of State for Planning and Finance. Although reminiscent of the Moroccan "superministry," the Tunisian organization differed in that it was given effective power. Later in the year its powers were made greater when portions of the Industry and Commerce Ministry were assigned to it, and the old ministry dissolved. Ben Salah was also permitted to draw upon the other ministries for key planning officials, many of whom had been his intellectual colleagues for years. An imaginative and devoted team was formed, and the full authority of the president was behind their work. Although evading emphatic references to socialism, Ben Salah made it clear that the plan was to embrace all sectors of the economy and would draw on earlier planning drafts.[24]

PROFESSIONAL PLANNING IN PAKISTAN

Economic planning was certainly familiar to the Pakistani officials, although planning activity has gone through much more administrative reorganization than in either Morocco or Tunisia. At the time of partition, development planning was not advanced beyond the design of individual projects by the respective provincial governments. Although a Department of Planning and Development had been set up by the British immediately after the war, the operating agencies were the provincial governments.[25] Lists of projects had been prepared by 1947, but were, of course, useless with partition. No large-scale development effort was begun after the war, no doubt because the British Indian government realized that its days were numbered and that no plans could be made until the future of India was decided.

With independence the Pakistani central government set up a Development Board to assess the projects which applied to the regions falling within the new country. The board was placed under the Ministry of Economic Affairs, had no powers, and was generally neglected. The new government also established a Planning Advisory Board of private entrepreneurs, which was concerned largely with industrial goals and policies.[26] Between 1948 and 1950 it managed to produce 112 schemes, mostly for industrial purposes, which were approved. Until the early

[24] *Afrique Action*, January 10, 1961, p. 11. This newspaper is the successor of the old *Action Tunisienne*, suspended in the fall of 1958 for criticizing presidential policy. In the spring of 1962 it was again involved in a dispute over the president's *pouvour personnel*, and has changed its name to *Jeune Afrique*, thereby totally removing a party slogan from its title.

[25] S. M. Akhtar, *Economics of Pakistan*, rev. edn., Lahore, Publishers United, 1961, p. 407.

[26] Albert Waterston, *Planning in Pakistan: Organization and Implementation*, Baltimore, Johns Hopkins Press, 1963, p. 13. The author is indebted to this study and to conversations with Dr. Waterston for much of the material on Pakistani planning. See also Clair Wilcox, "Pakistan," in Everett E. Hagen, ed., *Planning Economic Development*, Homewood, Irwin, 1963, pp. 52-79.

1950's the government was heavily occupied with absorbing the millions of refugees from India and with erecting a minimal administrative structure for the new country. There were no statistics applying to Pakistan, and available administrative talent had to be channeled into offices concerned with the exigencies of the moment. In addition, the country lost its chief mobilizing agent, Jinnah, and the Muslim League began to crumble under the irreconcilable demands of provincial rivals, linguistic controversies, and personal feuds.

The first stimulus for more comprehensive planning was the Colombo Plan in 1950, under which Pakistan agreed to prepare a Six Year Plan. However, it appears that the planning method remained one of *ad hoc* project formulation. Little attention was given to the rural populace. A third of the proposed investment dealt with agriculture, but there were no projects prepared. The Korean war brought an influx of foreign currency in Pakistan, as it did in many other developing countries, and planning was again reviewed in 1952. An Economic Council, comparable to the Superior Planning Council in Morocco and the National Planning Council in Tunisia, was appointed, and the first Planning Commission was created. Like many early planning attempts, it was the creature of the ministries, and its functional subcommissions were composed of representatives of ministries. A Two-Year Priority Programme was designed to utilize the supply of foreign currency, but the opportunity was greatly compromised with inflation at home and abroad. Professor Akhtar has described this planning as "merely an aggregate of the cost of approved schemes," with little attention to implementation "since the implementing bodies were composed either of politicans or general administrators with no experience either of planning or implementation of plans."[27]

Although a Planning Board was created in mid-1953 to prepare a more comprehensive plan using more reliable data, the turmoil within Pakistani politics in the 1950's made progress difficult. Like the present-day Moroccan planning group, the Planning Board was denied the permanent status needed to attract talented civil servants, and had only a handful of working members. Its purpose was not clearly defined; it had no explicit lines of authority in guiding ministries and no working relationships with ministries. The Ministry of Economic Affairs kept its own Planning Wing, which worked in competition with the Planning Board. Despite these obstacles the Planning Board produced the First Five Year Plan (1955-1960) with the assistance of a planning group from Harvard University. The Planning Board had a brief respite from politics in 1955, when a sympathetic prime minister took office. After his removal in late 1956, the board no longer had access to power and its influence steadily dwindled until the revolution. There were no

[27] Akhtar, *op.cit.*, p. 409.

avenues for regular policy discussion, ministerial consultation, or discussion of related problems of tariffs, credit expansion, or foreign-aid negotiation.[28]

The First Five Year Plan was completed by the fall of 1955, but its implementation was delayed because of fears that it would complicate East Pakistan's approval of the first constitution. Approved in early 1956, the plan was issued a year late, and had only two years of operation before the revolution. The Planning Board experienced some difficulty in getting what it considered sufficient attention to the problems of East Pakistan. Attempts to have advisers placed in Dacca were obstructed, although a bloc allocation of a billion rupees was made to compensate for the neglect of the eastern wing, then Bengal province.[29] The government was largely preoccupied with implementing the few projects on which all could agree, and the goals of the plan were so unreal that the deputy chairman later confessed they were designed "to keep despair away."[30]

The Waterston study neatly sums up the popular impact of the First Five Year Plan. "Although the Draft Plan was publicized by the press and widely discussed, there was little public participation in its preparation, revision and execution. In general the business community had had little to say about what went into the Plan. The majority of Pakistan's farmers, workers and villagers never grasped the purpose of the Plan, even if they were aware of its existence. Although the Plan had been approved by the National Economic Council, the controversial regional issue left the Plan with few political supporters. The failure of the Government to adopt it as its official development program and to provide it with organized political support greatly diminished such official and popular interest as the Planning Board had been able to arouse."[31] The irony of this judgment is that the conditions of planning changed little under the military-bureaucratic regime.

As might be expected, the professional orientation of the Ayub regime was a stimulus to planning, though it remains doubtful if much has been done to make planning more meaningful to the citizen. When Ayub came to power in late 1958, nearly six months' work had already been put into the Second Five Year Plan and working papers on the general features of the plan had been distributed to ministries and provincial governments. Under martial law the administrative deficiencies of the

---

28 Waterston, *op.cit.*, pp. 27-27.
29 David Bell, "Allocating Development Resources," *Public Policy: Yearbook of the Harvard Graduate School of Public Administration*, Cambridge, Harvard University Press, 1959, p. 105. Von Vorys notes that no projects were prepared during the First Five Year Plan despite the generous appropriation. Karl Von Vorys, *Political Development of Pakistan*, Princeton, Princeton University Press, 1965.
30 Waterston, *op.cit.*, p. 46.　　　　31 *Ibid.*, p. 65.

old planning organization were swiftly remedied. The Ministry of Economic Affairs was abolished, and planning was made directly under the supervision of the president. In June 1959 an Economic Council was formed to bring together the ministers most concerned with planning, the directors of public corporations involved with development, and the officials of the strengthened planning agency, now renamed the Planning Commission.

Under the reorganization the Planning Commission received sweeping and explicit directives: to prepare a national plan, to assess human and material resources, to prepare an annual development program, to stimulate and, where needed, to initiate projects, to advise on implementation and to assess progress, and to promote economic research.[32] With due regard for the need for strong support for planning activity, the Planning Commission tended to become involved in provincial and regional problems, and the authority over implementation sometimes meant that the commission operated at the expense of lower-level agencies, whose improvement and support were essential to effective planning in the long run. From time to time the commission was also involved in ministerial disputes.

Reportedly dissatisfied with the bureaucratic entanglements encumbering the Planning Commission, President Ayub made several important changes in early 1961. The commission was finally given full authority to draw personnel from other parts of the government. The Planning Commission's authority to evaluate progress was restored, and its stature further enhanced by making the president chairman. Under the new organization the commission was to have a secretary for planning and another for evaluation.[33] Each ministry was to create a "thinking cell" of its most able members to send recommendations to the commission. Although these organizational changes strengthened the commission for performing its immediate task, they did not constitute an effort to communicate the meaning of massive development to the people.

The Pakistani experience demonstrates the divorce of technically competent planning and popular impact that can easily overtake the professionally oriented regime. As in the case of the Basic Democracies scheme, the Ayub regime assumed that the virtues of professional competence were self-justifying and would be recognized in the mobilization of Pakistani society. The emphasis on rational behavior implied the exclusion of those who had not achieved the high level of rationality represented by the bureaucracy, and was reflected throughout the Basic Democracies scheme. Ayub himself expressed conflicting views

[32] Government of Pakistan, Planning Commission, *The Second Five Year Plan (1960-65)*, 1960, pp. 107-108.
[33] *Pakistan Times*, July 30, 1961.

on the nature of planning. Speaking before representatives of business, he would stress the plan's support for private enterprise.[34] However, he also saw that national development demanded popular support and was ultimately justified by the benefits it would bring to all Pakistanis.[35] The fatal handicap of the professional orientation to government is that it excludes the values that make possible the reconciliation of these two positions, or, more accurately, the stress on competence and reason tends to prevent the government from playing a role in forging shared beliefs to reinforce and sustain the developmental process.

The initial commitment to planning is only the first step in a development process destined to refashion not only the immediate environment of the citizen, but also his relationship to the political system as a whole. The success that a government may experience in the more complex task is to some extent denoted by the regime's reception of the planning challenge in early stages of the planning process. There is no reason to assume that failure in the early planning phase necessitates failure in the more complex task of integrating a population in a more advanced social structure. However, the pressures for radical social reform are so severe and the public commitment to rapid change so pronounced in most regimes that it is difficult to see how massive social change will be possible without a reasonably coherent approach.

The difficulties of forging a common attitudinal basis for social change is revealed in different ways in each regime, and the comparison of their early experience suggests the particular advantages and handicaps of each regime. In the monarchy the factional disputes of the parties and the hesitance of the Palace eroded planning efforts. Though it is extremely significant that all the governments discussed found it difficult to engage in planning activity, only in the case of Morocco did reluctance and confusion result in the complete debilitation of the planning agency. With all due regard to the complexities of Moroccan society, the monarchial system was not able to overcome the immediate challenge of new contenders for power in order to engage the country in a unified nation-building program.

Though the delay was as great in Tunisia as in Morocco, the single-party regime could not evade the pressures for a massive attack on poverty. Indeed, to permit the groups advocating energetic planning to disperse would constitute a threat to the regime. For an interlude there was a tactical isolation of the forces favoring massive change, but Bourguiba was at the same time formulating an approach amenable to the single-party regime and actively seeking a compromise among differing views. Most important, when the decision to plan was made, the new agency was given effective power and the social implications were pre-

[34] See Ayub's speech quoted in Von Vorys, *op.cit.*, p. 178.
[35] *Speeches and Statements*, Karachi, Pakistan Publications, vol. 1, 1961, p. 26.

sented publicly. Not only did the party fully exploit its organizational advantage, but it was able to make the values of national reconstruction part of the national ideology.

The professional orientation of the Pakistani regime was in many ways as much an obstacle to effective planning as it was a help. Ayub was determined to bring the common man into the developmental process, but he sought to do this in a way that would not jeopardize the values and habits of the military-bureaucratic alliance. Possibly his innate confidence in the peasant became a rationalization for the failure of the government to solve many basic planning problems. Clearly the civil service was able to place formidable obstacles in the path of the Planning Commission, which the extraordinary powers of the president could not easily remove. The sheer competence of Pakistani planning resulted in neglect of the way in which the plan was to be brought home to the peasant. In fact, planning in Pakistan has been more divorced from the populace than in either Morocco or Tunisia.

ON COMBINING PEOPLE WITH A PLAN

Compared to the problems of achieving a degree of popular involvement in planning goals, the organization of a planning agency is a simple task. The developing countries, and often the donors of developmental aid, have often proceeded on the assumption that a poverty-stricken people could not resist the temptations of increased wealth presented by the developmental process. Such an assumption attributes a degree of knowledge and confidence concerning national politics that is seldom found in Africa and Asia. The transformation affects the much more meaningful patterns of behavior engrained by village and family over centuries of deprivation and insecurity, stemming from both the impersonal forces of nature and the arbitrary intrusion of a variety of empire builders.

The planning process reveals, therefore, a country's capacity and intentions to diffuse power as well as to create the agencies needed to fulfill the formal requirement of planning. Planning is in many ways a microcosmic model of the development process in all its complexity. A plan cannot be made and forgotten without political risk. Furthermore, a plan put into effect begins to generate its own demand for more and better planning. Pakistan has entered its Third Plan cycle, Morocco has begun the second phase of wholly Moroccan planning, and Tunisia has completed the first phase in the Ten Year Perspective. The fact that the developing countries are inexorably committed to planning provides further justification for seeking better ways of evaluating the broad impact of the developmental process and the self-generated requirements of a less easily measured nature that appear as economic growth takes place.

The pressure for increasing participation in the three plans in the comparison offered in this study can be estimated in two ways. The first is simply the institutional repercussions of planning. Each of the political systems brought different institutional capacities to bear on the development process, as has been roughly sketched in previous characterizations of the three systems. The form of government is the primary determinant of what kind of array of parties, pressure groups, and individual expressions may be admitted in this early, highly formalized phase of national reconstruction. The second approach, and one for which the conventional institutional categorization of political science is inadequate, is the extent to which the relation between ruler and ruled is modified. The perception of government and modification of authority patterns is a critical aspect of the developmental process, and may be considered a prerequisite to the formation of more stable, effective patterns of institutional behavior.

The Moroccan monarchy has had the most difficulty of the three political systems in unleashing the developmental process from the concentration of power in the central government—in the Moroccan case, more specifically, in the royal Palace. The decisiveness of Hassan II was expressed at the expense of the other political forces in the country and culminated in the split between the king and the Istiqlal in 1963. The falling out between the monarchy and the historic nationalist party was perhaps the most dramatic evidence of an increasingly constricted view of the developmental process that appeared to predominate in Morocco. The Istiqlal could not manage to escape the dilemma of being caught between its loyalty to the Alaouite dynasty and its need to develop its own popular support. In the party congress of January 1960, planning was not even mentioned.[36] Some publicity was given to planning when the Superior Planning Council met, but it only revealed the party's secondary concern.

The Istiqlal's disinterest in planned development contrasted with the U.N.F.P.'s devotion to planning as the panacea for all national ills. Excluded from the seat of power, the U.N.F.P. and the U.M.T. concentrated their efforts in Casablanca, where they control the municipal council. Steps were taken to organize municipally owned corporations for public transport and electricity distribution. However, the progressives' experience in municipal enterprise has not served to tone down their vehemence in national affairs. The fear of the U.N.F.P. is that Morocco's development effort will become an interlocking structure of favored businessmen, wealthy landowners, and the Palace. In much less xenophobic form than his labor supporters, Bouabid also rejects

---

[36] *Al-Istiqlal*, January 16, 1960, special insert of party motions. For a review of Moroccan progress see Georges Oved, "Problèmes de développement économique au Maroc," *Tiers Monde*, tome II, no. 7, July-September 1961, pp. 355-398.

capital that would tend to entrench political groups or to sacrifice Moroccan control of her development.[37]

For a monarch confronted with two articulate and influential parties the prospect of diffusing power, whether in the form of new political activity or less directly in the form of new local responsibilities, presents obvious dilemmas. Nevertheless, the Five Year Plan contained a strong endorsement of regional planning.[38] But the endorsement was no substitute for purposeful action toward increased decentralization in planning. The need had been recognized long ago when the Superior Planning Council was established, and little had been accomplished by 1962. A special effort to raise the level of literacy in Beni Mellal province had been heavily concentrated in the hands of a trusted governor, as were additional projects to utilize better the agricultural potential of the region. A regional planning council was formed in Marrakech province under orders from the government, but local officials had little familiarity with its purpose and gave no indication that it had made a contribution to a variety of disconnected schemes to improve the province and stem the rural exodus. Under the provision of the law establishing the Superior Planning Council any local efforts would have to be reviewed by both financial and technical authorities in Rabat—a requirement which provided ample opportunity to muffle any spontaneous action that might be forthcoming.

Regional planning has been labeled "essential" by Douiri[39] as well as by his predecessor, Bouabid. Neither was ever given the necessary authority to create regional planning groups, and there is considerable evidence of intentional obstruction by other ministries who felt their interests would be slighted. Furthermore, the governors and provincial officials have remained so tightly under the control of the Minister of the Interior and so preoccupied with their policing tasks that they have little time or inclination to take on more onerous duties. Although there were reports that ministers were being sent out to solicit provincial programs in 1962,[40] they have had no perceivable effect on Moroccan planning.

The experience of the rural communes has been very similar. The law organizing the 800 local councils gave them the right to form *syndicats* or unions for developmental purposes.[41] In many provinces local problems can be handled only by coordinating the effort of several communes, and frequently funds must be pooled. While the Five Year Plan points with pride to the communal elections, which were to "produce

---

[37] *Al-Machahid*, October 1961.
[38] *Plan Quinquennal*, op.cit., pp. 351-76.
[39] *Compte Rendu* . . . , op.cit., p. 19.
[40] *Al-Istiqlal*, August 4, 1962, p. 3.
[41] *Bulletin Officiel du Maroc*, no. 2487, June 24, 1960, "Dahir no. 1-59-315 du 28 hija (23 juin 1959) relatif à l'organisation communale," pp. 1,234-1,235.

representatives of the local population and to facilitate their active participation in developmental actions,"[42] very little has been done to remove the communes from the close supervision of the Ministry of the Interior. Both the U.N.F.P. and the Istiqlal demanded increased budgetary and financial powers for the communes, no doubt to build local party strength as much as to increase developmental activity. Although some municipal councils under U.N.F.P. control engaged in enterprises already in operation, the government has done little to stimulate or to support more widespread, diffused interest in planning.

The handicaps for future Moroccan planners are not only the material losses of the years of inaction coupled with inflation.[43] The economic deterioration is accompanied with corresponding increments in popular distrust and disillusionment. The risk of the Moroccan approach is that with increasing individual skills and understanding the promises and plans of a hesitant monarchy will produce disinterest, and possibly rejection of planning. The danger was clearly posed by Bouabid several years ago in the following statement on mobilizing popular energies for development purposes: "There are mobilizations and mobilizations . . . those which come from a summit and which take the form of something imposed by a regime from which the people are excluded and which submit to no popular control, and result in a series of fruitless experiences demonstrating the corruption and incompetence of the administration; this form of mobilization cannot be taken seriously by the people."[44] Were it not that the Istiqlal has arrived at much the same position after an additional two years' cooperation with the monarchy, Bouabid's views might be more easily dismissed.

After the break between the king and the Istiqlal, the party became outspoken in its criticisms of the government's intentions. Indeed, the Istiqlal charged that the entire notion of planning was in jeopardy, and rushed to the defense of the conservative Five Year Plan, even though it was largely the product of the Ibrahim government. The party also revealed that Guedira, who criticized the plan for not having sufficient room for "private initiative," had worked to prevent the issue of the plan in 1960. More firmly than at any previous time, the Istiqlal defended comprehensive planning, and accused the government of favoring "simple budgetary programs."[45] Guedira was again bitterly attacked when he announced that a three year plan would be proposed in the fall

[42] Plan Quinquennal, op.cit., p. 22.
[43] The inflationary pressures increased greatly in Morocco over 1962 and 1963, sometimes estimated at 20 per cent. A study done in 1960 convinced the government that not only had the ministries fallen far behind in their projects but that financial disorder was so great that the plan had to be abandoned. See Division of Economic Coordination and the Plan, Ministry of the National Economy, La Situation Economique du Maroc en 1960, 1961; also, La Vie Economique, October 26, 1962.
[44] Al-Machahid, October 1961.   [45] Al-Istiqlal, May 12, 1963.

of 1963 to replace the excessively "ambitious" Five Year Plan which Douiri had labored to implement over the past years.

Compared to the sporadic activity to implement the Moroccan Five Year Plan, the purposeful effort of Tunisia and Pakistan takes on additional significance and suggests that both these materially less favored countries bring peculiar assets to the planning process. Their planning achievements are another indication that natural resources and careful calculations are but part of any plan hoping to achieve national integration. If these assets are in part the contrived harmony of the Socialist Destour and the aloof professionalism of the Pakistani civil servant and officer, one is still not obliged to conclude that the two more intent countries will persevere where Morocco may fail. No plan is a panacea, but neither is it devoid of some image of the social revolution, implicit or explicit, in the effort to reconstruct the developing country. From a political viewpoint the important point is not that any given political system has unique advantages, but that in no country undergoing rapid development have political solutions to the mobilization of the society been easy to find.

The Tunisian planning experience is especially instructive in this respect. In few countries have more imaginative persons been given the full governmental support and popular backing available to the Socialist Destour. The Tunisian Secretariat for Planning and Finance followed a carefully drawn schedule in preparing the *perspective* or forecast on which Tunisian planning was to be based. The team that Ben Salah assembled in the Planning Commission had almost exactly six months to prepare the first planning document, which was completed in September 1961. This permitted two months of discussion of the broad concepts of the *perspective*, which were to be followed up with a phased plan for the ten years beginning in 1962. The first phase of the plan for 1962-1964 was drawn up late in 1961 and presented publicly in early 1962. As it turned out, this was hardly enough time. The planning team did a good job, but the party and the country were not nearly so agreed on planning goals and methods as the uniformity of the single-party system suggests. The difficulties that the Tunisian officials had despite the political preparation provided by the party suggests how far Morocco has yet to go—and how many controversies remain hidden in Pakistani planning.

When Ben Salah was installed, the president began alerting high officials to the need to prepare the party's supporters and the people generally. In January 1961 the Economic and Social Council, an organ created by the constitution and seldom convened, was assembled.[46] The council was particularly well suited to its primarily political task, be-

[46] *Journal Officiel de la République Tunisienne*, no. 2, 104e année, "Décret-loi no. 61-4 du 16 janvier 1961 (28 redjeb 1380), instituant un Conseil Economique et Social," p. 69.

cause it brought together all the most influential Tunisians for the specific purpose of discussing economic proposals of all kinds. In the fall the party also enlisted its auxiliary organizations, which was a more confidential means of feeling out the party than the public meetings of the council. Through the extraordinary organization of the Socialist Destour, study commissions of party representatives were created at the level of electoral districts, and the leaders of the local National Front[47] met with municipal councils, local influentials of all kinds, and government officials to introduce the plan.

From the beginning Ben Salah had the support of the president. Bourguiba made it clear in his famous weekly speeches that the plan would be submitted to popular judgment and would not follow any doctrine except the well-worn goals of "Bourguibism," a mixture of political dexterity and compromise. Nevertheless, the president's speeches throughout 1961 explained more precisely the advantages of collective action in other spheres than agriculture. With characteristic skill he played on the beneficial results of nationalizing the *habous* land, while noting precedents for cooperative effort in Islam.[48] Gradually the new national goals took shape and emerged as "Neo-Destourian socialism." His presentation is a precise, reasoned case for planning in Tunisia, and at the same time acknowledges the hardships and conflicts that economic control and supervision will entail.

With great candor he called for "a true psychological revolution . . . to assure the success of the plan" and a purposeful campaign "similar to that which in the past allowed me to obtain the support of an elite and a considerable section of the population to whom I gave new conceptions and another scale of values."[49] Seldom has the problem been described so explicitly for public consumption. Bourguiba also again gave his public endorsement to Ben Salah and condemned those who charged the chief planner with too socialist ideals. The president acknowledged the historic importance of socialism, but sought to give planning much broader significance by appealing to national pride and individual self-respect. Rejecting Communism, he noted in closing that "Humanity's fate lies in the survival of the motives for collaboration among men." Few national leaders have given such unequivocal, cogent explanations for planning.

Despite the strong support given by the president there was increasing resistance to planning over the fall of 1961. Speaking to party militants,

[47] *Petit-Matin*, October 26, 1961, p. 1.

[48] Habib Bourguiba, *Bourguiba Addresses the Nation's Leaders (6 and 8 February 1961)*, Tunis, Secretary of State for Information, 1961. Also, his speech "Accent on Planning," March 28, 1963, Tunis, Secretary of State for Information, 1963.

[49] Habib Bourguiba, *Neo-Destourian Socialism (21 June 1961)*, Tunis, Secretary of State for Information, 1961.

the director of the Socialist Destour Political Bureau reassured the party that "the plan will be neither the work of a person nor a group of experts, but that of the party in its conception as well as its execution."[50] Shortly afterward Ben Salah received the ultimate expression of confidence by being restored to the Political Bureau. Nevertheless, newspaper reports acknowledged that the technical commissions of the Superior Committee of the Plan, the political advisory group to the Planning Commission, had expressed reservations on the prospective use of production cooperatives and tendency to restrain private initiative.[51] In a speech at Bizerte, Ben Salah publicly challenged the critics of the plan and presented it as part of the national effort to eliminate colonial influence.[52] Such public confessions of opposition are extremely rare in Tunisian politics. The opposition was especially strong from commercial interests, who suspected that Ben Salah's known antipathy for the merchants, new import and price controls, and suggestions for consumer cooperatives foretold their end.[53]

A Socialist Destour National Council meeting early in 1962 was very likely the critical hurdle for the party. It was reported that "it is not secret that in the party—and not only at the base—certain reserves, some reticence were sometimes manifested regarding the Plan."[54] The council's approval would mean that any subsequent opposition would encounter severe repression for "obstructing the nation." The party performed in its most persuasive manner for the meeting. Long, carefully prepared speeches were given by the president, Ben Salah, and Bahi Ladgham, his most trusted lieutenant, secretary general of the party and the vice-president. Bourguiba again gave an impassioned plea for "Neo-Destourian socialism," a doctrine that he called midway between anarchy and excessive state interference. Ladgham returned to the theme that the plan was only a new phase in the party's continuing struggle to liberate Tunisia, and did not represent a new orientation. Repeating a message he had often used in the regional and local meetings of the past six months, Ben Salah said that the plan was not directed against any class and was not designed "to annihilate" the merchants.

These elaborate preparations to enlist popular support did not eliminate opposition to planning. The small merchants, who had been an important source of local support for the Socialist Destour, actively

---

[50] *Petit-Matin*, November 18, 1961, p. 1.
[51] *Ibid.*, November 21, 1961, p. 1.   [52] *Ibid.*, December 16, 1961, p. 1.
[53] "Le Plan et les Commercants," *Jeune Afrique*, January 23, 1962, pp. 14-15. There may have been an element of passive resistance in a controversy shortly afterward over price controls placed on food imports. See "L'Affaire Tefaha," in *ibid.*, March 12-19, 1962, p. 12.
[54] *Jeune Afrique*, February 6-12, 1962, p. 6, and *ibid.*, March 26-April 2, 1962, p. 6. Summaries of the speeches are given in this issue. It is unusual for the party to display so forceful a battery of speakers except for congresses and major national holidays.

resisted price controls imposed on butter, meat, tea, and eggs. Bourguiba was serious in his pleas for austerity, and the state used its commercial controls to reduce food imports by a sixth in the first year of the plan.[55] The reorganization of the transport industry, which had been more or less allocated to the *fellagha* when Tunisia chose autonomy in 1954 and ended guerilla warfare, resulted in strikes and discontent; there were also strikes among the phosphate miners of the southern regions when the government imposed a "National Solidarity" levy on their wages. These repercussions indicate that the single-party regime had not been able to convince many Tunisians of the necessity of planned development. Indeed, after the attempt on Bourguiba's life, the president strongly denied charges that the Three Year Plan was of "Communist orientation," while trying to explain to the workers that the funds accumulated from their wages would be used to improve the productivity of their own enterprises.[56]

Concomitant with these crises, the Ministry of Finance and Planning took steps to regularize popular involvement in the planning process. Ben Salah had hoped in 1962 to appoint planning delegates to the provinces to supervise development and to explain the plan. These officials would be comparable to the party delegates. In early 1963 Bourguiba confessed that the scheme of dividing provincial authority between the governor and the party representative had led to confusion and inefficiency, and this experience probably discouraged adding another nationally appointed official at the provincial level. An entirely different policy was followed, similar to the old provincial committee that the Socialist Destour had used prior to the 1959 reforms. The Governors' Councils were no longer to be merely advisory bodies of local notables and party regulars. More important, the party cell's elective functions were to be restored in selecting some of the council's members. The controversial party *délégués* were abolished.[57] Through these committees the Ministry of Finance and Planning was provided with a new channel for popular involvement in national reconstruction, although the governor's position was still unchallenged in the administrative hierarchy. The reorganization is an illustration of how development places need requirements on the political system, culminating in important modification in the single-party regime.

The extent of the resistance to Tunisian planning suggests how the problems of the developmental process tend to multiply as progress is made and as more substantial adjustments in individual behavior are demanded. While one cannot place responsibility for the assassination attempt on the active development effort, the need to restrain commerce and to guide certain key services such as transportation no doubt

[55] *Jeune Afrique*, June 18-24, 1963 and October 29-November 4, 1963.
[56] *La Presse*, April 23, 1963.   [57] *Ibid.*, March 4, 1963.

contributed to the unrest leading up to the attempt. It is surely not wholly coincidental that the plot involved several ex-*fellagha*, and had support from some elements in the south of the country, as well as some of the more enthusiastic Islamicists, who resented the intensive secular reforms of the single-party regime.

The incident has greater significance in terms of the hypothesis being advanced on the relation of participation and the developmental process. In simplified form it appears that a single-party system may become so successful in manipulating the communications and administration of a developing country that political exchange may cease. The national political system may in fact be circumvented by party reliables to a degree that excludes the mass of participants. The insistence on pre-arranged harmony may simply contribute to the formation of a sub-society of persons who may not feel alienated from politics but simply see no way to relate their affairs to the national political system.

In Pakistan the restraints placed on party and group activity during Ayub's military dictatorship made much less information available on the popular impact, if any, of the Pakistani effort. Indeed, one of the shortcomings of the military-bureaucratic alliance was the inability of the regime to enlist support and understanding. Easing political controls in order to revive constitutional government unleashed a series of attacks on Basic Democracies and other aspects of Ayub's program for national reconstruction. Planning may be spared some of the accumulated hostility of the four years' autocratic rule because it dates from the prerevolutionary period and is even more pressing in Pakistan than in Morocco and Tunisia. Nevertheless, President Ayub has found it increasingly difficult to sustain the variety of reforms that supplement the formal planning process, and in 1963 he himself entered fully into party politics in order to protect the reforms of the military regime.

The problem was undoubtedly foreseen by some members of the Ayub government, and planning requirements alone demanded that an effort be made to involve more officials and citizens at lower levels in the political system. The first steps in this direction were taken with the reorganization of the central government. The report[58] suggested that the Economic Committee of the cabinet be abolished, and that the Economic Council of high officials concerned with development be transformed into the National Economic Council. This body was later incorporated into the new constitution (art. 145). New stress was placed on planning at the provincial level, where proposals affecting fuel and power, food, agriculture, health, labor, and industry were thereafter supposed to originate. The central ministries without provincial counterparts were to create planning groups, but were specifically denied plan-

[58] *Pakistan Times*, April 27, 1962.

ning facilities if their work was wholly delegated to the province for operational purposes.

In practice the staff of the Planning Commission often intervened as tactfully as possible to smooth the way for projects bogged down in ministerial and departmental procedures. The commission on reorganization of the central government acknowledged the officials' inability to allow administrative action within their purview to go unhampered. The central ministries having provincial equivalents (education, transportation, health, labor, and communications) were specifically cautioned against taking any operational role in the provinces' development in these spheres. Even in the case of planning there was to be only "broad scrutiny" of the provincial plan. The Ayub government made important changes in delegating other activities to the provincial level, e.g., railroads, over 1962, perhaps because the revival of constitutional government promised to complicate both planning and development. The president quite clearly was expressing his apprehensions when speaking to a divisional commissioners' conference in West Pakistan shortly after party activity returned in full force.[59] He asked that development activities be organized rapidly in such a way that they would be unaffected by "adverse political developments."

The subsequent reports for provincial reorganization of the two wings provide further evidence of how the Ayub regime hoped to improve planning and isolate development from political forces. The West Pakistan Provincial Reorganization Committee gave strong endorsement to more popular participation in planning. Aware of Ayub's hopes of preserving Basic Democracies in the parliamentary government emerging in the fall of 1962, the committee noted: "It is ignorance of the limited resources of Government that leads to unrealistic expectation and demands from the people. It is, therefore, necessary to take them into confidence and even to place the responsibility on them to plan within the resources available."[60] The report went on to advise that the division become the major level for consolidated planning, with the province serving in only a supervisory and support capacity.

The central government would be virtually removed from the details of the planning process, and sufficient development funds would be provided Basic Democracies to have a "definite impact" on local areas. Local development plans would become a separate section in developmental budgeting, and special attention would be given to community development projects. The reorganization proposals went on to suggest areas of obligatory consultation between various levels of local government, and gave strong encouragement to more spontaneous consultation

[59] *Ibid.*, August 29, 1962.
[60] Government of West Pakistan, *Report of the Provincial Reorganization Committee*, Part I—"West Pakistan," Lahore, December 1961, p. 38.

between officials and the Basic Democracies councils. The same expansion of local-planning activity was endorsed in the reorganization of East Pakistan,[61] where it was added that the Third Five Year Plan under preparation should make specific development allocations to Basic Democracies.

Although the intent of the reorganization proposals is quite clear as well as courageous, the Pakistani government has had great difficulty in fulfilling the aims of decentralized planning. Long before Basic Democracies and the Ayub regime, the First Five Year Plan acknowledged that "instead of being prepared and imposed from above, programmes—particularly in the sphere of rural development—should originate in the villages and proceed upward, so that their aggregate represents the needs, aspirations, and thinking of the people."[62] If the need had been long recognized, the reform had, nevertheless, been slow in coming. Neither the old parliamentary regime nor the Ayub government was able to break through the crust of administrative habit obstructing decentralized planning. The military regime had made the bureaucrats partners in government, and found their support essential. While the earlier parliamentary regime tended to leave the administrators to themselves, and by default tended to leave the management of the country in their hands, the military regime was more directly dependent on the officials' good wishes, and to that extent more vulnerable to them.

The force of the developmental process is seldom sufficient to override bureaucratic perfectionism and procrastination, although developmental needs are frequently evoked to justify major changes in the political system. The Pakistani government has done less than either the Moroccan monarchy or the Tunisian single-party system to create popular support for planning and understanding of planning aims. Indeed, the excessive compartmentalization of planning has succeeded in almost removing planning from the realm of political discourse, except, of course, for the distribution of investment funds between the two wings. The failure to diffuse the significance of the basic problems of national reconstruction was one of the major handicaps to Ayub's efforts to give Pakistanis a sense of local responsibility and confidence.

But a popular response to the challenge of development could not be forthcoming while plannning and development remained the province of a small number of centrally located administrators. Only with the revival of party activity did the challenge of development begin to be dis-

[61] Government of East Pakistan, *Report of the Provincial Reorganization Committee*, Part II—"East Pakistan," Dacca, April 1962.

[62] Government of Pakistan, National Planning Board, *The First Five Year Plan* (*1955-60*), Karachi, 1956, p. 103. In general the First Plan gave stronger support to rural development through local bodies than did the Second Plan. Compare *ibid.*, ch. 14, "Village and Rural Development," pp. 197-212, with *The Second Five Year Plan, op.cit.*, ch. 18, "Village Aid," pp. 393-396.

cussed in terms that might have popular impact, but by then there were a variety of additional, and more inflammatory, issues to distract political sensitivities. Ayub did not possess the instrument for escaping from the administration's designs, intentional or otherwise, until he joined the Muslim League early in 1962. The breach still remaining between popular politics and government was indicated in the ten "guiding principles" the president enunciated on the occasion. The first six points dealt with various aspects of development, and the remaining four with foreign policy and Islam.[63]

With the renewed party activity in Pakistan, President Ayub was directly confronted with the need to make his developmental effort meaningful to the villagers. When he formed his first parliamentary government in early 1962 he knew that his policies would face new challenges from the politicians, whose tactics and speeches had not changed much from the passionate and incoherent politics of pre-1958. Though always critical of "politicians," the president began to speak more comprehensively about planning and development. Development was portrayed less and less as a formal procedure under government direction, leading to a more bountiful era when paternalistic authority would mechanically dole out the produce of a modern society. With the Basic Democracies program already under attack, Ayub stressed the ways in which communities must take the lead in planning and development, and on one occasion even went so far as to suggest more welfare activities for the aged, orphans, and widowed. Though the appeal was similar to some of Ayub's earlier moralizing about Pakistani society, he coupled this observation with a clear warning to those industrialists and merchants who had amassed small fortunes under liberal development policies.[64] As the distribution of wealth became a legitimate subject for political discourse, the developmental process would inevitably become involved in parliamentary politics.

The experience of Morocco, Tunisia, and Pakistan provides impressive evidence of how difficult it has been to persuade many of the countries of Africa and Asia to commit themselves wholeheartedly to development planning. A well-documented and well-conceived plan does not guarantee energetic action toward development, and the comparatively elementary decisions needed to start effective planning have often proved too controversial to lead to well-defined planning procedures. Perhaps the most ironical aspect of the early phases of planning is that the most adamant resistance often comes from the ministries most involved with nation-building. Planning requires the phasing and coordination of efforts in education, public works, public health, and many other service activities of government essential to national reconstruction.

[63] *Pak Jamhuriat*, May 25, 1962.   [64] *Ibid.*, April 27, 1963.

In some countries, as has tended to happen in Morocco, planning becomes bogged down in the rudimentary phase of assigning competent personnel and establishing relations with nation-building agencies. There is evidence that this has also happened in other more traditional political systems—pre-Kassem Iraq, Iran, and Libya. Even where there is little or no popular participation in national political life, a plan that is to be more than a "shopping list" of schemes presses the government into defining the authority of the planning group and forcing the nation-building ministries to conform to the broad lines of the plan.

The stage of effective governmental coordination was reached in Pakistan only in the early 1960's, after several years of ineffective planning by the early parliamentary regime and several years of ministerial infighting under the military regime. The Ayub regime did not find it easy to rectify the planning inadequacies of the previous regime. Since they were heavily dependent on the bureaucracy, few changes could be contemplated that did not meet with the administrators' tacit, if not explicit, approval. Moreover, Ayub's determination to make Basic Democracies work did not have a clear relation to his similar determination to make planning work. Only in the second year of his rule did Ayub begin to clarify the planning relationship between Basic Democracies and planning, stimulated perhaps by his realization in 1961 that without his chairing the Planning Commission it would never have the prestige necessary in order to penetrate administrative resistance. The Second Five Year Plan gave more than lip service to the role of local government, barely mentioned in the Moroccan and Tunisian plans. Starting in 1962 the government began giving bloc grants for development support of Basic Democracies. Though the Pakistani government responded to the challenge of local reform organizationally, it did not create a durable national role for the new local authorities, and the future of decentralized planning as well as Basic Democracies in the new parliamentary regime is in doubt.

The formal planning requirements were probably filled most expeditiously in Tunisia, but only after nearly three years of carefully probing sentiment in the Socialist Destour and opinions throughout the country. Once a solution having minimal repercussions on the party is found, the single-party regime can manipulate administrators and resources with relative ease. Bourguiba was, of course, fortunate in having an unusually capable and hard-working minister for the planning position, who had already given much thought to national reconstruction in his previous positions as Minister of Health and Labor and secretary of the U.G.T.T. As a result, the Tunisian *perspective* had conceptual clarity and social purpose lacking in both the Moroccan and Pakistani plans. There were certainly economic objections to be made to the Tunisian plan, as well as to the other plans, but it was designed with full recognition of both political and economic circumstances affecting national development.

The great difference in the three planning processes—and particularly relevant to the problem of national development—was the way in which the three political systems acted as agents in creating popular support and understanding of planning goals. The *ad hoc* procedures of the monarchical system, combined with frequent changes of ministers and parties to meet royal desires, deprived the planning process of popular impact. There continued to be discussion of important broad reforms in landownership and cultivation, but the fanfare given Promotion Nationale, the rural communes, and other projects had too often raised excessive popular hopes. The monarchical system was in an especially difficult position. Just as independent ministries and agencies represented a threat to the pattern of Palace rule, so also did the creation of new national values and popular goals not dependent on the monarchy. The result was ministerial confusion on the one hand and popular confusion on the other. The planning process was seldom conceived in terms suitable for popular consumption. If substantial progress is being made, the less sweeping formulation of planning and development can be effective, but in Morocco it tended to be a rationalization for wasteful procrastination, poor coordination, and increasingly autocratic rule.

The impact of the military-bureaucratic regime is perhaps the most instructive on the critical relationship between planning and national integration. The specific reforms of President Ayub Khan cannot be denied: corruption diminished greatly in the upper ranks of the administration; important steps were taken to develop the Indus valley, increase power resources, et cetera; the morale of the military and their loyalty to the republic was reinforced at a time when Pakistan might have descended into the chaos of military cliques found in Iraq, Syria, and Indonesia under comparable conditions. It is then with no intent to disparage Ayub's accomplishments that one may also observe that the austere and compartmentalized rule of the military-bureaucratic alliance failed to capture the popular imagination in a way suitable to the development process, and possibly in a way capable of sustaining the regime's reforms. The most dramatic evidence in respect to planning is the great gap that continued to exist between political life in Pakistan and the endeavor to develop rapidly. Like the Moroccan king, Ayub made speeches promising a more productive society and outlining the specific achievements of the substantial economic progress under his direction. But it was difficult for the British-trained officer to descend to the popular level, and the planning process, for all the care lavished on it, was not accompanied with the aims or appeal appropriate to a national mobilization. The proof of the political inadequacies of the system was Ayub's own reluctant acceptance of party membership and the resurgence of party activity in Pakistan.

There is no doubt that the single-party regime in Tunisia was the most successful in arousing popular interest and stimulating a national response to the plan. Although some allowance must be made for the political advantages of operating in a smaller country and one already on the way toward political integration, the single-party regime was prepared to extract the maximum significance from planning and, indeed, was probably compelled to do this or else face the possibility of the plan's full implications being exploited by latent opposition groups. The Socialist Destour was accustomed to the methods of mass appeal, and Bourguiba argued the need for a popular mobilization in response to planning more energetically than either the Moroccan monarch or the Pakistani president. To facilitate the campaign for the plan Bourguiba devised the notion of Neo-Destourian socialism. He also encountered the first strong resistance to his regime, and contributed to the resentment climaxing in the assassination attempt.

Each political system brought its own limitations to the developmental process and, in turn, responded in characteristic ways to the tensions and challenges created as national reconstruction took place. In microcosmic form the planning process has provided an insight into the way in which obstacles to development may arise in the three political systems, and the difficulties each system has in creating patterns of political behavior appropriate to nationally sponsored development. Development cannot avoid having profound psychological and social effects, but it rests with the existing political system to determine the sequence, timing, and magnitude of these effects. The following chapters will explore some of the major areas in which development has more specific impact, and how the three political systems have responded to some of the more specific challenges of the developmental process.

CHAPTER 6

ORGANIZATIONAL RESPONSES TO RURAL RECONSTRUCTION

THE PEASANT OF AFRICA and Asia is caught in a precarious web of weather, subsistence, and fear. To change the physical forces isolating him from national life, and to reduce the social and psychological pressures confining him to the village environment, governmental action is required. There have been numerous studies of the technical problems of specific programs to reach the village, and many of these procedures have enjoyed a measure of success. However, the relationship of village to development will, above all, he influenced by the versatility and resourcefulness of the regime. As the rural populace enters a more complex world, the ability of the peasant to understand and to communicate with the array of nation-building agencies takes on great importance.

Although this study can deal with only the very early stages of effort to relate the villager to the more diverse environment of the modern world, the success of the over-all effort may well depend on the initial contacts and early relationships that are created. These depend as much on the existing political system as they do on the technical capacities and sheer physical circumstances at work in the new country. Land is the touchstone of the peasant's life. Thus it is not surprising that the first national issue of particular relevance to the locality is land distribution. The next is generally the way in which the resources of the central government will be channeled to the peasant. Both these problems will be considered in this chapter, and, as will be shown, involve decisions of critical import to the existing political system as well as the future of the villager.

Like most major reforms, agrarian reform can only be undertaken with help from the central government combined with action at the local level. The dilemma of decreasing yields, exhaustion of land supplies, excessive morseling of land, and demographic pressure is only the setting for the more complex, and essentially political, aspect of reorganizing the countryside. As the materials on Morocco, Tunisia, and Pakistan demonstrate, there is no panacea for the problems of undernourishment and underemployment. If there were, the determinist element of the argument for land and other rural reform would be compelling. In practice there are a multitude of alternatives open even to the governments having highly similar rural problems. A choice must be made, and this choice, in turn, reveals the new government's orientation and defines the avenues for participation offered the new citizens.

One of the most convincing proofs of the complexity of the rural-reorganization problem confronting most developing countries is the nearly universal failure of land redistribution alone to bring about noticeable changes in agricultural output and, more important, individual confidence in the chances of agricultural improvement. The first section of this chapter will deal with the approaches of the three governments to the land-reform question, and how their actions have been shaped by the political orientation of each government. On the whole, Western views on land reform in developing countries have been excessively colored by our own experience, and more subtly by our own convictions on the sanctity of private ownership stemming from the philosophers of classical liberalism. Where these notions were applied at an early period of colonial history, the tendency was to create a powerful landlord class. As Mukerjee noted a generation ago, "Every prejudice arising out of Western notions of property and the relations of landlord and tenant in Great Britain came to be entirely on the side of the *zamindars*."[1]

Not unlike many early notions of political power, the argument for land redistribution stemmed from an unidimensional concept of agrarian life. The farmer could be manipulated by simply changing the amount of land he owned, while the worker, on the other hand, could easily be transformed by manipulating his wages. It required nearly a century to break down these simplifications into less satisfactory but more realistic explanations allowing for the diversity of mankind. Nevertheless, patriotic pride and lack of explanations adequate to a more intricate vision of man often lead us into advocating direct transference of the American and European experience. Such simple notions have prevented us as well as many new governments from comprehending the full complexity of the development process and, in turn, advancing programs suited to the diverse needs of a developing society.

The importance of making individual contact in agrarian reform is especially important in the context of this inquiry, for it raises the issue of the peasant's psychological state in relation to political life. Though many programs for local improvement break down at this crucial point, it is seldom as dramatic as in the attempt to reorganize agriculture. Even the most remote official cannot ignore fertilizer left to deteriorate at the roadside distribution points by suspicious peasants, who refused to carry it the remaining few feet to their fields. Even the most masterful of mass orators among the city politicians will find his talents strained when thrust into a village council meeting to weigh the advantages of building a secondary irrigation channel through collectively owned lands. The obstacle to national integration, as well as national prosperity, is the mentality of the villager who cannot conceive of a multitude of new services stemming from government without the simultaneous arbitrary exercise of power associated with forces from outside the

[1] Radhakamal Mukerjee, *Land Problems of India*, London, Longmans, Green, 1933, p. 331.

village. The villager and tribesman must make his reconciliation with diversity just as the politician and official must become accustomed to the ambiguity of living in an intricate society.

Many of the early tasks of development are essentially attempts to establish working relations with the local level. The apathy and fear of generations must be overcome before more complex social and economic institutions can be formed. The new government encounters particularly difficult obstacles in the first stages of development because it must overcome the resistance of established, influential groups, while also opening the way for more diverse forms of political expression and social communication. The handling of the land-reform issue in the countries is, therefore, an important indication of how the government envisages the diffusion of developmental activity. The following discussion is not directed to the agricultural economics of land redistribution, but to the image of change projected in each political system. The same purpose directs the analysis in the later sections of the chapter, where the organizational devices for rural reorganization will be discussed. These are the first steps toward reaching the villager, and will play a critical part in the effort to integrate the peasant in a more productive and more satisfying life.

THE ILLUSION OF DEVELOPMENT THROUGH LAND REDISTRIBUTION

The history of the social science might be written around the theme of how sufficient conditions have been transformed into necessary conditions as our understanding of the world has grown. The experience of Morocco, Tunisia, and Pakistan suggests that land redistribution is only a step toward creating a more productive, vigorous life in the countryside. These are by no means the only cases. The long history of land reform and social change in Mexico, Egypt, India, and the Philippines represent only a few of the additional cases demonstrating the mixed results of reorganizing the pattern of land ownership.[2] In each of these countries the decision to divide the holdings of large landholders was only a first and relatively timid step in agricultural reorganization.

Land reform does not assure rural progress; it only makes easier subsequent actions to ameliorate the conditions of rural life and to further national integration. It has yet to be proved that a country could not enjoy the material benefits of a prosperous agrarian economy with heavy concentration of landownership. More pertinent to our present

[2] The role of land reform has been the subject of several specialized studies in other developing countries. See, for example, Clarence Senior, *Land Reform and Democracy*, Gainesville, University of Florida Press, 1958; Jose V. Abueva, *Focus on the Barrio*, Manila, Institute of Public Administration, University of the Philippines, 1959; Saad M. Gadalla, *Land Reform in Relation to Social Development, Egypt*, Columbia, University of Missouri Press, 1962.

concerns, however, is the observation that without some attempt to remove the gross inequalities in landownership, it seems most unlikely that the development process will begin on the scale needed to create a modern society. The diffusion of power concomitant with the creation of a more complex society threatens any person exercising such arbitrary authority over so many aspects of an individual's life as the huge land-owner in impoverished lands.[3]

The experience of the three subject countries contrasts greatly. The Moroccan monarchy has managed to make only token efforts at land distribution, and this from the more easily available categories of land. While Morocco often protests that more action was impossible because she lacked the cadre with which to manage and staff new types of farms, the fact remains that there has been only the most dim outline of what kind of agricultural enterprises the regime favors. Attention given to land reform, as to other important aspects of the developmental process, has been sporadic and seldom followed with effective action.

The Tunisian case also reveals the political interest of the regime. Land reorganization has been forcefully carried through, despite more severe lack of human and material resources than Morocco. However, Bourguiba has chosen to keep most of the released land in the hands of the state, where its distribution and exploitation is carefully managed by the joint hierarchy of the party and government. As in the case of the Tunisian municipal council, the approach has been experimental and at the convenience of the Socialist Destour; to that extent it may be jeopardized more by what has been left undone for political reasons than by the results achieved in the face of the extreme deprivation of the Tunisian economy and several poor agricultural years.

The Pakistani approach to land reform has also been cautious, and influenced by insistence on administrative order. The prerevolutionary parliamentary regime set the pattern for land reform under the military dictatorship. In 1949 the West Pakistan Muslim League Agrarian Reforms Committee made a series of proposals to eliminate the most abusive landowning practices.[4] There had also been studies of the tenancy conditions prevailing in the Punjab and the Sind, but action was effectively blocked by the large landowners dominating the Muslim League parties of the two former provinces. In Bengal the Permanent Settlement of 1793 produced an extremely unjust and unproductive landowning structure, which troubled the British for many years. In

---

[3] For many purposes the frequent analogy made to European nineteenth-century experience in the study of developing countries is misleading. For life in rural areas a much better comparison is the medieval period, as described in G. G. Coulton, *Medieval Village, Manor and Monastery*, New York, Harper, 1960 (first published in 1925).

[4] Government of Pakistan, National Planning Board, *The First Five Year Plan (1955-60)*, Karachi, 1956, p. 307.

1940 the Land Revenue Commission[5] finally recommended that the *zamindari* system, which sometimes put as many as fifty intermediaries between the cultivator and the owner, be abolished. These findings were confirmed after World War II, and legislation to remove the Bengali *zamindari* had actually been introduced into the provincial legislature prior to partition.

After partition the East Pakistan government again revived the issue, and a series of reforms were enacted under the East Bengal State Acquisition and Tenancy Act of 1950. The Permanent Settlement was abolished, and land taxes were to be paid henceforth directly to the government. Land holdings were limited to roughly 33 acres (100 standard *bighas*) or 3.3 acres per family member whichever was greater. Subletting was forbidden, and provision was made to recover land for consolidation. Some exemptions were made for commercial farms growing sugar, tea, rubber, and similar crops. Progress in transferring land rights was slow until 1956, when the government decided to ignore all claims by intermediaries, and moved to take over some 400 of the largest holdings immediately.[6] There was little the Ayub regime could do but facilitate the reforms already in motion in 1959, although there remain serious problems of morseling and the government can seldom collect more than about a fourth of the land taxes.

The Bengali experience in land reform provided the Ayub government with insights into the complexity of such reforms that has generally been lacking in North Africa. There were immense problems of compiling new land registers and calculating compensation, which was to start being paid in 1962. Under the new government a Land Revenue Commission was appointed to deal with some of these problems. In July 1959 it recommended that holdings per family be tripled, and that no parceling be permitted below three acres. It also suggested that the government continue to delay granting full land rights to the peasants because land taxes would bring only a fraction of the income now received as rent.[7] Under the military regime no changes were made in the 1950 act, and there is little doubt that East Pakistan has become an agrarian society composed of small proprietors, whatever may be the

[5] The British had been seriously studying land reform in Bengal since the turn of the century, but action was no doubt complicated by the communal tensions existing between the wars. References to the various commissions will be found in *Land Reforms in East Pakistan*, Government of East Pakistan, Director of Public Relations, n.d., pp. 1-5. Of the approximately one hundred million rupees (about twenty million dollars) in land revenue paid by the cultivators (*raiyats*), at that time under 20 million rupees were finally paid to the government by the *zamindars*, while the remainder was absorbed by the long chain of collectors.

[6] An account of progress in Bengal prior to partition is given in *The First Five Year Plan*, *op.cit.*, pp. 313-315.

[7] Government of Pakistan, Planning Commission, *The Second Five Year Plan (1960-65)*, Karachi, 1960, pp. 189-191.

legal conditions surrounding their ownership. With the revival of party politics the chances of curtailing the initial reforms seem most remote.

However, some additional steps toward consolidation and more productive land use will be imperative for East Pakistan. With virtually all the cultivable land under production, the population pressure has now approached the point where human reorganization can be achieved only by disaster. The land ratio of about half an acre per person is half that of West Pakistan. There are over six million holdings with an average of 3.5 acres per family, or roughly the suggested size for an individual holding under the 1950 act. Fully four fifths of these holdings are under three acres. There are over a million and a half landless.[8] The abolition of the *zamindars* has only put the government in the position to make the even more critical reforms required to alleviate the impoverishment of the villager. The most critical phase of agricultural development has yet to come.

TABLE V

Land Holdings in East and West Pakistan (1960)[a]

	East Pakistan Number (*mil.*) Per Cent		West Pakistan Number (*mil.*) Per Cent	
Owner-cultivators	3.8	62	1.5	42
Permanent tenants	2.2	36	.6	18
Tenants	.1	2	1.5	40
	6.1		3.7	
(Average Holding = 3.5 acres)			(Average Holding = 9.8 acres)	

[a] Figures taken from the 1960 Agricultural Census and published in the *Pakistan Times*, October 31, 1961.

The land-distribution problems of West Pakistan are complicated by tribal and regional differences. Like Bengal, much of the land in the former Sind was held under the *raiyatwari* system where ownership was technically still vested in the state and the *zamindars* acted as revenue agents.[9] The old Sind region was also heavily devoted to *jagir* lands, grants made to military lords prior to the British arrival and held without tax payments to the central government. An investigation in the

[8] Government of Pakistan, *Report of the Food and Agriculture Commission,* Karachi, 1960, p. 36. Hereafter cited as *F&AC Report.*

[9] An important qualification should be made on the role of the *zamindars.* In the late Moghul period they served, as in tenant systems in many ancient empires, to lighten the burden on the peasant when crops were poor. Despite the abuses that developed with time, the *zamindar* system had a flexibility that is important in precarious rural economies, and that is often lacking in modern commercial systems where prices and credit are influenced by many forces outside the agrarian economy. For more detail see *The First Five Year Plan, op.cit.,* pp. 307-308; and also S. M. Akhtar, "The Land Tenure System in Pakistan," in Parsons, et al., *Land Tenure,* Madison, University of Wisconsin Press, 1956, pp. 125-133.

Sind in 1946 showed that 30 per cent of the land was in the hands of one per cent of the owners, who had estates of over 500 acres each. Most of the land was farmed by tenants, who were at the mercy of their land-lords, although tenant rights were transferable and inheritable. In the Northwest Frontier and Punjab areas there remained the vestiges of communal land ownership, not unlike the collective tribal land of North Africa. However, large tracts of land were in the hands of the large landowners in the Punjab as well as near the frontier, where con-centration of holdings and abuse of tenants sometimes paralleled con-ditions in the Sind.

The early attempts at land reform in West Pakistan were to revise the Punjab Tenancy Act of 1887 and to take other steps to protect the tenant-cultivator from the landlord. In general these moves were success-fully defeated by the landlords or so ineffectively implemented that no change took place. In the Sind a provincial committee in close contact with the *zamindars* discredited the first postwar land inquiry. More vigorous efforts were made to protect tenants in the Punjab, but the variety of simple devices to coerce the peasant defied legislation. Under the *bargardar* system the landlord could simply fail to collect his share of the produce (placed at roughly 50 per cent of the farmer's pro-duct) or fail to provide a receipt, thereby fabricating grounds for evic-tion. Several attempts were also made to place ceilings on the amount of land an owner could cultivate while also renting land, and to force the landlords into making land declarations. Important as these early efforts were in laying the groundwork for the 1959 reforms, they tended to exacerbate relations between tenant and owner and increased the ruthlessness of the large holders.

The First Five Year Plan was outspoken in condemning these prac-tices, and served as the model for future reforms in West Pakistan. In-deed, it is reasonable to conclude that most of the groundwork had been done by the time that Ayub took office. The rapid completion of the Land Reforms Commission report suggests how much it relied on the inquiries and recommendations that had been made over the previous decade. The first plan did not conceal its distaste for the state of "feu-dalism" that was, for the most part, the lot of the peasant in the western wing, leaving him "no higher motive than to continue to exist as best he can with rights, without opportunities and without status or dignity."[10] Though reluctant to endorse the principle of state purchase used in the eastern wing, the group working on the first plan advocated ceilings of 150 acres of irrigated, 300 acres for partially irrigated, and 450 acres on unirrigated (*barani*) land.[11] The new distribution was to be accompanied

---

[10] *The First Five Year Plan, op.cit.*, p. 309.
[11] *Ibid.*, pp. 318-320. Though never enforced, much lower limits were placed on personal cultivation in the Punjab Tenancy Act of 1950, starting with twenty-

with provisions to prevent the emergence of a new landlord class, as has been done in the Bengali reform of 1950.

One of President Ayub's first acts on taking office was to appoint a Land Reforms Commission for the western wing. Their report[12] is one of the fundamental documents on the new government's efforts to reconstruct the country, and has provided the guidelines for land reform since it was submitted in January 1959. The fact that the commission required only three months to prepare its report indicates how much earlier studies assisted their work, and also the virtual unanimity that existed among high officials on the solution to West Pakistan's land problems.

The commission's recommendations were generally in line with the more cautious policy that has been associated with other aspects of the military-bureaucratic regime. Without bothering to argue the case for or against earlier recommendations for ceilings on holdings, the commission suggested that the maximum holding should be 500 acres of irrigated land, or 1,000 acres of unirrigated land. There were several exceptions to these limits. One might retain an additional 150 acres of orchards on the grounds that they require a long period of unproductive farming and would suffer from being divided. Exceptions can also be made for stud and livestock farming if the government considers it in the national interest. The 500-acre limit can also be lifted where the maximum acreage does not assure the landlord of the full quantity of production units, an index based on the productivity of the soil and used mainly for paying compensation proportionate to the owners' investment in the holding. The landlord could also make transfers of approximately half his maximum holding to any of his heirs,[13] and of about a sixth to each female dependent so entitled under Muslim law. The firmest policy was taken toward the *jagirdars*, who were abolished without compensation of any kind.

Compared to other land-reform programs, the proposal of the West Pakistan commission was generous, if not lenient. Land was recovered from only 6,061 persons. The social position of the large landowners was only slightly compromised, and their regional influence remains practically uncompromised until such time as new local leadership

---

five acres of irrigated land. More progress was made in the Northwest Frontier, where the law also applied and transformed nearly a quarter of a million of occupancy (permanent) tenants into full owners without serious conflict of landowners and cultivators.

[12] *Report of the Land Reforms Commission for West Pakistan*, Government of West Pakistan, Lahore, 1961.

[13] The transfers provision had an important qualification. Because many landlords in West Pakistan feared reforms similar to those pressed much earlier in East Pakistan following partition, the law was made retroactive to 1947. *The Second Five Year Plan, op.cit.*, p. 190, mentions some of the reasons the 1959 reforms placed relatively high ceilings. It was felt that lower ceilings would not "substantially" increase the number of peasants able to obtain land.

emerges. Even in the rich irrigated areas of the Punjab it was not difficult for some large families to retain control of 5,000 acres or more, and individual holdings of 800 acres or more remain common. Though there is no evidence of any direct collusion, it is certainly relevant that many of the Pakistani officers and high civil servants are members of the rural and tribal aristocracy that has dominated rural life in the western wing. Once allowance is made for the permanent tenants occupying much of the land acquired under the 1959 reforms, there will be little left for distribution.[14]

Allowing 750 acres as the average-size holding retained by most *zamindars* leaves a total of slightly over 3.6 million acres to distribute. If four acres of land is provided for each tenant, which is about half the average-size holding in West Pakistan, a total of roughly 900,000 peasants will acquire land as result of the reform. Farms will be sold first to peasants now living on the estates and holding some claims to their farms as occupancy tenants (as opposed to "tenants-at-will" who could be evicted). Since about 40 per cent of tenants have such claims, this leaves 540,000 farms to be distributed, which means that roughly 7 per cent of the rural populace could acquire land under the reform. It is not expected that the number of tenancy holdings in West Pakistan will be reduced by more than five per cent by the redistribution.

When the reforms of the Ayub regime are examined in terms of the over-all agricultural position of Pakistan, it becomes apparent that they are only an introduction to the profound reorganization needed in the countryside. Indeed, the actions in West Pakistan were extremely cautious compared to the policy of the premilitary government in Bengal. The Planning Commission and the Food and Agricultural Commission concur in the importance of following the initial reform with energetic programs for land consolidation and agricultural modernization. In East Pakistan the government has yet to deal with the issues raised by "population pressure, fragmented holdings, declining bullock power, poor yields, pathetically low incomes and the lack of a fair marketing system and good communications."[15] Although West Pakistan includes one of the largest irrigated areas in the world, salinity and waterlogging as a result of poor farming practices have made irrigation a necessary evil.

There are still opportunities to increase agricultural output, but this cannot be done unless the government is successful in reaching the peasant. In the debates of the West Pakistan Assembly in the spring of

---

[14] William Bredo, *Land Reform and Development in Pakistan*, Menlo Park, Stanford Research Institute, 1959, p. 9. Not all of the reclaimed land was arable, and there were also administrative limitations. *The Second Five Year Plan, op.cit.,* p. 185, notes that up to June 1960 the government had actually recovered 1.2 million of 2.3 million acres of cultivable land expected to be used for distribution.

[15] *F&AC Report, op.cit.,* p. 39.

1963, government officers confessed that much of the newly irrigated and reclaimed land was being sold to officials, because they had the funds to purchase and to exploit new land fully. If the economic pressure for development has been permitted to outweigh the need to integrate the peasant into modern agriculture, Ayub may well find his desires for local responsibility and local confidence disappointed. The 1959 reforms were well handled, but they accomplished much less in the reorganization of the rural economy than has often been suggested. Furthermore, they hardly represented a reorientation of agrarian politics. The landlord and official have tended to remain the handmaidens of government. Unlike the land transfer of the single-party regime in Tunisia, for example, the change of ownership was apparently not part of a larger design to mobilize the society. It was completed and ground into the administrative process before most Pakistanis had time to reflect on how auxiliary programs might utilize the leverage provided by the reforms. Comments on land reform in the Second Five Year Plan, issued under Ayub's auspices, were more concerned with the possible tax effects unlike the first plan, which liberally cited the broad impact to be derived from land reform and dwelt more on the personal vulnerability and hopelessness of the peasant. There was little coordinated attention to the support activities needed to make the peasant a more effective farmer, although these needs were covered in other documents on rural development. Though aware of the farmer's multiple needs, the military-bureaucratic alliance was timid in building other reforms into land reform, and highly concerned with tax collection.

POLITICAL REACTIONS TO LAND REDISTRIBUTION

The situation the British found in Bengal and the Indian subcontinent in the nineteenth century contrasts sharply with the more recent intrusion of French influence in North Africa. In Bengal most of the land was occupied, and the colonial regime had relatively few ambitions of putting land under cultivation by Britishers. Their interest was largely "law and order," the essential purpose being regular tax collection. Though unjust, the Permanent Settlement was a common-sense solution to an immensely complex problem. Land tenure was no less complex in North Africa, but the French arrived at a different stage in the struggle for empire and with fewer illusions about their ultimate purpose. While the need for land had brought most of the easily cultivable parts of India into production by the twentieth century, there were still large unoccupied, rich areas in North Africa.

The French found themselves confronted with at least three types of *habous* (religious foundations; *waqf* outside North Africa) property, several kinds of collectively owned tribal land, and a well-established system of individual ownership for *melk* or private land. In the words of the leading French expert on Tunisian land tenure, "The spirit of Descartes and that of the French capitalists accommodated itself poorly to this confused situation."[16] The French passion for order did much to prepare Tunisia and Morocco for later nationalist reforms, although the ironical purpose of the early French reorganization was to pave the way for the French settler and investor.

The presence of large numbers of French settlers (*colons*) in North Africa does not pose a serious obstacle to the comparative purpose of this inquiry. Like the large landholder in Pakistan, the French farmer in North Africa presents the government with a well-defined and vulnerable structure for rural reconstruction. Each lends himself to quick and relatively easy reorganization, compared to the more complex and less effective techniques that might be used to improve the small landholder's productivity. The economic justification for increased control and improved methods in agriculture is, if anything, greater in Pakistan than in Morocco and Tunisia. Pakistan depends on agriculture for about 80 per cent of her exports,[17] while Morocco and Tunisia depend on agriculture for about 60 and 40 per cent, respectively, for exports. In all three countries the large landholders are a natural political target, perhaps even more attractive in North Africa because about half of them are foreign nationals.

The French and other foreign holdings in Tunisia pose a more serious and pressing problem for the government than does the similar issue in Morocco. The reasons for this are apparent on an inspection of Table VI. There is much less cultivable land in Tunisia and great need to organize and modernize the remaining exploitable land as rapidly as possible.[18] The *colon* land dominated large highly productive areas in the north, and in many areas was exploited by large commercial farms. This is very different from Morocco, where most *colon* farms are individually owned and farmed by the owners. The Tunisian approach to land reform has been greatly influenced by the single-party system. The authority of the state could be brought to bear directly on some of the more intricate questions involved in modernizing agriculture on *habous* and collective land.

[16] Republic of Tunisia, Secretary of State for Agriculture, *Textes Legislatifs et Circulaires Concernant le Service des Affaires Foncières*, with commentary by Hervé Sicard, 1960, p. 19. Hereafter cited as *Affaires Foncières*.

[17] *F&AC Report, op.cit.*, p. 29. Pakistan is also typical of developing countries in exporting nearly three fourths of these products in raw form.

[18] Vigorous efforts to colonize land in Tunisia were made well before similar efforts could be started in Morocco. Sicard, *Affaires Foncières, op.cit.*, pp. 2-4, notes that nearly 853 thousand hectares, or about 2 million acres, had been taken before World War I. Before World War I in Morocco there were only several small commercial farms in Chaouia province outside Casablanca, and the bulk of the settlement took place after the war and by independent farmers.

TABLE VI

Classification of Landownership in Tunisia (1960)[a]

		Acres
Forest		2,500,000
Collective or tribal		3,750,000
Private or *melk*		5,875,000
State		
Consolidated	450,000	
Public *habous*	300,000	
Mixed *habous*	1,500,000	
Private *habous*	1,250,000	
Sequestered	375,000	
		3,875,000
Foreign		1,500,000
Total		17,500,000

[a] *Affaires Foncières*, Hervé Sicard, ed., Tunis, Republic of Tunisia, Secretary of State for Agriculture, 1960, p. 14. These figures are for land surveyed by the government. The total cultivable area of Tunisia is commonly given as 9 million hectares or roughly 22.5 million acres. Also the most frequent figure for collective lands is 6 million hectares or 15 million acres. However, large tracts of this land (most of the southern half of Tunisia) are not cultivable and remain unsurveyed. The table has been converted at 2.5 acres to the hectare.

Bourguiba's direct attack on the use of *habous* land is in many ways unlike his usual tactic of carefully laying the groundwork for a unanimous decision within the framework of the party. Clearly little rural modernization could begin until the wasteful and unjust practices possible under the religious foundations were terminated. But the underlying motives for this phase of land reform have an important political history, which personally involves the president of the republic. The vast proportions of *habous* land in Tunisia meant that much of the richest land was under the Islamic administration. The Protectorate took several steps to enable settlers to gain title to these lands, particularly in the case of the public *habous*.[19] Most of the transactions of desirable land under these provisions of Islamic law took place prior to World War I, and only later did the colonial regime begin to explore ways of transforming private *habous* property for more productive use. Under Islamic law all the beneficiaries of private *habous* property, which sometimes might be

[19] Under the practice of *enzel* the land could be perpetually assigned for a fixed rent, and under other circumstances public *habous* land could be exchanged for other forms of property. The practice of *enzel* tenure is comparable in some ways to the permanent tenants of Pakistan, though in the first case the land is in *habous* and in the second it is state-owned. Under the terms of an *enzel* transaction the tenant or other property user gains permanent access to the property in question. The handling of the *habous* problem is discussed by Leon Carl Brown in "Colonization—A Second Look," *Institute of Current World Affairs Newsletter*, mimeo., May 23, 1961, pp. 13-17.

several hundreds of persons, must give their consent. During the 1920's the regime began to seek ways of simplifying this process by gaining the sympathy of privileged Tunisians in control of *habous* property. Bourguiba first came into the public eye as a young lawyer defending less privileged Tunisians who saw their livelihood being taken away through the manipulation of *habous* property.

In attacking the *habous* institutions shortly after independence, the president was not only aggressively launching the Tunisian land-reform program but was also demolishing a center of power that had opposed the Socialist Destour, and was likely to continue to oppose it. Salah Ben Youssef, who led the opposition to Bourguiba in the Socialist Destour Congress in late 1955, had received support from Islamic conservatives as well as extreme Arab nationalists.[20] The first step was the dissolution of the public *habous* in March 1956. There were only about 300,000 acres of such lands, mostly devoted to aging olive trees that were seldom properly cared for. The assimilation of the public *habous* as state land also enabled the president to dissolve the governing committees appointed under Islamic law, an historic point of convergence of conservative opinion. The more drastic reform was the merger of the private *habous* lands with state land a year later. These lands constituted about nine tenths of the area under religious foundations and cultivated by beneficiaries and tenants whose "work consisted of scratching the soil with no valid notion of exploitation."[21]

The disposition of the private *habous* land created some delicate problems for the beneficiaries of the foundations. If the donors were still living, they were permitted to recover their property. Six months were given for any private transactions the occupants wished to make among themselves. The equitable division of the property then rested with Regional Habous Liquidation Commissions,[22] with an appeal commission sitting in Tunis. The original commissions were presided over by a judge designated by the Ministry of Justice, a representative of the governor, an agent of the Ministry of Finance, and also of the Ministry of Agriculture's Service Foncier. Although the commissions were supposed to complete their inquiries in six months, a large amount of un-

[20] This is one of many fascinating examples of the meeting of the extremes in Arab politics. The Islamic elements in Tunisia, more or less aligned with remnants of the old Destour Party, saw opportunities for revival by using pan-Arab doctrines and slogans emanating from Egypt. Nasser had also given strong support to the North African liberation fighters in Tunisia and Morocco, whose activities were curtailed with independence. Salah Ben Youssef was the organizer and main link between Cairo and Tunis.

[21] Habib Bourguiba, "La Bataille Economique dans le Domaine Agricole," speech delivered October 27, 1961, Secretary of State for Information and Touring, Tunis, 1961.

[22] The methods and regulations governing the operation of the Regional Commissions are given in *Affaires Foncières, op.cit.,* pp. 24-62.

cultivable or grazing land still remains unregulated. The immediate goal of the reform was to put the cultivated *habous* lands under private ownership where their improvement and use could be associated with the effort to modernize Tunisian agriculture.

Bourguiba's reform of tribal or collective lands was more controversial than the *habous* changes, and it is typical of the *ancien combattant* that he plunged ahead into the more intricate question of regulating the use of collective land. Nearly the entire southern half of Tunisia, composed largely of semiarid or arid steppes, is held as collective land. Although the Socialist Destour government repeatedly claims that tribal homogeneity no longer exists in Tunisia, there were enduring property rights attached to the area as well as some difficult problems in human reorganization as the nomadic peoples are placed on small farms. Estimates vary greatly, but it appears that roughly six million hectares or about fifteen million acres of Tunisian soil are collective land. Much of this land is unproductive, and most of it is in a region where rain is unpredictable.

The process of finding individual proprietors for collective land has obvious hazards, but the government initially set out on a policy of establishing small private holdings. With the renewed emphasis on economic planning in 1961, the goal of the reorganization shifted to the establishment of farm cooperatives. However, the president clearly felt in 1957 that the only way to make more careful regulation of tribal land palatable was to offer the material security of the small individual holding. The tribe's claim on its territory was firmly fixed. According to the law of September 1957 the collective land was "unseizable, unalienable and unprescribable."[23] The tribe was made a legal and financial entity under the tutorship of the state.

However, from the beginning of the transition the president made it very clear that unless the tribesmen settled on the new farms responded by observing their obligations and by improving agricultural methods, the state would reclaim their land. His famous tours of the central and southern regions nearly always touch on the integration of the tribesmen. Asserting the readiness of the government to assist, he warns the people against "avoiding work under the pretext that labor is unfamiliar," and notes that the uncooperative will be left to "a primitive life condemning them to vegetate on the margin of society."[24] Neither the exhortations of Ayub nor the promises of Hassan II have approached so firm a view on rural reconstruction.

[23] "Loi no. 57-16 du 28 septembre (3 rabia I 1377), fixant le régime organique des terres collectives," *Journal Officiel de la République Tunisienne*, October 15, 1957, pp. 250-251. The additional regulations appear in *Affaires Foncières, op.cit.*, pp. 123-166.

[24] Habib Bourguiba, "Fixer les hommes sur la Terre," speech of May 16, 1960, Secretary of State for Information and Touring, Tunis, 1960.

Visits to the southern governorates, as well as the circulars urging cooperation with the new regulations, suggest that the new law was not quickly or easily applied.[25] Several circulars urged the governors to proceed to select the local and regional councils, and stressed the country's great need "to improve the use of the collective lands, to add to their value through labor and investment, and to draw together the maximum resources for the profit of the tribe and the collectivity." In some cases it appears that the governors displayed inadequacies similar to those observed among Pakistani rural officials. The governor was told that his role was not "that of a passive President, but a tutor exercising permanent surveillance and animating the Council, without imposing his manner of viewing the Council."[26] There is no doubt that the reform was viewed with suspicion locally, and was occasionally neglected by the officials. Except for the collective lands that were included in the more intensively developed *cellules de mise en valuer*, there is little evidence that the collective-land reforms had meaningful consequences for the rural economy prior to 1963, when more vigorous action began under the Three Year Plan.

The difficulties of establishing effective contact with the rural segment of the population are well illustrated in the Tunisian experience with collectively held land. Several years passed while the state tried to create inducements and pressures to convert the tribes to private landholders. By 1964 it was apparent that this strategy was politically unworkable, and probably also uneconomic under such precarious conditions.[27]

[25] Unlike much of the rudimentary legislation found in other developing countries, the Tunisians had a clear notion of how the reorganization of tribal land would proceed. Each area would be supervised by a *conseil de gestion*, generally elected family heads of the tribe and limited to a *sheikhat*. The council acts under the "tutorship" of the Secretary of State for Agriculture, however, and in practice can do little without the consent of the governor and the central government. Nevertheless, it is a legal and financial unit, having its own budget and entitled to enter into legal actions. At the provincial level a tutorship is provided by a regional council under the governor, representing justice and agriculture officials. As a member of a tribal group makes improvements on his parcel, his rights can be transformed into private ownership with the accord of the *conseil de gestion* and the Secretary of State for Agriculture. This provision of the law was later changed by decree to give the governor's council the right to assign private holdings, to be determined in proportion to the farmer's family and the size of the collectivity.

[26] *Affaires Foncières, op.cit.*, pp. 144 and 150.

[27] There have in fact been two laws encouraging the effective utilization of the huge quantities of land held by the state. See "Loi no. 63-17 du mai 1963 portant encouragement de l'Etat au développement de l'agriculture," *Journal Officiel de la Republique Tunisienne*, May 31, 1963, p. 745ff. This law was the first legislation to implement resettlement of land recovered from France. A much firmer statement of state interest is found in the 1964 decree-law, "Décret-loi no. 64-11 du 26 Mars 1964 relatif aux associations de développement agricole," *op.cit.*, March 27, 1964, p. 380ff. Another account useful in connection with the growth of land-management offices is J.-M. Verdier, "L'évolution de la législation foncière depuis l'Indépendance," *I.B.L.A.*, vol. 24, nos. 95-96, 1961, pp. 399-404.

Shortly after seizing the remaining French land the government replaced its supervisory legislation with outright ownership of collective land. A decree law of early 1964 stated that all rural associations that did not succeed in converting to effective methods for full exploitation of the land at their disposal could be dissolved by decree and reorganized by the state. The abrupt reversal of the private holding policy, and the forceful nature of the new legislation indicates both the flexibility and concentration of power in the single-party regime.

The Socialist Destour has also been insistent in its negotiations for the return of French-held land. The issue was, of course, ideally suited for political exploitation in the party-oriented regime. Though political opportunity may have affected the timing of Tunisian pressure, it is also clear that the government has steadily pressed for return of the *colon* land. The first agreement, made between the Tunisians and the French in the fall of 1960, constitutes the diplomatic model for later acquisitions. Tunisia agreed to pay a million *dinars* or somewhat over two million dollars to reimburse French citizens for 250,000 acres. The government next negotiated the transfer of an additional 200,000 acres, on which agreement was reached early in 1963. It appears that several of the early efforts to recover *colon* land were made under pressure of the trade unions, and not too well planned. One informed observer notes that the first "movement for decolonization did not represent, due to inadequate technical means, a true economic reintegration."[28] The president later admitted that state lands were not fully exploited. The completed transaction would have given Tunisia about a third of the one and a half million acres of *colon* land in the country.

The eventual aim of the recovery of foreign-owned land was always clear, and it is therefore surprising that Bourguiba's seizure of all *colon* land in early 1964 should have created such a sensation. In May 1964 the president's announcement that all foreign-owned land would be taken over by the state in the coming year led to the suspension of French technical assistance.[29] The probable sequence was to recover first land held by French companies, then rented land, and lastly the 700,000 acres held in private ownership. This move would give the

[28] See M. Callens, "Cinq années d'action administrative dans le domain agricole," *I.B.L.A.*, vol. 25, no. 98, 1962, p. 116 and passim. First announcement appeared in the *New York Times*, October 11, 1960. The problem is also discussed in J. Kluytenaar and C. L. Pan, *La Gestion des Terres Agricoles par l'Office des Terres Dominales*, Rome, Food and Agricultural Organization, 1962. Tunisian self-sufficiency, and possibly political concern as well, is reflected in the decision not to have a land-tenure expert work on the above mission, which includes only an agricultural and an irrigation expert.

[29] See *Jeune Afrique*, May 25, 1964 and May 18, 1964. The seizure also evoked favorable comment in the Algerian revolutionary newspaper *Révolution Africaine*, May 23, 1964, where both Morocco and Tunisia had been chided for their reluctance to take over *colon* land. See also *Le Monde*, May 12, 1964. Bourguiba's action led to the suspension of French assistance to Tunisia at a critical point in her development program.

government full control of the rich lands in the north of the country, and virtually complete the process toward total state ownership of farmlands. How rapidly the government could convert these lands to cooperative use would be a severe test of the regime's effectiveness.

In most cases the recovered land became the property of the *Office de Terres Dominales* (O.T.D.), which, in turn, was to transfer the land to agricultural production cooperatives as envisaged in the Three Year Plan. The government had already been experimenting with production coops. Fifteen were formed in 1962, with a membership of over 500 families, occupying nearly 17,000 acres. Nearly 60 more were formed in 1963. As might be anticipated, the coops were attached to a carefully centralized organization which operated through Regional Cooperative Federations (Union Régionale de la Coopération), whose powers extended over all forms of cooperative enterprise in a province. The personally appointed governors act as chairmen, and the president of the Socialist Destour's provincial committee is included, as well as representatives of other auxiliary organizations of the party. The government has clearly embarked on a program of rural reorganization of major proportions, and it remains to be seen if the single-party regime can indeed adjust to the complexities of the reform.[30] With all due recognition of the energetic efforts of the Tunisian government, officials were candid in admitting that most cooperatives were still state farms, and that the members were in most cases still handled like salaried farm hands.

The Tunisian experience suggests the growing pressures for reform as a new country is more deeply involved in the developmental process. The commitment to active planning released cumulative forces in all areas of Tunisian life. Difficulties experienced in one aspect of national reconstruction served to increase pressures in other areas. Most important, the single-party regime could not isolate the national forces that had been unleashed with Destourian socialism, though an effort was still being made to compartmentalize the institutions for nation-building at various levels. This experience contrasts sharply with Pakistani land reform, which never took on a cumulative force in the society or had noticeable impact on political forces in the country. Likewise, the Moroccan land-reform effort had little political and social effect, and, like so many aspects of Moroccan reconstruction, became mired down in the inflammatory appeals of isolated political groups and the evasive tactics of the monarch.

[30] See particularly the assessment of Jean Poncet in *Paysages et Problèmes Ruraux en Tunisie*, Paris, Presses Universitaires de France, 1963, pp. 371-372. For background on the coops see Moncef Guen, *La Coopération et l'Etat en Tunisie*, Tunis, Editions de l'U.G.T.T., 1964; also, *La Voie Coopérative*, November-December 1963, the first issue of a journal published by the National School for Cooperation under the Ministry of Planning and Finance.

While Tunisia and Pakistan are confronted with situations that demand immediate action, Morocco has been able to indulge in considerable procrastination. Given the increasing demographic pressure and the static cereal yields over the past decade, it will not be possible to continue to neglect agriculture many more years without risking serious shortages. If Morocco's agrarian problems were not primarily those of human reorganization, a more sympathetic judgment on her progress might be possible. The country has over twice the cultivable area of Tunisia; estimates vary from 50 to 60 million acres. As in most cases, no more than half this area is suitable for intensive farming. The figure is generally placed at 20 million acres, of which roughly an eighth or two and a half million acres are farmed by *colons*. The remainder of the farm land is divided among some 900,000 Moroccan holdings.[31] One of the most serious agricultural problems is the severe morseling of these farms. There are roughly half a million landless Moroccan peasants, and, of course, the over-all rate of underemployment among the rural Moroccans represents a huge loss of labor. Though the average landholding is about 15 acres, similar to Tunisia and Western Pakistan, the pattern of distribution reveals inequities that are major obstacles to mobilizing the rural population.

Morocco is no better prepared to undertake programs to achieve more productive forms of land tenure than Pakistan, although the Tunisian example suggests what can be done with strong governmental support. The Protectorate established an Office Foncier, which has been largely confined to the management of state land. The amount of state land has not been made public. The collective land has been fre-

[31] Like Tunisia and Pakistan, the rural land census is in many respects still incomplete, and the task is divided among ministries having different interests. More recent Moroccan figures were released when the issue again attracted political interest. See *La Vie Economique*, April 20, 1963, for Guedira's proposal and figures; also, *Jeune Afrique*, August 3, 1964, for estimates of *colon* land and the over-all tenure problem. Earlier figures are sketchy and probably unreliable. See *Plan Quinquennal 1960-1964*, Division of Economic Coordination and the Plan, Ministry of National Economy, 1960, p. 175. These figures are substantiated and apply to approximately 16 million acres of arable land, although there has never been a complete land census in Morocco. The Ministry of Agriculture estimates about 13 million acres are sown to cereals, over 2 million to fallow lands, and about a million to fruit (including grapes and olives). See *Momento Pratique de l'Economie Agricole Marocaine*, Ministry of Agriculture, 1960, p. 6. Though no figures are available, a large proportion of Moroccan land is farmed under the traditional *khammes* (fifths) system, which is somewhat less prevalent in Tunisia and is comparable to the *bargadar* system in Pakistan. Commonly found among Muslim countries, the *khammes* system divides agricultural production into the contribution of animals, seed, water, land, and labor. The peasant, thereby, may end up with only a fifth of his crop (or less after various direct taxes), and has little inclination to improve the land or to farm methodically. Tables on declining cereal production can be found in Georges Oved, "Problèmes du développement économique au Maroc," *Tiers Monde*, vol. 2, no. 7, July-September 1961, p. 366.

quently estimated at six million hectares or about 15 million acres,[32] but no more than half of this has been surveyed. *Habous* land is much less important in the Moroccan agrarian economy than in Tunisia. For development purposes perhaps the most valid standard for judging a government's achievement is how much has been done with the land at its disposal. Although there has been no official estimate, the Minister of the National Economy announced that there were two million hectares or about five million acres prepared for development.[33] He claimed that this was composed of *habous*, state, and collective land which was surveyed and readily available for development.

Keeping in mind that land redistribution is, at best, only a first step toward the integration of the rural populace, one may inquire why the monarchy has been so slow to establish even the broad lines for land reform. The problem has certainly not been unknown to Moroccan politicians. When the late king distributed some small parcels of land in the Triffa plain of Oujda in 1956 he noted, "One of the most important aspects of the social revolution we propose consists of a vast agrarian reform, distribution of land to small *fellahs*, [and] the use of modern techniques and methods to exploit the soil."[34] Nor did the Istiqlal press for land reform until Moroccan politics became sufficiently competitive to compel them to make a stand. The party has received considerable support from large Moroccan landowners, especially in the Gharb, and the U.M.A. (Union Marocaine des Agriculteurs) has generally supported the Istiqlal. The first strong demands for land reform came from the U.N.F.P. and the U.M.T. after the split of the nationalist movement. Their public demands often border on demagoguery, although several of the U.N.F.P. leaders have more elaborate, reasoned proposals. The treatment of the issue in Moroccan politics is an intriguing example of the hazards as well as the advantages of handling complex problems under a traditional regime.

While the king refused to act, elements hoping to share the fruits of office, which are considerable in a developing country, were forced to follow suit. The first clear statement from the Istiqlal was early 1960, shortly after it went into opposition for the first time. The more progressive nationalist faction in office under Ibrahim was pressing for land reform within the government, and might thereby take public credit if the king decided to act. At the Istiqlal party congress the party came out against further morseling of land, the "concentration of land in the hands of a minority," and in favor of exploiting state, collective, *habous*,

---

[32] For a discussion of the variety of land-tenure methods used for the collective land see Jacques Berque, "Le système agraire au Maghreb," in Jean Dresch, et al., *Réforme Agraire au Maghreb*, Paris, François Maspéro, 1962, pp. 49-68.

[33] *Al-Istiqlal*, January 19, 1963.

[34] Quoted in Georges Oved, "Note sur la récente évolution économique du Maroc, 1949-1958," mimeo., Ministry of the National Economy, April-May, 1958.

and *colon* land in cooperatives.[35] There were few indications that the government was prepared for such sweeping reforms, or had any detailed notion of how they might be furthered. However, Ibrahim's Minister of Agriculture took the first concrete steps by negotiation with the French to repurchase certain categories of foreign-owned land.

The first attempt to recover foreign-owned land was made under the Ibrahim government early in 1959, and from that time there was increasing discussion of land reform. The first land to be repurchased was collective land that had been sold in such a way as to permit perpetual foreign ownership. Since this was some of the last Moroccan land to be occupied, and done under very doubtful circumstances, the French government was prepared to discuss restoration. The initial agreement with the Ibrahim government specified 100,000 acres that were to be returned in four lots as the Moroccan government was prepared to make the transfer. Moroccan officials report that only one group of farms, about 20,000 acres, were returned because the government was not prepared to exploit and manage the property. The first experiments demonstrated how rapidly the highly productive European farms could decline. Though Moroccan advisers urged that some method be found "to persuade the peasants to accept immediately collective forms of exploitation,"[36] the country lacked the necessary technical and managerial skills. Moreover, the peasants' idea of land reform was to secure their own parcels of land and thereby rapidly reduce valuable farms to traditional, subsistence agriculture.

Moroccan politics became increasingly embittered after 1962. Eventually both the Istiqlal and the U.N.F.P. found themselves in opposition to the monarch and, significantly, for many of the same reasons. In their opposition the parties began to discuss their earlier efforts. Ben Barka, a leading spokesman for the U.N.F.P., revealed in a study of Moroccan agriculture[37] that a land-reform scheme had been submitted as part of the Five Year Plan in 1960. The original draft of the plan allegedly conceded that attempts to redistribute farm income were doomed by the structural characteristics of Moroccan agriculture. Therefore, it was stipulated that an "agrarian reform" was needed, which would consist of new institutions to serve as a "liaison between the technical interventions

[35] *Al-Istiqlal*, January 16, 1960. See also the discussion of this problem in I. William Zartman, *Morocco: Problems of a New Power*, New York, Atherton, 1964, pp. 133-143.

[36] Oved in *Tiers Monde*, *op.cit.*, p. 377. There was, in addition, only the most perfunctory discussion of agriculture in the available minutes of the Superior Council of the Plan. In 1,931 pages of minutes there were only eight pages of discussion of agrarian problems. See *Compte Rendu de Délibérations du Conseil Supérieur du Plan*, Division of Economic Coordination and the Plan, Ministry of the National Economy, 1960, pp. 25-27 and 56-61.

[37] Mehdi Ben Barka, "Les conditions d'une véritable réforme agraire au Maroc," *Réforme Agraire au Maghreb*, *op.cit.*, pp. 119-123.

anticipated in the Plan and the agrarian structures in the process of transformation." Although the plan did note the necessity of cooperative farms to overcome the problem of excessively morseled land and to accustom the peasant to modern agricultural methods under state supervision, it did not specify how such action was to be taken or place responsibility for further action.

As the issue of agrarian reform began to gain attention, Hassan II spoke more openly about regulating agriculture. For some time comments centered on the foreign-held land, which provided an issue appropriate to the increasingly bitter politics of the country and meshed smoothly with the parties' concerns over "neocolonialism." In his report to the Istiqlal in April 1963, Al-Fassi dwelt at length on the *colon* land while slipping over the obstacles to agricultural production. Rumors were widespread that the king was considering a sweeping agrarian reform. In the spring Hassan II announced a "total reorganization of agrarian structures by a limitation on property, [and] a redistribution of land."[38] His announcement produced more detailed discussion of agrarian reform, and the next week the Istiqlal published the text of a proposed law.

The proposal was particularly interesting because it was the first detailed program to appear in Morocco, although officials of the Ministry of Agriculture asserted that drafts of such laws had been prepared for several years. The general lines of the law draft were harmonious with the new Moroccan policy of relying more heavily on semipublic corporations and concentrating on irrigated land for increased food production.[39] The political strategy was clever. Concentration on the more highly productive irrigated land would not affect the vast proportion of small peasant proprietors and olive growers on whom the Istiqlal depended for rural support, but would promise to increase yields. The proposal also had the practical advantage of concentrating on the type of land that posed no serious problems of ownership because of the country's long experience in irrigation for Moroccan use. Since the Palace was also trying to extract more aid from France, the strategy postponed the issue of *colon* land, too.

The Moroccan land-reform effort took another halting step in the fall of 1964, when each party proposed its alternatives in a parliamentary

[38] *La Vie Economique*, March 8, 1963. Guedira's early comment appeared in *ibid.*, February 22, 1963, and Al-Fassi's rejoinder in *Al-Istiqlal*, April 21, 1963.
[39] Réforme Foncière," in *Al-Istiqlal*, March 3 and 10, 1963. The regulations are curiously similar to those of the government in the Medjerda Project in Tunisia and the land ceilings are alike. The law was based on a graduated table for recovering a proportion of the income of holdings of over 30 hectares (about 75 acres), depending on the quality of the holding. Where the owner so desired he could give part of his land to the state and apply its value to his contribution. Payment in money was limited to those holding 50 hectares (about 125 acres) or less, which thereby effectively placed a limit on the size of irrigated farms.

debate. The Istiqlal favored limiting irrigated holdings to about 200 acres, and dry farmed holdings to roughly 1,000 acres. The details of the reform were only vaguely spelled out, but would include all *colon* land. The U.N.F.P. produced a detailed draft law, limiting irrigated holdings to 100 acres and dry farming to 500 acres. The proposal would affect all types of land—private, French-held, *habous*, tribal, and state. The proposal of the royalist group under Guedira accepted the more generous limitations of the Istiqlal, but excluded those categories of land closely associated with the Palace. Under Hassan II the government renewed the negotiations that had started in 1959. Late in 1964 the monarch announced that agreement had been reached to repurchase about 500,000 acres of French-owned land or about half the *colon* property. A new government agency was established to manage the transfer, and plans were announced to recover half of the agreed amount over three years[40] tenure and land-distribution policies demonstrates again the common problem of nearly every government in a developing country.

Possibly Tunisia had the strongest case for a sweeping reform because so much of her land was frozen in the framework of traditional and outmoded tenure systems. The fact that land was thereby also a source of influence for traditional elements opposed to the Socialist Destour might be passed off as fortuitous circumstance by those treating politics as a dependent variable. However, the timing of the land-reform effort in the very early phase of the country's reorganization and the energetic measures to concentrate control of released land under Bourguiba suggest that the needs of single-party system were not neglected. The president was so eager to take control of the land that the state acquired larger holdings than it could manage, and, in turn, was forced simply to rent the property until improvements could be made in farming methods. The policy certainly benefited the Socialist Destour, but it is questionable how much was done to improve agricultural production until the party had sufficient resources to embark on a serious, comprehensive program of reconstruction in 1962.

The Pakistan case is complicated by the prerevolutionary progress made in East Pakistan. The complication serves to underscore the extent to which the Ayub regime in fact depended on existing programs and sought to build on earlier achievements. This would be desirable if the earlier Bengali reforms had embodied provisions leading to increased food production and better farming methods. Essentially the same strategy was followed by the military regime in the western wing. The glaring inequality of land distribution and its wasteful exploitation in

[40] The 1964 agreement reveals the deceptive character of figures on French foreign aid. Nearly half the French assistance to Morocco in 1964 went to repay French *colons*. The party views on the agreement are found in *Jeune Afrique*, September 14, 1964. See also *Le Monde*, September 12, 1964, and the *New York Times*, September 19, 1964.

the Punjab had been the subject of historic concern, and had been actively considered since World War II. To a large measure Ayub simply followed through on a generally agreed course of action, which had minimal effect on village life and created minimal disruption in the life of the land aristocracy. The earlier parliamentary regime had been prepared to go much farther. There is no doubt that Ayub caught the imagination of the peasant, but one may question how much was accomplished in the countryside with this initial advantage. As politics at the center became increasingly complex, the Ayub regime turned over the complexities of agricultural reorganization to the bureaucracy, whose past record in the villages was something less than spectacular, and there were indications that new lands were falling into the hands of landlords who had historically dominated rural political life.

The Moroccan experience may reveal the influence of national politics on the development process more dramatically than the other two cases. The reasons for this are self-evident, for the monarchy permitted more criticism than either Ayub or Bourguiba have found useful or desirable. Nevertheless, Mohammed V, and even more forcefully Hassan II set the pattern of the discussion. The Istiqlal, in particular, was reluctant to raise issues that might create complications for the strife-torn nationalist movement, though this could not be avoided once the U.N.F.P. arrived on the scene in 1959, and made the first moves toward recovering *colon* land. The price of the relatively open monarchical system was that ministerial and personal rivalries throve at the expense of constructive social action.

THE PUBLIC CORPORATION AND HUMAN PROBLEMS

All three governments compared in this study have responded with great restraint to the challenge of agricultural reorganization. As in other aspects of the inquiry one must probe beneath the similarity to see how the political systems vary in other aspects of rural reconstruction. The creation of new agencies to do what government apparently is incapable of doing carries important implications for those concerned with the developmental process. The use of the public corporation for development purposes has become a widespread phenomenon in the developing countries, and its political implications deserve more careful examination than it has usually received. The large public agency with liberal government support may well become only another form of arbitrary and distant control in the life of the village populations of Africa and Asia.

Several general characteristics of the public-development agency must be noted in relation to the power structure of the new country. First, the new agency is in many respects very similar to the kind of government that most colonial regimes inspired, and which, in turn, was taken as a model by the new nations. With rare exceptions it preserves the tradition of highly centralized operations and priority for financial accountability. There is, perhaps, even less assurance that the peasant will find means of recourse for grievances. At the same time the public corporation holds obvious attractions for the politician. He can claim that authority is indeed being diffused, but often it is not diffused enough to escape his surveillance and occasional intervention on behalf of friends or pet projects. The political figure also finds it much easier to avoid responsibility for the failure of such an agency, but not too difficult to take credit for possible accomplishments. While no doubt filling important developmental objectives in a strictly material sense, the semipublic corporation may not succeed where government has failed for exactly the same reasons.

Tunisia has had considerable experience in using the semipublic corporation. The country's small size and the relatively small scale of most rural-development projects encouraged reliance on regionally located offices. There are four major public corporations involved in rural development schemes—Medjerda, Enfida, Souassi, and Sidi Bou Zid. The oldest of these is the Office de Mise en Valeur de la Vallée de la Medjerda (O.M.V.V.M.), whose authority extends directly over nearly half the irrigated land in the country and indirectly over the entire river basin of some 500,000 acres. The Protectorate first took an interest in developing the valley in 1946,[41] and a special office to manage development works was established in 1953. Although Tunisian officials have hopes of quadrupling the output of the valley, the project has proved more expensive than anticipated and more recently has been handicapped with salinity problems.

When the office was reorganized by the Tunisian government in 1958, each proprietor was obligated to contribute toward the cost of irrigating his land in proportion to his holdings. Where the landholder had over 50 hectares (about 125 acres) he was obliged to make payment in land held above this limit.[42] Land that is not being fully or properly exploited

---

[41] For a brief account of the early history of the project see Moncef Guen, *La Tunisie Indépendante face à son Economie*, Tunis, Cercle d'Etudes Economiques, 1961, pp. 239-244, and also *Medjerda 1960*, Tunis, O.M.V.V.M., 1960, pp. 5-7. In a speech of June 11, 1959, President Bourguiba acknowledged that 60 per cent of the funds for the project have come from the United States since independence. For additional information on the colonial impact on irrigation in both Morocco and Tunisia, following lines of evaluation similar to those suggested here, see Pierre Marthelot, "Les Implications Humaines de l'Irrigation Moderne en Afrique du Nord," *Annuaire d'Afrique du Nord: 1962*, Paris, Centre National de Recherche Scientifique, 1963, pp. 127-154.

[42] Three basic laws organized the project: Law no. 58-76 of July 9, 1958, reorganized the O.M.V.V.M.; Law no. 58-63 of June 11, 1958, placed the 70,000 hectares developed under the Protectorate under state control; and an order of June 15, 1953, was used to extend supervisory powers over 250,000 hectares in the entire basin. In 1959 the state recovered 86 properties, including 2,884 hectares for cooperative use, and the *Plan Perspectives* called for the recovery of 4,700 hectares in 1960.

can be seized by the office, including grants made in newly opened regions. The O.M.V.V.M. seeks to allocate some 12,000 additional acres of irrigated farmland each year, but has had some difficulty finding a sufficient number of skilled farmers to enable the full exploitation of the presently available water. When the 1958 law was passed many proprietors chose to leave rather than to submit to increased government controls. In some cases farmers were transplanted from other areas. To demonstrate the benefits of intensive agriculture the party has undertaken the operation of one group of lots using party youth. Nevertheless, there have been numerous complaints against the arbitrary procedures of the O.M.V.V.M., though these grievances may easily have been inspired by the rigors of more regular farming methods required by the office. Even the mobilizing energies of the Socialist Destour have not always been sufficient to overcome the fears created in a rural-modernization program.

The remaining offices are located in the semiarid reaches of the center and south. The Enfida office has the longest history of all the rural development agencies, dating from 1877 when an Ottoman official sold his holding of some 250,000 acres to the Société Marseillaise.[43] Much of the estate was too barren to cultivate, but the arable lands became one of the richest olive-producing regions in Tunisia. Shortly before France granted Tunisian autonomy the French company agreed to sell most of the land back to the Tunisian government, but kept about 12,000 acres of the best land. The Enfida office was established in February 1954, and the French company refused to sell any of more desirable land until after independence. The first but by no means the most difficult obstacle to profitable exploitation of the newly acquired land was the return of the families who had been forced off their property some hundred years earlier.[44]

Because the tasks of improving the soil and initiating cultivation are more difficult at Enfida than at Medjerda, there is more emphasis on cooperative effort. The model villages built at Medjerda have sometimes been left vacant, the small farmer preferring his own, less expensive hut.[45] At Enfida the government is working with many Tunisians who

[43] Habib Bourguiba, "Le Discours de l'Enfida," Tunis, Secretary of State for Information and Touring, 1959. The history of the Enfida property suggests how the premature reformer may do injury. The property was confiscated by the bey from rebellious tribesmen in 1841 and 1850, later to be given to Khereddine for his services in the early, abortive attempts to modernize Tunisia. When Khereddine was driven out of Tunisia in 1878 he sold his estate to the Société Marseillaise.

[44] At Enfida, as with several land-reform projects around Kairouan, the original owners of the land, though absent for a hundred years or more, often returned to submit their claims when the state became owner. In Kairouan feelings ran so high that serious riots broke out on several occasions.

[45] The Medjerda Office was working under considerably more pressure because

have never been fixed on the soil, and where the insecurity of the climate makes the monetary burdens of accepting a lot in the project seem less onerous. The agency has been assisted by United Nations experts in training village workers,[46] most of whom double as party organizers in the new villages. Housing subsidies have been provided for the villagers who previously rented land on the estate, and four model villages have been created.

The Enfida and Medjerda agencies are limited in size and in the number of persons they can introduce to modern agriculture. The other two offices, Souassi and Sidi Bou Zid, cover much larger areas, most of it composed of collective land nationalized under the procedures discussed above. Though located in even more precarious climates (Sfax and Gafsa, respectively) than the other two offices, they are an essential part of the Socialist Destour's aim to relieve the poverty of the south and central regions. Furthermore, they are the pilot projects for the future exploitation of the vast collective lands in Tunisia and serve as experiments in the settling of nomadic peoples on the soil. The Souassi and the Sidi Bou Zid domains each extend over 500,000 acres, though only small parts have been developed thus far. The Three Year Plan firmly cautions that the ultimate goal must be to create viable communities, and that "all action in physical areas should be accompanied with equally resolved action in human areas."[47] For the present it is difficult to foresee the future of these two projects, for the first villages in the area are very new and remain heavily dependent on the government for subsidies and technical assistance.

Given the central control of land, the convenience of the regional development agency is obvious. The state is able to retain title to the holdings while the conversion to more intensive farming methods is made. Budgeting and planning is greatly facilitated. The development corporation is especially well suited to the single-party system. The Socialist Destour provincial committees can be called upon to support and to encourage the new enterprises, and it is easy for locally rooted figures of national importance to make periodic visits to bring at-

---

of the large investment that had already been made, and also because of unanticipated obstacles that appeared as the project advanced. Uncultivated, potentially irrigable land represents a great loss once the basic installations have been made, and new lots are available in relatively large quantity as work proceeds. Enfida was planned from the beginning by Tunisians, and since it was dry farming, new areas could be opened up for exploitation as funds and occupants could be found.

[46] The Enfida project appears to be one of the few projects in North Africa where community-development methods have been successfully practiced. With the assistance of the United Nations "polyvalent" workers were trained to supervise new villages. See *La Mise en Valeur de l'Enfida et ses Goulots d'Etranglement*, Tunis, Office de l'Enfida, 1961, pp. 33-54.

[47] *Plan Triennal, 1962-1964*, Tunis, Secretary of State for Planning and Finance, 1961, p. 30.

tention to the efforts of the government and the party. Needless to add, the Tunisians have decided advantages in selecting and placing individuals in such a way as to serve the interest of both the party and the nation.

As in the case of land reform, Morocco has been much slower in creating rural-development agencies than Tunisia and Pakistan. Despite the repeated advice on the necessity for regional development from both Moroccan and foreign advisers,[48] the monarchy has lost valuable time, and, no doubt, even more valuable human resources, while equivocating over the organization of public corporations with agrarian functions. The roots of the conflict have a long history in the Protectorate administration, where the rivalries of the agricultural and interior services were never resolved. Even within the agricultural service there were controversies between the rual extension office (*vulgarisation*) and the rural engineering service (*génie rural*). The fact that the monarchy would seem better suited than other forms of government for the resolution of these rivalries makes their continuation in independent Morocco more curious.

The Moroccans have made two massive assaults on rural modernization, using large public corporations. The first of these date from the Protectorate, the Secteurs de Modernisation du Paysannat (S.M.P.).[49] After independence the S.M.P. stations were transformed into the Centres des Travaux Agricoles (C.T.A.) with little modification. However, as the country's agricultural problems became more pressing, there was continued discussion of how these organizations, which tended to become simply machine stations for wealthy Moroccan and European farmers, could be used in the rural-mobilization effort. The first effort to establish popular contact having both social and agricultural effects was the Operation Labour, which sought to combine the efficiency of massive cultivation methods with voluntary adaptation of improved methods among the peasants.

After a prolonged period of bureaucratic warfare and political sparring, the government decided to divide the country into those areas suit-

[48] Pressure for regional planning has a preindependence history, and it appears that the Protectorate shared the monarchy's apprehension for decentralization. See Frédéric Brémard, *L'Organisation Régionale au Maroc*, Rabat, Institute for Advanced Studies, 1949, pp. 158-165.

[49] Machine-tractor stations were tried out in Tunisia, but did not lend themselves to the structure of the rural economy. Machines were better exploited through the regional offices. In 1959 the few stations that existed were reorganized. "Loi no. 59-81 du juillet 1959 (15 moharrem 1379), portant création et organisation d'un Office National de Motoculture et de Mise en Valeur Agricole," *Journal Officiel de la Tunisie*, July 24, 1959, pp. 285-287. For additional information on early French efforts to reorganize Moroccan agriculture see Albert Guillaume, *L'Evolution Economique de la Société Rurale Marocaine*, Paris, Librairie Générale de Droit et du Jurisprudence, 1947, especially pp. 77-116 on rural credit and pp. 117-130 on the S.M.P.

able for dry and irrigated farming, and to establish a superagency to deal with the exploitation of each area. The fact that the independent government took so long to learn from the errors of the Protectorate, and, to some extent, to undo limitations intentionally placed on rural modernization, suggests how difficult the political reorientation of a developing country may be despite the symbolic achievement of independence. The new agencies, the Office National de Modernisation Rurale (O.N.M.R.) and the Office National d'Irrigation (O.N.I.), must still overcome the political restraints that have long handicapped rural modernization, and must face the same problems of gaining the peasants' confidence. Indeed, their problems are undoubtedly compounded by the earlier failures and injustices at the village level.

The early experiment in alerting the peasant to the possibilities of modern agricultural methods was part of the postwar impulse, supported by the brief epoch of effective, liberal government in Paris, to enlighten North Africa.[50] Conceived by Jacques Berque and Julien Couleau, the S.M.P. were organized on the principle that a multiple impact in the lives of the peasants would bring about desired results in his adaptation to modern life. The impact was not to be ruthless, however, and there originally were provisions for literacy programs, primary schools, and rural dispensaries to convey to the *fellah* the variety of benefits awaiting the Moroccan who would increase his farm production and contribute to the savings needed for rural modernization. In Berque's words, "Progress will be total, or it will not be." Important as the initial concept is, it remains to be seen if the S.M.P. became an appropriate vehicle to convey the meaning of modern agriculture to the mass of underprivileged Moroccan farmers and landless.

The machine-tractor stations were looked upon with increasing suspicion by conservative elements in the Protectorate administration, who were virtually in control of Morocco after 1951. Although the S.M.P.'s continued to perform important services in helping the more prosperous farmer get credit, mechanical assistance, and expert advice, the more ambitious social purpose of the stations was gradually forgotten. Eventually the S.M.P.'s were reduced "progressively to the role of service-stations performing work as needed for the middle-sized peasant.[51] Even under the most favorable circumstances the S.M.P.'s were

[50] For the early history of the S.M.P. see P. Marthelot, "Histoire et réalité de la modernisation du monde rural au Maroc," *Tiers Monde*, vol. 2, no. 6, April-June 1961, pp. 144-146; J. Célérier, "La modernisation du paysannat marocain," *Revue Géographique du Maroc*, 1947, pp. 3-29; and J. Berque and J. Couleau, "Vers la modernisation du fellah marocain," *Bulletin Economique et Sociale du Maroc*, no. 26, July 1945, pp. 18-26.

[51] Oved, *Tiers Monde, op.cit.*, p. 368. The problem was clearly foreseen by the early organizers of the S.M.P. See Yves Barennes, *La Modernisation Rurale au Maroc*, Paris, Librairie Générale de Droit et du Jurisprudence, 1948, and also Marc Bonnefous, *Perspective de l'Agriculture Marocaine*, Rabat, Institute for Advanced Studies, 1959.

unsuitable for programs extending beyond the partially commercialized sector of Moroccan agriculture, which included about a million acres of Moroccan-owned land (of which only two thirds was cultivated by machine). With independence there was virtually no change in their operation and little was done to relieve the rivalry between the services of the Ministry of Agriculture and the machine stations. As an instrument of broad impact they were further impaired when the few remaining social and educational facilities under the old S.M.P. were assigned to the specialized ministries concerned shortly after independence.

The number of C.T.A. expanded from 57 in 1955 to 108 in 1962, but the possibility of their having effect at the local level was further complicated as other programs aimed at the village were discussed. As the opportunities for a multiple impact on village life grew, effective action within the government became more difficult. The notion that the C.T.A. should be operated on a strict economic basis paralyzed efforts to have broader effects, and the C.T.A. "appeared in eyes of the *fellahs,* not as their device, but as one of several grand exploitations . . . confused with the administrative services . . . [and] often proposing divergent conception."[52] In the absence of clear agreement within the government the Ministries of Agriculture and National Economy began to cast about for a program that might enable the government to have a new kind of impact on the peasant. The basic idea of the new scheme, Operation Labour, was in many ways only an exaggeration of the C.T.A. experiment, and it is curious in retrospect to see the new Moroccan leaders embarking on a program that simply magnified the shortcomings of the earlier experience.

Because few projects to affect agricultural production have been undertaken on the scale of Operation Labour, the scheme merits special attention. In many respects it reflects a new country's eagerness to find spectacular and massive solutions to the highly individualized obstacles to development, although it is difficult to imagine either Tunisia or Pakistan embarking on so ambitious a program without more experimentation. The project involved the purchase of over 1,000 tractors and additional farm machinery which was to be used on consolidated lots of 400 hectares or 1,000 acres, though this optimum division of cultivation units was seldom achieved. The plan depended on the coordinated action of the Ministries of Agriculture and the Interior in order to persuade the peasants temporarily to remove the stones and paths marking the borders of their plots, which wasted large amounts of fertile land. In the first year of operations, 1957-1958, fertilizer was distributed gratuitously to the peasants working smaller tracts, and improved seed was made available at reduced cost. The machines returned

52 Marthelot, *Tiers Monde, op.cit.,* p. 147.

again in the late summer to reap the main crop and to plant cover crops. Leaving aside the more technical question of the economic feasibility of the scheme,[53] we can see that there were a multitude of problems in getting the villagers' cooperation, as has been suggested in the decline of cultivated areas given in Table VII.

TABLE VII

Areas Cultivated by Operation Labour (1957-1961)[a]

Year	Area (thousand acres)
1957-1958	394
1958-1959	751
1959-1960	481
1960-1961	400
1961-1962[b]	250

[a] Figures for 1957-1960 taken from Mohammed Fadli, *L'Operation Labour*, Rabat, Centre d'Etude du Développement Economique et Social, 1961, p. 26; figures for 1960-1962 based on interviews with C.T.A. headquarters officials. Slightly different figures are used by J. Le Coz, "L'Operation Labour au Maroc: tracteur et sous développement," *Méditerranée*, vol. 2, no. 3, July-September 1961, pp. 3-34.

[b] The 1961-1962 figure shows an additional decline because areas formerly under the C.T.A. were being transferred to the new National Irrigation Office. The total amount cultivated was probably close to the 1960-1961 figure.

The use of fertilizer was a key aspect of the scheme. In the second year of the program the *fellahs* were asked to pay for fertilizer, and many discontinued its use. In some cases fertilizer was simply left abandoned at delivery points near the fields because the peasants were not accustomed to its use, or suspected the ultimate intentions of the authorities. Without the regular use of fertilizer, of course, the cultivated areas failed to achieve their maximum yield and many small farmers were unnecessarily disappointed. Machine cultivation could only reach maximum effectiveness by the repeated cultivation of the same fields over several years. In many instances the participating farmers changed from one year to the next. The plan was clearly designed to make optimum use of very limited numbers of rural agents and monitors, who were fully occupied keeping land records and expense accounts. Very little was done, therefore, to keep the farmers from engaging in their usual habit of opening cultivated fields to livestock after the harvest and destroying much of the forage that should have been plowed back into the fields.

[53] See F. Clerc, "Rentabilité de l'Operation-Labour," *Bulletin Economique et Sociale du Maroc*, no. 82, 1959, pp. 105-172. Roughly, the cost of full cultivation for both cash and cover crops was 6,000 francs per hectare, of which peasants having under five hectares were charged 5,000 francs.

In some cases the mechanical plows were used without proper evaluation of the soil, and excessively deep plowing contributed to land erosion or covered topsoil. Without close supervision it was difficult to encourage proper crop rotation, which remained virtually impossible on the small, subsistence holdings. In areas where *khammes* farming prevailed, the tenants quite rightly saw that modern methods would eventually eliminate their livelihood, and they resisted land consolidation even more fiercely than the private farmer. Although adjusted in subsequent years, the prices initially made no allowance for the size of the harvest, and often left the peasant in greater debt than he would have been under normal conditions. Needless to add, being in debt to the government and subject to the local *caid* was more threatening than the much less arbitrary control of the local moneylender, whose excessive rate of interest was moderated by his inability to send the farmer to prison. These are only some of the obstacles that plagued the Operation Labour,[54] and greatly reduced both its agricultural and human effectiveness.

The success the program achieved was in no small measure due to the enthusiastic support given by Mohammed V, who visited the peasants in the fields and mounted the tractors in working clothes. He gave speeches in central points, assuring the *fellah* that the program was "in no way a threat to private property and presented the advantage of creating among the cultivators the spirit of cooperation and collaboration for the common interest."[55] The essential human vehicle for the program was the *comité de gestion*, which was supposed to be organized for each bloc of roughly 1,000 acres. If the committees had been the expression of more determined interest or had been used to build on the results of the initial experience, they might have had important effects in the modernization of the countryside. However, they were frequently appointed by the local *caid* and seldom received sustained assistance from the overburdened machine station, which was the only source of skilled technical advice. There were many reports of arbitrary organization by the local authorities, and in some cases the use of fertilizer, credit, et cetera, to favor the friends of the local official. The most careful study of the program concludes that the committees were "insignificant . . . often intervening only for the purpose of personal interest."[56]

[54] The problems of Operation Labour are most thoroughly analyzed in Mohammed Fadli, *L'Operation Labour*, Rabat, Centre d'Etude du Développement Economique et Social, 1961. See also Oved, *Tiers Monde, op.cit.*, pp. 373-375, and J. Le Coz, "L'Operation-Labour au Maroc: tracteur et sous-développement," *Mediterranée*, xv, 2, no. 3, July-September 1961, pp. 3-34.

[55] All the king's speeches on the occasion appear in *Operation Labour*, Rabat, Ministry of Agriculture, 1957. The quote is from the Sidi Hajjaj address.

[56] Fadli, *op.cit.*, p. 31. More political background on the *comités de gestion* can be found in the author's *Political Change in Morocco*, Princeton, Princeton University Press, 1961, pp. 382-384.

RESPONSES TO RURAL RECONSTRUCTION

The multiple human errors of Operation Labour serve as important instruction on the difficulties of extending the developmental process to the dormant rural population. It is not difficult to grasp the outlook of the small peasant as his morsels of land are consolidated and the machines swiftly pass over the new blocs of land. For him "a mound of earth or a clump of cactus, the work of many years, constitutes the sole security. . . . What will happen to his plot of ground when these limits disappear? . . . The tractor passes like a sponge on a puzzle made of small parcels in order to start an immense public project."[57] Another observer noted that "above all it did not touch the dimensions of property nor the dimensions of parcels. It is neither an agrarian reform, nor a reform of tenure, and, in addition, the enthusiasm was not easily supported, where it existed, because there was no change."[58] So long as the government could envisage mobilizing the villagers only through such impersonal, centralized programs as Operation Labour, there could be only mixed results and, in many cases, only further resentment and suspicion of the arbitrary hand of government.

Interest in fully exploiting irrigable land stems from the Five Year Plan. Although its comments on the future of the C.T.A. and "agricultural" (not "agrarian") reform were sketchy at best, there was a large section devoted to the organization of a new irrigation agency.[59] Irrigation does not have the primordial importance for the two North African countries that it has for Pakistan, but the ample water supplies of the Middle Atlas mountains were profitably exploited by the European farmers. In the Doukkala region and in the south there are numerous irrigated farms operated by Moroccans. The exploitation of irrigated lands, especially in the Beni Amir region, was poorly managed, and produced such severe abuses that much of the land went uncultivated. Figures vary on how much irrigated land was being effectively cultivated, but it seems that no more than 150,000 acres of well over a million acres of irrigable land were being used in 1958.[60]

---

[57] Fadli, *op.cit.*, p. 51.

[58] Oved, "Note sur le récente évolution économique du Maroc, 1949-1958," *op.cit.*, p. 72, and P. Marthélot, "Les expériences marocaines dans le domaine rural jusque l'indépendance," *Réforme Agraire au Maghreb*, *op.cit.*, pp. 80-81. An even more critical commentary, influenced in part by the writer's ideological convictions, was René Dumont, "Le Maroc doit apprendre à mériter ses tracteurs," *Terres Vivantes*, Paris, Plon, 1961, pp. 184-199.

[59] *Plan Quinquennal*, *op.cit.*, pp. 117-137, provided detailed cost estimates, draft laws, and organizational charts. Nothing comparable was provided in the plan concerning the rest of Moroccan agriculture.

[60] The regional breakdown can be found in *Tableaux Economiques du Maroc 1915-1959*, Rabat, Division for Economic Coordination and the Plan, Ministry of the National Economy, 1960, p. 50. The author was told on several occasions that it was not unusual for the local clan or tribal elder to remain in the mountains supervising the care of the flocks, while the excess population of the tribe was sent off to a "precarious" and less honorable existence on irrigated fields.

The economic attractions of intensive, irrigated farming are self-evident. The farm can produce two, and sometimes three, crops a year of products that are considerably more valuable than the prevailing cereal culture of most developing countries. Irrigation holds promise of relieving the chronic underemployment of the countryside, and may help stem the flow of the excess population to cities, where the costs of integrating them into modern life increase precipitously. As a rule of thumb, a farmer can work up to 200 days a year on irrigated land as opposed to the sixty or so days involved in dry farming; it is not unusual to multiply the monetary value of the crops by ten. The ancillary benefits derived from improved commercialization of agricultural commodities, light industry to process farm products, improved nourishment, and higher savings are difficult to calculate.

Although the law establishing O.N.I. appeared in the fall of 1960,[61] the new agency had done little more than organize its central offices two years later. The new office had many advantages over the old public agencies managing irrigated land. O.N.I. was able to hire (and presumably fire) foreign technical and professional staff freely, and at wages that would attract talented people. Moreover, the new office was generously financed; it was allocated approximately twelve million dollars in 1961 and eighteen million in 1962. In 1962 O.N.I. reportedly had 7,000 employees, nearly three times the staff of the Ministry of Agriculture. However, the new agency had considerable difficulty getting started, and its first director, though talented and imaginative, was not a good administrator. Early in 1963 he resigned in a dispute over the operation of a sugar-beet factory financed under the plans of O.N.I. for irrigated lands in the Gharb.[62]

As a development agency O.N.I. will have authority over roughly five million acres of the most fertile and productive land in Morocco. The new office faces some difficult obstacles in undoing the resentment accumulated in dealing with government officials under the previous organization. In Beni Mellal province, where the government has tried to encourage cotton production, the old office would sometimes seize the

[61] "Dahir no. 1-59-401 du 11 rebia I 1380 (3 septembre 1960) portant création de l'Office National des irrigations," *Bulletin Officiel du Maroc*, September 16, 1960, pp. 1,697-1,699. The ministerial struggle involved in establishing O.N.I. is indicated by the variety of offices merged in the new agency: thirty C.T.A. (roughly a fourth of the existing machine stations), the Irrigation Offices of Beni Amir and Beni Moussa, the Génie Rural Services in the affected areas from the Ministry of Agriculture, the Service Hydraulique from the Ministry of Public Works, and the Bureau d'Etudes Hydrogéologiques from the Bureau of Mines. See *La Vie Economique*, November 21, 1961.

[62] *Al-Istiqlal*, January 9, 1963. Tahiri was an Istiqlal militant, and no doubt the resignation of the Istiqlal ministers early in January contributed to his undesirability. For a summary of the early work of O.N.I. see J. Brunet, "L'Office National des Irrigations au Maroc: Deux Ans d'Experience," *Annuaire d'Afrique du Nord: 1962*, Paris, Centre National de Recherche Scientifique, 1963, pp. 249-268.

crop without providing an account for the farmer. Several farmers have complained that they have received no billing for water or supplies for two or three years; in other cases peasants have traveled thirty to forty miles to spend the day waiting outside an official's office in order to get the simplest information on their financial status. Possibly the most demoralizing experiences have been incidents where *colon* farmers have been able to receive preferential treatment, and in some instances less expensive assistance. "The peasant remained alone with himself, as before, but he found himself even more enmeshed in a network of constraints."[63]

Once the C.T.A. were virtually confined to areas suitable for dry farming, it was natural to augment their activity in a similar fashion, partly to improve dry-farming methods and partly to reconcile farmers whose lands would not benefit from the comparatively lavish resources of O.N.I. For these reasons the O.N.M.R. was established early in 1962, composed of the C.T.A. not merged in the new irrigation office. The new organization[64] emerged late in 1962, and placed more emphasis on rural-extension and improvement efforts than had the old agency. In addition to provincial headquarters there were three regional offices to coordinate work in depressed areas such as the Rif. The subsidy of two million dollars provided the old C.T.A. in 1961 was increased to nearly five million in 1962. On the whole, the O.N.M.R. appeared more cognizant of the problems of making contact with the villager than did the O.N.I.

The political significance of the Moroccan experience, as in the other cases involved in the inquiry, can be found on two levels. On the one hand, there is considerable evidence on the monarchical system at work. Although the style of governing under Mohammed V and Hassan II differs greatly, neither was particularly successful in untangling the rivalries of the ministries and independent agencies working in the countryside. As a result, the social and political impact at the local level was minimized. The gap between the spiritual authority of the monarch and the remote local economy could be closed only by modifying political patterns at both levels. Important as the new corporations and programs were in marshaling resources where they might have impact, the psychological links between the *douar* and the *maghzen* were essen-

[63] Yves Goussault, *Problèmes d'Animation dans le Périmetre Irrigué du Tadla,* Rabat, Institute de Recherche et d'Application des Methodes pour Développement (IRAM), 1961, p. 39.

[64] The law was promulgated on January 21, 1962. In interviews with officials of the C.T.A. in Rabat and in the field it appeared that they were aware of the need to make successful contact with smaller peasants, but not entirely clear how they intended to go about it. Organization chart appears in *La Vie Economique,* November 16, 1962. The C.T.A.-O.N.M.R. was also plagued with problems of finding a suitable director. In 1963 Messaoudi, the first director of Promotion Nationale, was appointed.

tially unchanged. Morocco was not alone in facing the dilemma of how to diffuse authority as development took place, but faced problems peculiar to the monarch's orientation to the development process. The Pakistan example demonstrates how a country with a presumably much more flexible form of government, and more pressing agrarian problems, had difficulties as great or greater than Morocco.

In West Pakistan the cultivated land is divided roughly equally between the irrigated Punjab and Sind regions, one of the largest irrigated areas in the world and also one of the least productive, and the dry farming and rangeland areas surrounding the irrigated portion. Two factors have contributed to the deterioration of the irrigated river basin. The British installations were designed, first, to cover the maximum acreage possible because less water was being utilized in the nineteenth century and investment funds were limited. Since then demographic pressures have forced the Punjabi farmer, and to a lesser extent the Sindi farmer, to spread the water even more thinly over larger areas by neglecting to leave a proportion of his fields fallow. The effect has been to raise the water level until approximately half the irrigated area, ten million acres, have become seriously waterlogged. An additional complication is that the highly saline soil was cultivable only so long as the water level kept the salts below root level. Two generations of irrigation have brought the salt to the surface and now destroy several hundred thousand acres of valuable farmland yearly.

Obviously massive measures must be taken quickly. The intricate structure of wells to flush the soils and improved drainage to control waterlogging are clearly beyond the capability of the peasant. Two large projects are already under way and will not concern this study directly. The Indus Valley scheme[65] is designed to provide better control of the watershed for both India and Pakistan, to improve drainage, and to increase power supplies needed to operate the thousands of pumps to be installed to reduce salinity. The Water and Power Development Authority[66] (WAPDA) has been given special funds and authority to improve power production and power distribution, and is an integral part of the over-all program. However, both these enterprises are new and,

[65] The Indus Basin Development Fund Agreement was signed on September 19, 1960, and is concerned largely with the economic infrastructure for better use of the water available to Pakistan and India. It will, therefore, not be elaborated on here, although considerable materials are available from the I.B.R.D.

[66] Pakistan has established a WAPDA for each wing, although the West Pakistan WAPDA got started first. These two agencies are concerned with all aspects of power production and distribution, including rural electrification. The plans to install thousands of pumps depend on increased electric power in rural areas. In some areas the WAPDA's have found themselves blocked by local companies and local disinterest. For example, a WAPDA power line had linked Comilla with the main grid and cheaper power for a year when the author visited there, but local disputes prevented attaching the line to the local network.

as is noted in the Food and Agriculture Commission report, "no organization yet exists to tell farmers what to do, to finance, where necessary, the field drains and to see that they do it."[67] In the absence of individual contact in the field the massive effort being made by the corporations concerned with agricultural infrastructure may be dissipated at the most critical point in the transformation of the rural economy.

The problems of East Pakistan are hardly less complex. With ground parched for six months of the year and subjected to torrential rain the other six months, the East Bengali peasant has been reduced to extracting a minimal existence from the soil. Although the soil is extremely fertile and water supply is plentiful in most places, less than a third of the region is double-cropped. Animals and men compete for nourishment in the overcrowded areas, so that pastures are inadequate and animals are too weak to provide either meat or power. The chronic poverty of the peasant forces him to sell his crop immediately at depressed prices to agents who virtually monopolize grain storage and handling, often selling the same rice back to the farmer at high prices during the dry season. Markets are totally unregulated, and there is no uniform standard of weights and measures and no official system of grading commodities.

Perhaps the greatest service of the Food and Agriculture Commission was that it spoke with great prestige on the attitudinal problems that had separated government from the villager. Noting "how very recent is the sense of urgency for any increased agricultural production," the report went on to urge government officers to "overcome attitudes arising from years of neglect and in part contempt of agriculture." The landlord and businessman were equally at fault in ignoring the need for new leadership and investment, so that "the farmer has come to be looked down on as an illiterate of little importance to the country's economy. Living at a mere subsistence level his resultant apathy has become identified with idleness, while his inability to take any risks has increased his conservatism and developed an attitude of complete dependence on government for any innovating action."[68]

After evaluating the various governmental agencies operating in the countryside, the commission went on to recommend the establishment of an Agricultural Development Corporation (A.D.C.) for each wing. The new organizations should be "comprehensive enough to be a force in the highest counsels in the nation, should have resources which permit the development of a program matching the immensity of the problem and flexibility enough to meet the variations inherent in the panorama of Pakistan's agriculture."[69] The basic concept of the proposal

---

[67] *F&AC Report, op.cit.*, p. 176.
[68] *Ibid.*, pp. 150-151.
[69] *Ibid.*, p. 213. The purpose and organization of the A.D.C.'s is laid out in

was that an integrated, forceful effort must be made to incorporate the farmer in modern life. The main administrative device would be the A.D.C.'s supply organization, which would produce, procure, and transport seeds, fertilizers, plan-protection materials, and farm implements to the entire country. Associated with the effort toward commercialization of farming is the other major operating wing for field activities, responsible for extending the use of credit, improved irrigation management, soil conservation and reclamation, increased crop rotation, and better marketing.

The commission is specific on the need to increase both the quantity and quality of staff working in the field—a problem that will be discussed further in the following chapter. The key field representative will be the project director, whose pay and status compares with that of the district officer. Rather than see the new agencies' resources dissipated, the report calls for the establishment of project areas similar to the old development areas of Village AID. Beneath the project director there are to be union agents, similar to the rural-extension agents used in part of Pakistan and familiar to many rural-development programs. The ultimate goal of the A.D.C. would be to persuade farmers to submit their lands to joint management. The report is emphatic in stating that this must be accomplished voluntarily, possibly using as test areas the 200 or so villages now organized on cooperative lines in the Punjab and the new irrigated lands being made available under the Ghulam Mohammed Barrage project.

The Ayub government moved quickly to put the Food and Agricultural Commission report into effect, although there were some delays in finding a high civil servant with sufficient stature to accept so difficult a task. The West Pakistan A.D.C. was established in September 1961, and the East Pakistan A.D.C. in October 1961. Three months later in West Pakistan the departments of agriculture, forestry, irrigation, animal husbandry, and cooperatives were disbanded at the provincial level and decentralized to divisional and district offices. Early in 1962 the Minister of Food and Agriculture, Lieutenant General Shaikh, announced a new policy for the encouragement of cooperative farming among small farmers. Preference in extending credit, the sale of state land, and the procurement of machinery was to be given to farmers prepared to establish joint management. Small landholders declining to accept measures for the improved use of land and water would be penalized. Though it is early to measure the results of the Pakistani effort in rural modernization, there is evidence that the govern-

---

great detail in *ibid.*, ch. 7, pp. 214-255. The commission was fully aware of the jurisdictional disputes that might plague such an organization and gives full attention to the role of local officials, related ministries, and the Basic Democracies program.

ment was seriously pursuing the aims set down by the Food and Agriculture Commission.[70]

The same trend toward increasing reliance on public corporations in agricultural development can be seen in all three countries, and has political implications that merit considerably more study. In Pakistan the reorganization of the central government, followed by the creation of the A.D.C.'s and the decentralization of provincial departments, left the governmental agricultural services with little more than planning and limited-service functions in seed production, breeding, and cooperative management. Similarly in Morocco the Ministry of Agriculture has been virtually divested of responsibility for direct contact with villagers through the *génie rural* and *vulgarisation,* whose activities will be carried on locally through the projects of O.N.I. and O.N.M.R. In Tunisia the new trend in agricultural organization has led to the creation of regional commissioners directly under the Secretary of State for Agriculture, who will have special powers in agricultural planning and improvement under the impulse of the Three Year Plan.[71] Their main interest will be to focus government efforts on the regional projects of Medjerda, Enfida, Souassi, and Sidi Bou Zid, and to assist in the creation of more coordinated, intensive farming schemes.

Undisputed as the priority placed on agriculture may be, the question remains whether or not the early steps toward mobilizing the rural population may have significant impact in integrating the peasant into the political and social system of the developing country. Delay and procrastination have characterized the approach to land reform in all three regimes. Intricate as the problems of land reform may be, the various approaches to land redistribution suggest how remote are the considerations of the social and political impact on the local level in most new governments. Unless the peasant can be persuaded that such changes are meaningful to him as well as to the over-all benefit of the country, agricultural reorganization through land reform is unlikely to have sustained effect in narrowing the gap between authority and village, as well as in increasing agricultural productivity.

The transformation of the peasant and the integration of local life with national affairs is equally crucial in the establishment of new organizations to provide essential services to the villager. Again, it can be seen that all three regimes have been slow to respond to the full complexity of

[70] On the cooperatives see *Dawn,* February 18, 1963. The efforts of the government appeared to have highly beneficial results in 1963-1964, when the Pakistani government exported a million tons of rice to India and was able to curtail sharply imports of American wheat. The sluggishness of the A.D.C.'s was discouraged by new regulations concerning the paying of commissions at fixed prices to independent distributors of agricultural supplies, seed, and fertilizer.

[71] Outlined in *La Presse,* April 5, 1963. The regional headquarters for the north, west, central, and south will be Tunis, Le Kef, Sousse, and Sfax, respectively.

mobilizing the rural populace. The regional agencies created in Tunisia have found it difficult to build local organizations without jeopardizing single-party supervision. The national agencies of the Moroccan monarchy have become entangled in feuds and rivalries at the center, while the Pakistan regime has placed responsibility in service-type public corporations. Each has encountered obstacles characteristic of the regime: the need to evade professional and bureaucratic stagnation in Pakistan, the imposition of national political ambiguities in rural planning in Morocco, and the hesitance to expand beyond the supervisory capacities of the single party in Tunisia.

The continuing interdependence of the political process and development is illustrated in the sporadic and incomplete efforts of the three regimes. From a political viewpoint it is apparent that the early concessions in land and organizational reforms do little to bring the villager into close contact with the government, and, in some ways, depend heavily on devices used by colonial administrations to assure central control. Thus Bouabid has wondered if the foreign *colon* is being removed only to be replaced by "another *colon*, but of Moroccan nationality . . . an agrarian feudal class which becomes an economic power by means of state funds."[72] The same theme has appeared in Bourguiba's speeches,[73] and more recently in Ayub's concern for more just distribution of not only the output but also the facilities for development. The inextricable meshing of opportunities and material gain in the developmental process provides the basis for political entrenchment as well as political adaptation.

[72] *Al-Machahid*, October 1961.
[73] *La Presse*, March 2, 1963.

CHAPTER 7

SELF-INTEREST AND NATIONAL
INTEREST IN THE VILLAGE

THE DEVELOPMENTAL process has contributed to the alienation of the rural mass in nearly every country of Africa and Asia. The colonial powers are sometimes blamed for the disproportionate stress placed on industry and commerce during the preindependence period, but the same stress can be detected in the planning policies of most new countries. The separation of the rural and urban communities is more than an economic division; indeed, one perceptive writer on North Africa has suggested that the difference may be one of "civilizations."[1] The new political leaders are mostly products of universities in Paris, London, and New York. While they may object to the segmentation of their economies, and sometimes exploit consequent injustices to good political advantage, it seems doubtful if they have grasped how profound a difference exists between the village and the city, much less the heroic effort that will be needed to close the gap.

Most governments of developing countries have unquestioningly accepted Western industrial methods. In this there has been little choice, but the pattern of reliance on social and political institutions, assuming an articulate, responsive population, is obviously ill-suited to the village problems of Africa and Asia. In some respects the Westerner is still better qualified to analyze the developmental obstacles of the new country, because the contrast of village and modern life strikes him so vividly. To the nationalist leader of the developing country, the gap between town and country may become simply a fact of life, and the problem of integration may become only an ill-defined ultimate goal, rather than a question demanding careful and constant consideration.

Integration is a constant problem of every society, and new social devices are being created in every society in response to new challenges to a harmonious and productive social order.[2] But the issues facing most industrial nations today—unemployment due to automation, conflict over racial and religious minorities, and the insecurity created in metropolitan life—are of a different order. The political system of the developed country is integrated in the sense that a common cognitive

---

[1] P. Marthelot, "Juxtaposition en Tunisie d'une économie traditionnelle et d'une économie moderne," *I.B.L.A.*, vol. 18, no. 4, 1955, pp. 481-501.

[2] Those concerned lest the mention of social order indicates unwarranted commitment to conservatively oriented social theory should be cautioned here that the author has purposefully tried to avoid the not too fruitful controversy over the latent meaning of social theory in order to focus attention on political participation in the development process. The tendency of the existing regimes to be extremely cautious in making such experiments has been frequently underscored.

framework exists despite the new challenges. The United States, for example, knows what should be done about integrating Negroes into American society, and a variety of specific actions have been undertaken to ameliorate the problem. The government of the developing country, in contrast, has seldom arrived at the point where it has some idea of what should be done, except in the simple, deceptive sense of making the peasant prosperous. But prosperity is no panacea, and certainly no substitute for a population able to attack social questions without the arbitrary intervention of authority or the massive subsidy to sooth the neglected parties.

The structure of integration in the developed society is undefined, and it is by virtue of its being undefinable that the individual responses can be forged into effective social action. It is quite possible that the extraordinary innovative quality of industrial societies is, in part, derived from the ambiguities surrounding the structure of integration. There is increasing evidence that this is indeed the case in political life.[3] The leader of the developing country has almost always been educated in societies where self-equilibrating and self-adjusting processes were at work. His notion of a modern society may very likely be wholly inadequate to the problems of the severely segmented society existing in his own country. His people do not acquire the framework for continued political and social action on the national level by adolescence.[4] The vast majority learn instead to suspect authority from outside the family and village, whether it is communicated in the form of modern machines, more education, or new local governments. Political integration of the country must be superimposed on the rural mass of the developing country. It is the unavoidably arbitrary character of the developmental process that may, in turn, represent the greatest threat to effective adaptation to modern life. Without constant and informed attention to the reconciliation that must take place at the local level, the massive efforts of many developing countries may be largely wasted.

The previous chapter has considered some of the direct assaults that the three subject countries have made on the rural populace. They are notable for the extent to which they do indeed perpetuate the colonial power's conception of rural improvement and continue the exercise of highly centralized authority. Morocco has probably been the most dependent on massive measures. As Marthelot has noted, "It is not that

[3] There are many indications of this in American political life, which will be explored in the context of political development in more detail in the concluding chapters. See, for example, Robert Dahl's comments on "free-floating political power" in *Who Governs?*, New Haven, Yale University Press, 1963, p. 305, and also Seymour Lipset's elaboration of the ambiguities of democratic political life in *Political Man*, New York, Doubleday, 1960, passim.

[4] Along with some important suggestions concerning broader questions of participation, this point is raised by Harry Eckstein, *A Theory of Stable Democracy*, Princeton, Center of International Studies, 1961.

the mechanical and hydraulic infrastructure that they have built is not valuable, but that it is not sufficient: the environment of technical materialism, and the technocratic ignorance of sociology, which has to a large measure surrounded the elaboration and the execution of these programs has made them miss their purpose for the large part."[5] In this chapter some additional means of reaching the rural population, largely in the agricultural realm, will be discussed, and in particular the various attempts to use the underemployed rural populace on public-works projects.

The idea of "labor investment" or "labor capital" has been popularized by the controversial experience of Communist China, though most leaders of developing countries tend, as the above comments would indicate, to disassociate the occasionally spectacular achievements of the Chinese experience from the rigid police methods which have, to a large extent, made such achievements possible. Perhaps the advocates most familiar in North Africa are René Dumont and Gabriel Ardant. The American wheat program has also made less ideological suggestions for the productive employment of rural people on public works. Certainly much has been done to bring more villagers into direct contact with government and its developmental potential through public works than in any other way. Other methods of making contact with the villager are rural credit, the organization of cooperatives, and rural monitors or extension agents—part of a more personal but no less direct effort to make individual contact at the village level.

INDIVIDUAL CONTACT AND RURAL DEVELOPMENT

The massive programs evaluated in the preceding chapter provide only a general framework for the integration of the rural populace. Essential to their success is the ability of the government to put into the field sufficient agents and to implement more individualized programs to meet a variety of specific needs. There is no single organizational model for accomplishing the variety of services needed to incorporate the peasant into a modern rural economy and, thereby, into important aspects of modern life. The missing facilities are numerous. The villager needs a place to store his seed, supplies of improved seeds, better methods of marketing what cash crop he may have, credit that will free him from the oppressive moneylender without putting him behind bars when crops are poor, simple instruments suited to his skills and situation, and inexpensive fertilizers suitable to his crops and soil. Agriculture is in fact an area in which the ability of a government to construct and to coordinate a complex program is severely tested.

Tunisia has devised what is probably the most complete program of

[5] P. Marthelot, "Histoire et réalité de la modernisation du monde rural au Maroc," *Tiers Monde*, vol. 2, no. 6, April-June 1961, p. 167.

agricultural education in coordination with changes anticipated in the rural sector. Her versatility in this regard is one aspect of a well-calculated estimate of educational needs in several fields, which will be discussed in more detail in the following chapter. Under the supervision of a capable Secretary of State for Education, Messadi, who has the full confidence of the president, Tunisia was able to formulate a ten-year educational perspective only three years after independence.[6] Since the plan was made, progress has been made in reorganizing agriculture, and the decision was made to engage in large-scale planning in all sectors. Bourguiba has also decided that those introduced to modern agriculture must do so under the supervision and management of cooperative farms in both irrigated and dry-farming regions.

Following the attempted coup of late 1962, the president confessed that the government was indeed having difficulty in farming all the state lands.[7] Until the country was able to supply the necessary agronomists, monitors, and technicians reforms could not get under way. The educational cycle for advanced cadre of these kinds takes from two to six years, and the more vigorous effort to train agricultural staff did not begin until 1960. Some officials in agriculture were frank in stating that Tunisia had lost valuable time in preparing personnel for modernized agriculture, although it should be noted that the Tunisian program compares favorably with accomplishments in both of the other countries. In 1962 the Secretary of State for Agriculture put the number of college-trained agronomists and agricultural engineers at 300, not including Frenchmen working on *colon* farms. There were also about 500 rural monitors or extension agents distributed among the various services of the ministry. Inadequate as these numbers appear, it will be seen that Tunisia's comparative position is by no means so desperate as that of Morocco or Pakistan.

Up to 1962 the Superior Agricultural School in Tunis had been able to train an average of 25 agronomists and agricultural engineers a year. Under the Three Year Plan its capacity will be tripled. In 1964, for example, 57 agricultural engineers graduated and nearly 200 were in training. The Secondary Agricultural School at Moghrane had a capacity of training 80 students a year, which will also be expanded under the plan.[8] Four more secondary agricultural schools have begun under the plan. In 1964 almost 2,000 students were in the first three-year cycle

[6] Secretary of State for National Education, *Nouvelle Conception de l'Enseignment Tunisien*, Tunis, 1958.

[7] Habib Bourguiba, "Towards True Socialism," Speech Delivered to the National Council of the Socialist Destour, March 2, 1963, Secretary of State for Cultural Affairs and Information, Tunis, 1963.

[8] For general background see Secretary of State for Agriculture, *Collège Secondaire d'Agriculture*, Tunis, n.d., which gives full course requirements and schedules, and *Les Centres de Formation Professionelle Agricole*, Secretary of State for Agriculture, Tunis, n.d.

and 334 were in the second or advanced cycle. The hopes for a broader impact at the local level rest, however, with eight technical agricultural schools at the high-school level, having a total of 814 students in 1961, and the nine Centers for Professional Agricultural Training. The former train semiskilled monitors, while the latter are regional schools to provide terminal, elementary courses for the sons of promising farmers. The candidates are selected, in part, through Socialist Destour channels and receive intensive indoctrination on modern agriculture. They are expected to return to their parents' farms to assist in improving farming methods. The centers had 475 students enrolled in 1961, and enrollment increased to 1,200 by 1964. The plan calls for a center for each province, and capacity will eventually be expanded to 1,500 students over a three-year cycle.

Although there are some ministerial disputes over the priorities in placing the students with agricultural education, the Tunisian government has a distinct advantage over the Moroccan and Pakistani governments by having a clear concept of agricultural reorganization. There are three reasons for this. First, the single-party regime cannot permit tensions to accumulate that might take the form of political opposition. The political system must perform in order to survive. Second, the government is in fact the owner of nearly half the best land in the country. Immediate pressures to sustain the productivity of this land are great, particularly because some 2,000 skilled French farmers departed in 1964 after land nationalization. More important, the Tunisian farmer will not respond to immediate needs, and will certainly not modernize, if he sees no opportunity of sharing the benefits of his effort. Third, agriculture is simply too complex and too vital a problem in Tunisian life to attack without some guiding principles.

Though each developing country must formulate its own solution, the Tunisian government has found a solution compatible with the political requirements of the regime in the cooperative movement. Bourguiba has been enthusiastic in the support of cooperatives in all sectors. The plan observes that the cooperative movement "responds best to the objectives of our economic and social beliefs and adapts perfectly to our conditions and our means." However, the cooperative system organized in Tunisia also meets even more critical political requirements, and has already had important political repercussions. Coops are obviously a convenient device to control and supervise the activity of thousands of Tunisians as the benefits of national development multiply. The entire cooperative movement has been centralized in Tunis, and is closely managed from the provincial level by the governors and the Regional Cooperative Federation composed of party reliables and high officials. The immediate political casualty in the expansion of the cooperative system was the U.G.T.T., which has pressed for more cooperative activity for many years and had taken the initiative in organizing some of the most successful cooperatives in the country. U.G.T.T. coops in fishing, construction, and agricultural supplies were absorbed into the new government organization, and contributed to the controversy between the union and the government during 1963 and 1964.[9]

The scope of the Tunisian approach to organizing cooperatives can be seen in Table VIII, which outlines the size and nature of coops

TABLE VIII

Agricultural, Consumer, and Manufacturing Cooperatives in Tunisia by Province (1964)[a]

	Agriculture		Consumer		Manufacturing[b]	
Governorate	Coops	Members	Coops	Members	Coops	Members
Tunis	32	8,338	11	5,931	36	5,270
Bizerte	9	853	2	269	11	748
Béja	61	3,940	4	760	1	121
Souk al-Arba	23	1,801	3	1,351	1	530
Kef	71	3,919	4	2,294	7	294
Kasserine	4	3,531	—	—	3	623
Gafsa	12	2,082	1	83	7	463
Médenine	2	276	4	433	12	414
Gabès	9	1,905	1	284	2	108
Sfax	3	540	3	1,097	13	3,154
Kairouan	15	1,861	31	8,040	10	541
Sousse	118[c]	35,784[c]	14	2,063	46	2,975
Nabeul	19[c]	3,615[c]	8	4,558	8	723
Totals	378	68,445	86	27,163	157	15,964

[a] Table provided the author by the Cooperative Division, Bureau of Regional Planning, Ministry of Planning and Finance. Nabeul's 8 credit coops, with 4,558 members, have been omitted.

[b] In Tunis manufacturing of office furniture, et cetera; in Médenine, Sfax, and Sousse, fishing coops; and in the remainder, handicrafts.

[c] In these two provinces most of the land was under productive use by Tunisian fruit and olive growers. They were organized into service coops for all supplying and marketing.

organized to the end of 1964. There are three basic types—production, consumer, and service coops—and all three types exist in agriculture. The most important of these are the agricultural-production coops, of which 86 were organized entirely in the north in 1963 and an additional 160 were formed in 1964.[10] They are generally ex-*colon* farms

[9] Government officials are reluctant to specify how many of the coops were in the hands of the U.G.T.T. However, official statements often referred to the poor management of coops prior to the official program, and the removal of Habib Achour as secretary general of the union in 1965 was allegedly prompted by his poor management. Why the government had not acted before was, of course, unmentioned. See *L'Action*, July 4, 1965.

[10] For the early experience of the coops see Moncef Guen, *La Coopération et*

that have been transferred to cooperative management under a local committee, the part-time advice of a monitor or extension agent, and the supervision secretary responsible to the Regional Cooperative Federation. Over a five-year period the production coops remain under the control of the government, but ownership may be transferred after this period with government approval. The government plans that a million acres or a third of the arable land in the north will be under cooperative management by 1968. Although the production coops accomplished little in preparing the peasants for self-management by 1964, they have prevented morseling of nationalized land and provide a semblance of financial accountability.

Two other forms of coops have been used to organize agriculture in other regions. In the Medjerda Valley the peasants hold individual title to their land, and work on relatively small irrigated plots of about 20 acres. The nature of intense irrigation places them under close supervision. In the olive-growing coastal plain, the Sahel, the farmers' individual ownership has not been questioned, but all have been required to join a regional service coop which manages all marketing, supplies, and exporting. Production in the once rich Sahel region has dropped because of poor care and exhausted trees. Because the new system also involved compulsory compliance with government agents who identified aged and worthless trees for destruction or severe pruning, the service coop met some stiff resistance. Several persons were killed in demonstrations in Msaken, but firm government action, involving the arrest of several hundred local citizens, has overcome opposition. The irony that the Socialist Destour has historic roots in the Sahel region is only another manifestation of how national development sets in motion more complex political relationships.

Although the coops in the extreme south are technically similar to the northern production coops, the local conditions impose very different conditions. The first coops formed here were based on the *cellules de mise en valeur*, and respond to the party's promise to help the impoverished peasant of this arid region. The most important affected regions in 1964 were Souassi, Enfida, Sidi Bou Zid, and Meknassi. The farms often run to a thousand acres with variations in crops as one works out from the central area irrigated by wells. The poverty of the region makes it very easy to obtain the peasant's consent and interest, but any form of real cooperative management is probably more difficult in the south than in the north, where peasants have been exposed to

---

l'Etat en Tunisie, Tunis, Editions de l'U.G.T.T., n.d. (1964?), and also Slahed-dine Ben Said, "Les unités coopératives d'exploitations et la réforme des structures agricoles," *La Voie Cooperative*, November-December 1963, pp. 31-42. The first coops in agriculture are discussed by Jacques Cherel in "Les unités coopératives de production du Nord tunisien," *Tiers Monde*, vol. 5, no. 18, April-June 1964, pp. 235-254.

aspects of modern agriculture much longer. A report on experiments in Gafsa province concludes, "The population installed there does not really participate in the improvement work, except perhaps as salaried persons."[11]

The president has been firm in his support of the coops, particularly since the attempt on his life, when it appeared that dissidents might exploit rural apprehensions over these reforms. He stated as early as 1959 that ineffective farmers might have their land seized by the state.[12] Legislation in early 1964 gave the Secretary of State for Agriculture authority to form regional associations and also where necessary to compel compliance with modern methods.[13] Land nationalization in 1964 was both a sequel and an impetus to further cooperative effort. The early coops were often inefficient because they were confined to the poorer lands under Tunisian ownership. The later coops were formed under the urgent need to keep additional land under cultivation and in good condition.

The full impact of the cooperative movement can be seen in visiting the new farms. Starting with the north again, each province began organizing service coops in 1964 as well as regional coops to service and maintain machinery. On the coops the new provincial consumer coop had often a small shop, which was supplied and supervised from the provincial capital. The major agricultural products for export are sold to large cooperative firms in Tunis, who manage foreign operations, storage, and transportation. The political implications should not be underestimated. Few developing countries have any organizational device comparable to the Tunisian coop system, which included twelve per cent of all active Tunisians by the end of 1964.[14] As the system grew, the

[11] S.E.R.E.S.A., *Région 08—Steppe Ouest-Gafsa*, Secretary of State for Agriculture, 1960, p. 58. Unlike the published studies of the Medjerda project, they are candid in discussing problems of participation. In the study *Région 05—Sahel de Sousse, ibid.*, p. 42, the group noted that U.N.A.T. and U.T.A.C., auxiliary organizations associated with the Socialist Destour, had ceased to make important contributions to local development, although they had members in most villages.

[12] Habib Bourguiba, "Dans dix ans, la Tunisie rénovée," Speech of March 2, 1959, Tunis, Secretary of State for Information. Also his speech "Production Units: First State of a Revolution in Agriculture," Speech delivered before the National Assembly, October 5, 1962, Secretary of State for Cultural Affairs and Information, Tunis, 1962, and "Transcending Individualism in Outlook," Speech delivered at Socialist Destour officials' school, Gabès, April 28, 1963, Secretary of State for Cultural Affairs and Information, Tunis, 1963.

[13] Loi no. 63-17 du 27 mai 1963 (4 moharrem 1383), portant encouragement de l'Etat au développement de l'agriculture," *Journal Officiel de la République Tunisienne*, May 24-31, 1963, pp. 745-753, and "Décret-loi no. 64-11 du 26 mars 1964 relatif aux associations de développement agricole," *ibid.*, March 27, 1964, pp. 380ff.

[14] These figures were given to the author by the Cooperative Division, Bureau of Regional Planning, Ministry of Planning and Finance, in the summer of 1965. More detailed studies of the Tunisian agricultural coops are being planned.

governmental controls also grew, and in late 1964 a law required that official approval be given for any expansion or extension of the coop into new areas of activity. The remarkable achievements of the single-party regime can never eliminate the fear that the diffusion of power may shatter the essential unanimity at the national level.

One of the most important support institutions for rural development is credit. Nearly all developing countries have experienced difficulty in persuading the peasants to accept modern credit agencies, and often agricultural credit has been neglected because of the difficulties in administering and collecting rural loans. Tunisia had a Caisse Mutuelle de Crédit Agricole and Sociétés Tunisiennes de Prévoyance, but their influence has seldom been felt beyond the restricted number of modern farmers. They were not prepared to make adjustments in loans, nor could they easily expand the volume of credit beyond conservatively fixed limits. After an investigation of the rural credit problems,[15] it was decided to form a new bank, the Banque Nationale Agricole, to expand the volume of available credit, and, as plans for the cooperatives advanced another bank, the Banque Coopérative, was organized for their assistance.

The demand for additional and more lenient credit was one of the major problems discussed in the first national meeting of all cooperatives, held in the summer of 1963.[16] The new credit institutions should benefit from the improved cooperative organization. Though delayed by the need to consolidate the power of the Socialist Destour, and handicapped by exceptionally poor harvests in the early 1960's, Tunisia has been able to formulate and to begin to put into effect a remarkably coherent plan to make contact with the peasant.[17] The relatively strong authoritarian strain in the program should not be concealed. The Socialist Destour has often used party militants to persuade and pressure farmers where programs began to lag. The government has not been reluctant to use its control of nearly half the best land to coerce the peasants into accepting new agricultural organizations; nor has it been soft-spoken in telling the reluctant participants in the new cooperatives that they would be permanently excluded. Where the regime has run into stiff opposition, the Socialist Destour readily evokes the superior claim of the nation, expressed largely in the designs of the president, but increasingly influenced by the plan and Ben Salah.

Morocco has, on the whole, been much less successful than Tunisia in providing the human infrastructure for agricultural mobilization. Her

[15] S.E.R.E.S.A., *Le Crédit Agricole en Tunisie*, Secretary of State for Agriculture, Tunis, 1958.
[16] "Le bilan des coopératives," *Jeune Afrique*, July 29-August 4, 1963.
[17] See the instructive review by M. Callens, "Cinq années d'action administrative dans le domain agricole," *I.B.L.A.*, vol. 25, no. 98, 1962, pp. 111-134.

problems are symptomatic of the government's general reluctance to resolve serious conflicts among ministries in order to supervise the training of professional and technical *cadre*. Seven years after independence there was still no organized liaison between the Ministry of the Interior, which had control of the rural communes, and the Ministry of Agriculture. The fact that from 1961 to late 1963 these two ministries were under the same man, who was simultaneously Director of Cabinet for the king, only added to the confusion and rivalry among the various services and divisions trying to reach the *fellah*. The contrast with Tunisia is clear. Whereas the phase of cooperative organization and expanded activity by public corporations represented a partial fulfillment of Tunisia's over-all design for rural modernization, the decentralization of the Moroccan Ministry of Agriculture into O.N.I. and O.N.M.R. was an admission of the incapacity of the government to deal with the complexities of the countryside. There were certainly many rivalries within the Tunisian ministry, but they were unable to obstruct effective action.

Although Morocco possesses agricultural training facilities comparable to those of Tunisia, very little has been done to expand their activity. Virtually nothing has been done to evaluate their curricula, methods, or recruitment in terms of the country's agricultural needs.[18] The nearly total neglect of agricultural education in Morocco will place severe restraints on the projected activities of the new agricultural-improvement agencies, and has made the country dependent on professional and technical assistants recruited at considerable expense abroad. Possibly the most alarming evidence of neglect is found in the Five Year Plan, which has only half a page of generalities on the subject. Noting that the "need for agricultural cadre is enormous," the plan admits that "until now the problem of professional training in agriculture has only been raised by the administration in respect to staffing [central offices] and agricultural extension [*vulgarisation*]."[19] In fact, there has been fierce competition among the agricultural services in distributing the pitifully small supply of Moroccan agricultural experts, and these quarrels have served only to exacerbate relations among rural services.

Morocco has one college to train agronomists and agricultural engineers, the Ecole Nationale d'Agriculture, at Meknes. The institution has a capacity of about 30 students a year; until independence the vast majority were French. From 1945 to 1957 the college trained 120 engineers, of whom two were Moroccan; of the 57 students in 1957 thirteen

[18] A study of agricultural education in Morocco has been done by P. Bourqui, *Rapport au Governement du Royaume du Maroc sur l'Enseignement Agricole*, Rome, Food and Agricultural Organization (Report P.E.A.T. No. 955), 1958. However, there were no indications in the plan or other statements of the Ministry of Agriculture that these suggestions were being applied.

[19] Division of Economic Coordination and the Plan, Ministry of the National Economy, *Plan Quinquennal 1960-1964*, Rabat, 1960, p. 327.

were Moroccan.[20] The few Moroccans who have received advanced education are thinly distributed among the large commercial cooperatives serving the large farmers; government offices controlling wheat-trading, tobacco, and rural-tax collection; and the various services of the Ministry of Agriculture and the C.T.A.

There are three secondary schools in agriculture, all built by the Protectorate before independence. As in Pakistan, most talented young Moroccans avoid agriculture, and there is little to indicate that many more than 50 Moroccans are being trained a year to work as technical experts and extension agents in the countryside. As in the case of the college graduates in agriculture, the effects of the skilled monitors are dissipated in the absence of plans or projects for their utilization. Most of them have been attached to the machine-tractor stations, where their services are available largely to those privileged farmers able to use the center. They have seldom been in a position to help small, traditional farmers. The figures from two studies on Moroccan agriculture place the number of locally installed, effective extension agents at about a hundred.[21] There is roughly an equal number of French extension agents.

There is no program designed to train rural youngsters at the level of the technical high school, comparable to the Centers for Professional Agricultural Training in Tunisia. The Protectorate instituted a program of agricultural training in 250 primary schools, but this effort has been broken up by the consolidation of primary education under the Ministry of National Education. Some training of the sons of local farmers was also undertaken at several regional centers, but these early projects to reach the *fellah* directly have apparently been discontinued with independence or only continued in an unofficial capacity where French teachers were available.

Jurisdictional disputes and personal rivalries also dissipated the effects on a promising program under private auspices to locate and encourage adaptive farmers.[22] The Institut de Recherche et d'Application des Methods de Developpement (I.R.A.M.) initially received support, especially in the Marrakech region, where about 200 promising farmers were put through short courses designed to simulate existing rural conditions. The trainees were then returned to their villages, where their success in adapting new methods would serve to identify the most

[20] Division of Economic Coordination and the Plan, Ministry of the National Economy, *L'Evolution Economique du Maroc*, Rabat, 1958, p. 97.

[21] Background on the schools is found in *Morocco 54*, special issue of the *Encyclopédie Mensuelle d'Outre-Mer*, Paris, 1955, pp. 120-121. *Jeune Afrique*, January 10, 1965, reported that discussions on the new Moroccan plan revealed that the country was training 50 agricultural engineers a year. There were 165 technical cadre to fill 1,000 posts and 450 extension agents for an estimated need for 2,000.

[22] See Yves Goussault, "La participation des collectivités rurales au développement," *Tiers Monde*, vol. 2, no. 3, January-March 1961, pp. 27-40.

talented for further courses. The scheme acknowledged that effective local impact depended on the extent to which "technical services and the state decide to utilize wholly the *animateurs.*"[23] In fact, no such coordinated effort was possible in Morocco. The trainees simply drifted back into village life, and the agency decided to concentrate its efforts in Senegal, where the scheme has received support and cooperation.

One other experience in expanding local opportunities deserves comment. In 1958 the Moroccan government requested three community-development experts from the United Nations. However, the government was unprepared for their arrival, and after six months of idleness it was decided to withdraw two of the advisers until the Moroccan government resolved internal conflicts over who was to utilize the experts and where they might be put to work. In mid-1959 it was finally decided that a Community Development Bureau would be established in the Ministry of the Interior and that a pilot project would be started at the village of Lalla Mimouna in the Gharb. Four cooperative weaving enterprises were started, and over $40,000 was raised by the community over two years to improve the village. There were also substantial contributions of wheat, money, and transportation provided by the government. In 1962 it was decided that a program would be designed to introduce similar techniques in three other test areas,[24] although it is still too early to judge the success of the expanded program. A similar project under United Nations assistance has been started in Targuist, a rural commune bordering on the Rif mountains.

Like Tunisia and Pakistan, Morocco inherited a rural-credit system devised by the colonial power, which had become the instrument of the small modernized segment of the rural economy. The Moroccan Sociétés Indigènes de Prévoyance (S.I.P.), established in 1917, soon became "enmeshed in a very rigid and very distant administrative system which forcefully limited their sphere of activity, while the terms of credit, the necessity of security and of individual guarantees, which the small *fellah* was far from being able to offer, prevented easy access beyond a small circle of notables and middle-sized cultivators."[25] The S.I.P. grew eventually into a national organization having 82 offices, the Sociétés de Crédit Agricole et de Prévoyance (S.O.C.A.P.) that provided the bulk of the rural credit available to the fortunate farmers who could meet the standards.

[23] *Les Animateurs Ruraux au Maroc: Etude Générales et Orientations Actuelles,* Rabat, I.R.A.M., n.d. (1960?), p. 22. See also *Problèmes d'Animation dans le Périmètre Irrigué du Tadla,* Rabat, I.R.A.M., 1961, and *Rural Animation Study in Morocco, ibid.,* n.d.

[24] *New York Times,* February 23, 1962.

[25] Marthelot, *Tiers Monde, op.cit.,* pp. 142-143. Articles on the reorganization of Moroccan rural credit are to be found in *La Vie Economique,* December 21, 1961, and January 12, 1961, with some financial data.

For many years the government submitted to the influential farmers, who found the system suitable to their needs, and, no doubt, had some apprehensions over the impact of more readily available, expanded credit for the small farmer and tenant. Nearly every survey of the Moroccan economy was unanimous in labeling the rural-credit system inadequate and antiquated. A new organization was finally begun in December 1961, the Caisse National de Crédit Agricole (C.N.C.A.),[26] but it remains to be seen if the heavy hand of the early administrators will defeat the purpose of the new credit system.

The Moroccan experience has hardly begun to fill the promise of the rich agricultural resources of the country and the fairly ample supply of funds to make a start on rural modernization. The monarchy, of course, is not alone in neglecting the countryside, for all the parties and leaders were equally familiar with the obstacles to integrating the *fellah* in political and social affairs at the national level. Nevertheless, policy was still subject to the monarch's consent, and where the king gave active support, as in Operation Labour, he could contribute materially to the success of the project. The hesitance of the monarchy appears to have come from an unwillingness to assign responsibilities and provide authority appropriate to rural-development tasks. Indecision created impatience, contributing to the splitting of the parties and also leading to the choice of massive programs to change agriculture. From the viewpoint of the eventual integration of the country both actions have the same fault in their failure to help political forces at the two levels to coalesce in a pattern of action that might sustain continued development.

Under British rule the Indian agricultural services stagnated to the point where effective action at lower levels was almost impossible. Each department (agriculture, animal husbandry, irrigation, forestry, fisheries, and game) followed different patterns of recruitment, pay, promotion, and field organization. None of these services were made sufficiently attractive to recruit more able staff, and over the years each tended to limit itself to areas and projects of special interest. A basic organization existed for placing extension agents at the level of the village, but was never fully exploited and in most cases seldom staffed. The idea of social action at the village level was never part of its overall purpose and, as noted in the Food and Agriculture Commission report, the Agricultural Department's "original purpose was that of a very attenuated advisory service confined mostly to demonstration to rural leaders and larger landlords."[27]

[26] *Bulletin Officiel*, no. 2564, "Dahir no. 1-60-106 du 25 joumada II 1384 (4 décembre 1961) relatif à l'organisation du crédit agricole," December 14, 1961, pp. 1777-1780.

[27] *F&AC Report*, Karachi, Government of Pakistan, 1960, p. 153.

The traditional organization left much to be desired. The front-line official in East Pakistan was the Union Agricultural Assistant with a Thana Agricultural Officer above him. At the union level there are about 10 villages and approximately 15,000 persons, so that the Union Agricultural Assistant might have become a reasonably effective rural agent with proper motivation and support. However, of the 4,000 Union Assistants available in East Pakistan, only some 1,700 have had a year of agricultural training, and the balance have been acquired from the now abolished jute regulatory service. Even if they had been trained, it seems unlikely that they could have had effect. "Low in status and pay, with no office and no transport and a purely nominal housing allowance, many of the Union Assistants cannot afford to bring their families with them and frequently live away from the Union in which they are supposed to work."[28]

In West Pakistan the situation has been worse, for there was no official supposedly working at the lowest or union tier until the Village AID program. The Field Assistant worked at a level corresponding to the *thana* official in East Pakistan, but his area was often larger (up to 100,000 acres). Like his opposite, he was usually without office, housing, or transport. Over every two Field Assistants there was an Agricultural Assistant at the district level, responsible for up to 30,000 farmers and 200,000 acres. He had an office, but no housing, and until recently no transport. As a result the villager seldom knew that the agricultural services existed, and work was confined to the more accessible farms. The agents often concentrated on assisting landlords, who sometimes provided free housing. The totally inadequate seed-storage, fertilizer, and other supply facilities alone would have crippled the system, but it was also encumbered with unbelievable administrative tangles. The Food and Agriculture Commission found cases where staff had not been paid for two and even four years.

These conditions were repeatedly found by the commission and explain why it decided to form an entirely new organization, the Agricultural Development Corporation, to supply and distribute seed, fertilizer, and implements. The Union Agents performing these functions under the A.D.C. would be supplemented by an improved extension service under the Agricultural Departments of the two wings, wholly devoted to demonstrating and assisting the local farmers. The District Agricultural Officer, renamed to indicate the additional powers and

---

[28] *Ibid.*, pp. 154-156. See also the table in *The First Five Year Plan (1955-60)*, Government of Pakistan, National Planning Board, Karachi, 1956, p. 273. The planning group found 586 extension workers available in East Pakistan (116 villages per worker) and 365 in West Pakistan (104 villages per worker). There were slightly less working in the extension service of the Department of Animal Husbandry. However, very few of the extension workers in either department were actually engaged in demonstrations and other local-level work.

broader role of the agricultural officer at that level, would have the authority to remove lower agricultural officers. Between the district and the union the commission would keep the present Agricultural Assistant in West Pakistan and Thana Agricultural officers in East Pakistan, whose main concern would be to evaluate work at the union level and to make sure that supplies and fertilizers reached the villages.

Services associated with agriculture, most of them under separate departments in the British tradition, were equally lacking. Animal husbandry was found to be strictly a veterinary department, seldom operating below the district and confined largely to breeding and inoculation.[29] Conditions were scarcely better in the more prestigious Irrigation Department, where meticulous attention to measuring the water flow and collecting fees was provided at the expense of performing any service to improve farming methods. Under comparable conditions in India it was estimated that fully half the water reaching the fields was wasted by faulty channels in the fields, and half again from watering without considering type of crops, optimum harvesting times, et cetera. The department still used a complex and outmoded system of charging for water, based on type of crop, which the commission recommended to be changed to a volumetric system. The tale of excessively centralized, inflexible organization at the expense of the individual farmer could be repeated for many other aspects of Pakistani agriculture.

In relation to the population Pakistani facilities for agricultural education are comparable to those of Morocco and Tunisia. The Second Plan called for over 1,000 college graduates in agriculture, a fourth of them simply to fill vacancies then existing in the provinces and at the center.[30] Half of them were assigned by the plan to the provincial services, but it seems likely that the newly created A.D.C.'s will impose higher priorities. The four universities existing in 1960 could admit 380 students a year. In West Pakistan the Agricultural College at Lyallpur was expected to train 400 during the plan period; the Tanodojam college, 210; and the new Peshawar college, 140. In addition, the Dacca Agricultural Institute, being converted into a full university at Mymensingh, was to train 200 in East Pakistan.

The rural-credit system preoccupied the British and, later, the Pakistanis for many years, but little has been done to alleviate the distress of

[29] Despite the shortages of technicians and facilities, some of the agricultural agents showed considerable ingenuity. The F&A Commission visited one district agent who had only a single refrigerator for the storage of vaccine, and had no way of distributing it safely to the animal-husbandry agents throughout the district. He arrived at a plan whereby each subagent brought a thermos bottle to the weekly meetings and carried his own vaccine to the substations. *F&AC Report*, *op.cit.*, p. 171.

[30] *The Second Five Year Plan* (1960-65), Government of Pakistan, Planning Commission, Karachi, 1960, p. 175.

the small farmer. Indebtedness has now reached such high proportions in East Pakistan that a large landless class is being formed as farmers are compelled to turn over land in payment of debts. The irony of the Pakistani farm debt is that it has been augmented and, in turn, become unmanageable as a result of the agricultural improvements made in British India. As land rights were defined and land values increased, moneylenders were prepared to extend much more credit than was formerly available. Moreover, much of the new money supply was used for family ceremonies or other unproductive purposes, while demographic pressure and poor farming methods reduced the farmer's ability to repay his loans. Darling estimates that the number of moneylenders and dependents increased nearly fourfold from 1868 to 1911.[31] The decline in agricultural prices between the wars multiplied the debt burden several times. After World War II the per capita debt of the farmer was estimated at about 500 rupees,[32] easily twice his annual income.

The British response to the peasants' indebtedness was to authorize the formation of credit cooperatives in 1904. The vast proportion of them have been organized with unlimited liability, and so have not been popular. Furthermore, with the passage of time the credit cooperatives have found more lucrative places to invest outside agriculture. With the virtual disappearance of the Hindus after partition, the banking business collapsed. Many credit coops found attractive opportunities making commercial loans and abandoned the farmer. Although supervised by a government department, the cooperatives worked without coordination or support from the agricultural departments. The government has not provided funds for the extension of the coops, and there has never been an attempt to involve the farmer in the operation of the coops. From 1948 to 1958 there was a small increase in the number and membership of cooperative-credit societies in West Pakistan, but their 1958 membership of about 375,000 was only a fraction of the needy. In East Pakistan nearly four fifths of the rural cooperative-credit societies disappeared in this period, and in 1958 they served only some 575,000 members.[33]

As is so often the case in working with major obstacles to national development, effective action must begin with the state. Credit in the amounts and under the terms needed to help the small farmer requires strong support from national banks oriented toward agriculture. For

[31] Sir Malcolm Darling, *The Punjab Peasant in Prosperity and Debt*, 4th edn., London, Oxford University Press, 1947, p. 208.

[32] S. M. Akhtar, *Economics of Pakistan*, Lahore, United Publishers, vol. 1, 1961, pp. 204 and 246-249.

[33] *F&AC Report*, *op.cit.*, pp. 178-183, and S. M. Akhtar, *op.cit.*, pp. 231-271. These figures on volume of credit vary slightly from those found in *The First Five Year Plan*, *op.cit.*, p. 283.

this purpose the pre-Ayub government established the Agricultural Development Finance Corporation in 1952, to provide more short- and medium-term credit, and the Agricultural Bank of Pakistan in 1956, to bolster credit supplies further and to encourage the construction of warehouses, supply depots, et cetera. To avoid overlapping, the two banks divided the two wings, and were obviously duplicating many activities needlessly. Little was accomplished in dealing with basic structural problems of the rural economy in marketing and transport, and no significant impact was made on the small farmer. The merger of these two banks was urged by every inquiry concerned with credit, most forcefully by the Credit Enquiry Commission itself,[34] and was finally accomplished in 1961.

The Agricultural Development Bank can be expected to improve the rural-credit system. Its bylaws enable it to make allowance for subsistence farmers, and it is more closely coordinated with other agricultural services. In its first full year of operation the A.D.B. sanctioned roughly twice the amount of credit that the other two banks had issued over a period of six years.[35] In East Pakistan assistance was directed in particular to the purchase of seed and improved draft animals; in West Pakistan, to well construction and mechanization. The A.D.B. is supposed to give preference to small borrowers, and has authority to see that loans are used for their stated purpose. Like the banks discussed in the Moroccan and Tunisian cases, however, the new Pakistani bank represents only a first step in reaching the villager, and cannot be fully effective until marketing practices and farm methods also begin to adapt to the structure of a more productive rural economy.

The efforts of the Pakistani government to grapple with agriculture at the national level contrasts sharply with an experiment at the local level in East Pakistan. The project was begun in 1961 at the Academy for Rural Development at Comilla, East Pakistan, then under the direction of Akhter Hameed Khan. The success of the experiment is in no small way due to his energy and persistence, but more recent expansions of the program show that the progress made in Kotwali *thana* was not wholly dependent on the skill of a single man. More recently the program has been expanded to include, first, the other *thanas* of the district and, then, to extend the Comilla experiment to the entire wing.

There are few local development programs that have started with as clear a notion of the requirements at the village level. Even the Tunisian program has depended heavily on the governor's initiative, and relied little on the municipal councils for proposals or support. Akhter Hameed started with a clear formulation of national development, which ac-

[34] *Report of the Credit Enquiry Commission*, Karachi, Ministry of Finance, Government of Pakistan, 1959, p. 76.
[35] *Dawn*, March 21, 1963.

knowledged the widening gap between city and village. The design never lost sight of the cost of replication, and took as a central principle the absolute necessity of local saving.[36] The huge cost of reaching the village through massive, central schemes was borne out when the government estimated the cost of improving a disastrously flooded *thana* in Khulna district of some 300 square miles at 10 crores of rupees. If this were done in all the *thanas* of East Pakistan, the cost would approach eight billion dollars. Even if the money were available, the injection of such large amounts of money would completely disrupt the rural economy, and very likely defeat the goal of development.

The Kotwali experiment made no attempt to conceal the painful adjustment that villagers would need to make. The essential aspects were training, demonstration, and saving. At first only a handful of farmers trusted the officials of the *thana* credit cooperative with their money. The cooperative has now grown to dimensions that make it an appropriate vehicle for expanding credit by farmers who understand that loans must be repaid. They are no longer dependent on moneylenders, and are beginning to accumulate money to enter additional cooperative enterprises to store and market their produce, pay for seed and fertilizer, and improve their villages. The agents of the technical or nation-building services were converted into teachers, and encouraged to make visits to the fields.

The striking quality of all three efforts to provide direct support to the villager is how slow all the governments were in recognizing the problem. Morocco has been the slowest to redirect governmental agencies, and probably has the weakest human infrastructure for rural modernization, even though Morocco is a wealthy country and has important precedents for rural modernization. The failure of the monarchy leads back to the monarchy's reluctance to establish clear-cut ministerial responsibilities, and also an apparent distrust of establishing self-regulated islands of social reform at the local level. The fact that the obstructions to improving agriculture in Morocco have often been the product of fruitless but easily regulated ministerial rivalries makes the Moroccan situation more discouraging. Tunisia and Pakistan have acted more firmly. The one-party system has given Tunisia a continuity that is lacking in both the other governments, but it has also been used to nationalize delay and to exploit agricultural problems to the advantage of the Socialist Destour. The benefits of the Tunisian regime are indisputable in the early phase of reorganization and reorientation of rural life, but the party's skill in mobilizing agreement on the national level weak-

---

[36] Many detailed reports on aspects of the Comilla experiment are found in the *Journal of the East Pakistan Academy for Rural Development.* The main principles of the project are set forth in two speeches of Akhtar Hameed Khan, "How Villagers are Creating Capital," mimeo., August 18, 1962, and "The Basic Principles of the Comilla Programme," mimeo., February 13, 1963.

ens when adapted to the locality and may, indeed, prove to be in conflict with the diffusion of power needed in a major rural-development program.

The discontinuity is of a different kind in Pakistan, though the country has also been slow to build on early efforts to assist the peasant. While working with a rural population that is more isolated from government than either Morocco or Tunisia, the military-bureaucratic alliance produced a highly compartmentalized program. This has, of course, been characteristic of Pakistan's entire administrative hierarchy, and it is, therefore, perhaps not too surprising to see the same structure reproduced in seeking to influence the villager. The great risk of such an approach is that there will be no over-all design and in practice none of the coordination of projects which the Ayub regime felt especially able to provide. The example of the Basic Democracies program in relation to rural modernization is instructive. Conceiving political problems as easily circumscribed and focused on national problems, they launched the program well ahead of other efforts to modernize the village, and without changes in social and welfare agencies essential to persuading the peasant that the political goals of Basic Democracy could take on local meaning in harmony with national goals. The result has been that the government turned to new agencies, like the Agricultural Development Corporation, to produce changes in local life that are closely related to national integration, but remain unrelated locally for bureaucratic reasons. While both Morocco and Tunisia may have serious administrative problems at the local level, it must also be recognized that their respective political systems can more easily contribute to the integration of local and national political life.

RURAL PUBLIC WORKS: DEVELOPMENT OR DOLE?

The three countries in this study were selected, in part, because each has used substantial quantities of American wheat to support public-works programs in rural areas. Pakistan has also taken large amounts of wheat to acquire counterpart funds for other development purposes. The response to the challenge of the public-works programs and how the various programs have worked out in each country provide further insight into each type of government as a mobilizing agent. The reader should be under no illusions that this type of program is a panacea for all national ills, although it is significant that one country, Morocco, presented its scheme for rural public works in this light. Furthermore, it should not be assumed that such programs have been received with uniform enthusiasm or produced success in every instance.

There are three easily distinguished aspects of the rural public-works programs. First, the government must have some conception of how the program will relate to its over-all developmental needs, and must translate the scheme into terms that have some meaning to the participants. The American government is, of course, in a poor position to influence this phase, which may be the most critical aspect in the creation of a program that will have productive and sustained results. The next phase is the implementation of the program, which provides another case study in the adaptability of administrative services and an indication of how well the government can coordinate activity at many levels of the society as well as in many distinct branches of the administration. As has been argued in other parts of the inquiry, the organizational response will be significantly influenced by the flexibility of the political system as a whole, and especially by its initial ability to conceptualize the developmental process in its full meaning and complexity. The last phase of the program is the evaluation of the results, although it is still too early to judge how the programs may ultimately work out as the governments make adjustments and modifications on the basis of their early experience.

A series of poor crops put Tunisia in desperate need of aid well before the political system was oriented to national planning. A succession of unusually dry years left hundreds of thousands of rural unemployed, and in many instances destroyed what meager savings the peasants had in animals and stores.[37] Under the impulse of the Secretary of State for Social Affairs, Ben Salah, now Secretary of State for Planning and Finance, the local authorities conducted a survey in 1955 to estimate how many rural employed would be willing to work on government-organized public works. A total of 335,000 persons were enrolled,[38] and a few *chantiers d'assistance* were formed early in 1956. The first projects were under French aid, which was being withdrawn, and in 1957 the public-works program continued to operate on a small scale in conjunction with American wheat made available under emergency famine conditions. The public-works program took on its present form in 1958, when about 30,000 persons were employed on the first *chantiers de la lutte contre le sous-développement* over the spring months, using American wheat.

The new projects were enthusiastically received by Bourguiba, who was, of course, encountering severe difficulties due to poor harvests and was also in the midst of making important political changes. He asserted,

[37] One of the factors facilitating land-reform operations in the south has been that the tribes lost most of their animals and, thereby, their savings in recent droughts. Thousands of animals were herded to water sources in Libya, but hundreds of thousands perished.

[38] See *Les Chantiers de Travail*, Tunis, Secretary of State for Cultural Affairs and Information, 1962, pp. 3-6, for a review of the development of the public-works projects. Actually the Tunisian legislation on *chantiers* dates back to earlier relief projects organized by the French. See the regulations on the transformed system outlined in the *Journal Officiel*, December 10, 1957, p. 512.

"Nothing prevents the realization of full employment in the framework of the vast programs that will be organized by technicians and accomplished by unemployed hand labor." On other occasions he appealed to national feelings by underscoring the need "to restore to the unemployed the dignity of real workers by employing them on productive jobs, which will increase the resources of the country."[39] The appeals were mixed with references to the threat from without, and sometimes the threat from within from conservative Islamic groups. It seems very likely that the president received his first insight into the possibilities of national planning in studying the early proposals for public-works projects.

Under the expanded program control shifted closer to the president's office and out of the hands of the controversial Ben Salah. The governors were put in charge of assembling projects for their provinces, and the proposals were then sifted by the Directorate of Planning in the president's office. The projects were also submitted to the Secretary of State for Public Works, who was to verify technical aspects of the projects and to provide logistical support in the field. To November 1959 from 50,000 to 70,000 workers were employed on a two-week basis, with a rotation system designed to distribute the wages. The pay was initially 100 *millimes* a day (roughly 100 francs or 35 cents), but was raised successively to 150 and then to 200 *millimes*. In addition, the workers received an allowance of semolina, which was reduced as the cash wage was increased so that employment on the works projects would not begin to attract paid labor from other jobs. Gratified with the first year of full-scale activity, the Tunisian government made plans to enlarge the works program to 120,000 men in 1960.[40]

The success of the program depended heavily on the strong support that could be mobilized from the locality to the capital, once the government and party were convinced of the *chantiers'* value. The governor was able to pick out those regions of the province in most dire need of relief and most suitable for the hand-labor projects possible under the scheme. The regional delegates of the governor, also Socialist Destour militants, were able to rally support from the party and the U.G.T.T. Very early in the program the government saw the potential mobilizing effects of the public-works program, and schools were held to train monitors. The monitors were generally local party militants, young Socialist

[39] Quotations taken from speeches of Habib Bourguiba, "Le gande bataille contre sous-développement," February 5, 1960, and "The First Duty: Conquer Underdevelopment," December 10, 1959, Tunis, Secretary of State for Information.

[40] Within the terms of the P.L. No. 480, Tunisia has become a model project in the eyes of the Agency for International Development. The procedures and operation of the program have been widely publicized in a memo, "Utilization of U.S. Surplus Commodities for Economic Development, P.L. 480, Title II, Section 202: A Summary of Experience in Tunisia," dated February 15, 1961. The report notes the importance of the party in putting the program to work, *ibid.*, pp. 8 and 13.

Destourians or union militants. Bourguiba was quite insistent that the workers improve "their intellectual level and civil conscience," even going so far as to suggest that an effort be made to control leisure hours for the ultimate benefit of the country.[41] The monitor program was enlarged in 1961, and special courses were again held for about 100 militants from the Socialist Destour and the U.G.T.T. In addition, the Secretary of State for Education provided literacy teachers, and the Secretary of State for Public Health and Social Affairs organized dispensaries for the larger projects. The entire program was a rewarding example of how the single-party regime could direct national energies to a common goal within the framework of national development.

The Tunisians had particular need for relatively large earthworks in the center and south to hold the sparse rainfall on the soil, and to prevent the floods that often followed the infrequent but torrential rains. In Sousse and Sfax provinces there were large reforestation projects, in some cases with several hundred workers living at the project sites. Employment on the *chantiers* varies seasonally with the demand for agricultural labor, and annually with the size of the harvest. For example, workers tended to leave the works projects in Sfax in 1961 because there were good olive crops. In visits to the provinces during the slack period of the spring of 1962 it appeared that the works program was making substantial reduction in unemployment; about 20,000 men were working in Gafsa province, 30,000 in Sousse, and 10,000 in Sfax.

The perennial difficulty of the works programs has been to judge the productivity of the project. Bourguiba has repeatedly insisted that the *chantiers* were making a substantial contribution toward economic recovery, but these hopes may well be exaggerated. Table IX gives the allocation of the labor by man-days among the different type of projects. Two fifths of the labor was expended on soil-reclamation projects, whose effects will only be felt over many years and about a fifth of the labor went into cleaning-up exercises that have relatively little productive effect. The type of project having more immediate effect, i.e., reforestation, roadwork, and waterworks, is more difficult to plan and to support and, therefore, has not expanded so rapidly as the program grew. However, Tunisia has been more successful with this type of program than most other developing countries, and has used the wheat program to make substantial inroads into rural unemployment.

As planned for 1961 the projects occupied about 170,000 men (50 million man-days of labor and involved the expenditure of about twenty-five million dollars in cash payments plus the seminola allowance.

---

[41] Habib Bourguiba, "A New Experiment: Work Site Monitors," Tunis, Secretary of State for Information, March 24, 1960. For more details on the transformation of the program see M. Callens, "Promotion-Emploi," *I.B.L.A.*, vol. 24, nos. 95-96, 1961, pp. 279-300.

Tunisian officials expected the level of activity to remain at about this level for the immediate future. Important as the extent of the relief may be, the critical long-run effects of the program will be felt only as the repercussions of the large-scale mobilization of the rural population are felt.[42] It is interesting to note that the single-party regime has used the works program to engage the workers more directly in national affairs, and especially in the aims of the Socialist Destour. Tunisian officials rarely expressed apprehension that the mobilization effects of the programs would have social or political effects that the government and party could not absorb. However, the fact remains that thousands of Tunisians are receiving basic education and political indoctrination, which places new requisites on future efforts toward national integration. The limitations of the public-works program had begun to appear by 1964, when the government placed more emphasis on the cooperative movement.

TABLE IX

Allocation of Public-Works Labor by Project in Tunisia (1958-1960)[a]

	Type of Project (thousands of man-days)						
	Soil Reclamation	Reforestation	Road-work	Sanitation	Water-works	Other	Total
1958	3,791	1,339	183	647	678	65	6,703
1959	8,079	1,408	2,577	5,195	815	241	18,315
1960	19,470	7,828	5,857	10,162	1,715	2,784	47,816

[a] Figures supplied by the Secretary of State for Public Works, Tunis. Totals corrected according to listed items.

Among the Moroccan development efforts few projects provide more dramatic evidence of the differences that exist in political systems in their approach to the challenge of modernization. The Moroccan program, the Promotion Nationale, has brought significant relief to the countryside, but also reveals some of the major obstacles to the effective use of labor capital that arise in many developing countries. The program further elaborates some of the peculiar characteristics of the monarchy as a vehicle for development. The proposal for using American wheat for an agricultural works program was not made until 1961, and, unlike Tunisia and Pakistan, the Moroccan government advanced an extremely ambitious program in a very short period of time. Even with

[42] Some of the long-range problems related to creating full employment are raised by Gabriel Ardant, *La Tunisie d'Aujourdhui et de Démain*, Paris, Calmann-Lévy, 1961, pp. 109-129; see also the article on the *chantiers* appearing in *Jeune Afrique*, February 20-26, 1962.

the full cooperation of the ministries and services involved, it would have been difficult to achieve the goals of the program.

The Promotion Nationale was launched with a massive publicity campaign in the summer of 1961. The major spokesman was Guedira, the king's Director of Cabinet, Minister of Agriculture, and Minister of the Interior. The economic basis for the use of the rural unemployed had been outlined in an earlier paper,[43] whose optimistic forecast concerning the possible developmental contribution of such a program may have misled high officials into thinking that all aspects of the scheme could be calculated and implemented with equal certitude. The fact that all the rural unemployed might be occupied for 30 years on reforestation and land-reclamation projects does not mean that a government can indeed prepare and carry out such a program.

Under the direction of a capable high civil servant a Superior Council for Rural Advancement was established by law (and was later authorized by the constitution), including all interested ministers and the directors of the rural services. The director was supplied with a technical committee to review projects and to ensure proper interministerial coordination, and also with provincial councils that were to be the source of projects and to organize the *chantiers*.[44] The rural communes were to have a voice through one communal president selected by all the commune presidents of each *cercle*. Thus the Moroccan scheme had an important initial advantage over the Tunisian program because local representatives were supposed to be directly involved, although it became apparent later that the communal officials had very little voice in selecting or supervising projects. Most were probably unqualified, and, in any event, were undoubtedly overawed by the governor and technical officials also sitting on the provincial committee.

The enthusiasm of the king's official and the energy of an able civil servant were not sufficient to set in motion a program that might eventually assist the estimated 500,000 underemployed and unemployed Moroccan villagers. In retrospect it seems doubtful that the government officials fully appreciated the rivalry and inflexibility of their own administrators. For the balance of 1961 projects were assembled to provide 18 million man-days of labor, of which seven million were performed; for 1962 the projects totaled some 20 million man-days of labor, of which 5 million were performed. The 1963 program was less ambitious, calling for 15 million man-days and the employment of

[43] Division of Economic Coordination and the Plan, "Note sur la politique agricole du plan quinquennal et le rôle de la centrale de travaux agricoles," mimeo., dated June 1961.

[44] The organization scheme for the Promotion Nationale (initially called Promotion Rurale) can be found in the *Bulletin Officiel*, no. 2543, "Dahir no. 1-61-205 du 1er safar 1381 (15 juillet 1961) rélatif à la promotion rurale," July 21, 1961, pp. 1,020-1,021.

approximately 115,000 workers.[45] Later figures are not available, but the Promotion Nationale employed an average of 60,000 men up to mid-1962.

The conflicts stemming from the Promotion Nationale scheme provide a microscopic version of the dilemmas encountered in nearly every developing country as it seeks to release the energies and talent of its neglected citizens.[46] Except for the initial law organizing the office, there was never any institutional adjustment to the needs of the program. In fact, the director was never given more than three skilled assistants in the central office and was, therefore, almost entirely at the mercy of the governors and the ministries as they chose to interpret and apply the program. In the absence of a major adjustment in the administrative system and a genuine effort to capture local interest, the Promotion Nationale risked becoming only another relief project, without making either the material or human contribution to the country's development that the early plans had promised.

The program was handicapped, in part, by the hasty preparations, but the experience of the first year created much graver doubts about its ultimate impact. In a review of the year's activities,[47] an inter-ministerial group noted that projects were seldom worked out with local authorities, and even more rarely with locally elected representatives. The projects were usually only "appendices" to the existing plans of each technical service at the provincial level and, with the exception of Beni Mellal, seldom held "promise of a true development program, integrated and planned, with projects of urgency and value differentiated." The technical services of each ministry jealously guarded their special interests, and refused to make compromises to provide cadre for other projects. There was general "incomprehension" of the financial require-

[45] The programs for 1961 and 1962 are reviewed in *La Vie Economique*, April 13, 1962, and February 8, 1963. The 1963 program in *ibid.*, May 8, 1963. Indicative of exaggerated hopes associated with the Promotion Nationale was the proposal to associate 900 community workers (presumably one per commune) with the local activities generated by the program. Morocco in fact had no corps of trained community workers at the time, nor was there any indication that the government intended to train them or utilize more talented communal officials. The Tunisians could at least call on local party militiants, but the Moroccans had no device at hand to give the program meaning at the local level.

[46] Most of the material in this and the following paragraphs is taken from a long report prepared by the director shortly before his resignation, entitled *La Promotion Nationale* and consisting of four parts, "But et Bilan," "Impératifs et Moyens," "Problèmes et Perspectives," and regional project summaries for 1962.

[47] These comments are taken from another report of the Superior Council for National Promotion, "Synthèse de l'examen des programmes provincials de Promotion Nationale," mimeo., dated January 5, 1962. One of the immediate major obstacles to the program was deciding how private landowners should compensate the government for improvements made on their land by public-works projects. Several proposals were made, and might also have served to give the government leverage in promoting agriculture generally, but no decision was made.

ments of the program, negligible local buying, wasted material, and virtually no phasing of one project into another to contribute to the over-all improvement of the province.

In defense of the provincial authorities and services it should be noted that they had indeed received little direction or additional support in the previous five years. The idea of suddenly decentralizing authority and actively coordinating technical services at the provincial level was, and largely remains, unheard of. Moreover, the Promotion Nationale conceived in its fullest perspective would have indeed become a super-ministry supervising regional development and regulating governmental services at the provincial level. The Ministry of the National Economy had already failed in its attempt to accomplish this through planning, and it may well have been naïve to hope that a freshly created agency would succeed where others had failed.

In practice, the different local services simply forwarded their respective claims on local labor to their own headquarters in Rabat, which, in turn, passed on the requirements to the Promotion Nationale office. In the field the program remained dependent on a group of royal army officers, who had been trained early in 1961 as coordinators, but tended to become simply the logistical agents of the various technical services at the provincial level. Nearly half of the projects in 1961 and 1962 were for roadwork under the Ministry of Public Works, which could use fairly large amounts of hand labor with a minimum of planning. O.N.I., which had initially refused to attend meetings of the Promotion Nationale, used about a fifth of the available labor; and quite large amounts were also occupied with reforestation. The workers were also used in several one-shot programs to build schools and communal houses, largely under the direction of the royal army, but heavily financed by the ministries concerned.[48]

As planned for 1963-1964, Promotion Nationale submitted to the demands of other ministries to keep operational control of public works, and achieved little toward making public works a device to stimulate civic awareness. A much publicized program to mobilize Beni Mellal province was not repeated, nor was there evidence of continued effort to build on the experiment. Most important, two thirds of the projected work was to be done directly under technical services and within their budgets. The remainder, representing about 7 million man-days, was to be performed under Promotion Nationale direction where community projects could be found in cooperation with local authorities of the Ministry of the Interior, very likely depending heavily on royal army support.[49] Though the goal of mobilizing local interest and participation

[48] See the issues of *La Vie Economique* cited above. Also, *Promotion Nationale au Maroc*, Rabat, Office de la Promotion Nationale, n.d. (1964?), p. 78.
[49] *Ibid.*, pp. 89-90.

has not been lost, the Moroccan public-works scheme has yet to relate itself effectively to the environment of the villager.

Pakistan's efforts to mount public works in the rural setting stem from the successful experiment in building rural credit cooperatives at Comilla. Impressed by the achievements in the Kotwali Thana, the Harvard Advisory Group made a proposal in 1961 to utilize the Comilla project in a large public-works program.[50] The planning paper noted that about a fifth of the East Pakistan rural labor force of 13 million persons was completely idle, and that during the slack season in the spring up to three fourths of the villagers were unoccupied. From the beginning of the study the necessity of meaningful participation at the village level, in conjunction with the aims of the Basic Democracies scheme, was kept in mind. The small-scale experiment under way at Comilla was an ideal test project to see how well a public-works program could be initiated at the village level.

Several features of the 1961-1962 pilot project demonstrate the effectiveness and ingenuity of the experiment, which, of course, profited from the previous year's work that had been done to build local leadership and create an interest in cooperative effort.[51] The stipulation was made that no earthwork could be done by contractors—the usual method of accomplishing district improvements. Furthermore, the contractors found the amounts available for subletting masonry work and sluice construction too small and refused to make bids. The Thana Council then proceeded to make their own drawings with the help of a Peace Corps engineer, and began to manufacture their own bricks. Special methods were designed to enable the local committees to calculate the amount of earth moved and to prevent cheating. Strict verification of payrolls and wheat distribution was maintained. Special arrangements were made to show the villager how to cook with wheat and to permit his children to join him according to custom for the large meal served at noon on the project.

[50] Planning Commission, Government of Pakistan, *Use of Resources Provided by Expanded P.L. 480 Aid*, June 1961, and Planning Commission, Government of Pakistan, *Memorandum on the United Surplus Agricultural Commodities Aid to Pakistan*, February 1961.

[51] The experience in 1961-1962 is presented in a *Report on a Rural Public Works Programme in Comilla Kotwali Thana*, Comilla, Pakistan Academy for Village Development, June 1962. From this work emerged the *Manual for Rural Public Works*, August 1962, which has served as the basic training document in expanding the project. The pilot project involved 250,000 rupees (about $50,000, half in wheat), and plans were solicited from the villages and assembled by the Union Councils. Project Committees were formed using the chairmen and vice-chairmen of the Union Councils, who were required to sign a bond for all materials or funds taken in advance. The program affected 158 villages and contributed some 45,000 work days. The major projects were the cleaning and improvement of thirty-seven miles of a large drainage channel, and the construction of twelve miles of embankments to protect against floods and enable better irrigation.

The Thana and Union Councils were indeed made the channel for the selection and presentation of projects, subject to the approval of the technicians. But the crucial change was one of attitude. Cheating was prevented, poor work was done over, and the local importance of the work was directly perceived. The villagers were spared none of the detailed requirements essential to managing a businesslike, modern enterprise. The government was sufficiently impressed to decide in favor of extending the scheme to the 54 *thanas* of Comilla district for 1962-1963.[52] An appropriation of 10 crores of rupees (about 20 million dollars) was made in wages and wheat, half to be distributed through District Councils and a fourth through the Thana and Union Councils.

The experience of the program's second year was encouraging. The academy arranged a crash program to provide several weeks' training for the 54 Circle Officers and prepared handbooks. Although late in starting, the 17,000 public-works projects organized in 1962-1963 employed some 250,000 persons. The reports suggest the hazards confronting any localized program when it is enlarged to the provincial or national level. Under the pressure of time and limited technical assistance, the newly added *thanas* concentrated on repairing roads and bridges, spending approximately two thirds of their funds and arranging two thirds of their projects for this purpose.[53] Though these projects will have some productive effects, much less was spent on new and improved waterworks, which are essential to bringing East Pakistan under full cultivation.

In 1963-1964 the government decided to expand the program to all the *thanas* of East Pakistan, with an appropriation of 20 crores of rupees; late in 1963 an appropriation of 10 crores of rupees was made for West Pakistan. Once again the Comilla academy prepared a compressed training program for 284 Circle Officers, and increased technical support was provided by the East Pakistan WAPDA. Although the variety and quality of the projects undertaken in 1963-1964 improved over those of the previous year, there were several changes that caused

[52] As the distribution of the wheat through higher tiers indicates, this phase was not wholly within the framework of the Comilla project. The expanded program is outlined in an order from the Basic Democracies Department, Government of East Pakistan, No. IV/NDO-39/62/1213 (180), "Works Programme through Basic Democracies," September 25, 1962. This regulation was later presented in more elaborated form in a brochure, *Works Programme through Basic Democracies, 1962-63*, Basic Democracies and Local Government Department, Government of East Pakistan, 1963.

[53] *An Evaluation of the Rural Works Programme, East Pakistan, 1962-63*, Comilla, Academy for Rural Development, 1964, p. 28. The sequence involved in spreading the program in East Pakistan has allowed the academy to compare many of the critical variables over a period of time.

[54] *An Evaluation of the Rural Works Programme, East Pakistan, 1963-64*, Comilla, Academy for Rural Development, 1965, especially pp. 15-20. See also *The Comilla Rural Administration Experiment: Annual Report for 1963-64*, Comilla, Academy for Rural Development, 1965.

anxiety among those concerned with the local impact of public works.[54] Though the amounts available to Thana and Union Councils tripled, much less was spent on small-scale waterworks for irrigation and drainage. The predominance of roadworks threatened to minimize local impact and to impair the agricultural effects of the program. The evaluation also showed that participation by villagers declined in 1963-1964. Many Union Councils did not even meet to discuss the audit report from 1962-1963, and officials frequently reported that they were too pressed to convene the local bodies.

Though the ingenuity of Akhter Hameed has had a great deal to do with the success of the Comilla experiment, the work that has been accomplished there has not required huge sums of money or depended on large numbers of technical staff supplied by special agencies or government. The project contrasts with both the Tunisian and Moroccan public-works projects in the way in which the Comilla group has built from the locality upward, rather than arriving on the local scene with the full authority of the central government. However, the directional difference, important as it may be in accounting for Comilla's success, does not alter the nature of the political integration viewed as a national problem. In fact, the East Pakistani villagers may remain as remote from the patterns of national politics as they were a generation ago, but the scheme has altered their position for the future by giving them increased material resources and understanding of modern organization.

In assessing the progress made under the three governments, three very different patterns emerge, and are to some extent repeated in many aspects of each government's developmental activities. The Moroccan monarchy has tremendous capacity to arouse rural interest, but has great difficulty in channeling this interest into constructive, institutionalized forms. The rural communes, the Promotion Nationale, and even the new constitution all caught the public eye, and in their early phase benefited greatly from the appeal of the monarchy. But the transformation of these affective reactions into sustained local activity has regularly proved to be a difficult hurdle. A pattern of influence that is to assist national development must have individual meaning and have high instrumental content. The locality must not only understand its potential in relation to the developmental process, but make substantial progress toward staking out a real claim in the expanded activity of the more productive society. Important as the many administrative and political shortcomings of the monarchy may be at the central level, the persistent pattern of exaggerated hopes and insufficient results represents a classic problem of converting highly affective political relationships into operational relationships.

An entirely different problem is found in Tunisia, where the existing political organization, by virtue of being identical to the Socialist Destour and encompassing all government, becomes almost indistinguishable from the national political system. The villager of Morocco and Pakistan is obviously left out of national affairs, but the Tunisian citizen may find it difficult to consider how he is indeed not involved. While we have no intent to belittle the accomplishments of the Tunisian government, it also appears that the citizen has had a relatively small voice in programs affecting the countryside. Mobilization of a government should not be confused with mobilization of a populace. The Socialist Destour's efforts to increase rural participation after 1962 suggests how the developmental process indeed creates new requirements to allow for individual choice and judgment of priorities. Important as Tunisian achievements have been, the real test of the regime will be its ability to absorb and accommodate the more articulate and responsive citizen now beginning to assert himself.

Although the Ayub government contrasts sharply with the prerevolutionary regime for its awareness of the need to reach the villager, it seems doubtful if the military-bureaucratic alliance has indeed made major progress in this direction beyond the reorganizational measures described in Chapter VI. The basic notions for the Ayub regime were taken from projects and plans under way in the prerevolutionary regime, and it might be argued that the discontinuity introduced in rural-reform projects by the abolition of Village AID, for example, represent a net loss. The alliance of military and administrator, however, had a realistic concept of the necessity of involving the villager, though the regime also had many problems in converting this concept into effective action. Like Tunisia, Pakistan responded to promising experiments in rural reform and could provide the administrative support at higher levels. But even as the Ayub regime began to find answers to the developmental problems of the countryside, it also began to lose its political appeal. The fruitful interplay of individual responses to the developmental challenge and to the political system became more difficult with time, in part, because the bureaucratic orientation of the government was itself inimical to joining the two processes.

CHAPTER 8

LEARNING TO WORK AND TO BELIEVE

THE INTANGIBLE quality of education means that discussions of the aims and achievements of education very easily become elusive, if not meaningless. Here, as in the case of agriculture, governments differ in their ability to reduce educational problems to manageable proportions. The comparison of what has been accomplished is often less significant in assessing the political system as a developmental vehicle than the way in which the various governments have gone about the task. In this context there is great contrast among the three political systems. The materials available on the Ayub regime suggest considerable dependence on the work of the previous regime, as in the case of agriculture. However, the reports show that the military-bureaucratic alliance has confronted some of the controversial alternatives although there remains a large quotient of elliptical discussion of Pakistani education. As might be anticipated, the Moroccan monarchy has found it difficult to make a clear statement on the objectives of Moroccan education and highly affective issues such as Arabization dominate educational exchanges. The single-party regime has acted with much more purpose, largely because the discipline of the Socialist Destour enabled it to reduce education to specific proportions early in the developmental process. It should perhaps be repeated that the purpose of the evaluation of the three systems is not to decide which has accomplished "more," but how the approach to the challenge of development is affected by the prevailing characteristics of the regime.

The developmental process involves the transformation of strong affective relationships to the nation into more rational form. The ultimate values governing the individual may remain the same as his highly affective image of the nation is adjusted to the needs of a more complex society, but the image becomes more articulate and more specific as development advances along the dimensions described in this study, and in many other ways as well. In building the national image the new governments have almost uniformly relied on emotionally charged devices to arouse the population, and the distinctions among more specific national goals is hard to maintain. Most leaders of developing countries, in practice, shift easily from one imperative to another. Indeed, they may do so with such ease that the subordinate areas of conflict are concealed, though at best this can be only a temporary solution. This problem is particularly acute in the case of education in the three countries considered herein, all of which are almost wholly Islamic and contain vestiges of Islamic educational institutions.[1] Education involves, there-

[1] The designation given the village Koranic schools, varies from country to

fore, an especially acute case of conflict of national values and local practice, which the new government can only treat with some jeopardy to itself. As will be seen in the following discussion, the reconciliation of developmental requirements and political orientation varies greatly.

The creation of a predominantly secular educational system raises two important questions in a developing country. At the lower level of primary and secondary education the problem is more technical and one of creating a balance within the educational system. In nearly every country of Africa and Asia the colonial regime took steps to educate, and hopefully to indoctrinate, an elite. There was relatively little attention given to basic education outside the cities and towns. Despite the implicit threat to religious values, the demand for primary education is uniformly high in most new nations, and it is important to remember that the demand for reconciliation with Islam, in most instances, originates from quarters other than the countryside. The peasant still needs the additional labor at certain times of the year, but he is also highly motivated to educate his children. Because he nearly always is without funds to build schools, pay teachers, and buy books, the burden falls entirely on government, which must reconcile these needs with the development of the country in many other areas that may hold more promise of immediate returns and for which there may be much more effective pressure.

The second aspect of education has less direct relation to the locality, but is nevertheless essential to local improvement, and represents the most important alternative strategy to mass education for educational improvement. The students in the higher schools, colleges, and universities must be guided into occupations appropriate to the developmental process. The advanced segment of the educational system is critically important in the development process for obvious reasons, and also the center of peculiar tensions that will be discussed in more detail below. The transitional educational generation has clear memories of colonial injustice, and is often fervent in its attachment to the new nation, a quality that can have mixed effects in their perception of the future and of the government. In addition, they have seen the best posts filled with persons who are often no better qualified than they are; though, coming five to ten years after independence, the present graduates must be satisfied with filling in the rapidly increasing number of less glamorous, more routine posts. The fact that young adults in developing countries

---

country. In Morocco they are called *musiid*; in Tunisia and in much of the Middle East, *kuttab*; and in Pakistan, *maktab*. In all these places each school is taught by the local religious figure, who has often attended an Islamic university for several years and is known as *fqih* in the Maghreb and *imam* or *mullah* in Pakistan. Frequently the only book used is the Koran, which is memorized, although the pupil may also receive some basics in arithmetic and history.

have such varied and such violent responses to political life is in itself an indicator of their unsettled frame of mind. Without their help no government of a developing country can reach the countryside. The success that the various regimes have in creating prestige for rural work and motivating young talent to engage itself in a truly national mobilization is an important indicator of the chances of a fruitful integration of the developing country.

PRIMARY EDUCATION AND THE BASICS OF NATION-BUILDING

No single aspect of Western culture took firmer grip in the developing nations of Africa and Asia than the belief in the inevitably enlightening effects of education. The West has unfortunately laid the basis for one of the most gigantic disappointments of the new nations. To acquire educational qualifications in a rapidly growing and an unusually prosperous society is very different from the protracted, tedious struggle to expand that most newly developing countries face. Faith in education has put most developing nations in a kind of double jeopardy. Not only must they divert considerable resources to ostensibly less productive forms of education, but the process of basic education seems to produce new demands before it achieves a level where the society benefits materially or where the subjects are able to act with self-restraint. The most obvious example of the much-labored "rise in expectations" is the nearly universal endorsement of massive primary-education schemes in the developing countries.

To ask whether or not universal primary education is desirable has become a truly academic question. Over the coming decade the three countries in question, and most other developing countries of Africa and Asia, are committed to providing five to ten years of education for every citizen. The human revolution that such an accomplishment suggests, even if done imperfectly, is only another reason why more attention should be given to problems of rural development and political integration. Given the rapid pace of events in developing countries, it may be advisable that, instead of concentrating on understanding the frustrated college student—a world-wide characteristic of advanced students—we might perhaps learn more from examining the transformation of the primary- and secondary-level student, still enmeshed in an illiterate, impoverished social structure of countless villages. The kind of detailed psychological and pedagogical studies this implies are not available for the present inquiry, but the scope of the transformation now taking place can be traced, and its possible relation to the political integration of the dormant populations can be examined.

To some extent the West has also had a distorted view of the impact of education, and the increased concern of the developing nations with the training of technical and professional cadre reflects their reevaluation of the problem. Most of the nations strongly committed to development are in a phase that is not considered in much of the writing on education alone. Thus it may well be correct that "when education has progressed so far that there is a handful of educated and politically articulate people, a tension invariably develops,"[2] but this observation tells us relatively little about political complexities of such tensions. There is little to suggest that a relatively high level of primary education, for example, contributes to political stability or to more rapid development. Moreover, by the time most developing countries have acquired the segment of educationally privileged people needed to propel an independent country, they have also generally made the decision to support universal primary education and to foster literacy programs. The educational build-up in most new countries follows at such a pace that the common-sense observations based on educational distinctions in advanced societies, and their relation to political life, can be extremely misleading.

The prospect of the developing countries' creating a slightly improved mass of less educated people still governed by an educational elite does not seem unlikely. The extent to which educational strategy reverts to earlier colonial patterns, for very different reasons, should not be concealed. The implications for the emerging power structure are comparable, and in some ways are even more explosive than the kind of educational self-interest that motivated the colonial regime in a very different kind of situation. These questions can be partially explored by following the experience of the three countries of the study. Possibly the most openly aristocratic educational system was laid down in British India, under the now famous directions of Macaulay.[3] In preparing an elite according to British standards, primary education was neglected and, as in the early educational history of England, was left to voluntary and local agencies. The result was that three historic forms of primary schools persisted, none of them appropriate for a national school system. There were, first, the traditional schools (*maktabs* and *madrasas*), confined largely to Islamic teachings and basic education. Attached to mosques there were also some Koranic schools, where one learned little more than phrases from the Koran. Lastly, there were a variety of

---

[2] W. E. F. Ward, *Educating Young Nations*, London, George Allen & Unwin, 1959, p. 17. See also James Coleman, ed., *Education and Political Development*, Princeton, Princeton University Press, 1965, and Hobert W. Burns, ed., *Education and the Development of Nations*, Syracuse, Syracuse University Press, 1963.

[3] For a Pakistani view of the early British policy see the study by the first Minister of Education, Fazlur Rahman, *New Education in the Making in Pakistan; Its Ideology and Its Problems*, London, Cassel, 1953, pp. 21-22; also, the Indian reaction, Humayun Kabir, *Education in New India*, London, George Allen & Unwin, 1956, pp. 44-45.

private primary schools, largely in more thickly populated and wealthier regions.[4]

Seventy years after Macaulay, Lord Curzon, one of the first governor generals to take an active interest in rural education, noted that "ever since the cold breath of Macaulay's rhetoric passed over the files of Indian languages and Indian textbooks, the elementary education of the people in their own tongue has shrivelled and pined."[5] The colonial administration did support some district-level schools, but they were often confined to teaching in English and thereby excluded the vast majority of the young people. Nevertheless, primary education expanded over the nineteenth century, and in 1892 there were over 14,500 primary schools and 639,000 pupils maintained by the districts, although a large proportion were in urban areas. In 1907 a fourth of the primary schools were under public sponsorship, and the rest under missionaries, local bodies, and other private auspices. Despite the encouragement given by Lord Curzon, not too much progress was made in reforming the complex and inadequate system by World War I. By then both Jinnah and Nehru were demanding free and compulsory primary education in the Imperial Legislative Council.

As in the case of local government, Bengal took the lead and the Bengal Primary Education Act of 1919 was extended to village councils in 1921. The act was amended in 1930 to transfer initiative in establishing compulsory schools to the provincial government, and to use district schools for the administration of primary education. The effects of more vigorous local bodies in East Pakistan can be seen at this earlier period. There were over 44,000 primary schools in 1919 with 1,384,201 pupils. Over nine tenths of these schools were locally supported, though of poor quality and unrelated to institutions for higher education. The intervention of the provincial government was not well calculated, although the schools did receive a portion of local taxes after 1930. Teachers were still unbelievably underpaid and untrained. About 60,000 of the 90,000 primary teachers in East Bengal in 1938 had no training, and it was not uncommon for a teacher to be paid 10 rupees a month. The effects of Bengal's comparative advantage in primary education under the British have now become a handicap. Though still more literate than West Pakistan, Bengal has inherited a poorly equipped and poorly staffed school system.

The progress of the Punjab under the British was much less promising than that in Bengal, but it has left West Pakistan in a position to produce relatively more persons with higher education, and has enabled

[4] Probably the most complete account of primary education in Pakistan is Muhammad Shamsul Huq, *Compulsory Education in Pakistan*, Paris, UNESCO, 1954, who discusses the varied background of primary schools, pp. 11-12.

[5] *Ibid.*, p. 27. A good brief account of progress under the British is given in *ibid.*, pp. 27-42.

the western wing to profit from building an entirely new school system from the ground up. In 1919 the former Punjab had only about 6,000 primary schools with 298,690 pupils. The Punjab Primary Education Act of 1919 anticipated compulsory primary education through free public schools, but was not widely applied. Since the creation of the schools depended on local contribution, education in the Punjab tended to be more selective and of higher quality, though more limited. Whereas the use of elected school boards in East Pakistan tended to reduce the quality of school administration, the subordination of the Punjab school boards to the district official produced better results where facilities existed. In brief, by 1947 there were three major policies in force: the Punjab had compulsory education as a local responsibility that was not widely enforced; the Sind was wholly dependent on the provincial government's initiative; and Bengal had a compromise between local and central responsibility that was stagnating under the outmoded and inadequate burden of a large primary-school system. Only token progress has been made in the other regions of West Pakistan.

In the period of parliamentary government prior to the revolution only minor progress was made. The rivalry of the two wings made central planning difficult, and the country was so fully occupied in looking after more pressing problems that little attention was given to the country's long-run educational needs. The Pakistan Education Conference of 1947 resolved that "free and compulsory primary education should be introduced for a period of five years." Each of the wings has a program for the introduction of compulsory primary education dating from 1951,[6] but there is no information available on how much has actually been accomplished, nor did the plans ever become the subject of public interest and concern. Under the Bengali scheme the schools under one Union Board in each *thana* or about 2,500 schools per year were to be put on a compulsory basis, requiring ten years to achieve fully compulsory primary education. The old West Punjab province approved a twenty-year program to build 1,200 schools a year. In 1952 the central government issued a Six Year Plan of Educational Development. Though it was the first effort to translate needs into concrete terms, it was, in the words of the First Year Plan, "not related to an overall plan for social and economic development." Reviewing the country's situation in 1955, the Planning Board noted that there had been a "comparatively sterile system of education that represented primary education at Independence, and no significant improvements had been made in it since."[7] Though the first planning group acknowledged

---

[6] The prepartition proposals for Bengal, Sind, and Punjab provinces are given in *ibid.*, Appendices I-III, 127-146.

[7] Government of Pakistan, National Planning Board, *The First Five Year Plan (1955-60)*, Karachi, 1956, pp. 543 and 545.

the importance of widespread primary education, they suggested that five years would be needed to reorient the entire system—an optimistic estimate—and added that fifteen years or more would be needed before universal primary education could be achieved.

The over-all position of Pakistani primary and secondary education has improved somewhat faster under the military regime, but the total figures conceal important differences between the two wings. In 1960-1961, for example, primary enrollment increased by some 400,000 pupils and included just over five million students or about a fifth of the 5- to 14-year age group.[8] Secondary-school enrollment, though somewhat inflated by the Pakistan classification system, reached almost one and a half million in 1960-1961, and displayed much larger increases than in previous years. The ratio of secondary to primary pupils is much higher in Pakistan than in Morocco and Tunisia—a fact which can be accounted for by the professional orientation of government still reflected in the military-bureaucratic regime. Education has yet to make a major contribution to social mobility in Pakistan and, thus, to increased participation. On the whole, West Pakistan has better schools, though they are not well distributed. A more important regional disparity is that nearly two thirds of the entering students in the west complete the primary cycle, where as few as 15 per cent of the entering pupils completed it in parts of Bengal.[9] The First Plan called for 4,000 new schools, of which about 2,500 were built, an increased enrollment of a million students, of which about half a million took place. With demographic pressures eating away the increased attendance, Pakistan had about the same proportion of her eligible students in primary school—about 40 per cent—in 1955 and 1960.

The problems of grass-roots change are suggested by the fact that only a bit more than two thirds of the funds allocated to education in the First Plan period (1955-1960) were spent. A new emphasis was made in the Second Plan, which was in harmony with the National Education Commission Report, issued in 1959 and, therefore, available for close coordination with the Second Plan. Though pleased with the improvement in secondary-school enrollment, the members of the Planning Commission noted that "no significant improvements in the quality of school

[8] For early figures see *ibid.*, p. 541, and *The Second Five Year Plan* (1960-65), Karachi, 1960, pp. 338-339. Since 1958, total figures appear in the *International Handbook of Education*, vols. 20-24, 1958-1962, Paris, UNESCO; but educational classifications were changed in 1958, so comparison with earlier performance is difficult. Age-group figures are taken from the *Population Census of Pakistan: Age, Sex and Marital Status*, Bulletin No. 3, Office of the Census Commissioner, Ministry of Home Affairs, Karachi, 1962, p. 2.

[9] Tables giving the distribution of pupils by classes from 1947-1948 to 1951-1952 for each of the major provinces will be found in Huq, *op.cit.*, pp. 148-149. In this period under a tenth of the Bengalis entering first grade continued to the fifth.

education was made."[10] Noting the great need for improved school buildings, the group hoped that Basic Democracies could be used to provide local support for building programs. About half the buildings in East Pakistan were to be improved, and about 15,000 new schools were planned for West Pakistan. Though stressing technical and vocational training, the Second Plan tripled the expenditures on primary education, and aimed at putting 60 per cent of the eligible children in school by 1965.

Though some exception may be taken to parts of the report of the Commission on National Education, it is a courageous and imaginative response to Pakistan's educational problems. Reminiscent of the quarrels that have begun to plague North African progress, the report noted that fundamental progress requires a revival of the solidarity Pakistanis felt in 1947. It condemned the reappearance of "the attitudes that had been absorbed into the bloodstream of the nation during the past century" to encumber reforms with "passivity, indiscipline, opportunism and regionalism."[11] Perhaps more clearly than in either Morocco or Tunisia, the notion of education as a process in which all must participate was underscored. The report frankly stated that education could not be accepted passively as a benefit of government, to which the people were not committed. Though giving recognition to the place of Islam in the national ideology, the group placed first importance on fostering a sense of national identity, and also gave preference to the immediate tasks of nation-building. Exactly how these lofty goals are achieved from one society to another remains unclear, but the commission stated the goals of education in a developing country in bold terms.

In line with these objectives the report advised that the districts of West Pakistan and the subdivisions of East Pakistan be expected to provide half the cost of primary education, double the standard contribution in 1959. Stress was placed on the need for strict enforcement of the rules of admission, promotion, and attendance, all of which had been relaxed to permit serious lowering of standards. While religious instruction would remain obligatory during primary school, the commission also hoped that steps would be taken to foster patriotic habits and good citizenship as well. With an eye toward the destructive prestige attached to education, it was suggested that a way be found for practical, manual experience in primary education, possibly by making certain handwork mandatory. While advocating more community participation in maintaining schools and providing for teachers, the report admitted

---

[10] Planning Commission, *The Second Five Year Plan, op.cit.*, p. 338. See also *ibid.*, pp. 341-342, for their estimate of primary education. As in the case of agriculture, the second planning group paid less attention to the rationale of the subject, and was more directly focused on the "hard" needs of development.

[11] *Report of the Commission on National Education*, Ministry of Education, Karachi, 1959, p. 6.

that administration had suffered under the decentralization permitted in 1921, and wanted supervision to remain at the district level.[12]

Because of the over-all superior quality of higher education in West Pakistan, certain disparities appear. For example, the western wing is to develop a training capacity of 7,000 primary teachers and 2,000 secondary teachers per year, as opposed to a capacity of 5,000 and 1,100 for the same categories in the eastern wing. While the literacy accomplishments of the eastern wing are impressive and higher than literacy levels in the west,[13] the more selective, higher quality system inherited in the Punjab has sent more students on to higher levels. West Pakistan has a larger number of students who have had secondary education, and double the eastern wing's number of students above that level. Though the Pakistani plans seem to have realistically evaluated the existing strengths and weaknesses of the educational systems of the two wings, the risk remains that the different levels will be magnified with time and contribute to additional regional rivalries. At the local level the villages remain heavily dependent on the caliber of district administration.

Tunisian educational reform at the lower levels has certainly profited from the comparatively small scale of the problems posed, but the reforms also reflect the purposefulness of the single-party regime. Tunisia has several historical advantages, which should be acknowledged. At a time when Morocco was still ruled by a sultan and limited to a strictly Islamic educational system, Tunisia was producing a young, urban elite under French auspices. In Pakistan the first effective moves toward providing educational opportunities specifically designed to prepare Muslims for modern life date from the founding of Aligarh University in 1875 and the appeals of Syed Ahmed to young Muslims to prepare themselves for higher posts in India. However, the same issue had been presented in Tunisia by the mid-nineteenth century by Khereddine,[14] and by the turn of the century there were sufficient numbers of French-trained Tunisians to form the original Destour Party. Though having little direct impact on education at lower levels, the relative advance

[12] Primary education is discussed in *ibid.*, pp. 171-185. The fact that the shortcomings of the primary-school system varied so much between the two wings made specific recommendations difficult.

[13] In the 1961 census the over-all literacy level was 19.2 per cent; regionally, 21.5 per cent in East Pakistan and 16.3 per cent in West Pakistan. However, 88.6 per cent of the East Pakistani literates were in rural areas as opposed to 33.1 per cent of West Pakistani literates. Two thirds of the male literates and three fourths of the female literates of Pakistan had attended primary schools in East Pakistan. See *Population Census of Pakistan 1961: Literacy and Education*, Bulletin 4, Office of the Census Commissioner, Ministry of Home and Kashmir Affairs, Karachi, 1962.

[14] For an account of late nineteenth-century reforms see Leon Carl Brown, "Education, 'Cultural Unity' and the Future," *Institute of Current World Affairs Newsletter*, December 1, 1960, pp. 8-14. Comparable early intellectual influence in Pakistan under Syed Ahmed is described in Richard Symonds, *The Making of Pakistan*, London, Faber & Faber, n.d., pp. 28-37.

of Tunisia provided her with a group of leaders of distinctly different orientation, revealed in many aspects of Tunisian life. Though quantitatively in a position similar to that of Morocco and Pakistan, Tunisia had a secular view of education by the time independence was achieved.

For the first two years of independence there was a general stock-taking of the country's educational system. The main effort was in the direction of subjecting the Islamic school system under the auspices of Zaitouna University to government control. Through a system of fourteen city and seven provincial centers, the ancient Islamic university drew students from the *kuttabs* for its religiously oriented program, which did little to prepare students for constructive roles in a modernizing Tunisia. The Tunisian government was quick to brand its methods as "archaic and medieval," and the first steps to merge the Islamic school system with the modern schools were taken promptly in the fall of 1956.[15] In two years the lower levels of the Islamic school system were wholly absorbed in the Ministry (later Secretary of State) for National Education. The fact that the Islamic centers had become a focus for agitation against the energetically secular policies of the president very likely influenced this action. At the primary level there were also private, Jewish, "French-Arab" or mixed, and purely French schools. One Tunisian noted in the fall of 1956 that the country's students were still studying the Jesuit-Jansenist controversy, while Arabic was being taught as in the "age of the camel."[16]

Unlike Morocco, Tunisia and Pakistan did not make substantial concessions to popular demands for widespread primary education. In many respects the Tunisian policy represents a compromise between Morocco, where the primary-school system was rapidly expanded, and Pakistan, where attention was focused on providing technical, skilled cadre for the development effort. To some extent each responded to its particular needs, but the important point in the political context of the inquiry is that in no case was the government concerned responding solely to popular pressure, but to its own vision of the developmental process as well. The single-party regime asserted its widely recognized virtue of decisiveness in the spring of 1958. The first Minister of Education was relieved of his job in order to appoint Mahmud Messadi, a talented and energetic teacher himself. The previous minister had brought the system under control from a political viewpoint, but progress

[15] See the discussion of the Tunisian situation in *Action Tunisienne*, October 5, 1955. Some 213 Koranic schools were immediately absorbed, *International Yearbook of Education*, Paris, UNESCO, vol. 19, 1957, p. 380.

[16] *Action Tunisienne*, September 3, 1956. See also Leon Carl Brown, "Tunisia," in Coleman, ed., *Education and Political Development*, *op.cit.*, pp. 144-168. See also the useful bibliography on many aspects of North African education, M. L. Tillet, A. Van Leeuwen, and A. Louis, "Eléments bibliographiques sur l'enseignment et l'education en Afrique du Nord, et particulièrement en Tunisie," *I.B.L.A.*, vol. 17, no. 67, 1954, pp. 285-307.

in providing the cadre needed for development, and even in admitting more pupils at the primary level, had not been distinguished.

In addition to his vigor, Messadi brought to education an unusual planning talent and an appreciation of the problems of bringing a French-oriented school system into harmony with the social requirements of the country. In the opinion of many Muslim countries, including Morocco, the Tunisians made disastrous concessions to modernity. The irony of the criticism is that as the result of careful planning and school integration Tunisia has made more progress toward Arabization of the school system than Morocco, and is probably less dependent on French support at higher levels despite the large number of French teachers. Indeed, the reforms adopted in Morocco several years later were essentially the same as those instituted by Messadi in 1958. Under his direction a ten-year plan for education was drawn up, based on estimated requirements for higher skills and knowledge, and with explicit cost provisions. The Secretary of State for National Education, like Ben Salah several years later, had the full support of the president and the Socialist Destour. Messadi, like the Moroccan and Pakistani officials, recognized that "educational development is part of the general development of the country, notably economic development."[17]

The basic elements of the reform involved converting the seven-year primary cycle to six years, followed by two three-year periods of increasingly selective advancement. This enables Tunisia to conform to French practice, while the Pakistani cycle of five years of primary education, followed by a three-year and lastly a four-year cycle is closer to American practice.[18] But the ideal phasing of primary and secondary education is not so important in educational development as the government's ability to make changes in the existing scheme, and it is in this respect that Tunisia has distinguished herself. At the primary level the important changes, which were in fact carried out, were to make the first two years of primary school half time, to concentrate on the children arriving at school age at the expense of those who failed or were over age, and to eliminate the seventh year of primary school. Though the country has fallen slightly behind its schedule (not forgetting that Tunisia is distinguished by virtue of even having one), the aim is to admit all newly eligible children to school by the fall of 1966, and to have

[17] *Action Tunisienne*, June 30, 1957. See also *Perspective Décennale de Scolarisation*, Tunis, Secretary of State for National Education, 1958; also, *New Conception of Education in Tunisia*, Tunis, Secretary of State for National Education, 1958.

[18] There is some confusion as to what kind of secondary cycle the Pakistani will settle on. The phasing given here is taken from the *Report of the Commission on National Education*, op.cit., pp. 117-119. The controversy centers over what role the colleges and universities should have in supervising higher sccondary education, which will be discussed further in the next section of this chapter. Practice varies from one part of the country to another.

universal and compulsory primary education by the fall of 1968.

The core of the plan was not only the achievement of compulsory primary education, but also the phasing of this expansion with secondary and university education. The government estimated that about 40 per cent of those completing primary school would be admitted to secondary or to intermediate schools, the latter being terminal and designed to fill lower-level commercial and managerial posts. In addition, it was determined that, of the roughly 200,000 students entering the full secondary cycle, about a fourth would become primary-school teachers, a fourth would enter universities, and half would become skilled technical cadre. The Tunisian approach is remarkable for its comprehensiveness and selectivity, but it is also apparent that the severe selection process could contribute to dissatisfaction among students and parents. In effect, a student was having his entire career plotted out by the government, and there were no educational opportunities outside of those controlled by the government. There is evidence that some discontent accumulated by 1961, and the Secretary of State for National Education expressed his hope that the proportion admitted to the secondary cycle might be increased in the later part of the Ten Year Plan.[19] Local admissions committees were instituted in 1960, but it is doubtful if local authorities would permit them to become an avenue for modifying state policy or adjusting planning requirements.

Messadi's work is particularly notable because he set the pace and style for later planning under the single-party regime. Ben Salah soon followed him by introducing comparable reforms and phased planning into public health, but the first indication of the party's capacity was the ten-year perspective for education. Moreover, Tunisia has come very close to filling its objectives, and admission at the primary level has been kept to the comparatively low and constant rate specified in the plan. Tunisia may well be unusual for the extent to which educational planning anticipated, and perhaps stimulated, planning in the society as a whole. In his *Ten Year Prospect* Messadi frankly recognized that the products of the scheme could be usefully absorbed into the society "only if the prospects of economic development over the same ten year period [could] be drawn with the same accuracy." The single-party regime squarely faced the alternatives of development: either the country prepared to undergo the strains of mobilizing its talent or it would remain impoverished and weak. The risk of overproduction of students

[19] The arbitrary advancement policy no doubt created some hardships, as well as inadequate resources. Messadi discusses modifications in the *Perspectives Décennales de Développement*, Secretary of State for National Education, Tunis, 1962, p. 251. Strained relations between parents and school authorities were noted in another article by Lelong, "L'Enseignment Tunisien en 1961: Bilan et Perspectives," *I.B.L.A.*, vol. 24, nos. 95-96, pp. 251-277.

with intermediate and advanced educations was present and acknowledged, but it is a risk inherent in the modernization process.

There is little doubt but that Tunisia's calculated and selective approach to the challenge of education offended the sensitivities of some Arab countries, who saw that such planning entailed narrowing the Islamic orientation of the educational system and making some very painful choices about the number of educational opportunities for young people. Morocco represents a middle course. It should be remembered that the Socialist Destour decided *prior* to these reforms that Islamic influence in education would be reduced. For example, "Koranic and moral studies" were given one hour a week in primary school, and at the secondary level an austere subject, "Philosophy and the Study of Islamic Thought," gave most of its time to philosophy. The solidarity of party leadership makes it difficult to detect reservations to this policy, but it is significant that some usually reliable party members objected on the floor of the National Assembly to the neglect of Islam.[20] No doubt with a very different orientation than the old Islamic instruction, steps were taken in 1961 to provide more teaching in Islam, national history, and Tunisian geography at the secondary level.

The advantage of any type of planning is that it enables a country to judge its own progress in explicit terms. Despite the highly relative, and occasionally distorted, conclusions of such estimates, the act of publicly evaluating performance is an important step along the road to modernization. When the ten-year economic perspective was being made, the Secretary of State for National Education was able to assess the progress of the first three years of educational planning. Though slightly short on the primary level, the more serious shortfalls had been in secondary education, where it appeared that there were serious shortages of teachers.[21] Steps were proposed to divert more capable students into teaching at the expense of other development needs. One of the encouraging aspects of the evaluation was that the Tunisian primary system had been praised by inspectors sent from France, who noted that

[20] Noted in an excellent summation of the Tunisian transition to secular education by Michel Lelong, "La Formation civique, morale et réligieuse dans l'enseignment tunisien," *I.B.L.A.*, vol. 25, no. 99, 1962, pp. 257-270. Bourguiba is also outspoken on this issue. See, for example, his speech, "La Réforme de l'Enseignment: Prémier Bilan," June 19, 1961, Tunis, Secretary of State for Information, 1961.

[21] Secretary of State for National Education, *Situation Scolaire: Trois Premières Années de l'Application du Plan Décennal de Scolarisation*, June 1961, pp. 19-20. It was, of course, wholly fortuitous that this evaluation of Tunisian progress, and the heavy continued dependence on French assistance, was made several months before the Bizerte crisis. Bourguiba's willingness to retreat was in no small measure dictated by the needs of Tunisian education. Tunisia is one of the few developing countries that prepares detailed reports on educational accomplishments. See also *Situation de l'Enseignment (1962-1963)* and *Deuxième Année d'Exécution du Plan Triennal (1963-1964)*, Tunis, Secretary of State for National Education.

some aspects of the Tunisian system were in fact superior to instruction in France.[22] However, Tunisia paid a price for quality education which few developing countries will accept. The country remained heavily dependent on France for secondary-school teachers, about half of them being under contract from the Metropole.

The review showed that the regional disparities in the numbers of pupils admitted from the eligible groups of various provinces still persisted. Though the "disinherited" regions of Kef, Kairouan, and Gafsa had made important progress, their level of attendance was only about a third of that in the more favored regions of Sousse, Tunis, and Sfax.[23] If the disparities were so great in the relatively compact country of Tunisia, they were very likely even greater in Morocco and Pakistan. The latter two countries do not publish appropriate data, but the differences in Pakistan are very large and can be detected in literacy and education figures published in the 1961 census.[24] To compensate for the lag in rural areas the Tunisian government began a scheme for subsidized school construction as part of the 1958 reforms, a plan that was partially adopted by Morocco several years later and used in some parts of Pakistan. The country was building over half its schools under this scheme in 1959 and 1960; but returned to full government financing in 1963 in order to regulate regional disparities.[25]

Tunisia represents a country where the political system made it possible for the leaders to define the "national imperatives" and to pursue them vigorously. The fact that this applied to nearly every aspect of the developmental process makes the country an important example for the study of the advantages and disadvantages of the single-party regime. The Moroccan monarchy represents an equally challenging alternative. Morocco was not occupied for a sufficient time for French educational methods to make the imprint they did in Tunisia, although most modern education was provided under French auspices or in France itself prior to independence. The first resident general, Marshal Lyautey, had rather aristocratic ideas about education, but was not opposed to widening educational opportunities and to creating a modern Moroccan elite. Recalling his experience in the use of officers as primary-school teachers

[22] *Situation Scolaire, op.cit.,* pp. 24 and 27. Francophobes will be pleased to note that the Tunisians were doing especially well in English instruction, and have in fact pressed the study of English since the Bizerte crisis. At the height of the crisis the government considered briefly the possibility of making English the second language, which would, of course, have caused serious dislocation in the educational system.

[23] For the comparison over a three-year period see *Action Tunisienne,* July 11, 1958, and *Situation Scolaire, op.cit.,* p. 10.

[24] Detailed results by district can be found in the *Population Census of Pakistan 1961: Literacy and Education, op.cit.,* pp. 160-331.

[25] *Deuxième Année . . . , op.cit.,* p. 4. Earlier figures are available in the *International Yearbook of Education,* Paris, UNESCO, vol. 21, 1959, pp. 394-395, and vol. 22, 1960, pp. 412-413.

in Madagascar, he noted that "we are in complete accord that there remains a great effort needed to develop primary education among the natives."[26] He made several suggestions on the way in which books and supplies might be donated by French publishers sympathetic to the Moroccan cause.

The timing of the colonial impact no doubt made a great difference in Morocco and Tunisia. The Tunisians were under the French regime long enough to see how French education, and modern ways in general, might be used to sustain Tunisia, and how it might be converted into a national blessing rather than a cultural insult. Arriving much later in Morocco, the Protectorate had no sooner pacified the tribes and united the country than a nationalist movement having strong pan-Islamic overtones began. The first Muslim secondary school was founded in Fez in 1926 by Mohammed Ghazi, a teacher for the young men then reacting against French rule. Unlike Sadiki College in Tunis and Aligarh in Pakistan, the first response of the local Muslim community in Morocco was to revive and to defend its culture by asserting the role of Arabic and Islamic principles. Their reasons for reacting against colonial methods are explained in part by the active effort to divide Morocco into Muslim and Berber regions after 1930, the date of the famous Berber *dahir*, which sought to preserve tribal customary law in a third of the country. Simultaneously there were more vigorous attempts to convert Berbers to Christianity.[27] Thus the early Moroccan nationalists were confronted with a more desperate situation than either the Pakistanis or Tunisians, where the Muslim elite, small as it might have been did not feel threatened culturally.

The outgrowth of this conflict, in addition to the great impetus it gave the nationalist movement, was that a distinct organization of Muslim schools was started by contributions from early nationalist leaders. These schools were heavily oriented toward traditional Islamic education, but there was also some instruction in modern subjects and an attempt to prepare young Moroccans to take responsible positions in the emerging society. The essential characteristic was to preserve Arabic instruction at all costs. During the 1930's "free schools," meaning schools free of French influence, were started in most of the cities and towns, and became a training ground for the future leaders of the Istiqlal.[28] With inde-

[26] Pierre Lyautey, ed., *Lyautey l'Africain*: *Textes et Lettres*, Paris, Plon, vol. 4, 1953-1957, pp. 172-174.

[27] The effects of the Berber *dahir* are described in the author's *Political Change in Morocco*, Princeton, Princeton University Press, 1961, pp. 34-56. Comparable efforts were being made in Algeria and Tunisia at this time, though on the whole less likely to succeed and with less ultimate political effect.

[28] For the early role of the free schools see Robert Rezette, *Les Partis Politiques Marocaines*, Paris, Colin, 1955, p. 312; also, Ashford, *op.cit.*, pp. 57 and 64. Rezette estimates that the free schools were training a total of 20,000 students at primary and secondary levels in 1952.

pendence Morocco not only had a large school system organized and financed apart from the government, but also had a large number of educational leaders committed to the principle of continuing instruction in Arabic and with strong Islamic emphasis. With Istiqlal leaders in most important government posts and in control of education until 1960, the country faced particularly difficult problems in renovating its educational system.

The emphasis given free and equal education throughout the history of the independence struggle meant that the Moroccan government was committed to increasing admission to primary schools rapidly. The first Minister of National Education, Mohammed Al-Fassi, a brother of the Istiqlal leader, proceeded to admit large numbers of new pupils before the country had prepared teachers, curricula, or materials. There was no attempt to unify the different primary and secondary schools operated by the French, the Jews, and the Muslims, both modern and traditional. With almost no preparation, enrollment in Muslim primary schools, many of them on the model of the traditional Koranic school, was over 300,000 by the fall of 1956, roughly triple the preindependence enrollment. While they neglected modern secondary education—largely controlled through the remaining French schools—they increased Muslim secondary-school enrollment also far beyond the capacity of the system,[29] The Islamic secondary-school system, operating under the aegis the Qarawiyn University in Fez and Ben Youssef University in Marrakech, was under a completely different series of phases and examinations than the modern system. Not only did each of the three systems operate independently of the others, but within any one system there was no coordination from one level to the next. The resulting chaos and deterioration in quality of instruction was unbelievable.

The first attempt to emerge from confusion was the establishment of a Royal Commission on Education Reform, which was to make suggestions for the fall of 1957. The mission of the group reflected the continued confusion, for it was asked to devise means of rapid Arabization, to consider ways of constructing a standard basic education for Moroccans, and to determine how Moroccan schools would relate to European education for advanced instruction. The fact that the three goals were contradictory in many ways apparently escaped notice. The report of the commission did little to clarify the problem, and admitted that there was no agreement on how modern and traditional Muslim education should be coordinated. It was suggested that the secondary cycle be unified "gradually," leading to specialization in Islamic studies, letters, science, or math in the final three years of the six-year cycle. The com-

[29] From the Moroccan report made in the *International Yearbook of Education*, Paris, UNESCO, vol. 20, 1958, pp. 234-235. The secondary-school figures appear in *op.cit.*, vol. 22, 1960, p. 258.

mission also discreetly noted that "we fear certain officials do not have the enthusiasm necessary to assure a good application of the reforms."[30]

After two years the indiscriminate expansion of the school system threatened to handicap the country's entire development effort. With the formation of the Balafrej government in the spring of 1958 it was decided to formulate a two-year estimate of national development needs, including education. The school system was losing skilled teachers to other ministries, and it was obvious that few steps were being taken to give young Moroccans the training needed to fill modern jobs. Under the new Minister of National Education a Royal Commission was again convened, and the group was given a courageously honest estimate of the country's educational situation. Benjelloun frankly stated that Morocco must not sacrifice "quality to quantity" by Arabizing the entire system with haste or by a "general lowering of the educational level of the primary cycle."[31] After bitter controversy within the commission it was decided to accept reforms similar to those adopted in Tunisia. The primary cycle was reduced to five years, with the first two years half time and elimination of students over fourteen. Morocco had a single primary- and secondary-education division for the first time in the fall of 1959.

But the repercussions on the secondary level were still severe, and were minimized in Tunisia in similar circumstances only be preserving careful standards of selection and promotion. Not until the fall of 1960 did the secondary schools begin to conform to a standard six-year cycle, including the Muslim secondary schools under the Islamic universities. There was nothing comparable to the Tunisian *Ten Year Prospect* for education, and the goals set down in the Moroccan plan were imperfectly enforced, although it was apparent that even by rough estimates the country was preparing little more than a fifth of the necessary skilled persons.[32] Even under the new secretary general of the ministry each division continued "to distinguish itself in order to prove its originality," while the tide of new recruits at the primary level meant that the deteriorating process could only be reversed with firm sacrifice. In 1963

[30] See *Al-Istiqlal*, February 9, 1957, and July 6, 1957. Also, I. William Zartman, *Morocco: Problems of a New Power*, New York, Atherton Press, 1964, pp. 170-174.

[31] *Al-Istiqlal*, August 30, 1958. See also the report in the *International Yearbook of Education*, *op.cit.*, vol. 21, 1959, pp. 304-306, and Zartman, *op.cit.*, pp. 185-188.

[32] The first national estimates appear in the *Plan Quinquennal*, *op.cit.*, pp. 334-344; see also *Al-Istiqlal*, September 19, 1959, and October 10, 1960, and Zartman, *op.cit.*, p. 173. Although not directly related to lower-level education, an early attempt was made by Abdallah Ibrahim when he was Minister of Labor and Social Affairs to start a coordinated plan for the training and placement of commercial, technical, and scientific cadre. Even this comparatively more manageable chore went undone because of ministerial rivalries, and the author was told in 1962 that nothing more had been attempted.

Morocco was prepared to establish compulsory primary education, but she also found that less than half the students entering higher levels could be accommodated.[33] The political system not only failed to respond to the obvious shortcomings of education, but acted to compound the problems.

The crux of the controversy remained the Arabization issue, called the "battle horse for all political propaganda" by a high official who resigned in disgust. The concessions to the Arabizing bloc were many, including special facilities for a Faculty in Islamic Law at Qarawiyn and the Royal Pedagogical Institute, later dissolved, to devise ways of giving instruction in science, math, geography, and related subjects in Arabic. The Law Faculty at the University of Rabat was divided into warring sections oriented to Arabic versus French instruction. Indirect efforts were made to convert the ancient universities by introducing new subjects and even women students. These changes did not affect the lower levels of the system, but they indicate how the intransigent views of the Arabizing faction obstructed changes in other parts of the educational system. Indeed, the Moroccans later reported to UNESCO that educational planning and coordination had been "ineffective" until the fall of 1961, when the three divisions of elementary, secondary, and higher education were finally put under a General Director of Education.[34] Furthermore, the pedagogical center, to which such high hopes had been attached, was converted to teaching secondary teachers, as a result of its "absurdly low" output.

The achievements of the Moroccans should not be ignored. Many thousands of schools have been constructed, and, whatever the sacrifice in quality, the number of Moroccan primary teachers more than tripled since independence. Many of these are Koranic schoolteachers who have been given short conversion courses. About a third of the new recruits are student teachers, many with only a year or two of secondary education. The country has also built a thousand or more schools each year, often calling on local contributions to construct the foundations and shell of the building. However, the voluntary program was organized

[33] *Jeune Afrique*, October 11, 1964. The figures on secondary education substantiate the alarm denoted in the report from which this quote came, "Note sur l'Education Nationale," mimeo., Ministry of National Education, June 22, 1961. The tardy attempt at reform is reflected in the sharp drop in secondary-school enrollment in the fall of 1959.

[34] *International Yearbook of Education*, op.cit., vol. 22, 1960, p. 249. At the height of the chaos in 1958-1959, the Moroccan report did not contain figures for secondary education. Prior to this the four (French, Jewish, modern Muslim, and traditional Muslim) kinds of schools were listed separately. Only in 1959-1960 did consolidated figures comparable to Tunisian and Pakistani reports begin to appear. In the fall of 1962 Moroccans received some distressing evidence of the price their children might pay for the deterioration of the educational system. About 90 per cent of the candidates for the baccalaureate failed, though there were later some reports of irregularities in the examining procedure.

on a crash basis, and succeeded largely because of the logistical support given by the royal army.[35] Again, this is not intended to minimize the value of these accomplishments, but to suggest that they have been achieved in unplanned and irregular fashion. Though Morocco began to appoint local admission committees in the fall of 1960, there is no single aspect of education on which the communities might focus, nor were there even reliable bureaucratic lines relating the towns and villages to the educational system. Moroccan education, like other aspects of her developmental activity, was caught in a twofold dilemma. Political confusion at the national level encouraged opportunism, while a growing sense of ineffectiveness at the local level produced apathy.

The large absolute gains in Moroccan primary education indicate that there will be a momentous increase in rural literacy in the next decade, and the beginnings of a similar effect can be seen in the literacy figures for West Pakistan. The future of the political systems of these countries will depend to a large extent on the way in which these increases were accomplished. Morocco has made widespread primary education an overriding national goal, and many citizens are likely to be disappointed when they learn that primary education does not prepare one for most tasks in a developing country. If anything, the effect is likely to increase expectations even more than the mobilizing action of the monarchy has already done and thereby to contribute to more dissatisfaction. Had the secondary system, or other aspects of Moroccan life, begun to make more preparation for the impact of increased lower-level education, more optimism could be expressed.

The course of Tunisia and Pakistan are both instructive in this regard. Bourguiba speaks frequently of the "cadres of the nation," but this emphasis denotes an entirely different view on the role of education in national political life. Without the dramatic effect of Bourguiba, Ayub has conceded to the same priorities in education. Both political systems show themselves to be more task-oriented, but relatively less has been done in Pakistan to communicate the over-all significance of the sacrifice at the primary level. As in the case of most developmental problems, the military-bureaucratic alliance had great difficulty in making its goals and achievements known to the local people,[36] and the task

---

[35] The Moroccans had a program for local contribution to school construction from 1958, but it was largely in the hands of the *caids* and regional school officials, like the Tunisian plan. Normally from 500 to 600 schools were built under this program. In 1961 school construction threatened to fall far short of the expected increase in enrollment, and "Operation School" was given a personal push by Hassan II. A total of 1,022 schools were constructed over the summer.

[36] There are, of course, a host of problems surrounding village schools per se, and this literature too is useful in evaluating a government's response to the developmental challenge. See, for example, Cole S. Brombeck, "Education for National Development," in S.M.Z. Rizvi, ed., *A Reader in Basic Democracies*, Peshawar, West Pakistan Academy for Village Development, 1961, pp. 81-99.

is now greatly complicated by the alarming actions of the revived political parties.

POLITICALLY OVERDEVELOPED YOUTH

There are two aspects of education that have particular significance in the effort to involve more persons in the developmental process. The question of raising the general level of education and providing the basic knowledge needed to become an active, responsible citizen has been discussed. The second aspect of rural mobilization is finding talented persons with higher education who are willing to work in the less attractive posts opened up in rural locations. In some respects this is only an aspect of the broader questions of how to provide the technical and scientific skill needed for the development process in any country. However, the requirements for the industrial sector can be more easily calculated, and persons can more easily be attracted to new jobs in urban centers. All three countries have given considerable thought to the subordinate aspect of the way in which the more easily measurable task of filling industrial, commercial, and scientific jobs will be accomplished. Despite the commonly recognized need, the success of the three governments varies greatly, and merits closer examination in the light of the capacity of each government to channel the energies of its young people into developmental posts.[37]

The uncertain image of the future that seems to influence the thinking of many college and university students in Africa and Asia is, after all, a small-scale version of the uncertainty which confronts the government itself. The fact that insecurity and apprehension among youth is often expressed directly, while governments act in more subdued terms, is accounted for by the extent to which the youth who has progressed toward a modern education cannot independently delay the process that is carrying him into a more complex world. As individuals the advanced students have a large investment in the creation of the more complex society promised through intensive development, but they share the entire society's apprehension over how they will fit into such a society. How they envisage this transformation relates directly to the success of the political system in creating confidence in the future and in

[37] All three governments have required periods of service for students accepting scholarships and training under public auspices. The essential distinction is that they vary greatly in their initial plans as to what kinds of training and specialization are needed. In Morocco, which the author knows best, these responsibilities are divided (and fought over) among the Ministry of Labor and Social Welfare, the Ministry of National Education, and the Ministry of Public Works. The closest Morocco came to having agreed priorities was when Ibrahim was Minister of Labor from 1956 to 1958. An estimate was made then, *Le Maroc au Travail*, Ministry of Labor, 1958, and for a time a commission on professional training existed. Laws were prepared in 1961, but no action was taken.

guiding them toward positions that will be both individually and socially rewarding.

The developmental process demands not only that more highly talented young people perceive places for their talents, but also that they are prepared to occupy the kinds of positions created in the emergent society. The over-all trend of the developmental process is to open up opportunities in service-type activities, while minimizing the importance of control-type posts in both relative and absolute terms. Thus the generation of university-educated people entering first into the developmental process are inextricably caught up in both the attitudinal and social aspects of building a new basis for social integration. Unfortunately, most of the studies of advanced students in developing countries have dwelt on how they perceive other countries[38] rather than their own. The research focus has been dictated in part by concern for the image of our own country abroad, and also by the reluctance of the new leaders to permit or to encourage examination of their own role in the country's social and political reconstruction.

The grievances of advanced students in most developing countries center on questions of education and politics, the two subjects being closely entwined partly because the educational system is often undergoing renovation. This problem is most dramatically illustrated in Pakistan, where higher education inherited some of the exclusiveness of the British system compounded with the limited aims of the colonial regime.[39] Higher education was divided into three phases: matriculation, corresponding roughly to the last two years of American high school; the bachelor's degree, given after two years' instruction in one of the 100 odd colleges loosely affiliated to universities; and the master's degree, given upon a third examination, usually after two years' additional instruction. The vast majority of Pakistani students went only as far as matriculation, which generally assured them of a secure position in the lower or middle civil-service ranks. The system has resulted in divided authority in the secondary schools, and has diverted the universities and colleges from their primary goal of producing imaginative and more specialized scholars.

Those familiar with the weight of prevailing opinion in the American

[38] See, for example, "Impact of Studying Abroad," in the special issue of the *Journal of Social Issues*, George V. Caelho, ed., vol. 18, no. 1, 1962; also, S. M. Zaidi and Mesbahuddin Ahmed, "National Stereotypes of University Students in East Pakistan," *Journal of Social Psychology*, vol. 47, 1958, pp. 387-395.

[39] The background to the British university system in India is given in *The First Five Year Plan*, op.cit., pp. 564-566. Some fascinating material on comparable planning for North Africa appears in *L'Enseignement aux Indigènes*, Paris, International Colonial Institute, 1931. Another frank discussion of the interplay of education and politics is Grant McConnell's "The Political Aims of Education in Developing Countries," in Burns, ed., *Education and the Development of Nations*, op.cit., pp. 39-55.

university will appreciate how difficult it has been to reorient the Pakistani universities. The problem had been recognized since the Pakistani Educational Conference of 1947, but almost nothing has been done to revise the system. The Inter-University Board created in the 1947 conference never became effective, and ten years later it was reported that "none of its specific functions [have] been effectively discharged."[40] Teaching remained at a low standard and uninspiring; final examinations were set and cumulative evaluation almost unheard of; research facilities, laboratories, and libraries were seriously deficient. Students rarely made contact with the objects of their study, and the learning process was reduced to furious cramming for set examinations in the final weeks of the school year.

Much of the student discontent in Pakistan today can be traced directly to the major overhaul of the university system stemming from the Report of the Commission on National Education, which laid down the lines for a renovation of higher education appropriate to the needs of a developing society.[41] The commission recommended that the universities and colleges leave secondary education to provincial boards of secondary education and concentrate on students having twelve years of preparation, allowing five years as a reasonable period for the shift. The bachelor's degree should, in turn, be extended to three years with pass and honors courses, depending on the student's long-range desires, and with examinations at the end of each term or at least the end of each year. The revision of the examination system struck directly at student interests.

The report noted that in the past students had often rebuked teachers who departed from the prescribed materials for the final examinations, neglecting "the more arduous but rewarding aim of mastering a subject, understanding its basic principles, and learning how to apply this understanding to real situations." Although there were some educational authorities who advised the commission to abolish all external, terminal examinations, the group decided that periodic internal examinations should be combined with the finals. Both grades would be calculated in the student's final standing, and the period before announcing grades—a source of dislocation in career planning as well as extreme tension for idle students—would be reduced to several weeks from the several months that often elapsed before the student knew his fate. Most important to the students, the commission aimed to revise the higher educational system so that the degree would, in its words, no longer be

[40] *The First Five Year Plan*, op.cit., p. 569. See also Karl Von Vorys, *Political Development in Pakistan*, Princeton, Princeton University Press, 1965, pp. 134-137.
[41] *The First Five Year Plan*, op.cit., pp. 17-54.

a "passport to government service," but a reliable criterion of academic achievement.

These reforms were clearly designed to orient higher education toward the requirements of a more complex society. However, the students, who have the greatest stake in the country's reconstruction, were caught in the immediate dilemma of the transition. With the revival of party politics in 1962 there was ample opportunity for subsequent discontent to be expressed. Commenting on the serious riots of the spring and fall of 1962, the Minister of National Education stood firm in defense of the reforms, noting that the students had attended only twenty-eight days of classes since February of that year. He added that the report aimed at creating more doctors, scientists, and technicians rather than "clerks for British viceroys."[42] President Ayub has also come to the defense of the commission's report, although his observation is hardly correct that "nowhere in the world" do advanced students dabble in politics.[43] Students are drawn into politics by the nature of the crisis they face, and also by the character of the political system itself in most developing countries.

The simple power structure of the developing country lends itself to student agitation. The small numbers of politically active persons focusing on the distribution of severely limited resources and opportunities gives a high value to student support, for these persons are, above all, the newly arriving contestants in the very restricted struggle for power that characterizes political life in the developing country. Pakistan has been especially disrupted because her political system, based initially on the intrigue of the Muslim League and other parties and later on the austere rule of the military-bureaucratic alliance, gives particularly high rewards to those who are successful manipulators. The Commission on National Education was no doubt correct in noting that the politician has "continually attempted to embroil the academic community in partisan politics . . . [putting] student against student, student against teacher, and, when it has suited his purpose, both against the lawful authority of the university."[44] In many ways the Pakistani political system has been more vulnerable to this kind of activity, but the cases of Morocco and Tunisia will show that they too are vulnerable to student agitation and have difficulties getting students to accept the vision of the future elaborated in the existing political system.

The view that continued growth will absorb the discontent among students is very likely incorrect. If anything, the importance of higher education in relation to primary and secondary education is likely to

---

[42] *Pakistan Times*, September 17, 1962.

[43] *Ibid.*, April 2, 1962.

[44] *Report of the Commission on National Education, op.cit.*, p. 39. An excellent account of student rioting in Dacca is given in Von Vorys, *op.cit.*, pp. 54-57.

increase as development proceeds. The requirements for highly trained people multiply rapidly, given the low level from which most newly developing countries start. There seems little doubt but that these specific requirements are likely to produce even larger numbers of advanced students before the majority of villagers and townspeople have a moderating effect on political life. The expansion of the Pakistani universities and colleges is indicative of this effect. From 1954 to 1960 primary-education enrollment increased by about 10 per cent, secondary enrollment by about 20 per cent, and university-college enrollment by almost 100 per cent. Eventually the political disequilibrium stemming from the rapid expansion of higher education will be overcome, but Pakistan had nearly 120,000 students in advanced institutions in 1960, not including specialized professional training.[45]

The scale is smaller, of course, in the other two countries, but they have experienced similar political tendencies among advanced students. The smaller scale does permit Moroccan and Tunisian students to consolidate their activities in a single organization, although, as might be anticipated, the Moroccan students are too divided politically to confine themselves to a single group. The solidarity of the Tunisian students has also been put under severe pressure as the complexities of political life multiply. The single-party regime does not hesitate nearly so much as the monarchy or the military in engaging the advanced students in political affairs. During the struggle for control of the Socialist Destour in late 1955, Bourguiba received strong support from the Tunisian student organization in Paris. The secretary of the Union Général des Etudiants Tunisiens (U.G.E.T.), Abdelmajid Chaker, has since become the secretary of the party, and many other prominent figures in the high ranks of government were Parisian students only a decade ago. Of course, the assimilation of students under such advantageous conditions cannot continue indefinitely, and it is probably not coincidental that student discontent has been more in evidence over the past four years than immediately after independence.

In the euphoria of the immediate postindependence period, the U.G.E.T. sounded very much like the alter ego of Bourguiba, calling for

---

[45] A comparison of the university and college population is given in *The Second Five Year Plan, op.cit.,* pp. 338-339. The number of colleges may be misleading, since many of them are substandard and offer only the matriculation certificate. The gross figures are misleading in another context because there are many more Pakistani with advanced education in the west than in the east, despite the higher level of primary education. The 1961 census showed 299,967 matriculates in East Pakistan, up only 6 per cent from 1951, and 28,069 graduates, down 32 per cent from 1951. In West Pakistan there were 584,181 matriculates, up 144 per cent and 54,000 graduates, up 21 per cent. The long-run effects of this disparity in higher education between the two wings might be very serious as the development process proceeds. See *Population Census of Pakistan 1961: Literaacy and Education,* Bulletin 4, Karachi, Ministry of Home and Kashmir Affairs, 1961, p. xx.

a constitution, rapid reform of the rural administration, and a "last assault on the Protectorate," foretelling the end of the bey. Their condemnation of the "theoretical studies so often the lot of intellectuals" sounded very much like Bourguiba's own distrust of an ideological appeal that might overshadow his personal strength,[46] and sounded not at all like students in most parts of the world. The U.G.E.T. soon came to have a voice in the assignment of state scholarships, though it is indicative of the uneasy association between party and students that the organization never became and never has been claimed as an auxiliary arm of the Socialist Destour. A society as sophisticated as Tunisia has difficulty in producing ideological agreement, which may be part of the party's strength, but in the student organization it meant that a variety of intellectual tastes had to be accommodated. In 1958 the U.G.E.T. had two Communists on its board, and was one of the public sources of criticism of Bourguiba's plan to appoint all regional party officials.[47]

Nevertheless, the single-party regime can reconstruct the country rapidly, and thereby make a continuing appeal to students. In their 1960 congress the students supported economic planning, economic mobilization, and agrarian reform, and in 1961 these aims were underscored with support for "draconian measures" against anyone obstructing the plan.[48] Bourguiba's most serious handicap in appealing to students was his foreign policy. During the Congo crisis a faction of the U.G.E.T. demonstrated with Algerian students in Tunis in opposition to the president's conservative policy. One officer was arrested, and in the following congress the protesting faction was excluded from office. No sooner did Bourguiba appeal to the students' nationalist sympathies in the Bizerte crisis, than he was in difficulty once again with the Paris section of the U.G.E.T.

The Parisian students objected to newspaper controls which had muffled reports on strikes in the phosphate mines in the south. There was also discontent over Bourguiba's self-indulgences, though they were certainly no greater than those of most heads of state, and over the pace of development. The dispute smoldered throughout the academic year 1962-1963, starting in the fall when a group of Arab socialists, Trotskyites, and Communists successfully challenged the leadership of the students sympathetic to Bourguiba.[49] Emissaries from Tunis were un-

[46] For reports on the early congresses see *Action Tunisienne*, August 1, 1955, and October 31, 1955.

[47] *Ibid.*, August 11, 1958, and September 8, 1958.

[48] For more details see *IXè Congrès national: congrès de l'evaluation*, Tunis, Union Générale des Etudiants Tunisiens, 1961, and *8è Congrès National*, Tunis, Union Générale des Etudiants Tunisiens, 1960.

[49] The dispute was well covered in *Jeune Afrique*, December 3-9, 1962, and May 13-19, 1963. It is interesting to note that U.G.E.T. was using an organizational tactic not unfamiliar to the Socialist Destour to minimize the influence of the more extreme students concentrated in certain fields. The dispute arose in

able to quell the revolt, and in the spring the Paris section was dissolved. At the Eleventh U.G.E.T. Congress in the fall of 1963 the student union was completely reorganized to restore the unanimity required in the single-party regime. The left wing of the group was consoled in seeing the term "socialism" replace "Neo-Destourian socialism" in the charter, but the new leaders soundly condemned "marginal citizens" who threatened to handicap the national struggle for social reconstruction.[50]

Actually, the U.G.E.T. and its Moroccan counterpart have never engaged more than about half the advanced students. In these two countries, like Pakistan, most students realize that their future employer will be the government, though it is indicative of the changing scene that the Tunisian students noted in the most recent controversy that the "epoch of easy honors" is over. The nature of the developmental process is such that government has a dominant role. The student reconciliation to the government, therefore, differs according to the political values involved. The basic similarity of the students' plight should not prevent observation of the very different form of reconciliation in the three systems. In Tunisia the student found the activist orientation of the single-party regime highly compatible to his outlook, and, in turn, the government has had very close relations with students. In Pakistan, by contrast, the student body has been more estranged from the political system, which itself is limited in its appeal because of the highly formal, professional orientation of the regime. Ayub has even expressed the view that students should remain "outside" politics, while Bourguiba's aim has been to politicize them to the advantage of the Socialist Destour. Morocco represents a third alternative.

Although the Moroccan independence movement had organized support from the students, the major student organization, the Union Nationale des Etudiants Marocains (U.N.E.M.), dates from 1956.[51] From the beginning the student organization reflected the diversity of political interest as well as the intransigence that has characterized political life in Morocco. A struggle took place during the spring of 1957 to eject the leaders of a minority party opposing the Istiqlal slate of officers. The U.N.E.M. sought to bolster its position among students by demand-

---

part because Tunis was trying to represent the students according to "corpos" or bodies in each field. For a more detailed inquiry into the organizations and attitudes of North African students see the author's *Second and Third Generation Elites in the Maghreb*, Washington, Department of State, 1963.

[50] *Ibid.*, September 2-8, 1963.

[51] The different origins of the U.N.E.M. and U.G.E.T. deserve mention. The U.N.E.M. has lines to the old North African student organization in Paris dating from the 1930's, the *Association des Etudiants Musulmanes Nord-Africaine*, in which some of the elder Istiqlal leaders had been active as Parisian students. U.G.E.T., like the Algerian student group, was originally an affiliate of the French National Student Union (U.N.E.F.), breaking off only in the 1950's when hostilities began.

ing representation in the distribution of scholarships. However, Moroccan students, like many other Moroccans, were uncertain about their future political interests, and hesitated to join. The Istiqlal managed to remove the opposition within the organization, but the new officers acknowledged that the students had not responded as had been hoped and that their "sense of syndicalism [was] not sufficiently developed."[52]

As might be expected, the students were most attracted by the younger officials of the Istiqlal, and were severely tried when many of these officials formed the opposition U.N.F.P. in 1959. Ben Barka had played an important role in getting the students organized, and gave them increased political prestige by having two officers appointed to the National Consultative Assembly. His hand was also apparent in the motions of the early U.N.E.M. congresses. Possibly participants were most outspoken at the Third Congress in the fall of 1958, when the students criticized the "colonial type administration," the police, and the royal army.[53] However, these statements frightened off less politically oriented students, and the organization continued to have difficulty. For a few months after the party split, the Istiqlal tried to restore a neutral quality to the U.N.E.M., but failed and eventually started its own group for university students. When the young Istiqlal minister, Douiri, was in Paris in the spring of 1961, the local U.N.E.M. section declined to hear him speak before the group.

The Moroccan students are caught up in the indecision of the political system, and students tend to rely more and more on personal contact and influential friends rather than organizations to represent their interests. The students are increasingly divided between those who decline to express views on the monarchy rather than risk their future chances, and those who are extreme and heavily politicized. Accepting the students' active political interests as a fact of life in developing countries, engendered by the power structure of the changing nation, one can thus pass on to the probable effects of the experience of each student group on the developmental process. The most obvious evidence is the career selection that takes place in higher education which is controlled by government in the three countries.

Evidence is lacking for the Pakistan case, but significant contrasts can be seen between the Moroccan and Tunisian students. The Tunisian educational plan lays down clear guidelines for the distribution of students among subjects of advanced study, and these proposals are supported in the priorities given to the construction of advanced institutions and in the assignment of scholarships.[54] The Tunisian

[52] *Al-Istiqlal*, April 27, 1957.
[53] *Ibid.*, August 16, 1958.
[54] See the *Plan Triennal*, Tunis, Secretary of State for Finance and Planning, p. 339, where the following breakdown of advancement from secondary school is given: 20 per cent to normal schools for teacher training; 20 per cent in eco-

students have been selecting careers in science and technology about twice as often as careers in law and letters. Indeed, their orientation to subjects needed in the developmental process can be traced to a time before independence, when there were 260 students studying law and letters in Paris compared to 687 in science and medicine.[55] The Moroccan plan has no comparable provisions to direct students into needed professions, but does show that there were over 2,000 Moroccans in law and letters in 1959, when 166 were studying sciences.[56] It is also important to note that the total advanced-student population of Tunisia is almost as large as Morocco's. Thus it appears that Tunisia has succeeded in accomplishing more in both absolute and relative terms. Certainly Tunisia will be much less dependent on French professional and technical assistance as development takes place, whereas Morocco is more likely to find that key posts in the developmental organizations remain in French hands.

The long-run effect of the various policies on higher education deserves more careful examination than it has usually received from political scientists, not only because the quantity and quality of advanced students places concrete limits on how much reconstruction can take place, but also because higher education instills attitudes about development itself. The Moroccan monarchy, as it has done in the case of primary education, has probably been the most reluctant of the three governments to influence the character of higher education. A great deal has been accomplished in the way of building new institutions for engineering and even medicine, but there is less relation between the country's long-range goals and student life than in Tunisia. In Pakistan, where the student-population ratio to the population compares with the North African countries, students appear to be even less cognizant of the country's reconstruction effort, and have often resorted to violence to express their views. If it were not that attitudes toward political life formed at this stage of life appear to be quite durable in later life,[57]

nomic studies; 20 per cent into higher technical schools, and 40 per cent into universities to be distributed among law, letters, and science.

[55] These figures are taken from Michel Lelong, "La jeunesse universitaire," *I.B.L.A.*, vol. 19, no. 74, 1956, p. 155. This issue is devoted entirely to the question of Tunisian youth. The proportions are unchanged in later figures appearing in Leon Carl Brown, "Education, 'Cultural Unity' and the Future," *op.cit.*, p. 23. However, it is interesting to note that even the firm policies and general good will of the students in Tunisia has not persuaded sufficient numbers of college graduates to become teachers. See *Deuxième Année d'Exécution . . . , op.cit.*, p. 22.

[56] *Plan Quinquennal, op.cit.*, p. 343. From interviews with Moroccan students and later figures appearing in the *International Yearbook of Education, op.cit.*, it did not appear that this trend had changed.

[57] See the materials related to education and political attitudes in Gabriel A. Almond and Sidney Verba, *The Civic Culture*, Princeton, Princeton University Press, 1963, and also the chapter on education among the Istiqlal cadre in the

there might be more grounds for hoping that the developmental process might overcome the political restlessness of the students.

One of the most curious aspects of the developmental activities in all three countries is the failure to impress advanced students with the complexities and realities of development. This shortcoming appears to be directly proportional to the ability of each political system to come to grips with the question of national reconstruction. Distress among advanced students seems to be magnified where governments themselves have felt threatened by the complexities and uncertainties of the developmental process. The students' relatively fruitless preoccupation with the direct influence of government and the manipulation of authority is only a microcosmic version of their elders' similar preoccupations, which so often handicap development. Were it not for the rapidly growing wave of more demanding, more articulate citizens, they could perhaps indulge themselves more safely in their very personalized notions of power and prestige.

There is a twofold stagnation effect in the educational process of the developing countries. The first is of a more quantitative nature, although we have as yet done relatively little to anticipate its form and magnitude. The massive primary-educational systems of the African and Asian countries represent an enduring commitment just as much as the more specialized training of advanced students. The dislocations and discontent that results from poor planning in education, and from failure to anticipate the relation between education and the expansion of the society envisaged under development, are not too difficult to identify.[58] Some of these dislocations in primary and advanced education have been noted in this chapter, and evidence on the more crucial agricultural sector of secondary and intermediate education was given in the preceding chapter. Similar analyses could be done for industrial and other technical fields, though these have been omitted here because they are on the whole more widely recognized as important to the developmental process and raise less difficult questions about political integration under intensive development.

But the question of whether or not the developing country has enough trained, responsive individuals for various phases of development, im-

---

author's *Perspectives of a Moroccan Nationalist*, New York, Bedminster Press, 1964. The suggestions made in this paragraph are derived largely from Eric Erikson, *Childhood and Society*, New York, Norton, 1963, pp. 262-263.

[58] The haphazard nature of educational change in developing countries has produced some concern about return for investment. See Theodore W. Schultz, "Reflections on Investment in Man," *Journal of Political Economy*, vol. 70, October 1962 supplement, pp. 1-8, and also Gary S. Becker, "Investment in Human Capital: A Theoretical Analysis," *ibid.*, pp. 9-49. For a general discussion of the issues see John Vaizey, *The Economics of Education*, New York, Free Press, 1962.

portant as it may be in preliminary planning, is only the first step. Many of the developing countries have not yet taken the first step, but this does not justify ignoring the more difficult phase to come, when the reconstructed society must integrate an infinite variety of new educational capabilities into political life and more advanced phases of the developmental process. As we look at the advanced group of students alone, it has become apparent that developing countries like Iran, India, and much of the Middle East have more highly specialized students than they can accommodate. By excessively segmenting the problems of development these countries have become only more vulnerable to the criticism of irresponsible and uninformed groups. In an unusually frank appraisal of the country's educational problems, an Indian scholar has noted that "by choosing to do the easiest things first one causes illusory satisfactions and stores up trouble, because one forgets the first aim of education: to equip young people to earn a living in some work of their own society."[59]

This kind of compartmentalization of development is a direct product of yielding to demands of influential groups in the existing political system who insist that the expectations of their children be filled immediately. Political systems vary in their readiness to respond to this type of pressure, but implications for the ongoing process of development are similar, whether such concessions are made in the field of education, public health, or public housing. Each of these activities, like every aspect of national reconstruction, has a part in bridging or widening the gap of authority between the fortunate and the less fortunate in the developing country. The reconstruction of the developing country takes place on all fronts, and it is for this reason that the chapter has placed primary education alongside advanced education.

The problem of devising new forms of political integration as societal complexities multiply can only be glimpsed if one is prepared to examine what are now in fact almost unrelated aspects of development. Just as the developing countries vary greatly in their conception of development as a whole, so also do they vary in their willingness and ability to integrate various sectors of development. Thus the Moroccan monarchy places great emphasis on massive primary education and does relatively little to guide advanced students, possibly hoping that their political fervor will be neutralized by the amorphousness of the educational as well as the political system. The Tunisian single-party regime has taken firm steps in both phases of education, but significantly still meets resistance among the more privileged students in higher institutions. The military regime in Pakistan barely managed to conduct an

---

[59] *Capital* (supplement), December 22, 1960. The author is indebted to the AID Educational Assistance Officer in Lahore, Dr. Grimes, for bringing this article to his attention.

overdue renovation of the entire educational system, but it too has produced violent reactions because of its failure to assure advanced students that social reconstruction is not a threat.

Since the three subject countries all are predominantly Muslim, the survey of education and development affords an opportunity to examine how each responds to the Islamic feelings related to education in each country. Admittedly, such a comparison depends on the differing degrees of vitality of Islam in each country, but there is also evidence that the latent influence of religion may persist long after the external religious obligations have been discarded—most notably in the case of Turkey.[60] The obviously critical place of Islam in the Moroccan monarchy accounts for the country's hesitance to evaluate its educational system in 1957 and 1958. As this was done later, Morocco gradually moved toward a primary-school system and a pattern of Arabization that was essentially the same as Tunisia's. However, the conversion of Qarawiyn was made much more slowly than the similar conversion of Zaitouna in Tunis. The potentially explosive lag that Islamic reverence can justify is revealed on the one hand by student strikes at Qarawiyn by young scholars who realize that they are not being prepared for positions in a modern society; while in Tunisia, in contrast, the students of Islamic law make the adjustment to development in metalworking schools.[61] The relation between religion and educational reform is much more ambiguous in the Pakistani case. The explicit requirements of Islam are acknowledged in compulsory Islamic instruction through secondary school, but there is the almost wistful hope that it will prove possible to "bring Islamic education closer to life."[62] Though it would be unfair and inaccurate to assert that the military-bureaucratic alliance is insensitive to Islam in the modernization effort, particularly as religious feelings are again exploited by politicians under the constitutional regime, they do not succeed in using Islam to support developmental changes in either the traditional context of the Moroccan *imam* or the more secular context of the Tunisian *combattant*.

[60] For an account of the vestiges of Islamic-inspired feeling in Turkey see Dankwart A. Rustow, "Politics and Islam in Turkey 1920-1955" and Howard A. Reed, "The Religious Life of Turkish Muslims," in Richard Frye, ed., *Islam and the West*, The Hague, Mouton, 1957, pp. 69-148. More material will be found in Robert E. Ward and Dankwart A. Rustow, eds., *Turkey and Japan: A Comparative Study of Modernization*, Princeton, Princeton University Press, 1964.

[61] *Jeune Afrique*, April 3, 1961.

[62] *Report of the Commission on National Education*, op.cit., pp. 212-213.

CHAPTER 9

ADMINISTRATIVE REFORM:
THE CONFRONTATION OF AUTHORITY
AND COMMUNITY

THE PAST decade has brought a great increase in American concern with administration in developing countries. Our interest has been stimulated in part by increased overseas commitments and in part by the developing countries' desire to find administrative solutions to pressing problems. This chapter will suggest that both may be misguided in looking to the manipulation of so small an elite for panaceas to development. Governmental reorganization and administrative efficiency are certainly crucial ingredients in the developmental process, but they remain at best only tools for attacking the more complex problems of popular involvement in development. In many ways the administrator is more poorly prepared than the villager and peasant, because his methods are often inappropriate and his motives are often doubtful when confronted with the bewildering task of relating millions of new citizens to the nation-building process.

The passing of administrative reform reflects many characteristics of the new nation's attack on material poverty and low productivity. Though a new nation may be fully aware of the injustices of the colonial administrative regime, obvious tasks and preliminary reforms take precedence with the coming of independence. Even the minimal reorganization of administrative services has been an uphill struggle in most developing countries.[1] The new governments of Morocco, Tunisia, and Pakistan are concerned with administrative reorientation, often perceive the requisites to such change, and make gestures of adaptation. But the final results are almost always confined to administrative reorganization in the narrow sense, and adjustments are forthcoming largely in areas where the minimal functions of government are involved.

In many new countries the drive for independence has produced an uncritical acceptance of Western procedures and methods. In the early years of independence the new state often lives on the borders of disaster and great emphasis is placed on control and order. For these purposes the unimaginative duplication of the colonial model of the local administrator may be sufficient, but does not lay the groundwork for a more productive association of villager and government in the locality. There are two reasons for this, which will be examined in this chapter.

[1] Some of the best materials on this problem have come from India's developmental experience, which has been ably recorded in the *Indian Journal of Public Administration*, itself a product of the reorientation program for civil servants.

The bureaucrat on the Western model is trained, first, to isolate himself from the political system of which he is a part and, second, to confine his activities to the specific responsibilities of his job description.

These characteristics are admirable in the highly developed society where national values are widely accepted and where a high degree of popular participation has been achieved. The civil servant himself is deeply immersed in the society as a complex working unit and he is surrounded by people whose understanding and involvement in the system are equal to his own. These happy assumptions do not apply in the developing country, where reconstructing the political system becomes a major focus of pressure as the development process occurs. Under these conditions the bureaucracy can indeed become a major obstacle to emergence of a more complex society, and a government's success in converting the administrator to new tasks may depend on the kind of system that seeks to permeate the entire country. The first section of this chapter outlines how the three governments in question have approached their civil servants as the developmental process has gradually changed the role of government.[2]

The direct transformation of administrator by the pressure of government is certainly a delicate process. An alternative sequence of change in the administrative system is considered in the second section of the chapter, where the impact of the villager on the civil servant as a feed-back effect will be analyzed for the three governments. Each political system has differing potentialities in mobilizing the remote populace outside the administrative process. Insofar as the government is able to modify the demands and expectations of the peasant outside the formal channels of government new local pressures will be felt by the administrator. The more circuitous device for modifying administrative behavior also implies, however, that the citizen is increasing his capacity to participate in the political system as a whole and may bring new pressures on the government itself. Thus the government hoping to reform the administrator by indirect means must also be prepared to accommodate new forces in political life itself.

Government by a bureaucracy was indeed the prevailing pattern in Africa and Asia long before the European intrusions.[3] In the static

[2] Several theoretical treatments of the developmental role of the administrator have appeared. See, for example, S. N. Eisenstadt, "Bureaucracy, Bureaucratization and Debureaucratization," *Administrative Science Quarterly*, vol, 4, no. 3, December 1959, pp. 302-320; Fred Riggs, "Bureaucracy and Political Development—A Paradoxical View," in LaPalombara, ed., *Bureaucracy and Political Development*, Princeton, Princeton University Press, 1963, pp. 120-167; and Robert V. Presthus, "Social Bases of Bureaucratic Organization," *Social Forces*, vol. 38, 1959, pp. 103-109.

[3] No attempt will be made here to cite the vast literature on the historic bureaucracies, but a recent study of S. N. Eisenstadt, *The Political Systems of Empires*, New York, Free Press, 1963, and also Clifford Geertz, ed., *Old So-*

societies of Ottoman and Moghul times, officials could maintain barriers between themselves and the masses, and justify their own positions in terms of the essential services provided. The contemporary citizen, however, is being asked to take a much more active role in political and social life. The complexities of nation-building outlined in the preceding chapters require his understanding and loyalty in numerous situations that cannot be constantly watched. The new participant will enter into a more active role under the guidance of government officials, but the developmental challenge to the administration, as to the government as a whole, is the way in which it will cope with forms of involvement that cannot be supervised constantly and that are indeed not amenable to administrative regulation.

ORIENTING THE CIVIL SERVANT TO DEVELOPMENT

Much of the literature on development administration deals with converting the existing administrative system to problems of national reconstruction. The nature of the conflict is undisputed, and those interested in political development are indebted to scholars in this field for underscoring the inadequacy of the civil service in many developing countries. After roughly a decade of various training operations to reorient administrators, it has also become apparent that preparing the officials of the developing country is only one step in creating a more vigorous environment for development. The official who has been so carefully nurtured at an enlightened public-administration institute in Bangkok, Manila, or Lahore can have no effect on the mobilization of his country without other adjustments in the political system over which he has little influence. Even the best-intentioned public servant must operate in the political environment of his country.[4]

While political leaders are assassinated, jailed, and exiled, the official simply begins to forward his reports and requests to new authorities. His immunity to the political process is indeed institutionalized in important ways in both modern and traditional societies. There is no doubt that the official's distance from the legitimate authority in any going political system is essential to performing his tasks, but the fact that administrative chores demand such remoteness and immunity suggests that the civil servant may not be nearly so important in political development as

---

cieties and New States, New York, Free Press, 1963, provide ample sources and suggestions for further reading.

[4] There is, of course, another alternative—not returning home, which is quite familiar in universities having large numbers of foreign students. With all the careful study of purely administrative problems in new countries, it is unfortunate that there is not more work done on how the administrator himself perceives his country. See, for example, Patricia L. Kendall, "The Ambivalent Character of Nationalism among Egyptian Professionals," *Public Opinion Quarterly*, vol. 20, no. 1, Spring 1956, pp. 277-292.

the quantity of literature on administration in new countries would indicate.[5]

The historic traditions of the old India Civil Service (ICS) have made it one of the favorite targets for those suspicious of bureaucratic influence in the developing countries. The now classic formulation of Macaulay, calling for a class of administrators "Indian in blood and colour, but English in taste, in opinions, in morals and in intellect," has become the focal point for countless inquiries into public administration in developing countries.[6] The I.C.S. tradition has been sharply attacked by some of its own members, whose criticisms bear out how well the British succeeded in establishing an elite. The I.C.S. officer became British in dress, speech, and manner. Indeed, it could be charged with some truth that the British managed to alienate the young Hindu or Muslim so successfully from their own culture that they were less effective civil servants.

Few Pakistani would question, however, the meritorious service of the higher civil service in establishing the independent country. In his admirably clear analysis of the early years of the I.C.S. officers inherited by the Civil Service of Pakistan (C.S.P.)[7] Braibanti has demonstrated how a small corps of 136 officers available for administrative duties became the foundation of the new government. By 1962 the elite corps was placed at 386 men. With the similarly recruited and distinguished civil servants in the other special services, finance, auditing, foreign service, and others, the country has depended on a small cadre of some 600 higher civil servants supported by approximately 5,000 additional officers in the Class I or executive category.[8] The country drew on this pool of talent for political purposes from roughly 1953.[9]

[5] The systematic alienation asserted, for example, by Masihuzzaman in "Public Service Tradition in Pakistan: A Case for Revision," in Inayatullah, ed., *Bureaucracy and Development in Pakistan*, Peshawar, Academy for Rural Development, 1963, pp. 285-298, may be more apparent in administrative behavior than in any other for the official involved. The unsuitability in the behavior of the official, severe as it may be, is only a matter of degree from that needed to run a bureaucracy, and the argument does not take into consideration how many officials must feel conflict and express their national ties in other ways. It seems unjust and possibly misleading to blame the official for acquiring characteristics essential to performing his task, though there is no doubt that the case of the I.C.S. tradition is an extreme one, and the authority tradition is often so deeply ingrained as to inhibit adaptation to new requirements.

[6] Quoted from Ralph Braibanti, "The Civil Service of Pakistan: A Theoretical Analysis," *South Atlantic Quarterly*, vol. 58, no. 2, Spring 1959, p. 265.

[7] Ralph Braibanti, "Public Bureaucracy and Judiciary in Pakistan," in *Bureaucracy and Political Development, op.cit.*, pp. 362-372. The disadvantage of the Muslims in the old I.C.S. is suggested by the fact that there were 1,157 members before partition. Most of the Muslims were from the Punjab, and only two from Bengal.

[8] *Ibid.*, pp. 381-382.

[9] For a more detailed account of the administrator's rise in Pakistani politics

Relatively early in the independent history of the Indian sub-continent, on the invitation of the governments the Ford Foundation sent two public-administration experts, Paul Appleby and Rowland Egger, to evaluate the services of India and Pakistan, respectively. The reaction to these two reports is in itself indication of the very different political environments existing in the two countries in the early 1950's. Though Appleby's report was stated in less severe terms and triggered fewer administrative defenses, the content of both reports was similar. Egger's report has never been published, but the available comments indicate some of the problems the Pakistani government had in converting to development administration in the narrower sense.[10]

In 1953 there were nineteen ministries, having from one to six secretaries or chief administrators.[11] In the years since independence, and to some extent from vestiges to the British system, the various ministries were often operating at different levels, had overlapping functional interests, and often were immobilized by cumbersome and confusing lines of authority to working officials. As might be expected, the Ministry of Finance pervaded the entire administrative system, having six secretaries and greatly complicating the effective operation of the rest of the administration. At that time the government still depended heavily on sixty directorates to communicate policy and supervise implementation to subordinate officials, but there was a paralyzing inability to delegate authority and to differentiate line and staff functions. The over-all picture is not unlike that of many administrative systems in new countries, but the Pakistanis have had great difficulty in reorganizing more effectively.

---

see Khalid Ben Sayeed, "The Political Role of Pakistan's Civil Service," *Pacific Affairs*, vol. 31, no. 2, June 1958, pp. 131-132. For more detail on the organization and role of the Pakistani civil service see Keith Callard, *Pakistan: A Political Study*, London, George Allen and Unwin, 1957, pp. 284-301; Khalid Ben Sayeed, *Pakistan: The Formative Phase*, Karachi, Pakistan Publishing House, 1960, pp. 383-405; Muzaffar Ahmed Chaudhuri, "The Organization and Composition of the Central Civil Services in Pakistan," *International Review of Administrative Sciences*, vol. 26, no. 3, 1960, pp. 278-292; and Karl Von Vorys, *Political Development in Pakistan*, Princeton, Princeton University Press, 1965, pp. 108-118.

[10] References to the reports will be found in the excellent accounts given in Braibanti's work. The published material appears in Rowland A. Egger, "Ministerial and Departmental Organization and Management in the Government of Pakistan," *Public Administration*, London, vol. 39, Summer 1961, pp. 149-172, and also a reply by G. Ahmed, "Changes in the Administrative Organization of the Government of Pakistan since 1953," *ibid.*, Winter 1961, pp. 353-360.

[11] One of the interesting ramifications of an elite civil service is that very fine lines come to be drawn between the higher posts. The elaboration of variously ranked secretaries in Pakistan is an example. When the official in charge of Village AID was lowered from a joint to a deputy secretary it indicated the end of the program for all practical purposes. See Masihuzzaman, "Community Development—The New Bureaucracy," mimeo., p. 83.

Because of the severely critical tone of Egger's report, the Ford Foundation sent another expert, Gladieux, to repeat the task. Though his report has also remained unpublished, it provided the basis for several recommendations in the First Five Year Plan. The plan stressed the importance of "a reorientation of attitude . . . necessary to bring the people and the administration closer to each other, to develop identity of outlook and purpose, and to create faith in the country's ability to achieve its goals." The plan was particularly explicit on the deplorable way in which nation-building departments were treated "as poor relations in the family of government organisations," often being supervised to junior officers and offering inferior pay and promotion opportunities to their lower officials.

The report in the plan went on to suggest that steps be taken to make the C.S.P. "broader-based, numerically stronger, less entrenched and self-regulating, more varied in talent, deeper in knowledge, and, last but not least, wider in outlook." To accomplish these ends it was recommended that a single examination and recruitment procedure be used for all the superior officers, that training and evaluation place more stress on performance, and that the central and provincial Public Service Commissions be given greater authority to equalize pay, promotion, and conditions in all areas.[12] Though some steps toward better handling the more tangible developmental problems of industry and commerce had been made by 1958, there had been few steps toward accomplishing the fundamental kind of reorientation described in these two studies.

The arrival of the military regime opened new opportunities for reform, but also created certain obstacles. Ayub was heavily dependent on the higher civil service to rule the country. Unlike the parliamentary regime, however feeble and corrupt it may have been, the military government is not permitted to select scapegoats among those performing essential services, and to this extent the power structure becomes even more concentrated than it was under the degenerating struggle between politician and official. In their basic agreement on the importance of orderliness and efficiency, the coalition of bureaucrat and military officer produces a situation where there may well be even less room for political adjustment outside the confines of government, so important to generating a continuing, self-supporting development effort. While the Ayub government has greatly improved Pakistan's administrative capability, it is also correct that few fundamental changes have been made, and the position of the elite higher civil service has been kept intact.

In the limited context of central reorganization, however, Pakistan has certainly accomplished a great deal compared to many developing countries, and the military has been able to acquire the confidence of the

[12] *The First Five Year Plan* (1955-60), Government of Pakistan, Planning Board, 1957, pp. 91-95 and 110-121.

administration for central reorganization that would have been resisted under the earlier regime. The first of these measures was a modification of the stringent procedures of financial control, which had required that funds already budgeted and authorized for expenditure had to receive approval once again. Control was to be exercised henceforth primarily through the budget, and annual budgets were to be prepared with a one-year leadtime. To ease ministerial actions the Ministry of Finance was to assign to each ministry a financial adviser who would have sufficient delegated authority to expedite financial matters and to advise on improved budgetary procedures.[13] This was the first reform enacted under the advice of the Administrative Reorganization Committee, whose full report was submitted in 1962.

Another major change came in January 1961 when it was announced that there would be a 20 per cent reduction in personnel at the central secretariat, which had 7,500 persons in 1958. The ministries would endeavor to confine their activity to policy-making, and the ministerial secretaries would be given additional powers by their respective ministers. Health and education were to be solely under technical officers. In an attempt to liberalize the exclusive character of the higher civil service, a section-officer system was initiated, which would have clearly defined staff responsibilities in order to keep a direct contact between the ministries and the provincial secretaries. There was provision for internal promotion by merit to section-officer positions, and presumably more section officers would be technically qualified personnel than had been possible under the old system.[14]

The third round of central administrative reorganization came a year later when the number of ministries was reduced to eleven, plus five secretariats to handle presidential matters. The secretariats were for planning, economic affairs, associated states and frontiers, cabinet or presidential administrative needs, and the establishment. The latter preserved the close association of the higher civil service with the country's chief executive,[15] and served to remove these matters from the expanded realm of discourse made possible by the return to constitutional rule. Once again it was reiterated that the ministries were not to become operational. Even in planning they were to rely on the proposals coming from lower echelons in the provinces. The ministers were

---

[13] *Pakistan Times*, August 27, 1960.

[14] The changes described in this paragraph are described in the *Pakistan Times*, January 27, 1961. For more information on the section-officer scheme see Braibanti in *Bureaucracy and Political Development, op.cit.*, p. 393, and G. Ahmed, *op.cit.*, p. 356.

[15] *Pakistan Times*, April 27, 1962. It is indicative of the difficulties in creating coordinated supervision of the civil service that the Public Service Commission remains weak and underused. See *The First Five Year Plan, op.cit.*, pp. 115-117, and also *The Second Five Year Plan (1960-65)*, Government of Pakistan, Planning Commission, 1960, p. 116.

never to engage in day-to-day administrative matters, leaving the major operations of government to the provinces.

In the preliminary phase of administrative reform Pakistan had certain advantages from being heavily oriented to the professionalist view on development. Ayub and his advisers knew that changes at the central level would have little meaning if provincial, divisional, and district procedures were left unchnaged. Hence the president appointed commissions to make similar reports for each province. The report on the administrative reorganization of the West Pakistan government appeared first and sketched the aim of the provincial reform. Like the earlier investigations, the provincial report started with an acknowledgment that "over-centralization exists side by side with inadequate supervision and control," and that departmental insularity resulted in "little accountability or sense of public service at the local levels."[16] The report distinguished between those activities of the provincial government that required continued centralized control and an administrative staff (attached department) for the departmental secretary; those where decentralization produced complications, given the present regional divisions; and those where the provincial secretariat would be confined entirely to policy-making, relying entirely on lower administrative echelons for the implementation and supervision of policy.

Except for a few specialized services, the matters falling in the first category were the conventional control activities of the police, legal affairs, corruption, the provincial Public Service Commission as well as industrial and labor affairs, which might directly affect broad policies of the province. Nearly all the nation-building departments were completely decentralized and without administrative staff from the provincial secretariat: irrigation, public works, education, health, cooperatives, agriculture, forestry, food, and several others, making a total of fifteen areas of decentralized activity. The report was outspoken in condemning the deceptive forms of delegation of authority that had made it almost impossible for divisional or district officials to perform developmental duties in the past.

The report on the administrative reorganization of East Pakistan continued along the same lines as the West Pakistan report, and noted that it too was addressed to the "familiar defects of over-centralization, absence of coordination, outmoded methods and procedures of work, delays and supplication, and inadequacy in tackling its new and enlarged responsibility."[17] The proposal elevated the rank of four secretaries of

[16] Report of the *Provincial Reorganization Committee*, Part I—West Pakistan, Government of Pakistan, December 1961, p. 5. See also the guidelines provided in Decisions of the Cabinet on the *Report of the Provincial Administration Commission (June 23, 1960)*, Karachi, Government of Pakistan, President's Secretariat, 1962.

[17] *Report of the Provincial Reorganization Committee*, Part II—East Pakistan, Government of Pakistan, April 1962, p. 1.

nation-building departments, and applied the financial-adviser scheme to the east wing as was being done in the west. Steps were taken to reduce the role of both the Home and Finance Departments, by assigning several of their auxiliary functions to offices more directly concerned. There was a noticeable effort to disperse the control activities of the police. As in the west, corruption investigations were placed under the General Services and Administration Department, and given additional staff. Some of the political investigatory powers of the Home Ministry were reduced, and the Bureau of National Reconstruction was moved to the Information Department.

The administrative reorganization underway in Pakistan is only a preliminary step in the developmental process as conceived here, but without bringing governmental authority closer to the community very little can be done of a more ambitious nature. The sheer inefficiency of many procedures must be recognized. In their inquiries the Pakistani investigators found, for example, that routine licenses had to pass through the hands of the divisional officer, that permission for minor ceremonial affairs at the village level worked their way to the district, and that the transfer of primary-level students sometimes went before district or divisional officials.[18] Obviously the villager felt remote from the process of government, and in many cases had good reason to express hostility and apathy.

The citadel of the administrative services is the Civil Service Academy, which has accepted 240 of 9,385 applications from 1950 to 1962. Under the Ayub regime the practice of sending the C.S.P. candidates to England was discontinued, and a year and a half is spent in practical training at the district level. Development has been given new importance in the curriculum, and the deputy director of the academy has made it clear that "development and not stability is now the main objective of government and all administrative effort has been subordinated to it."[19] An even greater innovation is the Administrative Staff College, founded in 1960, whose three-month course has become a requisite for appointment to higher secretary-level posts. In the six sessions held in 1963 a total of 128 higher civil servants and some officials from outside government underwent training. In addition, there are three National Institutes of Public Administration located in Lahore, Dacca, and Karachi, and begun in 1961.[20] Another program working with

[18] *Provincial Reorganization Committee*, Part I, *op.cit.*, p. 13.

[19] Rafiq Inayat, "The Civil Service Academy," in *Bureaucracy and Development in Pakistan, op.cit.*, pp. 405 and 411-412. In addition, see the frequent references to the Civil Service Academy in Professor Braibanti's work.

[20] See Abdul Qayyum, "The Administrative Staff College," in *Bureaucracy and Development in Pakistan, op.cit.*, pp. 416-424, and Inayatullah, "National Institute of Public Administration—Lahore," *ibid.*, pp. 425-432. See also *Pakistan Administrative Staff College: Interim Report on Activities*, Syracuse, Maxwell Graduate School of Citizenship and Public Affairs, June 30, 1963.

officers at the intermediate levels, and focusing on rural problems, is the work of the Academies for Rural Development at Peshawar and Comilla.[21]

The foregoing sketch of the adjustments made to fill developmental needs and to improve administrative organization represents a substantial concession by the Pakistani government, almost wholly achieved under the impulse of the military regime. Though the military and bureaucracy appear to have cooperated well from 1958 to 1962, it is also possible that the enthusiasm and purpose of the martial-law regimes may have represented a potential threat to some officials. In many ways their freedom of action was greater under the old parliamentary regime than under the watchful, impatient eye of the military. In any event, the Pakistani administration has been the least vulnerable to superior political authority of the three administrations under consideration. The accrued advantage of the Pakistani civil servant over the less well-prepared Moroccan and Tunisian official may easily have worked to the country's disadvantage. Few of the organizational changes described above have taken place without C.S.P. approval, and virtually nothing has been done effectively to break down the barriers between the C.S.P. official and the citizen.[22]

Both Morocco and Tunisia inherited the tradition of an administrative elite corps from France, but its conversion to the requirements of independence has posed a different kind of problem in North Africa. The notion of an all-purpose generalist to deal with native affairs was highly developed in the body of *officiers des affaires indigènes*, who are directly comparable to district officers of the Indian subcontinent. The tradition was perhaps most firmly implanted in Morocco, where Marshal Lyautey created a special training center for the rural-administration elite. He specified that they should be "young *contrôleurs*, newly recruited," and that their "education should be general matters: history of

---

[21] See the *Annual Reports* issued by both academies, as well as *Monthly Reports* from Comilla. The Peshawar Academy has been publishing a journal, the *Academy Quarterly*, and the Comilla Academy, the *Journal of the Pakistan Academy for Rural Development Comilla*. Also, Inayatullah, "Pakistan Academy for Village Development—Peshawar," in *Bureaucracy and Development in Pakistan, op.cit.*, pp. 433-453. As has been apparent in earlier references to the two academies, the emphasis at Peshawar has been more on training middle-level civil servants, while the Comilla Academy has tended to do more with actual experiments in rural reorganization.

[22] The Pakistani government is reported to be unaware of the total number of employees of both the provincial and central governments, nor has a breakdown by ministry of the central government been published. The most recent total figure is from Muzzaffar Ahmed Chaudhuri, "The Organization and Composition of the Central Civil Services in Pakistan," *International Review of Administrative Sciences*, vol. 26, no. 3, 1960, p. 278. He gives the 1950 figure as 236,444, a growth rate comparable to Morocco, but in over twice as much time. Braibanti estimates that the total in 1962 was about 330,000, *Bureaucracy and Political Development, op.cit.*, p. 381, footnote.

Morocco, law, education, finance, etc."[23] In practice there were not enough indigenous affairs officers to fill all the posts, and some military officers and regular civil servants were also used.

The failure of these officers to become the core of an elite civil service, like their Indian counterparts, requires some explanation. They were, first, almost all French. More important, the French overseas administrative system, much more highly developed and differentiated than the British, did not give them opportunity to move into high positions in all the vital services of government, although they were undoubtedly some of the most talented officials. Unlike India, the remnants of central authority in the Moroccan sultan and the Tunisian bey were still sufficiently strong to be maintained apart from the new colonial administration.[24] The effect was to make the French administration a complement, albeit a dominating one, to the historic Muslim regime. With the unification of the two administrative systems at independence, there was no doubt that the French-inspired organization was alien to the new political systems as well as the origin of considerable abuse in the closing years of the two Protectorates.

Thus at the time of independence in Morocco there were over 5,000 French officials of the executive classification compared to about 700 Moroccans. Since most of the Moroccans were in the civil-service reserve and seldom received additional training, probably only a small fraction had any experience in higher positions. The only comprehensive reform that the Moroccan monarchy has produced is the decision to merge the "mixed" and "reserve" services, which had been a French device to discriminate against Moroccan officials. The distinctions that had existed in regards to promotion and recruitment had disappeared, of course, with independence, and the remaining difference rested largely on different pay scales and allowances. Late in 1958 the Moroccan government decided that a standard system of family allowances would be used, and that the "reserve" category would be eliminated.[25]

By 1960 very little had been accomplished to relieve dependence on French civil servants, and there has been no new program or legislation since the evaluation at that time. The Five Year Plan noted that little progress had been made in transforming the administration to the needs of independence and added that "by the expansion of its numbers one has sought to build administrative efficiency while failing above all to adapt in conformity with new functions."[26] The estimates prepared for

[23] Pierre Lyautey, ed., *Lyautey l'Africain: Textes et Lettres*, vol. 4 (1919-1925), Paris, Plon, 1957, pp. 41-42.

[24] For an outline of the organization of the two Protectorate governments see Arthur Girault, *Principes de Colonisation et de Législation Coloniale (Afrique du Nord)*, vol. 3, Paris, Recueil Sixey, 1921, pp. 429-462 for Tunisia and pp. 592-610 for Morocco.

[25] *Al-Istiqlal*, October 18, 1958.

[26] George Oved, "Problèmes du développement économique au Maroc," *Tiers-Monde*, vol. 2, no. 7, July-September 1961, p. 390.

the plan showed that the Moroccan government still depended on Frenchmen for 47 per cent of its higher administrative officials, and for 89 per cent of its higher technical officials.

Since independence, questions of ministerial organization and civil-service structure have rested almost wholly with the Palace, which has been careful to guard its prerogatives. The direction of the *fonction publique* has been within the office of the president of the cabinet, except for two periods. From October 1956 until May 1958 a minister was appointed from the royalist group. The only period when the civil service was not directly controlled by the Palace was from May 1960 to June 1961, when Boucetta became Minister for the Civil Service as part of a compromise to preserve Istiqlal support for the cabinet. Because the monarch has been president of the cabinet since May 1960, and Hassan II has been particularly active in governmental affairs since he came to the throne in early 1961, the officials concerned with the administration have in practice been able to do little without royal consent.

Early in 1958 a civil-service statute was accepted, but it did little more than guarantee equal access to and treatment in the civil service for all Moroccans.[27] The new law was apparently modeled on French legislation of 1956, and left each ministry to continue to regulate all administrative and personnel matters within its jurisdiction. The most controversial part of the law was the accompanying decrees forbidding the police and auxiliary troops of the Ministry of the Interior (*gendarmerie*) to join unions, and other legislation forbidding strikes by civil servants.[28] The recruitment, examination, classification, promotion, and remuneration in the various ministries was decided entirely by each as it saw fit, with the judiciary, police, teachers, and armed forces exempt from even the vague protection and dispersed regulation contained in the 1958 statute.

The Istiqlal was especially disturbed as it became clearer that the monarch was not prepared to treat the parties seriously or to give ministers real delegations of power. Early in 1960 the party denounced the "anarchy" prevailing in the ministries, who freely raided one another and competed for recruits without regard for developmental or administrative needs. Possibly the most energetic effort to reorganize the administration came from Boucetta, who found himself completely

[27] "Dahir no. 1-58-008 du 4 chaabane (24 février 1958) portant statut de la fonction publique," *Bulletin Officiel*, no. 2372, April 11, 1958, pp. 631-636; also "Décret no. 2-57-1465 du 15 rejeb 1377 (5 février 1958) relatif à l'exercice du droit syndical par les fonctionnaires," *ibid.*, pp. 636-637. For other commentaries on this law see Jacques Robert, *La Monarchie Marocaine*, Paris, Librairie Générale de Droit et de Jurisprudence, 1963, pp. 149-161, and Jean Theis, "Les institutions publiques du Maroc indépendant," *Revue du Droit Public et de la Science Politique*, vol. 77, no. 3, May-June 1961, pp. 543-547.

[28] The monarchy has been in a running dispute with the U.M.T. over the civil servants' right to strike. In December 1961 the first of several very successful strikes was held, starting with the workers of the Post, Telegraph, and Telephone Ministry.

frustrated in an attempt to clarify personnel practices or organizational patterns in the government. He designed a proposal establishing standard educational requirements and an examination system for the civil service. The plan intended to reduce some 400 different but overlapping civil service ranks to 80, and would have organized administrative personnel by functional categories based on skill and experience.[29] When the discouraged minister left office, the party condemned the "furtive methods and underhanded tricks" that had been used to obstruct his work. Once the Istiqlal joined the opposition to the monarch, it was even more outspoken in protesting the "complicity and indulgence which appears to be the internal rule of the administration."[30]

The more active role of the monarch under Hassan II's reign has meant that administrative distinctions and responsibilities have, if anything, lost significance. From 1961 to 1963, for example, the Ministries of Agriculture and the Interior were under Guedira, who also served as the king's cabinet director. The concentration of economic affairs under the Ministry of National Economy, accomplished by Bouabid in 1956, was again dispersed in two ministries after 1961. Hassan II favored an economic "czar," Laghzaoui, who was particularly concerned with foreign industrial investment and ran the Sherifian Phosphate Office. The government established in 1963 was completely subordinated to the king, and had support from only those parties submissive to the monarch's wishes. All these actions made the question of ministerial and other administrative reorganization for developmental purposes superfluous.[31] Though possibly not the king's intent, the unavoidable effect was to make the official extremely sensitive to royal influence, and more apprehensive over any modifications not personally endorsed by Hassan II.

Mention should be made of the one institution in Morocco designed to

[29] Boucetta's proposal is outlined in some detail in *Al-Istiqlal*, February 25, 1961. As part of the proposal, the king agreed to suspend further recruiting until the new law was passed. The result was that the government did no recruiting for six months, and then returned to its former practices.

[30] The criticisms became outspoken after Boucetta was removed. See *Al-Istiqlal*, June 3, 1961; October 28, 1961; November 18, 1961; and October 13, 1962. The party had, of course, profited from the *ad hoc* procedures used immediately after independence and then continued. Most estimates calculate that three fourths of the civil servants are Istiqlal members, and large numbers were enlisted from Fez, a region of chronic unemployment and also Istiqlal strength.

[31] Total figures are not published, but interviews and the figures given for total authorized strength in *Finances Publiques du Maroc*, M. Champion, ed., Ministry of the National Economy, Rabat, 1961, p. 57, suggest that about 80,000 persons are employed by central and provincial governments. The 1960 figure represents steady expansion of civil service at the rate of about 10 per cent per year. However, Champion also notes that the government has generally been about 10 per cent understaffed. Late in 1961 it was revealed that the central government had 65,000 employees; up 7,000 from 1961 and 13,000 from 1960. See *Jeune Afrique*, November 19-25, 1962.

train higher civil servants, the Ecole Nationale d'Administration, patterned on the similar French institution and until 1962 under a French director. The school was created in 1948 to train an administrative elite, and accepted only more distinguished Moroccans with some advanced university education. In the first ten years of activity it turned out 182 civil servants, who became leading officials in the Moroccan superior civil-service category of about 3,000 persons. In 1957 the school conceded to strong pressure from the government to create a wholly Arabic section, and after 1960 plans were made to Arabize all instruction. The results may be more symbolic than effective because the civil service still depends heavily on French, while entailing somewhat lower standards at E.N.A. The experience of the school is another example of the strong drive in Morocco to accomplish token Arabization, while many fundamental problems remain unsolved.[32]

The response of the monarchical system to the more formal aspects of administrative reorganization has been cautious and tentative. Unless the first steps can be taken to organize the bureaucracy and to mobilize the existing administrative resources in a developing country, the more complex task of reorienting the administrative system to the developmental environment and increased participation can hardly begin. The substantial allocations to education, public health, and housing in Morocco should not be ignored, but the country was not benefiting from these contributions as much as would be possible in a better-integrated administration. The civil service was justifiably consumed with making its own way among a maze of regulations and protecting itself against the capricious effects of nepotism and favoritism. The curious result was that the king became increasingly dependent on his poorly organized administration as political life became more complex, and as the parties were driven into the opposition.

Working from a similar bureaucratic tradition, the single-party regime in Tunisia has gone about the problem of administrative reform very differently. French administrative practices were more deeply entrenched in Tunisia than Morocco, and the fact that there had been a politically active urban minority since World War I also contributed to greater familiarity with administrative and organizational procedures. Under Lucien Saint the Tunisian Protectorate had adopted the French system in 1926,[33] though many Tunisians had been familiar with modern administration even longer. Under Bourguiba's principles nationalists were not barred from governmental posts as they were under

---

[32] See *Al-Istiqlal*, March 5, 1960, and July 9, 1960, for more details.

[33] For additional information on some of the Protectorate reforms see Nicola Ziadeh, *Nationalism in Tunisia*, Beirut, American University Press, 1962, pp. 30-36, and André Pellegrin, *Histoire de la Tunisie*, Tunis, Librairie Namura, 1958, passim.

the Istiqlal, and it was not unusual for Socialist Destourians to accept ministerial posts before independence.[34]

The backlog of experience and familiarity facilitated the transition of the Tunisian administrative system, and probably helped minimize the kind of emotional but futile protest over French influence in the bureaucracy that was so common in Morocco. Tunisia was in a more favorable situation than Morocco in absolute terms. There were 9,750 Frenchmen in the Tunisian administration in 1956, and 9,566 Tunisians. In the highest category there were 1,960 Frenchmen and 1,190 Tunisians. They were certainly better prepared than the Moroccans, and in absolute terms possibly as well staffed as Pakistan, which had about twenty times more people.

All these factors combined to permit the Tunisians to eliminate French assistance more quickly than did Morocco. The Tunisians even managed to reduce the number of permanent civil-service appointments in the transition. By 1958 there were only 1,867 tenured French civil servants remaining, plus about 700 temporary, and about half the total number were teachers.[35] The accomplishment was in no small measure due to the businesslike attitude toward administrative reform that was made possible by the single-party regime. Like the Moroccans, the Tunisians first worked to remove Frenchmen from posts in the president's office, foreign affairs, police, and the military, which are now almost entirely staffed by Tunisians. A later effort was made to remove Frenchmen from the Ministry of the Posts, Telephone, and Telegraph after it was discovered that some French employees were tapping phone lines into Bourguiba's offices.

There is, of course, much less public discussion of administrative reform in the single-party system, where the officials tend to become an adjunct of the regime. Obviously no high civil servants could afford to neglect the party, although it is interesting that some officials felt that the imposition of party activities on government officials was handicapping the conduct of government business and an unfair criteria for advancement at higher levels. But the formal aspects of the adjustment to independence, and later to developmental needs, went smoothly under the firm direction of the Socialist Destour. Though Tunisian legislation on administrative organization did not appear much before the first statute of Morocco, the party did not stop with only a skeleton law. The basic law providing equal opportunity and assurances for all

[34] For details of Franco-Tunisian cooperation under the Chenik government see André Julien, *L'Afrique du Nord en Marche*, Paris, Julliard, 1952, pp. 199-216.

[35] Table provided by the Office of the President, Sous-direction de la Fonction Publique, entitled "Répartition des fonctionnaires français et tunisiens exerçant dans l'Administration Tunisienne au cours des vingt dernières années." Officials claimed that there were only 500 French civil servants remaining in 1962, plus about 1,000 teachers.

Tunisian civil servants appeared in early 1959,[36] and within a few months thereafter supporting legislation was decreed giving detailed instruction for the classification, pay, promotion, and other privileges of the officials in each category.[37] The new legislation built directly on the earlier administrative laws inherited from the Protectorate, and gave Tunisia an administrative system closely modeled on the French system.

With a high proportion of the articulate, highly educated populace working for the government, generally the case in all developing countries, it would be a mistake to assume that all these initial reforms were accepted without criticism or dissent. Until 1958 there was some mild criticism in the press, where it was noted that the problem of ministerial organization was being neglected. There were also complaints over efforts to reduce the allowances of civil servants.[38] In conversations with high officials of various ministries it became apparent that the ostensible harmony and order of the administration still concealed some very strong differences of opinion on the role of control and service ministries, and some pronounced, though suppressed, suspicion over the rapid growth of the nation-building ministries.

A Tunisian study, for example, raises real doubts over how appropriate the administration may be for the challenge of development. The paper alleges that civil servants have tended to protect "crumbling structures" inherited from the Protectorate; that the ministries have tended to erect impenetrable barriers among themselves; that the higher levels of the departments are overstaffed, duplicating and obstructing decisions on pressing matters; and that civil servants are underpaid in the lower ranks and too concerned with luxuries in the higher ranks. With the choice posts filled with Socialist Destour dependables shortly after independence, talented young persons are not being attracted to government, while some experienced officials are leaving government employment to take more rewarding posts in business and commerce.

The same charges have been made against administrative practices in

[36] *Journal Officiel*, "Loi no. 59-12 du 5 février 1959 (26 redjeb 1378) fixant le statut général des fonctionnaires de l'Etat," published in *Statut Générale des Fonctionnaires*, Tunis, 1959. For complete tables of salaries and details of fringe benefits see *Journal Officiel*, "Loi nos. 59-18 et 19 du 5 février 1959 (26 redjeb 1378) et textes complémentaires," published in *Régime des Retrailes Civiles et Militaires*, Tunis, 1959.

[37] *Ibid.*, vol. 103, no. 21, April 29, 1960, "Décret no. 60-142 du 26 avril 1960 (20 chaoual 1379) portant statut des Administrateurs du Gouvernement, Secrétaires d'Administration-Chefs de Groupe et Commis d'Administration." The three groups correspond to category A, B, and C in the Moroccan administration, and are roughly equivalent to Class I, II, and III officials in Pakistan. The new legislation was based on earlier administrative laws dating from 1949 and 1950.

[38] *Action Tunisienne*, November 11, 1957, and June 9, 1958. Tunisian officials also report that the civil service was actually reduced in the early months of independence. This appears to refer to the exodus of French officials, on the one hand, and the early retirement of 1,000 Tunisians within five years of retirement. See *Petit-Matin*, March 1, 1956.

Morocco and Pakistan, but in these two political systems the issues can at least be brought to the surface. In no developing country has administrative reform been easy, but the character of the threat to single-party hegemony has special political implications. Indeed, it is characteristic of many single-party regimes that the administrative arm of the state is above criticism.[39] Nevertheless, it must also be acknowledged that the Socialist Destour has found it possible to make some far-reaching organizational changes in ministerial organization in order to fill developmental requirements. How well these changes are received by the civil servants and how much resistance there may be from ministries concerned with control activities is not open to examination.

The Tunisian administration employed about 27,000 persons, according to high officials in 1962. This figure does not include police, military, or locally employed civil servants, but does include teachers. Compared to Morocco, roughly four times the size of Tunisia in population, the country does appear to have a large bureaucracy. However, it is important to add that the government also had laid down fairly specific lines for further growth in the Ten Year Perspective and the Three Year Plan. Unlike Morocco and Pakistan, the Tunisian government can specify approximately how many civil servants are needed for future growth, by both category and specialty.[40] The planned expansion includes about 17,000 persons in the Secretary of State for National Education, nearly all teachers; almost 5,000 for the Secretary of State for Agriculture, a large proportion of them engineers, veterinarians, and rural agents; and about 14,000 persons for general administrative positions.

The formal indicators of administrative change suggest that both Tunisia and Pakistan have surpassed Morocco. The single-party regime and the military-bureaucratic alliance have found it much easier to make organizational changes and to incorporate new activities. But it is also apparent that internal adjustment of administrative working conditions has been difficult in Pakistan, where the official elite remains, if anything, more firmly in control than in the parliamentary regime. This contrasts with Tunisia, where Bourguiba's dependence on the state machinery has not prevented creating a standard, more efficient way of classifying and evaluating the civil servants. Both these regimes are able to accept the colonial influence in the administration as a fact of life, and each in their own way have acted to remove it.

Tunisia's success could be more easily explained by the simple fact

[39] See, for example, Bernard Charles, "Un parti politique africain: le Parti Démocratique de Guinée," *Revue Française de Science Pölitique*, vol. 12, no. 2, June 1962, pp. 312-359; also, David Apter, *Ghana in Transition*, New York, Atheneum, 1962, pp. 350-351.
[40] *Perspectives Décennales de Développement, 1962-1971*, Tunis, Secretary of State for Planning and Finance, 1962, pp. 304-306.

of her small scale, if it were not that Morocco too had many of the same advantages and has failed to take her administrative problems in hand. The ironical result has been that Morocco has allowed herself to become transfixed over colonial influence in the administration, but has so suffered from her indecision that she remains much more dependent on French employees than Tunisia. The same general effect can be detected in the case of Arabization, which tended to become a *sine qua non* in Morocco and delayed simple administrative reforms. Tunisia now has an almost wholly Tunisian bureaucracy, and the language issue has resolved itself by a determined, explicit program for replacing Frenchmen.

In terms of organizational adjustment to developmental needs at the center, the single-party regime has clearly found it easiest to reconstruct ministries and shift personnel. The reforms planned for Pakistan, many of which have gone into effect, are also impressive. The Moroccans have, on the whole, had the most difficulty in gearing their governmental apparatus to development. But all these moves are preliminary steps toward a full-blown effort at national reconstruction, and very little can be accomplished through any of them without adjustments at the local level of administration.

ORIENTING THE CIVIL SERVANT TO THE LOCALITY

The feedback process from the governed to the government depends heavily on the local administrator's sensitivity to the local populace. In perfecting the administrative arm of the new nations of Africa and Asia, Western governments have generally asserted that the orderliness of our federal agencies should be duplicated throughout the administrative structure, down to the smallest unit of government. As a matter of fact, state and local administration has always been a rather disorderly business, especially in the United States. The operation of a complex political system may indeed require a loosening of the administrative process at lower levels, and, as has been argued by Merton and others, may even find that a measure of corruption and nepotism increases the system's flexibiliy and adaptiveness.

While it has been acknowledged that "participation at the village level [will be] quite different from the pattern adopted for the country,"[41] there is a great scarcity of literature suggesting how such patterns of participation may emerge and how they will impinge on the civil servant. Because the administrator is already firmly ensconced in the locality, it may well be that the significant pressures for administrative reform at lower levels will not come from government, but from individual citizens

[41] B. Mukerji, "Administrative Problems of Democratic Decentralization," *Indian Journal of Public Administration*, vol. 7, no. 3, July-September 1961, p. 307.

who find administrative processes unwieldy and inappropriate to new tasks in the developmental process. The extent to which any given political system can encourage such pressures raises again the central theme of the study. Feedback through the citizenry into the process of government is inherent in the developmental process, but also places new requirements on government.

To the extent that a new government can accommodate and integrate more articulate demands and greater frequency of interaction with its people, it will be more able to utilize its own populace in bringing indirect pressure for administrative reform. In this case the concessions will not be the formal manipulation of government discussed above, but gradual modification of administrative behavior to accommodate the locality, its habits, and its values. The meshing of the local administrative process and the locality itself is no doubt a subsequent step to central reorganization, but unless it can be done successfully, the chances of cumulative, sustained interest in development at the local level are indeed dim.

The first impulse, and in itself highly desirable, is to hope that, by improving the conditions of work for the local administrators, their increased satisfaction will translate itself into more constructive methods and greater efficiency in localized operations. Between 1958 and 1962, according to Tunisian officials, the lowest wage in the civil service rose from 28 to 50 *dinars* a month, although in the highest category a civil servant can be paid as much as 2,500 *dinars* a year, plus fringe benefits that are generally about equal to the base pay.[42] The lower categories of the Moroccan civil service benefited from the merger of the mixed and reserve components of the administration, when allowances were equalized. A second major raise was given in late 1961, when Hassan II decided to allocate three million francs to salary increases, making the minimum wage 275 *dirhams* or roughly the same as Tunisia in 1958.[43] The highly segmented civil service of Pakistan produces more severe differences, and the pay scale as a whole is lower than that of the two North African countries. A schoolteacher may receive as little as 70 rupees a month, while a C.S.P. officer starting at the district level receives 350 rupees and a similarly educated agricultural official, 200 rupees.[44]

Adequate pay is certainly an important prerequisite in the reform of the lower levels of the civil service. Local officials have probably been

---

[42] *Action Tunisienne*, June 16, 1958.

[43] These raises were given after the government had been severely handicapped after a successful strike by government workers. See *L'Echo*, December 19, 1961, and *La Vigie*, December 21, 1961. The latter reports that the new minimum was 315 *dirhams*.

[44] Braibanti, *South Atlantic Quarterly*, op.cit., p. 285. See also his comments on pay increases in *Bureaucracy and Political Development*, op.cit., p. 392.

the most prone to abuse their positions, and it is not unusual in Pakistan for lower civil servants to have second jobs. The problem of corruption and graft raises a host of problems beyond the concern of this analysis, but it is important to realize that so long as local officials are free to abuse their authority it will be difficult to communicate to the population the scope of the changes being introduced through governmental activity. There was a concentrated assault on corruption in Morocco in 1960 and 1961, but most observers agree that in the handling of permits, licenses, and tax assessments there remains great abuse.[45]

The Tunisian administration is regarded as generally free of corruption, though it must also be acknowledged that the workings of the single-party system provide an alternative avenue of approach for those seeking favors by more legitimate means. Pakistan has had a chronic problem with graft, nepotism, and corruption, although there have been stern measures to combat dishonesty in office from a time before the military regime. While the lead must certainly come from the central government, it is probably correct, as suggested by Professor Braibanti, that allowance must also be made for cultural differences between the two worlds in which the low-level official operates.[48]

Like the reorientation of the administration to nation-building tasks in general, the elimination of official abuse of office will probably come about as the civil servant himself is increasingly enveloped in an administrative system focusing on the more specific, constructive problems of the service agencies of government. Certainly the prevention of corruption does not in itself ensure administrative improvement of other kinds, nor does the meticulously honest official always find it easy to accomplish his mission where he is not supported by public morality and popular expectations. Concomitant with the more obvious reforms in local administration are the changes needed to place before the participant a more meaningful representation of what development means.

Because confessions of governmental inadequacy are extremely rare in single-party regimes, the case of Tunisia is particularly interesting. Moreover, the strains that have brought about modification of local administrative organization are closely related to the need to mobilize greater popular support for the development program. Beneath the

[45] An article in the *New York Times*, October 7, 1960, on Boucetta's campaign to reduce corruption gives several examples including the case of an official who diverted seven million francs of public funds. Hassan II sought to set a new standard by giving a high decoration to M'Hammed Bahnini, who had been secretary general of the government since independence. See *La Vigie*, October 19, 1961, for the praise given him as a loyal and honest official, which was widely interpreted as an indication of the monarch's growing concern over abuse of office. Once the Istiqlal left the government, it published more material on corruption. For example, *Al-Istiqlal*, January 26, 1963.

[46] Ralph Braibanti, "Reflections on Bureaucratic Corruption," *Public Administration*, London, vol. 40, Winter 1962, pp, 357-372.

governors, the Ministry of the Interior appointed 84 delegates (*déléguées*) and 700 *chioukh*, still the primary village or tribal officials. This lowest level of the rural organization was not reorganized until after the local elections of 1957, when Mehiri announced that 600 had been removed and that new *chioukh* would be selected in consultation with the local party cells and other national organizations. In an attempt to reduce abuse and inefficiency their pay was also increased from about 10,000 to 20,000 francs a month. The minister also indicated that these officials might be elected after a year or so, but this has not been done. Both the delegates and their subordinates are selected from among the most reliable young officials. There has been no announced recruitment system, and officials of the Secretariat of State for the Interior say that there are no special examinations.

The reorganization of the party in harmony with the local administration was a crucial turning point in Tunisian political history. Bourguiba has since acknowledged that the old regional party federations "hampered the administration on a regional scale,"[47] and it is entirely possible that as local representatives of the strong middle class they had resisted the developmental plans of the president. In addition, they were largely representatives of local interests first organized in 1937. Their demands for privileges and special consideration may have indeed become detrimental to national reconstruction and national planning. In proposing the party reorganization, which was delayed several months to overcome local resistance, Bourguiba often spoke of the "need for concentrated power which will not exhaust itself in multiple channels"[48] in order to hasten development. At the time it appears that Bourguiba shared the commonly found view in developing countries that the concentration of authority in a few persons was a requisite to development.

At the party congress in the spring of 1959, when the above changes were adopted, Bourguiba defended his reorganization by labeling the Socialist Destour as a "school for political education" in the developmental struggle, while the governor was "to eliminate bad habits of traditions and social customs which have hampered our march toward progress until now."[49] In the same speech he noted that "the Governor and the [party] delegate are the emanation of the Government and my person." The new scheme was perhaps too successful in representing only the government and the president, and after four years it was

[47] "Toward True Socialism," Speech to the National Council of the Socialist Destour, March 2, 1962, Tunis, Secretary of State for Information, 1963, p. 30.
[48] *Petit-Matin*, October 5, 1958. See also Bourguiba's speeches introducing the party reforms in *Petit-Matin*, October 7, 1958, and March 5, 1959. See also the report on the 1959 Socialist Destour meeting, *Les Congrès du Néo-Destour*, Tunis, 1959.
[49] *Petit-Matin*, April 10, 1959.

abandoned in the face of the many complications arising with the increased commitment to development. The adjustment made early in 1963 reveals both the dilemmas on insisting on highly central control as well as the risks of cutting the administration off from the local population.

Admitting that the "dualism" in administration between the party and the governor had resulted in provincial conflict, Bourguiba went on to describe new regional commissions, to be elected by sections of the party and to include representatives of the party's auxiliary organizations.[50] Although the governor's position is more exalted with the removal of the party delegates, he will now operate with a regional commission having elected party members and representatives of labor, commerce, farmers, and the women's organizations. In this way the party and the local administration will "no longer get in their own way." Instead, the authority vested in the governor will now be exercised simultaneously over party and government officials. The inclusion of representatives of the technical departments makes the Tunisian scheme comparable to the Pakistani Basic Democracies plan, and appears to be a compromise between the provincial representatives for planning, which Ben Salah had hoped to appoint, and the desire to preserve the governor's authority.

The tendency toward forming a closely coordinated hierarchy of party and government officials continued in the Seventh Party Congress in October 1964.[51] In addition to several measures to centralize power more effectively in Tunis, the governor was made chairman of provincial party commissions, partly elected and partly ex-officio members from auxiliary organizations. From the viewpoint of the local administrator the changes represent a net increase in his authority. The governor's *déléguées* no longer deal with opposites in party positions, and clearly enjoy more frequent and more direct access to the governor. The manipulation of the local administrative system in Tunisia reflects the single party's apprehension over the diversity of the developmental process. The local administrator's position is unchanged, but the orientation of power in the regime focuses his attention on the government and the party at the expense of the locality.

[50] "Toward True Socialism," *op.cit.*, p. 31. Since this speech there has been a major shuffling of governors and a new Director of Administrative Affairs has been appointed. To improve regional coordination a joint committee has also been formed for the provinces of Kairouan and Sousse. See *Jeune Afrique*, September 10-16, 1962.

[51] As is generally the case with one-party regimes, the constraints placed on local sources of expression was reflected throughout the system. An account of the centralization tendencies of the Seventh congress is found in *Jeune Afrique*, November 1, 1964. The subsequent efforts to restrict the party's auxiliary organizations are described in *Maghreb*, "Le parti socialist déstourien et les organisations nationales," no. 9, May-June 1965, pp. 19-25.

Development entails the performance of increasingly specialized tasks at the local level and with greater reliance on popular support and involvement in such tasks. Political systems vary not only in their ability to make adjustments directly in the administrative hierarchy in order to facilitate such activity, but they also differ in their ability to affect the local administrator indirectly by confronting him with a more alert, ambitious populace. The mobilization of popular energies poses serious threats to the fragile political systems of nearly every developing country, but it is indicative of force of the single-party regime in Tunisia that it has not faltered nearly so much as the other two regimes in bringing the citizen into localized development activities. It is also much more difficulty to arrest such a process in such a regime, because the highly personalized leadership is rationalized on the basis of the assured harmony between the leader's designs and the people's interest.

Although there have been few precise measures of the feed-back process in developing countries, the Tunisian experience demonstrates how the local official may be increasingly confronted with an articulate populace, and challenged by the diversity of development at the local level. When the Socialist Destour thought largely in terms of expressing authority locally through a powerful governor and an equally influential party delegate, the citizen not only felt estranged from the political system, but was also handicapped in his participation in developmental tasks locally. The rivalry of the two officers meant that further diffusion of power stopped, and that the individual was caught up in a fruitless jockeying for position between two officials. The administrative system was less adaptable to developmental needs, and popular energies tended to languish.

The Moroccan monarchy has done less to reform local administration than either Tunisia or Pakistan. The rural officials of the *makhzen* have been endowed with royal authority on a personal basis for centuries. Though the *caids* often came from the tribes which they supervised and taxed, they were, and remain, essentially agents of the king himself. For the single-party regime in Tunisia the termination of the "epoch of the *caids*" was synonymous with independence, and all the remnants of the bey's court was quickly removed. In Morocco, on the contrary, the future of the *caids* was never publicly questioned. There were, of course, numerous complaints in 1956 against those rural officials who had most actively collaborated with the Protectorate in the abuses of the years just prior to independence, and there were a few cases of summary justice at the hands of resistance fighters. The new Ministry of the Interior began immediately to remove the most objectionable.

With the shortage of officials qualified and willing to work in the remote posts of the Moroccan countryside, it was not easy to find a sufficient number of well-qualified *caids*. The new provincial organization of 20 provinces and 72 *super-caids*, who replaced the old *controlleurs civils* and the indigenous affairs officers, needed about 300 *caids*.[52] Many of them were abruptly promoted from lower rural administrative positions as translators, market inspectors, and village officials. In areas of the country where the resistance had been strong, guerilla fighters often filled *caid*'s posts, although this proved to be a major error. Unfortunately, no careful analysis of the local administration has been possible, but there have been repercussions from the poor administration. The tribal revolts in the eastern Rif in late 1958 and early 1959 were inspired, in part, by the harsh methods of local officials, while little had been done to improve conditions. At the time of the party split there were serious implications of local officials' complicity in the bloody disputes that arose over the handling of local property and favors formerly claimed by the Istiqlal alone.[53]

Like the governors, local officials were not governed by a civil-service code until early 1963, and were directly appointed by the king. There was one attempt to provide some special instruction for local administrators in 1957 and 1958, but it was directed at overcoming the basic inadequacies of the inexperienced officials, and could do little to instill new orientations toward development, which, at that time, was not a well-defined concern of the government. After an auspicious start the "*caid* school" was abandoned without explanation early in 1958 after about 150 local administrators had attended its four-week course.

Until early 1963 the only legislation defining the duties, authority, and rights of the local officials was a minor law forbidding the *caids* from assessing market revenues for their personal income, which had long been a source of abuse.[54] The Istiqlal pressed for the adoption of a law governing the Ministry of the Interior, but nothing was done. The law was originally submitted to the cabinet in May 1960, but was sidetracked and never received royal approval. The party was particularly outspoken on the injustices of the rural officials, charging that like the ancient *caids* the new officials, "suffering from complexes, and in order to demonstrate authority which they lack morally, intellectually or by experience, they tend to obstruct action and see spies, sabotage, and threats to the state everywhere."[55] Both major parties were further incensed when the rural administration played an active part in the national and communal elections of 1963 in order to secure support for the F.D.I.C. The Istiqlal was only further insulted when the law they had supported in 1960 was issued in 1963 after the party had been excluded

[52] For more details on the early provincial organization of Morocco, and a consolidation of provinces in 1958, see the author's *Political Change in Morocco*, Princeton, Princeton University Press, 1961, pp. 185-203.

[53] *Al-Istiqlal*, March 7, 1959.

[54] *Bulletin Officiel*, no. 2267, April 6, 1956, "Dahir no. 1-56-047 du 7 chaabane 1375 (20 mars 1956) fixant le statut des caids," p. 342.

[55] *Al-Istiqlal*, January 1, 1960.

from the cabinet, and without many of the guarantees the party wished to provide.[56]

Those who have expressed such grave doubts over the readiness of the rural official in Pakistan and the C.S.P. tradition pervading the district office may derive some consolation from the Moroccan scene. Rather than helping the local officials to define their new developmental roles, the struggle for power surrounding the Palace has immersed the local official in politics and local feuds even more than under the Protectorate. Using the local official as the manipulator of tribal loyalties and religious devotion in order to protect the monarchy against the increasing demands of modern segments of Moroccan society has only further reduced their usefulness in the developmental process.

To a large extent the task of the local administrator in the personalized regime of Hassan II has been to hold the line. Neither governmental reorganization for developmental purposes nor increased activity at the local level has placed the local official in a position where he needed to reassess his role. As the king depended more and more on personal emissaries and devoted high officials to run the government, the local administrator no doubt became increasingly suspicious of expressions of interest and priority from the locality. The rejection of party activity except by those previously committed to palace policies cut off a major alternative for stimulating local interest in development, and, thereby, for placing new requirements on the *caid*. Essentially the political system reinforced his role as a law-and-order agent and an official representing the personal desires of the monarch.

Organizationally the position of the district officer in the Asian subcontinent has not been unlike that of the regional official in North Africa. The imperatives of colonial administration were so much alike that authority was highly concentrated at approximately the same level, while there was so little developmental work being done prior to independence that the need to divide authority was seldom pressing. India has provided the prototype of the tireless, resourceful regional official who moves frequently among his people, avoiding local crises by his wit and wisdom, and sometimes by the superior communication and repressive capacities of the higher apparatus of the colonial regime.[57]

[56] *Ibid.*, February 16, 1963. The incident is reminiscent of the delay in approving the rural-communes law, and indicates how dependent the cabinets were in even putting agreed reforms into effect.

[57] There are numerous studies, both factual and fictional, of the old district official, of whom Brayne and Darling, already cited in this study, were examples. However, few had their innovative and research orientation. Perhaps the most revealing and well-written is Philip Woodruff, *The Men Who Ruled India: The Guardians*, London, Jonathan Cape, 2 vols., 1954. The glamour and versatility of the British district officer is indicated by the number of times the post has been portrayed in fiction. For additional references see Braibanti, *Bureaucracy and Political Development*, op.cit., p. 395.

But the basic technique has become vulnerable with independence and the growing complexities imposed by development. The British *raj* derived his superiority by his monopoly of the skills and resources enabling him to move quickly and easily between the tiny modern world of the colonial administration and vastly preponderant but inactive world of the villagers. The goal of development is to destroy the barriers between these two worlds, and it is, therefore, not surprising that the position of the district official has become the focus of reform in Pakistan.

Because Pakistan is perhaps the most determined in its drive toward national reconstruction, and more desperately in need of mobilizing the long-neglected rural population, the role of the local administrator has been subject to more examination than that of the comparable official in North Africa. Despite the estrangement inherent in the relation between the British official and the villager, the office was so critical of the colonial system in Asia that it has become the focus of concern in developmental planning. The major disadvantage has been that the stature of the office and its crucial role in the formation of an elite civil service have made it extremely difficult to reorient the local administration to developmental tasks. In both Morocco and Tunisia, moreover, the less exalted position of the local official has not provided comparable immunity to local political forces. Difficult as harmonious reconciliation may be, political and administrative elements will interact at the local level as the development process takes place. In this regard the Pakistani government's professional view has inhibited the emergence of more complex local patterns of interaction.

Indicative of the inherent weakness of the system was Canning's own admission in 1857 that the concentration of authority and duties was desirable in order to keep the local officials active and responsible to the government.[58] During the interwar period of this century the chores of the district official had become so numerous that he obviously could not perform them all adequately, and the result was that the "whole show [was] coming to be managed by clerks."[59] The local official was, and often remains, torn between the hundreds of forms, applications, and appeals awaiting his initials at the district office, and the need to make local visits and follow local political factions. As he lost the local influence which his power to grant titles and to make land grants gave him in an earlier age, he sometimes indulged in local and even national politics.

Local administration in Pakistan has suffered from the fact that the

[58] A. H. Aslam, *The Deputy Commissioner: A Study in Public Administration*, Lahore, University of the Punjab, 1957, p. 3. This is one of the most complete studies on the district officer in Pakistan. See also Inayatullah, ed., *District Administration in Pakistan*, Peshawar, 1964.

[59] Aslam, *op.cit.*, p. 25.

district officer's post was a proving ground for very young officials selected for the elite group, the C.S.P., and the resting ground for the
provincial officials, the P.C.S. There have been the historic problems of
finding enough officials to work at the local level. Thus, in 1957 the
C.S.P. had some 519 local government posts reserved to it, but was able
to provide only 248 officers.[60] At the district level in West Pakistan in
1956, 27 of 50 district officers were from the C.S.P. Another factor was
the high rate of transferal. While it was customary before 1947 for a
district official to remain in his post from two to four years, he seldom
stayed more than six months as the new country was being organized.[61]
The implications for development are clear. There was undoubtedly
much less time to become familiar with the more complex problems of
the region, while the temptation to deal with day-to-day problems with
authoritative dispatch was much greater.

Despite the broad powers of the district officials in matters of revenue collection and maintenance of order, the expansion of governmental
activity even before partition created additional confusion at the local
administrative level. A report issued toward the close of World War II
compared the district official to a "comic opera policeman," having
extraordinary powers wholly unsuited to the tasks of his post. The report
stated that though "responsible for stimulating the activities of the officers of other Departments . . . he has no real control over them . . .
even if they keep him informed of what they are doing. They are under
no compulsion to discuss their plans with him in advance."[62] Each new
organizational empire of government sprang up alongside a glorified
but increasingly distracted local authority. His situation changed relatively little over the next decade, and Gladieux, reporting in 1955,
wrote that "district officers, speaking generally, have played but a minor
role in the development programme thus far."[63]

The First Five Year Plan, much influenced by Gladieux's report,
acknowledged that "there has been a noticeable deterioration in the
quality of district personnel in recent years, owing to a general shortage of
mature and experienced administrators, made more acute by with-
drawals to the secretariat. . . . The effectiveness of district officers and the
unity of district administration have been impaired by the growing size

[60] Braibanti, *South Atlantic Quarterly, op.cit.*, p. 269.

[61] Aslam, *op.cit.*, p. 36; also, Braibanti, *Bureaucracy and Political Development, op.cit.*, p. 399. The same trend can also be distinguished in India, where
Braibanti notes that whereas the I.A.S. once provided 75 per cent of the district
officers, it now accounts for 40 per cent, *Administration and Economic Development in India, op.cit.*, p. 63.

[62] *Report of the Bengal Administration Enquiry Committee, 1944-45*, Alipore,
Government Printing Office, 1945, pp. 26-27.

[63] The Gladieux report has also remained unpublished, but has been used by
some public-administration specialists. The quote used here comes from an able
study by Richard W. Gable, *Introduction to District Administration*, mimeo.,
p. 103.

and importance of individual departments, each anxious to emphasize its own entity."[64] To provide coordination and coherence at the local level the first planning group suggested that the district official be given distinct supervisory control. In addition, he should be given a full-time district development officer, as well as assistants for tax collection and judicial matters as needed in larger districts. To accomplish a change in mentality both divisional and district officials were to be encouraged to attend mid-career courses in developmental problems at the Rural Development Academies, the Administrative Staff College, and other conferences and seminars. Much has been accomplished along these lines under the Ayub government.

There remain, of course, a host of problems in orienting the local officials to their new roles, and their confusion has by no means been alleviated. In a study of district and divisional officials attending courses at the Peshawar Academy, for example, it appeared that many thought the Village AID officials inadequately trained, but many also felt that training alone could not accomplish the tasks of development.[65] Some of the most careful survey work done in East Pakistan indicates that the ten departments usually represented at the *thana* level have yet to develop a working relationship with Basic Democrats, and that even Union Council chairmen had occasion to meet with only three departmental representatives over a year. In addition, District Councils were not performing planning and coordinating functions, nor did departments always present their schemes to the councils.

The ambiguity over the role of the Basic Democrats in development no doubt contributed to official cautiousness in working with them even before the revival of party activity. The paternalism of the entire scheme could be justified only if the government could initiate sufficient localized development work to provide a focus for local political activity prior to the renewal of highly inflammatory national party activity. Thus Ayub's professional orientation to government made him wholly dependent on the bureaucracy if he was to succeed at the local level.[66] His plan operated under double jeopardy. On the one hand, the local officials were

[64] *The First Five Year Plan, op.cit.*, pp. 101-102.

[65] The two positions are, of course, not necessarily contradictory and very likely influenced by official disapproval of Village AID from above that was widely known at the time of the study. See M. A. Sabzwari, *Administrator Reviews Rural Development*, Peshawar, Academy for Village Development, 1961, pp. 23 and 44, ms.

[66] *An Analysis of the Working of Basic Democracy Institutions in East Pakistan*, Comilla, Bureau of National Reconstruction and the Pakistan Academy for Village Development, 1961, pp. 121 and 135. See also A. T. R. Rahman, *Basic Democracies at the Grassroots*, Comilla, Pakistan Academy for Village Development, 1962. In an even more pessimistic assessment than this writer would make, Albert Gorvine concludes that the civil service has intentionally kept control of Basic Democracies. See his "The Civil Service under the Revolutionary Government in Pakistan," *Middle East Journal*, vol. 19, no. 6, Summer 1965, p. 332.

not attuned to development work at the local level, and, on the other hand, the professional regime was not suited to generating new local pressures that might indirectly guide the local official into reevaluating his role.

Professor Sayre has noted that the bureaucracy always has a "somewhat ambiguous role in the matter of innovation,"[67] and this is doubly true in the case of rapidly developing countries. The administrator must not only adjust to the immediate requirements of development, improved planning, and more careful budgeting, but he is also a crucial link in relating the mobilized nation to the activities of government. Even the initial increments in productivity and social complexity brought about by the obvious developmental tasks demand more effective administration. An airline, a port, or a railway cannot operate without skilled management. The authoritative aspect of administration rapidly loses its importance as a society orients itself to performing more specific, more intricate tasks.

Administration at the local level poses much more difficult problems of judgment and reorientation, which we have only begun to investigate. At the local level the importance of "organized adulation,"[68] characteristic of colonial administrative methods, is unavoidably eroded as the nation-building departments grow. The administrator can resist only at his own peril. In a highly inflexible and unresponsive administrative system he may soon find himself performing tasks irrelevant to the society, and out of a job. Although this writer concurs in Professor Braibanti's high estimate of the generalist in sustaining Pakistan through a period of extreme stress,[69] this should not become an argument for the preservation of an all-powerful higher civil service, or keeping villages under the benevolent hand of a philosopher-king.

There are two more important complications at the local level. The first is the nature of the transition toward more participation and self-control in the locality. The extent to which local participation and energies of the community are channeled into national reconstruction efforts depends not only on the receptiveness of the official, but on the political environment in which he works. As development advances beyond the phase of obvious necessities the administrator will be increasingly dependent on the individual citizen's capacity to organize his

[67] Wallace S. Sayre, "Some Problems of Public Administration in a Developing Economy," *Indian Journal of Public Administration*, vol. 8, no. 2, 1962, p. 143.

[68] Used by Mashiuzzaman, "Administrative Obstacles to Voluntary Organizations in Pakistan," in *Bureaucracy and Political Development in Pakistan, op.cit.*, p. 78.

[69] His balanced and documented appraisal will be found in *Bureaucracy and Political Development, op.cit.*, pp. 383-409.

work and to relate changes to social and political life in the village. Indeed, only when this begins to happen may one say that the developmental process has traveled its full cycle in the social system.

The second complication, and one which has received relatively little systematic study in our concern with higher administrative problems, is that the multiplication of administrators required at the local level will probably bring a deterioration in the quality of local administration. India has already suggested that more decentralization will bring officials with "less education, a narrower outlook and hardly any experience" to the villages.[70] If handled only as an administrative problem, improved local administration may result in even greater concentration of authority, perhaps accompanied with even greater inefficiency and disappointment for the peasant. One of the most critical decisions in the administrative development of the new country will be made by the local official of traditional stature and authority, who will unavoidably create the environment for the proliferation of local officials that has already begun in many countries. Once again the local authority is being asked to restrict his own authority in order "to accept fully, emotionally as well as intellectually, the importance of the technician."[71]

Concern with administration in isolation from the political environments in developing countries may, therefore, be somewhat misdirected. As in the case of development generally, we have concentrated on the most tangible and obvious of developmental obstacles in dealing with the central and higher administration. Though a logical starting place in orienting a new state to development, the narrower administrative framework does not adapt well to the analysis of development that involves a major societal revolution. In their response to the increasing capabilities of the villagers, the three political systems considered in this study display important differences. The Moroccan monarchy has done relatively little to change the dominant position of the local official or even to provide more effective local use of nation-building agencies. The single-party regime in Tunisia has made concessions to service agencies locally, but under the guidance of an extremely powerful governor, now buttressed with party representatives. The military regime of Pakistan has engaged in a major appraisal of its local administration, and has begun to focus developmental activity at the local level.

The administrative system is very likely more inclined to take its cue from the government's reception toward increased local participation than from increased interest at the local level. Posing the developmental problem on the national level enables one to compare how

[70] B. Mukerji, op.cit., p. 310.
[71] Douglas Ensminger, "Democratic Decentralization: A New Administrative Challenge," Indian Journal of Public Administration, vol. 7, no. 3, 1961, p. 295.

various systems may have affected their bureaucracies through other institutional change. In evaluating capabilities and potential for development it may be more important to assess correctly a government's views on increased involvement in political life than its more easily specified ability to handle funds, make plans, and market goods.

The elevation of administrators to high political office in the Moroccan monarchy, accompanied with very little internal reform or reorganization, very likely serves to reinforce more traditional views on administration in the colonial manner. While Bourguiba has done more to sustain the sheer efficiency of the administration, he has also made concessions to local Socialist Destour interests, and may be compelled to make more as development advances. The governor must at least work under the scrutiny of locally selected party members. The Ayub regime was, of course, highly dependent on the higher administrators, and their reluctance to accept the full implications of the national mobilization are evident in resistance to certain reforms and in the burning controversy over the role of the C.S.P. and the other superior services. Possibly the greatest irony of the developmental revolution begun under the military-bureaucratic alliance is that it must eventually yield to the administrative partner, while the military partner steps down voluntarily.

The developmental process is unidimensional only in the sense that it leads constantly toward a more complex society. But decisions are made from day to day by governments, which have the predominant role, and as the trends of government become apparent to the officials as well as to the people, a new set of conditions has been laid down for the next phase. For this reason it is wrong to ignore the developing country's early experiments in institutional reform of a distinctly political type. The new constitution, the experimental legislature, and the reformed judicial system are all part of the environment for development. The manner in which these early reforms take place shape the mind of the privileged civil servant as well as the isolated villager. Perhaps no part of the world is as rich in bureaucracies that have survived endless, sometimes monthly, changes of regime as the Muslim countries. The permanent officials react to government more promptly and more effectively than any other group in the developing country. If the national government indicates the path toward national reconstruction, the official will almost certainly be prepared to follow.

SECTION IV:

NATIONAL DEVELOPMENT AND ATTITUDINAL CHANGE

"Perhaps the greatest resistance force operating in small groups is the members' imperfect awareness of their own interpersonal processes and their lack of a frame of reference in which to judge their performances and their possibilities for improvement."[1]

In this section of the inquiry the discussion shifts from a consideration of the forces impinging on the new participant to the way in which he may indeed perceive and reconcile these forces. To facilitate conceptualization of the problem two aspects of change have been singled out: those tending toward elaboration of the individual's feelings and emotions about government and those tending toward improving the individual's understanding of his environment. The discussion in Section II dwelt on how the governing values of the three political systems, all of which acknowledge the importance of increased participation, have indeed been translated into patterns of participation at the local level. The discussion in Section III focused on the major programs of each government to teach the new citizen about the complexity of his environment and the way in which it might be managed to assist the developmental process.

Together these two sections characterize what has been referred to as the affective and cognitive elements of the individual undergoing rapid social change. On the one hand, he has intensely held beliefs and feelings about the new nation, which may be more or less transformed into new patterns of social action in the locality. On the other hand, he is being pressed in a variety of ways to learn more about his environment and, in so doing, to become a more productive person. The basic argument of this study is that the two processes are inextricably mixed, i.e., that we cannot begin to explain the instability of many new political systems without allowing for the multiplicity of new behavior the participant is being asked to perform in other contexts, and that we cannot fully appreciate the complexity of the developmental process without some consideration of how more general values about government are perceived. The purpose of this section is to elaborate how affective and cognitive elements appear to be reflected in behavior and, in conclusion, what their changing relationship may be as a more complex society emerges.

[1] Ronald Lippitt, Jeane Watson, Bruce Westley, *The Dynamics of Planned Change: A Comparison Study of Principles and Techniques*, New York, Harcourt, Brace, 1958, p. 181.

– 301 –

The reader should perhaps be warned against attaching concrete significance to the perceptual elements that have been distinguished for purposes of analyzing the developmental problem in attitudinal terms. In the study of an individual one cannot distinguish these qualities as they refer only to the perception of general values about the political system or only to specific actions that the government may be encouraging at the local level. In the early phases of a nationalist movement, of course, it may well be that new imperatives, however intensely held, are not seen in any association with community life. The three countries have been selected in part because they represent situations where national development has entered a phase where there is increasing need to articulate national values and loyalties. As much of the material on local reorganization suggests, a political system cannot advance very far in elaborating the meaning of these affections without also beginning to restructure behavior at the local level and to give the peasant new understanding and new responsibilities. Thus the affective dimension of developmental change soon shades into increased understanding and improved evaluative capacities, which are the origin of the cognitive dimension.

A similar line of reasoning applies to the direct impact of new programs for development. An individual is capable of learning a certain amount about more refined ways of dealing with his environment in agriculture, education, and administration without beginning to assess the relevance of these new areas of social interaction to his national values. In other words, there can be a degree of cognitive development in his outlook on the world without a major restructuring of his entire environment and value system. However, there is a good deal of psychological evidence, to be noted in the concluding chapter, that he can advance only so far without creating new frames of reference and perhaps making major adjustment in his closely held values. In this way cognitive elaboration produces pressures to reinterpret and reorganize old values, both traditional and newly acquired national values.

The process of reevaluating the nation can easily be thought of as a problem of attitudinal change, stemming from the pressures for both affective and cognitive reorganization. The ease and the success with which the restructuring process takes place, it is argued, will vary greatly according to capacity of the political system to deal with what, in effect, represents a more confident, more active citizen. Thus the affective orientation of the Moroccan monarchy is reflected in both the problems of establishing effective government at the local level and in the disjointed character of many developmental efforts. both of these factors contribute to the difficulty of the Moroccan citizen in defining his relation to government and to development. The cognitive orientation is strong in the Pakistani approach to both local reform and development programs, and the difficulty the regime has had in blending attitudinal components has also placed obstacles in the path of more meaningful participation. Tunisia represents an intermediate course, where cautious efforts have been made to reinterpret national values while also advancing developmental programs that enhance individual capacities and understanding. As the author has suggested above, the precise "mix" of these elements no doubt depends on many factors, such as the strength of traditional institutions, the over-all level of development, et cetera, but for an initial formulation of the developmental challenge attention has been confined to the relation between locality and government.

CHAPTER 10

THE AFFECTIVE VORTEX: MORAL
IMPERATIVES AND DEVELOPMENT

THE THEORY of attitudinal change casts the problems of national development into a new framework. The individual is not only being asked to use resources more effectively, i.e., change his social behavior to become more productive, and to operate in a new value system, i.e., relate the nation and its goals to his activity, but also to interrelate these two new demands. Admittedly a nation might make substantial progress, as some of the early and more responsive modernizers already have, without explicitly dealing with the transformation of the citizen's perceptual world. The theory does not make assumptions about the consciousness of undergoing attitudinal change in the broad sense, although it is hypothesized that the frequently observed tensions, defensive reactions, and emotional outbursts are a function of perceptual disparities. Essentially this study is suggesting that more attention be given to disparities on the grand scale as the new citizen is thrust into a new framework for social action.

Much of the early writing on development worked from models of human behavior that implied that change was linear, i.e., that a more or less complex, steadily accumulated quantity indicated how far a nation had moved along the path of development. Implicit in such a theory, of course, was also the assumption that such a path or delimitation of possibilities was a meaningful concept. Much of the earlier material in this study has been included to indicate the extent to which the intricacy of human behavior cannot be reasonably studied in such a context, and how the diversity of the developmental process may easily open up new ways to combine human activity in institutions and organizations undetected by more deterministic notions about development. Anticipating change of this kind in sociological terms is perhaps an unmanageable task at this stage of our knowledge, but we can begin to inject into the study of development some notions that allow for the versatility of human nature and seek to identify how some of the momentous structural changes in the way men see the environment take place.

The theory of attitudinal change, like several other theories of personality development, does not assume that the interaction of the individual and his environment, however defined, is a simple, additive process. People often refuse to acknowledge "realities," and they often attribute meaning to perceptions that is not "real." Without entering into the full controversy of the phenomenalist position in psychology,[1] common sense

---

[1] Those interested in the framework of this controversy in psychology per

suggests a multitude of ways by which this notion might reasonably apply to development. Most important, this notion shifts our attention from the ostensibly immovable limits to development to the multiplicity of possible combinations created by national reconstruction. The challenge of development is not only maximizing achievement under unfavorable conditions, but it is also creating new relationships and finding new solutions that may indeed disprove many notions of how to maximize.

The study of attitudinal change tries to deal with the problem of perception in such a framework, though psychologists have, by and large, confined themselves to the more favorable conditions of the laboratory. However, some work on attitudinal change has raised questions about the effects of major restructuring as a result of introducing what have been called new "terminal values."[2] The appearance of the nation-state and the intense feelings aroused in patriotic displays quite clearly represent values of this kind, though we know relatively little of how they operate in either advanced or less advanced nations. Strong feelings, deeply held beliefs, intense emotional attachment characterize the affective forces operating on a range of attitudes for every individual. The study of authoritarian personality has probably been the richest source of knowledge of how such feelings operate in our perception of the world and in making judgments about how to act.[3] As the critics of the early authoritarian studies observed, however, the conceptual framework did not allow for the way by which wider social conditions, organizational alternatives, and major restructuring of personality might modify or eliminate the aggressive behavior on which the authoritarian studies first focused.[4]

The national framework is in many ways an attractive one for finding new ways of formulating how personality reacts to new conditions. The new nation, or, indeed, any other nation, cannot continue to exist if it becomes simply the vehicle of Oedipal rage. Nor does the notion of emotional pressures in Freudian thought do full justice to refinement

---

se might read Gardner Murphy, "Social Motivation," in G. Lindzey, ed., *Handbook of Social Psychology*, Reading, Addison-Wesley, 1954, pp. 601-633; also, Martin Scheerer, "Cognition," *ibid.*, pp. 91-142. Some of the works stemming from this viewpoint that have influenced this study greatly are Milton J. Rosenberg et al., *Attitude Organization and Change: An Analysis of Consistency Among Attitude Components*, New Haven, Yale University Press, 1960; Leon Festinger, *A Theory of Cognitive Dissonance*, Evanston, Row Peterson, 1957; and Milton Rokeach, *The Open and Closed Mind*, New York, Basic Books, 1960.

[2] Rosenberg et al., *op.cit.*, p. 34. See also Milton J. Rosenberg, "A Structural Theory of Attitudinal Change," *Public Opinion Quarterly*, vol. 24, 1960, pp. 319-340.

[3] T. W. Adorno et al., *The Authoritarian Personality*, New York, Harper, 1950.

[4] R. Christie and M. Jahoda, eds., *Studies in the Scope and Method of "The Authoritarian Personality,"* Glencoe, Free Press, 1954.

of national values that had indeed occurred in many new and old nations. At the same time, no person could deny the intensity of the passions aroused by the contemporary nationalist movements, least of all in the Muslim world. They have indeed provided the motivating force for heroic sacrifice and the initial, sometimes the only, point of identification in the emergence of new nations of Africa and Asia. Political leaders have, of course, played on this emotional identity with the nation, though it is highly significant in the context of this inquiry to note the extent to which this identity soon takes on something more of the symbolic, exclamatory meaning as developmental problems multiply. Indeed, the history of modern nationalism could be written in terms of the transformation of an emotional identity into a working relationship between citizen and government—in other words, in the transformation of the affective orientation to national life into a more articulate, differentiated body of opinion and expectations that structure the relation of the new citizen to the new framework of action.

Nevertheless, the magnetic power of the symbol remains great, and certainly is not without some immediate form of gratification for the member of the chanting crowd. It should also be noted that in time of national crisis the advanced nations also manipulate national symbols in order to elicit uniform and sacrificial behavior from citizens. The developmental process, especially in the early stages, embodies a good deal of behavior of this kind, but it rapidly becomes less and less appropriate to the diverse tasks of nation-building. As argued in Section II in particular, the ease with which the value placed on the new nation may be transformed into more instrumental form varies greatly with the political system. The purpose of this chapter is to provide two examples of how affective forces in the three countries have been managed, the implication being that where they remain strongly symbolic the effort to relate them to the diversity of the developmental process will be inhibited. However, it is quite reasonable to expect that different governments will experience varying degrees of success in changing the affective orientation toward national political life.

ISLAM AND NATIONAL DEVELOPMENT

One of the frequently noted discontinuities in the life of the Muslim peoples is the ever-widening breach between Islam and modern life. Though we are not directly concerned with how the religion might be invigorated, it is indicative of the strong hold of Islam that so many millions have held fast to their religion despite the failures and inadequacies of the past five centuries. The multitude of disappointments and defeats endured by the Muslim world have probably served to reinforce religious devotion. The emotional bonds individuals feel for Islam may have become more intense, while Muslims were also seeking Islamic solutions to new problems. The ironic psychological effect may have been to make adjustment to new external forces more difficult, and to entrench defensive and basically rigid attitudes. As Wilfred Smith has noted, "Islamic backwardness implies that something has gone wrong not only with the Muslim's own development but with the governance of the universe."[5] Unable to make an appropriate response, Islamic leaders have tended to interpret the religion in intransigent and inflexible terms.

The alternatives for transforming Islamic ideologies have been well described by Manfred Halpern.[6] The interesting point of his inquiry in an attitudinal context is that each of the alternatives represents even greater stress on the affective role of the religion, and holds relatively little promise of converting Islamic values into a form enabling the individual to articulate the present-day world more meaningfully and more flexibly. Indeed, the political manifestations of most of the reform efforts over the past century have resulted in highly authoritarian expressions, highly unsuitable for the tasks of development. The Muslim countries appear to be drifting either in the direction of rigid interpretations to national ideology unsuited to nation-building, and giving Islam a less important role, or to founding the entire social system on Islamic principles, often interpreted with such compulsive literalness that social change becomes almost impossible.

Each country must start, of course, from an infusion of Islam that has different characteristics. For this reason a comparison based on Islamic principles alone is difficult and often misleading. The interest of the present investigation is to treat the religion as a dependent variable in national reconstruction, an analytical approach that reverses the priorities used in conventional studies of Islam. How the religion is to be affected by development varies greatly with the new demands that a government is prepared to make of its people, and with the way in which it wishes to guide the increased participation necessary to rapid development. The three countries selected for this study have responded very differently to Islam, and have dealt very differently with Islamic institutions. These actions have probably contributed more to the transformation of Islam than theological explorations, which provide the developing country with very few guideposts for social change. As each country responds to the problems of converting Islam to modern needs in the working situation of current development, the perplexing religious question may be dissolved in a multitude of individual reconciliations and adjustments.[7]

[5] Wilfred Cantwell Smith, *Islam in Modern History*, Princeton, Princeton University Press, 1957, p. 112.

[6] *The Politics of Social Change in the Middle East and North Africa*, Princeton, Princeton University Press, 1963, especially pp. 119-195.

[7] There is a variety of rewarding readings on the Islamic transition in Turkey.

The ultimate transformation of Islam will be the creation of a society where individuals find it possible to lead more fruitful, satisfying lives without abandoning their religion and also without making Islam the sole criterion of all human interaction. As in many other aspects of development, the initial decision as to whether or not Islam may be individually reconciled with modern life and how Islamic loyalties may be exploited for political purposes must be made by the government itself. There is no doubt that Islam can easily be made into a powerful emotional appeal, or that Islamic officials exercise great influence, often at the grass roots of the society. To forego the exploitation of these convenient devices for national mobilization requires a leadership that is prepared to refrain from exercising the control religious beliefs can provide, and that is ready to respond to the varied interpretations of the religion that any highly diverse population might make. The attitudinal relationship between a government's use of Islam and expanded development effort may become a critical turning point in the creation of a more complex society.

Perhaps the country that has most firmly rejected Islamic influences has been Tunisia. The Tunisian constitution acknowledges the importance of the "teachings of Islam" in the preamble, and gives Islam equal but not predominant recognition in establishing the country as a regime whose "religion is Islam, language Arabic and regime republican" (art. 1).[8] Bourguiba's views on Islam have been touched on previously in discussing his steps to abolish Islamic educational institutions and the rapid dismantling of the *habous*. In the single-party regime the appeal of Islam can be used to obstruct the government. There were indications that the bey had hopes of rallying conservative Islamic elements to bolster his position against the energetic president. These same persons sympathized with Ben Youssef's appeal to preserve stronger ties with the Arab world and to make Tunisia a more distinctly Muslim country.[9] The bitterness of the conflict was heightened by the reluctance of the single-party regime to acknowledge influence not subsumed within

---

See, for example, Howard A. Reed, "The Religious Life of Modern Turkish Moslems," in Richard N. Frye, ed., *Islam and the West*, The Hague, Mouton, 1957; Smith, "Turkey: Islamic Reformation?" in *Islam in Modern History*, *op.cit.*, pp. 161-205; and Robert E. Ward and Dankwart A. Rustow, *Turkey and Japan: A Comparative Study of Modernization*, Princeton, Princeton University Press, 1964.

[8] The Tunisian Constitution appears in Charles Debbasch, *La République Tunisienne*, Paris, Librairie Générale de Droit et du Jurisprudence, 1962, pp. 207-218.

[9] *New York Times*, November 21, 1955. See also the revealing article of Jean Tostain, "Tunisie: prémiers pas dan l'indépendence," *Esprit*, vol. 24, no. 240, Juillet-Aout 1956, pp. 133-140, and "Salah Ben Youssef contre Bourguiba," *ibid.*, vol. 23, December 1955, pp. 1897-1900.

the party organization. In this case the president used his own highly charismatic appeal to counterbalance the affective appeal of Islam.

The president has gone to remarkable lengths to portray the Tunisian Islamic figures as selfish and dishonest and—possibly most devastating of all—closely conspiring with the French in order to defeat the Socialist Destour in the struggle for independence. Although the French administration in Morocco was also able to manipulate the *ulama* of Qarawiyn to approve the installation of a puppet sultan at the time of Mohammed V's exile, and to issue statements supporting other abuses of Islamic property and practices, the Moroccan political system has not sought to restrain religious authorities; nor has there been an ideological breach between Islam and government in Pakistan comparable to the Tunisian situation. Bourguiba has given publicity to the *ulama's* refusal to support the Socialist Destour in its fight with the French, and has also criticized their inaction and conservatism in education.[10] The government has widely distributed documents showing how Islamic authorities coveted positions in the French administration, and Bourguiba has often referred in detail to the resistance of the religious officials in and around Kairouan, where opposition has lingered on in subdued form. In one of his most outspoken speeches, he proclaimed, "The Moslem religion does not need champions of proven duplicity, who only yesterday were in the service of Islam's enemies, hoping for some material gain, a post, a sum of money, a sinecure."[11]

Bourguiba is not suggesting that the Tunisian people abandon their religion, but that it must be combined with modern learning and reason. In the speech cited above he condemns Islam for becoming a "doctrine of intellectual asphyxia," and for branding any change in conservative Islamic practices as apostasy. His most sustained attack has been directed against Ramadan, which he considers "an excuse for idleness." Using the same theme of Islam's refusal to adapt to the demands of reason, he has noted how the religion became "an impediment, an excuse for laziness, a factor of Moslem regression and an obstacle to freedom of thought and creative action."[12] The Ramadan campaign was heightened in 1960, when only stringent concessions were made to civil servants

[10] Habib Bourguiba, "La Réforme de l'Enseignment: Premier Bilan," Speech delivered June 29, 1961, Tunis, Secretary of State for Information, 1961; also, "A Solemn Message for the National Assembly," Speech delivered November 20, 1959, Tunis, Secretary of State for Information, 1959.

[11] The quote is from his most outspoken attack in a speech of February 8, 1961, printed in Habib Bourguiba, *Bourguiba Addresses the Nation's Leaders,* Tunis, Secretary of State for Information, 1961, p. 49. The photographs of the documents revealing the Islamic officials' submissiveness to the French appeared in Habib Bourguiba, "General Mobilisation for Work," Speech delivered February 26, 1960, Tunis, Secretary of State for Information, 1960.

[12] Habib Bourguiba, "The Mouled Speech," Speech delivered September 3, 1960, Tunis, Secretary of State for Information, 1960.

wishing to fast and when the military continued to follow the normal eating and working schedule. His attempt to associate the developmental struggle to the *jihad* or holy war, which would, thereby, exempt the participants from fasting, generally fell on deaf ears. Although it was not unusual to find Tunisians breaking Ramadan in the capital city,[13] the president found it prudent to withdraw from the strong position of his first speeches and to reassure the populace that each would in fact be free to follow his religious conscience.

Bourguiba has never ceased in his criticism of the *ulama* for their "sterilizing complex" and "underemployment of intelligence"; nor has his attack on religious institutions been confined to the *habous* and Islamic schools. In the first months of independence the Sharia courts were simply closed down, and the entire legal system has been transformed along Western lines. When the new civil code was announced in the fall of 1956 the Secretary of State for Justice noted that the fundamental principles of Islam would be preserved, but suggested that the *ulama* might be best occupied in finding "legal principles permitting the operation of banking institutions necessary to improve the country's economy."[14] A year later the rabbinical courts were also merged with the Tunisian civil and criminal legal system. Bourguiba has also taken legal steps to protect women's rights, which have been given only qualified recognition in Morocco and have received little attention in Pakistan. A law on Tunisian personal status, issued only five months after independence, forbids polygamy outright. Repudiation was no longer an acceptable divorce procedure, women were guaranteed complete freedom in selecting a husband, and marriages could be performed only with the free and mutual consent of both parties. Legislation in 1959 went even farther in assuring offspring of equal inheritance rights.[15]

The Tunisian code on nationality of 1956 makes no mention of Islam, and starting in 1959 the president spoke out against the patronymic pattern of naming children. Bourguiba's repudiation of Islamic practices has been accompanied with increasing emphasis on one's obligations and duties to the state. The onslaught against Islamic institutions has no doubt tended to remove religious appeals from political life, and to that extent has provided the foundations for the elaboration of new attitudes prepared to cope with the requirements and diversity of

[13] Charles F. Gallagher, Jr., *Ramadan in Tunisia: Aspects and Problems of The Tunisian Republic*, New York, American Universities Field Staff Report, North Africa Series, vol. 6, no. 1, 1960.

[14] "Tunisian Code of Personal Status," George N. Sfeir, trans., *Middle East Journal*, vol. 11, no. 3, Summer 1957, pp. 309-318.

[15] For additional summaries of the reforms see Debbasche, *op.cit.*, pp. 173-174, and André Raymond, *La Tunisie*, Paris, Presses Universitaires de France, 1961, pp. 98-99. Also, Henri de Montery, *Femmes de Tunisie*, Paris, Mouton, 1958.

development. But the affective pitch has been sustained by transferring much of the arbitrariness of the Islamic conservative to the single-party regime. In the same speeches in which he condemned the *ulama*, Bourguiba went on to state he was "not prepared to show any consideration to anyone at all when it is a case of protecting the regime." While confessing that the state was using force to break the grip of Islamic practices, he also noted that his basic objection was that the religious officials and their views had committed the supreme offense of creating "a serious split in the nation."[16]

The transformation of affective orientations to politics rooted in Islam sprang from peculiar institutional problems confronting the Tunisian political system. Islam was not only a strongly held value, but it was also the organizational basis for opposition to the single-party regime. Nevertheless, the emotional value of the state has been transformed, which suggests that Bourguiba was not interested solely in eliminating ideological competition. The president has not refrained from making a religious appeal, but has sought ways to interpret Islam in the context of problems facing the country. This accounts for much of the organized opposition from Islamic groups, which was rapidly eliminated. Having achieved his immediate political objective, however, Bourguiba did not ignore the appeal of religion or the obstacle that religious belief might be in dealing with developmental problems. In fact, he took the offensive in urging the mobilization of popular energies on Islamic principles adapted to specific needs. To say simply that he advocated a more secular society does not do full justice to the attitudinal change implicit in his position. Islam was to remain a critical value in his view of the world, but it was to be integrated and related to other values and to coherent patterns of activity relevant to national reconstruction.

The role of Islam in the Moroccan transition appears much simpler, but in fact its relation to political change is infinitely more complex than in Tunisia. Bourguiba has, of course, always considered himself a devout Muslim. The conversion of his Roman Catholic wife in 1960 indicates that he wants to retain an image of a faithful Muslim. The constitution, written under his close supervision, provides that the president of the republic must be Muslim (art. 37). Morocco almost defies comparison institutionally because the political system is inextricably merged with ancient Islamic practices, and the Istiqlal has been the vehicle of a still active Islamic reformist movement. To millions of Moroccans the monarch's role as *imam* or spiritual guide is more significant, and possibly indistinguishable from, his role as *malik* or king. In the mixed Islamic expressions of the countryside, the king's *baraka* or

[16] See the speech of February 8, 1961, *op.cit.*, pp. 27-29.

blessing remains powerful, and his visits are the occasion of festivity and semireligious celebrations.[17]

The strength of the Islamic appeal in Morocco hardly requires documentation. All the existing political forces, with the exception of a few Communists and U.N.F.P. members in unguarded moments, have constantly given the monarchy unqualified support as a religious institution. Early in the century the Salafiya reformist movement, inspired by the teachings of Mohammed Abdu, took strong root among the *ulama* of Qarawiyn, and has remained the guiding purpose of the most dynamic Istiqlal leader, Allal al-Fassi.[18] But the simple existence of two sources of religious inspiration and interpretation has introduced complications into Moroccan religious life, which have, in turn, had unavoidable impact on political affairs. Indeed, one of the important early advocates of Salafiya reform, Moulay bel-Larbi al-Alaoui, left the select group of royal councilors appointed by Mohammed V shortly after independence to support the political opposition. Nevertheless, nearly all Moroccan political leaders continue to support the monarchy and to give strong endorsement to the Islamic character of Moroccan life.

The association of religious reform and political action in Morocco dates from the Berber *dahir* of 1930, though many *ulama* of Fez had long been disturbed over the lack of Islamic emphasis in the Protectorate, and had been advocating more rigorous application of Salafiya doctrines. In contrast, it is interesting to note that the Roman Catholic congress held in Carthage in the same year did not arouse comparable feelings among the Destourian leaders, nor did Bourguiba's defection to form the Socialist Destour in 1934 have similar Islamic inspiration. The *ulama* and other traditional officials of Tunisia were almost uniformly at the service of the French, while the Islamic universities and schools of Morocco became an integral part of the nationalist organization. The transformation of Islamic sentiment has never been attempted, and therefore the modification of attitudes and beliefs in response to development is in many ways a much more delicate and complex problem in Morocco.

[17] One of the few examples of the Istiqlal's adjustment to the demands of independence is the party's changed views on the holding of *moussems*, or tribal festivals often interlaced with Islamic practices considered heretical by more proper Sunni Muslims. They were condemned by Al-Fassi shortly after independence, but he later decided that the tribal rallies, which are good places to organize tribal support and to make political speeches, were acceptable. The *moussems* are now held on a highly organized basis for tourists and official visits to the countryside.

[18] See the excellent summation by R. Marston Speight, "Islamic Reform in Morocco," *Muslim World*, vol. 53, no. 1, January 1963, pp. 41-49. Possibly the most authoritative account in English on Morocco is Allal al-Fassi's *The Independence Movements of North Africa*, H. Z. Nuseibeh, trans., Washington, American Council of Learned Societies, 1954, passim. Islam in contemporary Morocco has been more recently examined in the works of Mohammed Aziz Lahbabi and Malik Bennabi.

The breakdown of Morocco's formula for Islamic reform was indicated by the need to give the state an explicit Islamic character in 1961 in the Charter of Fundamental Rights. Significantly, it was shortly after the death of Mohammed V and the transfer of his office to Hassan II that the affirmation was made. In its preamble the law stated that Morocco was to be "inspired by the spirit of authentic democracy which finds its foundation in the teachings of Islam." Not only did the document insist that political reform must be inspired by Islam, but following articles stated that "Islam is the official religion of the state" (art. 2) and that "the state must provide for instruction following an Arabic and Islamic national orientation" (art. 14).[19] These provisions were in part to pacify the Istiqlal, which was disturbed over the delay in establishing a constitutional monarchy as well as the secular influences being injected into Moroccan life by modernization. While the Istiqlal elders had no doubts over the intentions of Mohammed V, they made this pronouncement their price for support of Hassan II.

The difficulties of interpreting Islam are reflected in reforms touching civil law, the position of women, and inheritance. The hesitance of the monarchial system has already been reflected in the discussion of educational reform. Though Morocco has carried through a remarkably thorough reorganization of her courts, it is noteworthy that the contribution from Islamic teachings has been minimal.[20]

In fact, the ease of the judicial reforms in Morocco appears to have rested to a large extent on the reservoir of nationalist feeling against French intrusions more than on any positive notion of how Islamic law related to problems of national reconstruction. Under the chairmanship of Al-Fassi, the new legal codes governing marriage and inheritance were milder versions of rights given in earlier Tunisian legislation. Polygamy was not forbidden, but the wife has legal recourse where a marriage is threatened as a result of multiple wives. She may also stipulate on being married that she is to be the sole wife. The minimum age for marriage for women is fifteen, and her explicit permission must be given. Divorce procedures remain close to Islamic practice. Repudiations made in anger may be withdrawn, and there must be three successive statements. The most important protection for women is probably the

---

[19] *Bulletin Officiel*, no. 2537, June 9, 1961, "Dahir no. 1-61-167 du 17 hija 1380 (2 juin 1961) portant Loi fondamentale pour le Royaume du Maroc," pp. 801-802.

[20] See the minister's speech at the inauguration of the Supreme Court and also organizational diagrams in *Al-Istiqlal*, December 28, 1956. For discussions of the steps toward the reorganization see *ibid.*, May 25, 1957, and October 26, 1957. The new civil judge was to take over the judicial functions of the *caid*, and one was appointed for roughly each *cercle* or *super-caid*. Morocco made the final break with French legal influence early in 1965 when Arabic became the official language of all courts and legal procedures. The French judges on loan to Morocco were dismissed and several hundred French lawyers working in Morocco returned to France.

provision that a wife may seek divorce if deserted for over a year even if the husband has been providing support.[21] Given the high degree of Islamic devotion found in Morocco, the country's ability to carry through even these partial reforms has no doubt depended heavily on the concerted support of the monarchy as *imam* and the Istiqlal as the source of Islamic reformism.

Morocco, however, is still far from the articulation of Islamic principles that encourages the individual to make an independent reconciliation of his relgious beliefs and the requirements of modernization. Al-Fassi has called on all sincere Salafiya reformers to "devote themselves to cleaning up the corruption, enforcing the truth, putting an end to deviation, until Islamic thought returns to its pristine freshness and vigor."[22] But it seems unlikely that other changes in Moroccan life will halt until the Islamic reformers can produce a theologically acceptable compromise. Indeed, the pressure of social and political change has already caught up the Istiqlal, and placed them in opposition to the monarchy, which they had always considered as the prime mover in the transformation of Islam. In the Istiqlal congress of early 1962 the party repudiated the legal reforms which it had played so active a role in bringing about, and objected to the parallel existence of Islamic and modern courts.[23] The party received a great blow when an Istiqlal militant and respected *alim*, dean of the law faculty at Qarawiyn University, was removed in mid-1963 for his criticisms of Hassan II's constitution.[24]

The attempt to find a constructive role for Islam in the new Morocco has not been nearly so structured and explicit as it has been in Pakistan and Tunisia. The curious result has been that although the king exerts considerable influence as a religious figure, he has also found it increasingly necessary to restrain the excesses permitted in the name of Islam. The new constitution, for example, is not so firm in its support of the religion as the Charter of Fundamental Rights. The Kingdom of Morocco is called a "sovereign Muslim state" in the preamble, and the king is described as the "leader of the faithful" (art. 19), but the specifically Islamic provisions are qualified. Article 6 stipulates that "Islam is the religion of the state, which guarantees to all free exercise of worship." The much more militant view of the Istiqlal leaders was revealed in the Bahai controversy. Al-Fassi gave firm support to the

---

[21] *Ibid.*, December 7, 1957, for a full discussion of the marriage and divorce reforms.

[22] Quoted in Speight, *op.cit.*, p. 45.

[23] *Al-Istiqlal*, January 17, 1962.

[24] The *âlim* was removed at the same time as were two other high officials from the party. During 1963 most Istiqlal officials in high office were gradually removed. See *ibid.*, July 7, 1963. The Istiqlal was especially incensed because the *âlim* had been one of the few prepared to defy the French when Mohammed V was exiled in 1953.

regional court's decision to execute the offenders for treason, but Hassan II supported appeal to a higher court where the decision was annulled and the Bahai missionaries released. The royal decision to appeal the case was one of the major incidents leading to the resignation of the Istiqlal ministers in January 1963.[25] Shortly after Al-Fassi's departure from the government, the Ministry of Islamic Affairs, which was organized to his specific designs in 1961, was dissolved.

Despite the attempts to adapt Islamic principles to the needs of Moroccan political life, there is little evidence to suggest that Islamic feelings have been substantially transformed or that there are programs under way which will affect individual perception on the role of religion. When a peasant was asked for his opinion on the constitutional referendum in late 1962, he replied that there is "Allah, the King, and 'yes,' "[26]—an answer which indicates how closely the three issues were regarded in his perceptual world.

In their handling of affective forces in national attitudes the Moroccans have hardly broached the subject of reconciling Islamic values with new patterns of activity. A partial explanation might be sought by saying that Morocco is a more traditional society, but in the attitudinal context this is only to repeat the problem. Islam has indeed been used to elicit some new behavior, for example, when the monarch has appeared on a tractor or to dedicate a new school. But, like the developmental process itself, the impact of these isolated and momentary associations of religious prestige and new behavior is disconnected and generally infrequent. In effect, the religion continues to be used to underscore differences in politics and to reinforce the monarchy with very little attempt to elaborate its meaning in the broad context of development. The political system exploits old Islamic predispositions in the familiar context, and does little to channel them into new situations. The Moroccan is being asked to live a more complex life, but very little has been done to use his fundamental values to make the new life coherent and meaningful.

The role of Islam in the reorientation of Pakistani values is also complicated by social conditions in the country. Pakistan did not have the remnants of Umayyad and Ottoman institutions that existed in North Africa to help to give institutional structure to Islamic beliefs, and the religious identification might be called the only common quality of the Pakistani citizen. Much of the turmoil in prerevolutionary Pakistan revolved around giving this emotional identification meaning. In the words of Profesor Smith, since partition the Pakistanis have been "self-

---

[25] For background on the controversy, indicating that there were about 300 Bahaists in Morocco, see the *New York Times*, January 16, 1963. Possibly an even more dramatic example of how highly affective appeals can be manipulated is the rise of Mauritanian irredentism in Morocco, largely under the sponsorship of Al-Fassi.

[26] *Jeune Afrique*, December 17-23, 1962.

consciously and clamorously" committed to Islam.[27] The theory of attitudinal change would suggest that they may indeed have been so transfixed on their sole common quality that interpretation and elaboration was a painful process. As a symbol of national unity it may very likely have become too precious to jeopardize by examination and analysis.

The early leaders of the Muslim League were curiously insensitive to the Islamic complications of erecting the new state, but the country has been forced to make adjustments in even less time than was available to the North Africans, where religious and political forces were at play in nationalist movements since the turn of the century. The Lahore Resolution of 1940, generally taken as the first statement favoring an independent country for the Muslims, did not mention Islam. Some of the foremost Islamic reformers, including Mohammed Iqbal, came from the subcontinent. Their intellectualized reconciliation of contemporary society with Islam was accepted more or less without question by privileged Muslims prior to 1947. The fact that reformist thinking was virtually unknown in the countryside, and seriously in conflict with the Islamic principles of the *ulama* and other religious leaders, does not appear to have troubled the Muslim League in the hectic period leading to independence.

The paradoxical result, then, was that Pakistan was one of the few Muslim countries where the villager was probably more sensitive to Islamic influence than were the political leaders. The circumstances of village life obviously prevented the peasant from making a reconciliation, and Islam became even more important to him as a refuge from the arbitrary authority of the district official; but he did not live in two separate worlds like many politicians. The modernists and reformers, who became Pakistan's leaders and high officials, were a tiny minority in isolation from Islamic—and other—views of the people.[28] If the ease with which the reformist leaders passed off the conflict of Muslim law and the realities of contemporary science and technology represented only a discontinuity between leaders and followers, the Pakistani problem would be much simpler. In fact, there was a highly influential group, the *maulana* or *ulama*, who came much closer to the villager's concept of Islam and had great influence at the local level through the *mullahs*

[27] Wilfred Cantwell Smith, *Islam in Modern History*, Princeton, Princeton University Press, 1957, p. 206. His chapter 5, "Pakistan: Islamic State?" is an excellent statement of the Islamic implications of Pakistan's goal, indicating both the ambiguities and risks of the experiment. For a statement of the modernists' position see Ishtiaq Husain Qureshi, "The Background of Some Trends in Islamic Political Thought," in Braibanti and Spengler, eds., *Tradition, Values and Socio-Economic Development*, Durham, Duke University Press, 1961, pp. 212-242.

[28] See Keith Callard, *Pakistan: A Political Study*, London, George Allen and Unwin, 1957, pp. 194-231; also, I. H. Qureshi, "Islamic Elements in the Political Thought of Pakistan," in Braibanti and Spengler, *op.cit.*, pp. 212-242.

or local Islamic teachers and scholars. Had the political leaders and intellectuals of Pakistan cultivated local support, the political integration of Pakistan would today be a much easier task.[29]

The profound differences among Pakistani Muslims are indicated by the *ulama's* opposition to the very idea of forming an independent state. In reaction against the reformist notions of Sir Sayed Ahmed, the *ulama* formed their own association in 1875, and vigorous centers of fundamentalist Islamic study were formed at Deoband and Barelvi, now in India. Clinging to a literal interpretation of the Koran and the Sunnah, the *ulama* saw the erection of a modern state as a threat to Islam, and for many years worked more closely with the Indian congress than the Muslim League. The Islamic controversies involved in their position and the efforts made by the new country to win their support have been carefully analyzed by Professor Binder.[30] The theological aspects of the conflict do not directly concern this inquiry, but it should be noted that the Muslim League did succeed in bringing several important *ulama* to Pakistan. The most distinguished *âlim* to accept the "two-nation theory" was Maulana Shabbir Ahmad Usmani, who played a leading role in drafting the first constitution. Another important figure was Maulana Abul Ala Maududi, the founder of the Jama'at-i-Islami.

The conservative Muslim leaders did not remain wholly intransigent, however, and even compromised their position to the extent of suggesting a ministry of religious affairs at one time. The explosive force of the *ulama's* appeal and also their vulnerability to political maneuvering was exposed in the Ahmadi riots in 1953. The Ahmadiyya sect was regarded as heretical by Sunni Muslims, and riots in which the *ulama* conspired marked a decline in their influence in official circles.[31] The suggestions of the *ulama* in the Basic Principles Committee reveal how literal a translation of Islam they prefer. Among other things they favored compulsory prayers, the designation of the head of state as *amir* or *khalifa*, and the specific consideration of his pious qualities in selection. The 1956 constitution proclaimed in its preamble that "sovereignty over the

---

[29] Smith's work, *op.cit.*, pp. 225-227, is particularly good in pointing out that events do not stand still while Islamic solutions are hammered out, and that viewpoints often diverge even more in the course of such explorations. In contrast, it might be noted that the local Islamic teacher or *fqih* in Morocco was organized by the Istiqlal, then the Committee for Action, in the 1930's and was thereby politicized when independence took place. In Tunisia the politicization of religious officials has a much longer history. Sadiki College, a *lycée* with a large component of Muslim students, was founded in 1898.

[30] *Religion and Politics in Pakistan*, Berkeley, University of California Press, 1963. This study is devoted largely to the *ulama's* role in forging the first constitution, and is especially helpful in understanding how Islamic fundamentalists gradually made concessions to the state.

[31] For an account of the political intrigue in the riots see Callard, *op.cit.*, pp. 204-207; also *Report of the Court of Inquiry Constituted under Punjab Act II of 1954 to Enquire into the Punjab Disturbances of 1953*, Lahore, 1954.

entire universe belongs to Allah Almighty" and directed that Muslims should be enabled to order their lives in accordance with "the teachings and requirements of Islam, as set out in the Holy Koran and Sunnah." In addition, the president was directed to set up an Islamic research institute for "the reconstruction of Muslim society on a truly Islamic basis" (art. 197) and no law was to be passed that was "repugnant to the injunctions of Islam" (art. 198). Though far from the Islamic state envisaged by the fundamentalists, Pakistan made more explicit concessions to Islam in government than any other Muslim country.[32]

The digression into the Islamic background of Pakistan prior to the revolution of 1958 is essential to understanding the magnitude of the adjustment yet to be made. The military regime of 1958 was not basically different in its estimate of Islam than were the modernists and intellectuals who had played a dominant role in the earlier parliamentary regime. Without our questioning the sincerity or devotion of Pakistan's leaders, it can be observed that religious feelings at Sandhurst and Oxford are essentially the same. When President Ayub speaks of religious principles as "out of step with the pace of changing times" or of the need to "discover fresh avenues" for the application of Islam,[33] he is only rehashing viewpoints that Pakistani modernists have discussed for many years without reaching the population. Both the monarchy and the single-party regimes have tools to attack the chasm of belief between modern and traditional segments of society, but the highly professional outlook of Pakistani officialdom provides only the platitudes that have served to reinforce the Islamic extremists in their resistance to government and the reforms associated with development.

The military regime could neither disassociate itself from Islam nor use it to the advantage of the society. The constitution of 1962 indicates how little the relation between Islam and politics has changed. The new constitution dropped "Islamic" from the "Republic of Pakistan" and also the specific reference to the Koran and Sunnah in living in accordance to Islamic principles; but otherwise it is the same as the 1956 constitution.[34] The new constitution reiterates the need for an Islamic

[32] The extreme case is, of course, Saudi Arabia, where Islamic injunctions are directly and literally enforced and there is virtually no political activity outside the lines prescribed in Islam, except, of course, for rather crucial negotiations with oil companies. Under these conditions there is no room for political development or social change within the political system. Saudi Arabia is under the influence of the Wahabi fundamentalists' reform movement in Islam, which is also subscribed to by many more conservative Istiqlal elders.

[33] From Field Marshal Mohammad Ayub Khan, *Speeches and Statements*, vol. III (July 1960-June 1961), Karachi, Pakistan Publications, 1961, pp. 80 and 134.

[34] The new constitution differed substantially from the parliamentary regime suggested in the *Report of the Constitution Commission*, Karachi, Government of Pakistan Press, 1961. The constitution will be discussed further in the following chapter, but it is relevant to note that the commission, whose report was submitted

Research Institute (art. 207), and also organizes an Advisory Council on Islamic Ideology (arts. 199-206). Under Article 6, the assembly, the president, or a governor may refer to the council questions of lawmaking involving principles of Islam. The council may also make recommendations as it sees fit, but the government is not obliged to accept its advice. The council was a compromise with fundamentalist opinion which wanted Muslim legal scholars to exercise the right of review over all legislation. The stipulation that no law should be "repugnant to Islam" has been included as a principle of lawmaking (art. 6). Among the principles of policy (art. 8) are the provisions that Muslims should be provided with facilities to encourage their understanding of Islam, and that instruction in the Koran and the Sunnah (given as "Islamiat") should be compulsory for Muslims.

The operation of the affective appeal derived from religion is well illustrated in the reaction to the 1962 constitution. The reaction was comparable to events in 1953, when Islamic feelings were easily inflamed to do violence against the Ahmadi, but were complacent when Nazimuddin, a sincere supporter of Muslim concerns, was abruptly dismissed a few months later. Islamic feelings were again outraged in 1962, and one of the first actions of the new National Assembly was to revise the Islamic provisions of the constitution. In the summer of 1962 a bitter battle was waged to pass a Fundamental Rights Bill which would make the injunctions of the Koran and Sunnah binding on all existing legislation, and would direct the Islamic Council to compile all injunctions for reference in all future legislation. A bill was passed in late 1963, but did not yield to the Islamic demands of the opposition.[35] There was no doubt that the politicians were exploiting the Islamic issue in Pakistani political life with an energy that the military had been unable to mobilize. The fact that this was being done at the expense of many less moving but pressing developmental problems indicates the difficulty of reorienting political attitudes in Pakistan.

In fact, the president had tried to put forth several basic laws to focus Islamic questions on problems at the grass roots, and to pave the way for a social revolution. The Family Laws Ordinance was one such attempt,[36] and it was also one of the first laws from the martial-law

---

in May 1961 and not released until March 1962, was strongly in favor of incorporating all the Islamic features of the 1956 constitution, *ibid.*, pp. 114-120.

[35] *Pakistan Times*, July 3, 1962; *New York Times*, November 26, 1963.

[36] The full text of the Family Laws Ordinance and the provincial rules can be found in *Noorani's Compilation of The Muslim Family Laws Ordinance (and Two Allied Acts)*, Karachi, Pakistan Publications, 1961. The Conciliation Courts Ordinance appears in *The Pakistan Law Reports*, West Pakistan, Part II, November 1962, pp. 358-369. Further protection of inheritance for women is contained in the West Pakistan Muslim Personal Law (Shariat) Application Act, 1962, to be found in *The Pakistan Law Rports*, West Pakistan, Part II, February 1963, pp. 6-8.

period to be attacked in the new National Assembly. Ayub received a group of Basic Democrats shortly after the constitution was released who protested that the inheritance provisions of the ordinance were against the Koran. Another early action of the assembly was to introduce a bill to repeal the Family Laws Ordinance despite the majority Ayub could generally muster. The Islamic Council was asked to pronounce judgment on the law as one of its first opinions, and the law was upheld by Ayub's assembly majority late in 1963.

The naïveté of the government's approach is suggested by Ayub's placid affirmation that "the resuscitation of Islamic spirit in its true perspective [could be] the panacea of all problems in the country." But the professionally oriented regime had few workable suggestions, and Islam was used through the elections of 1964 to exacerbate political feelings with little relation to specific issues in the country. The opposition of the well-organized Jamaat-i-Islami became so troublesome and inflammatory that the leaders were finally arrested for subversive activity.[37] Compared to Morocco and Tunisia, then, it is clear that religious sentiment was expressed almost entirely outside any framework of action relevant to the development of the new nation. Ayub was fundamentally correct in resisting the destructive force of Islam, but he had very little to say that contributed to a more effective interplay of religious ideas and national problems. He lacked Bourguiba's determination and also his organization to convert the meaning of affective appeals in political life, and he was denied the religious prestige of the Moroccan monarch. As we have suggested in the earlier discussion of Basic Democracies, the tragedy of Pakistani politics under the professional regime has been that there were indeed no values that the leaders could use in seeking to reconstruct the citizen's feelings about government.

If one compares trends in the three political systems, it appears that there are three distinct patterns of relating religious beliefs to the political life, and through politics to the tasks of national reconstruction. By far the simplest is the Tunisian approach of supplanting the affective power of religion with that of the state, simply destroying Islamic institutions and eliminating Islamic officials. When the manifestations of the religion are no longer to be seen, a people begins to reorient their values and beliefs. The intensity of religious devotion may be unchanged, and many of the contradictions of religious and secular life may continue to exist, but the affective focus in political affairs becomes the state. This is essentially the path that many European nations have followed,

[37] *New York Times*, January 7, 1964. For additional background on the Jamaat-i-Islami see Khalid Ben Sayeed, "The Jama'at-i-Islami Movement in Pakistan," *Pacific Affairs*, vol. 30, no. 1, March 1957, pp. 59-68, and Freeland Abbott, "The Jama'at-i-Islami of Pakistan," *Middle East Journal*, vol. 11, no. 1, Winter 1957, pp. 37-51. See also Khalid Ben Sayeed, "Religion and Nation Building in Pakistan," *Middle East Journal*, vol. 17, no. 3, Summer 1963, pp. 279-291.

and the pitfalls of magnifying the importance of the state are well known.

The Moroccan alternative is in many ways the most promising as a means of adjusting the participants' perceptual framework to developmental activities and eliciting a more comprehensive commitment to the country. Despite the fact that the monarchy has performed less well than either the Tunisian or Pakistani government as a vehicle for change, it remains a manipulable, easily discernible focus for transforming religious feelings. The major obstacle for Hassan II, and other Muslim monarchs, is that by transforming the affective appeal of their person and office in the Islamic framework they risk diminishing their own political influence. The monarch is a highly affective focus for Islamic emotions undergoing the stress of modernization, but insofar as attitudes are transformed the participants acquire the capacity to act outside this focus.

As has been suggested above, the most difficult attitudinal transition has yet to be made in Pakistan, where Islamic sentiments and the new nation exist in an almost purely symbolic, synonymous form. The efficiency and purpose of the military regimes have led us to accept them without questioning how well suited they may be in bringing about very basic attitudinal reorientations. The fundamental weakness of the Ayub regime in the case of Islam, very similar to the crucial weakness in Basic Democracies, is that it could not make an affective appeal except by reverting to the highly charged methods of earlier politicians. The various compromises and inroads toward reconciling Islam with national politics, and forcing religious spokesmen to deal with the concrete problems of operating a state, have had little effect.

INTERNATIONAL SUBSTITUTES FOR NATIONAL ACTION

In the participant's expanding world, Islam can be an extremely moving force, but it can also become a perceptual barrier as new behavior is learned. For many years the "reality" of Islam was so great that it indeed excluded detailed consideration of how nation-building tasks might be performed, and it remains a tempting devise to revive the highly affective orientation to national life that provided the militantly uniform response needed in the earlier nationalist phase of the new country. Though somewhat different in its source, the highly affective appeal of international affairs offers the same respite from national reconstruction. Like the Islamic issues, however, the attitudinal forces unleashed by foreign issues and international crises are difficult to translate into affective action at the local level, and may indeed become attitudinal obstacles to focusing on more prosaic matters.

The sequence of events in the establishment of most developing countries has often produced more familiarity and sensitivity concerning the international framework of activity than the national framework of activity. This is not to suggest that either is perceived with accuracy or is even the object of sustained interest; but contact on the international level has often preceded the acquisition of independence. For example, both Morocco and Tunisia had active groups at the United Nations from 1951. The organization of these offices was regarded in nationalist propaganda as a highly significant step toward liberation. Nationalists were able to have their problems aired before the International Court, and often received assistance from unofficial international agencies for youth, labor, and human rights. Pakistan and India were embroiled in a major international dispute over the partition of Kashmir from the moment of independence, and the issue continues to disrupt relations between them. No less significant is the international environment into which the new countries have entered, which raises the threat of world destruction for all peoples and makes the new country the object of international rivalries. Like Islam, these conditions are not pertinent to the present inquiry for their substantive meaning, but as forces shaping political perception at lower levels in the political system and establishing conditions which leaders must interpret while also engaging in national reconstruction.

As perceptual objects, the issues of international affairs, like the issues of Islam, are extemely remote from the individual, but impinge directly and forcefully on his national identification and pride.[38] The ways of diplomacy and the legal complications of specific problems escape the understanding of the citizen of Africa and Asia, just as they do the perception of many citizens in advanced countries. Unable to grapple with foreign issues in his own world, the new participant must rely heavily on national leaders to interpret foreign affairs and to provide evidence, if any is available, on how such issues relate to national political life. Often the goals of international activity are so vague or the issues so successfully defy solution acceptable to all parties that the instrumental significance of the questions is all but lost.

Again, it should be noted that international relationships, like Islam, can have cognitive impact. The Indus Valley agreement hopefully reinforced understanding between India and Pakistan, for example, and opened the way for increased cooperative activity in a much less in-

[38] See the findings on the significance of Islamic and other religious differences among students in Levon H. Melikian and Lufty N. Diab, "Group Affiliations of University Students in the Arab Middle East," *Journal of Social Psychology*, vol. 49, 1959, pp. 145-159; also, E. Terry Prothro and Levon Melikian, "Social Distance and Social Change in the Near East," *Sociology and Social Research*, vol. 37, no. 1, October 1952, pp. 3-11; the author's "Political Usage of 'Islam' and 'Arab Culture,'" *Public Opinion Quarterly*, vol. 25, no. 1, Spring 1961, pp. 106-114; and the chapter on religious differentiation in the author's *Perspectives of a Moroccan Nationalist*, New York, Bedminster Press, 1964.

flammatory situation. But the operational, more concrete forms of international relations have been discouragingly slow to expand, even among such fervently united countries as those of the Arab world. As the new citizen becomes involved in the more complex perceptual framework of politics outside the village, foreign affairs appear to have a predominantly affective impact.

With the notable exception of the studies conducted by Hadley Cantril and Lloyd Free,[39] which are confined to international perceptual problems among the more modern elements of developing countries, there has been relatively little research into the questions raised above. The incidents described below in the experience of the three subject countries do not require a great amount of documentation, but are intended to illustrate the type of issue that often arises in the course of intensive development efforts. Precisely how these incidents have affected the formation of national attitudes and national integration requires additional inquiry of a specialized kind, but attention can at least be drawn to how these events may have shaped ongoing programs for development, and the attitudinal transformations that such programs entail. Even a cursory review of the press and statements of national leaders during any of these incidents reveals the highly emotional environment for national action that was created.

The single-party regime as it is found throughout much of Africa and Asia has often displayed a remarkable capacity to mobilize popular support for foreign issues. The Socialist Destour government and similar governments have, of course, unusually effective organizations and full control of internal communications to build such support. Perhaps the most revealing incident in Bourguiba's foreign relations has been the Bizerte affair. The brief struggle for Bizerte in the summer of 1961 dramatically indicates how the leader of a single-party regime can go so far as to reverse his policies by generating affective support. This inquiry is not concerned with the justification for Tunisian action, though it should be noted that France had agreed in the independence treaty to negotiate the Bizerte question and had repeatedly postponed discussion. Bourguiba himself had suggested that Bizerte be internationalized by becoming part of the NATO base framework, and had also proposed a western Mediterranean defense pact. Under fire from Radio Cairo and under pressure from other Arab states, his compromising position indicates the grip on popular opinion provided by the regime.

The president's attempt to dramatize his extreme pro-Western posture was doomed, in part because international affairs are so highly emotional and because, therefore, even more impassioned views could penetrate

[39] See Lloyd A. Free, *Six Allies and a Neutral*, Glencoe, Free Press, 1959, and Hadley Cantril and William Buchanan, *How Nations See Each Other*, Urbana, University of Illinois Press, 1953.

the party's appeal from external sources. Bourguiba raised the Bizerte issue in more intransigent terms before the National Assembly in early 1960.[40] He continued to pose the issue as a possible means of seeking compromise in the Algerian war, a strategy that never attracted sympathy from the Algerians, and to merge the Bizerte issue with the determination of Tunisia's southern boundaries. These attempts to justify his procrastination by appeal to other national goals failed, and became doubly embarrassing over 1960 and early 1961 when Morocco made agreements for the withdrawal of American and French troops from her territory. Bourguiba gave new stimulus to the "battle for evacuation" in early 1960, and scheduled demonstrations and strikes for the anniversary of the Sakiet-Sidi Youssef raids, but backed down when De Gaulle was threatened by the revolt of the French army in Algeria. These reversals and delays, combined with growing sentiment in favor of the Algerians, meant that the president was under great pressure to justify his policy, as was indicated by the attempts to rationalize "Bourguibism" in his speeches of the period.

In February 1961 Bourguiba met with General De Gaulle at Rambouillet, and again posed Tunisian demands for negotiation on an evacuation schedule. Tunisia received no indication of France's willingness to negotiate, and in June found French forces at Bizerte extending runways to accommodate larger aircraft. In retaliation the Tunisians forbade unauthorized flights of foreign aircraft over her territory, and fired on French military planes that continued to use the base. After a brief but bloody battle, French paratroopers occupied most of Bizerte and its environs. Tunisia went to the United Nations Assembly, where she received support from the Soviet Union and most African and Asian countries.[41] Relations with the U.A.R. were quickly patched up, and offers for military support came from several Arab and Communist countries. Diplomatic relations were broken between Tunis and Paris for a year while France was preoccupied with the Algerian negotiations. Evacuation finally took place in October 1963. The formal opening of the installation under Tunisian control became the occasion of a triumphant reunion of Ben Bella, Nasser and Bourguiba.[42]

The internal aspects of the Bizerte issue are more relevant to present concerns. It should be recalled that at this time Bourguiba was experienc-

[40] Habib Bourguiba, "*The Battle for Evacuation: Bizerte and the South,*" Speeches of April 7, 1960, July 17, 1960, and July 14, 1961, Tunis, Secretary of State for Information, 1961. Also, Bourguiba, "*Nous Libérer de Toute Dépendence,*" Speech of October 12, 1961, Tunis, Secretary of State for Information, 1961.

[41] *New York Times*, July 29, August 22 and 23, 1961.

[42] *Jeune Afrique*, December 23-29, 1963. Plans had already been made to make Bizerte a northern industrial center when France formally withdrew on October 15, 1963. One of the early projects was a refinery under an agreement with E.N.I. of Italy. See *ibid.*, December 2-8, 1963.

ing resistance to his development plans, and trying to mobilize popular support for Destourian socialism. One of the most striking indications of Bourguiba's insight is his apparent realization that to succumb to the full emotional impact of the incident would mean committing the regime to continued reliance on highly affective devices to mobilize opinion. Once the reorientation of a developing country is enmeshed in inflammatory issues, real and imagined, identification with national politics takes on a new form, and one that is very likely incompatible with the attitudinal adjustment needed to accomplish the prosaic, tedious chores of handling internal developmental problems. The Tunisian stand is consistent with policies noted in earlier chapters indicating the Socialist Destour's reluctance to disperse control in development. The aroused passions of a people having little knowledge of how to implement their values and, in the case of international situations, having virtually no awareness of intricacies and conditions bearing on issues can become an overriding and possibly inhibiting commitment.

It would be too simple to argue that Bourguiba has opted for a "rational" approach to national development, and it remains uncertain if the cautiousness of the Socialist Destour will be able to prevail indefinitely with detachment and compromise revealed in the Bizerte incident and other international problems. From a political viewpoint the Socialist Destour has been consistent in its desire to make political situations calculable and to pursue only foreseeable solutions to political conflict. The Islamic question may appear at first glance to be an exception, but it should be noted that by eliminating Islamic institutions with the overwhelming popular support at his disposal on the eve of independence, Bourguiba removed another incalculable source of affective appeal from the national scene. The single-party regime in Tunisia differs greatly from the highly volatile and impassioned methods of some single-party systems, but is alike in its insistence that political relationships be specifiable and therefore open to manipulation by central authority.

One of the most dramatic illustrations of the compelling force of highly valued international goals is the Moroccan irredentist movement aimed at recovering Mauritania. Indeed, the Mauritanian campaign reached its peak shortly after the country achieved independence, and produced such severe complications in Morocco's foreign relations that Hassan II began to withdraw from his extremely awkward position. The example underlines the great potential appeal of highly affective issues in national politics because initial support for the Mauritanian cause did not come from the government, but was successfully created by the Istiqlal. Where sufficient emotion can be aroused, even legitimate authority cannot resist. The monarchy was doubly vulnerable. In addition to Mohammed V's desire to keep Istiqlal support, the Mauritanian issue played heavily on Islamic ties and historic factors.

Even before the Franco-Moroccan treaty for independence in 1956, Allal al-Fassi indicated that he would consider North Africa liberated only when Algeria was free and Morocco had been restored to her historic boundaries. When the Istiqlal leaders returned to Morocco, they made only vague reference to "territorial unity" in the party congress of December 1955. Al-Fassi remained in Cairo for some time, and in the midst of negotiations for independence defined his claim in terms of the expanse of the Almoravide empire.[43] In the eleventh century the Moroccan dynasty was recognized by tribes from Saint-Louis in the south all the way across the Sahara to Lybia. Some of these tribes still worship in the name of the Moroccan monarch. In establishing French rule in North Africa, several centers, such as Tindouf, Tlemcen, and other border points, had been arbitrarily placed in surrounding territory. Thus there was sufficient historical truth in Al-Fassi's claim to make it attractive to attach the issue to loyalty toward the monarch and faith in Islam.

Although Al-Fassi returned to Morocco after independence, he continued to wage the irredentist battle almost singlehandedly. In the summer of 1956 he further inflamed the issue by traveling to Cairo with a Mauritanian exile, Horm Ould Babana, and seeking Arab League support. When the delegation returned from Cairo, Mohammed V had little alternative but to receive the Mauritanian group, though he made only the most equivocal statement of Moroccan interest in recovering lands to the south. The king was quite clearly embarrassed by the excessive claim. In memorial ceremonies to the resistance movement in the summer of 1956 he skirted the question, while Al-Fassi, speaking in Tangier, made irredentism the new mission of the guerilla fighters, who had been recently subdued after delicate talks with the monarch himself. However, Al-Fassi was the dynamic leader of the Istiqlal and his colleagues were forced to take some note of his campaign. In Istiqlal meetings of late 1956 the moderate Balafrej advocated steps to restore independence to "the tribes to the south" still recognizing the king.[44]

But Al-Fassi was not to be satisfied with these palliatives, and in the winter of 1957 spent several months barnstorming among the border towns and villages in the south. Almost the sole theme of his long, impassioned speeches was recovery of Mauritania and the Spanish

---

[43] *L'Express*, December 5, 1955. It is indicative of Al-Fassi's strained relations with party leaders accompanying the king in France at this time, and also his own charismatic appeal, that he refused formal office in the party, keeping the honorific title of Leader (*zaim*). He continued to remain aloof until the split of the Istiqlal.

[44] *Al-Istiqlal*, August 24, 1956.

territories to the south. In his words, "The battle for the Sahara has begun. . . . We will not consider ourselves independent while the Sahara is not free. . . . Our soul is the Sahara, our culture and religion emanate from the Sahara."[45] Simultaneously, steps were taken to organize remnants of the Moroccan guerilla forces in the borderlands, initially under the control of the Istiqlal. The brief fight to recover Ifni, a Spanish enclave in southern Morocco, took place in the fall of 1957, while the king was in the United States. The hostilities served to magnify the issue further, and officially involved the Moroccan government.

As the Moroccan irregulars extended their operations, the government took a more active part and a Directorate of Saharan Affairs was organized in the Ministry of the Interior under Al-Fassi's brother. The guerilla bands were largely wiped out in a joint French and Spanish operation early in 1958, but Morocco, represented by the Istiqlal, took its cause to the Tangier meeting of North African states that spring, where the delegates agreed to initial a statement acknowledging Moroccan interest in Mauritania and her concern for "the historic and ethnic unity" of the region. Shortly afterward a more significant Mauritanian delegation, led by the Amir of Trarza arrived in Rabat, and was warmly received by Mohammed V. By then Moroccan fears were further aroused over French plans to seek I.B.R.D. support for mining operations in Mauritania, and over rumors that the predominantly Negroid southern part of Mauritania might be attached to Senegal.

In February 1958 the monarch traveled to the Moroccan Saharan outpost, M'Hamid, and ceremonially received a number of tribal representatives from the region beyond Moroccan borders. Though the king refused to endorse the vast claim of Al-Fassi, he stated that Morocco would continue to press her Saharan claims in accordance with the popular and historic wishes of the tribesmen. Mohammed V appointed a Frontiers Commission under Al-Fassi, whose verdict might easily have been anticipated, and organized a Mauritanian congress in the fall of 1958 in Rabat, where Prince Hassan presided. These efforts, coupled with an appeal to the United Nations, were of no avail, and the Islamic Republic of Mauritania was established after the French colonial referendum of September 1958.[46]

By the fall of 1958 Moroccan foreign policy was entirely oriented to the Mauritanian issue, and the irredentist campaign became the predominating theme of political discussion within the country. Though many Istiqlal leaders, most notably the progressive wing of the Istiqlal, gave the issue only lukewarm support, and the monarch himself appeared loath to be encumbered with the full claim of Al-Fassi, the Mauritanian

[45] *Al-Alam*, January 13, 14, and 27, 1957.

[46] For details on the joint military operations of the French and Spanish see *Le Monde*, March 4, 1958. Also, Jean Serjuc, "Mauritanie et Maroc," *L'Afrique et l'Asie*, no. 45, 1959, pp. 11-21.

appeal swept aside all other considerations. Like many other highly affective questions in politics, involvement in one tends to produce involvement in others, raising the emotional pitch of political life even more. By late 1960 France was prepared to give full independence to her colonies. Morocco received Arab League support, and began to speak of the "Palestinization" of Mauritania. Her effort to keep the Islamic Republic out of the United Nations succeeded because of a Soviet veto,[47] and the monarch spoke of the Mauritanian issue as part of Morocco's "sacred combat" to liberate Africa. With some of the most progressive African nations in the Casablanca group, Mohammed V pledged support for Nasser's Israel campaign in return for recognition of Moroccan claims. Momentarily Moroccan intransigence was only further inflamed with the *fait accompli* in Mauritania, but the complications of her quixotic mission started to become unbearable in 1961.

Although Al-Fassi continued to declare, "The independence of Morocco will be incomplete so long as Mauritania and the Sahara are not integrated into the country," the government found its relations with the Algerian revolutionaries, Tunisia, and many African states under strain.[48] The new constitution specifies that the king will assure the country's independence within "authentic frontiers" (art. 19), but Hassan II has gradually withdrawn from the rigid position the issue entailed. Over 1962 the royalist front under Guedira's direction challenged the Istiqlal policy, and Hassan II noted late in 1962 that there was no legal solution.[49] His new approach, involving a *rapprochement*

---

[47] Morocco also received a letter of support from Hanoi. Her drift toward closer relations with the Communist world dates from this time, and she received Soviet MIG fighters in 1960. Paradoxically, the government was stiffening its policy versus the local Communists at this time. Nevertheless, the Moroccan Communists followed the party line. See Ali Yata, *La Mauritanie: Province Authetiquement Marocaine*, Rabat, 1960. The full Moroccan position is given in *Livre Blanc sur la Mauritanie*, Rabat, Ministry of Foreign Affairs, 1960. See also Jamal Sa'd, *The Problem of Mauritania*, New York, Arab Information Center, 1960. The complications produced in relations with other African powers are outlined in I. William Zartman, "The Sahara—Bridge or Barrier?" *International Conciliation*, no. 541, January 1963, and in George Liska, *The Greater Maghreb: From Independence to Unity?*, Washington, Washington Center of Foreign Policy Research, 1963.

[48] An agreement was signed with the Algerian revolutionaries in July 1961, stating that their conflicting claims would be negotiated after Algerian independence. Morocco broke relations with Tunisia over Bourguiba's refusal to support the Moroccan position. Among the meetings boycotted in 1961 by Morocco because the Mauritanians were attending the United Nations were: the Economic Commission for Africa, the World Health Organization, and the Conference of Independent African States on Radio and Television. Even as late as December 1963, Hassan II felt he could not join the chiefs of state at the Addis Ababa meeting, and Morocco was one of the few represented by foreign-office officials.

[49] See the excerpts from both party publications, and map of the "Greater Morocco," in *Jeune Afrique*, April 15-21, 1963. Hassan II's statement appears in *Le Monde*, December 27, 1962.

with the Mauritanians for mutual exploitation of the Sahara, was one of the major causes of the Istiqlal resignations from the cabinet in January 1963. Subsequently the Amir of Trarza and his colleagues returned to Mauritania to seek a compromise, which prompted the Istiqlal to note that the government was considering "dangerously compromising solutions," which might amount to treason.[50]

As in the other instances of highly inflammatory foreign issues, it is impossible to measure the attitudinal effects without more field study. However, for at least five years Mauritanian irrendentism has been a major theme of the government radio station, directed part of this time by a Mauritanian exile, and for several years Al-Fassi published an Arabic paper devoted to the Saharan campaign. Mohammed V and, for a time, Hassan II have been closely associated with the issue, and their religious position was one of the major rationales for reclaiming the Saharan territories. It is noteworthy that the campaign was at its peak at the time Morocco was making its first major developmental effort in organizing rural communes and designing a national plan. These more complex, less attractive problems were certainly more difficult to bring to the attention of the Moroccan people in the midst of the irredentist campaign, whose intimate relation to overpowering national values and pride could be communicated so much more easily.

Like most highly affective appeals in politics, the Mauritanian issue was a two-edged sword. Though the monarch could not afford to resist a national issue bearing so directly on his position, the commitment to an irreconcilable question gave him no alternative but to assume an increasingly rigid posture. The government could modify its position only by exposing to attack its own legitimacy, as has already been suggested in Istiqlal publications. Though Bourguiba moved much more slowly on the Bizerte question, he too was open to severe criticism when the Tunisian adventure failed to produce results. Indeed, one of the most objectionable characteristics of the highly charged participation engendered by such issues is that they preserve the atmosphere of the nationalist struggle in which political relationships were focused on survival rather than constructive compromise toward a negotiable solution.

With the breakdown of universal agreement, which such issues demand as part of the participant's national loyalty, there are no alternative courses of action, for government or the citizen. He is indeed left

---

[50] *Al-Istiqlal*, March 31, 1963. See also *New York Times*, April 14, 1963. Events late in 1963 suggested that the king was not so concerned over the nature of the Saharan campaign as what it might be used for. The hostilities at Hassi Beida, and the strategy aimed at cutting off Tindouf and its alleged mineral resources, was a clever adaptation of the old theme to some very practical goals. The battle also served to identify the king once again with irredentist sympathies, thereby undercutting Istiqlal criticism of the monarchy and further glorifying the king.

in a void, where other highly affective issues are the only alternative substitutes. It is by no means coincidental that the most serious incidents of anti-Semitism in both Morocco and Tunisia arose when popular feelings reached a peak over these foreign issues. In the Moroccan political system the undesirable effects are more easily identified. The monarchy has been alienated from existing political organizations, most notably the Istiqlal, in seeking a compromise, and has been forced to resort to increasingly arbitrary methods to deal with political opposition. Thus political relationships between the participant and his government have tended to become more treacherous at a time when individuals need to develop flexible working relationships. As in every developing country, the government has the dominant role not only in laying down the physical conditions and priorities for development, but in creating a perceptual framework for the new citizen to relate himself to the more intricate society emerging from this effort.

Pakistan presents one of the most dramatic examples of how aroused feelings over foreign issues may relate to the political reorientation of nations committed to rapid development. As in several other matters, the Ayub regime inherited the Kashmir problem, whose history embodies a series of doubtful acts on the part of both Pakistan and India.[51] The relevance of the issue to Ayub's internal efforts toward national reconstruction has long been established in the mutual interest of Pakistan and India in exploiting the Indus basin. One of the most far-reaching of Ayub's accomplishments for development was to conclude an agreement for better use of the Indus waters. The following discussion is not intended to conform to all the complexities of Pakistan's relations with India, nor is it intended as a judgment on the Pakistani case. However, starting from the accord so highly favorable to both countries' development, relations have steadily deteriorated since 1961. In this same period the military regime was no longer free to operate in the austere environment of martial law, and Ayub was forced to seek internal political support.

While the two trends may not be directly related, exacerbated relations with India took place at a time when the regime was taking important steps toward institutional reorganization and increased participation in the newly revived legislatures. Though there were certainly an ample number of highly sensitive questions crippling the new national and provincial assemblies, the introduction of the Kashmir issue served to distract popular attention from the new legislatures, and to confirm

[51] There have been several good books on the Kashmir issue, which will not be explored in detail here. See Michael Brecher, *The Struggle for Kashmir*, New York, Oxford University Press, 1953; Lord Birdwood, *Two Nations and Kashmir*, London, Robert Hale, 1956; Josef Korbel, *Danger in Kashmir*, Princeton, Princeton University Press, 1954; and M. M. R. Khan, *The United Nations and Kashmir*, Djakarta, J. B. Wolters, 1955.

Ayub's feelings that more substantial concessions to self-rule would be dangerous. He also needed popular support, and took the first moves toward a more neutralist position, which enabled him to exploit the Indian conflict with Communist China in order to raise outstanding problems with the former. Nehru and Ayub agreed to a new round of talks on the Kashmir question at the same time that Pakistan was exploring closer ties to Communist China.[52] Before the National assembly, Foreign Minister Mohammed Ali, who had led Pakistan into her close alliance with the West in 1953, announced, "There are no eternal friendships in international relations and there is no eternal enmity." The statement was designed in part as a reply to growing opposition criticism of Pakistan's excessive reliance on her Western pacts as the United States shipped arms to India.

Always an inflammatory issue in West Pakistan, the Indian position on Kashmir merged with East Pakistani feelings when communal riots broke out on both sides of the eastern wing over 1962 and 1963. The attempt of Secretary of State Rusk to arrange for mediation of the Kashmir problem during CENTO meetings in Karachi early in 1963 failed, although Pakistan did go through with a series of steadily deteriorating talks with Indian delegations. Popular pressure and national interest converged in agreeing to closer relations with Communist China, and accords were signed on air communications, trade, and frontiers. After talks with India had collapsed, Zulfikar Ali Bhutto, the new Foreign Minister of known neutralist sympathies, stated in the National Assembly that Pakistan "would not be alone" in the event of hostilities with India, and blamed the United States for not using arms shipments to India as a lever to achieve Kashmir self-determination.[53]

National feelings were further inflamed in August 1963 when thousands of Muslim refugees arrived after renewed communal rioting in India along East Pakistan borders. Ayub then publicly returned to the old Pakistani position that no resolution of the Kashmir problem could be considered that did not involve a referendum, and Nehru retaliated by withdrawing the "concessions" that India had presumably been prepared to make earlier. Soon afterward India took another step toward the

[52] The effort to patch up Indo-Pakistani relations appears to have been the inspiration of British Commonwealth Secretary Sandys and American Undersecretary Harriman, and essentially an offshoot of the crisis in India. That two such experienced diplomats would seek reconciliation of such a bitter quarrel under conditions that were already deteriorating in late 1961 indicates how alarmed the United States was. See the comment of Selig Harrison in the *Washington Post*, May 18, 1963. However, the crisis contributed naturally to improved relations with Iran and to resuming diplomatic ties with Afghanistan. Mohammed Ali's statements appear in the *New York Times*, November 23 and 25, 1962.

[53] *Dawn*, July 16, 1963. Pakistan reinforced her friendly gestures toward Communist China by establishing new ties with Albania. In Cairo, Gen. Chen Yi spoke out against India as a threat to Pakistan and other peaceful Asian nations, *ibid.*, July 24, 1963.

merger of Kashmir with India by giving the regional officials titles corresponding to those of the other Indian states. Relations with the United States deteriorated further when plans were made known to enlarge the Srinagar air base, in the heart of Kashmir and only a hundred miles from the Pakistani capital at Rawalpindi. Like Morocco, Pakistan found herself confronted with a *fait accompli*, but the international situation in Asia offered compensations to Pakistan that did not exist in Africa for Morocco.[54] The continued deterioration throughout 1964 and the resort to war in 1965 are the tragic results of unleashing emotional political forces.

It should be recognized that Pakistan did not choose to revive the Kashmir problem, but that it inescapably became part of Pakistan grievances once the Chinese infiltration of Indian borderlands of Ladakh, north of Kashmir, necessitated United States' assistance to India. The chances of moderating the issue internally through traditional East Pakistani reluctance to support a purely West Pakistani cause were lost after communal rioting in Assam and Tripura of West Bengal, as well as in Khaipur and other Indian cities. As the sense of national emergency spread, East Pakistan demanded more troops along her borders and charged that the military, largely composed of officers and men from West Pakistan, had neglected the defense of Bengal. Passions were also aroused when the Jamaat-i-Islami was outlawed, in part because of its lukewarm support for Kashmiri irredentism. The crisis also provided some justification for continuing close supervision of the press and political organizations in Pakistan. Even though Ayub had not stimulated the crisis, and, on the contrary, had worked to resolve some important Indo-Pakistani differences, the inflamed sensitivities created a crisis atmosphere.

The adjustments in Pakistan's foreign policy over the past two years are indicative of the regime's increasing need for affective ties with the people. As has been mentioned before, the military regime was not particularly skilled at appealing to popular feelings, though the officers were, on the whole, respected. Unlike the other political systems described in the study, the military-bureaucratic government was isolated from the people by its own structure. Ayub showed great restraint in not converting the regime into a massive one-party system along the lines of

---

[54] Though not primarily concerned with U. S. policy, this is an obvious case where the extreme position imposed on a developing country by our defense alliances contributed directly to political instability. The efforts of Undersecretary Ball, *New York Times*, September 5, 1963, and General Taylor, *ibid.*, October 6, 1963, could not restore confidence, and Pakistan became a potential backer of Chinese membership in the United Nations, and also her inclusion in any further disarmament talks. The risk of building foreign policy on so shaky a foundation as the Kashmir problem might be defended if the United States could be assured that it would only collapse when equally critical issues were dormant, e.g., Indo-Chinese relations. Diplomatic history suggests that the converse seems to be much more the pattern.

Nasser's republic, which would have enabled him to make the emotional appeal needed to rally popular support under highly affective conditions. So long as martial-law powers existed, popular support and participation were secondary. The revival of parliamentary politics exposed Ayub's vulnerability, and also indicated how little had indeed been accomplished during the "housecleaning" to enable Pakistanis to identify with government in more constructive ways.

The curious dilemma of Basic Democracies as a tool for fashioning new political participation is again revealed at a higher level of generalization in reviewing the Kashmir issue. The feelings of hostility and insecurity associated with such appeals on the national level are difficult to direct toward constructive ends, particularly when such goals are virtually unattainable as in many foreign problems. Unless such devices are guided by a leader having great personal appeal, like Bourguiba, and carefully controlled through a single-party system, other political forces can make similar or even excessive claims to national virtue using the same terms. The uncompromising character of every question involving national survival makes it the vehicle for mobilizing popular attention in essentially rigid form, inviting more authoritative action on the part of government. The price paid in lost opportunity to convert popular energies into a form applicable to development is twofold. Attitudinal reorientation to developmental problems is forestalled, and subsequently there may be as yet unmeasured problems in converting sensitive and impassioned views of national political life to the tasks of nation-building.

The affective aspect of attitudinal formation is widely documented in the literature of psychology, partly because the study of personality stems directly from the first great psychological theorists, whose discoveries focused on the individual's internally determined drives and needs. As applied to social relations the approach has probably reached its fullest development in the work of Adorno and others.[55] Despite the limitations of Freudian analysis in handling social relations, the inquiry into authoritarian personality has underscored the relation of personal insecurity to perceptual distortion and inflexibility. But the relation of the individual qualities associated with the authoritarian syndrome has been difficult to relate to social action, and later critiques have noted that those exhibiting extremes in personality may find either a highly totalitarian or an extremely radical social pattern harmonious with their feelings and beliefs.[56]

[55] T. W. Adorno et al., op.cit. Also, Frankel-Brunswick, "Intolerance of Ambiguity as an Emotional and Perceptual Personality Trait," in J. S. Bruner and D. Krech, eds., Perception and Personality: A Symposium, Durham, Duke University Press, 1949, pp. 108-144.

[56] Edward Shils, "Authoritarianisms: 'Right' and 'Left,'" in R. Christie and

Many of the limitations of authoritarian personality theory still apply in the attempts to relate personal insecurity and tensions to political life in developing countries. This is not to suggest that personality factors are irrelevant to development, but that as conceived in much early work they are difficult to relate to political and social change except in the relatively obvious way in which the individual may prefer no change rather than modify values to which he attaches excessive importance. The work of Hagen has made an important contribution along these lines, but, like the body of theory from which it stems, the authoritarian approach applied to developing countries leaves the analyst in an impasse, except, of course, for the possibility of reorienting the insecure but influential persons who appear to prevail in many developing countries. Though not a major concern of this inquiry, much of the evidence accumulated here indicates that the influential extremist may have only short-term value in a changing society. He can choose not to commit his country to the tasks of reconstruction, and thereby expose himself to external threats and perhaps materially weaken his country, or he can set in motion forces for change that tend to become a greater and greater challenge to his very restricted, if not distorted, view of the world.

There is a great danger that, in pointing out the limitations of theory stressing affective personality aspects, a reverse and equally serious error may be made. The notion that an intricate, modern society is somehow equivalent with healthy personality is obviously just as misleading as the notion that mental illness is the equivalent of social tension and inflexibility. There is, indeed, no easy or systematic theory for handling the interrelations of society and personality. The present analysis suggests only that much more can be done with more comprehensive psychological theory that enables the investigator to make more explicit allowance for perceptual and environmental factors. To conclude that personality traits independently determine social patterns leads to the same logical problems as concluding that social patterns, imagined here in the form of a more complex society, will produce healthy personalities.

There is a substantial body of findings from learning theory that indicate the kinds of perceptual problems to be encountered under threatening and highly uncertain environmental conditions. Although there has been a great deal of laboratory study of how emotional stress relates to perception,[57] very little has been done to relate these findings to

---

M. Jahoda, eds., *Studies in the Scope and Method of "The Authoritarian Personality,"* Glencoe, Free Press, 1954, pp. 24-49. For an examination of differing views on psychological theory inherent in the controversy see Jerome S. Bruner and Robert M. White, *Opinions and Personality,* New York, Wiley, 1956, pp. 1-47.

[57] For example, see, Robert E. Murphy, "Effects of Threat, Shock Distraction and Task Design on Performance," *Journal of Experimental Psychology,* vol. 58, August 1959, pp. 134-141; Albert Pepitone and Robert Kleiner, "The Effects of Threat and Frustration on Group Cohesiveness," *Journal of Abnormal and Social*

political attitudes and more general problems of participation. Froman has indicated a broad framework for relating affective and cognitive attitudinal components in political life,[58] and there is some evidence that symbolic associations tend to reduce the participant's sense of effectiveness and cognitive skill in dealing with political problems.[59] In addition, the voting studies have helped us understand the complexity of the voter's perception of his role in elections, suggesting too that those who bring emotionally laden views to the electoral process have the most difficulty in finding satisfying ways to participate.

There are two major studies that introduced cognitive-affective analysis in large samplings of participants. A Swedish study has found that participants having highly "expressive" perception of politics, in the author's terms, tend to be repetitive and unchanging in the perception of political life.[60] More recently, the Almond-Verba survey compared political perception in one developing country, Mexico, with several European countries and the United States. The study revealed a marked discontinuity between the Mexican's identification with national politics and pride in governmental institutions generally as opposed to his confidence in operating institutions at the local level and actual use of such institutions. The authors conclude that the Mexican appears to maintain a "revolutionary or aspirational orientation to politics,"[61] enabling him to express enthusiasm and pride in his country even though the indications are minimal that he understands the political process or receives meaningful benefits.

There is no doubt that very general values about the worth of the

---

Psychology, vol. 54, 1957, pp. 192-199; John T. Lanzetta, "Group Behavior under Stress," *Human Relations*, 1955, pp. 29-52; Robert Meresko et al., "Rigidity of Attitudes Regarding Personal Habits and its Ideological Correlatives," *Journal of Abnormal and Social Psychology*, vol. 49, January 1954, pp. 89-93; M. Rokeach, "Generalized Mental Rigidity as a Factor in Ethnocentrism," *Journal of Abnormal and Social Psychology*, vol. 43, 1948, pp. 259-278; Sidney Palley, "Cognitive Rigidity as a Function of Threat," *Journal of Personality*, vol. 23, 1955, pp. 346-355; and C. D. Smock, "The Relationship between Test Anxiety, Threat Expectancy and Recognition Threshold of Words," *Journal of Personality*, vol. 25, 1956, pp. 191-201.

[58] Lewis A. Froman, Jr., "Learning Political Attitudes," *Western Political Quarterly*, vol. 15, 1962, pp. 304-313.

[59] M. Edelman, "Symbols and Political Quiescence," *American Political Science Review*, vol. 54, no. 3, September 1960, pp. 695-704. See also his book, *Symbolic Uses of Politics*, Evanston, University of Illinois Press, 1964.

[60] Ulf Himmelstrand, *Social Pressures, Attitudes and Democratic Processes*, Stockholm, Almquist and Wiksell, 1960.

[61] Gabriel A. Almond and Sidney Verba, *The Civic Culture: Political Attitudes and Democracy in Five Nations*, Princeton, Princeton University Press, 1963, p. 252. The Mexican expressed more pride in governmental institutions than either the German or the Italian, *ibid.*, p. 102, and still believed national government could improve his situation, *ibid.*, p. 82, but on several questions showed that he had less personal familiarity and less direct recourse to government nationally and locally.

nation are an essential component of every participant's view of political life in the nation. Where large numbers of immigrants have arrived, their failure to share such general values has obstructed their assimilation into the society.[62] The notion of a hierarchy of values, some having very vague behavioral implications, and others suggesting forms of expression and participation which the individual may manipulate himself, is closely related to cognitive theory. The subsidiary values cannot be acquired and individually elaborated in the early phase of nation-building, when national identity may be very weak in some segments of the population, and remains highly emotional, though intense, among those taking an active part in liberating the country. Deciding that such affective devices are not in themselves sufficient to transform the developing nation is only a preliminary step in the attitudinal transformation of the new nation. It may well be a most difficult one, and there are discouragingly few countries of Africa and Asia where leaders have indeed been prepared to forego the self-justifying technique of appealing solely to the citizen's patriotic loyalty.

In dealing with the attitudinal transformations attendant on rapid development, there has been a tendency in many disciplines to concentrate on what is in fact only the first step, i.e., how a country actually makes the decision to engage in a major national reorientation. Analytically such inquiries are treacherous because they may become mere reifications or depend on deterministic assumptions. In the real world they are elusive because it is not clear when a country "enters" a phase of development apart from the actual observations of social and psychological phenomena used in any given inquiry. Development is a state of affairs to which a new country may be more or less committed, whose "requirements" vary greatly over time.

In each country the government will greatly influence the way in which the new citizen's perceptual world will be changed. The limiting conditions are not particularly helpful in anticipating how political life will change, because they reduce the analysis to survival conditions. Despite the poverty of many new countries, relatively few are without choice in shaping new forms of participation and understanding of politics. A new nation that finds itself without a widely accepted fundamental belief in the worth of the new nation can hardly be considered an independent country, though some exist by simply manipulating

---

[62] Though it does not involve the emergence of attitudes appropriate for developmental tasks, some of the most helpful studies on the role of national values in political integration have been done with Israeli immigrants. See S. N. Eisenstadt, "Studies in Reference Group Behavior: I Reference Norms and the Social Structure," *Human Relations*, vol. 7, no. 2, 1954, pp. 191-216; Ronald Taft, "The Shared Frame of Reference Concept Applied to Assimilation of Immigrants," *Human Relations*, vol. 6, no. 1, 1953, pp. 45-56; and S. N. Eisenstadt, "Reference Group Behavior and Social Integration: An Explorative Study," *American Sociological Review*, vol. 19, no. 2, April 1954, pp. 175-184.

traditional values of tribal or religious groups to the government's convenience, unknown to the citizenry at large. This is obviously a transient and fragile form of national existence. In the three countries of this study, and in most other developing countries, there is a widely shared belief in the virtue of independent government and a shared national identity, however rudimentary and emotional it may be.

Not only may countries achieve comparable levels of development in material terms while very different attitudinal structures appear, but it should also be recognized that in any one country certain attitudinal components may prevail in political life and be excluded from other areas of activity. There are, again, probably limitations as to how great the discontinuities in various areas of development may become, but the limits of variation should not become the framework of analysis. The obvious example is the need to exercise more individual judgment and self-control as the economy becomes more complex, illustrated in reforms in the Soviet Union. Another form is the different degrees of competence in political and administrative activities noted in the Almond-Verba study, in which they suggest that familiarity with administration may precede the acquisition of confidence and skill in manipulating more complex political problems.[63]

The cognitive components of attitudinal change will be treated in the next chapter, but it is important to analyze more carefully the affective appeal of the three governments briefly. The Tunisian single-party regime has a virtual monopoly of affective appeal on the national level, and there is hardly any aspect of development that does not make a claim on patriotism or speculations about national disaster. The Moroccan monarchy also has strong affective appeal, but it has experienced difficulty in translating this appeal into political forms without becoming vulnerable to the claim that others have on national virtue. The Pakistani military regime has found it almost impossible to construct an appeal that compares with the intense but confused and amorphous emotional version of political life advanced by religious and political leaders. The full meaning of these three situations can only be explored by going on to the differing cognitive content on political life in the three countries, and how this appears to be affected by the different kinds of political systems.

An analysis of attitudinal change in developing countries must allow for the fact that national values are not the only ones entering into the new citizen's reorientation. There are similarly charged opinions emanating from religion, communal and linguistic differences, international crises, and contrived plots against the state.[64] However,

[63] *Op.cit.*, p. 221.
[64] A very similar argument in anthropological terms is advanced by Clifford Geertz in "The Integrative Revolution," in Geertz, ed., *Old Societies and New*

very few highly charged subjects can arise that the government is not able to affect in some way, and the more farseeing governments will very likely take steps to remove social differences and to placate inflamed feelings that may be exploited in such ways. This suggests that the turbulence that the world has so recently witnessed in the formation of a multitude of new nations has only begun unless the new governments can exercise great self-restraint. The new governments of Asia and Africa tend to become the sole guardians of the national values in a way that never occurred in the history of Europe and North America. The commitment to development only makes more pressing the central government's need to control affective aspects of the participants' perceptual world.

In early 1961 Bourguiba himself identified this trend and the pitfalls therein when commenting on extremist trends in Africa coming from the Casablanca group, and the frequent use of "plots" to mobilize a people. "This psychosis accepted, the people remain in a permanent state of mobilization. They believe in combatting the enemies. One gives them no respite. They cannot become fully aware of their misery, of their rags, of the hunger which gnaws at them. . . . But beside the mystique of struggle without end and against imaginary enemies, there is the mystique of unceasing new victories to the point that one asks himself why continue the battle after so many victories. . . . In spite of all these victories, the nerves of the people remain taut, however one distracts himself from the internal problems."[65]

States, New York, Free Press, 1964, p. 111, where he notes how social relationships in the new states tend not to be viewed as "self-standing, maximal social units, as candidates for nationhood," but become, instead, the focus for "terminal" conflict because such patterns do not have "alternative definitions of what the nation is, of what its scope of reference is."

[65] Habib Bourguiba, speech of January 12, 1961, published in *La Semaine en Algérie*, no. 113, February 1-8, 1961, p. 16.

CHAPTER II

THE COGNITIVE COMPONENT: INSTITUTIONAL ELABORATION

As HIGHLY formalized patterns of behavior to achieve widely supported goals, the simple existence of new national, regional, and local institutions in a developing country indicates progress toward greater individual involvement in political and social life. Section III focused on how rapidly new governments proliferate institutional relationships, no doubt much faster than most new citizens can comprehend. The developing country is characterized, in a sense, by the proliferation of new agencies and offices to perform tasks that are themselves poorly understood by the populace. A good deal of effort has gone into demonstrations of the inadequacy and distortion involved in the ordinary citizen's perception of these institutions, so much so that it is easy to overlook the fact that most institutions in advanced countries are perceived with considerable inaccuracy.

The attitudinal approach takes attention away from what is indeed perceived in the diversity of institutional involvement and places emphasis on how the individual perceives his institutional environment. The proliferation of new roles, the formulation of subordinate goals, the sheer complexity of human behavior present the new citizen with a world that is changing along many dimensions in every activity. Indeed, the process is so complex in institutional terms that it seems doubtful that sociological concepts can manage such a multidimensional problem. By focusing on the individual and his perception of the new environment the investigator avoids the self-defeating assumption of dealing with only one "typical" institution or of dwelling on a single institutional dysfunctional relationship, however revealing it may be. The fact of the matter is that the new citizen's world no longer has "typical" institutions and that he is confronted with numerous dysfunctional situations, which he is left to sort out with his own devices.

Attitudinal analysis makes a virtue of institutional complexity by suggesting that diversity itself may characterize the individual's view of the world. The development of more complex attitudes provides the citizen with concepts and principles adequate to the flexibility and uncertainty of a modern society. Relatively little is known of the way in which individuals acquire the capacity to view the world "more relativistically and less stereotypically," but this process is directly analogous to the institutional change taking place. The attitudinal component most relevant is cognition, not in the simple sense of increasing individual capacities to receive and utilize information, but in the sense of making substantial change in attitudinal structure based on new ways of ordering and organizing perceptions. The new citizen is being asked to acquire new concepts to "serve the critical cognitive function of providing a system of ordering by means of which the environment is broken down and organized, is differentiated and integrated into its many relevant psychological facets."[1]

In creating a perceptual world where the participant's feelings and understanding focus on new political and social problems, the governments of the developing countries are contributing to a vast experiment in attitudinal change. Indeed, as has been argued before, they have the major voice in this process. Cognition involves the acceptance of information, its manipulation and evaluation, and its application in problem-solving situations. Our civilization has placed such a high value on education and understanding that the specific advantages of acquiring cognitive skills and capacities are generally taken for granted. However, there is carefully accumulated evidence to show that such skills enable the individual to deal with the complexity of his environment, reduce his need to relearn for each new situation, direct his instrumental activity in a way enabling him to judge his own performance, and permit him to engage in future-oriented activity.[2]

Again, it should be noted that the line of inquiry is not intended to suggest that attitudes can be neatly categorized as solely affective or cognitive. On the contrary, the dynamic relations of these components in attitudinal analysis rather than their fixed proportions or requisite character is what makes the approach appropriate to developmental problems. Most new participants entering into governmental and other activities outside the village operate with an emotional identification with political life. The image of government, however distorted and inaccurate, is almost certain to be highly affective. There are many forces to persuade leadership in a developing country to perpetuate, if possible, the highly charged national image. But the emotional image may inhibit the participant's attitudinal organization to deal with other areas of activity where diverse, sustained reactions are needed. The villagers and peasants, not to mention urban workers and civil servants, are not only being asked to make greater sacrifices for their country, but to take a more active role in bringing about the social revolution. To be devoted and loyal is not enough. Institutions that simply magnify predetermined national virtue do not make significant choices, assign controversial priorities, and resolve social differences. If the country hopes to have articulate, self-supporting participation, the new institutions must en-

---

[1] O. J. Harvey, David E. Hunt, and Harold M. Schroder, *Conceptual Systems and Personality Organization*, New York, Wiley, 1961, p. 3.

[2] Jerome S. Bruner, Jacqueline J. Goodnow, and George A. Austin, *A Study of Thinking*, New York, Wiley, 1956, pp. 12-14.

courage the individual adaptation and attitudinal reorganization that is part of the developmental process.

The institutional concessions that are made in the enthusiastic atmosphere of the immediate postindependence period may later complicate political life. On the whole, however, the Western powers have been very fortunate that the newly independent nations have been eager to erect new institutions to regulate political life. The complications and disappointments inherent in the new legislatures and constitutional controversies of the developing nations represent a step toward modernization just as much, and perhaps more than, more specific institutions for banking and communications. Institutionalizing the comparatively simple patterns of behavior appropriate to a production line or importing firm is relatively easy compared to the institutions needed in a modern society to define goals more precisely and to make choices among conflicting goals.

If the developing countries were regularly thrown into the chaos of the Congo, for example, political decisions would be much simpler. The sole and inescapable desire would be to bring the parts of the country back together. The problem becomes infinitely more difficult in the Congo, because highly affective differences tend to become the sole means of differentiating alternatives. For this reason rudimentary institutions are probably more vulnerable to severely conflicting national values and to irreconcilable views than established institutions. But the tendency to discuss the emerging institutions in terms of a political system oriented solely to survival has tended to reduce the study of new institutions to self-evident terms, and little attention has been given to alternative strategies for assessing the developing country's readiness for elaborate political and social institutions.

CONSTITUTIONS AND POLITICAL UNDERSTANDING

Although the study of constitutions has become less fashionable in comparative politics, the fact remains that formulating a constitution is one of the first major tasks of most new countries. Obviously, they do not have the same significance in internal political affairs, nor do they represent similar commitment to Western institutional forms. The analyst would also be greatly in error to make predictions about a government in Africa or Asia—or Europe—based solely on a reading of its constitution. However, the drafting process focuses on the basic values the new country aspires to inject into political life, and is in fact one of the first "tasks" of an emergent political system. By simply observing the priorities given to constitutional drafting, one can note some revealing contrasts in the operation of new governments.

The previous chapter indicated that the single-party system was quite possibly the most sensitive of the three political systems to values and goals outside the party framework. The Socialist Destour has certainly worked to eliminate Islamic influence on government, and, except for the Bizerte crisis, used foreign issues with restraint. However, the affective orientation to political and social affairs differs in Tunisia in that feelings have been manipulated with a purpose in mind beyond the immediate goal of eliciting mass approval. Despite the fact that the party penetrates into nearly every aspect of Tunisian life, the party has maintained a remarkable level of exchange and controversy at lower levels.[3] Morocco, by contrast, enjoys more formal liberty of expression, as even a cursory glance at the press will confirm, but this expression is not effectively oriented to real problems in Moroccan development and politics. Indeed, Moroccan behavior does not appear to reflect a more involved populace, but one still related to the political system by relatively strong emotional ties having little articulation and meaning in the operation of government.

Tunisia represents an interesting reversal of this relationship. The government is highly alert to emotional appeal, but is also sensitive to individual and group interests generating and structuring such expressions. Historical experience should not be overlooked, and Bourguiba himself often refers to the constitutions of 1857 and 1861 to underscore his country's unity.[4] The Grand Council established by the second of these documents was hardly a working body, consisting of twenty officers and civil servants and forty members of outstanding families, all selected by the bey. The innovations came so late in the decline of beylical rule that little could be done to restore political unity or strength. French penetration of Tunisian life had already reached such proportions that officials could do little to invigorate the country's institutions.

Unlike Morocco, formulating a constitution was one of the highest orders of business for the Socialist Destour regime. The Sfax congress in December 1955 pledged the party to a constitutional monarchy, although the convention voted against the idea of a crown council to draft the new constitution. Plans were made for a National Constituent Assembly from early 1956. It is now clear that Bourguiba intended to use the new institution to remove the bey and make himself virtually undisputed head of state. The president's determination to proceed with his plan when under fire from both Ben Youssef and Ben Salah suggests how early the decision was made to install an effective single-party system. Although there was still severe fighting in parts of the south against Ben Youssef's guerilla bands, and signs of a serious break with the

---

[3] Clement H. Moore, "Politics in a Tunisian Village," *Middle East Journal*, vol. 17, no. 5, Late Autumn 1963, pp. 527-540.

[4] Habib Bourguiba, "Une Constitution par le Peuple et pour le Peuple," Speech of June 1, 1959, Tunis, Secretary of State for Information, 1959.

unions under Ben Salah, Bourguiba went ahead with his plans for the Constituent Assembly.

In January 1956 an electoral law was decreed, establishing a majority-list ballot system. The country was divided into eighteen districts, each assigned from four to nine seats.[5] As in the case of the municipal councils, leading Destourian Socialists figured in the lists from most districts. Although the U.G.T.T. was severely criticizing Bourguiba's failure to deal with economic problems, it decided to participate in a National Front with the other party auxiliary organizations. The Front served to remove organizational and doctrinal differences among the various groups associated with the Socialist Destour, although there were still serious disputes going on between several, particularly the merchants and workers. Bourguiba probably took the greatest risk of his career in opening the way for organized expression of the differences existing in 1956. His close colleague, Mehiri, virtually admitted that opposing parties would be formed within the new assembly.[6]

In March 1956 three quarters of a million electors, not yet including women, were eligible to vote, and over 610,000 supported the National Front. The Front was opposed only by two Communist lists and one independent list, neither of which received seats. However, several leading party members still expected divergent views to emerge in the assembly, and Ben Salah assured reporters that "the notion of a right and a left are going to appear in Tunisia and will be consecrated in the organization of the assembly."[7] But the Constituent Assembly was only a weapon in the new president's battle to consolidate power in the single-party regime. The opposing views were never expressed as he waged a campaign against the bey and Ben Youssef. He realized that the left-wing elements would not oppose enlarging the assembly's powers.

Within a few months of the Assembly's formation Bourguiba began the dismantling of the privileges of the bey, culminating in charges that the bey had conspired against independence with the French and benefited materially by favoring French influence. Of course, exactly the same charge could be made against almost any leading family of Tunisia, most of whom had been closely involved with French commercial and industrial enterprises in Tunisia.[8] The Constituent Assembly

---

[5] Details of the law and electoral plans appear in *Petit-Matin*, March 3, 1956. Although Ben Salah later decided to become a candidate, it is interesting that his differences at one time indicated that he would not participate, *ibid.*, May 13, 1956. Figures of registered, participating, National Front, and Communist voters appear in *ibid.*

[6] Charles Debbasch, *La République Tunisienne*, Paris, Librairie Générale de Droit et de Jurisprudence, 1962, p. 43.

[7] *Le Monde*, March 28, 1956.

[8] This is precisely what happened in September 1958 when Bourguiba insisted that Ben Ammar, a leading figure under French rule, should be indicted for

was convened long enough to agree on the preamble of the constitution in July 1957, which made Tunisia a republic and gave Bourguiba the pretext for exiling the bey.

For the next two years the Constituent Assembly remained dormant, although its commissions were presumably drafting the various sections of the new constitution under Bourguiba's watchful eye. The assembly met several times for expressions of unity in the struggle for Algerian independence and after the Sakiet-Sidi Youssef bombing by France. In explaining the new constitution over the summer of 1959 the president admitted that the executive had been given a "certain autonomy," but assured the Tunisian people that this would lead to more effective government. He compared a system having balanced legislative and executive powers to the monarchial regime from which Tunisia had just freed herself, and called for the people to express their "maturity" on election day.[9] There was only token opposition in the 1959 national elections, although the National Front majority in Tunis continued to be noticeably lower than that in the rest of the country.[10]

The formal provisions of the constitution are not so important as what has been done with the rights established by it and the powers given the new legislature.[11] In practice, the National Assembly has remained a symbol of national unity. Limited to 90-day sessions twice a year, the unicameral body sometimes meets only to hear the president speak. The president may issue decree-laws in its absence—a system which has become the main source of Tunisian legislation. Although the assembly can pass a law by a two third's majority over the president's veto, this has never happened. However, there have been occasions when mem-

---

treason under the purge law. See *Journal Officiel*, August 27, 1957, "Loi 57-13 du 17 aout 1957 (20 moharrem 1377), portant confiscation des biens mal acquis," pp. 83-86. The purge was never so great an issue in Tunisia as in Morocco, and in most instances Bourguiba was willing to overlook the abuses which did in fact implicate nearly every leading family in Tunisia. The Ben Ammar crisis led to the suppression of *Afrique Action* for criticizing the president and to Masmoudi's resignation from the cabinet.

[9] Habib Bourguiba, "8 Novembre 1959: Elections Générales," Speech of July 30, 1959, Tunis, Secretary of State for Information, 1959.

[10] For figures on electoral participation in 1959 see *Petit-Matin*, October 27 and November 11, 1959.

[11] In addition to the commentary and text given in Debbasch, *op.cit.*, pp. 41-82 and 206-218, there are several articles on the Tunisian constitution. See Victor Silvera, "Le régime constitutionnel de la Tunisie: La Constitution de 1èr Juin 1959," *Revue Français de Science Politique*, vol. 10, no. 2, 1960, pp. 336-394; Charles Debbasch, "La constitution de la République tunisienne du 1èr juin 1959," *Revue Juridique et Politique d'Outre-Mer*, vol. 13, 1959, pp. 573-590; Charles Debbasch, "La constitution du 1èr juin 1959 de la République tunisienne à l'épreuve des faits (novembre 1959-décembre 1960), *Revue Juridique et Politique d'Outre-Mer*, vol. 15, no. 1, 1961, pp. 145-155; William Lee, "The Government of Tunisia since Independence," *Parliamentary Affairs*, vol. 13, no. 3, Summer 1960, pp. 374-385; and Keith Callard, "The Republic of Bourguiba," *International Journal*, Canada, vol. 16, no. 1, Winter 1960-1961, pp. 17-36.

bers of the National Assembly have voted against a bill of the president, and such subjects as social security and birth control have produced lively debates.[12] The budget sessions are frequently used to voice minor grievances, and there are usually some complaints from conservative quarters about motion pictures and alcohol. One can hardly disagree with Professor Debbasch's conclusion that unity within the Tunisian constitutional system is one of "the most remarkable phenomena of unity in constitutional life."[13]

Bourguibism had depended heavily on exercising influence in elusive form in order to preserve party hegemony. However, the Bizerte incident and the new controversies aroused by vigorous planning produced a widely noted and fascinating quarrel over *pouvoir personnel* in Tunisia. Under a photograph of King Faruk, the weekly *Afrique Action* questioned the arbitrary aspects of the regime and its ability to transfer power peacefully. It protested the "fragility and precariousness" of power concentrated in the hands of a single man, noting that Bourguiba once told the assembly he could establish a dynasty if he wished, but that he preferred a republic, which, the journal added, now gave the powers of the old bey and the French resident general to one man.[14] The charges led to one of the first public discussions of the advantages and disadvantages of the single-party regime.

The reply came from the editorial columns of *Al-Amal*, a party paper, and in a speech Bourguiba made to the Political Bureau.[15] Bourguiba revealed some fundamental differences between politicians of developed and less developed countries when he claimed that "clear situations are indispensable for internal state policy." Collective endeavor in the state was the product of technical and engineering decision as to the best course, and when "fog clouds the horizon, work can only suffer." It is doubtful if Bourguiba himself finds the world so clear-cut or subscribes to so rational a notion of statecraft, and his comment on the controversy itself played heavily on the implied dis-

---

[12] See the full accounts of the debates given each year in the press, and also Debbasch, *op.cit.*, pp. 72-73. Sometimes the debates appear contrived if one knows the parties. For example, in 1961 Mehiri was carefully questioned by his own ministry's legal adviser on why the government had delayed expanding the powers of the municipal councils, *La Presse*, December 21, 1961.

[13] Debbasch, *op.cit.*, p. 81.

[14] See *Afrique Action*, October 7-13, November 7-13, and 21-27, 1961.

[15] The president's speech appears in *Petit-Matin*, November 21, 1961, and notice of Masmoudi's exclusion appeared in *ibid.*, November 18, 1961. The articles in reply in *Al-Amal* were also printed in *Petit-Matin*, November 1, 2, 3, and 4, 1961. The incident is another fascinating demonstration of Bourguiba's skill in keeping potential opponents from forming a coalition. Ben Salah had, of course, already been largely reconciled to the Socialist Destour, but it was at this time that Bourguiba chose to restore him to full party prestige by incorporating him in the Political Bureau. For a full account see the author's "Tunisian Leadership and the 'Confiscated Revolution,'" *World Politics*, vol. 17, no. 2, January 1965, pp. 215-231.

loyalty of the party regulars and danger of controversy during a "crisis" with France. The president went on to say that the regime would welcome criticism when it did not produce "tendencious interpretations that introduce doubt into [public] spirits." There are few moments in Tunisian life that so neatly summarize how the single-party regime views the power structure of a state.

Most important for evaluating the attitudinal problem is the tendency to give the regime a monopoly of *both* national virtue, which it has in every country, and policy formulation, whose relation to national values may often be doubtful in dealing with many subjects. One cannot enter into the latter realm without bringing upon himself complete responsibility for national dignity and security. The highly affective interpretation of national political life is perpetuated by the regime, and critics can enter into decision-making only by accepting these laudable but arbitrary and unreal conditions in political life. Bourguiba has seized the essence of modernization in noting that decisions now become more rational, but he has refused to accept the consequences, which are that estimates, assessments, and alternatives in politics become in fact more subject to human preference and individual evaluation.

A major change takes place in the developmental process when leadership begins to advance arguments of rationality and specific goals to justify governmental decisions. The participant is no longer governed by his fragile but intense loyalty to the new nation. The political system begins to make political participation meaningful not only by talking about known problems, but by admitting that known problems are relevant to abstract notions of national virtue. The void between feelings and understanding is gradually overcome as new activities for developmental purposes, e.g., the controversial replacement of exhausted olive trees, are no longer disagreeable tasks dictated by expert advice, but choices that are relevant to a wide panorama of change throughout the nation. Developmental demands and participation in the political and social life of the nation have, then, begun to merge in Tunisian life. This change represents a revolutionary change in attitudes toward the outside world among the peasants and workers which cannot be described by the substance and content of isolated viewpoints. There is evidence that Tunisians are indeed beginning to think differently, to apply widely applicable principles in assessing their needs, and to generalize about the bewildering, and once fearful, diversity introduced by the modernizing forces.

The country's developmental efforts in planning, agriculture, education, and other fields have been well organized and, on the whole, appear to be effectively laying the groundwork for major changes in Tunisian life. More than Morocco or Pakistan, Tunisia has reached a point in the developmental process where earlier slogans and promises about participation are being translated into new organizations and opportunities. The country is now committed to development projects and social reorganization that contribute greatly to eliciting individual skills, capacities, and knowledge. As earlier chapters have outlined, the government depends more and more on the individual citizen's readiness to accept new methods and new information to keep the developmental process in motion. Although there have been certain misgivings in the Socialist Destour, the emergence of a more complex social and economic structure has already entailed major reforms within the party in order to give the local committees a voice in regional party affairs. These early adjustments indicate that the cognitive articulation of attitudes in the less overtly political areas of human behavior are beginning to influence attitudes in politics.[16]

The Moroccan monarchy has been committed to a constitutional system since Mohammed V announced his intentions in 1955. However, the political system has experienced much more difficulty in establishing constitutional institutions than Tunisia. The difference can, of course, be explained solely in terms of leadership and highly organized political forces. However, there were, and remain, peculiar problems of political participation in Morocco. Whereas Bourguiba had an organized instrument in the Socialist Destour to construct and channel participation, the monarchy was more exposed and, for all its traditional influence, more helpless in situations requiring additional participation. The paradox applies equally to many developmental problems, but is most acute in the elaboration of political institutions.

In the monarchial regime the attitudinal aspects of institutional elaboration are elusive, but essential to understanding the frequently observed immobility of more traditional regimes. The theory of attitudinal change does not state that new cognitive elements must be introduced, nor does it deny the possibility of relatively stable attitudes with different mixtures of affective and cognitive elements. In the developmental context the question is, To what extent can the individual whose national orientation remains largely affective begin to acquire cognitive capacities needed to involve himself more effectively in the developmental process, and even to acquire the margin of manipulative and managerial skill

---

[16] This represents the major shortcoming of the cognitive measures used in Gabriel A. Almond and Sidney Verba, *The Civic Culture*, Princeton, Princeton University Press, 1964. Cognitive skills are not represented solely by possessing information no matter what the subject, but by the individual's capacity to manipulate and generalize, using information. Moreover, cognitive skill may be applied to politics, using powers generated in other kinds of activity, e.g., development projects. Though less easily conceived, affection may also be transferred as one "learns" that gratification may be derived from more remote objects. Hence the affective-cognitive relationship may be developed and reoriented outside the formal political system, which becomes, as represented in this study, only a sounding board for emergent attitudes.

needed for sustained development? Of course, as the Tunisian case illustrates, considerable development can take place within the context of fairly rigid political institutions, though it is notable that even in Tunisia steps have been taken as development proceeds to make participation a more meaningful experience. The limitations of the Moroccan orientation would be less convincing were it not that Morocco has been handicapped in a number of more specific developmental situations, already described, in bringing the citizen into an effective, growing relationship to government.

The rather tortuous experience in establishing institutions in Morocco suggests how difficult the transformation has been. Like Tunisia and Pakistan, there was never any doubt as to the ultimate purpose of the regime. Mohammed V noted early in 1956 that the constitutional regime could be accomplished only "when conditions permit a free consultation of public desires." However, the progressive faction in the Istiqlal was eager to have at least partial recognition of their desires. In the fall of 1956 a National Consultative Assembly[17] was convened. The experimental legislature was entirely the creation of the monarchy. Parties, unions, and other groups were asked to submit a list of candidates to the king, and he then selected the members personally; but there is no indication that he deferred to the suggestions of the various groups.

The National Consultative Assembly, though always confined to an advisory role, was very appropriate to the conversion of popular opinion needed in order to introduce more formal political institutions in Morocco. The body had two sessions a year, one devoted to the budget and another to foreign policy. Mohammed V was scrupulous in the respect and attention given the National Consultative Assembly. The experiment broke down with the break in nationalist unity early in 1959. The monarch could not appropriate to himself the authority to determine party popularity and still maintain the semblance of a popularly determined assembly. The best course would probably have been to arrange for the election of a Constituent Assembly after the new left-wing party, the U.N.F.P., of Istiqlal progressives and trade unionists had had a few months to organize. For reasons that have never been entirely clear, the king decided that local elections, which had already been delayed several times by the Ministry of the Interior, should be held before a national ballot of any kind. The National Consultative Assembly was dissolved in 1959.[18]

[17] For a summary of the organization and sessions of the National Consultative Assembly see the author's *Political Change in Morocco*, Princeton, Princeton University Press, 1961, pp. 344-355.

[18] The experimental assembly had been established for two years, and the question of renewal inescapably raised a variety of questions about its composition. The meetings in the fall of 1958 were very stormy. Ben Barka and Ben Seddik were almost defeated for reelection to the offices of president and

Where the reorientation of the political system to wider participation and development activity is ambiguous, there is corresponding difficulty in deciding how the regime might willingly compromise its position. The Moroccan case had multiple difficulties because the progressive government under Abdallah Ibrahim, which accomplished a great deal in paving the way for more rapid economic development, was associated with the U.N.F.P. Moreover, Ibrahim was summarily dismissed on the eve of the rural-commune elections, although he had done more than any previous government to make the local elections possible. The fact that this was reportedly done on Prince Hassan's advice to his father made the new urban, worker party even less receptive to subsequent suggestions for for constitutional reform. Unwilling to subject the regime to popular vote in the form of electing a Constituent Assembly, the monarch sought to form a Constitutional Commission representing all political viewpoints. The commission was formed in the summer of 1960 under the chairmanship of Al-Fassi. Its efforts were doomed, because the U.N.F.P. refused to participate and the representatives of the minor parties soon walked out.[19]

King Hassan II took pains to assure the people that he intended to fulfill his father's promise to make Morocco a constitutional monarchy. Although the transfer of power might have excused some delay, he also promised that the draft would be submitted to the Moroccan people by the end of 1962. The Charter of Fundamental Rights[20] issued in June 1961 was a stopgap measure to reassure the Istiqlal. The new monarch proclaimed that the kingdom was "nearing the point for the institution of a regime of constitutional monarchy [permitting] representative institutions to select the proper means for the realization of important national objectives." Both the Istiqlal and the U.N.F.P. had been pressing for a constitution, the latter insisting that it must be the product of a freely elected Constituent Assembly. The Istiqlal was willing to com-

---

vice-president because the predominantly conservative Istiqlal membership knew they were scheming to bring more pressure on the party to back reforms. See *Le Monde*, October 21 and November 9-10, 1958.

[19] The U.N.F.P. never participated. Dr. Khatib, the Mouvement Populaire leader, and Mohammed Wazzani, of the Constitutional Democrat Party (the remnants of a schism in the nationalist movement in 1934), left early in 1961. The Constitutional Commission was not appointed until the fall, although announced in the summer. For the membership see *Bulletin Officiel*, no. 2507, November 11, 1960, "Dahir no. 1-60-318 du 13 joumada I 1380 (3 novembre 1960) portant nomination de membres du Conseil constitutionnel et du secrétaire générale permanent de ce conseil," p. 1930.

[20] *Bulletin Officiel*, no. 2537, June 9, 1961, "Dahir no. 1-61-167 du 17 hija 1380 (2 juin 1961) portant Loi fondamentale pour le Royaume du Maroc," pp. 801-802. Hassan II repeated his promise to present the Moroccan people with a constitution by the end of 1962 in his speech on the anniversary of the independence declaration. See *L'Echo*, January 12, 1962.

promise this point, and as it turned out no one knew who wrote the Moroccan constitution.[21]

The constitution that was announced in November 1962 was a great disappointment to all the parties except the royalist group, and did very little to present a new image of the monarch to the Moroccan people. Not only was the National Assembly virtually without power, but the new institutions were hedged in with a number of Superior Councils and other agencies that made the institutional structure needlessly complex. The powers of the king were so embracing that it is difficult to foresee a role for the Moroccan legislature that will be any more constructive or meaningful than that seen in the even weaker Tunisian legislature. Indeed, were it not dominated by the Socialist Destour, the latter might become an important political body and could easily play an important legislative role. In Morocco the king presides over the Council of Ministers (art. 25), appoints the ministers, and may dismiss them individually or collectively (art. 24). His position is fortified against solid opposition from the assembly by the provision that Morocco cannot have a single-party regime (art. 3). The monarch may submit any question he wishes to a referendum (art. 72). Where the referendum is held because of conflict with the Chamber of Representatives, the body is automatically dissolved if the monarch is upheld. He can also dissolve the body on his own desire after consulting a constitutional advisory group, appointed by him, but this power cannot be exercised more than once a year (art. 77).[22]

There is extemely little opportunity for the Chamber of Representatives, or the indirectly elected Chamber of Councilors, to engage in national affairs without royal approval. The king's annual message to the legislature may not be debated (art. 28). The vast domain of regulatory powers (*le pouvoir réglementaire*) is reserved to the king (art. 29). The government may act by decree-laws when the legislature is not in

[21] The reports were that King Hassan, himself a lawyer trained in Paris, took an active part. The government had also called on Duverger and on Labaudère, the constitutional law expert, for advice.

[22] For a thorough discussion of the constitution see Jacques Robert, *La Monarchie Marocaine*, Paris, Librairie Générale de Droit et de Jurisprudence, 1963, pp. 270-307, and the constitution, *ibid.*, pp. 328-345. See also Nevill Barbour, "Le problème constitutionnel au Maroc," *Politique Etrangère*, vol. 26, no. 2, 1961, pp. 110-123; Jacques Robert, "Le problème constitutionnel au Maroc," *Revue du Droit Public et de la Science Politique*, vol. 77, no. 5, 1961, pp. 959-1003; and W. A. Beling, "Some Implications of the New Constitution in Morocco," *Middle East Journal*, vol. 18, no. 2, Spring 1964, pp. 163-179. An interesting complication in the religious position of the monarch is the provision for hereditary male rule through the Alaouite dynasty (art. 20). Islamic practice is to have the *ulama* select the new king, who is, according to the constitution, "leader of the faithful" (art. 19) and whose person is "inviolable and sacred" (art. 23). While Morocco remains in an early stage of political integration, there is little chance that the implicit contradiction will take on much significance in the popular mind.

session (art. 58), and its business takes precedence in the agenda (art. 59). The legislature meets twice a year at specified times, but after thirty days in either session may be prorogued by the Council of Ministers (art. 52). Both the electoral law and the procedures for financial legislation are to be defined in later organic laws. A censure motion can bring down a government, but such a motion can be entertained only once a year (art. 81). The new Moroccan constitution is very reminiscent of the Fifth Republic of France, and King Hassan's sympathy for De Gaullist methods has been widely noted.

Though the more traditional character of Morocco may account for some of the conservative features of the Moroccan constitution, it is also clear that little ingenuity or care has been exercised to use the constitution as a means of enlarging popular understanding of government, nor is it likely that the image of the king as ruler and *imam* will be impaired with the numerous checks and alternatives open to the monarch. As might be expected, the reaction of the U.N.F.P. was adamant rejection without a constituent assembly. The party regarded the document a "prefabricated constitution elaborated in secret in the collaboration of foreign technicians."[23] Though the Istiqlal was disappointed, it had supported Hassan II throughout 1962 and participated in the preparations for the constitution. Despite reported defections in party ranks,[24] the Istiqlal joined in the constitutional referendum with enthusiasm.

The referendum showed that 80 per cent of the eligible voters favored the constitution, although the U.N.F.P. advised its members to abstain. In the cities there was a noticeable drop in voting, but not so large as might have been anticipated.[25] Only a month after their campaign on behalf of King Hassan, the Istiqlal found themselves in an untenable position in a cabinet reshuffle, and decided to resign from the government. After the stormy elections to the Chamber of Representatives in May 1963, the Istiqlal found that the young king was prepared to use every device at his disposal to cripple the opposition parties. Al-Fassi warned that the "king is chief of the community in the Muslim sense," in itself an unusual qualification to come from the *zaim* of the Istiqlal, and added that Guedira was no more than "a representative of France inside the government."[26]

Although the needs of this inquiry do not necessitate a lengthy analysis of the constitutional process in Morocco, the ensuing elections pro-

[23] *Le Monde*, November 17, 1962, quoting Ben Barka. On a later occasion Bouabid made the interesting observation that the constitution never mentions the "people" but only the "nation." *Ibid.*, November 27, 1962.
[24] See *Jeune Afrique*, December 10-16, 1962, and reports from *At-Tahrir* appearing in *Le Monde*, November 28, 1962.
[25] Robert, *op.cit.*, p. 307.
[26] *Jeune Afrique*, April 29-May 5, 1963.

vide interesting evidence of the maturity and independence of the Moroccan voter, and, therefore, relate directly to the difficult task of judging how much the new institutions may contribute to the reorientation of the Moroccan people in both political life and in their developmental effort. The election results were a surprise to all, including the Front for the Defense of Constitutional Institutions (F.D.I.C.), which lacked a majority of the 144 seats until by-election victories late in 1963.[27] The Istiqlal once again demonstrated its historic strength in the Jebala region in the northwest, pre-Riffian area of the country. The U.N.F.P. also reasserted its control of the cities, gaining about ten more seats than were generally expected. The F.D.I.C. strength came from the least advanced regions, to some extent from administrative manipulation in areas where the *caid* had always represented authority, and to some extent from tribal areas under the Mouvement Populaire. Subsequent by-elections gave the F.D.I.C. a slim majority of 79 in a body of 144 members.[28]

As an indication of the attitudinal development of the Moroccan people, the elections reveal generally unsuspected powers of political discrimination and much stronger loyalties than were thought to exist. Despite the rather heavy-handed tactics of the Palace to obstruct the opposition and the blatant use of administrative officials to direct voting in rural areas, the elections passed off peacefully and the concerted effort of the government did not suppress an affirmation of party loyalty and party differences. The fact that this was possible at all indicates that Moroccans may share a degree of attitudinal sophistication that few have suspected. The monarch's complacency in permitting the manipulation, and, for practical purposes, the political isolation, of the more remote areas is a distinct loss in the slow process of individual politicization to which these elections, like those in 1960, could have contributed. In a very real sense Hassan II was making the gap between the more and less privileged areas of the country only greater because the attitudinal disparities of Moroccans became, to some extent, more pronounced.

The brief description of institutional elaboration in Morocco has

---

[27] For reports on the 1963 national elections see *New York Times*, April 28, May 18 and 21, 1963; *Le Monde*, May 15, 18, 19-20, 21, and 23, 1963; and *Jeune Afrique*, May 13-19, 20-26, and May 26-June 2, 1962. One of the most surprising events of the election was that seven of eight ministers running for office were defeated. Guedira did gain a seat, however, in the heart of the Casablanca working district.

[28] *Le Monde*, January 5-6, 1964. By the end of 1963 the government was involved in considerable and costly harassment of the parties. The Istiqlal was brought into court for charging that American wheat had been used to buy votes. The U.N.F.P. was under more severe charges of conspiring to overthrow the king. After the national elections all the parties tended to withdraw in the face of increasing official manipulation of nominations, election procedures, and local publicity.

distinct parallels to earlier Moroccan experiences in areas of more specific developmental interest. The decision to construct new representative institutions was repeatedly presented in a favorable light, but constantly delayed. Popular interest was repeatedly aroused, but little was built on the monarch's appeal. The constitution that finally emerged after six years was probably more conservative than what Mohammed V would have accepted, but, in any event, it gave political representatives only minimal importance, and their rights within the legislature are overshadowed by the king in many ways. Though certainly not entirely of Hassan II's own choosing, the new constitution came about in an atmosphere in which political forces were dichotomized over the role of the monarchy—a fact which made political choice and compromise difficult for most Moroccans.

The behavior of the Moroccan voters in 1963 does not mean that their capacities to operate in an abstract framework and to consider remotely placed problems is suddenly perfected, but only that, whatever the various intervening variables of party and tribal manipulation, the society does have a capacity to relate spatial and policy differences to the process of government. These qualities, however imperfectly formed, represent emergent cognitive skills making the political process relevant to life in the village and, in turn, contributing to cognitive skills that might contribute materially to the developmental process. As attitudinal changes of this kind take place, the monarchy becomes less important in a relative sense, i.e., it has less directly exercised power of making decisions, but it also is increasingly the focal point in an emergent pattern of participation that relates to the monarch in ways encouraging more responsible action and greater individual initiative. Perhaps these qualities can be elicited in the Moroccan people without giving them comparable attachments to political life, but there is little to support hopes of perpetual fragmentation of views on government in the history of the industrial nations.

Few countries have endured as prolonged and exhausting struggles to formulate a constitutional basis as Pakistan. The great tragedy of Pakistan's monumental effort is that it has done little to bridge over the chasm between the people and their government. As a contributing factor in national integration, the constitutional debates of Pakistan have been the source of continued bitterness among politicians, and the excuse for their continued estrangement from local affairs. Writing the constitution has placed burdens on the Pakistani political system that have and continue to threaten to paralyze political exchange and expression. The Ayub regime has not been able to escape the emotionally charged atmosphere of institutional reform, nor has it been able to take command in the manipulation of symbols and values that have asphyxiated Pakistani political life at lower levels since partition.

The simple fact that Pakistan's early constitutional experience can be almost wholly described in terms of the religious conflict, so well outlined by Binder,[29] suggests the historic focus on the most inflammatory aspect of Pakistani life, and the one that is perhaps least suited to introducing cognitive adjustments appropriate to intensive development. If one accepts legal documents as evidence of national change, there is much to indicate that Pakistan should be the most advanced, rather than the least, in fashioning nationally meaningful institutions. The long series of India Acts supposedly accustomed the subcontinent to parliamentary forms. When the country tumbled into being an independent state in 1947, few educated Muslims, except the Islamic fundamentalists, had ever thought of any alternative.

In the eleven years before military rule Pakistan was in fact ruled by constituent assemblies. The first Constituent Assembly worked until 1954, and passed a total of 54 acts amending the India Government Act of 1935. These laws had constitutional force, though they were passed under less stringent conditions than ordinary bills, which had to be submitted to the governor general.[30] The first Pakistani constitution was agreed upon in 1956, after several years of active political intervention by civil servants. Limitations of space prevent a full exposition of the first parliamentary experiment in Pakistan, but it is important to recall that only the most feeble effort was made to adapt institutions to the needs of the villagers.[31] The politicians spent most of their time settling their own quarrels, and the two provincial elections that took place hardly compare with the political opportunity given North Africans under regimes which have far fewer pretensions about conforming to democratic principles.

Ayub never wavered in his determination to give Pakistan a workable constitution, although he was often subjected to pressure from military and civil servants to establish an authoritarian regime. That he resisted such temptations is often forgotten by the new wave of politicians, whose driving motive has been to wipe out the vestiges of martial law. Despite the shortcomings of the military-bureaucratic regime, the

[29] *Religion and Politics in Pakistan*, Berkeley, University of California Press, 1963. See also *Report of the Constitution Commission*, Karachi, Government of Pakistan Press, 1961.

[30] Keith Callard, *Pakistan: A Political Study*, London, George Allen and Unwin, 1957, p. 107. It has been estimated that the provincial assemblies forming the electoral body for the first Constituent Assembly represented no more than 15 per cent of the Pakistani population. By the time provincial elections were held in the mid-1950's, the provincial assemblies had sat for nearly a decade and corresponded in no way to the changing party structure.

[31] In addition to the account of drafting the constitution in Callard, *op.cit.*, see Khalid Bin Sayeed, *Pakistan: the Formative Phase*, Karachi, Pakistan Publishing House, 1960; Mushtaq Ahmad, *Government and Politics in Pakistan*, Karachi, Pakistan Publishing House, 1959; Ian Stephens, *Pakistan*, New York, Praeger, 1963; Wayne Ayres Wilcox, *Pakistan: The Consolidation of a Nation*, New York, Columbia University Press, 1963.

Ayub government saw clearly that the local community must be brought into political life at higher levels if representative institutions were to succeed. After winning a massive majority of the votes from the Basic Democrats, Ayub proceeded to appoint a Constitutional Commission in February 1960, noting that he hoped for constitutional rule in eighteen months.[32]

Like the other Pakistani commissions, the constitutional study group prepared a thorough and balanced report, involving over 6,000 widely distributed circulars and over 500 interviews with leaders in both wings. The report reveals, of course, how Ayub differed from the highly distinguished group appointed to investigate Pakistan's failure under the earlier constitution, but it also reveals how educated Pakistanis hope to build new institutions. The commission fervently reaffirmed Pakistan's devotion to the advancement of representative government, and was severe in condemning those who used religious values to supplant civic loyalty and obligation.[33] The commission favored a strong presidential system, though they also felt the president should be directly elected by universal suffrage rather than indirectly by the Basic Democrats. The most revealing discussion concerned the role of parties because it shows how Pakistani faith in institutional solutions is combined with an almost naïve notion of how such forms of behavior take on meaning and are widely accepted. In the post-mortem on the old regime the group speaks of parties as "interfering" with the administration and, conversely, of the administration "interfering" with the parties.[34]

While this was a perfectly accurate thumbnail sketch of political life in prerevolutionary Pakistan, the observers could hardly have made a more telling confession of how institutional patterns of behavior fail to take root in developing countries. The commission also reported that they had been asked to consider some form of loose association to be formed only at election time, and to serve the institutional need of

[32] *Pakistan Times,* October 16 and November 14, 1959; January 25, 1960. The report was submitted a year and a month later, in April 1961. Ayub was reportedly dissatisfied with the commission's suggestions, and the final draft was not announced until March 1962, although its general lines were known earlier. Martial law terminated in June 1962 when the National Assembly met for the first time.

[33] *Report of the Constitution Commission, op.cit.,* pp. 14-17. The report provides useful evidence on the Islamic fundamentalists. Throughout there is a firm minority of about 3 per cent of those interviewed adhering to rigid interpretation of Islamic principles.

[34] *Ibid.,* p. 6. The poor relations between administrators and politicians are curious, because there are many informal ties between the two groups. As a whole, they represent the minority of educated, informed persons; they are often of the same ethnic and geographic origins; and most upper-class Pakistanis have extensive family ties. The work of the Constitution Commission was followed by a series of studies by presidential committees, whose views were even less real. See Karl Von Vorys, *Political Development in Pakistan,* Princeton, Princeton University Press, 1965, pp. 208-229.

selecting representatives without lasting political organization.[35] There is probably no more impressive revelation of the Ayub government's fatal dilemma, and the simple bureaucratic solution he thought possible. Disregarding the obvious difficulty of making such a scheme workable, it suggests how absurdly simple were Ayub's associates in their estimate of the way in which persons perceive politics and involve themselves in national affairs. The commission came out strongly in favor of parties, although Ayub tried to discourage them until the revival became overpowering and threatened to isolate him fatally from new political forces.

The controversy over the role of political parties is important in the context of this inquiry because it shows how the military regime, having foregone the opportunity to set up an authoritarian regime of some kind, was without means to guide renewed political activity at the national level into more constructive channels. Shortly after the constitution had been proclaimed, Ayub issued an ordinance forbidding any organization to "propagate political opinions or otherwise to indulge in political activity" until a law on parties was passed by the National Assembly.[36] In the clamor to revive parliamentary life the new parties quickly passed a law in November 1962, though the law retained a highly controversial provision that the president could bar ministers from political activity for five years for gross misconduct. When the parties returned in full force, Suhrawardy spoke of reconsidering the unification of West Pakistan, and a National Democratic Front was formed of groups bitterly opposed to presidential rule.

The challenge to the new constitutional regime was too great. Suhrawardy was arrested early in 1962, and Khan Abdul Qayum Khan was detained in mid-1962 for inflammatory speeches against the new constitution. Very quickly political exchange at the national level returned to its earlier form of impassioned, bitter criticism followed by doubtful legal action to restrain the opponent. When parties became legal, Ayub bolstered his position further by issuing a new ordinance barring any person disqualified for political party membership from "otherwise associating himself," speaking at a public meeting, or issuing a press statement on behalf of the party.[37] Several months later the

[35] *Report of the Constitution Commission, op.cit.*, p. 79.

[36] "The Political Organisations (Prohibition of Unregulated Activity) Ordinance, 1962," *Pakistan Law Reports*, Part II, July 1962, pp. 74-75. The final law is "The Political Parties Act, 1962," *ibid.*, November 1962, pp. 175-179.

[37] "The Political Parties (Amendment) Ordinance, 1963," *ibid.*, March 1963, pp. 43-45. This ordinance provided the grounds for the arrest of the National Democratic Front politicians, who were some of the least scrupulous and many of whom had been barred from party membership, including Bashani, the left-wing, East Pakistani. The arrests of the National Democratic Front leaders included Lari, leader of the Councilors' Muslim League in Karachi; Mahmoodul Huq Usmani, former secretary of the National Awami League; Mian Qasuri, another National Awami League leader; and Tufail Mohammed of the Jama'at-i-Islami. See *Dawn*, May 8, 1963.

leaders of the National Democratic Front were arrested. Despite the careful reforms and progress of the military regime, the military and the politicians were essentially alike in their inability to make fundamental changes in Pakistani politics.

The idea of imposing administrative checks on party activity had been frequently supported by Ayub's foreign minister, Manzur Qadir, over the spring and summer of 1962. His notion of "structuring" party activities received support in Ayub's statements favoring a single "broad-based" party.[38] However, the vigor of renewed party activity forced the president to give way, although he has been quoted as saying that parties leave the people vulnerable to the "unscrupulous and demagogues."[39] For understandable reasons Qadir came under fire from the new National Assembly, convened for the first time in June 1962, and he was soon replaced. However, he was reportedly influential in stiffening the proposals of the Constitutional Commission. Though much more detailed than the Tunisian constitution, the Pakistani document gives virtually the same powers to the president.

The president selects his ministers and the provincial governors, and approves provincial ministerial appointments. The president may dissolve the National Assembly at his pleasure (art. 21), but must also stand for reelection within three months when this power is used. In the event of a conflict between the National Assembly and the president, he may hold a referendum (art. 24), but a favorable result does not carry the punitive measures found in the Moroccan constitution. The president is given broad administrative and financial powers, the assembly being permitted to alter only additions over the previous year's budget. The president convenes and prorogues the National Assembly. A third of the members may ask the speaker to convene special sessions, but they may be prorogued by the speaker. The president may veto constitutional amendments from the assembly twice and, if still defeated, may call for a referendum (art. 206).

The National Assembly consists of 156 members, six of them women selected by the members. Perhaps the most controversial aspect of the constitution was the indirect election of the members using the Basic Democrats. Two Muslim League parties were formed—the Conventionists, supporting Ayub, and the Councilors (Pakistan), who were the major opposition group. Among their leaders were Nazimuddin and the onetime prime minister Chaudri Mohammed Ali, both of whom campaigned for restoring direct elections.[40] The dispute brought new criticisms on Basic Democracies as a subtle "caste system" and the

[38] See *Pakistan Times*, April 14, June 12, and August 2, 1962.
[39] G. W. Choudhury, "Democracy on Trial in Pakistan," *Middle East Journal*, vol. 17, no. 1, Winter-Spring 1963, pp. 1-13.
[40] *Dawn*, April 7 and May 2, 1963.

creature of foreign imaginations, threatening to debase Islam. The virulence of the attack could not be moderated, although another study group was working on the franchise question.

The Franchise Commission reported in favor of direct elections after the next national election, scheduled for early 1965. It was problematical if new rolls could be prepared by then. An expanded electorate of 120,000 Basic Democrats was suggested, to be created by the replacement of the nominated members with elected members. The report tended to compartmentalize Basic Democracies, giving as its "sole object [the] management of purely local affairs."[41] The Franchise Commission also advised against a constitutional provision that presidental candidates be limited to two. Since this is the second special study group to repudiate Ayub's hopes of giving Basic Democracies a role in national affairs, there seems no doubt but that these recommendations will be accepted.

Two other disputes, less directly related to the villager's involvement in national politics, demonstrate how Ayub was forced to give more attention to domestic affairs as interpreted by the successors to the old party system. The first of these quarrels suggests how national politics soon became entangled with the feuds of the politicians. A Supreme Court decision upheld a case judged against the government in the Dacca high court, which held that ministers were obliged to give up elected office in any of the assemblies under a constitutional provision (art. 115) barring them from any other office. Though entitled to speak in the National Assembly, six ministers of the central government, seven ministers of West Pakistan, and all but two ministers of East Pakistan were forced to vacate their seats in the assemblies.

A more bitterly fought battle involved civil rights, which the opposition held should be enforceable through court action and should not be qualified by the restrictive ordinances established during martial law. Against the advice of the Constitutional Commission the Ayub government excluded the courts from protecting the fundamental-rights section, which was taken over nearly intact from the 1956 constitution. After very successful by-elections in late 1963 Ayub was able to increase the slim majority of the Conventionist Muslim League. By persuading fifteen members of the opposition to defect momentarily, he was able to get the necessary two-thirds majority, and passed a Fundamental Rights Act allowing the major ordinances of the martial-law period to remain, while opening fundamental-rights issues to judicial settlement.[42]

[41] "Franchise Commission Report," *The Gazette of Pakistan*, August 23, 1963, p. 637w.

[42] On the decision to remove ministers from representative office see *Dawn*, May 14, 1963, and *Pakistan Observer*, May 15, 1963. The latter reported that Ayub originally permitted ministers to seek elected office in order to please Mohammed Ali, a prerevolutionary politician. See also the discussion of the

Despite the violent protests of the opposition political groups, Ayub proceeded to use the Basic Democrats as the electors in the 1964 elections. The president has formidable opposition from Fatima Jinnah, the sister of Pakistan's founder and national hero, Mohammed Ali Jinnah. Indicative of the low level of political institutionalization still persisting in Pakistan, neither candidate was thought to have had well-organized party support. Ayub ran as the nominee of the Conventionist Muslim League, renamed the Pakistan Muslim League, and Miss Jinnah had a loose coalition of small parties and splinter groups.[43] Elections for the 80,000 Basic Democrats were held in November, followed by the indirect election of the new president on January 2, 1965. There is little evidence that Pakistani political behavior changed greatly from the pre-Ayub period. However, the impact of development on the operation of political institutions was seen in East Pakistan. The fact that Ayub was able to gather a small majority in the eastern wing is generally credited to the benefits of the rural public-works program. Whether his strength represented a simple appreciation for material favors or a fuller understanding and informed approval for effective government cannot be determined from the available data.

Nevertheless, the parties are again active and using many of the same highly affective appeals that distorted political life in the prerevolutionary period. If the values so emotionally forwarded by politicians were related to identifiable interests of the locality or held some meaning in the perceptual world of the villager, it would be more difficult to manipulate popular feeling irresponsibly. By foregoing these tactics Ayub sacrificed an important device for political control. He seems to have realized that such controls place limits on the diversity of behavior to be elicited and tend to reduce the individual's capacity to evaluate political situations unless compelling national values are constantly invoked. Lacking the charismatic appeal of Bourguiba and the Islamic legitimacy bestowed on the Moroccan monarch, the military government had to choose between a military dictatorship and the turbulent political life of Pakistan before 1958.

Conceptualizing more articulate forms of cognition in political life is clearly a more difficult task than identifying the many, almost limitless appeals that might be used for mobilizing attention and awareness. The difficult hurdle in the attitudinal changes occurring in developing countries is not the emotional identification with politics, so readily adapted

---

major legal decisions limiting the Ayub regime under the new constitution, Ralph Braibanti, "Pakistan: Constitutional Issues in 1964," *Asian Survey*, vol. 5, no. 2, February 1965, pp. 79-87.

[43] On the elections of late 1964 and January 1965 see Von Vorys, *op.cit.*, pp. 269-290. See also Jacques Nevard, " 'Zindabad!' for Miss Jinnah," *New York Times Sunday Magazine*, November 8, 1964, pp. 36 and 120-124, and *New York Times*, January 3, 1965.

from the European nation-state experience, but the way in which persons will relate their understanding of a more complex, intricate world to politics. The early experiments with institutional elaboration are useful indicators, and provide concrete evidence, of how the government hopes to extend a more meaningful, flexible image to the local level. The ability of the military to do so is severely limited because the political virtues of the officer are not very different from those of any loyal government servant, and sheer patriotism is difficult to monopolize. The monarchy finds that the articulation of national values unavoidably compromises other affective appeals, while the Socialist Destour finds the task of being the sole judge of national virtue more difficult as the complexities of the developmental process diffuse political understanding more widely.

Though it is clearly absurd to interpret the rash of new constitutions in Africa and Asia as commitments to democratic institutions, the new constitutions and the representative institutions they introduce are important components of a new perceptual world for the participant. They bring the operations of government a little closer to the village and, in doing so, challenge the exclusive concept of political authority fostered by countless colonial regimes. The new legislatures provide opportunity to discuss issues, grievances, and problems that were formerly concealed in the unknown labyrinths of the administration. This is not to suggest that developing countries are in some way compelled to elicit informed, responsive views, but only that new institutions may assist in attitudinal articulation.

VILLAGE DISINTEGRATION AND NATIONAL INTEGRATION

Although the required surveys have yet to be made, it has become apparent that the developmental process involves a major reorientation of political and social relationships at the local level. The village is in many ways the basic unit of change in most rural-development programs, although many tensions and adjustments might also be studied in terms of the family. But the institutional unit reacting to the challenge of development via the political system is generally the village, and the village is often the administrative unit for introducing change and calculating achievements of national significance.

One of the stumbling blocks to village analyses applicable on the national level has been the difficulty of reconstructing the data from local studies in a form permitting statements about national development. Political scientists are quick to assess the government's impact on the community, and anthropologists are confident of their estimates of the resistance to be found in the village. Neither viewpoint is appropriate to an analysis of the way in which institutional patterns are reshaped under the impact of developmental activities, because neither suggests that the changing pattern of village political and social life will indeed be a blend of forces emanating from government and the community. The purpose of this section is to suggest some of the ways in which villages do begin to orient themselves to national political life, and to present some of the materials indicating that the encounter must be conceived in terms of a dynamic transformation affecting both parties.

To make village studies meaningful for the analysis of national political change the investigator must work at a level of generalization that may appear to inflict severe injustice on the complexity of village life. The analytical problem exists for anyone wishing to deal with more than one example of the object under examination. When the reconstruction of village society becomes a pressing necessity for the developing country, it is not uncommon for nationalist leaders to soften the implied criticism of their society by extolling ancient and often long forgotten virtues of the village. Al-Fassi's statements on the tribal *jemaâ* reflect resistance to the notion that Moroccan society may, in some sense, be poorly prepared for developmental change. The same tendency is observable in the early programs for village government in Indonesia, where stress was placed on the use of general agreement of *mufakat*. As Legge has noted, the obvious defect is the "putting aside of problems where general agreement cannot be reached."[44]

The Indian community-development and national-extension service is the best example of government miscalculation of the integrative aspect of village reorganization. An Indian evaluation team in 1955 found that "the emphasis on organizational compliance and official responsibility is threatening to turn a state-induced popular movement of rural regeneration into an official program of tasks."[45] While Indian scholars soon discovered that the program "lacked a sense of direction,"[46] they were also reluctant to see national political differences enter into village life. Thus in 1958 an evaluation notes that "elections to the *panchayat* should be free of considerations pertinent to wider party politics and should be influenced by purely local issues and the merits of individual candidates."[47] The Indian response was to intro-

[44] J. D. Legge, *Central Authority and Regional Autonomy in Indonesia: A Study in Local Administration 1950-1960*, Ithaca, Cornell University Press, 1961, p. 141.

[45] Program Evaluation Organisation, Planning Commission, Government of India, *Evaluation Report on the Second Year's Working of Community Projects*, New Delhi, 1955, p. 27. This shortcoming is by no means confined to developing countries. Precisely the same criticism has been made of the American poverty program.

[46] S. C. Dube, *India's Changing Villages: Human Factors in Community Development*, London, Routledge, Keegan-Paul, 1958, p. 48. This study is an excellent summary of the findings of the Program Evaluation Organisation, and is also fully aware of the broad problems of integration facing the Indian community program.

[47] Program Evaluation Organisation, Planning Commission, Government of

duce the *panchayat samiti* scheme whereby higher tiers, comparable to the Pakistani Union Councils, have been introduced with planning and supervisory functions over the villages. The plan is an institutional response to what was both an organizational and a psychological inadequacy of the previous system, which are in fact two ways of considering the same problem.

Though village-level studies are few for North Africa, there is some evidence pointing to similar problems in the Basic Democracies scheme. Most members of Union Councils still felt isolated from officials, and few had acquired confidence in challenging official advice on budgets, planning, and other local changes. In the Comilla survey over two thirds of the Basic Democrats interviewed felt that the scheme was largely for administrative purposes.[48] While this feeling persists, it will probably be difficult to reconstruct the villager's concept of politics outside the village, and the notion of the omnipotent official will survive. The first step is no doubt to involve the villager in projects of immediate benefit to the locality, and this has been done with some degree of success in parts of all three countries under study. The next step, and a more difficult one, is to move beyond the simpler, motivational framework for development commitment, and to construct the concepts and understanding permitting the villager to deal with the outside world on his own terms.

Pye's study of political change in Burma suggests that the peasant may know a good deal more about politics outside the village than is often recognized by observers. "Peasants and villagers often engage in prolonged discussions on matters related to the political world outside their immediate lives, but they rarely seem prepared to translate the information they receive into action that might influence the course of national politics."[49] To assume that village differences defy reformulation in terms of national and regional politics is, of course, an extremely pessimistic conclusion, and one that would imply trouble for the extended programs of rural mobilization under way in Africa and Asia.

The sentimental version of community life under primitive conditions generally concludes with the suggestion that there are few relationships in village life that can be extended to more remote frameworks of activity, sometimes implying that the village will collapse if tampered with. More recent analyses suggest otherwise, and provide the inspiration for more useful analyses of how village qualities support the

India, *The Fifth Evaluation Report on Working of Community Development and N.E.S. Blocks*, New Delhi, 1958, p. 106.

[48] Bureau of National Reconstruction and the Pakistan Academy for Village Development, *An Analysis of the Working of Basic Democracy Institutions in East Pakistan*, Comilla, 1961, p. 36.

[49] Lucian W. Pye, *Politics, Personality, and Nation-Building: Burma's Search for Identity*, New Haven, Yale University Press, 1962, p. 25.

transformation of the isolated community into a part of a national and regional system for developmental and political activity. McCormack has noted, for example, that the factional divisions of Indian villages may operate as easily for the removal of traditional village leadership as for its entrenchment. Singh goes even farther and suggests that factional differences may help to produce new leadership at the village level.[50] That these differences are often exploited by local forces in development is widely recognized, but it appears equally correct that they by no means necessarily inhibit effective action at the village level, and may make important contributions in creating a more diverse society.

In addition to the structural characteristics of villages that may facilitate political participation, other social characteristics embodied in village life may help the new participant orient himself to new activities. Thus the Rudolfs have argued that caste associations have "absorbed and synthesized some of the new democratic values" by making modern political processes "comprehensible in traditional terms to a population still largely politically illiterate."[51] Retzlaff has taken the factional difference even farther in suggesting that whether factions are used to build other factional support or to ally forces outside the village such as parties or new associations, the familiarity with more complex relations in seeking political influence and compromise will have beneficial effect.[52] Similar conclusions are drawn by Hollensteiner in examining the highly personal loyalties that intrude into local political life in the Philippines.[53] There is no reason to assume that the dynamics of village life are incompatible with increased participation, and increasing evidence that once villages are encompassed in a developmental effort local forces may find the shifting, impersonal political arena reasonably familiar.

As has been suggested early in the book, the villager is highly moti-

[50] William McCormack, "Factionalism in a Mysore Village," in Richard L. Park and Irene Tinker, eds., Leadership and Political Institutions in India, Princeton, Princeton University Press, 1959, pp. 438-444, and Baij Nath Singh, "The Impact of the Community Development Program on Rural Leadership," ibid., pp. 358-371.

[51] Lloyd I. Rudolf and Susanne Hoeber Rudolf, "The Political Role of India's Caste Associations," Pacific Affairs, vol. 33, no. 1, 1960, pp. 5-22; also, Rudolf and Rudolf, "Toward Political Stability in Underdeveloped Countries," Friederich and Harris, eds., Public Policy, Cambridge, Graduate School of Public Administration, 1959, pp. 149-178.

[52] Ralph H. Retzlaff, Village Government in India, London, Asia Publishing House, 1962, p. 10. This study also presents an excellent account of the national implications of the panchayat raj scheme.

[53] Mary R. Hollensteiner, "The Development of Political Parties on the Local Level: A Social Anthropological Case Study of Hulo Municipality, Bulacan," Philippine Journal of Public Administration, vol. 4, no. 2, 1960, pp. 111-131. For a divergent view from Indonesia see Barbara S. Dohrenwent, Some Factors Related to Autonomy and Dependence in Twelve Javanese Villages, Ithaca, Cornell Modern Indonesia Project, Interim Report Series, 1959.

vated to change, but has been without the resources and knowledge to bring about change. Because the village has remained unchanged for years, or appears so to the scholar dwelling on more specialized developmental questions, the assumption has been made that villages resist change. The result has been that governments have sometimes argued "that villagers can be trusted to exercise their franchise . . . but are unfit to choose a committee to look after the parish pump."[54] In fact, the villages have very likely already made considerable adjustment to forces from outside the village and to new conditions within, if only in response to the population explosions of the past century. To identify poverty with incapacity to grow is to make the same determinist error that was noted in developmental plans based solely on massive injections of wealth.

The evidence suggests that there are indeed important social forces in the village that are amenable to the kind of combination and expression found in more privileged societies. The critical decision in tapping the local capacity for articulation and adaptation rests with the government, and the various hazards to be encountered in different political systems have been explored in the early chapters of this inquiry. The interesting common quality of the various rural mobilization schemes is that none of the governments appear to be making maximum effort to invigorate and revive community life. The most serious obstacle to local reform may not be the impoverishment and isolation of the village, but the reluctance of the new middle and upper classes to share power. The struggle for power in Western industrial development, despite the high productivity and natural wealth of European countries, suggests that the modern segments of the developing country's populace may be even more apprehensive over the diffusion of power.[55]

The vast differences between urban and rural life, and the frequent concentration of organizational skills in one part of the country,[56] permit delay and procrastination. The constructive exploitation of the differences and tensions that may exist in village life rests, to a large extent, on the political system's own capacity to tolerate differences and to adjust to changes at the local level. It seems unlikely that a country will

[54] J. G. Drummond, *Panchayat in India*, London, Oxford University Press, 1937. Another study anticipating the merger of Western institutions and Asian culture expresses similar views in J. S. Furnivall, *Progress and Welfare in Southeast Asia*, New York, Institute of Pacific Relations, 1941. See also John J. Honigman, *Three Villages in India*, Chapel Hill, Institute for Research in Social Science, 1958; Inayatullah, *Perspectives in the Rural Power Structure in West Pakistan*, Karachi, United States AID Mission, 1963; and Jacques Chérel, " 'De qui s'agit-il?' ou la mise en valeur agricole, problèmes d'ensembles humaines," *Les Cahiers de Tunisie*, vol. 8, nos. 29-30, 1960, pp. 17-49.

[55] Clement Henry Moore, "Politics in a Tunisian Village," *Middle East Journal*, vol. 17, no. 5, Late Autumn 1963, pp. 527-540.

[56] Douglas E. Ashford, "National Organizations and Political Development in Morocco," *Il Politico*, vol. 28, no. 2, June 1963, pp. 360-374.

be able to accept the uncertainties of comprehensive, locally supported development until it is also prepared to make similar concessions in the political realm. The two problems are only different aspects of attitudinal transformation, because the individual acquiring familiarity and confidence in the handling of developmental problems is also learning how to manipulate persons and issues in ways highly applicable to politics.

How these two trends, increased local development and awareness of more complex political relationships, interrelate in modernization is only dimly understood. What can be seen with much more clarity is that unanimity at the local level often means apathy, or at best a readiness to embark only on those ventures creating least village disruption and requiring minimal local sacrifice.[57] But massive uniformity in relation to distant political and social environment has kept the villagers isolated from affairs outside the community and its immediate surroundings for centuries. The material presented in Section III indicates that such isolation will be broken down in a multitude of ways during the coming generation. The projects and programs described above are clear statements of governmental commitment to hasten village disintegration by creating more diverse and more intricate activities at the local level.

How the transformation of village institutions relates to national politics may be more difficult to conceptualize than how national institutional change relates to politics. As was noted above, however, the modification of national institutions can be a misleading indicator of political development where there is no corroborative evidence that individual capacities and differences find expression in such institutions. The same process of institutional elaboration viewed at the extreme of the locality seems more difficult to imagine in relation to politics, in part, because political science as a whole is deficient in conceptualizing highly complex power relationships. But where it is possible to discover shifts in the villager's capacity and confidence to exploit processes and organizations outside the community, one is very likely dealing with more reliable indications of political and social advancement.[58] Moreover, once these capacities are generated, as they inescapably are in large development programs, the government can only repress them by foregoing the individual skill and self-control that has been created.

When speaking of village disintegration as a function of national integration, it is common to note the state of "amoral familism" described by Banfield.[59] There appear to be very different problems of integration

[57] S. K. Dey, *Community Development*, rev. edn., Allahabad, Kitub Mahal, 1962.
[58] For recognition of this shift in anthropological research see Oscar Lewis, *Life in a Mexican Village: Tepoztlán Revisited*, Urbana, University of Illinois Press, 1963, pp. 422-426, for his discussion of "public and private personality."
[59] Edward C. Banfield, *The Moral Basis of a Backward Society*, Glencoe,

in the emergent country and the advanced one, which has undergone severe depression after enjoying success. The integration process in the developing society is perhaps best described as a relaxation of relations between the community and the political system unaccompanied with the loss of confidence or disinterest seen in parts of Italy and France. The developing country can usually inspire strong affection and loyalty, though often without the cognitive skill needed to translate affectivity into effective action. As relations between peasant and politician become adaptive rather than rigid and essentially authoritarian, there is a corresponding relaxation of the defensive posture of the village, once encouraged by the isolated citizen's apprehension of the outside world.

Although limited to fragmentary data, there is an increasing amount of evidence that the ostensibly timeless institutional differences of the village may take on new cognitive significance. Differences created by caste, faction, and land tenure can be manipulated in new ways and in more extended frameworks as the peasant begins to operate in the expanded universe of developmental activity. At the other extreme of the political system the formal institutions of representative government may also acquire cognitive significance for the new participant. This does not necessarily mean that the political system will have become a model democracy, but it does mean that the participant has internalized certain notions about the structure of power in which his influence and importance is specifically provided for. Moreover, the internalization process is not wholly emotional, but the sentiment toward the nation has been elaborated cognitively and becomes part of the citizen's mental process for ordering a complex world.

The creation of more complex institutions is both a product and a reflection of attitudinal change. They are indeed separate levels of generalization about the development process, generally neglected in the available literature on developing countries. However, the pioneering studies that have appeared provide some notion of how individual transformation relates to more intricate problems of nation-building. Lerner's concept of "empathy" is a latent attitudinal quality enabling the individual to imagine himself in many roles.[60] Though not broken down into

---

Free Press, 1958. Other cases of a highly developed society declining are in Laurence Wylie, *Village in the Vaucluse*, Cambridge, Harvard University Press, 1957; O. A. Oeser and F. E. Emery, *Social Structure and Personality in a Rural Community*, New York, Macmillan, 1954; Richard W. Poston, *Small Town Renaissance*, New York, Harper, 1950; and J. T. Reid, *It Happened in Taos*, Albuquerque, University of New Mexico Press, 1946. These cases appear to differ greatly from the integration of communities where there is little awareness of central government and minimal development of cognitive attachments to government.

[60] *The Passing of Traditional Society*, Glencoe, Free Press, 1958. Although Lerner identified a highly important quality in attitudes, his method did not

attitudinal components, the capacity of the highly empathetic individual to move from one frame of reference to another involves both the aquisition of new values about political life and of vastly expanded skill in manipulating information about his environment. Such an individual may still have strong feelings about his community and nation, but they are feelings moderated by a large number of concepts and imaginative powers enabling the person to participate without being present.

Some of the important cognitive qualities of the participant in modern societies have already been singled out, although relatively little is known of their operation in developing countries. Participants in American political life have varying degrees of trust in both the candidates and the institutions of the democratic process. The citizens of highly developed countries are not only optimistic about the future and confident about their government, but they can generally state specific reasons why they are so attached to political and social life. The central quality of the individual high in cognitive skill is very possibly his enhanced capacity to live with uncertainty, a very different kind of uncertainty than that existing in the villages of Africa and Asia.

The peasant untouched by the development process, though he may have learned to manipulate many aspects of his environment, is still at the mercy of both natural and human forces that he cannot calculate. The peasant undergoing attitudinal change of the kind examined in this inquiry learns about an entirely new kind of uncertainty. The physical environment no longer represents a setting of minimal opportunity and a backdrop for capricious forces. The human environment is no longer sharply demarcated at the end of the village land, with all else beyond identified as untrustworthy and uncontrollable. Most important, and the underlying hypothesis of this study, learning about these two areas provides the individual with constructs and concepts that makes the uncertainty of probable alternatives and relative satisfaction acceptable. The new citizen has not lost his values, but he has learned to use them to make his life more rewarding and to extend the range of his imagination to situations as yet unknown.

---

permit him to describe the structural qualities of empathetic persons. Thus, as argued by both Pool and Mosel in Pye, ed., *Communication and Political Development*, Princeton, Princeton University Press, 1963, this kind of conceptual skill is not necessarily brought to bear on political and social problems. For this reason it is essential that studies of attitudinal change in developing countries deal with *how* conceptual skills and new values are joined perceptually.

CHAPTER 12

ATTITUDINAL CHANGE AND DEVELOPMENT

ALTHOUGH SYSTEMATIC inquiry into the relationship between participation and involvement in political life is fairly recent, this study has sought to underscore the changing nature of this relationship in countries of which comparatively little is known. In political science the tendency has been to assume that behavior outside the political realm is irrelevant to changing views on politics. The purpose of Section III was to indicate how comprehensive were the efforts to change behavior in areas intimately associated with the individual citizen. "Nonpolitical" participation is certainly going to increase at a phenomenal rate over the coming decade in all countries seriously intent on development. Whether or not such participation becomes "political" is a matter of definition, and those concerned with development both within and without the new nations would be poorly advised to accept definitions of growing participation because they appear politically feasible at the moment or because they support policy positions of narrow interest.

Treating the various aspects of development as neatly divided compartments only blinds the nation-building agency to the cumulative effects of increased participation. Indeed, the planner may sometimes fail to observe new opportunities and new human talent as a result of his concentration on specific developmental goals. On the other hand, the political leader is usually most sensitive to opinion in his country and to trends that might suggest a redistribution of power. The illustration of this sensitivity that is closely associated with development is local government. The politician sees the new agencies for the organization and expression of emerging views on national government in various ways from one political system to another. The purpose of Section II was to illustrate how increments in participation of a distinctly political nature were shaped by the dominant values of the three political systems. Thus the second and third sections of the book represent opposing methods of assessing a people's readiness to participate in political life.

Perhaps the central issue in developmental studies is how much new behavior of the kind described in Section III can be performed without becoming simultaneously performance of political significance. The argument has been repeatedly presented in the inquiry that the government itself will be the major determinant in the way in which new behavior will be permitted to acquire political significance. Conceivably a country may achieve a high degree of material advancement without there being major concessions to new forms of political participation. Conversely one might also imagine a situation with a great deal of citizen participation in governmental decision-making while the people were still at a very low level of development. The logical extremes, however, are less important in the actuality of the developmental process than they are for analytical clarity. At best one can speak of prevailing views, represented by the orientations of the three regimes, where a new balance between political participation and developmental behavior is sought from day to day.

The fact that governmental decisions about the development process are made in the context of ever-increasing complexity hopefully justifies the detail provided in Sections II and III. The developmental process might be simplified by making broad distinctions among phases of development or among varieties of leadership,[1] but the sociological categories have, at best, provided only a descriptive shorthand which the initiated may use to study a particular problem area or to identify a given dysfunctionality in the political system. Important as these contributions have been in helping scholars find their way through the complexities of the developmental process, they generally do not provide the conceptual precision needed to make more specific observations about a given country. For this reason the present inquiry has sought to focus conceptualization on the role of the citizen in the rapidly developing country, and has neglected the society as a unit of analysis.

The psychological orientation of the study has been derived from recent work on problems of attitudinal change, which enable the investigator to measure the changing views of the citizen as he acquires new behavior and, in turn, more knowledge about his environment (Section III) and as the prevailing political values of the system are interpeted at a level more accessible to him (Section II). As was noted before, developmental activity in either of these areas should not be viewed as purely affective or cognitive in its impact on the citizen, which would constitute a reification of the attitudinal framework of analysis. Equally misleading would be assumptions that similar behavioral change in two political systems tends to encourage comparable change in the application and articulation of national political values by the citizen. The attitudinal framework can make sense only when much more research is done on how attitudinal components are indeed combined under governments with varying orientations and varying degrees of developmental activity.

Most of the research to date on attitudinal change has been done

---

[1] There are now a variety of such typologies. Leadership distinctions are stressed in Edward A. Shil's, "Political Developments in the New States," *Comparative Studies in Society and History*, vol. 2, 1960, pp. 265-292 and 379-411. A functional model has been suggested by Gabriel Almond and James Coleman, *The Politics of the Developing Areas*, Princeton, Princeton University Press, 1960, pp. 3-64, and also by Fred R. Riggs, in William J. Siffin, ed., *Toward the Comparative Study of Public Administration*, Bloomington, Indiana University Press, 1957, pp. 23-116.

under laboratory conditions, where subjects would be hypnotized or put into carefully contrived situations of conflict.[2] Clearly these avenues of investigation are closed to the social scientist interested in the developmental process. In an attempt to formulate new general theories of attitudinal change appropriate to the problems of developing countries it is important to have a general model of the kind of change anticipated in the individual. Such a model has been drawn in Diagram 1. The horizontal axis represents time, with developmental phases roughly marked off as prenational, national, and postnational. The precise location of the two curves is, of course, unknown without further empirical study, although there is some evidence of their relationship in the postnational phase from studies done in more advanced nations. The important aspect is their changing relationship to each other as the individual operates in increasingly complex societal environments.

Diagram-1: Perception of National Development

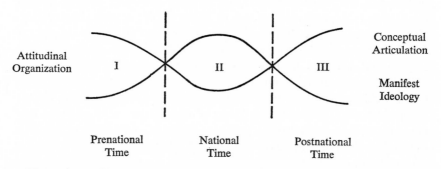

For schematic purposes the two curves will be referred to as conceptual articulation and manifest ideology, partly because these two aspects of attitudinal structure should not be confused with the assumptions about affective and cognitive orientation of political systems, nor with the affective and cognitive components of attitudes in the psychological literature. In fact, it would be anticipated that an affectively oriented political system, e.g., Morocco, would tend to stress national values at the expense of increasing understanding of national affairs, which is much like conceptual articulation in the model. A separate consider-

---

[2] Among the many works to which this inquiry is indebted are Milton J. Rosenberg, *Attitude Organization and Change*, New Haven, Yale University Press, 1960; Leon Festinger, *A Theory of Cognitive Dissonance*, New York, Row Peterson, 1957; Jack W. Brehm and Arthur R. Cohen, *Explorations in Cognitive Dissonance*, New York, Wiley, 1962; Milton Rokeach, *The Open and Closed Mind*, New York, Basic Books, 1960; and Nathan Kogan and Michael A. Wallach, *Risk Taking: A Study in Cognition and Personality*, New York, Holt Rinehart and Winston, 1964. Those interested in a good summary of recent changes in psychological theory are directed to M. B. Smith, J. S. Bruner, and R. W. White, *Opinions and Personality*, New York, Wiley, 1956, pp. 1-47.

ation, however, is estimating the suitability of stressing either attitudinal component in governmental policy at various stages of development. As has been suggested throughout the study, such emphasis is in many ways a constant in the developmental process, i.e., governments change very slowly in their orientation to participation.

Although the schematic formulation applies to individuals, it was thought best not to apply the psychologist's terms directly. Ideological manifestation refers to the individual's direct reliance on national values in ordering and explaining changes in his environment. One study of this kind has been done, which will be outlined below, and some material related to this problem has been presented in the Almond-Verba study. The curve representing conceptual articulation is closely related to the individual's cognitive skill, but has been labeled to indicate his ability to interrelate his information and to generalize about his knowledge as environmental changes occur during development. These modifications of the affective and cognitive components as they appear in psychological studies have been made partly for methodological reasons, and also because the knowledge we most sorely need is how the new citizen perceives remote frameworks of activity where the basic elements of perception are difficult to distinguish.

Several reservations should be made to clarify the meaning of the attitudinal variables traced in the diagram. First, conceptual articulation involves more than simply receiving and acting on information. Many villagers have begun to do this in Africa and Asia, but they have yet to acquire the conceptual skill in using information needed to support sustained development and, as will be argued below, the ability to evaluate the political system in relation to development. As Geertz has pointed out, "Things do not merely *seem* jumbled—they *are* jumbled, and it will take more than theory to straighten them out."[3] A degree of development is clearly possible by sheer imitation, but the routinization of developmental behavior does not give the citizen the capacity to make adjustments to crises, new conditions, and locally derived innovation that can be reasonably considered part of creating sustained support for development. Imitation may well be a device to persuade the villager to commit himself more wholeheartedly to developmental activity, but the intricacies of living in a more complex society can hardly be mastered by memorizing complete performances for every situation confronting the individual.

Ideological manifestation, secondly, is not meant to convey only intensity of nationalist conviction. The patriotic demands on the citizen, though they may be severe in times of national crisis, are very much alike from nation to nation. While there are some countries that have

---

[3] "Ideology as a Cultural System," in Apter, ed., *Ideology and Discontent*, New York, Free Press, 1964, p. 70.

sought to identify nearly all behavior with national loyalty, there are important reasons to doubt the individual's capacity to endure such an experience, and also the sheer feasibility of such a political system.[4] Though few cross-national studies have been done of intensity of national convictions, the available evidence suggests that citizens of both more and less advanced nations perceive national values with comparable intensity. The important differences are how well the individual can put these values to work and relate them to the problems encountered from day to day.

Perhaps a corollary of the above qualification is that ideological manifestation is intended as a characterization of one aspect of the way in which the individual sees his country, and is not meant to imply that nationalism is necessarily destructive.[5] Earlier comments on the problems of political communication in Pakistan should have assured the reader that nationalism—placing supreme value on the existence of the nation—has been accepted as an important aspect of nation-building. Though the problem requires much more empirical investigation, the diagram suggests that it is difficult and perhaps impossible to move laterally across the schematic drawing, even though conceptual articulation is pictured as reaching a high level of importance in a prenational phase, when ideological manifestation is relatively unimportant.

The fourth reservation also relates to the prenational phase, which is of secondary importance to the present inquiry. The scope of the perceptual world is growing during the nation-building process. The conceptual skill of an individual in the prenational phase may involve only those skills needed to live in a restricted environment, i.e., a social unit that is something less than a nation. It may even be doubtful if manifest ideology should be pictured as originating as early as the cognitive component of the diagram. The more important point, however, is that there is a secular effect through time as the citizens who assert some ideological convictions apply their attitudes to a wider scope of activity. The secular effect cannot be drawn easily, but it helps to explain why cognitive skills, consciously or unconsciously applied, from

[4] Perhaps the most persuasive evidence on this point is the decreasing commitment to extreme or rigid positions as one reaches higher levels of political leadership. See, for example, Samuel A. Stouffer, *Communism, Conformity and Civil Liberties*, Gloucester, Peter Smith, 1953.

[5] On the whole, the political scientist has neglected the role of national values in building national solidarity, though it has often been assumed that identification with the country tends to be constructive. The book argues, of course, that it may be either, depending on the orientation of the system and the complexity of the the behaviors being related to governing values. See, for example, Leonard W. Doob, *Patriotism and Nationalism: Their Psychological Foundations*, New Haven, Yale University Press, 1964; Murray Edelman, *The Symbolic Uses of Politics*, Urbana, University of Illinois Press, 1964; and David E. Apter, "Political Religion in the New Nations," in Geertz, ed., *Old Societies and New States*, Glencoe, Free Press, 1963, pp. 57-104.

the early phase are difficult to transfer directly, i.e., laterally, to the postnational phase.[6] Likewise, it also helps to explain why the rise in significance of manifest ideology in the perception of national affairs plays what may be a critical part in getting the individual to widen the scope of his perceptual world. Put very simply, attitudinal structure in the early prenational phase and in later national phases may be very similar, but this does not enable the individual to move suddenly from a tribal life to national participation.

The independent variable in the diagram is the creation of a more intricate society, generally referred to as the developmental process.[7] The major concern is the changing structural interdependence of cognitive articulation and manifest ideology as societies become more complex. The national phase is most important, and the rise in manifest ideology is suggested by the fervor of nationalist activity commonly observed throughout Africa and Asia. In this period the citizen is still operating with conceptual tools that may be adequate to his immediate needs, but that are initially quite unrelated to the existence of the nation. There are certainly qualitative changes in cognitive articulation alone as the society becomes more complex, but the most important point is that the citizen vis-à-vis the national framework of activity starts out with very little notion of how his conceptual tools relate to the existence of the country.

Political science has generally been concerned with only one component of attitudinal organization in this period, the highly emotional form of national identification. Because of our singular notion of how values relate to behavior, we have failed to note that highly emotional behavior is indeed a function of the way in which the new citizen goes about his daily tasks. The political scientist's prescription then becomes, "Be less emotional!" with little appreciation that it is the tenuous affective identity that holds the new country together and with even less

[6] Recent studies on the emergence of civic sensitivities touch on this point. See, for example, Reinhard Bendix, *Nation-Building and Citizenship*, New York, Wiley, 1964, and also the suggestive work of F. G. Bailey, *Politics and Social Change: Orissa in 1959*, Berkeley, University of California Press, 1963.

[7] Because of the level of generalization given priority in the study, i.e., the individual, attention has not been focused on how the independent variable might be fixed in order to perform cross-cultural studies. Certainly initial attempts of this kind would have to rely on the conventional demographic indicators as most inquiries up to now have done. See, for example, Almond and Coleman, *The Politics of the Developing Areas*, op.cit., pp. 532-576; Phillips Cutwright, "National Political Development," *American Sociological Review*, vol. 28, 1963, pp. 253-264; and Theodore Caplow and Kurt Finsterbusch, *A Matrix of Modernization*, mimeo., Columbia University, Bureau of Applied Social Research, 1964. The major shortcoming of all these attempts is that they unavoidably conceal structural change by their dependence on distributive variables. See S. F. Nadel's treatment of the ascriptive-achievement distinction in *Theory of Social Structure*, London, Cohen and West, 1957.

appreciation of the crucial role of values in the individual's perception. We are, in effect, asking the new citizen to destroy himself so that he may then be just like us. Even if such transformation were possible, it remains highly egocentric. Development consists of bringing cognitive tools into some working relationship with national values or, as noted by Geertz, of fashioning "maps of problematic social reality and matrices for the creation of collective conscience" from ideology.[8] This study has dwelt on the two major forces bringing about such a reconciliation, namely, the proliferation of new activity requiring the citizen to reorganize his immediate perceptual world (Section III) and the government's concern that new forms of political participation conform to the prevailing orientation of the government (Section II). It is not suggested, of course, that development must take this course, and there are in fact a number of pitfalls, alternatives, and escapes.

The three political systems studied were selected because they represented three very different orientations to change, which has been shown to have had direct impact on local reform, while they have also been committed to bringing about major changes in the citizens' environment. The three countries have been deeply concerned with reconciling the elaboration of national values and the relationship of new learning through development. Not every country has followed such a path, and most of the alternatives might be imagined in terms of the suggested model. The many obstacles to making some reconciliation of enhanced cognitive skill and national values open the very tempting alternative to make the gap wider by intensifying national fervor, thereby increasing the disparity by making minimal cognitive skills more inadequate to the perceived tasks of the nation, as outlined in Chapter x. Another possibility is to try to isolate growing cognitive capacities from the political process, though this is clearly only a stopgap alternative and one risking major upheavals as the enlightened populace realizes that its activities are indeed disconnected from the political system. The national phase is clearly the one with maximum instability, for the citizen and the government are in fact searching for ways to bring their understanding and values into harmony.

Before relating the model of attitudinal change to the three cases reviewed in this study, it may be helpful to survey the literature relevant to the components portrayed on the diagram. Most of the research on political perception has been done in more advanced nations, so this reservation applies to all the following work. A great deal of energy has gone into the study of authoritarian personality, and most of this research considers the individual's assertion and interpretation of national values. Despite the many controversies surrounding the study of authoritarian personality, fundamental agreements seem to exist on the

[8] *Op.cit.*, p. 654.

extent to which the person holding strong ideological views tends to perceive situations inaccurately and to resist learning about situations involving severe conflict with these values. The heightened importance of ideological manifestation in the emergence of the modern nation is clearly related to this kind of behavior, and there is, indeed, persuasive historical evidence that strongly held nationalist opinions in European nations and the United States contributed to prejudice and other perceptual rigidities.[9]

One of the major criticisms of the early work on authoritarian personality was that the expression of intensely held values might vary greatly with environmental conditions. This is why intensity alone was not considered a sufficient indication of the ideological component on attitudes toward the nation. Unfortunately the effect of this valid and penetrating objection has been to drive psychologists toward observing the effects of intensely held values under more highly controlled conditions, thereby making it even more difficult to generalize from their work. However, much of this work corroborates the argument being made for the significance of ideological manifestation in attitudinal change. When the individual must learn under situations of stress his efficiency decreases, he tends to respond compulsively, and his ability to recall earlier experience is greatly reduced. Such a person tends to place less value on himself as an agent of change, and tends to be "dependent on external criteria in defining his reality and evaluating his surroundings."[10]

In a more closely related context recent investigations into American political perception suggest the minimal significance attached to national values in political participation. V. O. Key advances the opinion that fundamental political values in modern societies are accepted, rather than agreed upon and purposefully manipulated.[11] This notion has been studied with imagination by McClosky, whose findings indicate that "a democratic society can survive despite widespread popular misunderstanding and disagreement about basic democratic and constitutional values."[12] Another study into the perception of political values in the United States also demonstrated how easily Americans express ideological agreement, while also advocating very different political policies

---

[9] For a cross-cultural application of the Adorno scales see Bradford B. Hudson et al., eds., *Journal of Social Issues*, vol. 15, no. 3, 1959, where authoritarian tendencies in Egypt and the United States are compared.

[10] Milton J. Rosenberg et al., *Attitude Organization and Change*, New Haven, Yale University Press, 1960, p. 34. See also O. J. Harvey and George D. Beverly, "Some Personality Correlates of Concept Change Through Role Playing," *Journal of Abnormal and Social Psychology*, vol. 63, 1961, pp. 125-130.

[11] "Public Opinion and the Decay of Democracy," *Virginia Quarterly Review*, vol. 37, 1961, pp. 481-494.

[12] "Consensus and Ideology in American Politics," *American Political Science Review*, vol. 58, June 1964, p. 376.

and supporting different issues.[13] Though these investigations tell us little about how the United States arrived at its happy situation, they do provide strong evidence for the argument that citizens of more advanced societies do in fact find many ways of expressing views and interests without raising ideological arguments.

The voting studies also provide some interesting evidence on the role of ideology in the perception of the electoral process in the United States. It is significant, first, that very few Americans occupy what the voting studies have labeled "ideologically pure" situations. Ideology may be used in an expressive manner to relieve tensions and pressures the voter feels during the election, but even this is a relatively rare phenomenon. Most American voters tend to form "ideological proxies" or more pragmatic views through which their ideological convictions are filtered and moderated. From a behavioral standpoint it is also important to note that those voters who take the purer ideological positions in assessing the election are least likely to vote, i.e., they inhibit their own capacity to act in an institutional context. Removed as these investigations are from the developing country, they provide some of the best evidence available on the way in which the citizen of the more advanced nation creates conceptual tools and generalizations in order to make his political act meaningful and effective.[14]

Another rich source of data is the Almond-Verba study of political attitudes in five democracies. Their "systems affect" is analogous to ideological manifestation in the proposed scheme, although they derived their affective attitudinal dimension from aggregate data. For this reason it is not possible for them to estimate how much the individual relies on national values, which may vary greatly among persons indicating the same degree of pride in the nation. For reasons that are not entirely clear, the study also overlooks the possibility of a construct that might be called "systems cognition," i.e., the extent to which perception of national politics assists organizing and interrelating the individual's cognitive skills. If the participant society is indeed a blend of affective and cognitive elements shaped by the political system, it is important that we generate (or borrow from psychologists) concepts that enable us to describe how the elements interact. However, the research design does demonstrate how perception of various levels of political participation may vary from nation to nation, and includes crude cognitive indicators as well as affective indicators. The fact that countries do place different emphases on these attitudinal dimensions suggests the

[13] J. M. Prothro and C. M. Grigg, "Fundamental Principles of Democratic Bases of Agreement and Disagreement," *Journal of Politics*, vol. 22, 1960, pp. 276-295.
[14] The notion of political efficacy was first introduced in Angus Campbell et al., *The Voter Decides*, New York, Row Peterson, 1954, and is more fully explored in Angus Campbell et al., *The American Voter*, New York, Wiley, 1960. See particularly ch. 9.

complexity of political behavior in the advanced nations, which we have often assumed simply does not exist in the less advanced nation.

In order to measure political cognition Almond and Verba relied heavily on indices derived from direct contact with officials and the respondent's information about government. For this reason their cognitive dimension falls short of demonstrating how individuals may use this information or contact to order their lives more generally. This limitation was imposed largely because of the aggregate nature of the analysis, which precluded individual analysis. The cognitive-articulation dimension suggested above would involve possessing information and establishing contact, but it is important to go a step farther and show how the citizen may use this experience in organizing his perceptual world. For example, the extremely high national pride of the Mexican discloses a condition pictured in the national phase of the diagram on the affective dimension, but the material on the Mexican's understanding of government, interesting as it is in revealing possible perceptual discontinuities, does not enable the analysis to specify how these cognitive qualities may be determined or influenced by the affective component.

Perhaps the most important work seeking to overcome this problem has been done by Himmelstrand, who set out to show that less overt concern with ideology did not necessarily mean that a people were not influenced by ideology in organizing their thoughts about government.[15] His analysis of the salience of ideology is analogous to the cognitive-articulation component on the above diagram. In showing how general values provide latent structure for political attitudes in Sweden, Himmelstrand concluded that the feeble manifestation of ideological difference in Swedish politics was indeed misleading. In his words, Sweden represents a case of "spurious depolitization," where national values still have an important role in orienting the citizen to government despite the fact that they do not become the focus of strong partisan views.

His findings are perhaps the strongest evidence for portraying the postnational phase of attitudes toward development in the form shown. There is, of course, a good deal of prima facie evidence that individual concern with ideology does decline in more advanced societies, but this does not permit the conclusion that such values then become irrelevant to political attitudes. Himmelstrand's further analysis of how ideology structures attitudes provides additional evidence of great importance in describing the transition shown in the scheme. He suggests that the individual still attached to ideology in a literal way will experience more difficulty in finding new goals as immediate aims are accomplished,

[15] *Social Pressures, Attitudes and Democratic Process*, Stockholm, Almquist and Wicksell, 1960. For a shorter presentation see his article, "A Theoretical and Empirical Approach to Depolitisation and Political Involvement," *Acta Sociologica*, vol. 6, fasc. 1-2, 1962, pp. 83-110.

that he will tend to organize his behavior to accomplish only the specified goal with less attention to other goals that might also be achieved, and that the direct form of gratification derived from such a commitment will tend to diminish over time, leaving the citizen detached and disorganized for the given area of endeavor. The more instrumentally oriented individual, i.e., the one possessing more elaborate attitudes toward the problem, tends to find "goals being established over and over again on the basis of previous attainments since the barriers met and the errors and the discoveries made in the flow of instrumental action usually present new problems projecting the goals of action further into the future."[16]

Though directed toward a very different problem, Shuval's study of assimilation in Israel also deals with the acquisition of new values about the society in terms of the "narrowness or broadness" of the recipient's cognitive organization.[17] In writing about the changing significance of mass media in developing countries, Pool also notes the need for "internal change in the latent structure of attitudes that would produce self-sustaining movement toward modernization."[18] Thus there is a large body of writing that suggests the less immediate role of ideology as people become involved in more complex patterns of behavior. This is not to say that ideology is less important, but only that national values become less controversial by in fact being elaborated to deal with the multiplicity of problems to be found in an intricate society. Cognitive articulation enables the individual to live in a world where symbolic certainty becomes less important than articulated views enabling him to weigh alternatives, accept calculated risk, and postpone immediate gratification.

The structural change in attitude organization depicted in the diagram has immediate relevance to the developmental process. The nations of Africa and Asia are asking their citizens to perform a wide variety of actions, described in Section III, that must be reconciled and organized through individual perception. They are at the same time also faced with the problem of how national values will be translated into a form permitting the citizen to see how his national identity may indeed affect the way he lives, described in Section II. Neither of the forces

---

[16] *Social Pressures . . . , op.cit.*, p. 51. Almost exactly the same terms are used by O. J. Harvey, David E. Hunt, and Harold M. Schroder, *Conceptual Organization and Personality*, New York, Wiley, 1961, in discussing the differences between highly literal, concrete forms of conceptualization and more abstract forms. Moreover, their conclusions on personality are very similar to Himmelstrand's observations.

[17] "The Role of Ideology as a Predisposing Frame of Reference for Immigrants," *Human Relations*, vol. 12, 1959, p. 53. See also her later book, *Immigrants on the Threshold*, New York, Atherton, 1963.

[18] "The Mass Media and Politics in the Modernization Process," in Pye, ed., *Communications and Political Development*, Princeton, Princeton University Press, 1963, p. 249.

impinging on political perception are located wholly in the developmental process or in local-government reform, which was used largely because it is a revealing example of how governments react to the challenge of elaborating the meaning of newly acquired national values. However, it has been argued that in the early part of the national phase governments may determine the extent to which attitudinal reorganization may be encouraged, and that their affective or cognitive orientations will provide some clues as to how successful they may be in creating attitudes more appropriate to rapid, sustained development. This question may be clarified by reviewing the experience of the three political systems in terms of the attitudinal-change model.

The following diagram places the three countries on the diagram of attitudinal change in the approximate positions suggested by the materials assembled in the study. Obviously a more precise location could only be found after careful interviewing and more research of an attitudinal nature. The vast majority of the Pakistani peasants and farmers still see little relationship between life in their village and the nation. As has been suggested several times before, the violence and instability of political life in Pakistan can be explained by the great disparity between individual understanding and the perception of national values. Comparable disparity continues in the Moroccan case, but her developmental advancement suggests that cognitive articulation has begun to take place and the diversity of political life has opened up many opportunities to bring individual capacities and national values into a more active relationship. Morocco is in a very real sense at an attitudinal turning point in her development. Tunisia represents a slightly more advanced case, where individual understanding of the political process

Diagram-2: Attitudinal Structure in Morocco, Tunisia, and Pakistan

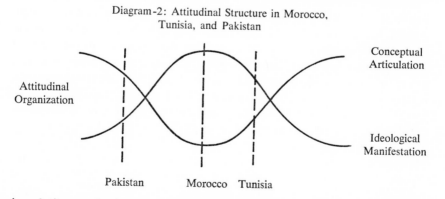

in relation to the locality and of developmental questions has probably advanced beyond the other two countries. There have been several attempts to reformulate national values in a form that is harmonious with the growing complexity of Tunisian society.

One of the most misleading assumptions in the study of political participation in developing countries has been the assumption that the act of achieving independence creates a new framework for relating the citizen to government. The attitudinal model makes no such assumptions. An individual may hold attitudes defined as prenational on the ideal model given in Diagram 2, but the country may have achieved independence, however ambiguous such an achievement might be in political life. Clearly this is a factor over which political scientists have little control, and they should not be expected to provide rationalizations for the institutional and perceptual shortcomings of trying to erect a national framework before a populace is, in this limited sense, ready for independence.

Pakistan would appear to be such a case. The unreality of the highly cognitive orientation of the military-bureaucratic alliance may be underscored by noting how the Basic Democracies scheme calls for the kind of conceptual skill that has generally emerged only after a country has effectively linked its ideology to a more intricate social structure. On this score the efforts of the Ayub regime have been sorely deficient, and their inadequacy can be partially explained by their apparent assumption that learning capacities operate independently from governing values in political life and in many other endeavors. The structural similarity of the late prenational and early postnational phases of attitudinal structuring are clear in the diagram, but it is doubtful if a society can leapfrog from one situation to the other. However distasteful it may be to the regime, the heightened importance placed on ideology in contemporary Pakistan is part of the attitudinal-change process and gives the new citizen a new set of values relating to the nation.

The professional orientation of the Ayub government has made it extremely insensitive to this point, although the situation is complicated greatly by the tendency of Islamic fundamentalism to impinge itself on national values and thereby create uncertainty over the meaning of a new national identity. The most persuasive evidence of the Ayub regime's inadequacy has been its inability to stimulate strong feelings of loyalty comparable to those generated by the competing political forces. The Basic Democracies experiment and the variety of intensive development efforts in the past five years have been a calculated risk. The detachment of the Pakistani peasant, deceptively comparable to the detachment of the citizen in a complex society, might be unchanged during the transformation of cognitive components of individual perception of political life. This is what has made the Pakistani experiment, and comparable efforts to mobilize dormant populations in other parts of the world, such fascinating experiments. They are more intelligible to the Western observer because this is in fact how we change our own society. Such a notion, of course, is not likely to appeal to leaders who have broken away from their European heritage as definitively for example, as, Nasser or Sukarno.

The critical role of government is basically the extent to which the political orientation of government determines how ideological manifestation will occur. Ayub is one of the few examples of national leaders choosing not to manipulate the ideological component, although this position has been modified as political competition is revived and as Pakistan seeks to establish its identity in foreign affairs. The moves to establish relations with Communist China, et cetera, can be regarded as indications of Pakistan's return to the basic model of attitudinal change wherein ideological manifestation takes on more importance, while the new behavior generated by development is simultaneously, rather than independently, intertwined with new values about national political life. The model would also suggest that Pakistan is only entering the period of maximum instability insofar as individual difficulty in reconciling values and behavior has only begun. Few experts on Pakistan would disagree with the view that the past two decades of political experimentation have been so divorced from real, i.e., behavioral, change at the local level that it is difficult to regard this period as anything but the preliminary efforts to establish working relations among a small, essentially modern group.

As the diagram suggests, Morocco is at a turning point in devising new formulas for political participation. The peasant has been propelled farther into the developmental process than is the case in Pakistan, largely because the monarchy has served as an institutional focus for traditional political values—a highly useful device for political communication denied to Pakistan. The prevailing Islamic nature of the Moroccan political system has, therefore, given the country a vehicle for relating traditional and modern values. The way by which such institutions may operate to give new meaning to ideological manifestation has been noted many times before, but much less attention has been given to the way in which the transferal relates to the individual's perception of political life and his cognitive skill in working in a rapidly changing environment.[19]

For purposes of the present inquiry, no distinction has been made between countries having a high degree of ideological manifestation under different kinds of institutions, though some implications might be drawn from the Tunisian case. Egypt, Indonesia, Ghana, and Guinea are

---

[19] A revealing empirical study of how great the discontinuity between perceived problems and their solutions can become, in Patricia L. Kendall's "The Ambivalent Character of Nationalism among Egyptian Professionals," *Public Opinion Quarterly*, vol. 20, no. 1, Spring 1956, pp. 277-292. The author has tried to relate these and similar problems to development in the Middle East in "Nationalism and Nation-Building in the Muslim World," *Middle East Journal*, vol. 18, no. 4, Autumn 1964, pp. 421-430.

all cases where similar ideological emphasis has been achieved while rejecting traditional institutions, and it is as yet by no means clear which type of institution will accomplish the transition to new attitudinal forms with more success. There are some indications, however, that the traditional vehicle meets certain kinds of obstacles as it seeks to elicit more informed, active opinion in political life and in the developmental process, precisely because affective attachments are more easily manipulated. Despite this institutional advantage, the injection of emotional appeal that seems to be part of the nation-building process is not radically different in traditional and so-called secular systems for purposes of assessing the nature of participation.

For purposes of comparing change in attitudinal structure the traditional society is a special case rather than a unique situation. The great confusion introduced into the analysis of political development by the charisma concept recommends this solution.[20] Personalized legitimacy is only an extreme form of legitimacy that exists to some extent in every new nation. Hassan II has, therefore, a special advantage in manipulating affective attachments to political life, but he exercises it only at the risk of diminishing his personal power. The obvious implication is not so important as the less obvious one that, by seeking to enhance the citizen's cognitive capacities in isolation from national values, the monarchy takes on great risk that the entire developmental process will be distorted and limited. Like all political leaders he can undermine himself unintentionally as well as intentionally. In any event, the psychological evidence is overwhelming that attitudinal change involves forming more abstract concepts to deal with more complex problems, and that affective components are to some extent farther removed, though no less "essential."

There may, however, be very different kinds of opportunities to introduce cognitive skills into participation in the traditional and secular political systems achieving ideological awareness in their people. The conventional form of this observation has been simply that a traditional institution cannot aggressively modernize without losing its legitimacy, but the same applies to the secular regime prepared to moderate and blend its ideology with the increased capacities of its people. The dismantling of the secular regime is simply not so easy to follow, though the refusal of such a regime to introduce new attitudinal components in the perception of politics—in the case of Indonesia, for example—is every bit as obvious as the reluctance of the Iranian or Moroccan monarch. Attitudinally these cases are all very similar and represent essentially a

[20] The most careful examination of the psychological and social implications of charisma has been conducted by Edward A. Shils, "The Concentration and Dispersion of Charisma," *World Politics*, vol. 9, October 1958, pp. 1-19, where the individual's readiness to believe in his own capacity is distinguished.

country where new values (or old values transferred) are widespread in popular perception of the governing process.

The tendency of the Moroccan monarch has been to ignore opportunities to build on the important step already taken toward forming a vigorous nation. As has been noted in Chapter XI, the intermediate organizations for political articulation have found their role in government diminishing steadily. The planning process has failed to take effective form and the organization of services directly affecting citizens leaves much to be desired. The rural-commune program had encouraging beginnings, but has not received coordinated support from other agencies of government and was quite effectively discredited at a crucial stage of its development by the flagrant manipulation of elections in 1963. Morocco may be approaching another kind of crisis in participation, pictured by the rising importance of cognitive articulation in attitudinal change in the diagram, and already experienced to some degree in Tunisia.

The schematic drawing does not suggest how long a country may take in any particular phase, but it does indicate that higher levels of developmental activity depend on the citizen's capacity to manipulate his environment and to exercise initiative to some degree. Research does not permit any neat pin-pointing of when a country may lose developmental opportunities failing to give the participant conceptual tools to operate in larger, more complex frameworks. However, some of the clinical material cited earlier in the chapter suggest the kind of crisis Morocco and other countries at comparable stages might experience. The complex patterns of behavior being encouraged need some kind of organization in the mind of the performer. A good many of the developmental efforts undertaken by the Moroccan government, described in Section III, have begun with exaggerated hopes and ended with disappointing results. Both these reactions to the developmental challenge suggest that values and skills are poorly related in Moroccan political life, and, in turn, ways to bring about some reconciliation in the mind of the citizen are not being encouraged.

For those interested in the dynamics of development, Tunisia may be the most intriguing case. While the personal attractiveness of the president should not be discarded as a device to elicit political support in the charismatic form, there are many indications that Tunisians are acquiring considerable sophistication about the political and social development of their country. On the one hand, the emotional appeal of the Socialist Destour has been relied on less and less, while the party has also made some specific organizational adjustments to local interests. In the 1964 party congress party doctrine was further refined, and has become virtually synonymous with the government's serious effort to rebuild the nation. Political controversy in Tunisia has shifted away from the sheer assertion of patriotic fervor and become a dialogue over the best ways to achieve the social revolution. For these reasons Tunisia has been portrayed in a position bordering on the postnational phase of attitudinal structuring.

How this has been achieved is less important than the opportunities it offered for the future. However, much of the material in Section III underscores the experimental and determined approach of the Tunisian government. The Bizerte incident might even be thought of as a relapse to prenational forms of building attitudes toward development, and one which many Tunisians would agree hurt the developmental process in their country. The overt and direct manifestation of ideology has gradually lost its overriding significance in the formation of Tunisian views, while various unusually effective programs to build individual understanding have begun to take hold. The comparison with Morocco and Pakistan is instructive. It is difficult to imagine any combination of forces building on grass-roots support in Pakistan in order to form a workable government to replace Ayub, and the chances of an effective government emerging in Morocco under less direct supervision of the monarch are doubtful. In Tunisia the orderly transfer of governmental authority seems possible, and it may be that Bourguiba's disinterest in the details of economic and social reform, for which he has sometimes apologized, has encouraged the formation of institutions capable of standing alone.

The Tunisian case illustrates another aspect of the developmental process, which provided some of the inspiration for focusing on attitudinal change. In the national phase it is difficult to use institutions to build participation and involvement precisely because individual understanding of the political process and the intricacies of development are rigidly associated with national values, i.e., there is a high degree of ideological manifestation. As cognitive skills multiply in the developmental process, institutions acquire individual meaning much more easily and hence can be used to channel particular forms of participation. Attempts to trace patterns of institutionalization through the entire development process have suffered from the assumption that the individual was perceiving or should perceive institutions in the same way throughout the process.

Though yet to be well established, the evidence gathered here suggests that capacity to institutionalize is heavily dependent on the kind of attitudinal structures that characterize the population. Tunisia is distinguished by the readiness of the government to build new kinds of understanding in many fields of endeavor tied to development, with one important exception. The one-party system experiences difficulty in applying these skills to political life, as has been suggested in Section II by the minor role given to local government. There remains a single framework for regulation and reconciling political relationships, sustained, in party, by the dual role of most high officials at the center and the minor role given to less easily supervised agencies of potential political importance at lower levels. Thus as development advances, the single party finds its capacity to use all kinds of institutions to encourage change enhanced, except for political institutions. The crisis of transforming political institutions remains in Tunisia and is much more complex than simply finding another president of Bourguiba's stature.

To see how a country embarks on the formation of more flexible attitudes, attention must return to the Moroccan case, and what is perhaps the central policy concern of this study. Learning about the environment and the acquisition of new conceptual tools is determined largely by the capacity of the government to immerse citizens in new kinds of behavior. The developmental process represents the tide of new experience engulfing the village, and the many ways by which this is occurring were sketched in Section III. For this reason government becomes the independent variable in the developmental process. The peasant cannot transform his perceptual world in isolation, and in very few instances will he be allowed to preserve his isolation. How this world is shattered will be determined largely by the impersonal and determined needs of the developmental process, which takes very similar form from one country to another. The extent to which the social and psychological upheaval can be restructured by the individual citizen, however, will depend most heavily on the capacity of the political system to restructure the individual attitudes with a new balance of cognitive and affective elements.

Thus the primacy of politics in the developmental process, which has become more widely acknowledged in the past decade, does not depend simply on the material monopoly of resources and skills of the new government. Material wealth is a necessary but not a sufficient condition for development. As has been shown in Section III, the basic needs are very similar for all three political systems, even though the effectiveness and imagination in applying resources vary from country to country. But involvement in a more complex world cannot be separated from the formation of new attitudinal structures about many facets of national life. It is in this respect that political systems meet their most severe tests, and reveal significant differences in the articulation of conceptual skill, illustrated in the response to local reform given in Section II.

If there are any altruistic designs in this study, they simply are to demonstrate that each nation must determine its own destiny. There is no ideal mix of attitudinal components, but one which must be found, given the stage of development and the readiness of the government to elicit new forms of participation. Second, there is no comfort to be taken in watching a developing country stand still, for this most likely means that it is moving backward in the process of forming new outlooks on political and social affairs. Third, and contrary to many popular notions about political life in both advanced and less advanced nations, national virtue does not evaporate when citizens learn more complex ways of adapting to their environment. National identity is clearly an important step toward building a new nation, but an identity which transfixes the believer will not enable him to live in a world of choice and uncertainty. Development means making uncertainty a manageable quantity, and the most creative acts of the new nations will be forging new ways for man to deal with this most central of human problems.

BIBLIOGRAPHY

NEWSPAPERS

Afrique Action
Al-Istiqlal
Dawn
Jeune Afrique
New York Times
Pakistan Jumhuriat
Pakistan Times (Lahore)
Petit-Matin
La Vie Economique

OFFICIAL DOCUMENTS

KINGDOM OF MOROCCO

Bureau of Communal Affairs, Office of the Governor, Fez, 1962. "List des travaux inscrits aux budgets primitifs et additionnels 1961 des communes rurales de la province de Fes" (mimeo).

Conseil Supérieur du Plan. *Exposé de M. Bouabid, Vice Président du Conseil* (mimeo.). Rabat, November 23, 1959.

Division de la Coordination Economique et du Plan, Service Central des Statistiques. *La Situation Economique du Maroc en 1961.* 1961.

Division of Economic Coordination and Planning, Ministry of the National Economy and Finance. *Compte Rendu des Déliberations du Conseil Supérieur de Plan* (mimeo.). Rabat, August 1-5, 1960, p. 19.

————. *Plan Biennal d'Equipment, 1958-1959.* Rabat, 1958.

————. *Plan Quinquennal, 1960-1964.* Rabat, 1960.

————. *Tableaux Economiques du Maroc 1915-1959.* Rabat, 1960.

Division of Economic Coordination and the Plan, Ministry of the National Economy. *L'Evolution Economique du Maroc dans le Cadre du Deuxième Plan Quadriennal (1954-1957).* Rabat, 1958.

Journal Officiel, 1956-1964.

Ministry of Agriculture. *Memo Pratique de l'Economie Agricole Marocaine.* 1960.

Ministry of Finance. *Elements d'Information: Finances Publique 1949-1959.* Rabat, 1961.

Ministry of Foreign Affairs. *Livre Blanc sur la Mauritanie.* Rabat, 1960.

Ministry of the Interior. *Décision de ministre portant délegation de pouvoirs au profite des Governeurs des Provinces* (mimeo.). September 12, 1960.

Ministry of Labor. *Le Maroc au Travail.* 1958.

BIBLIOGRAPHY

Ministry of National Education. *Note sur l'Education Nationale* (mimeo.). June 22, 1961.

Office de la Promotion Nationale. *Bute et Bilan.* 1962.

————. *Impératifs et Moyens.* 1962.

————. *Problèmes et Perspectives.* 1962.

————. *La Promotion Nationale au Maroc.* n.d. (1963?).

Office National d'Irrigation, Bureau de Récherche Générale. *Les Structures Agraires dans le Tadla.* 1961.

Office National des Irrigations, Bureau de Récherche Générale, Direction des Etudes Generals. *Les Structures Agraires dans la Base-Moulouya.* 1961.

————. *Les Structures Agraires dans le Rharb.* 1961.

————. *Les Structures Agraires dans le Tadla.* 1961.

Superior Council for National Promotion. *Summary Report* (mimeo.). October 20, 1961.

————. *Synthèse de l'examen des programmes provincials de Promotion Nationale* (mimeo.). January 5, 1962.

REPUBLIC OF PAKISTAN

Government of Bengal. *Report of the Bengal Administration Enquiry Committee, 1944-45.* Alipore, Government Printing Office, 1945.

Government of East Bengal, Department of Health and Local Self-Government. *Rules for Direct Election to District Boards.* Dacca, 1951.

Government of East Bengal, Home Department. *Election Manual.* vol. I, Rules, and vol. II, Appendixes. Dacca, 1953.

Government of East Pakistan, Department for Basic Democracies and Local Government. *Five Year Financial Plan for Basic Democracies* (mimeo.). September 28, 1961.

————. *Report on Activities and Achievements of Basic Democracies.* Monthly Reports, 1961-1962.

————. *Scheme for Supervisory Staffs for Basic Democracies and Provincial Advisory Councils* (mimeo.). September 28, 1961.

————. *Works Programme through Basic Democracies.* No. IV/NDO-39/62/1213 (180). September 25, 1962.

————. *Works Programme through Basic Democracies, 1962-63.*

Government of East Pakistan, Department of Health, Social Welfare and Local Government. *Annual Report on Basic Democracies in East Pakistan.* 1960.

Government of East Pakistan, Director of Public Relations. *Land Reforms in East Pakistan.* n.d.

Government of Pakistan. *The First Five Year Plan (1955-60).* Karachi, 1956.

————. *Noorani's Compilation of the Muslim Family Laws Ordi-*

nance (and Two Allied Acts). Karachi, Pakistan Publications, 1961.

―――. "Relationship between the Provincial Government and Local Bodies," *Local Government Reforms Committee Report*. vol. 2. Lahore, 1952.

―――. "Reorganization of the Structure of Local Government," *Local Government Reforms Committee Report*. vol. 1. Lahore, 1952.

―――. *A Report in Agricultural Extension Work in the U.S.A. and Reorganization of Extension Service in Pakistan* (Sufi Report). Karachi, Government of Pakistan Press, 1952.

―――. *Report of the Constitution Commission*. Karachi, Government of Pakistan Press, 1961.

―――. *Report of the Court of Inquiry Constituted under Punjab Act II of 1954 to Enquire into the Punjab Disturbances of 1953*. Lahore, 1954.

―――. *Report of the Food and Agriculture Commission*. Karachi, 1960.

―――. *Report of the Provincial Reorganization Committee*. Part I. (West Pakistan) Lahore, December 1961.

―――. *Report of the Provincial Reorganization Committee*. Part II. (East Pakistan) Dacca, April 1962.

―――. *Village Aid—Five Year Plan*, Karachi, 1956.

―――. *Village Aid—Some Articles and Reports*, Lahore, 1960.

Government of Pakistan, Bureau of National Reconstruction and Pakistan Academy for Village Development (Comilla). *An Analysis of the Working of Basic Democracy Institutions in East Pakistan*. Dacca, 1961.

Government of Pakistan, Local Government Reform Committee. *First Interim Report*. Lahore, Government of Pakistan, 1951.

Government of Pakistan, Ministry of Education. *Report of the Commission on National Education*. Karachi, 1959.

―――. *Report of the Commission on National Education*. 1959.

Government of Pakistan, Ministry of Finance. *Report of the Credit Enquiry Commission*. Karachi, 1959.

Government of Pakistan, Ministry of Health and Social Welfare. *Report on the Conference on Training for Basic Democracies*. Dacca, November 21-23, 1959.

Government of Pakistan, Ministry of Home and Kashmir Affairs, Office of the Census Commissioner. *Population Census of Pakistan 1961*. Karachi, 1962.

Government of Pakistan, Ministry of National Reconstruction and Information. *Scope and Function of Basic Democracies and their Contribution to Development*. 1961.

―――. *Annual Report on Basic Democracies, October 1959-October 1960*. 1960.

BIBLIOGRAPHY

Government of Pakistan, Planning Commission. *Memorandum on the United Surplus Agricultural Commodities Aid to Pakistan.* February 1961.

———. *The Second Five Year Plan (1960-65).* Karachi, 1960.

———. *Use of Resources Provided by Expanded P.L. 480 Aid.* June 1961.

Government of Pakistan, President's Secretariat. *Decisions of the Cabinet on the Report of the Provincial Administration Commission June 23, 1960.* Karachi, 1962.

Government of Pakistan, Program Analysis Unit, National Development Organization. *Evaluation Report: Chichawatni Development Area, Montgomery District, West Pakistan.* 1961.

———. *Evaluation Report: Tangail Development Area, Mymensingh District, East Pakistan.* 1961.

Government of West Pakistan. *Report of the Land Reforms Commission for West Pakistan.* Lahore, 1961.

———. *The West Pakistan Basic Democracies Election Report, 1959-1960.* Lahore, 1960.

REPUBLIC OF TUNISIA

Convention sur la Situation des Personnes et Convention entre la France et la Tunisie. Paris, 1955.

Direction Générale de l'Intérieur. *Monographie des Services.* Tunis, 1931.

Journal Officiel, 1956-1964.

Office de l'Enfida. *La Mise en Valeur de l'Enfida et ses Goulots d'Etranglement.* 1961.

Office de Mise en Valeur de la Vallée Medjerda. *Medjerda 1960.* 1960.

Régime des Retraites Civiles et Militaires. Tunis, 1959.

Secretary of State for Agriculture. *Les Centres de Formation Professionelle Agricole.* Tunis, n.d.

———. *Collège Secondaire d'Agriculture.* Tunis, n.d.

———. *Terre de Tunisie Indépendant.* Tunis, 1958.

———. *Textes Legislatifs et Circulaires Concernant le Service des Affaires Foncières* (Commentary by Hervé Sicard). 1960.

Secretary of State for Cultural Affairs and Information. *Les Chantiers de Travail.* Tunis, 1962.

Secretary of State for Information. *Le Conseil National du Plan.* Tunis n.d. (1958?).

Secretary of State for the Interior. *Loi Municipale* (2d edn.) Tunis, 1960.

Secretary of State for National Education. *Nouvelle Conception de l'Enseignment Tunisien.* Tunis, 1958.

————. *Perspectives Décennales de Développement*. 1962.

————. *Situation Scolaire: Trois Premières Années de l'Application du Plan Décennal de Scolarisation*. June 1961.

————. *A Ten Year Prospect of School Attendance*. 1958.

Secretary of State for Planning and Finance. *Perspectives Décennales de Développement 1962-1971*. Tunis, 1962.

————. *Plan Triennal, 1962-64*. Tunis, 1961.

Service des Statistiques. *Annuaire Statistique de la Tunisie*. 11ᵉᵐᵉ vol. Tunis, 1959.

————. *Recensement Général de la Population de la Tunisie (Répartition Géographique de la Population)*. Tunis, 1956.

Services des Statistiques, Secretary of State for Planning and Finance. *Structure Agricole en Cap-Bon en 1956*. March 1961.

Société d'Etudes et de Réalisations Economiques et Sociales en Agriculture (S.E.R.E.S.A.). *Le Crédit Agricole en Tunisie*. Tunis, Secretary of State for Agriculture, 1958.

————. *Région 08—Steppe Ouest-Gafsa*. Tunis, Secretary of State for Agriculture, 1960.

————. *Région 08-Sahel de Sousse*. Tunis, Secretary of State for Agriculture, 1960.

Statute Générale des Fonctionnaires. Tunis, 1959.

BOOKS

GENERAL

Abueva, Jose V. *Focus on the Barrio*. Manila, Institute of Public Administration, University of the Philippines, 1959.

Adorno, T. W., Frankel-Brunswick, Else, Levinson, Daniel J., and Sanford, R. Nevitt. *The Authoritarian Personality*. New York, Harper, 1950.

Allen, H. B. *Rural Reconstruction in Action*. Ithaca, Cornell University Press, 1953.

Almond, Gabriel A., and Coleman, James S., eds. *The Politics of the Developing Areas*. Princeton, Princeton University Press, 1960.

Almond, Gabriel A., and Verba, Sidney. *The Civic Culture: Political Attitudes and Democracy in Five Nations*. Princeton, Princeton University Press, 1963.

Appleby, Paul H. *Public Administration for a Welfare State*. London, London Asia Publishing House, 1961.

Ardant, Gabriel. *Le Monde en Friche*. Paris, Presses Universitaires de France, 1959.

Ashford, Douglas E. *The Elusiveness of Power: The African Single Party State*. Ithaca, Center of International Studies, 1965.

————. *The Politics of Planning in Morocco and Tunisia*. Syracuse, Syracuse University Press, 1965.

————. *Second and Third Generation Leaders in North Africa*. Washington, Department of State, 1963.

Association of Voluntary Agencies for Rural Development. *Panchayat Raj as the Basis of Indian Polity* New Delhi, 1962.

Austruy, Jacques. *Islam en Face au Développement Economique*. Paris, Les Editions Ouvrières, 1961.

————. *Structure économique et civilisation*: *l'Egypte et le destin économique de l'Islam*. Paris, Société des Etudes de Développement Economique et Sociale, 1960.

Baden-Powell, B. H. *Origin and Growth of Village Communities in India*. New York, Scribner, 1899.

Bailey, Frederick G. *Politics and Social Change: Orissa in 1959*. Berkeley, University of California Press, 1963.

Banfield, Edward C. *The Moral Basis of a Backward Society*. Glencoe, Free Press, 1958.

Batten, T. R. *Communities and their Development*. London, Oxford University Press, 1957.

Benham, Frederic. *Economic Aid to Underdeveloped Countries*. New York, Oxford University Press, 1961.

Bennabi, Malik. *Vocation de l'Islam*. Paris, Edition du Seuil, 1954.

Bennis, Warren G., Benne, Kenneth D., Chin, Robert. *The Planning of Change*. New York, Holt, Rinehart & Winston, 1961.

Berque, Jacques. *Etudes d'histoire rurale maghrebine*. Tangier-Fes, Editions Internationales, 1938.

————. *Structure sociales du Haut-Atlas*. Paris, Presses Universitaires de France, 1955.

Billerbeck, Klaus (Jean Bollkämper, trans.). *Mobilization of Manpower Potential in Africa and Asia*. Hamburg, Hamburg Archives of World Economy, 1961.

Black, Eugene R. *The Diplomacy of Economic Development*. Cambridge, Harvard University Press, 1960.

Black, Max, ed. *The Social Thought of Talcott Parsons*. New York, Prentice Hall, 1961.

Bosquet, G. H. *L'Islam Maghrebin*: *Introduction à l'étude générale de l'Islam*. Alger, La Maison des Livres, 1944.

Bracey, H. E. *English Rural Life: Village Activities, Organizations and Institutions*. London, Routledge and Kegan Paul, 1959.

Brehm, Jack W. *Explorations in Cognitive Dissonance*. New York, Wiley, 1962.

Bruner, Jerome S., Goodnow, Jacqueline J., and Austin, George A. *A Study of Thinking*. New York, Wiley, 1956.

BIBLIOGRAPHY

Bruner, Jerome S., and White, Robert M. *Opinions and Personality*. New York, Wiley, 1956.

Campbell, Angus, et al. *The American Voter*. New York, Wiley, 1960.

Cantril, Hadley, and Buchanan, William. *How Nations See Each Other*. Urbana, University of Illinois Press, 1953.

Clairemonte, F. *Economic Liberalism and Underdevelopment: Studies in the Disintegration of an Idea*. London, Asia Publishing House, 1960.

Coombs, Arthur W., and Snygg, Donald. *Individual Behavior: A Perceptual Approach to Behavior* (rev. edn.). New York, Harper, 1959.

Coulton, G. G. *Medieval Village, Manor and Monastery*. New York, Harper, 1960 edn. (first published in 1925).

Dahl, Robert. *Who Governs?* New Haven, Yale University Press, 1963.

Dey, S. K. *Community Development* (rev. edn.). Allahabad, Kitub Mahal, 1962.

——. *Panchayat Raj*. Bombay, Asia Publishing House, 1961.

Dohrenwent, Barbara S. *Some Factors Related to Autonomy and Dependence in Twelve Javanese Villages*. Ithaca, Cornell Modern Indonesia Project, Interim Report Series, 1959.

Drummond, J. G. *Panchayats in India*. London, Oxford University Press, 1937.

Dube, S. C. *India's Changing Villages: Human Factors in Community Development*. London, Routledge-Kegan-Paul, 1958.

Dumont, René. *Terres Vivantes*. Paris, Editions Plon, 1961.

Dumoulin, Roger. *Les Structures Asymétrique de l'Economie Algérienne*. Paris, University of Paris, 1959.

Eckstein, Harry. *A Theory of Stable Democracy*. Princeton, Center of International Studies, 1961.

Eisenstadt, S. N. *The Political Systems of Empires*. New York, Free Press, 1963.

Fazlur, Shah. *Science, Islam & Basic Education*. Dacca, Islamic Academy, 1959.

Festinger, Leon. *A Theory of Cognitive Dissonance*. Evanston, Row Peterson, 1957.

Flory and Miège, eds. *Annuaire de l'Afrique du Nord*. Tome I, 1962. Paris, Centre National de la Recherche Scientifique, 1963.

Food and Agriculture Organization. *Cooperatives and Land Use*. Development Paper No. 61, Rome, 1957.

France, President of the Council, General Commissariat of the Plan, Deuxième Plan de Modernisation et d'Equipment. *Rapport Général de la Commission d'Etude et de Coordination des Plans de Modernisation et d'Equipment de l'Algérie, de la Tunisie et du Maroc*. Maroc, 1954.

Furnivall, J. S. *Progress and Welfare in Southeast Asia.* New York, Institute of Pacific Relations, 1941.

Gadalla, Saad M. *Land Reform in Relation to Social Development, Egypt.* Columbia, University of Missouri Press, 1962.

Galissot, René. *L'economie de l'Afrique du Nord* ("Que-sais-je?" Series). Paris, Presses Universitaires de France, 1962.

Geertz, Clifford, ed. *Old Societies and New States.* New York, Free Press, 1963.

Gibb, H. A. R. *Modern Trends in Islam.* Chicago, University of Chicago Press, 1947.

Girault, Arthur. *Principes de Colonisation et de Législation Coloniale (Afrique du Nord).* Vol. 3. Paris, Recueil Sirey, 1921. Tunisia— pp. 429-462; Morocco—pp. 592-610.

Gordon, David C. *North Africa's French Legacy 1954-1962.* Cambridge, Harvard University Press (Center of Middle Eastern Studies Monograph IX), 1962.

Gorst, Sheila. *Cooperative Organization in Tropical Countries.* Oxford, Blackwells, 1963.

Government of India, Planning Commission. *The New India: Progress Through Democracy.* New York, Macmillan, 1958.

Government of India, Program Evaluation Organization, Planning Commission. *Evaluation Report on the Second Year's Working of Community Projects.* New Delhi, 1955.

———. *The Fifth Evaluation Report on Working of Community Development and N.E.S. Blocks.* New Delhi, 1958.

Government of India. *Report of the Team for the Study of Community Projects and National Extension Service* (Mehta Report). Three vols. New Delhi, 1957-1958.

Griffiths, Sir Percival. *The British Impact on India.* London, MacDonald, 1952.

Hagen, Everett E. *On the Theory of Social Change.* Homewood, Dorsey Press, 1962.

———. *Planning Economic Development.* Homewood, Irwin, 1963.

Hahn, Lorna. *Nationalism and Nationhood in North Africa.* Washington, Public Affairs Press, 1960.

Halpern, Manfred. *The Politics of Social Change in the Middle East and North Africa.* Princeton, Princeton University Press, 1963.

Hart, Henry C. *Campus India: An Appraisal of American College Programs in India.* East Lansing, Michigan State University Press, 1961.

Harvey, O. J., et al. *Conceptual Systems and Personality Organization.* New York, Wiley, 1961.

Hicks, Ursula. *Development from Below.* London, Oxford University Press, 1961.

BIBLIOGRAPHY

Himmelstrand, Ulf. *Social Pressures, Attitudes and Democratic Processes.* Stockholm, Almquist and Wiksell, 1960.

Honigman, John J. *Three Villages in India.* Chapel Hill, Institute for Research in Social Science, 1958.

Hoselitz, Bert F. *Social Aspects of Economic Growth.* Glencoe, Free Press, 1960.

Hudson, Geoffrey, Sherman, A. V., Zauberman, A., and Eckstein A. *Chinese Communes: A Documentary Review and Analysis of the "Great Leap Forward."* New York, Institute of Pacific Affairs, 1960.

Humes, Samuel, and Martin, Eileen M. *The Structure of Local Governments Throughout the World.* The Hague, Martinns and Nijhoff, 1961.

Infield, Henrik F. *Cooperative Communities at Work.* London, Kegan, Paul, 1947.

Inkeles, Alex. *Public Opinion in Soviet Russia.* Cambridge, Harvard University Press, 1950.

International Bank for Reconstruction and Development. *Economic Development in Lybia.* Baltimore, Johns Hopkins Press, 1960.

International Colonial Institute. *L'Enseignement aux Indigènes.* Paris, 1931.

Johnson, John J., ed. *The Role of the Military in Underdeveloped Countries.* Princeton, Princeton University Press, 1962.

Julien, Charles-André. *L'Afrique du Nord en Marche.* Paris, Julliard 1952.

———. *Histoire de l'Afrique du Nord.* Paris, Payot, 1956.

Kabir, Humayun. *Education in New India.* London, George Allen & Unwin, 1956.

Karim, Abdulkhair Mazuml. *Changing Society in India and Pakistan.* Dacca, Ideal Publications, 1961.

Karve, Irawati, and Damle, Yashwaut Bhaskar. *Group Relations in Village Community.* Poona, Deccan College Monograph Series, 1963.

Katz, Elihu, and Lazarsfeld, Paul F. *Personal Influence.* Glencoe, Free Press, 1955.

Kornhauser, William. *The Politics of Mass Society.* Glencoe, Free Press, 1959.

Kuo-Chun, Chao. *Agrarian Policy of the Chinese Communist Party 1921-1959.* London, Asia Publishing House, 1960.

Lagos, Gustavus. *International Stratification and Underdeveloped Countries.* Chapel Hill, University of North Carolina Press, 1963.

Lasswell, Harold D., and Kaplin, Abraham. *Power and Society: A Framework for Political Inquiry.* New Haven, Yale University Press, 1950.

Laugier, H., ed. *La promotion humaine dans les pays sous-développés.* Paris, Presses Universitaires de France, 1960.

Leduc, Gaston (Introduction). *Industrialisation de l'Afrique du Nord.* Paris, Armand Colin, 1952.

———. *Le sous-développement et ses problèmes.* Paris, Domat Montebrétien, 1952.

Legge, J. D. *Central Authority and Regional Autonomy in Indonesia: A Study in Local Administration 1950-1960.* Ithaca, Cornell University Press, 1961.

Levy, Marion. *The Structure of Society.* Princeton, Princeton University Press, 1956.

Lewis, John P. *Quiet Crisis in India.* New York, Doubleday, 1954.

Lippitt, Ronald, Watson, Jeane, Westley, Bruce. *The Dynamics of Planned Change: A Comparative Study of Principles and Techniques.* New York, Harcourt, Brace, 1958.

Lipset, S. M. *Agrarian Socialism: the Cooperative Commonwealth Federation in Saskatchewan.* Berkeley, University of California Press, 1950.

———. *Political Man.* New York, Doubleday, 1959.

Liska, George. *The Greater Maghreb: From Independence to Unity?* Washington, Washington Center of Foreign Policy Research, 1963.

Loomis, Charles P., and Beyle, J. Allan. *Rural Social Systems.* New York, Prentice Hall, 1950.

McClelland, David C. *The Achieving Society.* Princeton, Van Nostrand, 1961.

McConnell, Grant. *The Decline of Agrarian Democracy.* Berkeley, University of California Press, 1953.

Maddick, Henry. *Democracy, Decentralization and Development.* London, Asia Publishing House, 1963.

Malenbaum, Wilfred. *Prospects for Development in India.* Glencoe, Free Press, 1962.

Mansur, Fatma. *Process of Independence.* London, Kegan Paul, 1962.

Marriott, McKim, ed. *Village India: Studies in the Little Community.* Chicago, University of Chicago Press, 1955.

Mason, Edward. *Economic Planning in Underdeveloped Areas.* New York, Fordham Press, 1958.

Mayer, Albert, et al. *Pilot Project, India.* Berkeley, University of California Press, 1958.

Meyer, A. J. *Middle Eastern Capitalism.* Cambridge, Harvard University Press, 1959.

Montgomery, John Dickey, *The Politics of Foreign Aid.* New York, Praeger, 1962.

Moore, W. E., and Freedman, A. S., eds. *Labor Commitment and Social Change in Developing Areas.* New York, Social Science Research Council, 1960.

Moreland, W. H. *The Agrarian System of Moslem India.* Cambridge, W. Heffer and Sons, 1929.

Moussa, Pierre. *Les Nations Prolétaires.* Paris, Presses Universitaires de France, 1960.

Mukerjee, Radhakamal. *Land Problems of India.* London, Longmans, Green, 1933.

Nurullah, S., and Naik, J. P. *History of Education in India during the British Period* (2d edn.). Bombay, Macmillan, 1951.

Oeser, O. A., and Emery, F. E. *Social Structure and Personality in a Rural Community.* New York, Macmillan, 1954.

Opler, Morris E. *Social Aspects of Technical Assistance in Operation.* Paris, United Nations Educational, Scientific and Cultural Organization, 1954.

Organization for Economic Cooperation and Development. *Intellectual Investment in Agriculture for Economic and Social Development.* Document in Food and Agriculture #60. Paris, 1962.

Plamenatz, John. *On Alien Rule and Self Government.* London, Longmans, 1960.

Planhol, Xavier de. *Nouveaux Villages Algérois.* Paris, Presses Universitaires de France, 1961.

Ponsioen, J. A. *The Analysis of Social Change Reconsidered.* The Hague, Mouton, 1962.

———. *Social Welfare Policy.* The Hague, Mouton, 1962.

Poston, Richard W. *Small Town Renaissance.* New York, Harper, 1950.

Pye, Lucian W. *Politics, Personality, and Nation-Building.* New Haven, Yale University Press, 1962.

Qureshi, I. H. *The Muslim Community of the Indo-Pakistan Subcontinent 610-1947.* The Hague, Mouton, 1962.

Rambhai, B. *The Silent Revolution* (2d edn.). New Delhi, Jiwar Prakashan, 1959.

Redfield, Robert. *The Primitive World and its Transformation.* Ithaca, Cornell University Press, 1953.

Reid, J. T. *It Happened in Taos.* Albuquerque, University of New Mexico Press, 1946.

Retzlaff, Ralph H. *Village Government in India.* London, Asia Publishing House, 1962.

Riggs, Fred W. *The Ecology of Public Administration.* London, Asia Publishing House, 1961.

Rokeach, Milton. *The Open and Closed Mind.* New York, Basic Books, 1960.

Rosenberg, Milton J., et al. *Attitude Organization and Change: An Analysis of Consistency Among Attitude Components.* New Haven, Yale University Press, 1960.

Rostow, W. W. *The Stages of Economic Growth*: *A Non-Communist Manifesto*. Cambridge, Harvard University Press, 1960.

Rostow, W. W., and Blackmer, Donald. *The Emerging Nations*: *Their Growth and United States Policy*. Boston, Little, Brown, 1961.

Roy, Naresh Chandra. *Rural Self-Government in Bengal*. Calcutta, University of Calcutta, 1936.

Rustow, Dankwart. *Politics and the Westernization in the Near East*. Princeton, Center of International Studies, 1956.

Sanders, Irwin T. *The Community*: *An Introduction to a Social System*. New York, Ronald Press, 1958.

Schultz, Theodore. *The Economic Organization of Agriculture*. New York, McGraw-Hill, 1953.

Schuster, Sir George, and Wint, Guy. *India and Democracy*. London, Macmillan, 1941.

Sen, J. M. *History of Elementary Education in India* (2d edn.). Calcutta, The Book Co., 1941.

Senior, Clarence. *Land Reform and Democracy*. Gainesville, University of Florida Press, 1958.

Siffin, William J., ed. *Toward the Comparative Study of Public Administration*. Bloomington: Indiana University Press, 1957.

Smith, M. Brewster, Bruner, Jerome S., and White, Robert W. *Opinions and Personality*. New York, Wiley, 1956.

Smith, T. E. *Elections in Developing Countries*. London, St. Martins Press, 1960.

Smith, Wilfred Cantwell. *Islam in Modern History*. Princeton, Princeton University Press, 1957.

Southall, Aidan, ed. *Social Change in Modern Africa*. London, Oxford University Press, 1961.

Spicer, E. H., ed. *Human Problems in Technical Change*. New York, Russell Sage Foundation, 1952.

Spitz, Allan A., and Weidner, Edward W., eds. *Developmental Administration*: *An Annotated Bibliography*. Honolulu: East-West Center Press, 1963.

Tanham, George K. *Communist Revolutionary Warfare*: *The Vietminh in Indochina*. New York, Praeger, 1961.

Tourneau, Roger Le. *Evolution Politique de l'Afrique du Nord Musulmane 1920-1961*. Paris, Colin, 1962.

Turnbull, Colin. *The Lonely African*. New York, Simon and Schuster, 1962.

Ulich, Robert. *Education of Nations*. Cambridge, Harvard University Press, 1961.

United Nations. *Structure and Growth of Selected African Economies*. New York, 1958.

BIBLIOGRAPHY

United Nations, Department of Economic Affairs. *Progress in Land Reform*. New York, 1954.

United Nations, Department of Economic and Social Affairs. *Community Development and National Development*. New York, 1963.

————. *Decentralization for National and Local Development*. New York, 1963.

————. *Local Government in Selected Countries: Ceylon, Israel, Japan*. New York, 1963.

United Nations, Economic and Social Council. *A Note on the Utilizations of Agricultural Surpluses for Economic Development in Pakistan* (prepared by the Economic Commission for Asia and the Far East [ECAFE]) (mimeo.). Bangkok, 1961.

————. *Report of the Second Session of the Standing Committee on Social Welfare and Community Development*. February 16, 1963, E/CN.14/187.

————. *Report of the Standing Committee of Social Welfare and Community Development at its First Session*. February 18, 1962, E/CN.14/142.

United Nations Educational, Scientific and Cultural Organization. *International Yearbook of Education*. Paris, vol. 19 (1957) to vol. 24 (1962).

United Nations, Office of Public Administration. *Public Administration Aspects of Community Development Programs*. New York, 1959.

United Nations, Secretary General. *The United Nations' Development Decade: Proposals for Action*. E/613, 1962.

United States, Agency for International Development, Special Advisory Committee on Cooperatives. *Cooperatives and Democratic Institutions for Economic and Social Development*. Washington, 1961.

Vaizey, John. *The Economics of Education*. New York, Free Press, 1962.

Ward, Robert E., and Rustow, Dankwart A., eds. *Turkey and Japan: A Comparative Study of Modernization*. Princeton, Princeton University Press, 1964.

Ward, W. E. F. *Educating Young Nations*. London, George Allen & Unwin, 1959.

Woodruff, Philip. *The Men Who Ruled India: The Guardians* (2 vols.). London, Jonathan Cape, 1964.

Wylie, Laurence. *Village in the Vaucluse*. Cambridge, Harvard University Press, 1957.

Younger, Kenneth. *The Public Service in New States*. London, Oxford University Press, 1960.

Zikria, Niaz Ahmed. *Les Principes de l'Islam et le Démocratie*. Paris, Presses Universitaires de France, 1958.

Zink, H. *Comparative Study of Rural Local Government in Sweden,*

Italy and India. London, International Political Science Association, Stevens Press, 1957.

PAKISTAN

Academy for Rural Development. *An Evaluation of the Rural Public Works Programme, East Pakistan, 1961-1962.* Comilla, East Pakistan, 1962.

Academy for Rural Development. *An Evaluation of the Rural Public Works Programme, East Pakistan, 1962-1963.* Comilla, East Pakistan, 1963.

Ahmad, Mushtaq. *Government and Politics in Pakistan.* Karachi, Pakistan Publishing House, 1959.

Akhtar, S. M. *Economics of Pakistan* (rev. edn.). Lahore, Publishers United, 1961.

———. *A Report on the Contribution of Community Development to National Economic Development Particularly in Agriculture.* Lahore, University of the Punjab, 1960.

Andrus, J. C., and Mohammed, A. *The Economy of Pakistan.* London, Oxford University Press, 1958.

Ansari, M. A. Salam. *Assistant Directors in Basic Democracies.* Peshawar, West Pakistan Academy for Village Development, 1961.

Aslam, A. H. *The Deputy Commissioner: A Study in Public Administration.* Lahore, University of the Punjab, 1957.

Barth, Fredrik. *Political Leadership Among the Swat Pathans.* London, Athlone Press, 1959.

Beg, Aziz. *Grass Roots Government.* Rawalpindi, Pakistan Patriotiz Publishers, 1963.

Ben Sayeed, Khalid. *Pakistan: The Formative Phase.* Karachi, Pakistan Publishing House, 1960.

Binder, Leonard. *Religion and Politics in Pakistan.* Berkeley, University of California Press, 1963.

Brecher, Michael. *The Struggle for Kashmir.* New York, Oxford University Press, 1953.

Bredo, William. *Land Reform and Development in Pakistan.* Menlo Park, Stanford Research Institute, 1959.

Birdwood, Lord. *Two Nations and Kashmir.* London, Robert Hale, 1956.

Brayne, F. L. *Better Villages.* London, Oxford University Press, 1937.

Callard, Keith. *Pakistan: A Political Study.* London, Allen & Unwin, 1947.

Campbell, Robert D. *Pakistan: Emerging Democracy.* Princeton, Van Nostrand, 1963.

Caroe, Sir Olaf. *The Pathans.* New York, St. Martins Press, 1958.

Choudbury, Golam W. *Constitutional Development in Pakistan.* New York, Institute of Pacific Relations, 1959.

Committee for Restoration of Democracy in Pakistan. *Betrayal in Pakistan.* London, 1962.

Darling, Sir Malcolm. *At Freedom's Door.* London. Oxford University Press, 1949.

———. *The Punjab Peasant in Prosperity and Debt* (4th edn.). London, Oxford University Press, 1947.

———. *Rusticus Loquitur or the Old Light and the New in the Punjab Village.* London, Oxford University Press, 1930.

Douie, Sir James M. C. *Punjab Land Administration Manual* (5th edn.). Lahore, Government Printing Office, 1961.

Eglar, Zekiye S. *A Punjabi Village in Pakistan.* New York, Columbia University Press, 1960.

Fairchild, Henry W., and Huq, Shamsul. *A New Rural Cooperative System for Comilla Thana.* Comilla, Academy for Village Development, 1961.

Feldman, H. A. *A Constitution for Pakistan.* Karachi, Oxford University Press, 1956.

Gupta, Rai M. N. *Land System of Bengal.* Calcutta, University of Calcutta, 1940.

———. *The Multan Municipal Committee Development Plan 1961-65.* Lahore, Government of West Pakistan, 1961.

Haider, S. M. *Case Studies in Community Development.* Peshawar, Academy for Village Development, 1960.

———. *Decision Making in Administration.* Peshawar, Academy for Village Development, 1962.

Hassan Masudul. *The Multan Municipal Committee Development Plan 1961-65.* Lahore, Government of West Pakistan, 1961.

———. *Preliminary Report on the Development Plan for District Council Lyallpur.* Lahore, Government of West Pakistan, 1961.

Haydar, Mohammed Afak. "Basic Democracies in Pakistan," Master's Thesis, Southern Illinois University, Department of Government, June, 1961.

Huq, Muhammad Shamsul. *Compulsory Education in Pakistan.* Paris, UNESCO, 1954.

Husain, A. F. A. *Human and Social Impact of Technological Change in Pakistan.* Dacca, Oxford University Press, 1956.

Inayatullah. *An Analysis of the Functioning of Seven Union Councils in Peshawar Tehsil* (mimeo.). Peshawar, West Pakistan Academy for Village Development, 1960.

———. *Basic Democracies, District Administration and Development.* Peshawar, Academy for Rural Development, 1964.

————, ed., *Bureaucracy and Development in Pakistan*. Peshawar, Academy for Rural Development, 1963.

————, ed., *District Administration in West Pakistan*. Peshawar, Academy for Rural Development, 1964.

————. *Perspectives in the Rural Power Structure in West Pakistan*. Karachi, United States AID Mission, 1963.

————. *Study of Selected Union Councils in Rawalpindi Division* (mimeo.). Peshawar, West Pakistan Academy for Village Development, 1961.

————. *Study of Union Councils in Nowshera Tehsil* (mimeo.). Peshawar, West Pakistan Academy for Village Development, 1961.

Islam, Serajul. *Report of the Training Programme for Circle Officers (Development) in Rural Public Works Programme*. Comilla, Pakistan Academy for Rural Development, 1963.

Jennings, Sir Ivor. *Constitutional Problems of Pakistan*. London, Cambridge University Press, 1957.

Khan, Field Marshal Mohammed Ayub. *Speeches and Statements* (July 1959-June 1960). Vol. 2. Karachi, Pakistan Publications, 1961.

————. *Speeches and Statements* (July 1960-June 1961). Vol. 3. Karachi, Pakistan Publications, 1961.

Khan, Masudul Hasan. *Financial and Development Problems of Basic Democracies*. Lahore, Government of Pakistan, 1962.

Khan, M. M. R. *The United Nations and Kashmir*. Djakarta, J. B. Wolters, 1955.

Korbel, Josef. *Danger in Kashmir*. Princeton, Princeton University Press, 1954.

Maine, Sir Henry Sumner. *Village-Communities in the East and West*. New York, Henry Holt, 1889.

Malik, Hafuz. *Moslem Nationalism in India and Pakistan*. Washington, Public Affairs Press, 1963.

Masihuzzaman. *Community Development—The New Bureaucracy* (mimeo.). n.p., n.d.

Masud-ul-Hasan. *Law and Principles of Basic Democracies*. Lahore, Pakistan Social Service Foundation, 1960.

Maxwell Graduate School of Citizenship and Public Affairs. *Pakistan Administrative Staff College: Interim Report on Activities*. Syracuse, June 30, 1963.

Mezirow, Jack D. *Dynamics of Community Development: A Case Study of Pakistan*. New York, Scarecrow Press, 1963.

Mohsen, A. K. M. *Report on a Rural Public Works Programme in Comilla Kotwali Thana*. Comilla, Pakistan Academy for Rural Development, 1962.

Nath, Amar. *The Development of Local Self-Government in the Punjab (1845-1900)*. Lahore, 1930.

BIBLIOGRAPHY

Pakistan Academy for Village Development. *Report on a Rural Public Works Programme in Comilla Kotwali Thana*. Comilla, 1962. 1963, 1964.

Parnwell, M. *Organization and Methods in the East Pakistan Government*. Dacca, Government of East Pakistan, 1958.

Peace, W. N., Uzair, Mohammed, and Ruetter, George W. *Basic Data of the Economy of Pakistan*. London, Oxford University Press, 1959.

Qureshi, I. H. *The Muslim Community on the Indo-Pakistani Subcontinent*. Leiden, Mouton, 1962.

Rahman, A. T. R. *Basic Democracy at the Grassroots*. Technical Publication No. 3. Comilla, Pakistan Academy for Village Development, 1962.

Rahman, Fazlur. *New Education in the Making in Pakistan: Its Ideology and its Problems*. London, Cassel, 1953.

Rahman, Hafiz Habibur. *Pakistan Economics* (2d edn.). Dacca, Ideal Publications, 1962.

Rizvi, S. M. Z. *Reader in Basic Democracies*. Peshawar, Academy for Rural Development, 1961.

Sabzwari, M. A. *Administrator Reviews Rural Development*. Peshawar, Academy for Village Development, 1961, ms.

Shafi, I. Q. M. *Dynamics of Development in a Pakistani Village*. Peshawar, Academy for Rural Development, 1961.

Sajid, Muhammad. *A Review of the Orientation Courses for Tehsil Council Chairmen*. Peshawar, Academy for Village Development, 1960.

Social Sciences Research Center, University of Punjab. *A Study of Knowledge and Attitudes towards Basic Democracies*. Lahore, 1960.

Social Sciences Research Center, University of Punjab. *The Expanding Role of the Public Servant in Pakistan's Democratic Structure*. Lahore, 1960.

———. *Village Life in Lahore District (A Study of Selected Political Aspects)*. Lahore, 1960.

Stephens, Ian. *Pakistan*. New York, Praeger, 1963.

Symonds, Richard. *The Making of Pakistan*. London, Faber & Faber, n.d.

Tafri, M. H., Bauer, Elizabeth K. and Keddie, Mikki R. *The Economy of Pakistan*. Berkeley, H.R.A.F., 1950.

Tinker, Hugh. *The Foundations of Local Self-Government in India, Pakistan and Burma*. London, University of London Athlone Press, 1954.

United Nations. International Labor Organization. *Report on Labour Conditions in Agriculture in Pakistan*.

Von Vorys, Karl. *Political Development in Pakistan*. Princeton, Princeton University Press, 1965.

BIBLIOGRAPHY

Waterston, Albert. *Planning in Pakistan: Organization and Implementation.* Baltimore, Johns Hopkins Press, 1963.

Wilcox, Wayne Ayres. *Pakistan: The Consolidation of a Nation.* New York, Columbia University Press, 1963.

MOROCCO

Al-Fassi, Allal. *The Independence Movements of North Africa* (H. Z. Nuseibeh, trans.). Washington, American Council of Learned Societies, 1954.

Ashford, Douglas E. *Perspectives of a Moroccan Nationalist.* Totowa, Bedminster Press, 1964.

————. *Political Change in Morocco.* Princeton, Princeton University Press, 1961.

Barennes, Yves. *La Modernisation Rurale au Maroc.* Paris, Librairie Générale de Droit et de Jurisprudence, 1948.

Berque, Jacques. *Le Maghreb entre Deux Guerres.* Paris, Esprit, 1962.

Bertrand, Pierre. *Dix Ans d'Economie Marocaine (1945-1955).* Paris, Institut National de la Statistique et des Etudes Economiques, 1957.

Bonjean, Jacques. *L'Unité de l'Empire Chérifien.* Paris, Librairie Générale de Droit et de Jurisprudence, 1955.

Bonnefous, Marc. *Perspective de l'Agriculture Marocaine.* Rabat, Institute for Advanced Studies, 1959.

Bousquet, G. H. *Les Berbères.* Paris, Presses Universitaires de France, 1957.

Brémard, Frédéric. *L'Organisation Régional au Maroc.* Rabat, Institute for Advanced Studies, 1949.

Champion, M., ed. *Finances Publiques du Maroc.* Rabat, Ministry of the National Economy, 1961.

Continental Allied Co., Inc. *Une Strategie Economique pour le Maroc.* Washington, 1960.

Cowan, L. Gray. *The Economic Development of Morocco.* Santa Monica, Rand Corporation, 1958.

Drague, G. *Esquisse d'Histoire Religions du Maroc: Confreries et Zaouias.* 1951.

Dresch, J., et al. *Industrialisation au Maghreb.* Paris, Editions Maspéro, 1963.

Durand, Emmanuel. *Traité de Droit Public Marocain.* Paris, Librairie Générale de Droit et de Jurisprudence, 1955.

Encyclopedie Mensuelle d'Outre-Mer. Morocco 54 (Special Issue). Paris, 1955.

Fadli, Mohammed. *L'Operation Labour.* Rabat, Centre d'Etude du Développement Economique et Sociale, 1961.

BIBLIOGRAPHY

Fazy, Henry. *Agriculture Marocaine et le Protectorate.* Paris, Lecante, 1947.

Gadille, J. *Exploitations Rurale Européennes.* Rabat, Comité Géographique du Maroc, 1958.

Goussault, Yves. *Problèmes d'Animation dans le Périmetre Irriqué du Tadla.* Rabat, Institut de Recherche et d'Application des Méthodes pour Développement (IRAM), 1961.

Guiho, Pierre. *La Nationalité Marocaine.* University of Rabat, Collection de la Faculté des Science Juridiques, Economique et Social, n.d.

Guillaume, Albert. *L'Evolution Economique de la Société Rural Marocaine.* Paris, Librairie Générale de Droit et du Jurisprudence, 1947.

Institut de Recherche et d'Application des Méthodes pour Développement. *Les Animateurs Ruraux au Maroc: Etude Générales et Orientations Actuelles.* Rabat, 1960.

————. *Rural Animation Study in Morocco.* Rabat, n.d.

Jean, Raymond. *Problèmes d'Edification du Maroc et du Maghreb: Quatre Entretiens avec Mehdi Ben Barka.* Paris, Plon, 1959.

Lacouture, Jean and Simonne. *Le Maroc à l'Epreuve.* Paris, Editions du Seuil, 1958.

Lahbabi, Mohammed Aziz. *De l'être à la personne.* Paris, Presses Universitaires de France, 1954.

————. *Du Clos à l'Ouvert.* Casablanca, 1961.

————. *Le Gouvernment Marocain à l'Aube du XXè Siècle.* Rabat, Editions Techniques Nord-Africaines, 1957.

Lyautey, Pierre, ed. *Lyautey l'Africain: Textes et Lettres.* Vol. 4. Paris, Plon, 1953-1957.

Montagne, Robert. *Les Berbères et le Makhzan dans le Sud du Maroc.* Paris, Alcan, 1930.

————, ed. *Naissance du Proletariat Marocain.* Paris, Peyronnet and Cie, n.d.

————. *Villages et Kasbahs Berbères.* Paris, Alcan, 1930.

Mourer, Henry. *Les Problèmes Administratifs de le Urbanisation au Maroc.* United Nations, Department of Economic and Social Affairs, 1962.

Oved, Georges. *Note sur la récente évolution économique du Maroc, 1949-1958* (mimeo.). Rabat, Ministry of the National Economy, April-May, 1958.

Plantey, Alain. *La Réforme de la Justice Marocaine.* Paris, Libraire Générale de Droit et de Jurisprudence, 1952, p. 197.

Rezette, Robert. *Les Partis Politiques Marocaines.* Paris, Colin, 1955.

Ripoche, Paul. *Problèmes Economique au Maroc.* Rabat, Imprimères Françaises et Marocaines, n.d.

BIBLIOGRAPHY

Robert, Jacques. *La Monarchie Marocaine*. Paris, Libraire Générale de Droit et de Jurisprudence, 1963.

Romieu, Capt. Jacques. *Les Jemmas depuis le dahir de 1951*. Rabat, Service des Affaires Indigènes, 1953.

Sa'd, Jamal. *The Problem of Mauritania*. New York, Arab Information Center, 1960.

Tiano, André. *La Politique Economique et Financière du Maroc Indépendant* (Special Issue: Tiers-Monde). Paris, Presses Universitaires de France, 1963.

Union Marocaine de Travail (U.M.T.). *Sur le Dur Chemin du Développement*. Rabat, n.d. (1960?).

———. *Les travailleurs et le plan*. Casablanca, April 1960.

———. *L'U.M.T. rejette le Plan gouvernemental*. Casablanca, August 1960.

United Nations, Food and Agricultural Organization. *Maroc: Rapport National* (Mediterranean Study). Rome, 1959.

Waterston, Albert. *Planning in Morocco*. Baltimore, Johns Hopkins Press, 1962.

Westermarck, Edward A. *Ritual and Belief in Morocco*. London, Macmillan, 1926.

Yata, Ali. *La Mauritanie: Province Authentiquement Marocaine*. Rabat, 1960.

TUNISIA

Ardant, Gabriel. *La Tunisie d'Aujourd'hui et de Demain*. Paris, Calmann-Lévy, 1961.

Debbasch, Charles. *Le République Tunisienne*. Paris, Libraire Générale de Droit et de Jurisprudence, 1962.

Fitoussi, Elie, and Benazet, Aristide. *L'Etat Tunisien et la Protectorate Française 1825-1931*. Tome I. Paris, Librairie Arthur Rousseau, 1931.

Ganiage, Jean. *Les Origines du Protectorat Français en Tunisie (1861-1881)*. Paris, Presses Universitaires de France, 1959.

Garas, Félix. *Bourguiba et la Naissance d'une Nation*. Paris, Julliard, 1956.

Guen, Moncef. *La Coopération et l'Etat en Tunisie*. Tunis, Editions de l'U.G.T.T., 1964.

———. *La Tunisie Indépendante face à son Economie*. Tunis, Cercle d'Etudes Economiques, 1961.

Holm, Henrietta M. *Agriculture in Tunisia: Organization, Production and Trade*. Washington, Department of Agriculture, 1964.

Micaud, Charles, Brown, Leon Carl, and Moore, Clement Henry. *Tunisia: The Politics of Modernization*. New York, Praeger, 1964.

Montety, Henri de. *Femmes de Tunisie*. Paris, Mouton, 1958.

Moore, Clement Henry. *Tunisia Since Independence: The Dynamics of One-Party Government*. Berkeley, University of California Press, 1965.

Neo-Destour Party. *Les Congrès de Neo-Destour*. Tunis, 1959. Esp. pp. 89-91.

Pellégrin, A. *Histoire de la Tunisie depuis les Origines jusqu'à nos Jours*. Tunis, Libraire Namura, 1948.

Poncet, Jean. *La Colonisation et l'Agriculture Européenne en Tunisie depuis 1881*. Paris, Mouton, 1962.

————. *Paysages et Problèmes Ruraux en Tunisie*. Paris, Presses Universitaires de France, 1963.

Raymond, André. *La Tunisie*. Paris, Presses Universitaires de France, 1961.

Senoussi, Mohamed. *Les Collectivites Locales en Tunisia*. Tunis, 1958.

Silvera, Victor. *Organisation Politique et Administrative de la Tunisie*. Tunis, Ecole Nationale d'Administration, n.d.

Union Générale des Etudiants Tunisiens. *8é Congrès National*. Tunis, 1960.

————. *IXé Congrès National: Congrès de l'Evaluation*. Tunis, 1961.

Union Générale des Travailleurs Tunisiennes, *Rapport d' Activité: 8ème Congrès National*. April 1-3, 1960. Tunis.

————. *6ème Congrès National de l'U.G.T.T.* September 20-23, 1956.

Union Tunisienne de l'Industrie et du Commerce. *Vème Congrès National: Rapport Economique*. October 28-30, 1960. Pp. 10-15.

United States Government, Agency for International Development. *Utilization of U.S. Surplus Commodities for Economic Development, P.L. 480, Title II, Section 202: A Summary of Experience in Tunisia*. (mimeo.). February 15, 1961.

Ziadeh, Nicola. *Nationalism in Tunisia*. Beirut, American University Press, 1962.

ARTICLES

GENERAL

Aggar, Robert E., and Ostrom, Vincent. "Political Participation in a Small Community," in Eulau, ed. *Political Behavior*, Glencoe, Free Press, 1956, pp. 138-148.

Apter, David. "Nationalism, Government and Economics," *Economic Development and Cultural Change*, vol. 7, 1959, pp. 117-136.

Arensberg, Conrad M. "The Community as Object and Sample," *American Anthropology*, vol. 63, 1961, pp. 241-264.

BIBLIOGRAPHY

Arnold, G. L. "Communism and the Intelligentsia in Backward Areas: Some Recent Literature," *Problems of Communism*, vol. 4, no. 5, Sept.-Oct. 1955, pp. 13-17.

Ashford, Douglas E. "The Last Revolution: Community and Nation in Africa," *The Annals*, vol. 354, July 1964, pp. 33-45.

———. "Local Reform and Social Change in Morocco and Tunisia," in *Emerging Africa*, W. H. Lewis, ed., Public Affairs Press, 1963.

———. "Nation-Building and Nationalism in the Middle East," *Middle East Journal*, vol. 18, Autumn 1964, pp. 421-430.

———. "Patterns of Consensus in Developing Countries," *American Behavioral Scientist*, vol. 4, 1961, pp. 7-10.

Bachrach, Peter, and Baratz, Martin S. "Decisions and Non-Decisions: An Analytical Framework," *American Political Science Review*, vol. 57, no. 4, September 1963, pp. 632-642.

Baron, Anne Marie, and Pirot, Henri. "La famille proletarienne," *Les Cahiers de Faits et Idées*, no. 1, 1955, pp. 26-54.

Batten, T. R. "Social Values and Community Development," in Phillips Ruop, ed., *Approaches to Community Development*. The Hague, Van Hoeve, 1953, pp. 80-86.

Becker, Gary S. "Investment in Human Capital: A Theoretical Analysis," *Journal of Political Economy,* vol. 70, October 1962, pp. 9-49.

Beers, Howard. "Social Components of Community Development," *Rural Sociology,* vol. 23, no. 1, March 1958, pp. 1-12.

Bendix, Reinhard. "Public Authority in a Developing Community: The Case of India," *Archives Européennes de Sociologie*, vol. 4, no. 1, 1963, pp. 39-85.

Benkirane, Ahmed. "Considerations d'ordre théorique sur investissements groupés et investissements diffus," *Cahier de l'Institut de Science Economique Appliquée*, no. 109 (ser. F, no. 16), January 1961, pp. 85-109.

Berelson, Bernard. "Democratic Theory and Public Opinion," *Public Opinion Quarterly*, vol. 16, 1952, pp. 313-320.

Bettelheim, Charles. "Sous-développement et planification," *Politique Etrangère*, vol. 22, 1957, pp. 287-300.

Bousquet, G. H. "Islamic law and customary law in French North Africa," *Jour. of Comparative Law*. London, 1950, pp. 57-65.

———. "Une élite gouvernantes de l'Afrique du Nord depuis la conquête français," *Le Monde de l'Islam*, vol. III, 1955, pp. 15-33.

Caelho, George V., ed. "Impact of Studying Abroad," *Journal of Social Issues,* vol. 18, no. 1, 1962.

Chakravarti, Shri S. "Community Development, Planning and Administration at the Local Level in India," *Journal of Local Administration Overseas*, vol. 2, no. 4, October 1963, pp. 212-221.

Charles, Bernard. "Un parti politique africain: le Parti Démocratique de

BIBLIOGRAPHY

Guinée," *Revue Française de Science Politique*, vol. 12, no. 2, June 1962, pp. 312-359.

Cowan, L. Gray. "Local Politics and Democracy in Nigeria," in Carter and Brown, eds., *Transition in Africa: Studies in Political Adaptation*. Boston, Boston University Press, 1958, pp. 44-61.

Dahl, Robert A. "The Concept of Power," *Behavioral Science*, vol. 2, no. 3, July 1957, pp. 201-215.

Davison, W. Phillips. "On the Effects of Communication," *Public Opinion Quarterly*, vol. 23, 1959-1960, pp. 343-360.

Doob, Leonard. "Attitude and the Availability of Knowledge Concerning Traditional Beliefs," *Journal of Abnormal and Social Psychology*, vol. 59, 1959, pp. 286-290.

Dotson, Arch. "Democratic Decentralization in Local Self-Government," *Indian Journal of Public Administration*, vol. 4, no. 1, 1959, pp. 39-50.

Edelman, M. "Symbols and Political Quiescence," *American Political Science Review*, vol. 54, no. 3, September 1960, pp. 695-704.

Eisenstadt, S. N. "Internal Contradictions in Bureaucratic Politics," *Comparative Studies in Society and Culture*, vol. 1, no. 1, October 1958, pp. 58-75.

————. "Political Struggle in Bureaucratic Societies," *World Politics*, vol. 9, no. 1, October 1956, pp. 15-36.

————. "Reference Group Behavior and Social Integration: An Explorative Study," *American Sociological Review*, vol. 19, no. 2, April 1954, pp. 175-184.

————. "The Role of Ideology as a Predisposing Frame of Reference for Immigrants," *Human Relations*, vol. 12, 1959, pp. 51-63.

————. "Studies in Reference Group Behavior: Reference Norms and the Social Structure," *Human Relations*, vol. 7, 1954, pp. 191-216.

Ensminger, Douglas. "Democratic Decentralization: A New Administrative Challenge," *Indian Journal of Public Administration*, vol. 7, no. 3, 1961, pp. 287-296.

Figueras, Garcia T. "The Participation of the Native in the Evolution of His Country," *Civilisations*, vol. 6, no. 2, April-June 1956, pp. 193-206.

Fisher, Jack C. "The Yugoslav Commune," *World Politics*, vol. 16, no. 3, April 1964, pp. 418-441.

Fisher, M. J. "New Concepts of Democracy in Southern Asia," *Western Political Quarterly*, vol. 15, December 1962, pp. 632-634.

Fosket, John M. "Social Structure and Social Participation," *American Sociological Review*, vol. 20, 1955, pp. 431-438.

Frankel-Brunswick, Else. "Intolerance of Ambiguity as an Emotional and Perceptual Personality Trait," in J. S. Bruner and D. Krech, eds.,

Perception and Personality: A Symposium. Durham, Duke University Press, 1949, pp. 108-144.

Frey, Frederick W. "Political Development, Power and Communications in Turkey," in Lucian W. Pye, ed., *Communications and Political Development.* Princeton, Princeton University Press, 1963, pp. 298-305.

Froman, Lewis A., Jr. "Learning Political Attitudes," *Western Political Quarterly*, vol. 15, 1962, pp. 304-313.

Galbraith, John K. "The Non-Affluent Society," *AID Digest*, July 1962, p. 16.

Gales, Edwin. "Political Implications of Community Development Programs in the Newly Developing Areas of the World," *Community Development Review*, vol. 6, no. 3, September 1961, pp. 4-13.

Gallagher, Charles F., Jr. "North African Problems and Prospects: Part I: Rural Reform and Revolution," *American Universities Field Staff Reports*, North Africa Series, vol. 10, no. 2, 1964.

Gans, John M. "An Approach to the Study of Government in Rural Communities," in *Public Policy: Yearbook of the Harvard Graduate School of Public Administration*, Cambridge, Harvard University Press, 1960, pp. 1-15.

Girod, Roger. "Sous-développement, stratification sociale et évolution politique," *Revue de l'Institut de Sociologie*, vol. 1, 1959, p. 12.

Hagen, Everett E. "The Process of Economic Development," *Economic Development and Cultural Change*, vol. 5, no. 3, April 1957, pp. 193-215.

Hawley, Amos H., Mariano, L. C., and Jacobini, H. B. "National Planning and Administration," in Stene et al., eds., *Public Administration in the Philippines.* Manila, Institute for Public Administration, 1955, pp. 263-288.

Herson, Lawrence J. R. "The Lost World of Municipal Government," *American Political Science Review*, vol. 51, 1957, pp. 330-345.

Himmelstrand, Ulf. "A Theoretical and Empirical Approach to Depolitization and Political Involvement," *Acta Sociologica,* vol. 6, 1961, pp. 83-110.

Hoffer, Charles R. "Social Action in Community Development," *Rural Sociology,* vol. 23, no. 1, March 1958, pp. 43-51.

Hollensteiner, Mary R. "The Development of Political Parties on the Local Level: A Social Anthropological Case Study of Julo Municipality, Bulacan," *Philippine Journal of Public Administration*, vol. 4, no. 2, 1960, pp. 111-131.

Honigman, John J. "Field Research in West Pakistan," *Research Previews*, vol. 6, 1959, pp. 20-24.

———. "Relocation of a Punjab Pakistan Community," *Middle East Journal*, vol. 8, Autumn 1954, pp. 429-444.

BIBLIOGRAPHY

Hoselitz, Bert F. "Levels of Economic Performance and Bureaucratic Structures," in LaPalombara, ed., *Bureaucracy and Political Development*. Princeton, Princeton University Press, 1963, pp. 181-182.

Hyman, Herbert, Payaslioglu, Arif, and Frey, Frederick W. "The Values of Turkish Youth," *Public Opinion Quarterly*, vol. 22, no. 3, Fall 1958, pp. 275-291.

Issami, Charles. "Economic and Sociological Foundations of Democracy in the Middle East," *International Affairs*, vol. 32, January 1956, pp. 27-42.

Jones, Earl. *A Review of Some Agrarian Reforms*. Turrialba, Costa Rica, Department of Economics and Social Sciences, Inter-American Institute of Agricultural Sciences, Organization of American States, 1961.

Kendall, Patricia L. "The Ambivalent Character of Nationalism Among Egyptian Professionals," *Public Opinion Quarterly*, vol. 20, 1955-1956, pp. 277-292.

Kerblay, B. "L'impact des modèles économique, sovietiques et chinois sur le Tier Monde," *Politique Etrangère*, vol. 25, 1960, pp. 332-354.

Kilson, Marton. "Authoritarianism and Single-Party Tendencies in African Politics," *World Politics*, vol. 15, no. 2, 1963, pp. 262-294.

Knight, Eleanor G. "Education in French North Africa," *Islamic Quarterly*, vol. 2, December 1955, pp. 294-308.

Lanzetta, John T. "Group Behavior under Stress," *Human Relations*, 1955, pp. 29-52.

Lawrence, A. "Les préoccupations de la jeunesse d'outre-mer," *Nouvelle Revue Française d'Outre-Mer*, vol. 49, no. 5, May 1957, pp. 239-242.

Lewis, A. B. "Local Self-Government: Key to National Economic Advancement and Political Stability," *Philippine Journal of Public Administration*, vol. 2, no. 1, January 1958, pp. 54-57.

Maddick, Henry. "Decentralization in the Sudan—II," *Journal of Local Administration Overseas*, vol. 1, no. 2, 1962, pp. 75-83.

————. "Decentralization in the Sudan—I," *Journal of Local Administration Overseas*, vol. 1, no. 2, 1962, pp. 71-74.

————. "Panchayat Raj," *Journal of Local Administration Overseas*, vol. 1, no. 4, October 1962, pp. 201-212.

Magnin, J. "L'Epargne et l'ouvrier rural," *I.B.L.A.*, vol. 17, no. 65, 1954, pp. 93-98.

March, James G. "An Introduction to the Theory and Measurement of Influence," *American Political Science Review*, vol. 49, no. 2, June 1959, pp. 431-451.

Mayer, Adrian C. "An Indian Community Development Block Revisited," *Pacific Affairs*, vol. 30, no. 1, March 1957, pp. 35-46.

————. "Some Political Implications of Community Development in

India," *Archives Européennes de Sociologie*, vol. 4, no. 1, 1963, pp. 86-106.

McCormack, William. "Factionalism in a Mysore Village," in Richard L. Park and Irene Tinker, eds., *Leadership and Political Institutions in India*. Princeton, Princeton University Press, 1959, pp. 438-444.

Melikian, Levon H., and Diab, Lufty N. "Group Affiliations of University Students in the Arab Middle East," *Journal of Social Psychology*, vol. 49, 1959, pp. 145-159.

Mello, Lordello de. "Decentralization for Development—I," *Journal of Local Administration Overseas*, vol. 2, no. 1, January 1963, pp. 24-26.

Mellor, John W. "The Process of Agricultural Development in Low-Income Countries," *Journal of Farm Economics*, vol. 44, no. 3, August 1962, pp. 700-716.

Meresko, Robert, et al. "Rigidity of Attitudes Regarding Personal Habits and Its Ideological Correlatives," *Journal of Abnormal and Social Psychology*, vol. 49, January 1954, pp. 89-93.

Mosel, James N. "Communication Patterns and Political Socialization in Transitional Thailand," in Lucian Pye, ed. *Communications and Political Development*. Princeton, Princeton University Press, 1963, pp. 184-228.

Mouton, Georges G. "Le développement communitaire, espérance des pays insuffisamment développés," *I.B.L.A.*, vol. 22, 1959, pp. 441-473.

Mukerji, B. "Administrative Problems of Democratic Decentralization," *Indian Journal of Public Administration*, vol. 7, no. 3, July-September 1961, pp. 306-319.

Murphy, Robert E. "Effects of Threat, Shock Distraction and Task Design on Performance," *Journal of Experimental Psychology*, vol. 58, August 1959, pp. 134-141.

Noureddine, Ben Khader. "Le Parti Unique—Est-il une Solution?" *Jeune Afrique*, December 16-22, 1963.

Opler, Morris E. "The Problem of Selective Culture Change," in Hoselitz, ed., *The Progress of Underdeveloped Areas*, 1952, pp. 126-134.

Opler, Morris E., and Singh, R. D. "Economic, Political and Social Change in a Village of North Central India," *Human Organization*, vol. 2, 1952, pp. 5-12.

Oppenheim, Felix. "An Analysis of Political Control: Actual and Potential," *Journal of Politics*, vol. 20, no. 3, August 1958, pp. 515-534.

Osgood, Charles E. "Cognitive Dynamics in the Conduct of Human Affairs," *Public Opinion Quarterly*, vol. 24, 1960-1961, pp. 341-365.

Palley, Sidney. "Cognitive Rigidity as a Function of Threat," *Journal of Personality*, vol. 23, 1955, pp. 346-355.

BIBLIOGRAPHY

Pauker, Guy, "Southeast Asia as a Problem Area in the Next Decade," *World Politics*, vol. 9, no. 3, 1959, pp. 325-345.

――――. "The Indonesian Eight Year Plan," *Pacific Affairs*, vol. 34, 1960, pp. 115-130.

Pepitone, Albert, and Kleiner, Robert. "The Effects of Threat and Frustration on Group Cohesiveness," *Journal of Abnormal and Social Psychology*, vol. 54, 1957, pp. 192-199.

Polson, Robert A. "Theory and Methods of Training for Community Development," *Rural Sociology*, vol. 23, no. 1, March 1958, pp. 34-42.

Presthus, Robert V. "Weberian and Welfare Bureaucracies in Traditional Society," *Administrative Science Quarterly*, vol. 6, no. 1, June 1961, pp. 1-24.

Prothro, E. Terry, and Melikian, Levon. "Social Distance and Social Change in the Near East," *Sociology and Social Research*, vol. 37, no. 1, October 1952, pp. 3-11.

Prothro, James M., and Grigg, Charles M. "Fundamental Principles of Democratic Bases of Agreement and Disagreement," *Journal of Politics*, vol. 22, 1960, pp. 276-295.

Pye, Lucian W. "Communications and Political Articulation," *Communications and Political Development*. Princeton, Princeton University Press, 1963, pp. 58-63.

――――. "The Non-Western Political Process," *Journal of Politics*, vol. 20, no. 3, August 1958, pp. 468-486.

Reed, Howard A. "The Religious Life of Turkish Muslims," in Richard Frye, ed., *Islam and the West*. The Hague, Mouton, 1957, pp. 69-148.

Rétif, A. "La Leçon des romans nord-africains," *L'Afrique et l'Asie*, 1ᵉ trim., no. 33, 1956, pp. 20-23.

Retzlaff, Ralph, "Panchayati Raj in Rajasthan," *Indian Journal of Public Administration*, vol. 6, 1960, pp. 141-158.

Riggs, Fred W. "Economic Development and Local Administration: A Study in Circular Causation," *Philippine Journal of Public Administration*, vol. 3, no. 1, 1959, pp. 46-86.

――――. "The 'Sala' Model: An Ecological Approach to the Study of Comparative Administration," *Philippine Journal of Public Administration*, vol. 6, no. 1, 1962, pp. 3-16.

Rocher, Léon. "Perspectives d'évolution politique en Afrique du Nord," *L'Afrique et l'Asie*, no. 12, 1950, pp. 5-36.

Rokeach, M. "Generalized Mental Rigidity as a Factor in Ethnocentrism," *Journal of Abnormal and Social Psychology*, vol. 43, 1948, pp. 259-278.

BIBLIOGRAPHY

Rosenberg, Milton J. "A Structural Theory of Attitudinal Change," *Public Opinion Quarterly*, vol. 24, 1960, pp. 319-340.

Rosenberg, Morris. "Some Determinants of Political Apathy," *Public Opinion Quarterly*, vol. 18, 1954-1955, pp. 349-366.

Rudolf, Lloyd I., and Rudolf, Susanne Hoeber. "The Political Role of India's Caste Associations," *Pacific Affairs*, vol. 33, no. 1, 1960, pp. 5-22.

————. "Toward Political Stability in Underdeveloped Countries," in *Public Policy: Yearbook of the Harvard Graduate School of Public Administration*. Cambridge, Harvard University Press, 1959, pp. 149-178.

Rustow, Dankwart A. "Politics and Islam in Turkey 1900-1955," in Richard Frye, ed., *Islam and the West*. The Hague, Mouton, 1957, pp. 69-148.

Sady, Emil J. "Improvement in Local Government and Administration for Development Purposes," *Journal of Local Administration Overseas*, vol. 1, no. 3, July 1962, pp. 135-148.

Sanders, Irwin T. "Theories of Community Development," *Rural Sociology*, vol. 23, no. 1, March 1958, pp. 13-24.

Sarnoff, Irving, and Katz, Daniel. "The Motivational Basis of Attitudinal Change," *Journal of Abnormal and Social Psychology*, vol. 49, 1954, pp. 115-124.

Sautoy, Peter du. "A Guide for the Administration to the Principles of Community Development," *Journal of Local Administration Overseas*, vol. 2, no. 4, October 1963, pp. 204-211.

————. "Some Administrative Aspects of Community Development," *Journal of Local Administration Overseas*, vol. 1, no. 1, January 1962, pp. 39-46.

Sayre, Wallace S. "Some Problems of Public Administration in a Developing Economy," *Indian Journal of Public Administration*, vol. 8, no. 2, 1962, pp. 137-152.

Schultz, Theodore W. "Reflections on Investment in Man," *Journal of Political Economy*, vol. 70, October 1962, supplement, pp. 1-8.

Shils, Edward A. "Authoritarianism: 'Right' and 'Left,' " in Christie and Jahoda, eds. *Studies in Scope and Method of the Authoritarian Personality*. Glencoe, Free Press, 1954.

————. "The Concentration and Dispersion of Charisma," *World Politics*, vol. 11, 1958, pp. 1-19.

————. "Demagogues and Cadres in the Political Development of the New States," in Lucian W. Pye, ed., *Communications and Political Development*. Princeton, Princeton University Press, 1963, pp. 64-77.

————. "The Intellectuals and the Powers: Some Perspectives for

Comparative Analysis," *Comparative Studies in Society and Culture*, vol. 1, no. 1, October, 1958, pp. 5-22.

————. "The Intellectuals in Political Development of New States," *World Politics*, vol. 12, no. 3, 1960, pp. 329-368.

Simon, Herbert A. "Notes on the Observation and Measurement of Political Power," *Journal of Politics*, vol. 15, no. 4, November 1953, pp. 500-516.

Smith, Wilfred Cantwell. "Turkey: Islamic Reformation?" *Islam in Modern History*. Princeton, Princeton University Press, 1957, pp. 161-205.

Smock, C. D. "The Relationship between Test Anxiety, Threat Expectancy and Recognition Threshold of Words," *Journal of Personality*, vol. 25, 1956, pp. 191-201.

Somjee, A. H. "Forms and Levels of Political Activity in Indian Villages," *Political Studies*, vol. 9, no. 1, February 1963, pp. 1-10.

Sower, Christopher and Freeman, Walter. "Community Involvement in Community Development Programs," *Rural Sociology*, vol. 23, no. 1, March 1958, pp. 25-33.

Spengler, Joseph J. "Public Bureaucracy, Resource Structure, and Economic Development: A Note," *Kyklos*, vol. 11, 1958, pp. 459-489.

Stouffer, Samuel A. "An Analysis of Conflicting Social Norms," *American Sociological Review*, vol. 14, no. 6, December 1949, pp. 707-717.

Taft, Ronald. "The Shared Frame of Reference Concept Applied to Assimilation of Immigrants," *Human Relations,* vol. 6, no. 1, 1953, pp. 45-56.

Tevoedjré, Albert. "Pour où Contre le Parti Unique," *Jeune Afrique*, November 11-17, 1963.

Thoung, U. "Decentralization for Development—II," *Journal of Local Administration Overseas*, vol. 2, no. 1, January 1963, pp. 27-30.

Tillet, M. L., Van Leeuwen, A., and Louis, A. "Eléments bibliographiques sur l'enseignment et l'éducation en Afrique du Nord, et particulièrement en Tunisie," *I.B.L.A.*, vol. 17, no. 67, 1954, pp. 285-307.

Tinker, Hugh. "The Village in the Framework of Development," in Braibanti and Spengler, eds., *Administration and Economic Development in India*. Durham, Duke University Press, 1963, pp. 94-133.

Tuma, Elias H. "The Agrarian-Based Development Policy in Land Reform," *Land Economics*, vol. 39, no. 3, August 1963, pp. 265-274.

Udy, Stanley H. " 'Bureaucracy' and 'Rationality' in Weber's Organization Theory: An Empirical Study," *American Sociological Review*, vol. 24, 1959, pp. 791-795.

Villenauva, Buenaventura M. "The Community Development Program of the Philippine Government," *Philippine Journal of Public Adminis-tration*, vol. 1, 1957, pp. 144-153.

Von Vorys, Karl. "Some Political Incentives for Economic Develop-ment in India, Pakistan, Burma and Ceylon," *Western Political Quarterly*, vol. 12, December 1959, pp. 1057-1074.

Wilbern, York. "Losing the 'Human Touch,' " *National Municipal Review*, vol. 39, no. 9, October 1950, p. 14.

Williams, Oliver P. "A Typology for Comparative Local Government," *Mid-West Journal of Political Science*, vol. 5, May 1961, pp. 150-164.

―――. "The Yugoslav Commune," *International Social Science Journal*, Special Issue, vol. 13, no. 3, 1961.

PAKISTAN

Abbott, Freeland. "The Jama'at-i-Islami of Pakistan," *The Middle East Journal*, vol. 11, 1957, pp. 37-51.

Ahmad, Brig. Gulzar. "Basic Problems Related to the Evaluation of Extension and Rural Development Activities in Pakistan." Paper read to I.C.A. Regional Seminar, New Delhi, January 11-23, 1960, p. 13.

Ahmad, Kazi S. "Agricultural Development of West Pakistan," *Pakistan Geographical Review*, vol. 2, no. 1, 1956, pp. 1-16.

Ahmed, G. "Changes in the Administrative Organization of the Government of Pakistan since 1953," *Public Administration* (Lon-don), Winter 1961, pp. 353-360.

Akhtar, S. M. "The Land Tenure System in Pakistan," in Parsons et al. eds., *Land Tenure*. Madison, University of Wisconsin Press, 1956, pp. 125-133.

Bashir, M. "The Scholar and Society in Pakistan," *The Scholar and Society*, Bulletin of Committee on Science and Freedom, Manchester, 1959.

Bell, David. "Allocating Development Resources," in *Public Policy: Yearbook of the Harvard Graduate School of Public Administration*. Cambridge, Harvard University Press, 1959, pp. 84-106.

Ben Sayeed, Khalid. "The Jama'at-i-Islami Movement in Pakistan," *Pacific Affairs*, vol. 30, 1957, pp. 59-68.

―――. "Pakistan's Basic Democracy," *The Middle East Journal*, vol. 15, no. 3, 1961, pp. 249-263.

―――. "Pakistan's Constitutional Autocracy," *Pacific Affairs*, vol. 34, no. 4, Winter 1963-1964, pp. 365-377.

―――. "The Political Role of Pakistan's Civil Service," *Pacific Affairs*, vol. 31, no. 2, June 1958, pp. 131-132.

―――. "Religion and National Building in Pakistan," *Middle East Journal*, vol. 17, no. 3, Summer 1963, pp. 279-291.

BIBLIOGRAPHY

Braibanti, Ralph. "The Civil Service of Pakistan: A Theoretical Analysis," *South Atlantic Quarterly*, vol. 58, no. 2, Spring 1959, pp. 258-304.

————. "Pakistan: Constitutional Issues in 1964," *Asian Survey*, vol. 5, no. 2, February 1965, pp. 79-87.

————. "Public Bureaucracy and Judiciary in Pakistan," *Bureaucracy and Political Development in Pakistan*. Peshawar, Academy for Rural Development, 1963, pp. 362-372.

————. "Reflections on Bureaucratic Corruption," *Public Administration* (London), vol. 40, Winter 1962, pp. 357-372.

————. "Reflections on Bureaucratic Reform in India," in Spengler and Braibanti, eds., *Administration and Economic Development in India*. Durham, Duke University Press, pp. 3-68.

————. "Transnational Inducement of Administrative Reform: A Survey of Scope and Criticism of Assumptions" (mimeo.).

Brombeck, Cole S. "The American Education in the Underdeveloped Lands," *The Academy Quarterly* (Peshawar), vol. 1, no. 2, December 1961, pp. 107-111.

————. "Education for National Development," in S. M. Z. Rizvi, ed., *A Reader in Basic Democracies*. Peshawar, West Pakistan Academy for Village Development, 1961, pp. 81-99.

Brown, James D. "An Experiment in Basic Democracies," *Muslim World*, vol. 51, no. 2, April 1961, pp. 99-106.

Chaudhuri, Muzaffar Ahmed. "The Organization and Composition of the Central Civil Services in Pakistan," *International Review of Administrative Sciences*, vol. 26, no. 3, 1960, pp. 278-292.

Chaudri, Faqir Mohammed. "Administrative Structure in Pakistan," in S. M. Z. Rizvi, ed., *A Reader in Basic Democracies*. Peshawar, West Pakistan Academy for Village Development, 1961, pp. 39-58.

Choudhury, G. W. "Democracy on Trial in Pakistan," *Middle East Journal*, vol. 17, no. 1, Winter-Spring 1963, pp. 1-13.

Courbe, N. "L'administration centrale et l'administration provinciale au Pakistan," *Revue Administrative*, vol. 16, no. 96, November-December 1963, pp. 616-622.

"The Educational Plan for Pakistan, £115,000,000 Scheme," *The Asiatic Review* (new series), vol. 48, no. 175, 1952, pp. 211-215.

Eggar, Rowland A. "Ministerial and Departmental Organization and Management in the Government of Pakistan," *Public Administration* (London), vol. 39, Summer 1961, pp. 149-172.

Etienne, Gilbert. "Quelques observations sur l'économie du Pakistan," *Tiers Monde*, vol. 3, no. 11, July-September 1962, pp. 479-491.

Friedman, Harry J. "Pakistan's Experiment in Basic Democracies," *Pacific Affairs*, vol. 33, no. 2, 1960, pp. 107-125.

BIBLIOGRAPHY

Gable, Richard W. *Introduction to District Administration* (mimeo.).

Gilbert, Richard U. "Works Programme in East Pakistan," *International Labour Review*, vol. 89, March 1964, pp. 213-226.

Gorvine, Albert. "The Civil Service under the Revolutionary Government in Pakistan," *Middle East Journal*, vol. 19, no. 3, Summer 1965, pp. 321-336.

Green, J. W. "Success and Failure in Technical Assistance—A Case Study," *Human Organization*, vol. 20, no. 1, Spring 1961, pp. 1-10.

Habib-ur-Rahman. "Basic Democracies as Institutions of Local Government in Pakistan—I," *Journal of Local Administration Overseas*, vol. 1, no. 4, October 1962, pp. 231-238.

Haider, S. M. "Social Implications of Civil Services in Pakistan," *The Academy Quarterly* (Peshawar), vol. 1, no. 2, December 1961, pp. 131-133.

Haquim, Ibn Azzuz. "La administration local en Marruecos antes y después del Protectorado," *Revue de l'Administration Publique*, vol. 3, no. 7, January-April 1953, pp. 261-279.

Homji, H. B. Minocher. "Community Development and Local Government," in S. M. Z. Rizvi, ed., *A Reader in Basic Democracies*. Peshawar, West Pakistan Academy for Village Development, 1961, pp. 186-212.

Honigmann, John J. "Relocation of a Punjab Pakistan Community," *Middle East Journal*, vol. 8, no. 4, 1954, pp. 429-444.

Inayat, Rafiq. "The Civil Service Academy," in Inayatullah, ed., *Bureaucracy and Development in Pakistan*. Peshawar, Academy for Rural Development, 1963.

Inayatullah. "National Institute of Public Administration—Lahore," *Bureaucracy and Development in Pakistan*. Peshawar, Academy for Rural Development, 1963, pp. 425-432.

————. "Pakistan Academy for Village Development—Peshawar," *Bureaucracy and Development in Pakistan*. Peshawar, Academy for Rural Development, 1963, pp. 433-453.

Khan, Akhtar Hameed. "The Basic Principles of the Comilla Programme," *Journal of the East Pakistan Academy for Rural Development* (mimeo.), February 13, 1963.

————. "How Villagers are Creating Capital," *Journal of the East Pakistan Academy for Rural Development* (mimeo.), August 18, 1962.

Masihuzzaman. "Administrative Obstacles to Voluntary Organizations in Pakistan," in Inayatullah, ed., *Bureaucracy and Development in Pakistan*. Peshawar, Academy for Rural Development, 1963, pp. 57-78.

————. "Basic Democracy and Community Development," *Community Development Review*, vol. 6, no. 1, March 1961, pp. 82-89.

————. "Basic Problems of Rural Development in South East Asian Countries," *Chanpal*, vol. 1, no. 1, 1961.

————. "From Village to Basic Democracies," *Community Development Review*, vol. 5, no. 1, March 1960, pp. 20-27.

————. "Public Service Tradition in Pakistan: A Case for Revision," in Inayatullah, ed., *Bureaucracy and Development in Pakistan*. Peshawar, Academy for Rural Development, 1963, pp. 285-298.

Newman, K. J. "The Constitutional Evolution of Pakistan," *International Affairs*, vol. 38, July 1962, pp. 353-364.

————. "Pakistan's Preventive Autocracy and its Causes," *Pacific Affairs*, vol. 32, no. 1, 1959, pp. 18-33.

Page, Alex. "Asytasia or Learning Attitudes in Pakistan," *The Educational Record*, vol. 43, 1962, pp. 269-271.

Power, John K. "Ten Years of Pakistan's Second Plan," *The Pakistan Development Review*, vol. 3, no. 1, Spring 1963, pp. 118-133.

Prause, François. "La démocratie de base au Pakistan: faillité d'une politique," *L'Afrique et l'Asie*, no. 63, 1963, pp. 8-16.

Qayyum, Abdul. "The Administrative Staff College," in Inayatullah, ed., *Bureaucracy and Development in Pakistan*. Peshawar, Academy for Rural Development, 1963, pp. 416-424.

Qureshi, Ishtiaq Husain. "The Background of Some Trends in Islamic Political Thought," in Braibanti and Spengler, eds. *Tradition, Values and Socio-Economic Development*. Durham, Duke University Press, 1961, pp. 212-242.

Raper, Arthur F. "A Report on Comilla," *International Development Review*, vol. 6, no. 2, June 1964, p. 2.

Rushbrook-Williams, L. F. "Basic Democracies as Institutions of Local Government in Pakistan—II," *Journal of Local Administration Overseas*, vol. 1, no. 4, October 1962, pp. 247-256.

Schuler, Edgar A. "The Origin and Nature of the Pakistan Academies for Village Development," *Rural Sociology*, vol. 29, no. 3, September 1964, pp. 304-312.

Shorter, Frederick C. "Planning Procedure in Pakistan," *The Pakistan Development Review*, vol. 1, no. 2, 1961-62, pp. 1-14.

Sufi, M. H. "Conditions of Farming in Pakistan," in Kenneth H. Parsons, Raymond J. Peach, and Philip M. Raup, eds., *Land Tenure*. Madison, University of Wisconsin Press, 1956, pp. 123-125.

Syed, Anwar. "The Teaching of Public Administration in Pakistan," *Philippine Journal of Public Administration*, vol. 2, April 1958, pp. 109-114.

Taylor, Carl C. "National Development Organization and V-AID," in *Village Aid: Some Articles and Reports*. Lahore, Village AID Administration, 1960, pp. 139-149.

Wheeler, Richard S. "Changing Patterns of Local Government and Administration in Pakistan," *South Atlantic Quarterly*, vol. 62, 1963, pp. 67-77.

————. "Pakistan: New Constitution, Old Issues," *Asian Studies*, vol. 3, February 1963, pp. 107-115.

Wilcox, Clair. "Pakistan," in Everett E. Hagen, ed., *Planning Economic Development*, Homewood, Irwin, 1963, pp. 52-79.

Wilcox, Wayne, "The Economic Consequences of Partition: India and Pakistan," *Journal of International Affairs*, vol. 18, no. 2, 1964, pp. 188-197.

————. "Nation-Building: The Problem of Pakistan," *Asia*, vol. 1, Spring 1964, pp. 75-92.

Zaidi, S. M., and Ahmed, Mesbahuddin. "National Stereotypes of University Students in East Pakistan," *Journal of Social Psychology*, vol. 47, 1958, pp. 387-395.

MOROCCO

Adam, André. "Le bidonville de Ben Msik à Casablanca (Contribution à l'étude du Proléteriat musulman au Maroc)," *Annales de l'Institut d'études orientales de la Faculté des Lettres*, tome VIII, années 49-50.

————. "Naissance et développement d'une classe moyenne au Maroc," *Bulletin Economique et Sociale du Maroc*, no. 68, 4ᵉ trim., 1955, March 1956, pp. 489-492.

————. "Le proletarisation de l'habitat dans l'ancienne medina de Casablanca," *Bulletin Economique et Sociale du Maroc*, XII, no. 45, 1ᵉ trim., and XIII, no. 46, 2ᵉ trim., 1950.

————. "La société rurale et la societé urbaine au Maroc: deux leçons de sociologie marocaine pour la classe de Première," *Bulletin de l'enseignement publique au Maroc*, no. 227, Avril, Mai, Juin 1954.

Al Fassi, Mohamed. "Le problème des cadres au Maroc," in Incidi, ed., *Problème des cadres dans les pays tropicaux et subtropicaux*. Brussels, 1961, pp. 41-51.

Ammonn, André. "Les F.A.R. et le trône Marocain," *Etudes Mediterranées*, no. 8, 1960, pp. 59-66.

Ashford, Douglas E. "National Organizations and Political Development in Morocco," *Il Politico*, vol. 28, no. 2, June 1963, pp. 360-374.

————. "The New Irredentism: Morocco and Mauritania," *The Western Political Quarterly*, vol. 15, Winter 1962, pp. 641-651.

————. "Political Usage of 'Islam' and 'Arab Culture,'" *Public Opinion Quarterly*, vol. 25, no. 1, Spring 1961, pp. 106-114.

————. "Transitional Politics in Morocco and Tunisia," *Princeton Conference Series*, no. 20, 1959, pp. 14-35.

BIBLIOGRAPHY

Barbour, Nevill. "Le problème constitutionnel au Maroc," *Politique Etrangère*, vol. 26, no. 2, 1961, pp. 110-123.

Barka, Mehdi Ben. "Les conditions d'une véritable réforme agraire au Maroc," *Réforme Agraire au Maghreb*. Paris, François Maspéro, 1962, pp. 119-123.

Bastide, Henri de la. "Les civilisations dans le 'Promotion National' au Maroc," *L'Afrique et l'Asie*, no. 63, 1963, pp. 2-7.

Bauchet, P. "Note relative aux investissements groupés et diffus au Maroc," *Cahiers de l'Institut de Science Economique Appliquée*, no. 109 (ser. F, no. 16), January 1961, pp. 77-83.

Beling, W. A. "Some Implications of the New Constitutional Monarchy in Morocco," *Middle East Journal*, vol. 18, no. 2, Spring 1964, pp. 163-179.

Berque, Jacques. "Le système agraire au Maghreb," Jean Dresch et al., *Réforme Agraire au Maghreb*. Paris, François Maspéro, 1962, pp. 49-68.

Berque, J., and Couleau, J. "Vers la modernisation du fellah marocain," *Bulletin Economique et Sociale du Maroc*, No. 26, July 1945, pp. 18-26.

Bertrand, Pierre. "Aperçu sur les mouvements migratoires (1936-1949)," *Bulletin Economique et Sociale du Maroc*, 1è trim., 1950, pp. 381-384.

———. "Le recensement de la population du Maroc de 1951-1952," *Bulletin Economique et Sociale du Maroc*, no. 68, 4è trim., 1955, March 1956, pp. 469-488.

Bourqui, P. "Rapport au Governement du Royaume du Maroc sur l'Enseignement Agricole," *Food and Agricultural Organization* (Report PEAT, no. 955). Rome, 1958.

Brunet, Jean. "L'office National des Irrigations au Maroc, deux ans d'expérience," *Annuaire d'Afrique du Nord: 1962*. Paris, Centre National de la Recherche Scientifique, 1964, pp. 249-268.

Buttin, Paul. "L'evolution du fellah et la modernisation de l'agriculture marocaine," *Confluent,* no. 5, February 1960, pp. 30-75.

———. "La relève au Maroc des cadres Français par les cadres Marocains," *Civilisations*, vol. 11, no. 1, 1961, pp. 57-60.

Célérier, J. "La modernisation du paysannat marocain," *Revue Géographique du Maroc*, 1947, pp. 3-29.

Chambergeat, Paul. "Les élections communales Marocaines en 29 mai 1960," *Revue Française de Science Politique*, vol. 11, no. 1, March 1961, pp. 89-117.

———. "Le référendum constitutionel du 7 décembre 1962 au Maroc," *Annuaire d'Afrique du Nord: 1962*. Paris, Centre National de la Recherche Scientifique, 1964, pp. 167-206.

Chapelle, Frederic de La. "La formation du pourvoir monarchique dans les tribus berbères du Haut-Atlas occidental," *Hesperis*, VIII, 1928, 3 and 4ᵉ trim., pp. 263-284.

――――. "Les tribus de haute montagne de l'Atlas occidental; organisation sociale et évolution politique," *Revue des Etudes Islamiques*, III, 1928, pp. 339-360.

Clerc, F. "Rentabilité de l'Operation-Labour," *Bulletin Economique et Sociale du Maroc*, no. 82, 1959, pp. 105-172.

Dresch, Jean. "Proletarisation du masses indigènes en Afrique du Nord," *Chemins du Monde*, Oct. 5-6, 1948, pp. 57-68.

Fauquenot, Emile. "La jeunesse et l'enseignement au Maroc," *L'-Afrique et L'Asie*, 1ᵉ trim., 1956, pp. 14-16.

Gallagher, Charles F., Jr. "Two Tunisias: The Plan for the Development of the Center-South," *American Universities Field Staff Reports,* August 15, 1956.

――――. "Ramadan in Tunisia: Aspects and Problems of the Tunisian Republic," *American Universities Field Staff Reports*, North Africa Series, vol. 6, no. 1, 1960.

Gellner, Ernest. "The Far West of Islam," *British Journal of Sociology*, vol. 9, no. 1, March 1958, pp. 73-82.

――――. "Patterns of Rural Rebellion in Morocco: Tribes as Minorities," *Archives Européennes de Sociologie*, vol. 3, no. 2, 1962, pp. 297-311.

Goussault, Yves. "La participation des collectivités rurales au développement," *Tiers Monde*, vol. 2, no. 3, January-March 1961, pp. 27-40.

Grimaud, N., and Le Pecq, F. "Cheminement constitutionel et premières élections legislatives Marocaines," *Il Politico*, vol. 29, no. 2, June 1964, pp. 475-483.

Hahn, Lorna. "Tunisia: Pragmatism and Progress," *Middle East Journal*, Winter 1962, pp. 18-28.

Lablow, A. "La bourgeoisie, symbole et reflet direct de l'occidentalisation de la société Marocaine," *Civilizations*, vol. 14, nos. 1-2, pp. 62-80.

Lahbabi, Mohammed Aziz. "Pluralisme Ethnique et Culturel au Maroc," *Confluent*, vol. 3, no. 18, 1958, pp. 7-11.

――――. *Confluent*, vol. 3, no. 19, 1958, pp. 40-41.

Lawson, Richard B. "Administrative Patterns in Morocco before and during the French Protectorate," *International Review of Administrative Sciences*, vol. 23, 1957, pp. 166-176.

Le Coz, J. "L'Operation-Labour au Maroc: tracteur et sous-développement," *Mediterranée*, XV. 2, no. 3, July-September 1961, pp. 3-34.

Le Tourneau, Roger. "Evolution de l'enseignement en Afrique du Nord," *Rythmes du Monde*, no. 4, 1950, pp. 16-24.

————. "Le Développement d'une Classe Moyenne en Afrique du Nord," *Développement d'une Classe Moyenne dans le Pays Tropicaux et Sub-Tropicaux*, Brussels, International Institute of Differing Civilizations, 1956, pp. 103-111.

————. "Social Change in Muslim Cities," *American Journal of Sociology*, vol. 60, no. 6, May 1955, pp. 527-535.

Lewis, William H. "Feuding and Social Change in Morocco," *Journal of Conflict Resolution*, vol. 5, no. 1, March 1961, pp. 43-54.

Marais, Octave. "La classe dirigéante au Maroc." *Revue Française de Science Politique*, vol. 4, no. 4, August 1964, pp. 709-737.

————. "L'élection de la Chambre des Représentants du Maroc," *Annuaire de l'Afrique du Nord: 1963*, Paris, Centre National de la Recherche Scientifique, 1965, pp. 85-106.

Marthelot, P. "Les expériences marocaines dans le domaine rural jusqu'à l'indépendance," *Réforme Agraire au Maghreb*, Paris, François Maspéro, 1962, pp. 80-81.

————. "Histoire et réalité de la modernisation du monde rural au Maroc," *Tiers Monde*, vol. 2, no. 6, April-June 1961, pp. 144-146.

————. "Les implications humaines de l'irrigation moderne en Afrique du Nord," *Annuaire d'Afrique du Nord: 1962*, Paris, Centre National de la Recherche Scientifique, 1964, pp. 127-154.

Martinet, Guy. "La famille bourgeoise marocaine," *Les Cahier de Faits et Idées*, no. 1, 1955, pp. 55-71.

Mas, Pierre. "L'urbanisation actuelle au Maroc: les 'Bidonvilles,'" *Vie Urbaine*, 1951, pp. 185-221.

Massignon, Louis. "L'Islam et le témoignage du croyant," *Esprit*, 21e année n206 (Sept. 1953), pp. 378-388.

Maurice, Flory. "Consultation et représentation dans le Maghreb indépendante," *Annuaire d'Afrique du Nord: 1962*, Paris, Centre National de la Recherche Scientifique, 1964, pp. 11-34.

M. E. L. "Les institutions au Maroc indépendant et le 'modèle français,'" *Tiers-Monde*, vol. 2, 6, 1960-1961, pp. 169-182.

Milleron, J. "La mise en valeur du nouveau Maroc," *L'Afrique et L'Asie*, 1e trim., no. 33, 1956, pp. 5-13.

Montagne, Robert. "Naissance du prolétariat marocain," *L'Afrique et l'Asie*, 1e trim., no. 13, 1951, pp. 6-23.

————. "Où en est l'évolution sociale au Maroc," *L'Afrique et l'Asie*, n9 (1950), pp. 52-65.

Mouiller, Henry. "Etudes sur l'évolution du paysannat au Maroc," *Cahier de la Modernisation Rurale*, Rabat, Société d'Etudes Economique, Sociales et Statistiques, May 1954.

Nicolas, Georges. "La sociologie rurale au Maroc pendant les cinquante dernières années," *Tiers Monde*, vol. 2, no. 8, Oct.-Dec. 1961, pp. 527-543.

Oved, Georges. "Problèmes de développement économique au Maroc," *Tiers Monde*, vol. 2, no. 7, July-September 1961, pp. 355-398.

Papy, L. "Une réalisation française au Maroc: les secteurs de modernisation rurale," *Cahiers d'Outre-Mèr*, no. 36, 1956, pp. 325-349.

Pierre, Ebrard. "L'Assemblée nationale consultative marocaine," *Annuaire d'Afrique du Nord: 1962*, Paris, Centre National de la Recherche et Scientifique, 1964, pp. 35-80.

Pirot, Renne. "Les jeunes marocaines musulmans et la stabilité professionelle," *Bulletin Economique et Sociale du Maroc*, XVIII, no. 61, 1ᵉ trim., 1954, pp. 65-70.

Plantey, Alain. "La justice coutumière marocaine," *Revue Juridique et Politique de l'Union Française*, vol. 6, no. 1, January-March 1952, pp. 20-56.

———. "Le Plan Triennal Marocain (1965-1967)," *Maghreb*, no. 10, July-August 1965, pp. 49-54.

Robert, Jacques. "Le problème constitutionnel au Maroc," *Revue du Droit Public et de la Science Politique*, vol. 77, no. 5, 1961, pp. 959-1003.

Serjuc, Jean. "Mauritainie et Maroc," *L'Afrique et l'Asie*, no. 45, 1959, pp. 11-21.

Speight, R. Marston. "Islamic Reform in Morocco," *Muslim World*, vol. 53, no. 1, January 1963, pp. 41-49.

Tahiri, Mohamed. "L'Agriculture et l'Economic de Maroc," *Confluent*, vol. 2, no. 15, 1957, pp. 321-331.

Theis, Jean. "Le contentieux administratif au Maroc," *Revue du Droit Public et de la Science Politique*, vol. 74, no. 3, May-June 1958, pp. 401-407.

———. "Les institutions publiques du Maroc indépendant," *Revue du Droit Public et de la Science Politique*, vol. 77, no. 3, May-June 1961, pp. 543-547.

———. "Le statut communal Marocain," *Revue du Droit Public et de la Science Politique*, vol. 76, no. 5, September-October 1960, pp. 929-934.

Tiano, A. "Une experience de mobilisation du travail au Maroc," *Cahiers de l'Institut de Science Economique Appliquée*, no. 122 (Series AB, no. 2), February 1962.

Zartman, I. William. "Farming and Land Ownership in Morocco," *Land Economics*, vol. 39, no. 2, 1963, pp. 187-198.

———. "The King in Moroccan Constitutional Law I," *Muslim World*, vol. 52, no. 2, April 1962, pp. 129-136; Part II, July 1962, pp. 183-188.

———. "The Sahara—Bridge or Barrier?" *International Conciliation*, no. 541, January 1963.

Zemmouri, Hasan. "Operation 'Communes,' " *Confluent*, vol. 2, no. 22, 1958, pp. 242-247.

TUNISIA

Abdallah, Ridah. "Le Néo-Destour depuis l'indépendance," *Revue juridique et politique d'Outre-Mer*, no. 4, October-December 1963, pp. 573-657.

Ashford, Douglas E. "Tunisian Leadership and the 'Confiscated Revolution,' " *World Politics*, vol. 17, no. 2, January 1965, pp. 215-231.

Barré, Raymond. "L'Economie de la Tunisie: problèmes et perspectives," Part I, *I.B.L.A.*, vol. 17, no. 67, 1954, pp. 2-3-224 and Part II, no. 68, 1954, pp. 353-368.

Barthelem, Marcel. "La solution de problèmes de l'Enfida Tunisienne," *Economie et Réalités Mondiales*, no. 48, 1954, pp. 114-123.

Bernis, Gérard Destanne. "Les investissements en Tunisie," *Cahiers de l'Institut de Science Economique Appliquée*, no. 109 (Series F, no. 16), January 1961, pp. 31-53.

Bourguiba, Habib. "La Bataille Economique dans le Domaine Agricole" (Speech of October 27, 1961), Tunis, Secretary of State for Information and Touring, 1961.

———. "The Battle for Evacuation: Bizerte and the South" (Speeches of April 7, 1960, July 17, 1960, and July 14, 1961), Tunis, Secretary of State for Information, 1961.

———. "Bourguiba Addresses the Nation's Leaders" (Speeches of February 6 and 8, 1961), Tunis, Secretary of State for Information, 1961.

———. "Une Constitution par le Peuple et pour le Peuple" (Speech of June 1, 1959), Tunis, Secretary of State for Information, 1959.

———. "Dans dix ans, la Tunisie Rénovée" (Speech of March 2, 1959), Tunis, Secretary of State for Information, 1959.

———. *Le Discours de l'Enfida*, Tunis, Secretary of State for Information and Touring, 1959.

———. "Le Discours de Victoire" (Speech to the Sousse congress of March 1959), Tunis, Secretary of State for Information, 1959.

———. "8 November 1959: Elections Générales" (Speech of July 30, 1959), Tunis, Secretary of State for Information, 1959.

———. *Electoral Campaign Speeches*, October 26-November 5, 1959, Tunis, Secretary of State for Information, 1960.

———. "The First Duty: Conquer Underdevelopment" (Speech of December 10, 1959), Tunis, Secretary of State for Information.

———. "Fixer les hommes sur la terre" (Speech of May 16, 1960), Tunis, Secretary of State for Information and Touring, 1960.

———. "La grande bataille contre sous-développement" (Speech of February 5, 1960), Tunis, Secretary of State for Information.

————. "General Mobilisation for Work" (Speech of February 26, 1960), Tunis, Secretary of State for Information, 1960.

————. "The Mouled Speech" (Speech of September 3, 1960), Tunis, Secretary of State for Information, 1960.

————. "Neo-Destourian Socialism" (Speech of June 21, 1961), Tunis, Secretary of State for Information, 1961.

————. "A New Experiment: Work Site Monitors" (Speech of March 24, 1960), Tunis, Secretary of State for Information, 1960.

————. "Nous Libérer de Toute Dépendance" (Speech of October 12, 1961), Tunis, Secretary of State for Information, 1961.

————. "Production Units: First State of a Revolution in Agriculture" (Speech delivered before the National Assembly, October 5, 1962), Tunis, Secretary of State for Cultural Affairs and Information, 1962.

————. "La Réforme de l'Enseignment: Premier Bilan" (Speech of June 19, 1961), Tunis, Secretary of State for Information, 1961.

————. "A Solemn Message for the National Assembly" (Speech of November 20, 1959), Tunis, Secretary of State for Information, 1959.

————. "Towards True Socialism" (Speech Delivered to the National Council of the Socialist Destour, March 2, 1963), Tunis, Secretary of State for Cultural Affairs and Information, 1963.

————. "Transcending Individualism in Outlook" (Speech delivered at Socialist Destour Officials' School, Gabès, April 28, 1963), Tunis, Secretary of State for Cultural Affairs and Information, 1963.

Brown, Leon Carl. "Colonization—A Second Look," *Institute of Current World Affairs Newsletter*, May 23, 1961, pp. 13-17.

————. "Education, 'Cultural Unity' and the Future," *Institute of Current World Affairs Newsletter*, December 1, 1960, pp. 8-14.

————. "The Quiet Revolution—Education in Tunisia from Protectorate to Independence," in James S. Coleman, ed., *Education and Political Development*. Princeton, Princeton University Press, 1964, pp. 144-168.

Callard, Keith. "The Republic of Bourguiba," *International Journal* (Canada), vol. 16, no. 1, Winter 1960-1961, pp. 17-36.

Callens, M. "Cinq années d'action administrative dans le domain agricole," *I.B.L.A.*, vol. 25, no. 98, 1962, pp. 111-134.

————. "Conditions de vie matérieles et sociales de la jeunesse étudiante," *I.B.L.A.*, vol. 19, no. 74, 1950, pp. 125-131.

————. "Education du milieu rural," *I.B.L.A.*, vol. 22, no. 88, 1959, pp. 401-418.

————. "La Planification Tunisienne," *I.B.L.A.*, vol. 26, no. 101, 1963, pp. 63-73.

————. "Promotion-Emploi," *I.B.L.A.*, vol. 24, nos. 95-96, 1961, pp. 279-300.

Camilleri, M. C. "Etude comparée des goûts en lecture en milieu familial des jeunes tunisiens cultivés," *I.B.L.A.*, vol. 25, 1962, pp. 1-22.

Cherel, Jacques. " 'De qui s'agit-il?' ou la mise en valeur agricole, problèmes d'ensembles humaines," *Les Cahiers de Tunisie*, vol. 8, nos. 29-30, 1960, pp. 17-49.

―――. "Les unités cooperatives de production du Nord tunisien," *Tiers Monde*, vol. 5, no. 18, April-June 1964, pp. 235-254.

Debbasch, Charles. "La constitution de la République tunisienne du 1er juin 1959," *Revue Juridique et Politique d'Outre-Mer*, vol. 13, 1959, pp. 573-590.

―――. "La constitution du 1er juin 1959 de la République tunisienne à l'épreuve des faits (novembre 1959-decembre 1960)," *Revue Juridique et Politique d'Outre-Mer*, vol. 15, no. 1, 1961, pp. 145-155.

De Bernis, G. "Comment peut-on analyser le Chomage en Tunisie?" *I.B.L.A.*, vol. 18, no. 4, 1955, pp. 437-460.

Demeersman, André. "Aux frontières de la psychologie rurale," *I.B.L.A.*, vol. 28, no. 109, 1965, pp. 1-34.

―――. "Un grand témoin des premières idées modernisantes en Tunisie," *I.B.L.A.*, vol. 19, no. 76, 1956, pp. 349-374.

De Montmarin, A., and De Bernis, G. "Industrialisation et plein emploi en Tunisie," *I.B.L.A.*, vol. 18, no. 4, 1955, pp. 395-436.

Filali, M. "Difficultés et insuffisances de l'économie tunisienne: essais de solutions," *Cahiers de l'Institut de Science Economique Appliquée*, no. 109, (Ser. F, no. 16), January 1961, pp. 55-73.

Gallagher, Charles F., Jr. "Tunisia," in Gwendolyn Carter, ed., *African One-Party States*, Ithaca, Cornell University Press, 1962, pp. 11-86.

Kluytenaar J., and Pan, C. L. "La Gestion des Terres Agricoles par l'Office des Terres Dominales," *Food and Agricultural Organization*, 1962.

Lee, William. "The Government of Tunisia since Independence," *Parliamentary Affairs*, vol. 13, no. 3, Summer 1960, pp. 374-385.

Lelong, Michel. "L'Enseignment Tunisien en 1961: Bilan et Perspectives," *I.B.L.A.*, vol. 24, nos. 95-96, pp. 251-277.

―――. "La Formation civique, morale et réligieuse dans l'enseignment tunisien," *I.B.L.A.*, vol. 25, no. 99, 1962, pp. 257-270.

―――. "La Jeunesse Universitaire," *I.B.L.A.*, vol. 19, no. 74, 1956, p. 155.

―――. "Les movements de jeunesse," *I.B.L.A.*, vol. 24, no. 93, 1961, pp. 61-64.

―――. "Quelques problemès de la jeunesse étudiante à travers les revues et périodiques tunisiens," *I.B.L.A.*, vol. 18, no. 70, 1955, pp. 273-278.

BIBLIOGRAPHY

"Les chantiers de la lutte contre le sous-développement," *Bulletin Mensuel de Statistique*, Tunis, no. 90, May 1962.

Louis, André. "La jeunesse tunisienne et les études." *I.B.L.A.*, vol. 16, no. 61, 1953, pp. 1-46.

Lunet, P. "Aspects sociaux du Sahel de Tunisie," *"L'Afrique et l'Asie*, no. 28, 1954, pp. 55-63.

Marthelot, P. "Juxtaposition en Tunisie d'une économie traditionnelle et d'une économie moderne," *I.B.L.A.*, vol. 18, no. 4, 1955, pp. 481-501.

Moore, Clement Henry. "The Neo-Destour Party of Tunisia: A Structure for Democracy," *World Politics*, vol. 14, no. 3, April 1962, pp. 461-482.

————. "Politics in a Tunisian Village," *Middle East Journal*, vol. 17, no. 5, Late Autumn, 1963, pp. 527-540.

Nicolaï, André. "Tunisie: fiscalité et développement," *Tiers Monde*, vol. 3, no. 11, July-September 1962, pp. 429-478.

Nouira, Hedi. "Le Néo-Destour," *Politique Etrangère*, vol. 19, July 1954, pp. 317-334.

Rondot, Pierre. "Le functionnement de l'opinion et l'ijma 'moderne' en Tunisie," *L'Afrique et l'Asie*, no. 60, 1962, pp. 17-24.

Sfeir, George N. "Tunisian Code of Personal Status," translated in *Middle East Journal*, vol. 11, no. 3, Summer 1957, pp. 309-318.

Sicard, Hervé. "La politique agricole de la Tunisie indépendante," *Revue des Sciences Humaines Appliquées à l'Agriculture*, no. 2, 1963, pp. 155-176.

Silvera, Victor. "Le régime constitutionnel de la Tunisie: La Constitution de 1er Juin 1959," *Revue Français de Science Politique*, vol. 10, no. 2, 1960, pp. 336-394.

Verdier, J. M. "L'évolution de la législation foncière depuis l'Indépendance," *I.B.L.A.*, vol. 24, nos. 95-96, 1961, pp. 399-404.

Zarka, Claude. "L'économie tunisienne à l'heure de la planification impérative," *Annuaire d'Afrique du Nord: 1962*, Paris, Centre National de la Recherche Scientifique, 1964, pp. 207-242.

INDEX

citizen, 7, 8, 11, 18-19, 20, 49-50, 58, 70, 74, 108, 115, 122, 304, 311, 315, 325, 330, 339, 359, 376. *See also* citizen power orientation

citizen power orientation: 17, 114, 168, 230, 272, 287-88, 292, 306, 311, 330, 347, 369-86; affective, 16-17, 91-92, 137, 301, 306, 311, 320-21, 325; cognitive, 16-17, 138, 301, 306, 322, 347

civil liberties, *see* political expression

Civil Service Academy, 278

Civil Service of Pakistan (C.S.P.), 151, 273, 275, 278, 294, 296, 300

Clerc, Françoise, 199n

coercion, v, 9, 96

cognition, 6, 15, 49, 58, 74, 103, 122, 301-303, 307, 322, 336, 339, 347, 353, 359, 362, 365, 369-86

cognitive articulation, 370-86

cognitive skill, 15, 16, 92, 304, 333, 335, 371-72, 376, 381

Cohen, Arthur R., 370n

Coleau, Julien, 28, 197

Coleman, James S., 5n, 19n, 24n, 242n, 248n, 369n, 373n

colonial administration: French, 27-30, 35-36, 44, 48, 56, 64-69, 72, 98, 103, 141-42, 181, 194, 253, 280, 284-85; Spanish, 42; *colon*, 69, 180; British, 95, 98, 103, 105-107, 173, 221, 242-44, 273

Comilla, 127, 130n, 225, 235-37, 362; Academy for Rural Development, 225-26, 279

comité de gestion, 200-201

Commission on National Education, 246

Committee of Public Instruction (1832), 98

Communism, 58n, 160, 211, 263, 312, 324, 328n, 343

Communist party, 76, 79

community, 12, 90, 102. *See also* locality

community development: 76; Pakistan, 102-103, 105-110, 362; polyvalent workers, 195n; Morocco, 220, 233n

comparative analysis, 12, 13, 17, 21, 32, 38, 51, 92, 97, 104, 106, 118, 128, 137, 139, 301, 307, 341, 360. *See also* system power orientation

conceptual skill, 18, 339

Consultative National Assembly, 51

consumer cooperatives, 214, 216; Table VIII, 214

contrôleurs civiles, 279

Conventionist Muslim League, 131, 357, 359

Coombs, Arthur W., 16n

cooperative farms: 83, 183, 189, 193, 211, 215; Tunisia, 186, 213-17; Table VIII, 214. *See also* credit cooperatives, service cooperatives

coops, *see* credit, consumer, farm, and service cooperatives

Cornwallis, Lord, 105

corruption, 85, 124, 289

Coulton, George G., 173n

credit cooperatives, 211, 217, 220-21, 224-26; Table VIII, 214

culture and development, 6, 102-103, 115

Curzon, Lord, 100, 243

Cutwright, Phillips, 5n, 19n, 373n

Dacca, 278

Dahl, Robert, 210n

Darling, Sir Malcolm, 102-103, 224n, 294n

Debbasch, Charles, 308n, 310n, 343n, 344n, 345

decentralization, 10, 88, 101

De Gaulle, General Charles, 324, 351

délégué, 290-91

democratic centralism, 61

de Montery, Henri, 310n

de Planhol, Xavier, 94n

Deputy Commissioner, *see* district administration

Destour, *see* Socialist Destour

Destourian Socialism, 62. *See also* Socialist Destour

Deutsch, Karl W., 19n

development administration, *see* local administration, provincial administration, public administration

development process, 32, 62, 70, 80, 84-85, 90, 92, 94, 128, 131-34, 163, 165, 168-69, 173, 208, 248, 259, 268-69, 271, 288, 298-99, 301-303, 304, 306, 346-47, 369, 373

Dey, Surendra K., 94n, 365n

Diab, Lufty N., 322n

dirham, 41n

district administration, 97n, 100, 106-107, 116-18, 130-31, 288, 294-97, 313n; early boards, 100, 123; district council, 117-18, 236, 297; District Magistrate, *see* district administration

District Agricultural Office, 222-23

District Magistrate, *see* district administration

divorce, 310, 313, 319